MEXICAN LITERATURE

The Texas Pan American Series

MEXICAN
LITERATURE

A HISTORY

Edited by

David William Foster

UNIVERSITY OF TEXAS PRESS
Austin

Copyright © 1994 by the University of Texas Press
All rights reserved
Printed in the United States of America
First edition, 1994

Requests for permission to reproduce material from this
work should be sent to Permissions, University of Texas
Press, Box 7819, Austin, TX 78713-7819.

∞ The paper used in this publication meets the
minimum requirements of American National Standard
for Information Sciences—Permanence of Paper for
Printed Library Materials, ANSI Z39. 48–1984.

Library of Congress Cataloging-in-Publication Data
Mexican literature : a history / edited by David William
Foster. — 1st ed.
      p.   cm. — (The Texas Pan American series)
  Includes bibliographical references and index.
  ISBN 0-292-72482-9 (alk. paper)
  1. Mexican literature—History and criticism.
I. Foster, David William. II. Series.
PQ7111.M49   1994
860.9'972—dc20   93-40185

Contents

Preface

DAVID WILLIAM FOSTER

Despite the enormous production of interpretive criticism on Latin American literature since midcentury, the lack of adequate historical and bibliographic control is really quite surprising. This is true not only of what is available in English, but also, and more significantly, what is available in the specific languages of Latin American literary production. Although some excellent preliminary attempts at bibliographic control exist and one can point to a number of standard secondary-school manuals of literary history, comprehensive treatises of either Latin American literature in general or the various national literatures are notably lacking, and even more so when the emphasis shifts from the historical registries of names and titles to analyses based on theoretically explicit principles.

Following the pattern of *A Handbook of Latin American Literature* (New York: Garland Publishing Company, 1987; 2d ed., 1992), the present volume represents the attempt to provide Mexican literature with something like an adequate coverage of significant literary production from the specific point of view of detailed analyses of major texts. Rather than merely survey canonical authors and works, this literary history pretends to offer instead fairly detailed commentaries on those works that may be considered to define the parameters of Mexican literature. As such, these works are both the entries in a time-honored canon and texts that may, under a scrutiny dictated by alternative critical practices, emerge as contenders for privileged positions in a recasting of the canon. Such works emerge with a shift in focus based on historical principles (the recovery of pre-Columbian literature as an integral part of what is only, strictly speaking, a Mexican literature after independence in the nineteenth century), on social principles (the recovery of a silenced tradition of feminine or homosexual writing; the conjugation with Mexican literature of a Mexican-American production in both English and Spanish), or on generic principles (the inclusion in a global definition of cultural text of forms of expression not ordinarily considered properly literary—the journalistic essay, the historical chronicle, or literary criticism itself).

Inevitably, such a representation of a major national literature can only be undertaken as a collective project. The reasons for this are many, the most obvious one being the scope of material to be covered. Despite the devastating effects of current national and economic circumstances on cultural production in Mexico, publishing output continues to be extensive, and in any one genre there is virtually more than even the most industrious scholar can reasonably be expected to keep track of. This is especially true in the area of contemporary fiction, where the production seems to grow geometrically from one generation to the other. But this expansion is also a dimension of other genres. For example, although actual theatrical production may constitute an easily assimilable block of material (assuming that one is able always to actually see the plays performed), the sociocultural backgrounds of theatrical activity in modern Latin American societies extend significantly the range of other materials the scholar must be conversant with. Concomitantly, while poetry may strike one as almost a microgenre (especially alongside the sort of vast novelistic project someone like Carlos Fuentes engages in), the artistic seed bed, so to speak, of poetry is complex and requires constant and intense scrutiny. Finally, the ways in which multigeneric writing figures prominently in contemporary Mexico means that one cannot be content merely to limit scholarly focus to traditional genres like poetry or the novel: individuals like Elena Poniatowska, María Luisa Mendoza, and José Joaquín Blanco are not simply writing in several genres. Rather, their writing demands examination as a single, coherent textual project in which generic variations are secondary to the overall cultural principles that guide the production of their variegated works. In the context of such an intense modern literary productivity such as one finds in Mexico, only a collaborative effort can hope to represent adequately what needs to be considered a representative inventory of literary activity.

Such a circumstance extends also to critical focus and analytical methodology. Although the contributors were originally set the goal of providing an ideologically framed interpretation of the material assigned to them, it quickly became apparent that no unified orientation, ideological or otherwise, could legitimately be hoped for. In the first place, ideological approaches to Latin American literature mean many different things, even if, from the perspective of the United States, there may appear to be something like intellectual unanimity among researchers in Latin America as to what an ideological agenda for the study of Latin American literature and its national manifestations should be. The fact that different critical voices are involved is reflected in different perspectives on the same phenomenon. Therefore, the reader will find varying dates given for literary movements like modernism or conflicting accounts regarding its development. It is no longer possible to aspire to unitary interpretations of cultural phenomena, and the divergences to be found among the scholars whose work is represented here must be taken as an index of the interesting points of debate about Mexican literary history. If there was anything approximating such an agenda in the late 1960s or 1970s, multiple circumstances have contributed to fragmenting it substantially.

The result is that, while few scholars of Latin American literature, in either Latin America or the United States, would subscribe to anything other than the belief that literary production is intimately related to sociohistorical parameters, the actual models and methodologies employed vary significantly. Thus, representing the sustained commitment to examine literature as part of larger sociohistorical manifestations, the essays assembled here nevertheless constitute diverse emphases in how that examination is to be executed. Inevitably, historical and generic considerations of a rather traditional nature serve as basic organizing principles of the volume and of individual essays, principally because, despite the influence of innovative critical classifications, our courses and our general perceptions continue to subscribe to these principles. Yet, within this framework, one should be able to consult textual readings that are underlain by the attempt to explore production in Mexico as part of a comprehensive cultural dynamic in that country.

Finally, the specific research commitments of each scholar determine significantly the way in which each section is organized. In contrast to an encyclopedic approach where each entry demonstrates approximately the same organization of material, contributors were given considerable latitude in the structuring of their contributions. The only guiding injunction was to ensure that interpretive comments adhered to the principle of placing literary production in its sociohistorical context. This meant that a conventional historical registry was to be forfeited, that only a tightly defined inventory of significant texts was to be dealt with, and that principled critical analysis was being called for. The result is a volume that should be of use to both the specialist seeking a fresh interpretation of major texts and the general user (including students) requiring an informed discussion of the primary texts they are likely to find cited as exemplary of Mexico's literary production. Each essay closes with an annotated, selective listing of major critical sources that, when taken together, constitute a basic bibliography of extant criticism.

I cannot help but take advantage of this preface to make some comments about what I have learned about Mexican literary scholarship in the United States in the preparation of this volume. There is much valuable literary scholarship on Mexico that emerged in roughly two generations of industrious Latin American research in this country, and the reader will find the best of such work represented in the annotated bibliographies that accompany each essay. Yet, at the same time, there is a considerable asymmetry to this scholarship when placed alongside either the criticism being written in Mexico or alongside the scope of Mexican literary production. It is impossible not to be struck by the relatively small numbers of individuals who have anything approximating a comprehensive research program devoted to Mexican literature, in the sense of scholars producing a steady output of path-breaking interpretations. Concomitantly, one is frequently overwhelmed by the enormous concentration of effort on a few giants of contemporary Mexican letters and an attendant inattention to many other valuable figures who in various ways are making highly singular and original contributions to the growing stature of Mexican literary culture. It would be arrogant of me to cite names of those contemporary authors I feel are overstudied, but a simple check of the MLA *International Bibliography,* the *Hispanic American Periodicals Index,* or the

Year's Work in Modern Language Studies will show what I mean about what may be considered to be an imbalance in the coverage of Mexican literature on the part of the American academy. Another aspect of this circumstance are the gaps in our consideration of earlier periods of Mexican literature. The 1992 phenomenon has brought with it an enormous increase in the study of conquest and colonial topics through the seventeenth century. But the eighteenth century remains understudied, and there are many topics in the literature of the decades preceding the 1910 Revolution that seem to be perennially ignored. One has no pretense of contributing to bringing about a reorientation of the history and criticism of Mexican literature in the United States with this compilation, but it should have some value in assisting users in determining where they might do well to invest their intellectual efforts toward a more comprehensive understanding of literature in Mexico over five hundred years.

A final note: more specific bibliographic information on the topics and authors covered in this volume may be found in the new edition of my *Mexican Literature: A Bibliography of Secondary Sources* (Metuchen, N.J.: Scarecrow Press, 1992).

I am grateful to Katharine Kaiper Phillips for her editorial assistance, to my research assistants Roselyn Costantino, Melissa Lockhart, and Salvador Oropesa for their numerous contributions to the execution of this project, and to the various research programs of Arizona State University which have always endorsed my research efforts.

MEXICAN LITERATURE

1

Pre-Columbian Literatures

JOANNA O'CONNELL

I

A critical question facing the first Mexican literary historians in the late nineteenth century was where to begin their stories of Mexican literature. Their goal was to create a national literature through which to imagine the new nation, and their intellectual project of unification and construction, undertaken in response to independence and the prolonged struggles that ensued, was motivated by the desire to affirm, in the words of Angel Rama, "independence, originality, representativity" (11). Asserting originality as difference from Spanish metropolitan culture was a contradictory task; it meant coming to terms in some way with colonial society's foundation in a violent encounter between two radically different cultures, one of almost cataclysmic proportions for indigenous civilizations. The colonization and subjugation of many different indigenous peoples by the Spaniards were prolonged in a colonial society characterized by cultural heterogeneity and ethnic conflict rather than unity and continuity. After independence, the efforts of Mexican intellectuals and politicians to fashion a story of unity from this complex history of colonial dominance and enforced difference grew from a colonial Creole intellectual tradition in which the indigenous was always thought of as Other even as that same tradition worked to appropriate a pre-Columbian past as its own.

The field of what some scholars have called "pre-Columbian literature of Mexico" emerges from this rich and polemical history of representing the civilizations of Mesoamerica that begins with the conquest itself. Tracing its constitution requires us to read through the tension between official history—the voices of the conquerors—and the disappearance and silencing of the voices of indigenous peoples (Pastor).

For colonial Spanish administrators and evangelizers, the act of writing the indigenous Other was quite openly the act of constructing a colonial subject. Sixteenth-century historians and ethnographer-missionaries represented and inscribed "Indians," their culture and history, in order to control, manipulate, or even destroy them, often in the name of salvation. Even such an ardent defender of indigenous people as Fray Bartolomé de las Casas assumed that their transformation into Christians was necessary for their own good. The first move of most of these writers was to take one people, the Mexica, or Aztecs, as they are more commonly known,[1] as "the Indian," suppressing the diversity and conflict among Mesoamerican societies, and then to construct that Indian as existing *for* the colonial administrator-observer, cast as instrument of Providence. Benjamin Keen's *The Aztec Image* traces some of the ways these often-conflicting versions of the history and people of pre-Columbian Mesoamerica were at once responses to an encounter with a vastly different culture and products of the interests and modes of thought of European observers.

By the eighteenth century and after three hundred years of colonial rule, an important shift has occurred in colonial accounts of pre-Columbian history in New Spain. A Creole intellectual tradition develops that now claims a tie to an indigenous past; the perspective of the writer toward Mesoamerican peoples has shifted from seeing that culture as "Other" to calling it "ours" (Brading; Pacheco). The narrations of ancient Mexican (Aztec) history by the Jesuit Francisco Clavijero or Fray Servando Teresa de Mier are part of the project known as Creole patriotism, the assertion of a separate identity for the colony that justifies its difference from the metropole by a link to a pre-Columbian legacy. This intellectual tradition, which D. A. Brading has called "historical indigenism," will serve Mexican nationalists in their efforts to elaborate a collective national identity.

The place accorded to what we now call pre-Columbian literature will be a key factor in the partial literary histories that begin to appear in late nineteenth-century Mexico, written by such figures as Ignacio Altamirano, Francisco Pimentel, and José María Vigil. The existence of what we would recognize today as literary history assumes the existence of a separate class of texts marked as "literary" and also the special role of aesthetic works in the expression of the character of a people. The eighteenth-century Creole José Eguiara y Eguren undertook his *Biblioteca mexicana,* a compendium of writers of New Spain, in order to refute the European Enlightenment contention of the inferiority of colonial culture (González Peña, 160–161); the difference between such a list and a literary history is that the latter narrates literature as a story. The "end" of the story is the existence of "Mexicanness" while the story's beginning, its figures, and its emplotment turn upon a set of questions (whether explicitly formulated or not), such as whether Mexican literature should be said to begin with the conquest or with independence, and what the role and importance of indigenous peoples should be in the constitution of contemporary Mexican identity.

While many intellectuals in search of Mexicanness have invoked the Indian as a part of Mexican national character, most Mexican literary histories in the twentieth century, at least until recently, followed the lead of Francisco Pimentel and dismissed pre-Columbian culture from consideration as literature altogether. Carlos González Peña, for example, whose *Historia de la literatura mexicana desde los orígenes hasta nuestros días* (*History of Mexican Literature*) has gone through several editions since it was first published in 1928, calls Mexican literature a "branch" of Spanish literature. He begins his story of Mexican literature with the arrival of the Europeans, and the first moment studied is that of evangelization described as the providential arrival of Spanish culture to transform an "indigenous Babel." The organic trope of literary history as a tree resolves the exclusion of those cultures originally inhabiting Mexico by locating continuity not in a territory, but in the Spanish language and cultural legacy.

And yet, returning to the nationalist political necessity for originality, what could that original element be that would differentiate the colony from Europe if not the indigenous presence in this place now called Mexico? The question for the nation-builders has thus been how to use this presence: How will the Indian be incorporated into the social body? How will the story of the indigenous past be part of the narrative of the body of the nation? A statement by José Luis Martínez in *De la naturaleza y carácter de la literatura mexicana* (On the Nature and Character of Mexican Literature; 1960) characterizes another response:

> Pre-Hispanic literature was the expression of various autochthonous peoples who would later form—together with those others that would populate Mexican territory—one of the constitutive branches of our nationality. But it could not have, either through language or through culture, any immediate continuity in following eras; the only relation that would remain alive was of a spiritual kind or one of emotional affinities, a kind of synchronism of the fatal rhythm of blood. (38)[2]

Inverting the trope, the indigenous past is called a branch of Mexican nationality, while the metaphor of "blood" takes up another figure widely used to define Mexican identity: the Mexican as mestizo offspring of the sexual union— at times seen as marriage, at others as rape—between the Spanish father and the Indian mother. This alternative to the Hispanist exclusion of the indigenous posits collective identity as *mestizaje,* as cultural synthesis, but still locates pre-Columbian cultural expression outside Mexican literary history. And if the metaphor of Mexican culture as evolutionary tree acts to suppress the contemporary indigenous presence from the official story, these metaphors of consanguinity leave the same problem unresolved, that of the persistence of an indigenous cultural presence that is an alternative to the official national culture (Bonfil, 133–145).

In the last generation Mexican literary histories (and their more overtly didactic counterparts, school textbooks) are marked by another ideological shift. Pre-Columbian cultures are now regularly included in the story of national literature, and the trajectory of Mexican literature is now contextualized in its relation to Latin American literature. The reevaluation of the place of pre-Columbian cultures in literary history arises from two projects which are not necessarily in harmony with each other. One is the utopian desire for cultural synthesis given most vivid expression in José Martí's manifesto "Nuestra América" (Our America; 1891). For Martí, the study of the entire range of Latin American literature has an important role to play in the construction of collective identity: "The European university must give way to the American university. The history of America, from the Incas to now, must be taught to the letter, even if we don't teach that of the Greek archons. Our Greece is preferable to a Greece that is not ours. It is more necessary to us" (29). The new way of locating pre-Columbian culture in the story of Mexican national culture also stems from a more recent, radical critique of this century's social policies of assimilationist indigenism and a healthy suspicion of a nationalism that seems to require the disappearance of indigenous culture in the name of a mestizo Mexican identity (Warman et al.; Barre).

Creole colonial scholars and nineteeth-century literary historians wrote from the perspective of nonindigenous people, and their various ways of constituting the indigenous as object are clearly in the service of political agendas not elaborated by indigenous people from their own point of view. Theirs are not the stories that indigenous peoples have told about themselves, either then or now. But how can we know what those stories were?

One pre-Columbian story of origins, recorded after the conquest by chroniclers like Fray Diego Durán, was the Mexicas' own story of who they were and where they came from. According to their official history, the Mexica came out of their place of origin, Aztlán, and were led by their priests and their principal god, Huitzilopochtli, to the place where they would found Tenochtitlán, the seat of their divinely proclaimed empire. However, another version of this history has been pieced together from other surviving accounts and material artifacts. In this version, the one told today by historians and anthropologists, the Mexica were the latest in a series of waves of Nahuatl-speaking peoples to come down from the north to settle in central Mexico. Seen as rude and barbaric by the city dwellers who continued the legacy of the Toltec empire, they were allowed to settle in an undesirable swamp where they served as mercenaries to other cities as they assimilated that culture, eventually growing in power to become the rulers of a great empire (Caso, *The Aztecs,* 93–94; Keen, 3–48). The Mexica, like the Spaniards later, were expansionist and imperialist; they destroyed earlier records in order to present a version of history that glorified their origins and justified their practices of war and human sacrifice with a story of divinely guided foundation (Anderson and Dibble, 165). One of the tasks facing scholars of Mexican literature today is to try to reconstruct—often in what can only be an effort of the imagination—how Mesoamerican peoples before the arrival of European invaders told stories about themselves and their world and how they understood these stories and other acts of verbal creation. To do so we must sort out how their words have been not only transmitted, but also suppressed, lost, or transformed in the texts of the new empire and the Mexican state.

II

What *can* we mean by "pre-Columbian literature of Mexico?" We must examine some assumptions about writing and literacy, as well as the terms that make up such a category. The Spaniards named all of the peoples they encountered "Indians," uniting with this name a number of separate societies with different languages and cultures engaged in power struggles of their own. The terms *pre-Hispanic* or *pre-Columbian* perform a similar gesture for they constitute an identity retrospectively; knowledge of the existence of indigenous cultures passes through the lens of the conquest, the moment identified as foundational. The same can be said of the use of the name *Mexico* since national boundaries do not coincide with precolonial territories. For this reason many prefer to use the name *Mesoamerica* to designate the region occupied by ancient indigenous cultures because it includes the southern territories of the Maya in Central America as well as Mexico. Retaining the names *pre-Columbian* and *Mexico,* however, reminds us of the lens of nationalism through which literary historians have viewed these cultures.

A trickier problem is just exactly what it is we are going to call literature in cultures that did not have alphabetic forms of writing. Our modern generic assumptions about literature must be reexamined when we turn our attention to the texts, signs, and images that transmit the knowledge and heritage of Mesoamerican peoples. The idea of literature as a certain class of written texts already depends on culturally specific assumptions such as, for example, the differentiation of the written from the oral and of works deemed to have a primarily aesthetic function from other kinds of writing. These categories are already unsatisfactory when we are dealing with the colonial period and works such as Hernán Cortés's *Cartas de relación* (Letters of Account), written 1519–1526, or Fray Bernardino de Sahagún's *Historia general de las cosas de Nueva España* (*General History of the Things of New Spain*), the revised Spanish version of the Nahuatl texts of the Florentine Codex: neither of these colonial texts was written for primarily aesthetic purposes, and Sahagún's work, because of its incorporation of the oral traditions of the Nahuatl-speaking people of central Mexico, challenges the distinction between written and oral. Another assumption that must be set aside is the idea of an evolutionary scale of literacy and literature that reinforces Eurocentric (and often racist) notions of cultural superiority. A crucial difference between literary history and anthropology as disciplines is that literary history traditionally takes as its object a certain class of texts examined for their aesthetic functions and presumed to belong to a unified, evolving culture. Anthropology, on the other hand, has been historically the study by Westerners of "other" cultures, cultures of the past, or contemporary "preliterate" or "primitive" cultures. To take pre-Columbian verbal expression as the object of literary history is an inclusive gesture, but we should be wary of the many presuppositions that accompany it.

Miguel León-Portilla, one of the most important scholars in the field of pre-

Columbian culture and literature in particular, has defined his object of study as "the ancient and new word of Mesoamerican man" and as "the transmission of the word" ("La palabra antigua"; 345). In fact, orality was central to pre-Columbian verbal creation, and the oral traditions of contemporary indigenous cultures in Mexico are now being recognized as an important part of our understanding of those processes (Tedlock; Burns). Those who study "the transmission of the word" from pre-Columbian peoples must become familiar with the work being done in many disciplines toward reconstructing indigenous social systems, history, institutions, and practices. The resources of art history, archaeology, linguistics, anthropology, and historiography, as well as the skills of reading and interpretation that come from the study of modern texts, are being applied to any traces of those civilizations: monuments and artifacts, inscriptions, statues, paintings, pottery, books, and the collective memory passed down in the oral history and practices of the descendants of these peoples.

Studying pre-Columbian texts—both those books produced before the conquest and postconquest texts that contain transcriptions or traces of pre-Columbian verbal creation—as objects of a literary history, as opposed to anthropology, means a shift from treating texts as documents of a non-European culture's history and institutions to taking them as aesthetic objects and privileging a focus on how they manifest the ideas and values of that culture, including ideas about art and verbal creation. Moreover, by looking at them as "literature," and as part of Mexican literature, we can both extend and reevaluate the Mexican tradition of representations of pre-Columbian cultures as "Other" and as "ours."[3]

III

The earliest evidence of writing in Mesoamerica that we have available to us today dates back to 600 B.C. Inscriptions in and near Monte Albán in the state of Oaxaca contain glyphs that attest to a writing system already in existence by that time. Although many of these Zapotec glyphs have yet to be deciphered, the inscriptions accompany figures formerly called "los danzantes" (the dancers) but now thought to be images of slain captives; many appear to narrate the triumphs of the rulers of Monte Albán (Marcus, 44–45). The importance of the relation of image to text will be constant in Mesoamerican writing.

Joyce Marcus describes the four major writing systems in ancient Mesoamerica. The earliest are the Zapotec and the Mayan, in use between 600 B.C. and around 900 A.D.; they survive primarily in the form of inscriptions on stone, ceramic, or bone. Only three, perhaps four, of the Mayan paper books known as codices are known to have survived. The Mixtec and Mexica writing systems, in use mainly in the Post-Classic period (around 900–1600 A.D.), are also found in inscriptions but survive in a larger number of these pictorial-glyphic codices (36–37).

The Mesoamerican cultures that used writing were sedentary, agricultural, and increasingly urban. A laboring class supported a class of nobles and priests, and literacy was the province of the elite. Groups of intellectual specialists, often priests, maintained and transmitted the knowledge and traditions of their people through the use of writing in combination with the systematic preservation of an orally transmitted corpus. Spanish observers such as Bernal Díaz del Castillo and Fray Toribio de Benavente (also known as Motolinia) describe schools where such learning took place. They also testify to the existence of libraries, called *amoxcalli* in Nahuatl, or "houses of books," which were all destroyed with the conquest.

The emergence of writing and of the calendar in Mesoamerica are closely related. The bar-and-dot numbering system common throughout Mesoamerica is vigesimal, based on twenty rather than ten as in our decimal system. The glyphs used for the day-names, months, and years, signs that take different forms in various Mesoamerican cultures, are part of the earliest inscriptions and an integral part of each of the different writing systems. At first it was believed that Mesoamerican writing was mainly used to convey myths or astrological-prophetic knowledge, but we now know that many of the texts on monuments and in books in fact relate history, the deeds of people as well as the gods. Joyce Marcus points out that while the earliest writing in the Old World seems to have had an economic function, in the New World writing was an instrument of political legitimation: "A major theme of early Mesoamerican writing seems to have been the presentation of political knowledge in calendrical form" (43). In this capacity, writing—whether in books or on public monuments—did more than record; it was a necessary part of the ritual performance that ordered the world. "Writing was a sacred proposition that had the capacity to capture the order of the cosmos, to inform history, to give form to ritual, and to transform the profane material of everyday life into the supernatural" (Schele and Freidel, 55).

What distinguishes forms of writing from other sign systems used to communicate information is some relationship to spoken language. Marcus characterizes a sign system as writing when it displays the following criteria: it is recognizable by its format, has some kind of linearity that orders reading, bears some relation to the spoken language, and uses a limited number of conventional signs (38–39). At least four kinds of writing are distinguished by scholars (whether or not these can be considered chronological phases is debatable). In pictographic systems, an image of a thing stands for that thing; for example, a circle can be used to represent the sun. In ideographic writing, that image can stand for an idea or even a word, as when the sun sign is used to represent the ideas of "day" or "light" or the word *day* itself. In phonetic writing, signs are used to represent syllables. This kind of system is language specific (Marcus, 38). The fourth type of writing, which was not a part of Mesoamerican scripts but was introduced by the Spaniards, is alphabetical writing in which a sign represents a sound—a vowel or a consonant. Mesoamerican writing systems were heterogeneous; that is, they combined the use of pictographic, ideographic, and phonetic signs. They also, as already mentioned, most often incorporated a relation to an image and relied on the knowledge of a carefully preserved oral tradition to complete the reading process. The fact that the same sign could be used as pictographic, ideographic, or phonetic, depending on context and convention, makes attempts to read these texts more difficult. "Literacy" in these systems assumes more than knowledge of the signs themselves; it also requires the conventions necessary to read these signs (Mignolo, 65).

The latest breakthrough in deciphering Mayan writing, held by many to be the most sophisticated because it is capable of representing all elements of a Mayan language, came about when inscriptions were taken not as codes to be broken but as texts whose meaning depends on shared knowledge that may not be represented in the text itself. Using techniques of discourse analysis that consider both the linguistic conventions of Mayan languages and the relation of texts to the images they accompany, scholars are now making rapid progress in reading Mayan inscriptions (Schele and Freidel; Ayala Falcón).

This approach makes sense because it has long been known that the images and glyphs in inscriptions or books were used as keys to the recitation of an oral tradition transmitted by systematic memorization in schools and temples, especially in the central Mexican Nahua cultures. For the ancient Mesoamericans, the transmission of the word through written texts went hand-in-hand with careful fostering of oral traditions of history, ritual, astronomy, prophecy, poetry, and narratives of the deeds of gods and humans. Reading was also a performance, a recitation keyed to the visual suite of a text that combined images and written signs that were themselves an integration of word and image (Coe, *The Maya*, 178–187). Writing and painting were thus not separate forms of signification in Mesoamerica. A Nahuatl song gives a graceful image of the act of reading:

> I sing the pictures of the book
> and see them spread out;
> I am an elegant bird
> for I make the codices speak
> within the house of pictures.
>   (León-Portilla, *Pre-Columbian Literatures*, 11)

If we were to define pre-Columbian literatures of Mexico only in terms of written texts produced before the conquest, then the inscriptions and the codices—the objects themselves—are those texts. Yet clearly they are only a part of the practice of "the transmission of the word." Much of what survives in written form of the accompanying oral tradition—and especially the kinds of compositions we most readily identify as "literary" such as the songs and poetry, the tales, legends, and history of pre-Columbian peoples—is recorded in alphabetical writing in texts produced after the arrival of the Spaniards. We will consider later some of the questions raised by these hybrid texts, but first let us turn our attention to the codices themselves.

IV

Many of the Spanish chroniclers, beginning with Cortés, mention the presence of books among both the Maya and the Mexica; most of these were destroyed when their cities were burned or razed by their conquerors. Zealous priests such as Fray Juan de Zumárraga and Diego de Landa, later to be named bishop of Yucatán, gathered and burned codices as dangerous instruments of heretical beliefs. It is a terrible irony that the same man who destroyed so many of the Maya's own texts should also prove to be one of our principal sources of knowledge about Mayan cultures and tradition: Landa's book *Relación de las cosas de Yucatán* (Relation of Things in Yucatan), where he sets down what he observed and what was told to him by "native informants," is a graphic illustration of why most of what we know of Mesoamerican culture through texts has to be filtered through acts of destruction and appropriation of indigenous discourses for other purposes.[4]

The term *codex* actually refers to a manuscript sewn up along one edge and is thus not completely accurate as a name for surviving Mesoamerican texts which have different forms, but its use since the nineteenth century has come to signify the painted books themselves (Gutiérrez Solana, 8). Surviving codices were first collected and studied by missionaries in New Spain during the sixteenth century, and later generations of colonial scholars were able to consult them as well, but most were dispersed and lost from sight until the nineteenth century. They first came to the attention of the general public in Europe through the work of Alexander von Humboldt, whose thirty-volume work included reproductions of pages from codices (Gutiérrez Solana, 46). Most of the remaining pre-Columbian codices are now to be found in libraries and collections outside of Mexico and Guatemala. It is another irony that these books bear the names of European libraries or owners, names that have nothing to do with their content (Sten).

Of the almost five hundred codices known to exist, only fourteen are considered pre-Hispanic. The rest were made after the conquest, primarily in the sixteenth century (Aguilera, 12–13). The classification scheme elaborated by John B. Glass in the *Handbook of Middle American Indians* groups the codices by theme.[5] One group is primarily concerned with religious practices, the calendar, divination, ceremonies, and the representation of the gods, while another set has historical themes. A third type contains genealogical records, many of them made after the conquest to defend hereditary rights such as those of the descendents of Cuauhtémoc, the last Aztec king. Maps, a fourth category, can also contain historical or genealogical information, as do those codices that primarily treat economic matters. Finally, some of the codices elaborated after the conquest under the direction of the Spanish missionaries can be thought of as ethnographic records.

Codices are painted on three kinds of material: animal skins, paper made from bark or plant fibers, and, in the case of a postconquest codex, cloth. The paper, called *amate* in Nahuatl, was made of bark soaked and pounded flat into sheets, then covered with a lime solution to give it a smooth surface. Paper was used in rituals and was an important item of trade and tribute; instruments for making paper have been found that date back to the first century B.C. (Aguilera, 11). Many of the codices are accordion-pleated in what is called a screenfold and are often painted on both sides. This means that when they are unfolded the reader can either see many of the pages at once or even fold them so as to place images from different parts of the text next to each other, something that is impossible to do with the modern bound book.

Images and glyphs were painted with brushes and colors made from earth pigments. The wealth of detail and the skill displayed in the painting make it clear that the artists must have been selected and especially trained in their art. As many of the codices preserve ritual iconography, these painters must also have possessed specialized knowledge of rituals and the significance of the details and the colors they used.[6]

The Mesoamerican calendar is a signifying system in and of itself that forms the basis of the sign systems used in codices and also structures their content and that of later texts such as the Books of Chilam Balam and the Popol Vuh. More accurate than the Gregorian calendar in use in Europe at the time, the Mesoamerican calendar combines two forms of reckoning the year: a solar year and a ritual year. The solar year has 365 days: eighteen months of twenty days each give a total of 360 days, with five days left over that were considered a period of bad luck. The ritual year of 260 days was called the day-count (*tzolk'in* in Maya and *tonalpohualli* in Nahuatl) and combined thirteen number signs and twenty signs called day-names to give 260 different possible combinations of signs. Because each of these signs and their various combinations had meanings that were associated with a particular god or kind of luck, the calendars were used as tools of divination and prophecy. The signs for a person's birthday were thus extremely important and were one of that person's names. The solar calendar and the day-count calendar were geared together to reckon the days over periods longer than a year, such as the Mayan *katun* of twenty years or the cycle of fifty-two years. The Mayas had evolved a long-count that was extremely elaborate; they had the concept of zero and had fixed a date of origin for their calendar. The sophisticated astronomy of the Meso-americans allowed them to calculate the cycles of Venus and the moon as well.

Only three Mayan codices survived the Conquest and Landa's pyre. The three are the Dresden Codex, the Paris Codex (also called the Peresiano), and the Madrid Codex (which survives in two pieces known as the Troano and the Cortesiano). The Grolier Codex has not yet been authenticated. All three are screen folds made of bark paper, painted primarily in red and black, unlike the more colorful codices of the central highlands. All present aspects of the ritual calendar, providing material for the all-important divination that linked the social world with the supernatural.[7]

The Dresden Codex, made some time around the thirteenth century, appears to be a copy of an older book. It displays the styles of at least eight different artists. Eric Thompson classifies its contents as almanac-calendrical images, the tables of the cycle of Venus, calculations of eclipses, and the prophecies for years and *katuns* (twenty-year units). Because the codices were "read" when the images and script were used to provide the basis or the thread for the recitation of the oral tradition, the images themselves tell only part of the story. The Books of Chilam Balam, a group of parallel and overlapping texts written down separately in several Mayan towns after the conquest and in Mayan languages but using the Latin script, record part of the oral tradition correlated with the Mayan codices (Alvarez).

Pre-Columbian codices of other cultures have also survived. The five codices of the Borgia group from the central highlands—Puebla, Oaxaca, Tlaxcala—date from the Late Post-Classic period (c. 1200–1300 A.D.) before the Mexica came to dominate the region.[8] All are screen folds painted on animal skins, and all are related to the *tonalpohualli,* the 260-day calendar used for divination. The thirty-nine pages of the Borgia Codex are painted on both sides; all sections but one present calendar images and predictions.

The creation stories of both Mayan- and Nahuatl-speaking peoples attribute the origin of all things, including the gods, to a dual creator force or spirit called "our mother, our father." Duality was an important part of Mesoamerican religions. The gods could have many aspects or could be aspects of other things, and the representations of deities in the codices convey this multiplicity. The signs for the days and images of their reigning gods along with the appropriate rituals and sacrifices are represented in incredible pictorial detail: the twenty day-signs, the nine lords of night, the phases of Venus (Quetzalcoatl in his form as the evening star), the cycles of agriculture, and the six regions of the world (the four cardinal points plus up and down). The one exception is a sequence of fantastic images that may represent rituals of human sacrifice or dreams, perhaps even hallucinations. The principal deity in this sequence is the Toltec god Tezcatlipoca, or Smoking Mirror, always recognizable because his missing left foot is replaced by the mirror of his name.

Thirteen Mixtec codices from the region west of Oaxaca came to be considered as a group when it was discovered that they contained not divinatory explanations but rather historical or genealogical narratives: the births, deaths, marriages, wars, and conquests that relate the history of this region's people from the tenth century to the seventeenth century A.D. (after the conquest). The images are of great clarity and detail, with many more colors than the Mayan codices. As oral commentaries would have completed the readings of these texts, what we have in these codices is a kind of summary of this history.[9] J. Cooper Clark showed that many of the Mixtec codices contain stories about an important Mixtec ruler named Eight Deer (the name is taken from the number and the day-sign of his birthday) who lived from 1011 to 1050 A.D.

Recent research in the state of Oaxaca involves collaboration with Mixtec speakers who are generating new understanding of these texts.

A later group of codices—the Bourbon Codex, the Tonalamatl de Aubin, the Magliabecchiano, and the Tira de la Peregrinación—were made around the time of the Spanish conquest but record the preconquest history of the Mexica; the Tira de Peregrinación (also called the Boturini Codex) gives the history of the Mexica from their perhaps mythical origins in Aztlán around the twelfth century to about 1355. The Bourbon Codex displays the gods, their attributes, and the rituals and festivals associated with them; the vision of the cosmos in these codices is very close to that represented in the Borgia group.

Another group of codices, postconquest because painted on European paper, would appear to be a series of copies of a text set down by an anonymous Mexica very shortly after the conquest (Boone). The surviving copies use the indigenous style of representation with images but also record in Latin script some of the oral commentary that would have accompanied them. The Magliabecchiano Codex, the best known of the group, displays images of ceremonial mantles used in festivals and presents the deities and ceremonies of the eighteen-month solar calendar, including the "four hundred" (numberless) gods of pulque. This hybrid text, a copy of a lost transcription, combines the two cultures' forms of signification and ways of seeing the world in a literal fashion; such texts can serve as points of departure for reflections on the process of cultural heterogeneity and synthesis that took place in centuries to follow as well.

V

The codices do not stand alone as the means of transmission of pre-Columbian knowledge. To understand and complete our interpretations of them we must turn to the oral traditions as they are preserved in texts produced after the conquest, whether as transcriptions or reconstructions of pre-Hispanic traditions or as ethnohistorical observations by Spaniards. The two cultures whose legacies have best survived in this fragmentary fashion are the Maya and the Nahuatl. One text from the Purepecha (Tarrascan) culture of Michoacán has been handed down to us; it was transcribed under the direction of a priest shortly after the particularly brutal conquest of the region, but it is not certain whether or not this people used books before the arrival of the Spaniards (Le Clézio).

In the face of the destruction of their sacred texts and the persecution of those who tried to preserve their people's ways, some Maya used their new instruction in European forms of literacy to write down and preserve their beliefs and traditions. Twenty-four Mayan languages are spoken today, and Mayan texts survive in five of them: Yucatec Maya, Quiché, Cakchiquel, Chontal, and Pokonchi. The Spanish missionaries who studied Mayan languages wrote grammars and dictionaries and invented a system for representing their sounds, thus unintentionally enabling Mayan writers to preserve their heritage secretly in texts written in their languages but using the Latin alphabet. In these new kinds of texts they brought together the knowledge handed down through the codices themselves and the oral tradition that was their necessary complement. These postconquest texts almost always combine many different kinds of material; many of them present myths, history, maps, and genealogies together because they were written to preserve the claims of a community to a particular territory.

Literatura maya (Mayan Literature) is a critical anthology that assembles the most important Mayan texts recorded after the conquest. It is worth reviewing the criteria that editor Mercedes de la Garza presents concerning her selection of texts, for it brings us back to the question of what we might identify as Mayan literature or Mesoamerican literature in general. Interestingly enough, Garza classifies the pre-Hispanic codices as archeological material rather than literature because, although they are the only texts actually elaborated before the conquest, our ability to "read" them is still limited by the as yet partial decipherment of Mayan glyphs. Instead she classifies as Mayan literature only texts written by the Maya in their languages using alphabetic script and containing knowledge and traditions from before the conquest, acknowledging the fact that these texts do display varying degrees of Spanish or Western influence. She thus specifically excludes texts in Mayan languages whose content is not indigenous, such as sermons, catechisms, and other texts written to serve the administrative and proselytizing purposes of the conquerors; she also excludes chronicles written by Spaniards for whatever reason, although the material in these texts may be invaluable as secondary sources on the historical and social context of Mayan texts. Finally, she does not include ethnographic material collected in the last two centuries, except where it clearly shows elements that have survived from ancient Mayan culture. Those documents whose function was primarily legal—titles and claims—may have information of value but are not considered of interest to us as literature.

Another way to approach the issue of what constitutes pre-Columbian verbal art when most of the legible texts were elaborated after the conquest is to think about current Mayan verbal practices. In his discussion of "kinds of speech" in Mayan oral performance today, Allen Burns points out that these often represent performance "across cultural boundaries" (17) whereas texts transmitting pre-Columbian Mayan words represent Maya talking/writing among themselves.

The most important surviving Mayan texts are the Popol Vuh, the Books of Chilam Balam, and the Annals of the Cakchiquel. The language used in these texts is poetic and formulaic, but their main function is narrative. They tell stories of the creation of the universe, of the origins of human beings from corn and other tales that express the Mayan cosmovision; they also reveal a foundation of beliefs shared with other Mesoamerican cultures such as the dual nature of a supreme creator, the four (or five) successive ages of creation, and the important figure of Quetzalcóatl (Kukulkán to the Maya) as both god and culture-hero from the time of the Toltecs.

The desire to record their history and preserve their culture in the aftermath of the conquest motivated their writing down of many Mayan texts, but this effort must be understood as a continuation of a rich practice of recording history and understanding the future. The parallels and congruencies between the many Mayan texts of historical nature have allowed scholars to piece together the history of the Post-Classic Maya. Genealogies are an important part of these histories, even those not directly related to establishing legal claims, and genealogy appears to have been an important branch of knowledge for the priests before the conquest; the history of the people was the history of the rulers.

The highly symbolic language used in these myths, tales, and prophecies relies on metaphors drawn from nature to express ideas. Mayan expression is dominated by natural images, leaving us with a vision of the world based on the union of human beings with their environment. The intimate relation of the plastic arts with the word is also conveyed in images drawn from the natural world.

Some of the most notable characteristics of pre-Columbian verbal art, as recorded in Maya, Nahuatl, or other indigenous languages, arise from the oral and performative nature of this discourse. The Mayan delight in riddles and wordplay, still a part of their everyday speech, is evident in the visual punning of pre-Columbian writing as well (Roys, *The Book of Chilam Balam of Chumayel,* 73, 125; Burns, 226). The Books of Chilam Balam is a group of seventeen similar books which receive their individual names from the towns where they were found. Like the better-known Popol Vuh, these books survived underground as the Maya sought to preserve their culture in the face of oppression. The first one may have been written in Maní, but one of the best known is the Book of Chilam Balam of Chumayel. Chilam Balam is the name of a priest (*chilam,* priest; *balam,* jaguar) whose prophecies shortly before the arrival of the Spaniards were said to have predicted the arrival of strangers and a new religion. These texts, many of which repeat the same material, are compilations of myths, rituals, sacred hymns, prophecies, and chronologies related to the Mayan calendar, astronomy, and historical relations. In his studies of contemporary Mayan oral narrative Allen Burns has shown that for the Maya speech and communication are conceived of as dialogic; any act of tale telling involves the active participation of others in addition to the primary narrator. In public readings of the Chilam Balam, still performed annually in some towns, it is significant that the text is read by at least two people. The book is integrated into a tradition of performance and cultural memory that makes it an important instrument of maintaining cultural identity (Burns, 23, 71–72).

The Anales de los Cakquiqueles (the Annals of the Cakchiquel, also called the Memorial de Sololá, Memorial de Tecpán-Atitlán, and Anales de los Xahil de los indios Cakchiqueles) was written down in Sololá, Guatemala, around the end of sixteenth century by the descendants of the Xahil lineage of Cakchiquel kings. Several members of the family contributed to it over the years in a collective historical enterprise.

While the Books of Chilam Balam and the Anales de los Cakchiqueles are "compilations" or anthologies of fragments of a diverse nature, the Popol Vuh is a unified text, apparently set down by indigenous authors in the 1550s (Tedlock, 59–62). More than a transcription, it is an artistic composition telling the history of the Quiché Maya from the beginning of creation itself. The Quiché manuscript was seen by Fray Ximénez around 1701–1703, who copied it and translated it into Spanish. Also known as the Libro de consejo (Book of Counsel), it includes stories of the creation of the cosmos and of human beings and the deeds of the hero-twins Hunahpú and Ixbalanqué. It then relates the history of the Quiché people: their origins, migrations, cities, and rulers, their beliefs and social organization, and their conquest by the Spaniards and important events after it. Dennis Tedlock's translation of the Popol Vuh into English is the result of his apprenticeship and collaboration with a Quiché Mayan daykeeper (diviner, custodian of custom and ritual) in Momostenango, Guatemala. This man, Andrés Xiloj Peruch, read the text with Tedlock and taught him how to interpret it through Mayan forms of knowledge.

A few examples of other genres of pre-Columbian Mayan verbal art have survived in manuscript form. The most important collection of Mayan song and poetry is the Cantares de Dzitbalché (Songs of Dzitbalché), copied in the eighteenth century in the town of Dzitbalché in Campeche. It is a collection of songs of different types, some religious, some used in ritual dances or curing ceremonies, others of a more lyrical nature. The language of these songs is simpler than that of the myths and prophecies but maintains the use of parallelism, repetition, and variation that is such a striking feature of Mesoamerican verbal art. Names, ideas, or verses are often repeated in a different form, usually in pairs but sometimes in threes as well, with an extraordinarily rich range of effects. The repetition can be formulaic, as of the names of gods or rulers; at other times it gives another view or aspect of a thing. Sometimes the effect is of the rhythmic accumulation of details. In their study of variants of Nahuatl song-poems Frances Kartunnen and James Lockhart observe how the use of repetition and variation orders the compositions themselves:

> Nahuatl poems of the kind seen in the Cantares and Romances, then, are accretions of a number of verse units, arranged in more or less symmetrical patterns. The rearrangement of the order of verses in variants is one clue to an important aspect of the structure that can also be seen through direct inspection: most Nahuatl poems are not built hierarchically; they do not have a line of logical or narrative development in which each verse is the necessary antecedent of the next. Rather, it is as though the verses were arranged around a center—a theme, mood, character, or all of these—to which they relate directly in a comparable way, rather than to each other, so that the order of the verses is far less important than their relevance to a common theme and their pleasingly symmetrical arrangement. (2)

The Rabinal Achí is the best-known (if perhaps not the only) surviving example of what was a rich pre-Columbian Mayan tradition of ritual drama that involved song, dance, masks, and costumes (Acuña). Ritual drama is still a very important part of Mayan culture, but the forms it takes today are the products of cultural syncretism or transculturation (Bricker). Transmitted orally before being transcribed in Quiché in 1850, this work was still performed in 1856 in the village of San Pablo de Rabinal in Guatemala. The drama, also called the Baile del tun (The Dance of Tun), represents the ritual sacrifice of a Quiché warrior by the people of Rabinal. Like the Popol Vuh, it is a unified work. Abundant repetition and highly elaborate formulaic language make it rather monotonous to read, but it is of great dramatic and poetic force nonetheless. Ritual drama was also an important part of Nahuatl culture, as observed by Fray Diego Durán. As well as specifically ritual drama, he reports public comic entertainments that involved dialogue, masks, and acrobatics; unfortunately, only fragments of one such farce survive in the Cantares mexicanos (Songs of the Mexica).

VI

Much more of the pre-Columbian Nahuatl culture survived the destruction of the conquest because more immediate efforts were made to preserve it. This process began in 1528–1530 when, with the collaboration of the first twelve Franciscans to arrive after the conquest, some Mexica intellectuals or scholars recorded some of their commentaries in the Anales de Tlatelolco (Annals of Tlatelolco). This work contains the genealogies of ruling families in various cities, an account of the conquest, and some songs and poems. Many such chronicles would be written during the colonial period with varying degrees of collaboration with indigenous sources.

It is to Fray Bernardino de Sahagún that we owe the preservation of much of the Nahuatl legacy. Aided by students from the Colegio de Santa Cruz de Tlatelolco, the school where sons of native nobility were educated in the European subjects of rhetoric, grammar, logic, mathematics, geometry, music, astronomy, and theology, Sahagún set out to interview those whose memories preserved the oral history of their people; he was also able to consult the surviving codices. He describes his systematic compilation of material, a process that involved extensive interviews in a number of different towns over a period of decades. The material was transcribed in Nahuatl, edited and translated into Spanish, and illustrated with images drawn from the cultural repertory of pre-Columbian manuscripts. The original Nahuatl material was shaped into what is now called the Florentine Codex and later rewritten in Spanish by Sahagún as the *Historia general*. The material covered in the twelve books ranges from accounts of the gods and creation to descriptions of plants and animals; Sahagún's informants related to him the divine and moral order of Mexica society, ending with narrations of the Spanish conquest.[10]

The colonial genre of "indigenous chronicles," texts written by Nahuatl speakers such as Fernando Alvarado Tezozómoc, Chimalpahin Cuautelhuanitzin, and Fernando de Alva Ixlilxóchitl, reproduce (with varying degrees of internalization of a Europeanized perspective) much of the pre-Hispanic history and form of history telling. These writers also defend, albeit in a restricted fashion, the value of their ancestors' culture and history. While these texts expand our knowledge of pre-Columbian values and conventions and may contain embedded in them transcriptions or translations of Nahuatl verbal art, they represent writing across cultural boundaries, and it is often difficult to distinguish the pre-Columbian elements from the matrix. But such efforts provide a welcome corrective to constructions of Mexican history and letters from a Eurocentric perspective: Miguel León-Portilla's book *El reverso de la conquista* (The Other Side of the Conquest) draws on material gleaned from Nahuatl and Mayan texts to give a narrative of the conquest in the words of the vanquished.

In *Literaturas de Mesoamérica* (1984), León-Portilla distinguishes two main genres of Nahuatl expression: the *cuícatl* (song, hymn, poem) and the *tlahtolli* ("words," discourses, relations, history, speeches). He describes the *cuícatl* as works of inspiration, sentiment, and memories that were probably accompanied by music.[11] In some of the transcriptions of these songs, syllables are included that may be indications of the notes and rhythm or perhaps the tones of the musical accompaniment. One of Sor Juana's *villancicos* (carols) calls this type of song a "tocotín sonoro" and contains a Nahuatl example.

In their manuscript form these songs are not arranged in verse, but marked by "unities of expression" like exclamations, indentations, or signs that indicate a new paragraph. One issue when translating them into European languages is the temptation to arrange texts recorded in continuous paragraphs into verses, strophes, or other units. When Angel María Garibay K. translated Nahuatl poems into Spanish, his distribution of the words into verses followed the strong parallelisms of ideas and sentences that is such a striking feature of Mesoamerican expression.

Teocuícatl are the divine hymns that were accompanied by music and were sung in festivals to give thanks to and praise the gods. One group of twenty hymns is preserved in Sahagún's early manuscript, the Códice Matritense de la Real Academia de la Historia (Madrid Codex of the Royal Academy of History). Because of their archaic language, it is believed that some of these songs survive from the earlier Toltec era and that one may even be from as early as the time of Teotihuacán (urban apogee ca. 350–650 A.D.).

Other *cuícatl* take up themes such as the joy of spring and of being alive; there are songs of flowers and friendship, of warriors and glory, and philosophical poems that include speculation on death and the transitory nature of life (often in the form of questions). In the manuscripts many of these compositions are anonymous, but authors are named for some of them. The most famous Nahuatl poet was the king of Tezcoco, Nezahualcóyotl (1402–1472). When his father was killed, he had to fight to regain his throne. Crowned in 1431, he entered into the Triple Alliance with Tenochtitlán, the alliance that enabled the Mexica to expand their empire to the extent encountered by the Spaniards. Nezahualcóyotl's forty-year reign was a time of great achievements

in architecture, engineering, laws, and art. Thirty of his songs survive, many
of them on the transitory nature of life and the inevitability of death; one song
recorded in the Cantares mexicanos asserts the hope that through poetry,
something of his presence might survive:

> They shall not wither, my flowers,
> they shall not cease, my songs.
> I, the singer, lift them up.
> They are scattered, they spread about.
> Even though on earth my flowers
> may wither and yellow,
> they will be carried there,
> to the innermost house
> of the bird with the golden feathers.
>
> (In León-Portilla, *Pre-Columbian Literatures*, 89)

Aquiauhtzin (born around 1430) has two poems attributed to him, one an
erotic composition, the other from the "dialogue of flower and song" held
around 1490. A "dialogue of flower and song" was a gathering of poets who
performed compositions inquiring into the nature of poetry itself. David Carrasco tells us that the Nahua poet-philosophers of the elite, the *tlamatinime*
(knowers of things), sought through their poetic inquiry to link the human
personality with the divine. The essential duality of the cosmos was given form
in the technique called *difrasismo*, in which a pair of metaphors is used to
designate a third term: *in xochitl, in cuícatl*, flower and song, mean poetry or
truth (80–81).

The other major category of Nahuatl discourse described by León-Portilla
is the *tlahtolli*, which he defines as expression that does not spring from inspiration but rather from various kinds of systematic inquiry. While meter was
sometimes indicated, music does not seem to have accompanied this type of
expression as is the case with the *cuícatl*. One significant genre is the *huehueh-
tlahtolli*, or "words of the ancients." Sahagún and Fray Andrés de Olmos wrote
down many of these discourses, such as the instructions of parents to children
and other kinds of moral teachings and instructions, often pronounced at important occasions such as births, deaths, and marriages. Their language is very
refined and makes use of many forms of respect as well as the kind of metaphors also found in the *cuícatl*.[12]

Like song-poems, this type of discourse is also characterized by the use of
pairs of metaphors and parallelism. Especially frequent is the grouping of images in a scene or the piling up of verbal predicates on one subject. Rhythm
and repetition characterize orally transmitted stories as well as songs, as do
the use of many details, piling up of images to convey many aspects of a thing,
and the use of concrete images to signify abstract ideas and feelings. These
ancient words are a rich compendium of the ideas and values of the Mexica,

their notions of the place of the human body in the world, of sexuality, of love and affection for children, and of the proper way to be in the world.

VII

One of the major issues arising from the study of material written after the conquest is to what extent its content can be attributed to a pre-Columbian worldview; some texts appear to be transcriptions or translations of orally transmitted material, such as of the commentary that accompanied codices or songs and poems performed in ceremonies or preserved by those specialists whose job it was to pass on the best compositions. But even these, like other texts written at a greater distance in time by mestizos or indigenous people educated in Christianity and the European traditions of the Colegio de Santa Cruz, manifest another kind of translation process: some would maintain that these texts are products of transculturation. This is a rich area for scholars to explore: How do we talk about "hybrid texts" and their "double-voiced discourse"? How do we represent their heterogeneity? What are the implications for the study of contemporary Latin American literature such as indigenist or testimonial writing?

Literary history is an instrument also used in the public schools for the formation of a national consciousness through the identification of the individual-as-citizen with a role in a story. In the case of Mexico, one part of this process has been that the indigenous peoples of Mesoamerica, constructed as "Indians," have been projected into a past, to be incorporated into the national story as part of a proudly claimed legacy while at the same time divorced from the living presence of indigenous cultures isolated and identified as underdeveloped, in need of assimilation into "national" culture. Indigenism is that complex set of ideas, institutions, and social and aesthetic practices through which the project of assimilation has been postulated and carried out in Mexico since the revolution. This current has had only limited success, however, and has been subject to harsh criticism, especially in recent years when it has been denounced as ethnocide. But indigenism also created the conditions of possibility for the radical critical posture that challenges an official nationalist discourse of identity by asserting the right of indigenous peoples to tell their own stories. It is in light of this critique but also of social and political movements by indigenous groups speaking and acting for themselves on the national and international level that we must reevaluate the place of indigenous culture in any story of national literature.

In a few areas the study of pre-Columbian literature can confront texts themselves directly: the codices, the inscriptions. But the problem of reading is already more than that of interpreting the signs themselves, for without knowledge of that necessary complement of oral commentary and the shared cultural discourses of a society, the interpretation of these texts remains tentative and approximate (Mignolo). As for those records we do have of pre-Columbian discourses, they are embedded in transcriptions into other sign

systems, other languages; they survive in faulty copies and approximate translations; they are transformed to a greater or lesser degree by other values and
discourses through which they are transmitted. Yet, they do survive, and pa-
tient and creative scholarly work along with the changes in our assumptions
about the study of texts and discourses have produced exciting results: new,
more accurate editions, translations, and facsimiles, as well as investigations
of the philosophy and aesthetic practices of these cultures on their own terms.
These efforts take place in the context of a growing participation of indigenous
peoples in movements for self-determination, social justice, and attempts to
make their own voices heard, to constitute their own identities through political organization, active resistance, and writing—efforts that cross national
boundaries and that present the challenge of new ways of imagining the national community in Mexico.

NOTES

1. Benjamin Keen reminds us that the term *Aztec* is perhaps not accurate but is
more generally recognized than *Mexica* (xvii).

2. Translation mine, as are all subsequent translations unless otherwise noted.

3. The need for such a critical stance is underscored by the debate surrounding
Tzvetan Todorov's book *La conquête de l'Amérique* 1982 (published in English in 1985
as *The Conquest of America*) which can be read as an unfortunate continuation of the
long Western tradition of constructing other cultures in terms of notions of Western
superiority and native "lack." In this case, Todorov posits the conquest as the result
not of particular historical circumstances such as military technology and Spanish alliance with rival indigenous powers, but rather of a deficient mode of signification
made manifest by the lack of a phonetic writing system. For a cogent critique of Todorov's book, see Deborah Root, "The Imperial Signifier: Todorov and the Conquest of
Mexico," *Critical Critique* 9 (Spring 1988): 197–219.

4. Landa wrote his book around 1570 while in Spain defending himself in an inquiry into his persecution of the Maya. See *Relación de las cosas de Yucatán*.

5. The Glass classification numbers are generally used as common reference points
by scholars studying the codices.

6. For detailed descriptions of the images of the most important groups of codices,
see Nelly Gutiérrez Solana, *Códices de México*. María Sten gives examples of color
symbolism.

7. For facsimile reproductions of the Mayan codices, see Thomas A. Lee, *Los códices mayas*.

8. The other four codices of this group are the Féjérváry-Mayer Codex (now in
Liverpool), the Laud Codex (in the Bodleian at Oxford), the Cospi (in Bologna), and
the Vaticanus B (in the Vatican, as is the Borgia Codex).

9. The Nuttall and Vindobonensis codices were finished before 1438; these may
have been the two codices Cortés sent to Carlos V in 1519. The Bodley Codex dates
from around 1519 and presents genealogies spanning seven centuries, while the Selden
Roll was made around 1546. The American anthropologist Zelia Nuttall provided the
key to reading this group around the end of the nineteenth century when she deter-

mined that they were historical relations. Alfonso Caso was later able to fix their origin and chronology through the use of a map whose place glyphs gave keys to some of the glyphs used in the codices.

10. Sahagún's original material is in Madrid and is known as the *Códices matritenses del Real Palacio y de la Real Academia de la historia* (The Madrid Codices of the Royal Palace and the Royal Academy of History). Some of Sahagún's indigenous students continued this project on their own. Their work includes the *Cuauhtitlán Annals,* an example of the type of commentary that accompanied the codices, including some songs and poems, while another is *Leyenda de los soles,* considered by Miguel León-Portilla to be one of the richest sources of Nahua thought and worldview.

11. Two important sources of Nahuatl poetry are the Colección de cantares mexicanos (Collection of Mexican Canticles), also known as *Cantares mexicanos,* which includes examples of various poetic genres, some anonymous and some attributed to authors; and *Romances de los Señores de la Nueva España* (Ballads of the Lords of New Spain; ed. Angel María Garibay K.), probably transcribed by the mestizo Juan de Pomar.

12. Other genres León-Portilla describes are the *teotlahtolli,* which have to do with the divine, the ages of creation, the origin of the fifth sun (the sun of movement); the *yeihuecauh tlahtolli,* or discourse on ancient things, stories, and legends; the *tlamachilliz-tlazolzazanilli,* or oral relations of "what is known," often mythological narrations; *ihtoloca,* or "that which is said about someone or something"; *in tonalli itlatlahtollo,* or divinatory revelations; *nahualli, tlahtolli,* or magical words and esoteric discourse.

BIBLIOGRAPHY

Acuña, René. *Introducción al estudio del Rabinal Achí.* Mexico City: Universidad Nacional Autónoma de México, Centro de Estudios Mayas, 1975. Provides social and historical context of Mayan dance drama, both pre-conquest and colonial, along with consideration of texts and music.

Aguilera, Carmen. *Códices del México antiguo.* Mexico City: Instituto Nacional de Antropología e Historia, 1979.

Alcina Franch, José. *Poesía americana precolombina.* Madrid: Editorial Prensa Española, 1968. Concise studies and anthology of lyric poetry in Maya, Nahuatl, and Quechua; bibliographies.

Alvarado Tezozómoc, Fernando. *Crónica mexicana.* Mexico City: Editorial Leyenda, 1944. Reprint of the 1878 edition of Manuel Orozco y Berra of a narrative of Mexica (Aztec) history written by a descendant of Mexican nobility.

———. *Crónica mexicana/Códice Ramírez.* Mexico City: Editorial Porrúa, 1975. Contains the 1878 editions of both the *Crónica mexicana* and an anonymous narrative of Aztec history known as the *Códice Ramírez.*

———. *Crónica mexicáyotl.* Trans. Adrián León. Mexico City: Universidad Nacional Autónoma de México, 1975.

Alvarez, María Cristina. *Textos coloniales del Libro de Chilam Balam de Chumayel y textos glíficos del Códice de Dresde.* Mexico City: Universidad Nacional Autónoma de México, 1974. Correlates the pre-Columbian glyphic text of the Mayan Dresden Codex with the oral tradition preserved in the Libro de Chilam Balam de Chumayel; for the specialist, but an excellent example of the work necessary to connect pictographic texts with transcriptions of oral tradition.

Anales de Tlatelolco (Annals of Tlatelolco). Ed. Heinrich Berlin. Mexico City: Editorial Porrúa, 1948.

Anderson, Arthur J. O., and Charles Dibble, ed. and trans. *General History of the Things of New Spain: Florentine Codex.* 12 vols. Salt Lake City: University of Utah, 1950–1953. Translation of the famous work by Fray Bernardino de Sahagún.

Annals of the Cakchiquels. Also known as *Memorial de Sololá, Memorial de Tecpan-Atitlán, Anales de los Xahil de los indios cakchiqueles.* See Brinton. For Spanish version, see Recinos, Anales de los Cakchiqueles.

Arias-Larreta, Abraham. *Literaturas aborígenes de América: Azteca, Incáica, Maya-Quiché.* Buenos Aires: Editorial Indoamérica, 1968. General introductory studies.

Asturias, Miguel Angel. *Poesía precolombina.* Buenos Aires: Compañía General Fabril Editora, 1960. Mostly Nahuatl, some Mayan, grouped according to four themes: the gods, their attributes, heroes, and humans.

Ayala Falcón, Maricela. *El fonetismo en la escritura maya.* Mexico City: Universidad Nacional Autónoma de México, 1985. An overview for the generalist on deciphering Mayan glyphs and the debate on phonetic elements; good introduction for situating more recent developments.

Azcue y Mancerra, Luis. *Códice Peresiano.* Mexico City: Editorial Orion, 1967. Study of one of the surviving Mayan glyphic texts, with drawings accompanied by detailed descriptions and explanations of images and glyphs; includes explanations of the calendar and chronological glyphs. Not to be confused with the Códice Pérez, a manuscript of one of the Books of Chilam Balam.

Barre, Marie Chantal. "Políticas indigenistas y reinvindicaciones indias en América Latina 1940–1980." In Bonfil et al., *América Latina: Etnodesarrollo y etnocidio,* ed. Francisco Rojas Aravena. San José, Costa Rica: Ediciones FLACSO, 39–82.

Barrera Vásquez, Alfredo, trans. and ed. *Códice de Calkiní.* Campeche: Biblioteca Campechana, 1957. Translation of a Mayan text similar to the Books of Chilam Balam.

———, trans. and ed. *El libro de los cantares de Dzitbalché.* Mexico City: Instituto Nacional de Antropología e Historia, 1965. This edition reproduces the Yucatec Mayan text of fifteen songs along with their Spanish translations. Reprinted in Garza, ed., *Literatura maya.*

Barrera Vásquez, Alfredo, and Sylvanus G. Morley. *The Maya Chronicles.* Publication 585. Washington, D.C.: Carnegie Institution of Washington, 1949.

Barrera Vásquez, Alfredo, and Sylvia Rendón, trans. and ed. *El libro de los libros de Chilam Balam.* 1948. Mexico City: Fondo de Cultura Económica, 1969. The introduction gives a history of the scholarship of this group of Mayan texts which preserved Mayan prophetic and historical traditions underground during the colonial period. The translations, accompanied by extensive notes, correlate versions of both history and prophecy that exist in more than one of the Books of Chilam Balam, providing a synthesis of the variants.

Benson, Elizabeth P., ed. *Dumbarton Oaks Conference on the Olmec, 1967.* Washington, D.C.: Dumbarton Oaks Research Library and Collection, 1968.

———, ed. *Mesoamerican Writing Systems: A Conference at Dumbarton Oaks, October 30th–31st.* Washington, D.C.: Dumbarton Oaks Research Library and Collection, 1978.

Bierhorst, John, trans. and ed. *Cantares mexicanos: Songs of the Aztecs.* Stanford: Stanford University Press, 1985. English translations of Nahuatl song and poetry.

Bonfil Batalla, Guillermo. "El etnodesarrollo: Sus premisas jurídicas, políticas y organizacionales." In Bonfil et al., *América Latina: Etnodesarrollo y etnocidio,* ed. Francisco Rojas Aravena. San José, Costa Rica: Ediciones FLACSO, 1982: 133–145.

Book of Chilam Balam of Chumayel. See Roys. For Spanish version, see Garza, ed., *Literatura maya.*

Boone, Elizabeth. *The Codex Magliabecchiano and the Lost Prototype of the Magliabecchiano Group.* Berkeley: University of California Press, 1983. Major study of the most important of a group of copies of a lost text painted by a Mexican artist between 1528 and 1553; the lost prototype was one of the earliest attempts to record Aztec religious beliefs and practices after the conquest. A new edition of the Nuttall facsimile of the Codex Magliabecchiano has been published in a separate volume.

Brading, D. A. *The Origins of Mexican Nationalism.* Cambridge: Centre for Latin American Studies, 1985.

Brasseur de Bourbourg, Charles Etienne. *Histoire des nations civilisées du Méxique et de l'Amérique Centrale.* 4 vols. Paris, 1857.

———, trans. and ed. *Popol Vuh: Le livre sacré et les mythes de l'antiquité américaine, avec les livres héroïques et historiques des Quichés.* Paris, 1861. Quiché text and French translation that first brought the Popol Vuh to the attention of European scholars.

Bricker, Victoria Reifler. *The Indian Christ, the Indian King: The Historical Substrate of Maya Myth and Ritual.* Austin: University of Texas Press, 1981.

Brinton, D. G., trans. and ed. *Library of Aboriginal American Literature,* 1882–1899. 8 vols. Philadelphia. Vol. 1, *The Maya Chronicles;* Vol. 6, *The Annals of the Cakchiquels;* Vol. 7, *Ancient Nahuatl Poetry,* earliest English translation of some of the Cantares mexicanos; Vol. 8, *Rig Veda americanus.*

Brotherston, Gordon. *Image of the New World: The American Continent Portrayed in Native Texts.* London: Thames and Hudson, 1979. An extremely valuable resource for the study of Native American cultures: texts and illustrations are drawn from indigenous cultures of all the Americas and include images from codices; chapters organized thematically rather than geographically around topics such as rituals, healing, the European invasion, calendars, etc.

Burns, Allen F., trans. and ed. *An Epoch of Miracles: Oral Literature of the Yucatec Maya.* Foreword by Dennis Tedlock. Austin: University of Texas Press, 1983. Study of contemporary oral culture of the Maya; considers the issues of cultural syncretism and the persistence of pre-Columbian elements.

Campa, Antonio R. de la, and Raquel Chang-Rodríguez. *Poesía hispanoamericana colonial: Historia y antología.* Madrid: Editorial Alhambra, 1985.

Cantares de Dzitbalché. See Barrera Vásquez. Reprinted in Garza, ed., *Literatura maya.*

Carrasco, David. *Religions of Mesoamerica.* San Francisco: Harper and Row, 1990. Excellent overview of Mesoamerican culture and beliefs; a good example of the "ensemble approach" to reading and interpreting Mesoamerican texts in conjunction with other kinds of evidence.

Caso, Alfonso. *The Aztecs: People of the Sun.* Trans. Lowell Dunham and illus. Miguel Covarrubias. Norman: University of Oklahoma Press, 1958.

———. *Los calendarios prehispánicos.* Mexico City: Universidad Nacional Autónoma de México, Instituto de Investigaciones Históricas, 1968.

———. "Un códice en Otomí." *Proceedings of the 23rd International Congress of Americanists,* 130–135. New York, 1928.

———. *Las estelas zapotecas.* Mexico City: Monografías del Museo Nacional, 1928. On stellae (carved stones) of Monte Albán. Earliest work on Zapotec writing by the anthropologist who excavated Monte Albán.

————. *El pueblo del sol: Figuras de Miguel Covarrubias.* 2d ed. Mexico City: Fondo de Cultura Económica, 1962.

Castillo Ledon, Luis. *Antigua literatura mexicana indígena.* Mexico City: Imprenta Victoria, 1917. Early anthology of Nahuatl poetry, interesting for introduction which claims pre-Columbian cultures as part of Mexican national heritage.

Clark, J. Cooper. *The Story of Eight Deer.* London: Taylor and Frank, 1912. Important work of early scholarship that brings together the different stories of the life of twelfth-century ruler Eight Deer contained in the Mixtec group of codices. Beautiful color drawings.

Coe, Michael. *The Maya.* 4th ed. London and New York: Thames and Hudson, 1987. Beautifully illustrated overview of Mayan culture, incorporates recent scholarship; has sections on Mayan calendar, writing, and literature.

————. *The Maya Scribe and His World.* New York: Grolier Club, 1973.

Cornyn, J. H. *The Song of Quetzalcoatl.* Yellow Springs, Ohio: The Antioch Press, 1930. English versions of Nahuatl poetry recorded by Sahagún and his Aztec informants; bear an unfortunate resemblance to Longfellow's "Song of Hiawatha."

Cortés, Hernán. *Cartas de relación* (1519). Mexico City: Editorial Porrúa, 1971.

Dark, Philip. *Mixtec Ethnohistory: A Method of Analysis of Codical Art.* London: Oxford University Press, 1950.

Dibble, Charles E. *Historia de la nación mexicana: Reproducción a todo color del Códice de 1576 (Códice Aubin).* Madrid: J. Porrúa Turanzas, 1963.

————. "Writing in Central Mexico." In *Handbook of Middle American Indians* 10 (1971): 322–331. The evolution of glyphic writing in Nahuatl-speaking societies of Central Highlands of Mexico.

Durán, Fray Diego. *Historia de las Indias de Nueva España y islas de Tierra Firme.* Mexico City: Editorial Porrúa, 1967.

Eguiara y Eguren, José. *Prólogos a la Biblioteca Mexicana.* Ed. Agustín Millares Carlo. Mexico City: Fondo de Cultura Económica, 1944.

Garibay K., Angel María. *Historia de la literatura nahuatl.* 2 vols. Mexico City: Editorial Porrúa, 1953–1954. Important work by major scholar of Nahua culture.

————. *La literatura de los aztecas.* Mexico City: Editorial Joaquín Mortiz, 1970.

————. *Poesía nahuatl.* 3 vols. Mexico City: Universidad Nacional Autónoma de México, 1964–1968.

————, ed. *Romances de los Señores de la Nueva España: Poesia Nahuatl I.* Mexico City: National University of Mexico, 1964.

————. *Veinte himnos sacros de los nahuas.* Mexico City: Universidad Nacional Autónoma de México, 1958. Nahuatl songs recorded by Sahagún.

————. *Xochimapictli: Colección de poemas nahuas.* Mexico City: Ediciones Culturales Mexicanas, 1959.

Garza, Mercedes de la. *La conciencia histórica de los antiguos mayas.* Introduction by Ruz Lhuillier. Mexico City: Universidad Nacional Autónoma de México, 1975. Important study marking the recognition that Mayan writing, both in codices and on monuments, represents recording of history as well as calendar/prophetic discourse.

————. *El hombre en el pensamiento religioso nahuatl y maya.* Prologue by Miguel León-Portilla. Mexico City: Universidad Nacional Autónoma de México, Centro de Estudios Mayas, 1978.

————, ed. *Literatura maya.* Chronology by Miguel León-Portilla. Caracas: Biblioteca Ayacucho, 1980. Contains Spanish translations of the most important Mayan texts: Popol Vuh, Memorial de Sololá, Libro de Chilam Balam de Chumayel, Rabinal Achí, Libro de los cantares de Dzitbalché, Título de los Señores de Totonicapán, Las historias de los Xpanzay, and the Códice de Calkiní. The introductions, notes, bibliographies, and chronology make this volume an essential source for the scholar of Mayan literature.

Gillmor, Frances. *The Flute of the Smoking Mirror: A Portrait of Nezahualcoyotl, Poet-King of the Aztecs.* Albuquerque: University of New Mexico Press, 1949.

Glass, John B. *Handbook of Middle American Indians.* Robert Wauchope, general editor. Austin: University of Texas Press, 1964–1976.

Goetz, D., and S. Morley, ed. and trans. *Popol Vuh: The Sacred Book of the Ancient Quiché Maya.* Norman: University of Oklahoma Press, 1950. English version from the translation by A. Recinos.

González Peña, Carlos. *Historia de la literatura mexicana desde los orígenes hasta nuestros días.* 7th ed. Mexico City: Editorial Porrúa, 1960. English translation: *History of Mexican Literature,* trans. Gusta Barfield Nance and Florence Johnson Dunstan. Dallas: Southern Methodist Press, 1968.

Gutiérrez Solana, Nelly. *Códices de México: Historia e interpretación de los grandes libros pintados prehispánicos.* Mexico City: Panorama Editorial, 1985. Gives a general introduction to codices along with detailed descriptions of the four major groups: the Borgia, the Mixtec, the Maya, and the Mexica codices. Black-and-white photos.

Ixtlilxóchitl, Fernando de Alva. *Historia de la nación chichimeca.* Ed. Germán Vásquez. Madrid: Historia 16, 1985. History of Nahua peoples written between 1605 and 1614.

Kartunnen, Frances, and James Lockhart. "La estructura de la poesía náhuatl vista por sus variantes." *Estudios de Cultura Náhuatl* 14 (1980): 15–64.

Keen, Benjamin. *The Aztec Image in Western Thought.* New Brunswick: Rutgers University Press, 1971. Copiously illustrated volume begins with chapters on Aztec history and culture, then traces European responses to Aztecs from initial contact to 1960s; important as an account of scholarship of pre-Columbian texts.

Kelley, David H. *Deciphering the Maya Script.* Austin: University of Texas Press, 1976.

Kissam, Edward, and Michael Schmidt. *Flower and Song: Poems of the Aztec Peoples.* London: Anvil Press Poetry, 1977. Reprinted as *Poems of the Aztec People.* Ypsilanti: Bilingual Press/Editorial Bilingüe, 1983. English translations of Nahuatl poetry.

Landa, Fray Diego de. *Relación de las cosas de Yucatán.* Introduction by Angel María Garibay K. Mexico City: Editorial Porrúa, 1966.

————. *Yucatán before and after the Conquest, by Fray Diego de Landa.* Ed. and trans. William Gates. Baltimore: Maya Society, 1937. New York: Dover Publications, 1978.

Leander, Birgitta. *In xochitl in cuícatl: Flor y canto, la poesía de los aztecas.* Mexico City: Instituto Nacional Indigenista, 1972.

————. *La poesía nahuatl: Función y carácter.* Goteborg: Etnograf. Museet, 1971.

Le Clézio, J. M. G. *Relation de Michoacan.* Paris: Gallimard, 1984. French translation of an anonymous text in Spanish from around 1540; the only surviving book of the Porhé (Tarrascan) people of Michoacán, oral tradition recorded by Franciscan missionary after the conquest of Michoacán.

Lee, Thomas A., ed. *Los códices mayas.* Tuxtla Gutiérrez: Universidad Autónoma de Chiapas, 1985.

León-Portilla, Miguel. *Los antiquos mexicanos a través de sus crónicas y cantares*. Mexico City: Fondo de Cultura Económica, 1961.

———. *Aztec Thought and Culture*. Trans. J. E. Davis. Norman: University of Oklahoma Press, 1963.

———, ed. *The Broken Spears: Aztec Account of the Conquest of Mexico*. Intro. and notes by Léon-Portilla; translations from Nahuatl into Spanish by Angel María Garibay K. Trans. from Spanish to English by Lysander Kemp. Boston: Beacon Press, 1962. Translation of *Visión de los vencidos*.

———. *Cantos y crónicas del México antiguo*. Madrid: Historia 16, 1986.

———. *La filosofía náhuatl, estudiada en sus fuentes*. Mexico City: Universidad Nacional Autónoma de México, 1983.

———, trans. and ed. *Literatura del México antiguo: Los textos en lengua náhuatl*. Introductory studies by León-Portilla. Caracas: Biblioteca Ayacucho, 1978.

———. *Literaturas de Mesoamérica*. Mexico City: Secretaría de Educación Pública, 1984. Expands on material in *Literaturas precolombinas;* provides excellent overview with numerous examples.

———. *Literaturas precolombinas de México*. Mexico City: Editorial Pormaca, 1964. Major work on the subject. Translated as *Pre-Columbian Literatures of Mexico*. Expanded in 1984 as *Literaturas de Mesoamérica*. Chapters organized around genres.

———. *Nezahualcóyotl: Poesía y pensamiento, 1402–1472*. Facsimile edition of the 1972 edition. Mexico City: Enciclopédica del Estado de México, 1979. Study of the significance of Nezahualcóyotl both as ruler of Texcoco, whose figure assumed legendary dimensions in post-conquest chronicles, and as a Nahuatl poet. Contains texts of his songs in both Nahuatl and Spanish.

———. "La palabra antigua y nueva del hombre de Mesoamérica." *Revista Iberoamericana* 127 (1984): 345–366.

———. *Pre-Columbian Literatures of Mexico*. Trans. Grace Lobanov and Miguel León-Portilla. Norman: University of Oklahoma Press, 1969.

———. *El reverso de la Conquista: Relaciones aztecas, mayas e incas*. Mexico City: Editorial Joaquín Mortiz, 1964.

———. *Trece poetas del mundo azteca*. Mexico City: Universidad Nacional Autónoma de México, 1981.

———, ed. *Visión de los vencidos: Relaciones indígenas de la conquista*. Intro. and notes by León-Portilla; translations from Nahuatl to Spanish by Angel María Garibay. Mexico City: Universidad Nacional Autónoma de México, 1983. Compilation of accounts of the Spanish conquest drawn from various Nahuatl sources.

Leyenda de los soles. In Garza, ed., *Literatura maya*.

Makemson, Maud W. *The Book of the Jaguar Priest*. New York: H. Schuman, 1951. Translation of the Book of Chilam Balam of Tizimín.

Marcus, Joyce. "The Origins of Mesoamerican Writing." *Annual Review of Anthropology* 5 (1976): 35–67. Clear explanation of theories of writing systems and the evolution of writing among Mayans and Zapotec.

Martí, José. "Nuestra América." *Nuestra América*. Prologue by Juan Marinello; selection and notes Hugo Achúgar; chronology Cintio Vitier. Caracas: Biblioteca Ayacucho, 1977: 26–33. Martí's essay appeared first on January 30, 1891, in the Mexican newspaper *El partido liberal*.

Martínez, José Luis. *De la naturaleza y carácter de la literatura mexicana*. Mexico City: Tezontle, 1960.

Mignolo, Walter. "Literacy and Colonization: The New World Experience." In *1492–1992: Re/Discovering Colonial Writing,* ed. René Jara and Nicholas Spadaccini, 51–96. *Hispanic Issues,* vol. 4. Minneapolis: The Prisma Institute, 1989.

Monterde, Francisco, ed. *Teatro indígena prehispánico (Rabinal Achí).* Mexico City: Universidad Nacional Autónoma de México, 1955. Translation of the Mayan ritual drama, the Rabinal Achí.

Nicholson, Irene. *Firefly in the Night: A Study of Mexican Poetry and Symbolism.* London: Faber and Faber, 1959.

———. *A Guide to Mexican Poetry, Ancient and Modern.* Mexico City: Editorial Minutiae Mexicana, 1968.

Nicolau d'Olwer, Luis. *Cronistas de las culturas precolombinas.* Mexico City: Fondo de Cultura Económica, 1963. Anthology including selections from fifty chronicles representing European views of American indigenous peoples on first contact.

Nuttall, Zelia. *The Book of the Life of the Ancient Mexicans.* Berkeley: University of California Press, 1983. Facsimile of the Codex Magliabecchiano; in this anonymous sixteenth-century copy of an earlier, lost text, glyphs and images in the Aztec style are accompanied by a Spanish commentary.

———. *Codex Nuttall.* London: Dover Press, 1975. Reprint of a beautiful color facsimile edition, published in 1902 by the Peabody Museum, Cambridge, Mass., by a pioneering American scholar of Mixtec codices; introduction by Arthur G. Miller gives an excellent overview of codices, questions of style, iconographic conventions, and interpretation.

Orozco y Berra, Manuel. *Códice Ramírez.* Mexico City: Editorial Inovación, 1979. Reprint of the 1878 edition of an anonymous sixteenth-century manuscript entitled "Relación del origen de los indios que habitan esta Nueva España, según sus historias." The Spanish text is considered a translation of a lost Nahuatl original; Orozco y Berra's appendices discuss the chronology of ancient Mexican history and the colonial tradition of historiography in New Spain.

Ortiz de Montellano, Bernardo. *La poesía indígena de México.* Mexico City: 1935. Brief essay and anthology that claims a "purely aesthetic" approach to pre-Columbian culture while repeating exoticist clichés about the "oriental" nature of indigenous cultures.

Osuna Ruiz, Rafael. *Introducción a la lírica prehispánica.* Maracaibo: Editorial Universitaria de la Universidad de Zulia, 1968. Comparative study of Nahuatl and Quechua lyric poetry that uses a philological approach to examine questions of pre-Columbian aesthetic ideas, social roles of poets and poetry, and issues of translation.

Pacheco, José Emilio. *The Lost Homeland: Notes on Francisco Xavier Clavijero and the "National Culture" of Mexico.* Toronto: University of Toronto, Latin American in Residence Lectures No. V, 1975.

Pastor, Beatriz. "Silence and Writing: The History of the Conquest." In *1492–1992: Re/Discovering Colonial Writing,* ed. René Jara and Nicholas Spadaccini, 121–164. *Hispanic Issues,* vol. 4. Minneapolis: The Prisma Institute, 1989.

Pimentel, Francisco. *Historia crítica de la literatura y de las ciencias en México desde la conquista hasta nuestros días.* Mexico City: Librería de la Enseñanza, 1890.

Rabinal Achí. Also called *Baile del tun.* In Garza, ed., *Literatura maya.*

Rama, Angel. *Transculturación narrativa en América Latina.* Mexico City: Siglo XXI Editores, 1982.

Recinos, Adrián, trans. and ed. *Anales de los Cakchiqueles.* Mexico City: Fondo de

Cultura Económica, 1950. Also called Anales de los Xahil or Memorial de Sololá. Reprinted in Garza, ed., *Literatura maya.*

————, trans. and ed. *Popol Vuh: Las historias antiguas del Quiché.* Mexico City: Fondo de Cultura Económica, 1947. Reprinted in Garza, ed., *Literatura maya.*

Root, Deborah. "The Imperial Signifier: Todorov and the Conquest of Mexico." *Cultural Critique* 9 (Spring 1988): 197–219.

Roys, Ralph L., trans. *The Book of Chilam Balam of Chumayel.* Publication 538. Washington, D.C.: Carnegie Institution of Washington, 1933. Norman: University of Oklahoma Press, 1967.

————, trans. and ed. *Ritual of the Bacabs: A Book of Maya Incantations.* Norman: University of Oklahoma Press, 1965. Study of Mayan ritual songs, some of which were used in medical practices.

Sahagún, Fray Bernardino de. *Códices Matritenses del Real Palacio y de la Real Academia de la Historia.* Náhuatl texts of the indigenous informants of Sahagún.

————. *General History of the Things of New Spain: Florentine Codex.* Ed. and trans. Arthur J. O. Anderson and Charles E. Dibble. 12 vols. Salt Lake City: University of Utah, 1950–1953.

————. *Hablan los aztecas: Historia general de las cosas de Nueva España de Fray Bernardino de Sahagún y los informantes aztecas.* Ed. Claus Litterscheid. Prologue by Juan Rulfo. Barcelona: Biblioteca del Nuevo Mundo 1492–1992—Tusquets/Círculo, 1985. Profusely illustrated. Focuses on the contributions of Sahagún's Aztec informants in the Florentine Codex.

————. *Historia general de las cosas de Nueva España.* Ed. Angel María Garibay K. 4 vols. Mexico City: Editorial Porrúa, 1956. Edited by one of the foremost scholars of Nahuatl culture.

————. *El México antiguo: Selección y reordenación de la historia general de las cosas de Nueva España de Fray Bernardino de Sahagún y de los informantes indígenas.* Ed. José Luis Martínez. Caracas: Biblioteca Ayacucho, 1981. Introduction tells the story of the composition and subsequent editions of this encyclopedic work of colonial ethnography while the customary Biblioteca Ayacucho chronology focuses on the life of Sahagún. This edition uses Garibay's Spanish translations of the Nahuatl portions of the work.

Schele, Linda, and David Freidel. *A Forest of Kings: The Untold Story of the Ancient Maya.* New York: William Morrow, 1990. An important and fascinating book, the result of recent breakthroughs in deciphering Mayan script; leads the reader through the interpretation of glyphs, images, architectural symbolism, and archeological data to narrate the stories the Maya told in their public spaces.

Séjourné, Laurette. *Pensamiento y religión en el México antiguo.* Trans. Orfila Reynal. Mexico City: Fondo de Cultura Económica, 1957. Published originally in French as *La Pensée des anciens méxicains* (Paris: F. Maspéro, 1966); in English as *Burning Water: Thought and Religion in Ancient Mexico,* trans. Irene Nicholson. New York: Vanguard Press, 1957. Influential study of Aztec culture.

Sodi Morales, Demetrio. *La literatura de los mayas.* Mexico City: Editorial Joaquín Mortiz, 1964. An early anthology of Spanish translations, some by Sodi, of Mayan texts, including selections from the Popol Vuh, Books of Chilam Balam, Códice de Calkini, Anales de los Cakchiqueles, and the Rabinal Achí. In addition, Sodi includes contemporary oral tradition of Lacandón and Tzotzil Mayas of Chiapas, recorded by anthropologists, which demonstrates the persistence of pre-Columbian elements in contemporary indigenous culture.

Solís Alcalá, Ermilo. *Códice Pérez*. Merida: Imprenta Oriente, 1949. Translations of texts of the book of Chilam Balam of Maní.

Sten, María. *Las extraordinarias historias de los códices mexicanos*. Mexico City: Editorial Joaquín Mortiz, 1972.

Tedlock, Dennis, trans. *The Definitive Edition of the Mayan Book of the Dawn of Life and the Glories of the Gods and Kings*. New York: Simon and Schuster, 1985. This highly entertaining English translation of the Popol Vuh incorporates Tedlock's experience of study with contemporary Mayan daykeepers and represents a breakthrough in our understanding of the text and Mayan culture.

Thompson, J. Eric. *A Commentary on the Dresden Codex, a Maya Hieroglyphic Book*. Philadelphia: American Philosophical Society, 1972.

———. *Maya Hieroglyphic Writing*. Norman: University of Oklahoma Press, 1960.

———. *The Rise and Fall of Maya Civilization*. Norman: University of Oklahoma Press, 1966. A standard work on Maya culture and history by one of the major scholars in the field.

Todorov, Tzvetan. *La conquête de l'Amérique*. Paris: Editions du Seuil, 1982. Published in English as *The Conquest of America: The Question of the Other*, trans. Richard Howard. New York: Harper and Row, 1985.

Vaillant, George C. *The Aztecs of Mexico: Origin, Rise and Fall of the Aztec Nation*. Baltimore: Penguin Books, 1961.

Vigil, José María. *Estudios sobre literatura mexicana*. Ed. Adalberto Navarro Sánchez. 2 vols. Guadalajara: Tipografía Et Caetera, 1972. One of the earliest Mexican literary histories, by a scholar who promoted the inclusion of pre-Columbian cultures in Mexican literature.

Vila Selma, José. *La mentalidad maya: Textos literarios*. Madrid: Editorial Nacional, 1981. An essay on Mayan thought and worldviews introduces this anthology of Mayan texts organized thematically; includes passages from Landa and selections of nineteenth- and twentieth-century legends, songs, and stories as well as excerpts from the major Mayan literary texts in a somewhat confusing arrangement.

Warman, Arturo Guillermo, et al. *De eso que llaman antropología mexicana*. Mexico City: Editorial Nuestro Tiempo, 1970.

Wolf, Eric R. *Sons of the Shaking Earth*. Chicago: University of Chicago Press, 1959. The first chapters are a good introduction to Mesoamerican prehistory and pre-Columbian cultures.

2

The Colonial Period

LEE H. DOWLING

I EARLY SIXTEENTH CENTURY

Historical Writings

There is no question whether the historical writings of the sixteenth and seventeenth centuries constitute a part of Mexican literature: they do. Such is pragmatically the case, as a glance at most Mexican literary histories and anthologies instantly reveals. And because in our age the exclusively belletristic definition of literature has yielded to a vastly more encompassing concept by which virtually any document found to articulate the cultural rhetoric of a class, a country, a collectivity, or an age is fair game for literary critics, there is even more reason for including discussion of them.

Before continuing, it is well to consider briefly some of the reasons for current interest in colonial literature (the word *literature* will be used throughout this essay in its broadest sense). A flowering of nationalism in the 1940s inspired a number of Mexican scholars to accelerate the systematic reexamination of colonial archives. This movement produced, for example, Alfonso Reyes's *Letras de la Nueva España* (Letters of New Spain; 1946) and Pedro Henríquez Ureña's *Historia de la cultura en la América Hispánica* (History of Culture in Spanish America; 1947). Since then, publishers like the Universidad Nacional Autónoma de México (UNAM), Fondo de Cultura Económica, Secretaría de Educación Pública, and Editorial Porrúa have brought out hundreds of new and relatively inexpensive critical editions of significant early writings.

The 1960s witnessed the so-called boom and with it the introduction of Latin America's *nueva narrativa* (new narrative) to readers all over the world. Fictional works for the most part, these writings not only presented information about the region's past and present, but also did so within strikingly original narrative configurations that questioned both generic "logic" and the act of reading itself. In order to provide adequate interpretive strategies, literary theory underwent rapid evolution. Linguistically based structuralist/semiotic models of the seventies gave way in the eighties to those of poststructuralism

---

Translations are my own unless otherwise indicated.

and neo-Marxist approaches that attempted to deconstruct traditional philosophical oppositions in order to zero in on ideologies underlying texts, genres,
and discourse. As a result, representatives of almost all critical camps came
out in favor of subjecting "nonliterary" forms to literary analysis and expanding the "canon" to introduce works long excluded from mainstream
consideration.

This climate, prevailing since about 1975, is one in which Latin American
colonial literature, with Mexico and Peru as its production centers, has begun
to come into its own. The chronicles of Indies, a general heading that encompasses histories, *relaciones* (first-person reports), ethnographic compilations,
letters, and legal documents of various kinds, is unquestionably the dominant
literary type of the sixteenth and early seventeenth centuries. Because they
record both the earliest instances of New World opposition to European imperialism and the first stammering attempts of Amerindians and mestizos
(those of mixed blood) to resist effacement through the appropriation of their
own discursive space, chronicles are entailed by the very roots of Latin American culture. Recent literary scholars have focused on creative strategies elaborated by chroniclers to enable themselves to inscribe the new and to depict
the Other, given the theologicopolitical restrictions under which they functioned. Scholars have also begun to identify strategies with which colonial
writers sought to mitigate the effects of their own lack of political and cultural
authority. When approached on these grounds, among others, the chronicles
provide truly absorbing reading.

Since our purpose here, rather than providing more or less standard typolo-
gies of Mexican chronicles, is to summarize the reevaluative work scholars
have carried out or are in the process of carrying out to date, it is helpful for
the student of the period to keep at hand such encyclopedic manuals as Francisco Esteve Barba's *Historiografía indiana* (New World Historiography; 1964)
and Heriberto García Rivas's *Historia de la literatura mexicana* (History of
Mexican Literature; 1971). Yet it should be noted that the pace of reevaluation
is currently accelerating. Scholarship on the texts of the colonial era is now
entering a dynamic period, and each year sees significant advances not only
on canonical authors but also on the marginal and unknown.

It is important to remember that historical writings cannot be read adequately without an understanding of the historical and social realities of the
period from which they derive. A key concept toward understanding the Spanish rationale for conquest, for example, is that of providentialism—the idea
that all events taking place in the world were personally ordered and directed
by God in order to carry Christianity to as many human beings as possible.
The Spanish empire, undertaking crusades for which Catholic popes repeatedly provided blessings in the form of papal bulls, was seen as the only ideal
political structure for accomplishing such a goal. According to orthodox ideology, God's hand was discernible in the gradual shift of imperial power from
east to west—an argument that Mexican *criollos,* Spaniards born in America
or feeling themselves to belong to the New World rather than the Old, would

later seize as their own in an effort to establish a legitimate cultural identity. The Spanish exploration and conquest of the Indies, as Spanish America was then known, was thus seen to represent simply another chapter in the unfolding, providentially guided history of the universe, one affording an almost unparalleled opportunity to extend the message of redemption to masses of indigenous souls still mired in pagan idolatry.

This is not to say, of course, that Spanish intellectuals ever seriously maintained that all things done in the name of conquest would benefit Amerindians; on the contrary, debates and legal battles raged throughout the period on questions of natural law, natural slavery, the "just war," alleged massacres, and the institutional *encomienda* (the granting of Indians to a conquistador who was to instruct them in Christianity in return for labor and tribute), to name but a few. To deal adequately with such diverse themes, those undertaking the study of chronicles of Indies constantly confront issues associated with history, law, anthropology, economics, sociology, and philosophy, among others.

Another basic question concerns the exact connotations of the term *literacy* in the context of colonization. An examination of the diverse practices carried out by the Spanish missionaries in the name of literacy sheds light not only on the actions and reactions of these missionaries but also on the culturally based prejudices in favor of alphabetic writing that define our own disciplinary field today as well. Consideration of such a question leads us to rethink, in the words of Walter Mignolo, "both the field of literary studies and our conception of 'colonial letters'" (in Jara and Spadaccini, eds. 51–96).

All of this is not to deny the greater importance of poetics for literary scholars than for those laboring in other disciplines, nor to debate the sense in which, for the former, content is inseparable from form. Roberto González Echevarría has admirably perceived the challenge of this aspect of colonial writings in his statement that the richness of the chronicles can be found in the variety of forms possible within the rhetorical rules and conventions of the period and the way in which these came to be blended or modified by the social and cultural circumstances of each chronicler (16). It is to be emphasized, however, that a formalistically oriented analysis of isolated works will miss the more general discursive and interdiscursive factors that circumscribed the range of moves open to the colonial writer before he or she even began to wield the pen.

The case of Mexico is unusual in that the founding figure of its literature is none other than the man synonymous with its conquest, Hernán Cortés (1485–1547), still almost half a millennium later one of the most controversial figures in all of history. One difficulty resulting from such a dual role is that a critic's failure to take a stand on whether this man was admirably representative of the prevailing view of benign imperialism or, on the contrary, an insubordinate, immoral, and hypocritical opportunist may be interpreted as tacit approval of if not his means at least his ends. Yet without ever denying the vital stakes such a question implies, a literary scholar needs to focus on how effectively the writer Cortés—or any other—manages to wield his linguistic arms in order to win the battle of written communication with the addressee in question. For Cortés to win he must, in the words of Beatriz Pastor, transform his act of rebellion into one of service by endeavoring to depict the rebel (himself) as *model* (*Discurso narrativo*).

Cortés left five famous *Cartas de relación* (Letters of Report; 1519–1526) as well as other letters and documents. The letters from Mexico demonstrate the leader's familiarity, gained during his studies at the University of Salamanca, with the rhetorical conventions of his age and also, possibly, with the writings of Virgil, Julius Caesar, and the classical tragedians. Yet while respecting ancient precepts, Cortés also displayed strategic historiographical originality in responding to the dilemmas confronting him as he wrote. While continuing to assure the king that he, Cortés, posed no threat to Spanish authority, it was necessary for him to appear in every way essential to the defeat of the Aztecs. His status as an eyewitness historian living the events upon which he was reporting imposed clear limitations upon his knowledge of a comprehensive operation still in flux. Cortés's solution was to organize the narrative structure of his letters so as to distance Cortés the narrator as sharply as possible from Cortés the agent or subject. Such a strategy allowed him to deemphasize elements of contingency through *narrative* control. In other words, the *I* of the historian dominates, circumscribes, and even criticizes that of the acting commander of the expedition. While the latter may lose control from time to time, becoming unable to fulfill his promises, the former boldly claims foreknowledge of the outcome of any given course of action. He is thus able not only to portray his previous insubordination as a necessary response to overly restrictive rules and regulations, but also to attribute irregular procedure to the *legally* appointed imperial officers Diego Velázquez and Pánfilo de Narváez. Within Cortés's inscription of the conquest, temporal sequence is blurred as past and future are syntactically juxtaposed by means of such logical connectives as "therefore," "if," "although," and "as."

Providentialist assumptions overwhelmingly inform *Historia general de Indias* (General History of the Indies; 1552, the second volume containing an account of the conquest of Mexico) by Francisco López de Gómara (1511–1566) which records the multiple appearances in Mexico of Saint James the Apostle as well as the active help of the Virgin Mary (reported to have blinded the Indians during a battle by flinging dust in their eyes). López de Gómara's protagonist is clearly Hernán Cortés, and in fact he served the latter as chaplain and secretary for some seven years in Spain (Gómara was never in Mexico). An implicit assumption is also made in the work that history depends on great men and thus subsumes biography, an individualizing notion seemingly more in tune with renaissance thinking than is López de Gómara's reliance on providentialist metaphysics.

The best-known chronicle produced in the Mexican campaign is Bernal Díaz del Castillo's *Historia verdadera de los sucesos de la conquista de la Nueva España* (True History of the Events of the Conquest of New Spain; 1632), frequently referred to as "the popular chronicle." While Cortés strategically drafted his account on the spot, Díaz (1495–1583) waited some thirty years (until approximately 1551) to begin his own version, coming upon López de Gómara's history after completing only some seventeen chapters. Díaz's reaction to this work—and to several others composed entirely from secondary sources—gives rise to his repeated claims that (1) his is the "true history" by virtue of his eyewitness status, (2) the narrative eloquence of rival historians, while greater than his own, does not guarantee truth, and (3) the campaign's success was the product of concerted efforts and not of Cortés's genius alone.

While it is true that Diaz's prose lacks polish, his history is not short on dramatic tension turning upon such episodes as the emotional reunion with Aguilar, the long-anticipated face-to-face encounter with Moctezuma, the sudden arrival of Narváez's troops, the crushing defeat during the Noche Triste (Sad Night), and many others. Diaz's imaginative recourse to popular literary forms and archetypes like La Celestina, Amadís, and various epic heroes lends his work a semiotic richness no other chronicle can match. It is probably this aspect of the work that has most accounted for its undeniable appeal to literary critics, until very recently.

Building on a line of criticism initiated in the 1940s by Ramón Iglesia, however, a few scholars are now directing significant new inquiries to the question of Díaz's true purpose in becoming a historian relatively late in his long life. A comparison of the facts according to López de Gómara with those set forth in Díaz's "corrective" version showed Iglesia that there is little substantive difference between them. Díaz even occasionally accuses his "rival" of false allegations. If the oft-invoked correction of López de Gómara is actually a pretext allowing Díaz to present his own version of the conquest, what is the real message he seeks to convey and why must he conceal it?

Searching for an answer to these questions, Adorno ("Discourses on Colonialism") has recently compared the published version of Díaz's history with a hitherto unavailable earlier edition. Her findings lead her to suggest that the figure threatening Díaz's economic well-being as a successful conquistador is not López de Gómara alone, but López de Gómara reread in the light of Bartolomé de las Casas's recent indictments of Cortés's entire Mexican campaign. Fear that these allegations will undermine the notion of the "just war" legalizing the conquest of Mexico spurs Díaz to publish his own apologia at the same time that prudence makes him refrain from a frontal attack on a figure so powerful as Las Casas by pretending that López de Gómara is his only target. It should be noted that Adorno's unmasking comments run counter to the acclaim heaped upon Díaz through the twentieth century. Polemical responses to her work have already begun to appear, sparking a debate that promises to continue for some time to come.

The *Relación* (Report; 1542) of Alvar Núñez Cabeza de Vaca (1470–1557) has been one of the most commented on of all the chronicles during the last fifteen years. Written hastily by a man with little or no literary conditioning, this brief narrative documents meteoric changes in the fortunes of its author during the ten-year period from his embarkation in Spain as the treasurer of an expedition bound to explore and annex Florida (led by Cortés's old enemy Pánfilo de Narváez) to his return to "civilization" (a remote Spanish outpost) in the region of Sinaloa, Mexico. The actual events recounted—a hurricane in the Caribbean, the loss of the ships, the death of the bumbling Narváez and all but four of the men, capture and enslavement by Indians, cannibalism, escape, an almost fantastic flight through the Indian hamlets of Texas, Sonora, and Chihuahua in the guise of faith healer, and the final rescue—match exactly an archetypal adventure format popularized in countless works of fiction. Other factors mentioned by Núñez—for example, the accurate foretelling of disaster by an old Moorish woman—add to the dramatic tension and deepen the reader's sense of being on familiar literary ground in this narrative, for all its stylistic inelegance.

Recently Núñez's *Relación* has attracted the attention of ideological critics concerned with the "allegorization" of the conquest in the terms of a discourse monopolized by the agents of the conqueror with the intention of eliminating or at least circumscribing attempts by the conquered people to present alternative versions—a maneuver effectively supported by institutionalized Eurocentric assumptions regarding literary genre and style. According to his own testimony, Núñez, a noble Spaniard, finds himself suddenly divested of all the accoutrements of power and in a state of helplessness at the hands of his Indian captors. During their long struggle to survive, Núñez and his companions slowly come to recognize the humanitarian virtues of many of those who for most members of his own race will always remain Other. Reunited at last with his countrymen, the "Christians" he now sees terrorizing peaceful Indian villages in search of slaves, Núñez clearly undergoes an identity crisis that causes him, in a telling confusion of pronouns, to group himself *with* certain Indians while perceiving the hypocritical Christians as Other. But in doing so, as the rest of his life experiences bear out, Núñez finds himself in a state of cultural alterity or hybridization not supported by a single one of the institutions of his era.

In a seminal essay published in 1990, Juan Bruce-Novoa analyzes the *Relación* in the light of recent ideological advances and, following Luis Leal, claims it as the founding text of Chicano literature. Bruce-Novoa demonstrates convincingly that Núñez, like the Chicano, survives only by learning to operate on the frontier, where he is constantly translating for different groups whose cultural codes are mutually exclusive, and also hawking a syncretism officially opposed by everyone. Bruce-Novoa's essay is extremely significant vis-à-vis the current project of rescuing early U.S. Hispanic texts either from oblivion or from nationalistic bias on both the Mexican and the American sides. This ongoing project will undoubtedly throw new light during the 1990s and beyond on the fairly numerous early works written by Hispanics in various parts of what is now the United States.

Less studied than the histories of the New World's "discovery" and conquest are the numerous synchronically organized treatises that seek to provide Europe with accurate information on its lands and peoples (Pliny's *Natural His-*

tory is the usual model for such works). Official requests from the Crown as well as a body of European readers who doted on the novel if not the bizarre spurred important renaissance research in all areas of the natural sciences. Gonzalo Fernández de Oviedo's *Sumario de la natural historia de las Indias* (Natural History of the Indies; [1526] 1942) and the multivolume *Historia general y natural de las Indias* (General and Natural History of the Indies; [1535] 1851–1855), part of which deals specifically with Mexico, provide useful descriptions of American geology, flora, and fauna. In his depiction of the Amerindian, unfortunately, Fernández de Oviedo (1478–1557) is notably biased. His intransigence on this point provoked the voluble wrath of his adversary Las Casas, whose repeated references in his own writings to native Americans as "gentle lambs" present a sharp contrast.

It is important to remember in this regard that the period's ethnography was inevitably carried out within a rigid ideological framework upheld by the Church and was in fact known as "moral" history. Ethnographical "objectivity"—still much in question today—was then precluded even in cases in which the observer's orthodoxy was virtually unquestionable. Practically the only one of the colonial period's genres regularly incorporating the native American was the epic, where it was obligatory that the hero should encounter a worthy adversary. "Amerindian history" was almost an oxymoron for sixteenth-century historiographers who tended, with few exceptions, to assume that history properly consisted of chronologically ordered records of deeds performed by Europeans. Ethnographic compilations were problematic in a number of ways. First, they were by definition tales of *survival*. Second, they tended to treat such taboo subjects as sodomy (of which the Indians were constantly being accused). At the same time ethnographers were wont to conclude that Indians were *rational* beings; this presented a difficulty because it clearly called into question, if not official justifications of the conquest, certainly such entrenched institutions as the *repartimiento* (the feudal cession of Indians to Spaniards) and the *encomienda*. The Inquisition's censors, vigilant throughout the colonial centuries, were doubly so when the subject of a work was ethnography, meaning that few of the studies actually carried out saw publication until many centuries later.

Current colonial scholars, following a trend that has been clearly emerging since the sixties, are moving toward full consideration rather than exclusion, as has traditionally been the case, of these ethnographic compilations. Two of the earliest and most significant ethnographers of native Mexican culture are the Franciscan Fray Bernardino de Sahagún (1499–1590), author of the multi-volume *Historia general de las cosas de Nueva España* (General History of the Things of New Spain; completed around 1569 but not published until 1829–1830 in Mexico); and the Jesuit Fray José de Acosta (1540–1600), who wrote *De procuranda indorum salute: Pacificación y colonización* (On the Well-being of the Indians: Pacification and Colonization; [1590] 1962). Both stressed that the lore they had incorporated about Amerindian ways of life was valueless in moral terms but that a knowledge of it could help to advance and rejustify Christianity (and Sahagún likened the study of Nahua to a physician's analysis of a disease with the end of discovering its cure).

Having been a participant in the founding of Franciscan schools where Indian youths studied Latin and Spanish, Sahagún—himself fluent in the Nahuatl language—became an instructor at the Colegio (school) of Santa Cruz de Tlatelolco, founded in 1536. Aided by his own former pupils, he first prepared a collection of sermons in Nahuatl for use in proselytizing. His collaboration with his pupils thus established, Sahagún, beginning in 1547 and at times assisted by his colleague Fray Andrés de Olmos (?–1571), planned, organized, and edited data collected for a monumental study of the native culture. From Nahua elders of several towns, Sahagún requested and received explications of certain native codices as well as answers to a list of specific questions concerning cultural practices and religious beliefs. He even included a native account of the conquest, later published separately in English as part of the *Florentine Codex* (1982). Sahagún's most remarkable step, nevertheless, was to allow his informants to speak "for themselves" by transcribing more or less verbatim what they actually said (his assistants writing the information in Nahuatl using Spanish orthography). Successive stages of his work are described in the prologue to volumes 1 and 2, and some of his early drafts and revisions are also extant. Following the establishment of the Inquisition in Mexico in 1571, Sahagún's manuscripts were confiscated as the result of an ideological split among the Franciscans. They were returned to him in 1573 but collected again and ordered dispatched, in toto, to the Council of Indies in 1577–1578. Sahagún never learned either the exact reason for confiscation or the Council's reaction to his life's work.

His own role was always that of an intermediary between two cultures, even if the goal was to juxtapose voices rather than to foster cultural interaction (cf. Todorov). A major question continuing to preoccupy scholars is that of the extent to which such a role may have modified his informants' texts. His interventions certainly appear in the form of titles, notes, prefaces, digressions, and—occasionally—refutations and expostulations, though Todorov finds these remarkably free of value judgments, and others have called the Sahaguntine corpus the most thorough and objective study of another culture ever attempted up to its time. Nevertheless, Sahagún must be seen as a formal determinant of the Mexicas' discourse in the work. It is he, for example, who must ultimately decide whether the Nahuatl term for a deity is to be translated as "god" or as "devil."

The original draft of the Jesuit Acosta's *De procuranda indorum salute*, recently discovered, emphasizes the violence perpetrated upon the Peruvian people during and after the conquest, but the process of ecclesiastical and state censorship over a period of eleven years reduced it to, in Adorno's words, "a mere guide on missionary pedagogy" ("Literary Production and Suppression"). In his later widely read *Historia natural y moral de las Indias* (Natural and Moral History of the Indies; 1590), consequently, Acosta profited from the experience by repeatedly reminding his future readers that an understanding of native practices was essential to the eventual conversion not only of Amerindians, but of pagan Chinese, Ethiopians, and Hindus as well.

To a much greater extent than Sahagún, Acosta *framed* virtually all of his data with Biblical quotations and cultural comparisons, endlessly reiterating the precise ways in which his Christian readers would be strengthened by controlled exposure to heathen practices. He also explained how such exposure illuminated the providential plan for conquest and conversion. Nevertheless, Acosta also suggested that his eyewitness account of exotica could provide pleasure in the harmless way that the novels of chivalry had done. This strategy gained approval from the censors, and the *Historia* was in fact reprinted several times over the next decades. Acosta regarded the Indians as childlike persons of inferior mentality and, with Francisco de Vitoria (1492–1546), rejected the argument that they were natural slaves. Futhermore, he recognized that there were clear differences among Indians just as there were among various plant species. He classified the Mexicas as immediately preliterate since they possessed approximations to a written script. While deploring their idolatry, he also recognized an analogy between their structuring of religion around priesthood, temples, and rituals and the way in which the Christian religion did so. Their understanding of religious organization would, he thought, ultimately make their conversion possible, though the lack of sophistication of their language still presented problems.

A third figure in a position more or less analogous with that of Sahagún and Acosta is Fray Diego Durán (1537–1588), who came to Texcoco (Mexico) from Spain as a young child. Struck from the first by the beauty of the "promised land" and the admirable character of the Indians, in whose language he gained fluency, Durán became a Dominican priest at age nineteen, dedicating himself to the thorough conversion of the native population but convinced, unlike others, of the necessity of understanding their old religion in order to stamp it out. He therefore condemned the earliest evangelists for destroying virtually all of the codices encountered rather than seeking to discover their theological foundations, since his own awareness of the persistence of ancient practices convinced him that syncretism was everywhere present but usually went unrecognized. Durán's *Historia de las Indias de Nueva España y islas de Tierra Firme* (History of the Indians of New Spain and the Islands of Terra Firma; 1867), finished in 1589, consists of three parts, all of which have been translated into English (the first and second as *Book of the Gods and Rites and the Ancient Calendar* in 1971 and the third, abridged, as *The Aztecs: The History of the Indies of New Spain* in 1964).

In spite of his insistence on "pure" Christianity, Durán emphasizes analogies between Indian and European society and religion, describing an Aztec feast similar to Easter, rites resembling confession and baptism, and a concept not unlike that of the Holy Trinity. He believed the Amerindians to be descended from the lost tribes of Israel, and he is among the first to identify Quetzalcoatl with Saint Thomas, a dangerous notion that became a cornerstone of the doctrine known as syncretism, whose later *criollo* adherents would include Carlos

de Sigüenza y Góngora (1645–1700) and probably Sor Juana Inés de la Cruz
(1651–1695). He also held another heterodox notion to the effect that Cortés
had been providentially selected to open the way for conversion in the Indies.
Durán's sources seem to have been codices now lost as well as the oral testimony of Indian acquaintances and his own familiarity with dances, festivities,
and songs. Because his history of the conquest is told from the point of view
of the natives, Todorov classifies Durán as one of the first Mexicans, seeing
him as neither Aztec nor Spaniard but rather "that being who presents the
transition from one to the other."

Reevaluative study has already begun on the monumental *Veintiún libros
rituales de la monarquía indiana* (Twenty-one Ritual Books of the Indian Monarchy; [1612] 1943) by the Franciscan Juan de Torquemada (1557–1624),
highly significant for an important ongoing line of ideological inquiry. Writing
on the legends of Quetzalcoatl, Torquemada views the god, as had Sahagún,
as a "magician and necromancer." Nevertheless, Torquemada takes a significant step in his stated approval of a ritual exhortation to Aztec children chosen
to study at the *callmecac,* or elite schools of the Mexicas, to the effect that
these youths had been shaped by "an invisible god, creator of all things" and
that they had "come into the world by his will." The chronicler notes the
virtual identity between these words and those addressed to the Ephesians by
Saint Paul in the Christian Bible. He then quotes Saint Augustine to the effect
that Christians should abide by "whatever is good in the sayings of the gen-
tiles." Torquemada thus appears to advocate receptiveness to at least one aspect of the old religion. He also accepts the idea that Quetzalcoatl, though a
demon god, was white and that God had permitted the prophecy of his return
in order to facilitate the Spanish conquest, a providentialist interpretation giving structure and value to Aztec history even while Torquemada roundly condemned its theology and religious practices. Like Sahagún, Torquemada sub-
scribed to the notion of a series of correspondences between the Mexica god
Huitzilopochtli and Mars; Painal and Mercury, Tezcatlipoca and Jupiter, and
so forth. But he also seemed to admit the notion that there was *identity* between the Roman and Aztec deities, all of whom had been deployed by the
Devil for the same purpose.

Given this line of current inquiry, the texts actually written by mestizo and
native historians become the key ones in the reevaluation of the colonial period. Much less numerous than chronicles by Europeans, these tend to present
such obstacles as being inscribed in a native language or in imperfect Spanish
or, according to rhetorical or generic systems, difficult to interpret adequately.
Another problem has traditionally been their insistence on historical data generally accorded to be false. Three such texts in Mexican literature are the *Crónica mexicana* (Mexican Chronicle; 1848) of Hernando de Alvarado Tezozó-
maoc (1525?–?), various works including the *Historia chichimeca* (History of
the Chichimecas; [1608] 1985) of Fernando de Alva Ixtlilxochitl (1568?–
1648), and the *Descripción de la ciudad y provincia de Tlaxcala* (Description of
the City and Province of Tlaxcala; 1981) of Diego Muñoz Camargo (1526–

1614). The full incorporation of these texts into the mainstream of Mexican literature will clearly necessitate a degree of interdisciplinary expertise not required for the analysis of works by Europeans and *criollos*.

Belles Lettres

In attempting to determine a proper beginning for the poetry of New Spain, Alfonso Méndez Plancarte, compiler of what is still the most complete series of anthologies (*Poetas novohispanos* [Poets of New Spain], 3 vols.), emphasizes the confluence of Nahuatl and Maya traditions with Spanish, Portuguese, Italian, Latin, and even Arab elements. Like Méndez Plancarte himself, we will not deal in this essay with indigenous poetry, though its existence must be acknowledged as one of the embodiments of "the other Mexico" that has exerted an ever-increasing influence on the country's culture since independence from Spain in 1821.

With the important reevaluation of the indigenous heritage that would occur with the aid of Jesuit syncretism more than a century later not yet even visible on the horizon, the sixteenth century saw little significant interpenetration of indigenous and Spanish poetic traditions. Rapid Hispanization of the indigenous institutions remaining viable was of course the overriding concern of the Spanish Empire immediately following the conquest. The chief agencies in charge of implementing the task of *translatio imperii* officially held to have been "ordained by Providence" were the Church and the State, under whose auspices most Europeans arrived following completion of the conquest in 1521.

These immigrants along with the increasing number of *criollo* engaged to this effect in a virtually unending series of public acts and ceremonies, usually carried out with a maximum of pomp and pageantry. Literary culture under such circumstances served an ancillary purpose, that of moralizing, inculcating dogma, and institutionalizing official values, with little originality and no opposition allowed. The Royal and Pontifical University of Mexico was founded in 1553. Its students were required to master the rhetorical skills needed to produce verse commemorating such occasions as the "Departure of Our Lady of Guadalupe for Her Shrine in Tepeyac" or "Festival wherein the Colony of Jesuits Celebrates the Canonization of Saint Francis of Borgia." The frequent arrivals and departures of viceroys and Church officials offered fine pretexts for pageantry often including, in addition to bright costumes and original music, poetry contests, or *certámenes,* sometimes drawing hundreds of entries. But in each case the themes, most often taken from Greek and Latin mythology and held to signal key points of Christian dogma through figural typology, as well as the rhyme scheme to be employed by the contestants, were handed down from above, detailed prescriptions to be filled in order to keep the propaganda wheel turning and thereby stifle pockets of nascent social discontent.

To say that some of the conquistadors contemplated Mexico in poetic terms almost from their first inkling of its existence is not an exaggeration but rather a well-documented fact. One of the emblematic passages of Bernal Díaz del Castillo's *Historia verdadera de la conquista de Nueva España* evokes a scene on shipboard in the year 1519 in which several veterans of the two previous unsuccessful expeditions help to familiarize Hernán Cortés with landmarks along the Mexican coast. In a moment of exhilaration at their prospects under the leadership of an astute new captain, one of them recalls some appropriately optimistic lines from an old ballad of the Roldán (Roland or Orlando) cycle: "Cata Francia, Montesinos / cata París, la ciudad / cata las aguas del Duero / do van a dar a la mar" (Behold France, Montesinos / behold the city of Paris / behold the waters of the Duero / where they flow down to the sea). In Díaz's version (chapter 36), Cortés catches the intent instantly and responds with another ballad fragment that seems to function as an invocation for the remarkable events to follow: "Dénos Dios ventura en armas como al paladín Roldán" (May God give us good fortune in battle, as to the paladin Roland). Placed in the text just prior to the definitive landing on Mexican soil, these passages have been referred to as a sort of "literary shorthand" through which the Spanish are instantly transformed into analogues of the epic crusaders of an earlier period. The chronicles record literally dozens of other instances in which lines of poetry are hurled into the breach, forging a semiotically rich link between Mexico's founding texts and the heart of Spain's tradition of popular poetry.

On countless other occasions ballads are parodied or composed on the spot to encode the passions and humor of camp life, initiating the line of popular poetry, much of it satirical, that even today retains the same meter, rhyme, and framing devices as the *romance* (Spanish ballad), albeit with lexical, grammatical, and thematic innovations, out of which the modern *corrido* (Mexican street ballad) has evolved. A notion advanced by several critics suggests that Mexican folklore in contrast with Spain's is characterized by its tendency to gravitate toward the pole of the "literary" rather than the popular norm because during the Golden Age (sixteenth and seventeenth centuries) such masters as Lope de Vega (1562–1635) and Luis de Góngora (1561–1627) had begun to fuse forms and thematic material from the traditional ballad with the literary devices more commonly found in *poesía culta* (refined poetry). While on the Iberian Peninsula the Counter Reformation halted this process, in Mexico the trend toward fusion of the two norms has continued virtually uninterrupted, resulting in the tendency of Mexican popular poetry to display unusual refinement.

The ballad flourished in sixteenth-century Mexico despite the well-known royal edicts of 1531, 1536, and 1543 banning the importation of works of fiction in any form into the New World, since it was feared these might constitute a source of confusion to indigenous converts. Research into such documents as ship registries and trade receipts confirms the fact that dozens of *cancioneros* (collections of poems and songs) arrived in Mexico throughout the sixteenth century. The edicts were least effective in the viceregal court, whence the latest songs from Spain (including the intrigue-laden novelesque ballads) were soon transmitted to *criollos,* mestizos, and Amerindians, the receptiveness of the last group being enhanced by the analogous musical traditions of their own culture.

Aside from these popular transpositions, records show that much poetry of the *norma culta* (learned tradition) was also written in sixteenth-century New Spain, as attested in the eminently quotable line provided one of the dramatic characters of an early playwright, Fernán González de Eslava (1533?–1601?), to the effect that in the court of the viceroy "there are more poets than dung" (*Coloquio diez y seis,* 229). Examples may be adduced of narrative, epic, satiric, descriptive, and religious verse. The lyric manifested itself in both traditional and Italianate meters, the latter made popular in Spain by Juan Boscán (1493?–1542) and Garcilaso de la Vega (1501–1536) and introduced in the New World by such Spanish poets as Gutierre de Cetina (1520–1577?), Juan de la Cueva (1543–1610), Eugenio de Salazar (1530?–1605?), and various other Spanish-born poets who sojourned and in some cases succumbed there as well. Juan de Castellanos (1522–1607), a conquistador and poet of Nueva Granada (now Colombia), even makes mention in his heroic poem *Elegías de varones ilustres de Indias* (Elegies of Famous American Men; 1589) of a full-blown polemic taking place in the Spanish colonies during the early sixteenth century over which were superior—traditional Spanish verse forms or those borrowed from the Italian cities where humanistically inspired art flourished.

Virtually all anthologies of Mexican literature either begin with selections by the Spanish poets Cetina, Cueva, and Salazar or at least devote some discussion to their works. While none of these men was born in the New World, each made his influence felt during the period of time he spent in Mexico. Cetina, the most noted of the three, is not actually known to have written any of his poems in Mexico, but the discovery of an important manuscript entitled *Flores de baria poesía* (Flowers of Assorted Poetry), dated 1577, as well as other contemporary records, testify impressively to the influence of Cetina's knowledge of Petrarchan conventions on such *criollo* poets as Francisco de Terrazas (1525?–1600?). The *Flores* manuscript, whose complete contents were published for the first time in 1980 by Margarita Peña, contains 330 poems (some eighty-four by Cetina), most of which clearly display contemporary Italianate influence. The date of the earliest poem appearing in the collection is 1543. Among other Peninsular poets represented are Herrera, Cueva, Figueroa, and Hurtado de Mendoza; the *criollos* include Terrazas, Carlos de Sámano, Miguel de Cuevas, and even Don Martín Cortés, son and heir of the chief conquistador himself.

Scholarship on sixteenth-century Mexican poetry has generally been impeded by the following factors: (1) much of it has been lost; (2) Mexicans have tended until recently to regard New Spain's three centuries of existence as an atypical interregnum in their history, thus neglecting to study them thoroughly; and (3) early critics gave it a bad press. Marcelino Menéndez y Pelayo, for example, reportedly remarked in 1911 that nothing would be lost if the names of all Spanish American colonial poets were reduced to one—that of Sor Juana Inés de la Cruz. The historians who followed tended to reiterate his verdict, even though most did admit a more favorable disposition toward at least two others, Terrazas and Bernardo de Balbuena (1561?–1627). In retrospect it is clear that the merits of all three of these poets were relatively easy to assess since each excelled according to the prevailing contemporary *European* standards formerly held to provide the only valid measuring rod.

The first Mexican-born poet to write in Spanish is Francisco de Terrazas, five of whose sonnets appear in the *Flores de baria poesía* (several of his other lyric poems including a rhymed epistle and one epic work are also known). The well-to-do son of a conquistador, Terrazas is believed to have spent time in Spain mastering the Petrarchan poetics then in vogue among the Seville poets. He even gained admiring recognition by no less a literary light than Miguel de Cervantes (1547–1616), who mentions Terrazas with enthusiasm in the prologue to *La Galatea* (1585). Terrazas's reputation among peers in Mexico was equally exalted. While little significant critical work has been done recently on this poet, he is considered important for two reasons. First, his works demonstrate how rapidly the Italianate style of poetry, still relatively new on the Peninsula, took root in Mexico. Second, Terrazas was the first to attempt an epic poem, *Conquista y Nuevo Mundo* (Conquest and New World; [1604] 1902), glorifying Cortés.

Only fragments of this work have survived, discovered by Joaquín García Icazbalceta to have been intercalated within passages of the *Sumaria relación* (Summary Report; [1604] 1902), a chronicle by Baltazar Dorantes de Carranza (1550?–1610?). The traditional epic poem, a form currently (and for several centuries) perceived as archaic, ranked in the sixteenth century at the very top of the hierarchy of poetic types. With its elevated style and precise formal requirements, composition of an epic was a challenging undertaking. With verses of the classic epics of Virgil and Lucano as well as Juan de Mena's *El laberinto de la fortuna* (Labyrinth of Fortune; 1481) ringing in their ears, many of the conquistadors were fully aware of the epic quality of their own undertaking. In *Conquista,* Terraza's comprehensive plan was to commence with the two unsuccessful voyages to Mexico preceding Cortés's own and then carry the story forward to embrace such topical questions as the second-generation *criollos'* grievances against the Crown for dealing unfairly with them as the conquistadors' legitimate heirs. The work abounds in Biblical archetypes and allusions, with Jerónimo de Aguilar, the Spaniard who gave up his life among the Mayas of Cozumel to assume the important role of translator for Cortés, cast as the Prodigal Son. The slight unease with which Terrazas handles the requirement of a consistently elevated tone, a sine qua non of the epic, may be seen as a flaw. It is possible that the poet's birth in the New World rather than Spain resulted in an incipient divergence in values that could have been a factor in his failure to finish the poem. Whether or not such is the case, virtually all critics agree that *Conquista*'s most admirable passages are its lyrical ones, including the frequently anthologized idyll of the Indian lovers Huitzel and Quetzal. Some recent critics label Terrazas's lyric poetry as "mannerist," a term of European origin used to describe post-renaissance literature whose principal characteristics José Pascual Buxó ("Bernardo de Balbuena, o El Manierismo plácido") gives as refinement, hyperbaton, elusive or allusive metaphor, allegory, and so forth—all innovative in the works of Luis de Góngora but increasingly traditional and academic with the passing of time.

An epic poem of the Spaniard Gabriel Lobo Lasso de la Vega, *Cortés valeroso y Mexicana* (Cortés the Valiant and Mexicaniad; 1588), is rarely included in discussions of Mexican literature, though it seems likely to be reevaluated within the present current of interest in redefining the focus of Mexican literature. A later epic poem on the Mexican conquest is the criollo Antonio de Saavedra Guzmán's *El peregrino indiano* (The Pilgrim in the Indies; 1599), which has never lived down the scathing criticism delivered by a few of its early critics, even though Méndez Plancarte is not alone in praising the work. The firsthand information offered by the poet, a *corregidor* of Zacatecas (a magistrate or mayor-like official whose duties involved protecting the Indians), on Indian customs as well as the featured romance between a Spaniard and an Indian maiden, however, renders it ripe for reexamination. A revision of Gaspar Pérez de Villagrá's epic poem *Historia de Nueva México* (*sic*) (History of New Mexico; 1610) has already been called for, though in both of these cases length and the radical decline in appreciation of the epic form militate against substantial reintegration.

In Spanish America *mannerist* is the term many critics use to label the increasingly important literary theme of social problems, notably among whites, since it is almost exclusively they who act to produce and consume literature in New Spain. Growing resentment on the part of *criollos* against the Crown's preferential treatment of *gachupines,* or Peninsular Spaniards, is the grievance most often expressed, usually as satire. Three examples of poetic satire conserved in Dorantes de Carranza's *Sumaria relación* probably date from the end of the sixteenth century and are believed to have been written by the same hand. Composed in sonnet form, one voices the disgust of a newcomer from Spain at the crass commercialism and social disorder seen everywhere in Mexico City. In the other two a *criollo* speaker retorts by complaining of displacement by Johnny-come-latelys from Spain who take charge of colonial affairs, soon accumulating riches and honors in the New World despite their less than auspicious beginnings.

Pedro de Trejo (1534–1575?), born in Spain but in residence during most of his life in Morelia and Zacatecas, produced at least one satiric poem, "Canción de una dama" (A Lady's Song). Here the speaker is a woman expressing (in *redondillas,* or ballad-like lines) her prejudices against Mexican or *criollo* males (*atoleros,* or drinkers of *atole*) owing to their notorious deceitfulness. She claims to prefer Peninsular men, a typical attitude of *criollo* women constituting another frequently aired grievance. Trejo's works were discovered by chance among records of the Mexican Inquisition, which had sentenced him to labor as a galley slave after forbidding him to exercise his talents further in writing verse of this kind. Trejo's *Cancionero* (Songbook), written about 1570 but published for the first time in 1980, exemplifies the general characteristics of the era's poetry in religious, amorous, and elegiac as well as satiric verses.

The figure best known for satiric poetry in colonial literature is Mateo Rosas de Oquendo (1559?–1612?). A Spaniard who participated in European military campaigns, Rosas de Oquendo first passed to Córdoba del Tucumán (Río de la Plata), reportedly writing a long epic poem, now lost, on the conquest of this province. He next served the viceroy in Lima, where he resided for some time with his family. Toward the end of this period he wrote the *Sátira hecha por Mateo Rosas de Oquendo a las cosas que pasan en el Pirú, año de 1593* (Satire by Mateo Rosas de Oquendo on Things Happening in Peru, Year 1593), a *romance* of some 2,120 lines. Parodying the (oral) sermon but also the (written) testament or sworn statement, the narrator admonishes, informs, advises, exhorts, and apostrophizes a gallery of conventional types including "dirty old men," lustful women, adulterers, the cuckolded, false virgins, seducers, soldiers, slaves, and so forth, but especially the corrupt of the viceregal court. The complete version of this important poem, which employs techniques of Menippean satire and carnivalization, was not found until 1907 in the Biblioteca Nacional de Madrid, though Dorantes de Carranza had transcribed several excerpts in his *Sumaria relación*.

Rosas de Oquendo spent fourteen years near the end of his life in New Spain, where he continued to write verses. Some of these, though less mordant, are still satirical in intent. A well-known *romance* ("Romance del mestizo"; The Mestizo's Ballad) features a mestizo speaker who addresses himself to "señora Juana" (Madam Jane) and later to "Juanica mía, carita de flores" (my blossom-faced Janie), performing a number of self-ingratiating speech acts including cajoling, belly-aching, bragging about his tough constitution and hard life, and recommending his own diet of typical fare. He refers to himself as a coyote and claims to be, albeit in ragged clothing, of noble lineage and the son of conquistadors. At the poem's end the narrator enters to frame the parodied discourse with the ironic announcement that "All this was sung / by Juan Diego the noble, / while rolling a cigarette; / he took a puff on it and then fell asleep."

The poem is notable for several reasons. Every statement uttered by Rosas de Oquendo's subject highlights a key aspect of his psychological makeup, with the whole forming what in fact became an enduring stereotype of the Mexican male. The preoccupation with self-defense clearly stems from the mestizo's social insecurity as he insists on claiming a status his own words are made to refute. The narrator's final remarks carefully underscore what the speaker's verbiage represses: within his world he is at best ineffectual and at worst impotent. It is a succinct dramatization of the historical plight of the "new race" whose decline in fortune had already begun to accelerate.

Rosas's caricature of contemporary society in another of his New Spain poems, the "Romance a México" (Ballad to Mexico) has been quoted by virtually every Mexican historian and sociologist concerned with the turn of the sixteenth century. Here the speaker claims that in a moment of melancholy nostalgia "a great discourse came into my mind / pulling me along in its wake" thus introducing a kind of spontaneous, self-guided *sueño* (dream) that could almost be read as the dark side of Balbuena's *Grandeza mexicana* (The Grandeur of Mexico; 1604). What Rosas perceives, as in the "Romance del mestizo," are the exaggerated pretenses of a large and generally motley parade of social types, all of whom seem plagued by doubtful credentials and class instability. Rosas as satirist not only sees but hears; in addition to parodying the speech of mestizos and upper-class Mexicans, he is the first, according to Reyes, to attempt in another *romance* a written approximation of that of an "Yndio mexicano" (Mexican Indian).

While Fernán González de Eslava is best known for his theater, he was also a lyric poet of some renown, with two sonnets and a gloss on one of these in the form of a *lira* (poetic stanza with alternating seven- and eleven-syllable lines) appearing in the manuscript of *Flores de varia poesía* of 1577 (his other secular poems have been lost). The first six stanzas of the *lira* glossing the sonnet "Columna de cristal" (Crystal Column) could almost serve as an index of Petrarchan tropes idealizing woman; the melancholy tone of the lover in the second half recalls Garcilaso's eclogues. The *villancicos,* or Christmas songs, and *redondillas* (both forms of popular verse) making up a large part of González de Eslava's religious poetry (of which the first edition *Coloquios espirituales y sacramentales y canciones divinas,* or Spiritual and Sacramental Colloquies and Divine Songs, was published in 1610) tend to evoke in the opening line a bright visual image of something immediately at hand (a baby, a fountain, a mouthful of food, a star, a boat) and continue anaphorically, reminding the reader that González de Eslava was a priest conscious of the need to catch and hold the attention of an unsophisticated congregation. Easily grasped analogies serve to make his subject matter, often points of doctrine, accessible. The *adivinanzas,* or riddles, provide excellent examples of this. While many of his themes and motifs are traditional and traceable to medieval Spanish poets, González de Eslava's language identifies him as Mexican. In the often anthologized "Canción a nuestra Señora" (Song to Our Lady) he apostrophizes a *virgen morena* (dark virgin). His religious lyrics, unlike many of those by other sixteenth-century writers included in Méndez Plancarte's anthologies, are still enjoyable today. In their literary quality, these initiate in New Spain the line that will be extended some seventy-five years later in the *villancicos* of Sor Juana. González de Eslava, like Rosas de Oquendo a Spaniard without pretensions to a noble background, clearly displays empathy with the emerging *criollo* point of view.

Bernardo de Balbuena, like González de Eslava though in a different key, is bound to Mexican literature with the closest of ties. Born in Spain and later returning there for an interval in order to earn the degree of doctor of theology, Balbuena spent his boyhood and virtually all of his later life in the Indies, eventually becoming bishop of Puerto Rico. The poem for which he is most renowned today is the *Grandeza mexicana,* written in 1602–1603 and originally part of a letter to the poet's friend Isabel de Tovar y Guzmán. For some early critics, *Grandeza* represented the birth of American poetry. Though few would now accept a judgment so clearly reflecting European bias, it should be noted that among Mexican colonial writers only Sor Juana today evokes more critical commentary than Balbuena. *Grandeza*'s famous introductory stanza, in the form of an *octava real,* or "royal octave" (eleven-syllable stanzas rhyming *a b a b a b c c*), functions as a table of contents for the nine "chapters" (*cantos*) to follow. Each of these is made up of tercets rhyming *a b a b c b c d c* (etc.), the interlocking pattern (*rima abrazada*) of the terza rima eliminating the choppiness a series of short stanzas might otherwise convey. The final stanza of each chapter, a summation, is a quartet rhyming *a b a b*. The final chapter, corresponding to the phrase "todo en este discurso está cifrado" (all within this work is encoded), is given over to a metapoetics that reabsorbs the poem. The topics dealt with in *Grandeza* are the origin and topography of Mexico City, the grandeur of its buildings, its horses, the friendly relations among its citizens, the arts it boasts, occasions for celebration, and so forth. It is characterized throughout by enunciative exuberance, the poetic voice appearing to fill all available "space" by spilling out one image after another. Balbuena's imagination works metonymically, taking him laterally from one noun or adjective to another. His penchant for listing is one of the poem's most immediately identifiable features, and in fact this trait has led to the commonplace that *Grandeza mexicana* is a catalogue in verse. Nevertheless, a balance of sorts is offered by the metapoetic dimension of the last chapter, which is much the longest.

In a Marxist approach to colonial literature, Hernán Vidal has called *Grandeza* "the most conspicuous imperialistic poem of the colonial period"(120), pointing out that its false vision of an Arcadian paradise, in which the native American appears only once (with the designation "el indio feo," the ugly Indian), served to justify Spanish greed in the conquest and hardly impeded Balbuena's own rise within the ecclesiastical hierarchy despite the stain of his illegitimate birth. While Vidal's evaluation is accurate within his ideological frame, *Grandeza* may still be studied and appreciated as verbal art within a number of other perspectives that neither overlook nor deny its political bias. One of these, basing itself on the theories of Michel Foucault, would investigate the ways in which the notion of *territoriality* may manifest itself in literary discourse. Within such an approach Balbuena may be seen as one of those performing the essential (from the Spanish point of view) task of symbolically flushing out the "discursive space" of Tenochtitlán/Mexico, formerly the center of the Mexica world and a place where, in Balbuena's phrase, "nadie creyó que hubiese mundo" (no one believed a world to exist). Like Francisco Cervantes de Salazar (? – 1575), Juan de la Cueva, and Eugenio de Salazar, among others, he then sets out to fill this "empty" space with a new discourse—a poetic but orthodox portrayal of New Spain as the providential instrument of *translatio imperii*. Balbuena's attention in the poem's first chapter to the question of topography may be seen as his attempt to circumscribe the exact dimensions of the space to be appropriated and rechristened. Mexico is thus poetically "born again" as a mirror of Western culture.

Theater

Approaching theater in New Spain is easier if we first pause to remember what distinguishes drama from all other genres—its dual nature as literary form and spectacle. Because the initial impetus of Mexican colonial theater was the urgent task of evangelization following conquest, and because the racially diverse people involved in these events neither spoke the same language nor shared an alphabet, the fact spectacle clearly *preceded* text should not surprise us. As a result, critical discussion of the missionary theater depends largely on those descriptions of its manifestations that have been passed on to us by the period's chroniclers.

Simple processions in celebration of Corpus Christi and other religious occasions (and also, especially in sixteenth-century Mexico, in observance of state occasions) seem to have been the first step, with some representation carried out at various stops along the way. After the arrival in 1524 of the twelve Franciscan friars summoned by Cortés, performances dramatizing Bible stories and points of doctrine began to be organized. These productions were moved from the churches themselves to *capillas abiertas* (open chapels), the front patios of churches, and ultimately almost anywhere they could be staged to accommodate vast crowds of Indians. Later the infusion of profane carnivalesque elements was to become cause for concern on the part of ecclesiastical authorities. The first archbishop, Fray Juan de Zumárraga (1468–1548), made some provisional prohibitions, and dancing and the use of profane farsical elements and songs in the atria of churches were forbidden in 1585.

The one-act plays contrived by the missionaries were known as *autos*. This type of work, long common fare in medieval Europe, usually aimed at clarifying some aspect of the Eucharist through allegorical equivalence. The earliest ones produced in Mexico, brief and always featuring intervals of singing, dancing, and pantomime, were adaptations of already existing Spanish *autos* translated into one or more indigenous languages. The adapters and later the authors were the friars themselves, who quickly saw what great possibilities could be realized by substituting what they had to offer for the Mexica tradition of dramatic ritual. The actors in the first missionary *autos* were largely Indian males. The latter also contributed imaginatively to elaboration of the sets using many of their own skills as artesans.

The missionary Fray Toribio de Motolinia (?–1569), in his *Historia de los indios de Nueva España* (History of the Indians of New Spain; 1903), describes a dramatization of the sin of Adam and Eve in the Garden of Eden performed in Tlaxcala in 1538. The stage was arranged to represent a garden replete with replicas of fruit trees. Various kinds of birds and animals abounded, some of them artifacts made by Indians and others real, including parrots and ocelots. Motolinia notes that the Indians excelled at creating scenery and costumes and also at simulating many types of diseases.

Other popular themes included the adoration of the Magi (still pagans when they set out for Bethlehem) and of the shepherds, the Resurrection, the Last Judgment, and the striking dumb of Zacharias, which of course called for mime. *La destrucción de Jerusalén* (The Destruction of Jerusalem; in Rojas Garcidueñas, ed.), an anonymous *auto,* is one of the few of these early plays (some nine in all) whose texts remain extant, though the manuscript itself is of the next century. Here the emperor Vespasian is cured of leprosy upon accepting the gospel. He then lays siege to Jerusalem whose governor, Pilate, has not paid the required tributes to the Roman Empire. During the course of the siege, hunger causes several women—always played by boys or men—to "cook and eat their children" onstage. The *Destrucción* is believed to be based on medieval Provençal models though no actual European text of it is known.

Recent ideological considerations (see Shelly and Rojo) of the missionary theater have emphasized the extent to which drama constituted not only an educational tool of the Church but also an instrument of political control. The paternalistic propaganda served up in the guise of religion emphasized obedience, dependency, and the multiple virtues of poverty in order to produce ideal subjects for continuing Spanish domination. A particularly trenchant example of manipulation has recently been adduced by Ramón Gutiérrez. Toward the end of the sixteenth century the conquistador Juan de Oñate (1549?–1628?), in collaboration with Franciscan friars, used a dramatic representation of the 1521 conquest by Cortés and of the latter's reception three years later (1524) of the original twelve Franciscan missionaries in order to subdue the Pueblo Indians in what is now New Mexico. Oñate, who had even enlisted the aid of a second "Malinche" (a Pueblo woman baptized Doña Inés), himself took the part of Cortés, while a number of his soldiers impersonated conquered Aztec lords. In the most important scene of this drama, "Cortés" dismounted from his steed, fell on his knees before the friars, and kissed their feet, next ordering the lords to make a public acknowledgment of their conversion by doing the same. Once Oñate's drama ended, he insisted that the Pueblo people, who already knew something of the Aztecs' capitulation before powerful foreigners, repeat the acts of submission in real life. In subsequent presentations of this drama, Pueblo Indian actors were made to play all of the parts, reenacting over and over the rationale of their own defeat before the Spaniards.

The missionary theater is documented from 1529 until about 1572. Several years after the second date the Church initiated efforts to have existing texts of plays destroyed, the reason being the proliferation in dramatic productions of signs and practices pointing retrospectively to the paganism of the old religion. Nevertheless, there are reasons for supposing that performances of the early *autos* continued; scholars defending such an assumption (for example, Shelly and Rojo, 322) point to the fact that most extant texts seem to date from the later *seventeenth* century. There is no clear agreement on this point. It is a fact, however, that a dramatic tradition in Nahuatl continued through the colonial period involving representations of religious themes in plays employing devices identified with works of Spain's Golden Age dramatists. Several works by Lope de Vega and Calderón were also translated into Nahuatl by the versatile mestizo Don Fernando de Alva Ixtlilxochitl. This tradition existed apart from the so-called *neixcuitilli*—live tableaux functioning to illustrate some part of a sermon and carried out within the churches themselves—still seen today in some parts of Mexico.

By 1572 the Jesuits had arrived in New Spain, bringing with them a tradition of school or collegiate dramatic productions in Latin and Spanish. In 1577 according to the *Carta del Padre Pedro de Morales* (Letter from Father Pedro de Morales; 1579) written by the latter to the general of the Jesuit order, a series of plays was produced by several schools in order to celebrate the arrival of a collection of sacred relics sent by the pope. The most successful of these, whose text Morales includes integrally, was the *Triunfo de los Santos* (Triumph of the Saints; 1941), attributed to two priests. Consisting of a prologue and five acts and employing a variety of poetic meters, this rather static allegorical work, though of historical interest, has not inspired any recent scholarship.

González de Eslava is the first *criollo* dramatist whose plays were systematically collected, edited, and published (in 1610). González de Eslava was an able poet whose verses, including many appearing in his plays, are well crafted and enjoyable as popular literature. The plays are also well crafted *as plays*, though their purpose is always to catechize. Taking much from the medieval theater including a notion of fairly boisterous slapstick, González de Eslava clearly understood the importance of establishing a credible pretext for imparting the particular lesson to be dealt with in the comprehensive work to follow. This might be a fictional guessing game in which the character supplying the correct answer was to be rewarded. Or it might be a dispute in which some comically appealing individual learned in the course of the action why his interpretation of an idea relating to doctrine happened to be incorrect. González de Eslava's characters, even when allegorical, often traded graphic insults with one another; and though they did so in verse, it was through Mexican dialect and with reference to Mexican reality through topographical allusions and the like. In any conversation, even one conducted among "doctors of the Church," there might be witty repartee so that theology did not become oppressive. A balance is achieved, moreover, in the contrast between the lyric passages that refer to sacramental mysteries and the earthy vulgarity of the speech of the characters who provide the most direct bridge with the audience.

As the Spanish continued to expand the northern reaches of their empire into what is now New Mexico, Arizona, California, Texas, and so forth, new chronicles were produced by wave after wave of explorers on through the eighteenth century (see Esteve Barba, 237–268). On the whole, these writings have not been of great interest to recent Mexican scholars, but an important reevaluation of many of them by Chicano and other Latino scholars of the U.S. has now begun. The results of their efforts, in conjunction with the dialogue they have begun with Mexican intellectuals, will bear watching (see Gutiérrez; Bruce-Novoa).

II LATER SIXTEENTH AND SEVENTEENTH CENTURIES

Novel

Because the Spanish Crown was primarily concerned with inculcating Christian mythologies in the place of indigenous ones, it sought through specific legislation to prohibit subjects in the New World from reading such "profane and fantastic" works as chivalric novels or even those of the secular pastoral tradition. Even though officials failed to prevent large numbers of such books from being imported into New Spain, they did succeed in creating there a climate unpropitious for the writing of new ones. Years of research, along with a series of useful debates regarding the novel's defining characteristics, have resulted in the identification of a few candidates for the first Spanish American novel that predate Fernández de Lizardi's *El Periquillo Sarniento* (*The Itching Parrot;* 1816). An examination of these earlier texts reveals clearly that each escaped the ban by emphasizing Christian themes within the conventions of the pastoral novel *a lo divino* (set in a Christian frame).

The first is a combination of prose and (mostly) verse entitled *El Siglo de Oro en las selvas de Erífile* (The Golden Age in the Forests of Erífile), written by Bernardo de Balbuena and published in Madrid in 1608. The second is Francisco Bramón's *Los sirgueros de la Virgen sin original pecado* (Linnets of the Virgin without Original Sin), written in Mexico in 1620. There is very little action in either work, such dynamism as they do possess being generated by alternations between poetry and prose or, in the case of *Los sirgueros,* between straight poetry and the verse employed in the *auto,* or play, forming the third part. Balbuena's work is clearly an *imitatio* of *Arcadia* (1489) by the Italian Jacopo Sannazaro (1455–1530), whose vision of the city of Naples Balbuena reinscribes as a vision of Mexico City perceived from the depths of its lake. This is but one aspect of the "realism" not usually found in the Spanish tradition of pastoral literature (as opposed to the Italian) that critics have noted in the *Siglo de Oro,* which may be seen in some respects as prefiguring Balbuena's *Grandeza mexicana.* The poetry of the former work is highly regarded by critics, especially its eclogues, considered second only to those of the major Spanish poet Garcilaso de la Vega.

Bramón's work is more clearly allegorical, with the Golden Age representing Paradise and its disappearance ascribed to the Fall of Man. The imperfection of the world, which is given a Mexican landscape, serves as a contrast to the purity of the Virgin by virtue of her immaculate conception, which the work celebrates. The majority of the poems, dialogues, and descriptions (of arches, emblems, etc.) are panegyrical to the Virgin. Neither Bramón's "novel" nor the

several other minor works of the period in which critics have identified novelesque aspects have inspired any notable reevaluation, or even much in the
way of commentary (for the best summary see Cedomil Goic's essay in Iñigo
Madrigal, 369–406). By contrast, the *Infortunios de Alonso Ramírez* (Misfor-
tunes of Alonso Ramírez; 1690) by Sigüenza y Góngora (see below) continues
to attract critical attention.

Historical Writings

Reevaluative work has just begun on a line of chronicles by humanist scholars
who based their highly polished and officially sanctioned accounts of the conquest on the sometimes inelegant earlier ones authored by eyewitnesses. The
official versions, considered vital in countering the *leyenda negra* (black legend) given foundation principally by Las Casas, were rushed into print at
times even before they were finished, influencing the beliefs of thousands of
readers. Alternative versions, meanwhile, often lay collecting dust in library
archives when not destroyed, lost, or left unwritten for fear of retribution.

In his *Crónica de la conquista de la Nueva España* (Chronicle of the Conquest
of New Spain; 1552), Francisco Cervantes de Salazar shows himself, like
López de Gómara, clearly biased in favor of Hernán Cortés. In fact, the general
plan of his work and a large portion of the text coincide with López de Gómara's even though Cervantes did consult a few other written sources including some of Cortés's letters and the *Relación* (Report; 1868) of Andrés de
Tapia. While preferring not to cite López de Gómara even when the debt to
him is obvious, Cervantes de Salazar does, oddly, cite the missionary friar
Motolinia, not known to have left any work dealing specifically with the conquest. A distinctive feature of Cervantes's work is its largely trivial *amplificatio*,
often in the form of excessive passages of heroic discourse.

Next in this group is Antonio de Herrera y Tordesillas (1549–1652), author
of *Historia general de los hechos de los castellanos en las islas y Tierra firme del
mar océano*, usually referred to as *Décadas* (General History of the Deeds of
the Castilians on the Islands and Terra Firma of the Ocean Sea, or Decades;
1601–1615). Herrera, named as official chronicler of Indies by the king, freely
appropriated pages from the works of Díaz del Castillo, López de Gómara, and
Las Casas but chose to use Cervantes de Salazar's second-hand account as his
primary source. Some years later Antonio de Solís y Rivadeneyra (1610–
1686), Herrera's successor, began on a work entitled *Historia de la conquista
de México, población y progresos de la América Septentrional, conocida por el
nombre de Nueva España* (History of the Conquest of Mexico, Settlement, and
Advances of Southern America, known as New Spain; 1684) but actually treating only the conquest. Deeply influenced by the providentialist resolutions of
the Council of Trent, Solís believed that the true history of Spain's involvement
in the New World would consist of an account of what *should* have been done.
In other words, such a history must record inspiring epic deeds performed by
heroes in the name of religion and patriotism. Solís portrays a providentially

annointed Cortés devotedly overseeing the Christian baptism of his former enemies with no thought of material reward. Because López de Gómara's chronicle presents a heroic Cortés, Solís based himself on that version rather than the (slightly) corrective account by Díaz del Castillo. Solís justifies Cortés's treatment of Moctezuma by affirming that the latter refused baptism, even though none of his own sources upholds such an assertion. Guided by the inflexible principles set down by the architects of the Counter Reformation, principles that essentially reinstated medieval historiography, Solís conceived his task as essentially deductive, the result being a history that is largely fantasy.

Among the first *criollos* to record the history of the years immediately following the conquest was Juan Suárez de Peralta (1527–1590), a native of Mexico City. Suárez's *Tratado del descubrimiento de las Indias y su conquista* (Treatise on the Discovery of the Indies and Their Conquest; 1589), known since its publication in 1878 as the *Noticias históricas de la Nueva España* (Historical News of New Spain), carries an integral account of events actually witnessed by its author, a *criollo* aristocrat believed to have been a nephew of Cortés's first wife, Catalina Xuárez. These revolve around the alleged conspiracy of Hernán Cortés's legitimate heir, Don Martín, greeted in 1565 on his arrival in New Spain with a round of extravagant parties thrown in his honor by wealthy second-generation *encomenderos*—heirs of the original conquistadors. Though not all admired the somewhat feckless Don Martín, a number of these *criollos* were so disgruntled by the Crown's plan to deprive them of consignments of Indian laborers, without whom their lands would be virtually useless, that they began to lay plans to rebel against imperial authorities and elect Don Martín as their leader.

Since Suárez, according to his own account, never wavered in his support of the Crown (perhaps in part because he was a *segundón*, or second son), it is surprising for the reader to find that the emotional center of the *Noticias* would be the apprehension, imprisonment, sentencing, and ultimate execution of the aristocratic Avila brothers, Alonso Alvarado and Gil González de Avila, historical figures beheaded by imperial authorities for their alleged part in the 1566 *conjuración*, or conspiracy, of Martín Cortés. Yet such is unquestionably the case. The brisk pace of the report slows as the narrator offers a series of intense and lingering close-ups of the two foppish young men reeling incredulously before their fate. In the evocation of the men's—and Suárez's own—sense of strangeness and even of the monstrous, these passages not only dramatize the *criollo*'s emerging sense of cultural ambivalence, but also seem to foreshadow aspects of the baroque soon to become prominent in America.

The report of a slightly earlier analogous event in Peru—the full-fledged rebellion of Gonzalo Pizarro of 1544–1548—is *Historia de las guerras civiles del Perú (1544–1548) y de otros sucesos de las Indias,* usually referred to as the *Quinquenarios* (History of the Civil Wars of Peru (1544–1548) and of Other Events in the Indies, or Chronicle of Five Years; 1904–1929) of Suárez's contemporary Pedro Gutiérrez de Santa Clara (1525?–1603?), apparently a Mexican mestizo of whom almost nothing is known. In this extensive work Pizarro is dramatically cast as a Faustian figure who all but bargains with the devil in order to obtain political power but is defeated and like the Avilas ultimately beheaded in punishment for disloyalty and pride. Where Suárez's unexamined feelings appear to well up suddenly and move him to fashion second-rate journalism into literature, Gutiérrez de Santa Clara is heavy-handed in announcing his intention to produce an *enxiemplo,* or moral tale. Yet neither the heroes nor the villains of his piece behave as they should. The events, moreover, prove insufficient for filling up the five volumes allocated to their narration, and the result is work as intriguingly off balance as Suárez's. In both cases the authors' implicit identification with *criollo* values seems to create the need for a new kind of literary expression, one that cannot be accommodated within preexisting discursive frames.

Among late seventeenth-century historians Carlos de Sigüenza y Góngora must be included (discussed below under *Belles Lettres*) and also Fray Agustín de Vetancourt (sometimes appearing as Vetancurt or Betancur; 1620–1700), a native of Mexico City and the author of *Teatro mexicano: Descripción de los sucesos ejemplares históricos, políticos y religiosos del nuevo mundo occidental de las Indias* (Mexican Theater: Description of the Exemplary Historical, Political, Military, and Religious Events of the New Western World of the Indies; 1698), a chronicle of four volumes. The second of these, a history of Mexico up to 1519, provides a synthesis of Torquemada's *Monarquía indiana,* while the last, actually published separately in 1697 under the title *Crónica del Santo Evangelio de México* (Chronicle of the Holy Gospel in Mexico), is a history of the work of the Franciscans in Mexico from the arrival of the original twelve mendicant friars requested by Cortés. In the edition of 1698 the historian appended fifty-four additional pages including two intriguing treatises, one on Mexico City and the other on the municipality of Puebla. Vetancourt is one of the earliest Mexican historians to include a comprehensive listing of sources.

Belles Lettres

The comprehensive corpus of seventeenth-century Mexican poetry, available for analysis thanks in large part to the work of Alfonso Méndez Plancarte in his *Poetas novohispanos, segundo siglo* (Poets of New Spain, Second Century; 1944–1945), is still largely unexamined and its writers unknown. Most of these poems clearly reflect the influence of the Spanish poet Luis de Góngora, whose principal stylistic marks are listed by Carilla as highly Latinate syntax and vocabulary, frequent mythological allusions, hyperbole in description, and striking metaphor, with emphasis on elaborately decorative elements designed to contribute to an impression of fullness (*Barroco literario*). In the terminology many Mexican critics now prefer, Góngora is described not as a baroque poet, but as the foremost artist of the mannerist group noted for post-renaissance stylistic innovation in a variety of arts. As the novel devices Góngora introduced into poetry lose their freshness and become merely preceptive in the hands of scores of imitators, the writings in which they appear are relabeled baroque.

The American mannerist-baroque phenomenon emphasizes myth, magic, grotesque images pointing to the metaphysical, and a continuous tension between humanity and nature. Alfredo Roggiano holds that aspects of Mexico's indigenous arts happened to coincide with these in a number of important respects, including dynamism and tension, the tendency toward elaborate ornamentation and hyperbole, and a preference for asymmetry ("Acerca de los dos barrocos"). He sees the African roots of another growing segment of Mexico's population as also generating compatible paradigms, noting that the musical and dance forms they produced not only resisted obliteration at the hands of the hegemony but eventually left a permanent mark on the official culture as well. Others state simply that American baroque is the sign of *mestizaje* (the mixing of races).

Evidence of this last line of development is visible in a number of popular verse forms such as the *villancico*. Alfonso Reyes describes the seventeenth century as truly the "spring" of *villancicos,* observing that, in both anonymous ones and those of certain attribution, popular and learned elements, theological and scientific symbols, Latinisms and *aztequismos* (linguistic features of the Aztec language), the macaronic mode (in which words of modern languages are given Latin endings), and elements of Basque and Portuguese all coexist in mutual enhancement (*Obras completas,* 14: 358). The *tocotín,* originally an Indian dance form, was cultivated by Francisco Bramón in the verses of his *Los sirgueros de la Virgen sin original pecado* and also, notably, by Sor Juana Inés de la Cruz in a charming adaptation of an Aztec rite found in the *loa,* or prologue, to one of her masterpieces, *El divino Narciso* (The Divine Narcissus; 1692). In the attitudes evoked in much of this poetry, Campa and Chang-Rodríguez see not only a rejection of forced labor but also a deeper level of ideological questioning. The use of indigenous and African rhythms and music mark a means of cultural survival for ancestral traditions prohibited in their purer forms (28). These popular manifestations identified with Mexico's indigenous and Afro-American cultures present themselves as mannerist-baroque via two avenues: (1) disrealizing the logos itself and (2) dramatizing the logos so that the appearance of exotic characters hides the seams or ideological fissures creating tensions within colonial society.

The most thorough examination of Mexican mannerist poetry is Buxó's *Góngora en la poesía novohispana* (Góngora in the Poetry of New Spain) (see also Carilla's *El gongorismo en América;* Gongorism in America). Analyzing the particular ways in which Góngora's poetics were perceived by the poets of New Spain, Buxó emphasizes repetition of the same unusual words (*canoro, cerúleo, erigir, esfera, purpúreo,* etc.), the use of the verb *ser* (to be) to mean "cause," and a predisposition toward the Greek accusative, the ablative absolute, and elaborate hyperbaton. He also finds frequent examples of Góngora's well-known rhetorical formulas "A if not B" and "A if B," bimembration, allusion, and hyperbole. He views the results of his survey as proof that Mexican imitations of the Spanish "Angel-of-Light/Angel-of-Darkness" (i.e., Góngora) were not superficial but rather that Gongorism in New Spain had all of the characteristics of a literary movement in total sympathy with the aesthetic intent of its creator.

The anonymous sonnet "No me mueve, mi Dios, para quererte," (I Am Not Moved, My God, to Love Thee) was long attributed to the Mexican Fray Miguel de Guevara (1585?–1646?) since it was discovered along with others authentically his own in a manuscript dated 1638. Scholars now agree that he was not its author but have failed to reach agreement on any other attribution. The poem's two quartets affirm that it is neither hope of heaven nor fear of hell that moves the speaker to love God, to whom he speaks directly, but rather the recalled vision of Christ's bodily suffering and death upon the cross. The verb *mueve* (moves) is repeated here a total of six times. The tercets reiterate the original thought but intensify its expression by (1) declaring that even if heaven and hell did not exist the speaker would continue to love and fear God and (2) assuring the Creator that since love alone is enough, the speaker's love for God would remain the same even in the absence of any hope whatever.

In his pioneering efforts to stimulate critical interest in Mexican colonial poetry, Méndez Plancarte recognized early on (1937) the uncommon quality of the known works of Luis de Sandoval Zapata (1620?–1671), a *criollo* poet who lived his entire life near Mexico City. Sandoval Zapata's best-known poem up to the time of Méndez Plancarte's statement was a long *romance* entitled "Relación fúnebre a la infeliz trágica muerte de dos caballeros . . . " (Funereal Account of the Unfortunate Tragic Death of Two Gentlemen . . . ; 1608), the men in question being the brothers Alonso Alvarado and Gil González de Avila, beheaded by imperial authorities, an incident receiving a memorable description in prose by the Avilas' contemporary Juan Suárez de Peralta. The poem has long been of interest to historians for its portrayal of the increasingly bitter attitudes of *criollos* toward repressive government policies. Buxó recognized that Sandoval had indeed given significant expression to a political grudge in the "Relación" but that in addition he had skillfully interwoven mythic dimensions that allowed the poem to reverberate far beyond the bounds of one isolated case. In fact, he had written a tragedy. Following an invocation to the tragic muse, Melpomene, Sandoval presents the young widow of one of the condemned pair as the tragic figure. The poem's narration is masterful. In the last part, the *prendas* (family keepsakes) of the brothers are nostalgically enumerated in a way that seems to prefigure the later rococo. Sandoval takes full advantage of poetic license as he concludes the poem by having the king declare the brothers' innocence posthumously. His use of the *romance* meter in the poem's *planto*, or funeral lament, reflects the tendency toward synthesis of the learned and popular traditions already noted as a distinguishing characteristic of Mexican literature (see Méndez Plancarte, "Don Luis de Sandoval").

Matías de Bocanegra (1612–1688) is noted for one poem, "Canción a la vista de un desengaño" (Song upon Beholding a Disillusionment; before 1652; in Campa and Chang-Rodríguez, eds., 216–222), described by Alicia Colombí Monguió (1) as the "curious culmination" of one of the Siglo de Oro's (Golden Age's) richest series of imitations on a particular theme. The lengthy work (almost three hundred lines) with the once-famous opening phrase "Una tarde en que el Mayo / de competencias quiso hacer ensayo" (One Afternoon when May / Tried to Appear at Its Loveliest) uses a random pattern of seven- and eleven-syllable lines rhyming *a a, b b, c c, d d,* and so forth, and features a series of baroque commonplaces: sunset = maturity; *verde prado* (meadow green) = a reflection of heaven; flowers = reflections of the stars. The *monte* (woods) in the spring traditionally suggests erotic love, though the speaker in the poem who has wandered into this idealized setting is a religious. As the poetic voice drops references to the tragic figures Phaëthon and Ciarus, the unhappy cleric hears a *jilguero,* linnet or goldfinch (used to symbolize freedom), singing a song of "amores y celos" (love and jealousy). After addressing the bird enviously, the priest offers a soliloquy on freedom that paraphrases Segismundo's first-act monologue in Calderón's *La vida es sueño* (Life is a Dream; ca. 1635). The cleric concludes that although he is in one sense free, his vow of celibacy limits his exercise of free will. At this moment a *neblí* (hawk) suddenly swoops down from the sky, the ensuing battle in which the linnet is killed prompting some of the poem's liveliest verses. The moral extracted by the observing priest is that the bird's liberty has proved its undoing while he himself, though not free in the same sense, is protected by his habit. He therefore repents of impure thought and concludes with some moralistic generalizations in graceful ballad meter.

The one figure in Mexican colonial poetry who has never suffered from critical neglect is Sor Juana Inés de la Cruz, though prejudice against Góngora's influence on the *Primero sueño* (*First Dream;* 1692) did cause it to be set aside for a time. The volume of commentary on both the nun and her works has continued to increase during the present century. Some of this is of little value, consisting largely of "proprietary statements" attempting whimsical rationalizations of Sor Juana's genius that differ according to each critic's Weltanschauung and sometimes produce ludicrous results. Much recent scholarship, on the other hand, provides invaluable help in understanding the more difficult aspects of her art. Sor Juana's precociousness, affability, and beauty gained her an invitation at an early age to Mexico's viceregal court where she served as a favored lady-in-waiting to several vicereines. Both there and later in the convent she composed, at the request of her superiors, hundreds of poems in celebration of social, historical, and religious occasions, sometimes receiving pay for them. Unsurpassed in her time for the brilliance of her wit, Sor Juana excelled in her prodigious mastery of virtually all known verse forms and meters, as well as in her experimentation with new ones. Some of her finest works are theatrical pieces, both religious (*loas* and *autos sacramentales*) and secular (two *comedias*). In addition, she left several works in prose.

In order to be able to continue the scholarly and literary pursuits she valued above all else, Sor Juana at the age of seventeen became a postulate of the Hieronymite convent of Santa Paula, established in the capital some one hundred years previously. The Catholic Church has a long history of sheltering literati with doubtful vocations, and the customs of the period did not prevent her from conducting *tertulias* (literary circles) and receiving visitors, often illustrious personages, in her well-equipped "cell." For the next twenty years in addition to writing she read widely of works by ancient authors as well as such famous contemporaries as Lope de Vega, Quevedo, Góngora, Calderón, and Trillo de Figueroa (her own library was one of the largest in the hemisphere). High social connections made possible the publication of two volumes of her works during Sor Juana's lifetime, with a third appearing some five years after her demise. The first volume, *Inundación castálida* (Castalian Flood; 1689), saw nine editions. The standard modern critical edition of Sor Juana's *Obras completas* (Complete Writings) is that of Alfonso Méndez Plancarte in four volumes: 1. Lírica (Lyrics); 2. Villancicos y letras sacras (Songs and Sacred Poems); 3. Autos y loas (Sacred Theater); 4. Comedias, Sainetes y prosa (Secular Theater and Prose; edited by Alberto G. Salcedo after Méndez Plancarte's death). A recent translation into English of a selection of Sor Juana's works in all genres is Alan S. Trueblood's *A Sor Juana Anthology*.

Toward the end of her life a superior of Sor Juana's, the bishop of Puebla, Manuel Fernández de Santa Cruz, authorized publication of her scholarly refutation, based on an impressive command of current theological polemics, of the thesis of a sermon by the renowned reformist missionary-priest Father Antonio de Vieira, preached in Lisbon shortly before she herself was born. The title given by the bishop to Sor Juana's essay was the "Carta atenagórica" (Letter Worthy of Athena; 404), a reference linking her to the goddess of wisdom.* The point made in the document, of little interest to most modern readers, demonstrates its writer's agility in this kind of pedantic argumentation. What is of interest are the comments the bishop also published in a framing letter written by himself but signed, to protect his identity, with the fictional cognomen Sor Filotea de la Cruz (Sister Philothea of the Cross). Here the bishop mildly remonstrates with Sor Juana to remind her publicly that sacred issues as opposed to secular letters are a nun's proper concern, thus ambiguously praising but at the same time criticizing her.

Commenting on this exchange, Octavio Paz argues persuasively that the bishop's real motive was not to rebuke or even to admonish Sor Juana but rather to strike an indirect blow at his own archrival Francisco de Aguiar y Seijas, the man who had narrowly defeated him to become archbishop of Mexico in 1681, had been a supporter and even a personal friend of Vieira, and was a notorious mysogynist (551 ff.). In any case, Fernández de Santa Cruz's advice to Sor Juana publicly echoed numerous reprimands already issued by

---

*The number in parenthesis following initial mention of each of Sor Juana's works reproduces the numbering system introduced by Méndez Plancarte in the *Obras completas*.

clerical superiors who resented her for two principal reasons: (1) religion and
theology were not her primary interests, and (2) she was protected by high-
ranking admirers whose power rivaled and at times exceeded that of the
clergy.

Fortunately for posterity if not for herself, Sor Juana seized the opening
presented by the bishop's criticism to draft what has become her most famous
work, the so-called "Respuesta a Sor Filotea" (Reply to Sister Philothea; 405)
an apologia in which she claims to consider herself unworthy of discoursing
on theological issues and argues that her passion for acquiring secular knowledge cannot be wrong since it is God given. The wit for which Sor Juana was
so renowned in her day is not absent here. The reader will note, for example,
that by forcing her to address him informally and as a woman, the bishop has
unwittingly armed her with a weapon for occasionally mordant satire. The
passages in which Sor Juana seems to exhibit an innocent spontaneity toward
her addressee may mislead the unwary reader into assuming a confidentiality
between the two that could not have existed in reality. Studies have shown, in
fact, that much of Sor Juana's "spontaneity" derives from her use of the conventional rhetorical formulae contemporary manuals listed as appropriate for
the informal letter. Moreover, her argument is carefully organized into the
prescribed divisions of salutation, *captatio, benevolentiae, narratio,* petition,
and conclusion (Perelmuter Pérez).

It is nevertheless clear that in many passages Sor Juana forsakes this homely
style to flaunt her remarkable knowledge of patristics, even while claiming not
to possess any. However, a recent careful investigation of her sources has revealed the extent to which Sor Juana manipulated and even falsified many of
them to her own advantage (Scott). In the most widely anthologized parts of
the "Respuesta," Sor Juana narrates a series of charming scenes from her childhood that reveal her as a precocious scholar bent on acquiring knowledge
despite the many obstacles placed in her path. In a recent ground-breaking
essay, Jean Franco has argued convincingly that Sor Juana's autobiographical
statements wickedly parody the conventional hagiographical discourse in
which nuns typically described stumbling blocks placed in the path of pro-
fessing or living as a Christian, but hardly of learning!

It is difficult to imagine a document of this type more richly layered with
irony, parody, and satire than is Sor Juana's "Respuesta," but to forget that it
embodies the desperate rhetorical bricolage of one in full awareness that her
own fate as well as that of all her works are controlled by others would be to
miss the work's profound ideological significance. The "Respuesta" is not only
a strong *avant-la-lettre* statement of common-sense feminism, but also a remarkable metastatement in which Sor Juana explores strategies for seizing
openings within several of the entrenched hegemonic discourses of her day in
order to turn these back upon themselves, thus gaining a measure of freedom.

Only a few years following the writing of the "Respuesta," which was never
formally acknowledged by Fernández de Santa Cruz, history records that Sor

Juana renounced secular letters forever. Within a short time she died, victim of the plague that also killed many of her religious sisters. Paz doubts that any true conversion occurred as recorded, arguing that the language in her signed statements is atypical and in fact parodies the usual wording of such documents (596 ff). He holds that her boldness in defending her right to intellectual freedom in the "Respuesta" and elsewhere made her a target of the Inquisition which was at last able to gag her when, with the changing political scene, one after another of Sor Juana's secular protectors lost their influence.

The scholar who has never done so is strongly urged to examine firsthand the scope and variety of Sor Juana's writings as evidenced in the *Obras completas*. The modern reader will also profit from a contemporary (i.e., seventeenth-century) Spanish dictionary in order to capture the lexical subtlety of Sor Juana's art. Like Góngora's, her poems display abundant hyperbaton and periphrasis, and they overflow as well with literary topoi, Latinate phrasing, and tropes of all kinds. Yet while his reponse to the world is overwhelmingly sensual, Sor Juana's is mental and logical, displaying the keenest of wits (wit—intelligence combined with sensitivity—serves to discover hidden correspondences between things and ideas and to allow their expression in perfect form). Critics continue to emphasize the *spatial* dimension of intelligence underlying her frequent use of geometric configurations as a structural principle and the highly visual imagination that permits her to move laterally from emblem to emblem.

For Sor Juana's sixty-four sonnets Méndez Plancarte offers six thematic classifications: moral/philosophical (145–152), historical/mythological (153–157), satiric/burlesque (158–163), discrete love (164–184), honorific (185–205), and sacred (206–210). Among her most popular are several in the first category. "Este que ves, engaño colorido" (This Colored Lie You See before You; 145) is one of some sixteen poems in all that deal with the portrait, a traditional theme eminently suited to baroque conceits since it can be seen to epitomize self-deception and the futile struggle against mutability. An ecphrasis, the poem displays a superb syntactic/semantic structure. The first quartet is a single sentence; the second seems to well up and overflow into multiple anaphorical predicates climaxing in the tercets, as both portrait and poem dissolve away in the last line's graceful allusion to Góngora's "Mientras por competir con tu cabello" (While to Compete with Your Tresses). The enunciative structuring is notable as well. The speaker (the figure in the portrait?) explicitly addresses a *tú* (thou: the person gazing at the portrait?) in a play of perspective reminiscent of Velázquez's *Las meninas*.

In another moral/philosophical poem, "En perseguirme, Mundo, ¿qué interesas?" (What Do You Hope to Gain, World, in Pursuing Me?; 146), the poet defends intellectual propensities by pitting them against materialistic ones. Here Sor Juana skillfully manipulates the tropes of antimetabole, or *retruécano,* the inversion of the order of repeated words to sharpen meaning or display contrast, and antistasis, repetition of a word but in a different or contrasting sense, along with the rhetorical formula of "not A but B." These tropes are characteristic of Sor Juana, appearing in many of the *arte menor* (short line) poems as well.

The erotic poems (classified under "discrete love"), as well, several of which are among her most enduring, are full of distinctions, deductions, and corollaries. The disavowal is a frequent speech act. These poems speak of passion, jealousy, conflicting emotions, and death, following the traditions of Spanish verse originating in early Provençal love poetry but also revealing the influence on Sor Juana of scholasticism. It is believed that the erotic relationships referred to were fictitious, though this makes them no less poignant. The famous "Detente, sombra de mi bien esquivo" (Stay, Shadow of My Brief Contentment; 165), which, according to the gloss, "contains a fantasy content with platonic love," is perhaps her best-known sonnet, in part because it seems emblematic of Sor Juana herself. The theme is that of the erotic phantom trapped by the equally incorporeal fantasy of the speaking persona. The dominant images (shadow, projection, spell, illusion, fiction, phantom) deny the lover's incarnation, while those of magnet and steel on the contrary affirm it. For Sor Juana here as elsewhere love is primarily *awareness* followed by *reflection* during the lover's absence.

Of all her works the *Primero sueño* (216), a composition of some 975 verses, is the one Sor Juana herself considered the masterpiece. Critics now agree, but the work lay forgotten nevertheless during some two-and-a-half centuries until 1928, shortly after Góngora's rediscovery in Spain, when Ermilo Abreu Gómez republished the *Sueño* in the Mexican journal *Contemporáneos* (Contemporaries). It should be noted that even though *culteranismo* (euphuism, identified with Góngora) is apparent, all critics now recognize clear differences between his sensuous vision of nature and her more rational approach to all she came in contact with. Critics have disagreed as to the poem's divisions (not formally indicated) although many now see it as tripartite. Octavio Paz suggests that each of the three sections is multiple: (1) the sleep of the world/the sleep of the body; (2) the vision, the naming of categories of the great chain of being; Phaëthon as example; and (3) the awakening of the body and the world (483 ff.). Several traditions of the *sueño* as a literary form exist; Sor Juana follows that of the *sueño de anabasis,* or dream of ascent, in which the soul, freed from the body, acquires superior faculties allowing it to comprehend secrets of the universe otherwise hidden. The word *sueño* is used within the poem in several different senses.

Scholars have lately come to recognize the influence on the nun of elements of the so-called hermetic tradition introduced to her in the writings of the prolific Jesuit theologian Athanasius Kircher, and especially in his *Musurgia universalis* (1650). The term *hermetic* originally derives from Hermes Trismegistus, the Greek version of the Egyptian deity Thoth, associated with the search for wisdom believed to have originated in Egypt, which is one reference suggested by the poem's allusions to pyramids and obelisks. Hermetism views the human being as a microcosm reproducing the macrocosm. The upward flight of the soul as it escapes from the body is seen to correspond metaphysically to the purging of metals—a connection with alchemy that is typical of Kircher's thought. Many of the emblematic passages of Sor Juana's *Sueño* have been clarified by reference to his writings, in which hermetism and Neoplatonic elements were syncretized and assimilated to Christian doctrine. Most recently several other scholars have claimed to perceive a further hidden syncretism in the form of images strongly recalling Aztec myths of creation. Sor Juana shows creativity both in narrating her dream through poetry and in forgoing use of the traditional demiurge or heavenly guide. Striking originality is also seen in the fact that her dream *contains no vision.* The poem makes use, as Paz observes, of an old literary device—the feigned revelation of a revelation—in other words, literature (482). Allusion in the final passages to Phaëthon suggests the nobility of the unsuccessful attempt to comprehend the universe, the topos being that of eternalizing one's name through failure.

The religious poetry is most appreciated in Sor Juana's *villancicos,* which make up approximately one fourth of her writings; most though not all of these are sacred. The function of the eight or nine songs making up each cycle or set of *villancicos* was largely fixed by custom to emphasize dramatic contrast. The rhythms were those of popular songs and dances often performed with humorous stage effects, a sort of comic relief. Sor Juana's *villancicos* reveal her profound grasp of the purpose for which the Church employed them—to delight and instruct a popular audience through ritual, spectacle, and humor. But in addition, many also display their author's erudition and intellectual passion, as seen for example in the clearly profeminist thrust of the *villancicos* to Saint Catherine of Alexandra of 1691. The Asunción (Assumption) cycle of 1679 and that of the Natividad (Nativity) of 1689 include some of Sor Juana's most charming lyrics. Some of these foreground the Spanish dialects of blacks, Indians, Portuguese, and Basques, which may appear mixed with standard Spanish or even with Nahuatl. These verses, along with others incorporating African locutions and onomatopoeia, have been widely hailed as an early recognition of the racial diversity that would ultimately constitute Mexican society.

The seventeenth-century *auto* was a one-act religious spectacular written in verse of various meters. Subject always to Church approval, it was commissioned and funded by municipalities and enacted by theater professionals. Calderón had modified it from the simple dramatic representation of a miraculous tale into a coherent and symmetrical allegory foregrounding religious emblems, with each concept represented by a separate actor who usually spoke, sang, and danced. Sor Juana's best known *auto,* of a total of three, is *El divino Narciso* (368), an ingenious transformation of the Ovidian myth in which Narciso is made to represent Jesus Christ. Another character, the female Human Nature, has become disfigured because of her past sins. At a fountain where she is led by the character Gracia (Grace) so that she may regain her lost beauty through baptism, she encounters Narciso reflected as he drinks there. Narciso, falling in love with Human Nature's image combined in the reflection with his own, ultimately dies from his passion for her. In an interesting permutation of Sor Juana's, Eco, the nymph who loves Narciso in the original myth, comes to represent Satan.

The play is elaborately framed and highly self-aware, as the characters announce and reannounce the allegorical theme. While the drama is to provide *visual* proof of Christ's divinity for the indigenous nonbeliever and the characters interact with the visible/invisible as well as beautiful/disfigured, the audience is repeatedly enjoined to *listen* and *hear* the spoken word, which is conveyed through oratory, teaching, praise, prophecy, debate, singing, and other speech acts. The metaphoric text is to be given, in other words, through utterance. Whereas Narciso speaks truth of himself, Eco is conspicuously semi-mute and able to speak only through the poetic device of echo, or *recopilación*. Her sentences arise, that is, only by virtue of syntagmatic accumulation of the final words or syllables of each of Narciso's spoken lines. In the *loa* preceding the *Narciso* (367), Occidente (the Western World) and América are taken prisoners in battle by the European character Religión, who scolds them for continuing to worship the native (pagan) deity of seeds, Huitzilopochtli. The play to follow, they are told, will present visible proof of Christ's divinity in a manner they can understand. The play thus promises to be a didactic vehicle for an indigenous public. Critics have noted, nevertheless, that Sor Juana borrows elements from the preceding century's missionary theater in the interest of setting up distinguishing emblems of New Spain for educated *criollos*, who were becoming increasingly aware of their identity as different from that of Peninsular Spaniards.

Her best known *comedia* (play) is *Los empeños de una casa* (Pledges of a House; 388, 391, 394), with a cloak-and-dagger theme modeled closely on those of Calderón but possessing two distinguishing elements. First, the heroine, Leonor, in an eloquent act 1 defense of her intellectual proclivities, seems to speak for Sor Juana herself. Second, the work's *gracioso*, or comic, character, Castaño, in his clearly Mexican dialect, reverses the much-used device of featuring women disguised in men's clothing. A series of extremely humorous asides accompanies his donning of each article of feminine apparel in full view of the audience.

Sor Juana's genius, her singular life lived out in its particular time and circumstances, and her feminist perspective would probably suffice to ensure her historical immortality. The "Respuesta" will undoubtedly continue to be read as a key to these aspects of her life. Aside from this the *Sueño,* a number of her lyric poems, and *El divino Narciso* more than hold their own, notwithstanding the extraordinary richness of Hispanic Golden Age literature, of which Sor Juana is the last great representative. The most recent examinations of several *loas* and of the prose work *Neptuno alegórico* (400–402), moreover, strongly suggest the nun's creative participation in the intellectual redefinition of the significance of Mexico's pre-Columbian past. Finally, it should be noted that despite the hundreds of critical essays devoted to her in the past, some of the most suggestive work of all has been produced in the 1980s and 1990s.

The most acknowledged writer of seventeenth-century New Spain after Sor Juana is her friend and platonic admirer, the scientist-scholar Carlos de Sigüenza y Góngora, for many years professor of mathematics and astrology at the Royal and Pontifical University in the capital. Unlike the nun's works, unfortunately, all but one of Sigüenza's have failed until very recently to inspire any substantial literary scholarship. The newly begun global reevaluation of Sigüenza's writings stems from current attempts to place in sharper focus the particular outlines of a *barroco de Indias* (American baroque), as distinguished from the European baroque. Jacques Lafaye describes this polymath as "the great alchemist who presided over the mythological and historiographical transmutations that produced a new mentality" (67)—that of the Mexican.

For his part in the festivities organized to celebrate the arrival of the Marqués de la Laguna as viceroy in 1680 and the design of the festive arch erected in the square of Santo Domingo, Sigüenza composed an accompanying text entitled *Teatro de virtudes políticas que constituyen a un príncipe* (Theater of Political Virtues Constituting a Prince; [1680] 1984), in which he affirmed that the mythology most appropriate to such an event was Mexico's own, rather than Rome's. With the ancient "Mexican Empire" as his text, Sigüenza takes the remarkable step of proposing Aztec emperors and gods (Itzcoatl, Tizoc, etc.) as models for the new ruler in lieu of the traditional Graeco-Latin figures. His purpose, thoroughly explored by Lafaye, is to take advantage of the license allowed through syncretism in order to endow his country with a past reflecting *criollo* consciousness and difference. Unlike the Franciscans of the previous century, Sigüenza's Jesuit contemporaries wholeheartedly endorsed the notion that Jesus's original apostles had preached Christianity to all the heathen of the world *during their lifetime.* A careful revision of data allowed the conflation of the legendary Quetzalcoatl with the Apostle Thomas, thus facilitating the Aztec empire's transfiguration into an American Rome.

Parayso occidental (Western Paradise; 1684) is a work of layered narrative structure that had been almost totally overlooked up to the time of Kathleen Ross's important contribution. It consists of three *libros* (books) described as a history of the founding of the Convent of Jesús María in Mexico City. In fact, only the first of these, written entirely by Sigüenza, deals with this event. The second and third books incorporate the memoirs of confessors, conversations with the sisters themselves, and even one first-person account by Madre Marina de la Cruz, as well as other biographies. By compulsively rewriting the versions of events provided by the (female) primary sources, the male Sigüenza as narrator imposes a textual *encerramiento,* or cloister. Moreover, he depicts the convent as a *new* Eden where sin does *not* triumph—the locus, in other words, of a new Genesis. With his interpretation in the *Parayso* of Alva Ixtlilxochitl's version of the indigenous rites in which the "vestal" virgins of the Aztec religion prefigure the Jesús María virgins, the further outlines of Sigüenza's syncretic project become visible.

Another aspect of the same project may be seen in the poem *Primavera indiana* (American Spring; 1688), a sacred-historical poem of some seventy-nine royal octave stanzas that includes an ecphrasis of the icon that is the familiar image of the Virgin of Guadalupe. Sigüenza's lyric description of Mexico here does much more than merely continue the tradition of such portraits last seen in Balbuena's *Grandeza mexicana.* In another prose work, the *Glorias de Querétaro* (Glories of Querétaro; 1680), the appearance of the Virgin of Guadalupe–Tonantzin (Aztec goddess of fertility) to an Indian is taken as bringing finished expression to the idea of a Mexican (*criollo*) Paradise. That is, Mary's appearance to Juan Diego sanctifies Mexican history by signaling a new Eden in the New World.

In his *Alboroto y motín de los indios de México (Carta al almirante Pez)* (Uprising and Mutiny of the Indians of Mexico [Letter to Admiral Pez]; [1692] 1932), Sigüenza appears to turn against Mexico's indigenous subjects. Writing about a serious uprising in the capital (1692), he blames the city's "ungrateful" Indians for a whole series of natural disasters culminating in a food shortage. In this work, then, he clearly equates "*criollo*" with Mexican "Spaniard." Casting himself as hero as he narrates the daring rescue of the city archives from destruction by fire, Sigüenza underlines a parallel between Cortés's defeat during the Noche Triste 190 years earlier and the present crisis. This time, of course, the Spanish/*criollos* emerge victorious. As a baroque historian, Sigüenza feels compelled to embellish Cortés's writings, which by now have become classics, and thus improve on them.

Infortunios de Alonso Ramírez, the most studied of Sigüenza's works, is the story of a seventeenth-century Puerto Rican carpenter-turned-mariner captured by English pirates near the Philippines. After completely circumnavigating the globe from east to west, Ramírez is finally set adrift off the coast of Yucatán, whence he slowly makes his way, with little help from citizens of his adopted country, once again to the capital. The tale is apparently factual, but the first-person speaker, identifying himself as Ramírez, displays a certain resemblance to the traditionally untrustworthy picaresque narrator. This factor along with the rapid pace of the narration (the work is novella length) creates a significant interface with a well-known type of fiction. What have proven most attractive to semiotically minded critics, however, are the work's signs of what might be termed double inscription. The register of language attributed to the supposedly uneducated Ramírez, his display of cartographical virtuosity in chapters 1 and 2, and the oddly sophisticated treatment of the character's religious experiences (a hagiographical cliché) would tip the hand of Sigüenza's collaboration even if on the final page there were not an abruptly overt metamorphosis within the deictic *I.* Just as tellingly, the work encodes a dual act of requesting, as Ramírez pleads for the return of his booty while Sigüenza, on another enunciative level, solicits the viceroy's continuing patronage on behalf of his own scholarly pursuits.

The considerable volume of neo-Latin writings produced during the seventeenth and eighteenth centuries has been largely overlooked despite the energetic efforts of both Alfonso Méndez Plancarte and his brother Gabriel, who did much to foster interest in them. According to Ignacio Osorio Romero, theirs was a rather acritical enthusiasm tending to overlook the elitist nature of the phenomenon (in a predominantly agricultural colony like Mexico, writing in Latin was equivalent to writing in code). This is not the only negative value contemporary Mexicans associate with the language of Horace. Latin was strongly identified with the Counter Reformation, whose architects regarded the language as an atemporal medium representing eternal and unchanging values. The use of Latin tied the Mexican *criollo,* as Osorio points out, to a language as well as a system of values that were not wholly his own (12). Yet the fact remains that literature, scientific writings, and history appeared in both Latin and Spanish during the colonial centuries; to ignore the Latin corpus is to disregard entirely one of the faces of Janus.

We have already noted briefly the early contributions of Francisco Cervantes de Salazar and the importance of Latin in schools and universities. By 1599 the Jesuits had instituted their own brand of religiously orthodox and culturally elitist pedagogy. Neo-Latin writings of the last quarter of the sixteenth century include several letters written by missionaries who describe the native culture, including the *Carta del Padre Pedro de Morales.* A principal source for poetry is a manuscript in the Biblioteca Nacional of Mexico dated 1631. Bernardino de Llanos (1559–1639) and later Tomás González (1598–1659) published editions of an adaptation of classical rhetorical precepts widely used in Mexico through the eighteenth century. Osorio Romero's recent studies provide the best effort yet at reevaluation of the country's Latin literature.

Theater

While the missionary theater aimed at Indians and the dramatic productions intended for Spaniards and *criollos* represent two separate sixteenth-century currents in New Spain, no tradition of secular drama was actually established there since authorities feared its probable adverse influence on neophyte Christians. By 1597, however, a *corral de comedias* (open-air permanent theater) was built in the capital, and several others followed. During the seventeenth and eighteenth centuries the *criollo* tradition eclipsed all others. The plays presented were, in the great majority of cases, works of Spain's Golden Age dramatists, and productions staged by Peninsular companies were much preferred over local attempts as well. Secular theater in the seventeenth century was often supported by the viceroys and legitimated in part by the fact that hospitals and orphanages derived much of their support from it.

It would be a mistake to suggest that the *auto* died out after the initial missionary thrust; in fact, the *auto* thrived throughout the colonial period. This was in part the result of the Council of Trent's suppression (1545–1563) of the traditionally boisterous festivities associated with feast days, especially the celebration of Corpus Christi. The *auto,* with its Biblical or hagiographical themes, escaped censure and in fact became the theatrical form most favored during the period of the Counter Reformation. Official celebrations of various kinds were extremely numerous in New Spain, reflecting not only the religious calendar but also such secular occurrences as the arrival of a viceroy or a royal birth in Spain. All such festivities called for performance of one or more *autos,* with support coming from the *cabildo,* or municipal guild. Remuneration and prizes were often available for playwrights whose productions were successful. González de Eslava was one of the winners in his day, though the majority of *autos* were not in fact written by colonials, since Mexican audiences preferred those of Calderón de la Barca to all others. Still, even if a Peninsular playwright were responsible for the *auto* itself, a Mexican might be called on to contribute a topical *loa* or perhaps an *entremés* (playlet performed between acts of the featured work).

In the seventeenth century a "palace theater" grew up around the court since viceroys enjoyed inviting guests to join them in witnessing dramatic performances for entertainment. Eventually, small dramatic academies supported by the viceroys' largesse were established. A few local playwrights received payment for catering to a particular ruler's tastes, but earning a living at playwriting was never easy for *criollo* dramatists who were as a whole considered an inferior lot (the shining exception being of course Sor Juana Inés de la Cruz). The *criollo* public in New Spain was small and without influence except through the *cabildos.* For these reasons dramatic production was almost negligible during the first forty years of the seventeenth century.

The first baroque play by a Mexican is the *Comedia de San Francisco de Borja* (Play on Saint Francis of Borgia; [1641] 1944) by Matías de Bocanegra, in three acts and modeled on the plays of Calderón (a soliloquy delivered by the saint is clearly reminiscent of that of Segismundo in *La vida es sueño*). Written to celebrate a new viceroy's arrival, the play was presented by a Jesuit school group and is, as the name implies, hagiographical. Critics see it as well structured and generally admirable. Shelly and Rojo name the work as marking the beginning of a cycle of similar plays that would continue in Spanish America for some hundred years (329). These *comedias* feature high-flown language in the *culteranista* (euphuistic) mode, intrigue-laden plots, a usually hollow erudition, and subjects far removed in both time and space from colonial reality.

The most significant dramatist born in Mexico during the colonial period is Juan Ruiz de Alarcón (1581–1638), who went to Salamanca to study law at twenty, returned at twenty-eight to compete unsuccessfully for a chair at the Royal and Pontifical University, and five years later embarked once again for Spain to remain there through the end of his life. During a twelve-year residence in Madrid where he sought a government position through the Court, Ruiz de Alarcón wrote and succeeded in having produced some twenty *comedias* (five others are now attributed to him). He ceased writing after finally obtaining the post of court reporter at the Council of Indies in Seville in 1626. As the prologues to his collected works indicate, Ruiz de Alarcón's stint as a playwright was undertaken primarily to provide him a source of income, since the laws of primogeniture deprived him of family resources with which to live. There are many lacunae in Ruiz de Alarcón's biography. That he did establish himself in Madrid's literary circles is given purchase by the fact that a series of highly caustic attacks on him at the hands of contemporary writers created much publicity. These remarks, brought on by some inferior verses attributed to Ruiz de Alarcón, consisted of humorous jibes at his person (he was a hunchback), his character, and his social pretensions (he had recently begun to use the honorific *don* before his name). In spite of such ridicule his plays were largely successful, and he published the twenty of certain attribution in two volumes in 1628 and 1634, along with revealing prologues.

Ruiz de Alarcón essayed and mastered the *comedia* as defined by his contemporaries Lope de Vega and Tirso de Molina (?–1648). The majority of his plays involve themes of *enredo amoroso* (intrigues of love and courtship), but he also treats historic, semihistoric, national, and magical themes. No universally accepted chronology for the works has as yet been proposed. While critical commentary on a variety of the plays is regularly produced, it is one work, *La verdad sospechosa* (The Truth Suspect; 1619 or 1620) that continues to evoke the most spirited commentary and debate. In this play a second son, Don García, comes to Madrid from Salamanca upon the death of his older brother to take the latter's place as their father's heir. Both the title, which recalls several proverbs to the effect that "in the mouth of a liar even the truth is suspect," and a scene near the beginning between Don García's father, Don Beltrán, and a *letrado,* or intellectual, disclose at the outset the protagonist's flaw, that of being a chronic liar. In spite of this vice, critics agree that Don García is highly ingratiating, clever, and even wise. In fact, *La verdad* has been called the best play of character to be produced during the entire Golden Age cycle, with Don García's fame second only to that of Tirso's Don Juan.

As is the case with all classics, the play seems to invite diverse critical approaches. During the past decade exponents of speech-act theory and other linguistically based models have focused on the exact nature of the act of lying, noting that Don García makes a number of assertions that range from slight exaggerations to highly imaginative tall tales and downright falsehoods, all subtly shaded by the fact that he has also made an innocent mistake. The mistake, that of confusing the names of two young women, is ultimately the direct cause of the protagonist's comeuppance since he is in the end required to give up his true love and marry the other one. It is also the case, however, that all of the characters in the play utter falsehoods of one kind or another, the difference being that the lies they tell are socially permissible. Truthfulness thus stands revealed as relative, a question of social norms and belonging to the "in group." It is the precise nature of the social norms relative to his new status that Don García, who is not an insider, cannot quite grasp.

A recurring problem in the criticism of Ruiz de Alarcón's plays is that of the extent to which this writer should really be thought of as a Mexican, since he clearly functioned according to the conventions of the Peninsular milieu and rarely even mentions America. (It is interesting to note that both the U.S. Library of Congress and the Modern Language Association officially classify him as a *Spanish* dramatist.) The critic who has provided the most provocative recent insights into the question is Jaime Concha in a series of essays spanning the eighties. Refusing to consider either the author or the plays apart from one another, Concha sees Don García as struggling with the exact problems plaguing the life of Ruiz de Alarcón himself. These include overshadowing by an older brother, being different from his relations (an intellectual), coming from another place where behavioral norms are not the same, and being looked on as not quite a gentleman. In one of his lies Don García even claims to be, as Ruiz de Alarcón actually was, an *indiano,* or American. Concha sees in Don García as well as in various other "strangers," "newcomers," and "intruders" populating Ruiz de Alarcón's plays the quintessence of the role of outsider that the Latin American intellectual must still accept vis-à-vis Spanish and other established cultural traditions. The oppressive space confining these characters is also suggestive: a cave, the catacombs, a jail. Concha also sees in several of the plays an appeal to the possibility of magic as a means of escaping history. Thus even though Ruiz de Alarcón neither creates Mexican characters nor writes about his own place of origin, many aspects of the future discourse of the Latin American are already manifest in his protagonists.

III THE EIGHTEENTH CENTURY

Historical Writings

The eighteenth century in Mexico has been aptly described as projecting ideological ambivalence. On the one hand, a tired persistence of now institutionalized baroque precepts produced, unsurprisingly, no new major works in Spanish. Neo-Latin writing, on the other hand, reached its zenith. The majority of first-rate authors of Latin poetry and prose belonged to the Jesuit order, seen as elitist and ultraconservative throughout the New World but, at the same time, a real burden to the Crown as a result of both its wealth and its resistance to earnestly sought economic reform that might reverse the declining fortunes of the Spanish empire.

In 1767 King Charles III expelled the Jesuits permanently from the Americas. The majority of Mexican Jesuit literati repaired to Italy, where they continued to write and publish notable works on American themes. Many took an active part in defending the New World against the harsh accusations of several widely read representatives of the Enlightenment, including Cornelius de Pauw and Jean Louis Leclerc, Count of Buffon, who had made use of certain newly developed methods of scientific classification to conclude that Americans were biologically inferior to Europeans (the resulting polemics are known as the "dispute regarding America"). Both the nostalgic treatises the exiled Jesuits wrote concerning the Mexican landscape and their more objective ones dealing with aspects of New World history and literature not only helped to refute incorrect notions about America but also made these men direct forerunners of the proindependence writers whose cause picked up steam in the latter part of the eighteenth century.

Francisco Javier Alegre (1729–1788) is the author of *Historia de la Provincia de la Compañía de Jesús de la Nueva España* (History of the Province of the Jesuits of New Spain; 1841, not published until 1956–1960; and also of the seven-volume *Institutionum Theologicarum* (Theological Institutions; 1789). He translated into Spanish, with many modifications, Nicolas Boileau's *Art poétique*, a discourse upon the principles of Horace, which García Icazbalceta found still in manuscript form in 1889 and subsequently published in a limited edition. Alegre's critical notes and commentaries—longer than the translation itself—are considered the most valuable part of his work, which is on the whole favorable to the Spanish Golden Age tradition that had recently been maligned by Ignacio de Luzán in a book entitled *La poética, o Reglas de la poesía en general* (Poetics, or General Rules for Poetry; 1737). Though not opposed to neoclassical principles, Alegre, a moderate, condemns the excesses of *culteranismo, conceptismo,* and the "irreverent" Calderonian *auto* while arguing for the value of the Golden Age corpus, especially as compared to the literature of England and France.

The spirit of the Enlightenment soon forged new and radically different literary guidelines. Among eighteenth-century Mexican historians the Jesuit Francisco Javier Clavijero (1731–1787) became the best-known spokesman for modernity, arguing for "correct" historiography in which the personality of the historian does not color "objectivity"; commentary, in other words, must not degenerate into either hollow adulation or diatribe. Clavijero also objects to the inscription of history through the devices of literature, though today the elegance of his own "style" has come to be much admired by literary critics.

From Italy following the expulsion of his order in 1767, Clavijero wrote the *Historia antigua de México* (Ancient History of Mexico; 1780–1781), of which the most relevant part for today's researchers are the nine *disertaciones* (theses) on the land, animals, and inhabitants of Mexico since these actively join the argument initiated by the Europeans on the nature of the American. Clavijero rejected the Counter Reformation notion that the devil routinely intervened in the life and customs of the Indians, displaying a clear anti-Spanish bias as well as sincere admiration of preconquest Mexican culture, which he saw as relevant to the emerging Mexican nation whose basic *mestizaje* he recognized and accepted.

The Mexican José Eguiara y Eguren (1695–1763) is the author and publisher of the *Bibliotheca mexicana* (Mexican Library; 1755), written in Latin for the purpose of defending Mexican culture, including the pre-Columbian codices, against the attack of Luzán's widely shared views. Eguiara's effort was in many respects primitive; his strictly alphabetical classification did not differentiate, for example, between works produced before and after the conquest. Nevertheless, the study of literature as it was to be institutionalized in the late nineteenth and the twentieth centuries in Mexico would hardly have been possible without the pioneering efforts of Eguiara, as well as those of his contemporaries José Mariano Beristáin y Souza (1756–1817) and the Italian aristocrat Lorenzo Boturini Benaduci (1701–?).

The field of literary historiography is currently under reevaluation, since a growing number of scholars now recognize it as having been conceived according to narrowly Eurocentric and elitist guidelines. Even Eguiara and others of his generation are now seen to have exalted Mexico's indigenous heritage solely for the purpose of establishing *criollo* cultural and political identity. Given these insights, the problem for twenty-first century researchers will be that of elaborating a revised agenda capable of correcting traditional bias.

The most contradictory and intriguing figure of Enlightenment literature in Mexico is Fray Servando Teresa de Mier (1763–1827). A Dominican priest and noted orator, Mier claimed a dual ancestral nobility going back to both Europe and preconquest Mexico (his claim of kinship with Moctezuma was never substantiated). What he most desired was Mexico's independence from Spain, but as a state ruled by a privileged *criollo* aristocracy. His politics, expressed in a famous sermon of 1794 (published in 1968 as the "Apuntes para el sermón sobre la Aparición de Nuestra Señora de Guadalupe," or Notes for the Sermon on the Appearance of Our Lady of Guadalupe), caused him to run afoul of the Inquisition, as a result of which he was exiled but also enabled to travel widely in Europe and to make contact with several of the exiled Jesuit writers. He returned to Mexico at the moment of the definitive independence uprising of 1821.

Mier achieved literary fame for his work *Apología y relaciones de su vida* (Apology and Accounts of His Life; 1817), a biography of picaresque overtones that was later reissued by Alfonso Reyes under the title *Memoria* (Memoir; 1974). Recently, in the light of critical interest in the syncretism of Sigüenza y Góngora and the line of writers who followed him, the ideas Mier expressed in the sermon referred to above and in his *Historia de la Revolución de Nueva España, antiguamente Anáhuac* (History of the revolution in New Spain, Formerly Anáhuac; 1922) have begun to be reexamined.

Taking the already elaborated and officialized myths of the Virgin Mary's appearance to the Indian Juan Diego in 1531 and the residence of the Apostle Thomas in Mexico in the sixth and eighth centuries in the guise of Quetzalcoatl, Mier sought to revise them by claiming that the cloak bearing the Virgin's image, and produced by Juan Diego before a bishop, had actually belonged to Saint Thomas of Mylapore and that it was this saint who had evangelized Mexico in the sixth century. The purpose of such a move was to subvert the legal justification for the conquest in the form of Spain's "providential evangelical mission." It also enabled Mier to argue that Saint Thomas the *Apostle* (he upheld the notion of sojourn of two different saints of the same name in Mexico), whom he and others believed to have appeared some twelve years after the death of Christ, paralleled the appearance of the Apostle James, or Santiago, at an early time in Spain. Equally, according to Mier, the Virgin of Guadalupe's appearance paralleled that of Pilar de Zaragoza in Spain. Mexico thus was clearly Spain's equal before God.

Poetry

The man traditionally regarded as the most distinguished poet to write in Spanish in the period following Sor Juana and Sigüenza is the neoclassical Fray José Martínez de Navarrete (1768–1809), whose *Entretenimientos poéticos* (Poetic Entertainments) were published posthumously in 1823, though most of the poems had first appeared in newspapers. Menéndez y Pelayo (lxxxviii) and others have noted that Martínez de Navarrete's verse is clearly imitative of Meléndez Valdés (amorous), Garcilaso and Lope (bucolic), and Fray Luis de León (religious); indeed, it strikes the reader as *déjà lu.*

In the eighteenth century Latin was the language of all treatises on grammar and rhetoric. Its popularity among literati fed the mill that continued, as we have seen, to grind out imitations of Góngora. The neo-Latin poets of this period are virtually unstudied, though scholarship directed by Osorio Romero promises a long-delayed reevaluation. Of particular interest is José Villerías y Roel (1695–1728), a poet well known in his day but now almost forgotten. Villerías y Roel is the author of *Máscara* (Mask; 1721), *Llanto* (Lament; 1725), *Guadalupe* (1721), and several other works apparently now lost.

The *Rusticatio mexicana* (1782; translated as *Por los campos de México* [The Mexican Countryside] in 1942) of another Jesuit, Rafael Landívar (1731–1793), written from the author's long exile in Italy, extols rural scenes in Mexico and in his native Guatemala in verses declared by a number of critics to be superior to those of Balbuena. Landívar's intention is the defense of America. To this cause he cites Ruiz de Alarcón, Sor Juana, and Francisco Javier Alegre and urges his readers—especially the young—to "esteem highly your fertile lands, matchless blessings of heaven." The tone of pride in these statements may be interpreted as heralding the independence writers.

Theater

Other than Sor Juana, the seventeenth and eighteenth centuries boast no dramatists writing in Mexico who are now perceived as critically significant, with Spain's contributions maintaining a clear dominance in America through the eighteenth century and well into the nineteenth. Only the *loas, sainetes* (short comic pieces), and *saraos* (directions for festive music and dancing traditionally taking place following the main production) seem to be in any way connected to New Spain's historical situation. Scholars have directed attention to the second and third of these with somewhat disappointing results. The *sainete* does not seem to "reflect" colonial life in any direct sense, though it is more realistic than most of the plays themselves. The *sarao* often features a dance bearing the Aztec name *tocotín,* but this fact alone does not signal the *mestizaje,* or evidence of the blending, of Mexico's two major cultural traditions, actively sought by several earlier generations of critics.

The *loa,* or prologue, which died out in the eighteenth century, did offer a pretext for topical references, though in the preceding centuries these had served chiefly for pronouncing suitable encomia to patrons by way of a jungle of allusions equating the viceregal nobility with Mars, Venus, and a pantheon of other mythological figures. Toward the end of its existence the *loa* did in fact evolve into a vehicle for commentary on New World concerns, reflecting in some cases the emergence of new attitudes. Generally, theater flourished in the last half of the eighteenth century in the great metropolitan centers of Spanish America (especially Buenos Aires), but the plays bringing out patrons, most of whom belonged to the "middle nobility" or small upper-middle class, were overwhelmingly from the Peninsula and belonged either to the now cliché-ridden baroque tradition or the more current neoclassical wave. *Criollo* themes had not yet caught on in Mexico. The drama actually produced there during this period, with the exception of the *loa,* has not attracted any notable critical interest.

BIBLIOGRAPHY

Acosta, Fray José de. *De procuranda indorum salute: Pacificación y colonización.* 1589. Ed. Francisco Mateos. Madrid, 1952.

———. *Historia natural y moral de las Indias.* 1590. Ed. Edmundo O'Gorman. Mexico City: Fondo de Cultura Económica, 1962.

Adorno, Rolena. "Arms, Letters, and the Native Historian." In Jara and Spadaccini, eds., 201–204. Concerns the appropriation of discursive space by such traditionally marginalized mestizo chroniclers as Alva Ixtlilxochitl.

———. "Discourses on Colonialism: Bernal Díaz, Las Casas, and the Twentieth-Century Reader." *Modern Language Notes* 103.2 (1988): 239–258. A groundbreaking reevaluation of what were probably the true motives of Mexico's most popular chronicler.

———. "Literary Production and Suppression: Reading and Writing about Amerindians in Colonial Spanish America." *Dispositio* 28–29 (1985): 1–25. Contrasts Acosta's success with Sahagún's failure to win approval of censors; discusses successful vs. unsuccessful strategies in representing the native American in various genres.

Alegre, Francisco Javier. *Historia de la Provincia de la Compañía de Jesús de la Nueva España.* 1841. Ed. Ernest J. Burrus and Félix Zubillaga. Rome, 1956.

———. *Institutionum Theologicarum.* 1789. 7 vols. Unpublished? (Possibly in *Opúsculos inéditos latinos y castellanos del P. Francisco Javier Alegre.* Mexico City, 1889).

———, trans. *Art Poétique,* Nicolas Boileau. Annotated by Joaquín García Icazbalceta. In *Opúsculos inéditos latinos y castellanos del P. Francisco Javier Alegre.* Mexico City, 1889.

Alva Ixtlilxochitl, Fernando de. *Historia chichimeca.* Ed. Germán Vázquez. Madrid: Historia 16, 1985.

Alvarado Tezozomac, Hernando de. *Crónica mexicana.* Annotated by Manuel Orozco y Berra. Preceded by the *Códice Ramírez.* Mexico City, 1878.

Balbuena, Bernardo de. *Grandeza mexicana.* 1604. Preliminary study by Luis Adolfo Domínguez. Mexico City: Editorial Porrúa, 1985.

———. *El Siglo de Oro en las selvas de Erífile.* 1608. Ed. José Carlos González Boixo. Jalapa: Universidad Veracruzana, 1989.

Bocanegra, Matías de. "Canción a la vista de un desengaño." 1652. In Campa and Chang-Rodríguez, eds., 216–222.

———. *Comedia de San Francisco de Borja.* 1641. Prologue by José Juan Arrom. In *Tres piezas teatrales del Virreinato.* Ed. José Garcidueñas and José Juan Arrom, 237–379. Mexico City: Universidad Nacional Autónoma de México, 1976.

Bramón, Francisco. *Los sirgueros de la Virgen sin original pecado.* 1620. Prologue and selection by Agustín Yáñez. Mexico City: Universidad Nacional Autónoma de México, 1944.

Bruce-Novoa, Juan. "Naufragios en los mares de la significación." *Plural* 221 (1990): 12–21. A seminal essay using the well-summarized advances of ideological critics of Núñez Cabeza de Vaca's *Relación* to propose Núñez as the Chicano archetype.

Buxó, José Pascual. "Bernardo de Balbuena, o El Manierismo plácido." In *La dispersión del Manierismo,* 113–146. (No editor listed.) Mexico City: Universidad Nacional Autónoma de México, 1980.

———. "El *Sueño* de Sor Juana: Alegoría y modelo del mundo." In *Coloquio sobre la literatura mexicana,* ed. Merlin H. Forster and Julio Ortega. Mexico City: Editorial Oasis, 1986. Analyzes the influence of Kircher on Sor Juana's thought.

———. *Góngora en la poesía novohispana.* Mexico City: Imprenta Universitaria, 1960. An exemplary study of syntactical and lexical elements associated with Góngora and their presence in seventeenth-century Mexican poetry.

———. *Muerte y desengaño en la poesía novohispana (siglos XVI y XVII).* Mexico City: Universidad Nacional Autónoma de México, 1975. An innovative study using an ethnographic approach in the reevaluation of colonial poetry.

———. "Sobre la *Relación fúnebre a la infeliz, trágica muerte de dos caballeros,* de D. Luis de Sandoval Zapata." *Anuario de Letras* 4 (1964): 237–254. A fine introduction to the most important poem of an important but long-neglected poet.

Calderón de la Barca, Pedro. *La vida es sueño.* Madrid: Espasa-Calpe, 1955.

Campa, Antonio R. de la, and Raquel Chang-Rodríguez, eds. *Poesía hispanoamericana colonial.* Madrid: Editorial Alhambra, 1985. The introduction takes an ideological approach stressing contributions of marginalized groups.

Carilla, Emilio. *El barroco literario hispánico.* Buenos Aires: Editorial Nova, 1969.

———. *El gongorismo en América.* Buenos Aires: Universidad de Buenos Aires, 1946. A schematic but helpful listing of the characteristics associated with Góngora and their manifestations in New World poetry.

———. *Manierismo y barroco en las literaturas hispánicas.* Madrid: Editorial Gredos, 1983. Carilla joins other prominent scholars in accepting the new term *mannerism* as distinguished from *baroque;* a reclassification of colonial poets necessarily follows.

Castellanos, Juan de. *Elegías de varones ilustres de Indias.* 1589. 4 vols. Ed. Miguel Antonio Caro. Bogota: Editorial ABC, 1955.

Cervantes de Salazar, Francisco de. *Crónica de la conquista de la Nueva España.* 1552. First published in 1914. Prologue by Juan Miralles Ostos. Mexico City: Editorial Porrúa, 1985.

Cervantes, Miguel de. *La Galatea.* 1585. Prologue and notes by Juan Bautista Avalle Arce. Madrid: Espasa-Calpe, 1961.

Clavijero, Francisco Javier. *Historia antigua de México.* 1780–1781. 4 vols. Mexico City: Editorial Porrúa, 1958.

Coombí Monguió, Alicia. "El poema del Padre Matías de Bocanegra: Trayectoria de una imitación." *Thesaurus* 36 (1981): 24–43.

Concha, Jaime. "Juan Ruiz de Alarcón." In Iñigo Madrigal, coor., 353–365. A ground-breaking study—one of a series of essays by this critic on Ruiz de Alarcón—suggesting compelling reasons for considering him a Mexican playwright after all.

Cortés, Hernán. *Cartas de relación*. 1519–1526. Mexico City: Editorial Porrúa, 1963.

Cruz, Sor Juana Inés de la. *A Sor Juana Anthology*. Trans. Alan S. Trueblood. Cambridge, Mass.: Harvard University Press, 1988.

———. *Inundación castálida*. 1690. Facsimile of original, reissued and edited by Georgina Sabat de Rivers. Madrid: Castalia, 1979.

———. *Obras completas*. 4 vols. Ed. Alfonso Méndez Plancarte, vols. 1–3; Alberto G. Salcedo, vol. 4. Mexico City: Fondo de Cultura Económica, 1951–1957.

Díaz del Castillo, Bernal. *Historia verdadera de los sucesos de la conquista de la Nueva España*. 1632. Mexico City: Editorial Porrúa, 1955.

Dorantes de Carranza, Baltazar. *Sumaria relación*. 1604. Mexico City: Imprenta del Museo Nacional, 1902.

Durán, Fray Diego. *The Aztecs: The History of the Indies of New Spain*. Abridged translation of vol. 3 of *Historia*. New York: Orion, 1964.

———. *Book of the Gods and Rites and the Ancient Calendar*. Translation of vols. 1–2 of *Historia*. Norman: University of Oklahoma Press, 1971.

———. *Historia de las Indias de Nueva España y islas de Tierra Firme* [sic]. 1589. Mexico City: Editorial Porrúa, 1967.

Eguiara y Eguren, José. *Bibliotheca mexicana*. Latin edition 1755. Trans. Agustín Millares Carlo. Mexico City: Fondo de Cultura Económica, 1944.

Esteve Barba, Francisco. *Historiografía indiana*. Madrid: Gredos, 1964. A nearly complete listing of chronicles; useful although in need of updating.

Fernández de Lizardi, José Joaquín. *El Periquillo Sarniento*. 1816. Prologue by Jefferson Rea Spell. Mexico City: Editorial Porrúa, 1976.

Fernández de Oviedo y Valdés, Gonzalo. *Historia general y natural de las Indias*. 1535. Vols. 117–121. Madrid: Biblioteca de Autores Españoles, 1959.

———. *Sumario de la natural historia de las Indias*. 1526. Ed. Manuel Ballesteros. Madrid: Historia 16, 1989.

Flores de varia poesía. 1577. Ed. Margarita Peña. Mexico City: Universidad Nacional Autónoma de México, 1980.

Foucault, Michel. *Power/Knowledge*. Ed. Colin Gordon. Brighton: Harvester Press, 1980.

Franco, Jean. *Plotting Women*. New York: Columbia University Press, 1991. The first three chapters are relevant to Mexican colonial literature; the essay on Sor Juana is outstanding.

García Rivas, Heriberto. *Historia de la literatura mexicana*. Mexico City: Textos Universitarios, 1971.

Goic, Cedomil. *Historia de crítica de la literatura hispanoamericana*. Barcelona: Editorial Crítica, 1988. The single most important bibliographical tool for the colonial scholar; contains exhaustive annotated bibliographies as well as abridged versions of some fifty classic essays.

Góngora, Luis de. "Mientras por competir con tu cabello." In his *Obras completas*, 44. Study and notes by Arturo Marasso. Prologue by R. Foulché-Delbosc. Buenos Aires: Librería "el Ateneo" Editorial, 1955.

González de Eslava, Fernán. "Canción a nuestra Señora." In Campa and Chang-Rodríguez, 121–122.

————. *Coloquio diez y seis del bosque divino.* Ed. J. García Icazbalceta. Mexico City, 1877.

————. *Coloquios espirituales y sacramentales y canciones divinas.* Mexico City, 1610. Published as *Coloquios espirituales y sacramentales.* Ed. José Rojas Garcidueñas. Mexico City: Editorial Porrúa, 1958. Book 2 of the 1610 edition published as *Villancicos, romances, ensaladas y otras canciones devotas.* Critical edition, introduction, notes and appendices by Margit Frenk. Mexico City: El Colegio de México, 1989.

————. "Columna de cristal." In Campa and Chang-Rodríguez, eds., 120–121.

González Echevarría, Roberto. "Humanismo, retórica y las crónicas de la conquista." *La isla a su vuelo fugitiva,* 9–25. Austin: University of Texas Press, 1983. One of the best statements on approaching the chronicle of Indies.

Gutiérrez de Santa Clara, Pedro. *Historia de las guerras civiles del Perú (1544–1548) y de otros sucesos de las Indias (Quinquenarios).* Ed. Manuel Serrano y Sanz. Madrid: Librería General de Victoriano Suárez, 1904–1929. Also Madrid: Biblioteca de Autores Españoles, 1963.

Gutiérrez, Ramón. "El drama de la conquista de Nuevo México." *Gestos* 8 (1989): 73–86. Emphasizes how Oñate used proven aspects of the missionary theater to subdue and humiliate Pueblo Indians.

Henríquez Ureña, Pedro. *Historia de la cultura en la América Hispánica.* Mexico City: Fondo de Cultura Económica, [1947] 1970.

Herrera y Tordesillas, Antonio. *Historia general de los hechos de los castellanos en las islas y tierra firme del mar océano (Décadas).* 1601–1605. 5 vols. Prologue by A. Ballesteros. Madrid, 1934.

Iñigo Madrigal, Luis, coor. *Historia de la literatura hispanoamericana.* Vol. 1, *Epoca colonial.* Madrid: Cátedra, 1982. This essential work contains essays by outstanding scholars on many aspects of sixteenth- and seventeenth-century colonial literature.

Jara, René, and Nicholas Spadaccini, eds. *1492–1992: Re/Discovering Colonial Writing.* Minneapolis: The Prisma Institute, 1989. The most recent comprehensive study of the colonial period with essays by fifteen noted scholars; unlike most such collections it includes significant reevaluative work on the much-neglected eighteenth century.

Kircher, Athanasius. *Musurgia universalis.* Rome, 1650.

Lafaye, Jacques. *Quetzalcoatl and Guadalupe: The Formation of Mexican National Consciousness.* Trans. Benjamin Keen. Chicago: University of Chicago Press, [1974] 1976. An encyclopedic investigation into the roots of baroque syncretism; the starting point for subsequent research on this important issue.

Landívar, Rafael. *Rusticatio mexicana.* 1782. Trans. (from the Latin) Octaviano Valdés as *Por los campos de México.* Mexico City: Universidad Nacional Autónoma de México, 1942.

Lasso de la Vega, Gabriel Lobo. *Cortés valeroso.* Madrid: Pedro Madrigal, 1588.

————. *Mexicana.* Ed. José Amor y Vázquez. Madrid: Biblioteca de Autores Españoles, 1970.

Loesberg, Jonathan. "Narratives of Authority: Cortés, Gómara, Díaz." *Prose Studies* 6.3 (1983): 239–263. An exemplary comparison and contrast of three of the inaugural works of Mexican discourse.

López de Gómara, Francisco. *Historia de la conquista de México.* Prologue and chronology by Jorge Gurría Lacroix. Caracas: Biblioteca Ayacucho, 1979.

————. *Historia general de Indias* and *Vida de Hernán Cortés.* 1552. Prologue and chronology by Jorge Gurría Lacroix. Caracas: Biblioteca Ayacucho, 1979.

Luzán, Ignacio de. *La poética, o Reglas de la poesía en general.* Saragossa, 1737.

Martínez de Navarrete, Fray José. *Entretenimientos poéticos.* In his *Obras completas.* Mexico City, 1904.

Mena, Juan de. *El laberinto de la fortuna.* 1481. Edition, prologue, and notes by José Manuel Blecua. Madrid: Espasa-Calpe, 1968.

Méndez Plancarte, Alfonso. "Don Luis de Sandoval y Zapata (siglo XVII)," *Abside* 1, 1 (1937): 37–54.

———, ed. *Poetas novohispanos: Primer siglo (1521–1621).* Mexico City: Universidad Nacional Autónoma de México, 1942. Still an essential tool for research into sixteenth-century Mexican poetry; gives introductions and editorial comments on each writer and work.

———, ed. *Poetas novohispanos: Segundo siglo.* Mexico City: Universidad Nacional Autónoma de México, [1944] 1945. The most complete collection of seventeenth-century poetry; this is a corpus likely to draw critical attention in the nineties.

Méndez Plancarte, Gabriel, ed. *Humanistas del siglo XVIII.* Mexico City: Universidad Nacional Autónoma de México, Coordinación de Humanidades, [1941] 1979.

Menéndez y Pelayo, Marcelino. "Introducción." In his *Antología de poetas hispanoamericanos* [*sic*], i–clxxxii. 2 vols. Madrid: Tipografía de la "Revista de Archivos," 1927.

Mier, Fray Servando Teresa de. *Apología y relaciones de su vida.* In his *Memorias.* 2 vols. Ed. Antonio Castro Leal. Mexico City: Editorial Porrúa, 1946.

———. "Apuntes para el sermón sobre la Aparición de Nuestra Señora de Guadalupe." In *Colección de documentos para la Guerra de Independencia de México de 1808 a 1821,* vol. 3, 7–70. 6 vols. Ed. Hernández Dávalos, J.E., Mexico City, 1877–1882. Germany: Kraus Reprint, 1968.

———. *Historia de la Revolución de Nueva España, antiguamente Anáhuac.* Ed. André Saint-Lu and Marie Cécile Bénassy-Berling. Preface by David Brading. Série Langue et Langages 20. Paris: La Sorbonne, 1990.

Mignolo, Walter. "El mandato y la ofrenda: La *Descripción de la ciudad de Tlaxcala* de Diego Muñoz Camargo, y las relaciones de Indias." *Nueva Revista de Filología Hispánica* 35.2 (1987): 451–484. A model semiotic analysis of a long-neglected mestizo chronicle recently published in its first critical edition.

Morales, Pedro de. *Carta del Padre Pedro de Morales.* 1579. In *Colegios y profesores jesuitas que enseñaron latín en Nueva España (1572–1767),* ed. Ignacio Osorio Romero. Mexico City: Universidad Nacional Autónoma de México, 1979.

Motolinia, Fray Toribio de. *Historia de los indios de Nueva España.* 1903. Critical study, appendices, and notes by Edmundo O'Gorman. Mexico City: Editorial Porrúa, 1984.

Muñoz Camargo, Diego. *Descripción de la ciudad y provincia de Tlaxcala.* Ed. René Acuña. Mexico City: Universidad Nacional Autónoma de México, 1981.

"No me mueve, mi Dios, para quererte." In Méndez Plancarte, ed., *Poetas novohispanos: Primer siglo,* 166–167.

Núñez Cabeza de Vaca, Alvar. *Relación.* 1542. In his *Naufragios y Comentarios,* 13–97. Colección Austral No. 304. Madrid: Espasa-Calpe, 1971.

Osorio Romero, Ignacio. "Jano, o La literatura neolatina de México." In *Cultura clásica y cultura mexicana: Conferencias,* ed. Ignacio Osorio Romero, 11–46. Mexico City: Universidad Nacional Autónoma de México, 1983. The best recent attempt at a reevaluation of neo-Latin writers of New Spain.

Pagden, Anthony. *The Fall of Natural Man.* London: Cambridge University Press, 1982. A key investigation into the ideology of the sixteenth-century "ethnographers" Las Casas and Acosta.

Pastor, Beatriz. *Discurso narrativo de la conquista de América.* Hanover, N.H.: Ediciones del Norte, 1988. One of the most influential recent essays on the chronicle of Indies; uses an ideological model to trace the allegorizing New World discourse to favor the European while silencing the native culture.

Paz, Octavio. *Sor Juana Inés de la Cruz o las trampas de la fe.* Barcelona: Seix Barral, 1982. English version: *Sor Juana Inés de la Cruz or the Traps of Faith,* trans. Margaret Sayers Peden. London: Faber, 1988. An essential work for understanding Mexican culture of the sixteenth and seventeenth centuries; provides exhaustive analysis and information of Sor Juana's life, works, and milieu.

Perelmuter Pérez, Rosa. "La estructura retórica de la *Respuesta a Sor Filotea.*" *Hispanic Review* 51 (1983): 147–158. An illuminating exploration of the rhetorical devices underpinning Sor Juana's *Reply.*

Pérez de Villagrá, Gaspar. *Historia de la Nueva Mexico* [*sic*]. 1610. Ed. L. González Obregón. Mexico City: 1900.

Reyes, Alfonso. *Obras completas.* Mexico City: Fondo de Cultura Económica, 1960.

———. *Letras de la Nueva España.* In *Obras completas,* 12: 279–395. Mexico City: Fondo de Cultura Económica, 1960. One of the first complete narratives on colonial literature; a touchstone for virtually everything that followed.

Roggiano, Alfredo. "Acerca de los dos barrocos: El de España y el de América." In *El barroco en América,* 39–47. XVII Congreso del Instituto Iberoamericano de Literatura Iberoamericana. Madrid: Ediciones Cultura Hispánica del Centro Iberoamericano de Cooperación, 1978. Inaugural essay in an important collection bringing together many perspectives on the baroque.

Rojas Garcidueñas, José, ed. *Auto de la destrucción de Jerusalén.* In *Autos y coloquios del siglo XVI,* 1–36. Mexico City: Universidad Nacional Autónoma de México, 1972.

Rosas de Oquendo, Mateo. "Romance a México." In Méndez Plancarte, ed., *Poetas novohispanos: Primer siglo,* 140–142.

———. *Sátira hecha por Mateo Rosas de Oquendo a las cosas que pasan en el Pirú, año de 1598.* Critical edition by Pedro Lasarte. Madison, Wis: Hispanic Seminary of Medieval Studies, 1990.

Ross, Kathleen Ann. "Carlos de Sigüenza y Góngora's *Parayso occidental:* Baroque Narrative in a Colonial Convent." Unpublished dissertation, Yale University, 1986. The first exhaustive analysis of an important multifaceted baroque work for which no generic label is adequate.

Ruiz de Alarcón, Juan. *La verdad sospechosa.* 1619. In his *Comedias,* 349–441. Caracas: Biblioteca Ayacucho, 1982.

Saavedra Guzmán, Antonio de. *El peregrino indiano.* Madrid: Pedro Madrigal, 1599.

Sabat de Rivers, Georgina. *El "Sueño" de Sor Juana Inés de la Cruz: Tradiciones literarias y originalidad.* London: Tamesis, 1977. One of the three or four most enlightening studies of Sor Juana's masterpiece.

———. "Sor Juana Inés de la Cruz." In Iñigo Madrigal, coor., 275–293. An excellent introduction to Sor Juana and her comprehensive writings.

Sahagún, Fray Bernardino de. *General History of the Things of New Spain: Florentine Codex.* Trans. and ed. Arthur J. O. Anderson and Charles E. Dibble. Nos. 14, 13 parts. Salt Lake City: School of American Research and University of Utah, 1950–1982.

————. *Historia general de las cosas de Nueva España*. 1569. 4 vols. Mexico City: Editorial Porrúa, 1956.

Sandoval Zapata, Luis de. "Relacíon fúnebre a la infeliz trágica muerte de dos caballeros . . . ," 1608. In José Pascual Buxó, *Muerte y desengaño en la poesía novohispana (siglos XVI y XVII)*, 117–128. Mexico City: Universidad Nacional Autónoma de México, 1975.

Sannazaro, Jacopo. *Arcadia*. 1489. Introduction by Enrico Carrara. Torino: Unione tipografico-ditrice torinese, 1926.

Scott, Nina. "Sor Juana Inés de la Cruz: 'Let Your Women Keep Silence in the Churches. . . . '" *Women's Studies Institute Forum* 8.5 (1985): 511–519. Researches women mentioned by Sor Juana in the *Respuesta*.

Shelly, Kathleen, and Grínor Rojo. "El teatro hispanoamericano colonial." In Iñigo Madrigal, coor., 319–352. The best and most current guide to theater of the colonial period; uses an ideological approach to reevaluate several Mexican works.

Sigüenza y Góngora, Carlos de. *Alboroto y motín de los indios de México (Carta al almirante Pez)*. 1692. In his *Seis obras*, 95–141. Caracas: Biblioteca Ayacucho, 1984.

————. *Glorias de Querétaro*. 1680. Querétaro, Mexico: Ediciones Cimatario, 1945.

————. *Infortunios de Alonso Ramírez*. In his *Seis obras*, 5–92. Caracas: Biblioteca Ayacucho, 1984.

————. *Parayso occidental*. Mexico City: Juan de Ribera, 1684.

————. *Primavera indiana*. 1688. In his *Obras*. Ed. Francisco Pérez Salazar. Mexico City: Sociedad de Bibliófilos Mexicanos, 1928.

————. *Teatro de virtudes políticas que constituyen a un príncipe*. 1680. In his *Seis obras*, 167–246. Caracas: Biblioteca Ayacucho, 1984.

Solís y Rivadeneyra, Antonio de. *Historia de la conquista de México, población y progresos de la América Septentrional, conocida por el nombre de Nueva España*. 1684. Critical study, appendices, and notes by Edmundo O'Gorman. Mexico City: Editorial Porrúa, 1984.

Suárez de Peralta, Juan. *Tratado del descubrimiento de las Indias y su conquista: Noticias históricas de la Nueva España*. 1589. Preliminary study and notes by Teresa Silva Tena. Mexico City: Consejo Nacional para la Cultura y las Artes, 1990.

Tapia, Andrés de. *Relación*. 1868. In *Crónicas de la Conquista*, ed. Agustín Yáñez, 25–79. Mexico City: Universidad Nacional Autónoma de México, 1987.

Terrazas, Francisco de. *Conquista y Nuevo Mundo*. 1604. In his *Poesías*. Selection, prologue, and notes by Antonio Castro Leal. Mexico City: Editorial Porrúa, 1941.

Todorov, Tzvetan. *The Conquest of America*. Trans. Richard Howard. New York: Harper and Row, [1982] 1984. An often-criticized work that is a touchstone of current ideological criticism.

Torquemada, Juan de. *Veintiún libros rituales de la monarquía indiana*. 1557. 7 vols. Mexico City: Editorial Porrúa, 1975–1983.

Trejo, Pedro de. "Canción de una dama." In Méndez Plancarte, ed., *Poetas novohispanos: Primer siglo*, 9–10.

————. *Cancionero general*. 1570. Modern edition, introduction, and notes by Sergio López Mena. Mexico City: Universidad Nacional Autónoma de México, 1981.

Triunfo de los Santos. 1941. Ed. Harvey Leroy Johnson. Philadelphia: University of Pennsylvania Press, 1941.

Vetancourt, Fray Agustín [also Vetancurt, Betancur]. *Teatro mexicano: Descripción de los sucesos ejemplares históricos, políticos y religiosos del Nuevo Mundo occidental de las Indias.* 1698. Ed. José Porrúa. Colección Chimalistac de Libros y Documentos acerca de la Nueva España. Madrid, 1960.

Vidal, Hernán. *Socio-historia de la literatura colonial hispanoamericana: Tres lecturas orgánicas.* Minneapolis: Institute for the Study of Ideologies and Literature, 1985. A Marxist approach to the subject; what Vidal says is important even when it seems to lead to an impasse.

Villerías y Roel, José. *Guadalupe.* 1724. Unpublished.

———. *Llanto.* 1725. Unpublished.

———. *Máscara.* 1721. Unpublished.

3

Romanticism

MARGARITA VARGAS
Translated by David E. Johnson

"In mid-century mythology the worldly success of the male was deemed to
be inextricably intertwined with the self-denial of woman."

(Bram Dijkstra, 20)

Mexican romanticism, not having a neoclassicism against which to
rebel, proves to be "a literary school without violence, without a
radical break with its past. Romanticism passes through Mexico
with neither the noise nor the expectations with which it ran through Europe"
(Martínez, "Prologue," xxiv–xxv).[1] Therefore, in Mexico, romanticism is primarily a response to the country's particular political situation rather than an
aesthetic rebuttal. The authors of Mexican romantic literature fashioned their
response to Mexico's various political crises—both internal and external—in
a way that sought to unify the country. Put simply, the authors' predominant
ideological concern was to nationalize Mexican literature. A review of the
criticism of Mexican romanticism reveals at the very least that historically
the critics fretted the issue of one country, one literature. But the majority of
the authors themselves also consciously supported such an idea, and Ignacio
Manuel Altamirano (1834–1893) was one of its most fervent promoters. Altamirano believed that "our letters, arts, and sciences need to nourish themselves from our own themes and temperament and from our own reality in
order to become a true expression of the people and an active element of
national integration" (Martínez, "Mexico," 1054).

Altamirano's premises have been accepted almost without question and
have reproduced themselves in the texts of romantic criticism; in other words,
criticism of romanticism has allowed the romantics to establish the limits of
criticism, rather than the other way around. One of the few who has dared to
challenge Altamirano directly is Mariano Azuela (1873–1952). Referring specifically to *El Zarco*, he affirms:

To John S. Brushwood, for all he taught me and for the faith he showed in me.

[*El Zarco*] aspires to be a Mexican novel, its theme, its characters, the way in which they act, everything wants to be Mexican, but its content lacks what is authentically national. It suffers from the conventionalism of the European types to which José Ferrel refers in the prologue to *Tomochic* by Heriberto Frías. "Our literary types," he writes, "are the grossest falsification of the European types, frequently of the French; in other words, they are French characters in Mexican clothes who, blinded and stunned with their monumental, embroidered Mexican hats which slipped down to their moustaches, expressed themselves carelessly; their language is a mixture of vulgar Mexican expressions and a phraseology transcribed from the pages of imported pamphlets." (497)

In spite of the errors Azuela points out, it is undeniable that Mexican romantic writers sought to express in a sincere and conscientious way the reality of their country. Nevertheless, underlying the superficial or explicit ideology that manifested itself as the desire to nationalize literature, there exists an unconscious or hidden ideological level. This essay makes explicit what lies hidden in romantic literature; to unearth this hidden ideology, then, we have recourse to Engels, who asserts that

ideology is a process accomplished by the so-called thinker consciously indeed but with a false consciousness. The real motives impelling him remain unknown to him, otherwise it would not be an ideological process at all. Hence he imagines false or apparent motives. Because it is a process of thought he derives both its form and its content from pure thought, either his own or his predecessors'.

(*Letter to Mehring*, 1893, cited in Williams, 155)

Taking Engels's statement as a point of departure, and given the political, socioeconomic, and religious situation of Mexico at the time, it becomes obvious that the large majority of romantic works contain an underlying ideology which is not readily apparent to the reader. Even though, publicly, the writers claimed that their main purpose was to nationalize Mexico's literature, scrutiny of their works shows an ideology consisting of a surreptitious repression that restrains women both physically and verbally.[2] To understand the necessity of repressing women's voices and denying their bodies, besides studying certain works that clearly exemplify the phenomenon, it is also necessary to fix Mexico's political situation during the nineteenth century.

In 1810, Mexico, tired of living under Spanish rule, began its search for independence. After many years of struggle, the Vatican finally recognized Mexico's autonomy in 1836, even though legally Spain's dominion over Mexico ended in 1821 (Vázquez, 743). At the same time as Mexico was seeking recognition of its independence from Spain, Texas wanted to emancipate from Mexico. Problems between Texas and Mexico began in 1829 and were not resolved until 1836 with Texas's declaration of independence. In 1837 the

United States recognized Texas as an independent nation; France and Great Britain followed suit in 1839 and 1840, respectively. Meanwhile, in spite of opposition from various European countries, Mexico continued its own struggle for recognition. France is one of the countries that refused to acknowledge Mexico's independence "because of a series of demands, including the compensation owed to French citizens for damages caused during a particular revolutionary movement, and the claim that they be extended a series of privileges such as the country's retail business" (Vázquez, 808). Since they were unable to arrive at an agreement, France assaulted the port of Veracruz in November 1838, but in March 1839 England intervened in order to impose peace between the two countries.

Owing to its vast and unpopulated territory and the weakness of its army, Mexico's vulnerability became more and more apparent. Taking advantage of the country's deplorable situation, James K. Polk, president of the United States, petitioned Congress in May 1846 to declare war on Mexico with the intention of obtaining part of her territory. Congress agreed with the request, and the United States invaded Mexico. After almost two years of struggle, on February 2, 1848, a treaty was signed in which Mexico "acceded to the cession of New Mexico and Upper California . . . in exchange for an 'indemnization' of 15 million *pesos*" (Vázquez, 818).

With the signing of the treaty, the new Mexican government, headed by General José Joaquín Herrera, had to confront not only a strong economic crisis, but also various groups that accused him of betraying the country for having sold the northern lands. In addition, he had to take charge of the Indian insurrections, especially in Yucatán. In 1851 Herrera surrendered the leadership to Mariano Arista, who inherited a multiplicity of problems. Lilia Díaz offers a graphic description of the country's predicament at this time:

From the first year of his [Arista's] government, the national panorama could not have been more depressing. Tehuantepec threatened by the president of the United States, Millard Fillmore; Sonora invaded by Gaston Raousset de Boulbon, helped by French and North American adventurers in connection with a mining company in Arizona. Chihuahua at the point of revolt against the Federation and invaded by nomadic tribes of Comanches and Apaches; Tamaulipas besieged by José María Carbajal with an auxiliary band of mercenaries of unknown nationality. Other freebooters commanded by José María Canales inspired the proposal of separating a new portion of territory and creating the Republic of the Sierra Madre inside the state of Tamaulipas in order to annex it to the United States. Mazatlán rose in arms against the fiscal dispositions of the state authorities. Durango found itself invaded by indigenous nomadic groups, Yucatán was unable to extinguish the embers of the caste war; Michoacán, disturbed by the sect of the Piedad de Cabadas, placed itself against Governor Melchor Ocampo because of the reform legislature that imposed religious freedom and attacked the parochial privileges by preparing daring systems for the nationalization of Church property. (823)

Between 1850 and 1867 Mexico suffered several internal conflicts and an attack by the French in 1863 known as the French Intervention. The internal struggles resulted in the constant changing of governments—in which political power alternated between the conservatives and the liberals—and the French Intervention meant that from 1864 Mexico was ruled by the monarchy of Ferdinand Maximilian, archduke of Austria. In 1867 republican forces destroyed the government of the monarch, and once again President Benito Juárez governed the country until his death in 1872. Sebastián Lerdo de Tejada, Juárez's friend, succeeded him as president; during these two administrations the country enjoyed at least the semblance of peace. According to Luis González, during the decade 1867–1876, the country

> depended on a team of civilizers and patriots small in number but large in enthusiasm and intelligence; on a program of action which was multiple, lucid, precise, and vigorous; and on a national climate adverse to democratic, liberal, economic, scientific, and nationalist prosperities. Given the ideal circumstances under which they governed, they were able to plant the seeds of modernization and nationalism. (924)

Mexico ended the century under the rule of Don Porfirio Díaz, an epoch of progress but also of immeasurable repression.

Therefore, the nineteenth century represents in the history of Mexico a stage of great social, economic, and political instability. Moreover, the country's demographic situation added to its problems. The country was underpopulated not only from the losses it suffered with each conflict, but also from the epidemics of typhus, small pox, and cholera as well as the natural catastrophes, such as earthquakes and floods, that plagued the country during the thirties and forties (Vázquez, 799). The population increased very little during the Restored Republic (1867–1876) because "malaria and pneumonia and the frequent epidemics of yellow fever and small pox" were often fatal (González, 919).

With such a somber history, it is not difficult to imagine that most of the writers felt a moral obligation to improve the conditions of their country. This is evident in the large number of writers who participated simultaneously in some of the battles or held high offices within the government. Among the best known were Manuel Payno (1810–1894), Guillermo Prieto (1818–1897), Ignacio Ramírez (1818–1879), Ignacio Manuel Altamirano, and Vicente Riva Palacio (1832–1896). Juan Díaz Covarrubias (1837–1859) did not participate directly in any struggle, but he was a medic for the liberal troops during one of the internal conflicts. Together with the soldiers for whom he was caring, he was executed on April 11, 1859 (Díaz y de Ovando, 32–33).

Criticism of Mexican romantic literature focuses on its nationalist function and ignores one of the fundamental elements of the romantic work: the role of woman. The conscious desire to create a literature of "national character" does not automatically exclude an underlying effort to formulate a series of moral and physical characteristics that women should adopt. Grounding our-selves in the established premises of Marx and Engels in *The German Ideology*, in the ideas that Edmond Cros proposes in his *Théorie et practique sociocri-tiques*, in the historical investigations of Silvia Marina Arrom in *The Women of Mexico City, 1790–1857*, and in Bram Dijkstra's *Idols of Perversity: Fantasies of Feminine Evil in Fin-de-Siècle Culture*, we can surmise that the portrait of women in Mexican romantic works had a political and economic purpose. Within the chaotic political situation of the epoch it is not surprising that the governors looked for a way to placate an entire segment of the population in order to be able to carry out their governmental plans. Arrom suggests that in times of prosperity there is a greater tolerance of change, which is not the case during times of economic stress:

When the burgeoning economy of the late colonial city had promised enough jobs so that women need not compete with men, and when the reformers' ambitious plans required that women take on new responsibilities, many men were confident that they could adjust to whatever changes in sex roles might result. After indepen-dence, as the plummeting economy and failure to establish a viable government dashed the earlier optimism, most men felt threatened by incipient changes in women's roles. (266)

Therefore, given the economic and political conditions of the country, it was necessary to establish certain guidelines that women should follow to assure the tranquility of men's intimate life. Bram Dijkstra locates a similar situation in France around the same time. Dijkstra claims that "driven by the ever-increasing pressures of economic survival," men developed "the myth of the self-effacing sacrificial woman, the undemanding household nun," to escape from "the all too insistent demands related to sexual performance which had figured so largely in their grandfathers' and even in their fathers' smoking room and tavern conversations" (68). Also, in an analysis of *The Bostonians* (1886), Dijkstra asserts that what Henry James saw in Verena Tarrant, his heroine, was "the woman who could fulfill the male dream of the wife as household nun, for in her passivity she represented the soft, gentle, nonvio-lent, 'humane' values he longed for and could not find in the male world" (17). What a man wanted then, was a "gentle oasis of household peace presided over by his modest mate" (65). Edmond Cros suggests that such enterprises are carried out in the following manner:

Every society produces behavioral models through which it materializes the evolu-tion of appropriate values (son, mother, daughter, father, well-brought-up young lady, *femme fatale*, liberated woman, secretary, boss, . . . etc.) and which constitute *social roles* in terms of which each individual defines himself or herself. These be-havioral models, which subsume individual subjects under the category of same-ness, also create certain behavioral expectations; it is, of course, because I know a certain attitude is expected of me that I adopt it, and in so doing I am the victim of

what might be termed an "ideological interpellation." The decoding and the reproduction of these social roles are ensured by a whole syntax of signs that permit
their transmission to the nonconscious level, and that program the whole of our
social life. (46–47)[3]

The assumption, then, is that literature functions ideologically, that it establishes a range of possible characterizations from which its female readers will
choose the proper model to follow. Romantic literature, in fact, reduces the
complexity of women's choice by severely limiting their options. Typically,
female characters fall within the frame of the binary opposition angel/demon.
In other words, if the reader from the romantic epoch were to identify herself
with one of the characters, she ineluctably had to choose between the femme
fatale and the good woman; there did not exist a middle term. As this essay
will show, the dichotomy's intention was to produce women who accepted and
followed the example of the good woman; this choice would guarantee men a
privileged place in society. Therefore, what we want to investigate is the way
in which, within the parameters of romanticism's nationalization of Mexican
literature, a "syntax of signs" works to repress women.

THE SHORT STORY

The short story captures the ideal feminine by means of the establishment of
a dichotomy based on two religious symbols: the Virgin of Guadalupe and
Eve, although frequently the Malinche is substituted for Eve.[4] To approximate
the image of the Virgin, one must be beautiful, young, pure, fragile, and serene. Women who possess such characteristics inspire the most pure love in
sensitive men. The second is a voluptuous, capricious, and boisterous woman
who disturbs man's tranquility. They frequently appear in the same story and
inadvertently create a tension in the gullible and inexperienced young man.
The use of the Virgin of Guadalupe fits perfectly well within the nationalist
ideals of the Mexican romantics, as Luis Leal affirms:

> She is identified with what is truly Mexican as opposed to what is foreign. If *la
> Malinche* sided with the foreign invader and helped him conquer her own people,
> the Virgin of Guadalupe protects the Indian, the Mestizo, and the Creole, that is,
> the representatives of the new Mexican nation. (229)

The image of the evil woman arises at the beginning of the nineteenth century. It can be traced back as early as 1818 in José Joaquín Fernández de
Lizardi's *La Quijotita y su prima* (Little Miss Quixote and Her Cousin) and in
Jicotencal, an anonymous novel published in Philadelphia in 1826.[5] According
to Jean Franco, Fernández de Lizardi's novel "was paradigmatic not only because it presented the Utopian ideal of the new post-Independence family but
also because the novel created two female paradigms—the good and obedient
Prudenciana and the evil 'little Miss Quixote.'" (83). To show that the di-

chotomy was not restricted to Mexico nor to the romantic period, Franco goes on to say that "in writing the novel, [Fernández de] Lizardi drew freely on the vast literature on this subject, particulary French literature," and points out that his sources included Abbé Fénélon, Jean Baptiste Blanchard, and Antoine Leonard Thomas. The last two "belonged to a tradition of conservative thought that grounded women's subordination in their physical weakness and the need to protect them for childbirth" (83). In his discussion of *Jicotencal* Leal also marks the dichotomy good/evil and emphasizes its long tradition:

> In this historical novel Doña Marina represents the forces of evil and is characterized as wily, perfidious, deceitful, and treacherous. Her mythical nature is strengthened by the association that the author makes between Marina and the serpent, which placed her under the light of two feminine archetypes, one European and the other Mexican; that is, Eve and Coatlicue, an Aztec goddess. (228)

> Thus, we arrive at two contrasting types, the good woman and the bad woman, which have their origins in antiquity. In Mexican literature, recalling again the novel *Jicotencal,* we find Teutila, an angelical Indian woman who is virtuous, honest, and faithful as a wife, as opposed to *la Malinche.* The former is called "angel bajado del cielo" [an angel descended from heaven] (II.174), is characterized as the innocent victim of the tyrant Cortés, and is contrasted to Marina, "una astuta serpiente" [an astute serpent] (I.190). (231)

In his essay, Leal traces the female archetypes through all of Mexican literature in order to argue that because of their long tradition it is extremely difficult to get rid of them, but he does not comment on the politics of an epoch's assumption and reinvestment of the archetypes. He does concede, however, that "considering the fact that society changes, it is to be supposed that literary types will also change" (241). Leal then documents the changes at the end of his essay by citing various examples of the archetypal transformations.

This essay, then, examines how the two images of woman are presented in romantic prose and makes explicit the repercussions of such representation. Since we are dealing with a romantic and not a realist movement, we can presume that the intention is not to depict, in any factual sense, contemporary women; rather, the intention is to create an image. In an epoch in which the idea of nationalizing literature was emphasized, it is valid to explore the conscious or unconscious act of establishing role models for the reading public. Given the precarious state of the country, we contend that it was necessary to subjugate any element of society that posed a threat. Therefore, to suppress the power of women, not only were certain literary archetypes created, but in addition a rigorously limited and ideologically sexist education was imparted to women:

> An 1852 "Discourse on the Influence of Public Instruction on the Happiness of Nations" plainly stated the purpose of female schooling: it was not meant "to ele-

vate women to the level of competing with men and taking part in their delibera-
tions;" it was strictly designed to make women "good daughters, excellent mothers,
and the best and most solid support of the goals of Society." (Arrom, 23)

That men dictated what women were allowed to learn reflects only part of the
problem; even worse was the manner in which society labeled those few
women who chose not to follow the norm. According to Arrom,

> Even as Mexican writers affirmed the mental capacities of women, they ridiculed
> those with extensive learning. The intellectual woman, the *literata* who spent her
> day reading to the neglect of her personal appearance and home, the *talentacia* who
> made a fool of herself with her pedantry (*bachillerías*), was a stock comic character
> in newspaper satires by the 1840's. (24)

A possible explanation for this attitude toward women is found in the fact
that a large number of the romantic writers were high officials in the government, which reaffirms that the ideology hidden in their works owes itself to
their political involvement.[6] Carlos Monsiváis's stimulating essay, "Clasismo y
novela en México" (Classicism and the Novel in Mexico), supports such an
assertion:

> The dominant classes are prudish and sexist: they bring to literature their ideology
> of exploitation of women as a class: the exaltation of monogamy, the unconditional
> eulogy to the harem mentality, the prostitute as counterweight/savior of matri-
> mony, euphemism as the most adequate sexual description, the physical and pys-
> chological submission of women as the indispensible affirmation of the maturity of
> men. Although it is not exclusive of capitalism and it devastates powerfully all
> classes, machismo is a substantial part of bourgeois ideology. Literature has invig-
> orated and sanctified the process of the inferiorization of one sex, or of those who
> deviate from the norm. (177)

Tied to the *machista* problem that Monsiváis comments on is the fear of losing
power and control over women. Arrom notes that "individual freedom, another tenet of liberalism, was not directly extended to women either, since
liberals feared what women might do with too much freedom" (264).
    With the objective of verifying the presence of the ideas exposed by Arrom
and Monsiváis, we have chosen the most representative examples from the
collection entitled *Cuentos románticos* (Romantic Short Stories), edited by David Huerta (1949). Thematically, most of the stories follow a pattern similar
to that established by European romanticism: namely, unrequited love. Although there do exist minor variations, the fact that a single pattern remains
constant suggests that, rather than a concern for artistic creation in itself, the
stories' significance lies in the advocation of the predominant ideology. Curiously, the majority of stories do not take up, either in terms of theme or
environment, issues related to the authentically Mexican identity. Although

the majority of critical studies have emphasized Mexican romantics' promul-
gation of a national literature, few stories actually follow such precepts. If we
accept that nationalizing literature means "exposing the flowers of our gardens
and the fruits of our delicious orchards," as Guillermo Prieto proposes, then
clearly these are nationalist stories (Martínez, "Mexico," 1040). But these
qualities appear (literally) only in those stories set in Mexico, and of the thirteen stories in David Huerta's anthology only four take place in Mexico; the
others are set in Italy or in an unspecified place. Two frequent elements that
support the idea of nationalization are the incarnation of the Virgin—even
though she is not always dark like the Virgin of Guadalupe—in the good
woman and the foreignness of the evil woman.

Juan Díaz Covarrubias exploits the opposition between the two visions of
woman in "La sensitiva" (The Delicate Flower). The difference between Luisa
and Isabel implicitly remarks the romantic's ideological program to repress
women. Luisa exemplifies the model of perfection: she is "pure as a drop of
dew . . . innocent and simple as a child's first smile, tender and delicate as that
plant the poets call *sensitiva*, . . . with a heart that harbors exquisite treasures
of sensibility and tenderness" (Huerta, 214). As if the previous adjectives were
not enough, the narrator continues describing her as "one of those children,
always pale and sick, yet always affable and endearing; who die with a smile
on their lips without exhaling a single complaint . . ." (Huerta, 215). On the
other hand, Isabel typifies the woman with

> a soul of slime beneath the figure of an archangel whose memory horrifies, but
> whose presence attracts and fascinates with a mysterious magnet. [She was one of
> those] women who speculate on the sentiments of the soul, who tread upon the
> heart, and who can spoil an existence with the most frightful cynicism; who make
> men miserable, turning into hell what yesterday was paradise.
>
> (Huerta, 220)

The contrast between their personalities could be neither more opposed nor
more apparent. Luisa calls to mind the virginal qualities of innocence, purity,
resignation; Isabel is a type of monster or serpent who terrifies, poisons, fright-
ens, and transforms heavens into hells. Besides the physical and spiritual descriptions of the characters, the narration of their daily activities also distinguishes between the two types of women. While women like Luisa dedicate
themselves to the "cultivation of their flowers" and to walking in the country,
the Isabels spend their free time at evening parties and other similar diver-
sions. These "orgies," as the narrator calls them, are full of women with "naked
breasts of marble" and "alabaster foreheads" (Huerta, 223).[7] The cold and stiff
materials used to describe the evil women sharply contrast with the images of
fragility and tenderness attributed to the benevolent women. With regards to
the image of woman as flower, Dijkstra points out that "in her very essence,
her fragility, her physical beauty, her passivity and lack of aptitude for practi-

cal matters, woman was virtually a flower herself" (15). Responding to comments made by Jules Michelet and to such paintings as Robert Reid's "Fleur de
Lys" and Edgard Maxence's "Rosa Mystica," Dijkstra contends that "it is clear
that most nineteenth-century males would have liked their women to take a
few pointers from the flowers and learn to be silent too" (16), which applies
to male nineteenth-century Mexican writers as well.

When the heroines do not have a garden to care for or any needlework to
do, they assiduously attend Mass. A good example is María, the protagonist of
"Botón de rosa" (Rosebud) by Florencio M. del Castillo (1828–1863). The
narrator tells us that "every morning the young woman is there [at Mass],
fresh, beautiful, pure" (Huerta, 144). To her beatitude are added the familiar
characteristics: María is blond and also "a simple girl, candid and pure; one of
those women who, upon seeing them, inspire the idea of a flower" (Huerta,
145)—in other words, silence and prudence.

While the separation of this fragile woman and her secret admirer occurs
because of her death, the separation of the lovers in "El amor frustrado" (Frustrated Love) by José Joaquín Pesado (1801–1861) results from the discovery
at the story's conclusion that they are brother and sister. This impediment
represents a tragedy for the male protagonist because Isabel Gallardo inspired
"the pure and perfect love": she was between "twelve and fourteen years old,
beautiful, tender, graceful. . . . An angel on earth." Her hair was blond, her
color "fresh and rosy," an "elegant body," a "precious mouth," and "divine eyes"
(Huerta, 32). In addition to her earthly qualities, Isabel is accorded the honor
of being the niece of the parish priest, which indirectly secures the male spiritual well-being.

The image of the kind woman in the story "Buondelmonti" by José María
Roa Bárcena (1827–1908) differs little from that of the characters already
described. María Amidei is distinguished by her youth, her beauty, by belonging to a noble house and by having an excellent heart. She is also portrayed as
being "charitable toward the poor, loving with her family, religious beyond
comparison, and endowed with an elevated spirit" (Huerta, 121). On the other
hand, Constanza Donati (the woman who steals María's future husband) possessed only the "vulgar" qualities preferred by the majority, a dazzling beauty
and youth.

The juxtaposition of the two types of women makes evident the difference
between the eternal and the ephemeral. The bad woman is always presented
in terms of what impresses but does not last; the good woman has virtues that
remain even after her death. Moreover, that the good woman is associated with
nature and religion guarantees her resurrection.

It may seem paradoxical that the model that the reader should follow always
dies, but an examination of the unstated ideology makes the purpose of the
protagonist's death clear. Although during the nineteenth century it would
have been a contradiction for a liberal to be religious, that did not mean that
the majority did not retain the teachings their parents had instilled. Consequently, their vision of the perfect woman included images of religious figures.

As we have already noted, one of these figures is the Virgin of Guadalupe. Within the religious paradigm, the death of the benevolent women makes sense. It would, in fact, have been an aberration if these virginal women were to have consumated their love. Implicitly, then, it was suggested to the reader that it was preferable to die a virgin, which would guarantee perdurance among the living as a sanctified image, than to lead a life deprecated by every-one.[8] In *Mujer que sabe latín* (A Woman Who Knows Latin), Rosario Castel-lanos (1925–1974) proposes that fear brings men to create such virtuous images:

> Simultaneously, fear engenders propiciatory acts toward and violence against whatever causes it.
>
> Thus, woman, for centuries, has been elevated to the altar of the deities and has inhaled the incense of the devout. . . .
>
> This ambivalence of masculine attitudes is nothing more than superficial and apparent. If we examine it well, we will find an indivisible and constant unity of purposes that manifests itself masked in multiple ways.
>
> Let's suppose, for example, that woman is exalted for her beauty. Let's not for-get, then, that beauty is an ideal that man both composes and imposes and that, by strange coincidence, corresponds to a series of requisites that, upon being satisfied, turn the woman who encarnates them into an invalid. (8–9)

Castellanos cites numerous examples, such as the emphasis placed on the size of a woman's foot, to show the way in which men literally impede women's movement. She says that it was declared that, for women, big and vigorous feet were ugly, while for men they were admissible, obligatory. She gives the example of China where they would bind women's feet in order that they would not grow. She also focuses on fashionable shoes, an indispensible ac-coutrement for the elegantly dressed woman, suggesting that they possess "all the characteristics that define an instrument of torture" (10). Castellanos cites other examples pertinent to the romantic presentation of women:

> There are other more subtle and equally efficacious methods for reducing her to ineptitude: those that would like to transform women into pure spirit.
>
> While that spirit is not keeping the angels company in the ethereal realm, it is quartered in the jail of the body. But to ensure that the grief of that transitory state does not destroy its victim, one must procure for her a body that is as fragile, as vulnerable, as inexistent as possible. (10)

With these words Castellanos seems to direct herself specifically to romantic literature, but actually she refers to history in general. Her essay begins: "Throughout history . . . woman has been more than a component of society, more than a human creature, a myth" (7).

Thus, in romanticism, the bipolar myth, Virgin/Eve, works to emphasize the virtues to which all women should aspire and to denigrate those women who fail to conform. In either case, the mutual exclusivity of the two options, the lack of any medial ground, restricts the possible lives for women: on the one hand, although to live as a Virgin integrates a woman into society, it denies a large part of her being; on the other hand, to lead the free life of the Malinche automatically ostracizes her from society.

One story that does not follow the pattern of the preceding ones but which exposes the sexist ideology nonetheless is "Atenea" (Athena), by Ignacio Manuel Altamirano. Considering that Altamirano promoted a national literature, the story surprises because it is not situated in Mexico and the protagonist, Atenea, is not Mexican; her mother is from Buenos Aires and her father from Venice. Atenea was educated in London and Paris, which in part explains the difference between her and the protagonists of other stories, although she, too, is described as "almost timid, benevolent, sweet . . . like the virgins of our America" (Huerta, 191). Unlike the American virgins, however, Atenea did not spend the hours of the day cultivating gardens or attending Mass; yet, the narrator does not consider her frivolous either. A friend of the narrator describes her as "a strange dreamer," as someone with "an irregular character for a woman, but surprising as a thinker." "Irregular," he says,

> if you want to judge her according to the norm. She is exceptional. Her organization, her high talent, her truly extraordinary education, her travels, the type of studies she undertook, all of these have given her an independent character, so rare, but so adorable in its rarity, that if you deal with her you will go from one surprise to another, as if you were walking through a new and extraordinary country. . . . Atenea is a star that does not follow the ordinary orbit, but that has a brighter light than the others. (183)

Atenea's singularity and the positive tone with which the friend describes her characteristics could lead readers astray and make them believe that in Atenea Altamirano created the figure of an emancipated woman. However, Atenea's vision of love destroys this possibility:

> I thought that in our century [love] existed only in the poets' imagination. But you Americans have new things; you are primitive; one has to know you to believe in emotions that have disappeared from our old European ground, exhausted by civilization. (196)

The epoch's prejudices become evident when the narrator assures Atenea that "love lives even in Europe, and everywhere else," and he attributes the error of her vision to "your youth and perhaps your lofty education, to the environment in which you have lived, to your inexperience complicated by your instruction" (196–197). The emphasis on the detrimentality of education for the understanding of love reveals a negative stance toward the education of women.

The story ends with a long letter in which the narrator, with a superior air, explains to Atenea the particulars of love, abstaining from remarking on certain details because he is aware "that she is just a young girl" (202). He must hold back because he knows her "white and virginal soul should be respected, like a young flower" (203). The narrator refuses to accept that Atenea is a cultured woman and that her education and experience allow her to analyze rationally any information he gives her. Nothing in the story indicates that Atenea is a fragile woman; it is rather the narrator who wants to confine her to a specific mold. He is dazzled by her beauty and prefers to highlight her benevolence, youth, and sweetness, while the friend—who is both mature and uninterested in her—emphasizes her education and her talents.

Unfortunately, "the story seems to have formed part of a novel that is not extent or that, perhaps, [Altamirano] did not continue writing" (Huerta, 160). Owing to this, we do not know Atenea's reply to the narrator's excessively condescending letter. The work, as it stands, though, is valuable for daring to include a different vision of woman, although in the end it disparages her education.

In the same collection there is another story that, like Altamirano's "Atenea," neither establishes the opposition Virgin/Eve nor does it have a Mexican protagonist. In his story "Euclea, o La griega de Trieste" (Euclea, or The Greek of Trieste), the Count of Cortina (José Justo Gómez, 1799–1860) sketches a character that does not agree with the typical image of woman. The narrator, as witness and character, describes her in the following manner: "Her face and her figure seemed to me the type of ideal beauty, and in her features I saw, animated by all the fire of life, the divine forms that the models of Greek sculpture present to us" (Huerta, 11).

This description could fit any of the other virginal women we have seen before, but Euclea's experiences and her vision of marriage are far from theirs. At the age of fifteen Euclea kills a man of "corrupt and scandalous" habits who attempted to abduct her. Her action warrants for her "a just celebrity; but at the same time it brought her many griefs" (16), including the death of her adoptive father. She abandons the place of her misfortune and goes to live with a friend of the family; there she meets and falls in love with Alberto Mancel. Her relationship with Alberto cannot be consummated in matrimony because of Alberto's meager fortune, but this is not important to her because

> she had always seen matrimony with disgust, she had always believed that the chains imposed by duty remove the brilliance of love; that the pleasures a woman gives to a man cannot be but insipid and cold because the law prescribes it so; and that it is impossible for the sacrifices made unwillingly ever to substitute those made freely by the will. (18)

Although during the time that Euclea lived with her adoptive father she led "a pure life, tranquil and dedicated only to the domestic offices proper to her sex" (15), during her secret relationship with Alberto one could have written her off as a bad woman, an Eve-like figure. Euclea and Alberto's trysts took

place in either her house or "in the hovel of a poor woman of the village whose
deference they bought with money, and who looked at them with some interest, because she, too, had once been the victim of an obstructed love" (19).
One day before sunrise and after having spent all night with Euclea, "Alberto
retired from that mansion of love and delights, leaving Euclea surrendered to
a thousand pleasing illusions, which very soon were to become feelings of pain
and despair" (20). Her anguish results from Alberto's death; one of Euclea's
rejected suitors kills him. After this incident Euclea returns to Trieste where
once again she finds herself pursued by another man whom she also disdains.
Tired of petitioning her, the admirer "preferred to deprive himself of life rather
than suffer the prolonged martyrdom of preserving it with neither hope nor
illusions" (21–22). It is after this last misfortune that the narrator meets her
in Trieste.

In comparison to the other stories of the period, this one surprises for the
audacity and strength of the female character. Equally surprising is the attitude of the village toward her. Instead of being repudiated by others, she holds
the admiration of all those present:

> I saw Euclea coming, supported by the arm of an Englishman, . . . and accompa-
> nied by other persons that formed a rather numerous party. Their dances were in-
> terrupted; various young Greeks ran to her to welcome her, and everyone showed
> the pleasure that her presence gave them. (11)

Fascinated like everyone else by the image of Euclea, the narrator remains
at her side for seven months. During that time Euclea recuperates her capacity
for love and eliminates the fear of a new disgrace that might taint her happiness. Unfortunately, at the end of those seven months, Euclea's health begins
to fail and she dies shortly thereafter. She dies resigned to and believing in
God's precepts:

> Why was I born into this world? . . . What has been my existence? I was born
> among tears and afflictions; I have lived among horrors and disasters, and I am
> going to die like the shipwrecked person who perishes within sight of the har-
> bor. . . . If Providence so disposes, what judgement will I be able to form of its
> omnipotent power? (24)

Of all the characters we have seen, Euclea is undoubtedly the most interesting
because of her complicated persona: her character combines respect for God
with liberal ideas about the sacrament of matrimony. Also, she is presented as
a strong and courageous woman who is able to kill a man, find consolation
after her lover's death, and endure the suicide of an admirer. Nevertheless, and
in spite of all she experiences, at the end—like the majority of the heroines—she dies without having reached complete happiness.

Before such a conflicting character, one who does not conform to the established rules, it behooves us to ask about the reactions both of other writers

and of the readers of the epoch toward her. We wonder if stories that establish the duality Virgin/Eve were not in fact written as a reaction to stories like this one. It does not seem likely that a country suffering so many political conflicts could afford, from an ideological point of view, to allow the development of internal conflicts which such stories might cause. A work in which the woman is neither archetypically good nor bad a fortiori raises many issues, two of which might be the value of the dominant literature and women's role within society. A story such as "Euclea," then, leaves many doubts concerning its proper place within Mexican romantic literature: perhaps it was tolerated precisely because it was an anomaly. Or it is possible that the audience emphasized Euclea's good qualities and ignored the bad ones, attributing these latter to the fact that she was a foreigner.

THE NOVEL

Unlike the short story, the novel provides sufficient space to develop more thoroughly the Virgin/Eve duality. While the short story principally avails itself of the characters' portrayal in order to establish the dichotomy, the novel adds narrative and linguistic techniques to achieve a similar but more sophisticated effect. In addition to the distinguishing physical characteristics that the novel grants to women, it makes a distinction between them through the suppression of their voices, the negation of their bodies, and the emphasis placed on their ability to wait. Principally, the novel permits the good woman to speak only to defend the man she loves; it represses her sensuality by turning her into an angelic figure without any earthly vices and by either killing or marrying her off without her previously having known the pleasures of the body. These aspects of the romantic novel are best illustrated in works like *El Zarco* by Ignacio Manuel Altamirano and *Gil Gómez, el insurgente* (Gil Gómez, the Rebel; 1858) by Juan Díaz Covarrubias. Other novels which would substantiate our argument include Nicolás Pizarro Suárez's *La coqueta* (The Coquette; 1861), Manuel Martínez de Castro's *Una hija i una madre* (A Daughter and a Mother; 1875), and Pedro Castera's (1838?–1906) *Carmen* (1882). The last, however, emphasizes the impossibility of a love affair rather than the dichotomy angel/devil. Yet Carmen epitomizes the perfect romantic figure; she has nothing but angelic characteristics, is sickly, and dies a virgin.[9]

El Zarco marks the line between the two feminine images with the terms *angel* and *demon*, although the word *virgin* is also used to distinguish the good from the bad. Faithful, in this case, to his idea of nationalizing literature, Altamirano exalts the figure of the woman representative of the "true" Mexican. It is not by mere chance that he concedes the angelical characteristics to Pilar and the diabolical ones to Manuela, even though the former is a dark young woman "with that soft and delicate tone of the Creoles, which distances them from the Spanish type without confusing them with the Indian, and which reveals the humble daughter of the village" (315). Following the romantic precepts, she is also "beautiful and good"; she has a "fragile body," almost "sickly" (315), and a "tender and soft heart like a sensitive plant" (369). She is considered a "modest flower" (362) and the "pearl of the village for her character, for her beauty and her virtues" (414). To her beloved she is "the good angel of his existence" (369).

Manuela is exactly the opposite: her complexion is white and there is something "contemptuous and haughty" about her; her smile is more "mocking than benevolent" (314). Like Pilar, Manuela, too, is compared to a flower, though not to a sensitive or modest flower, but rather to a "poisonous flower" (362). While Pilar is the good angel, Manuela is the bad one, the demonic one. Nevertheless, on two occasions the narrator refers to a past in which, at least on the surface, Manuela demonstrates having been good. The first time, we are told that Nicolás (Pilar's beloved and, earlier, Manuela's admirer) realized he "had been loving a demon believing it to be an angel" (369). The second reference to her past occurs in a conversation between Manuela and a woman; this woman informs her, "I met you two years ago, . . . so beautiful! So decent! So well dressed! You looked like a Virgin" (390). Both citations, as well as the events of the novel, indicate that Manuela is a type of fallen angel. Manuela comes from a decent family, and she is judged the most beautiful woman of the village, but precisely for this reason, she is always exposed to danger. The warnings of the villagers, who had predicted her fall, become reality and Manuela loses her social position when she joins some bandits.

To maintain the parallel development of the two characters, Pilar also experiences a transformation. In both cases, the change depends upon the two women being in love. In Manuela

> it was the love, it was the fascination, it was a type of vertigo, that made her mad and abandon everything: mother, home, honor, all that is respectable and sacred, to follow that man [el Zarco] without whom, . . . she couldn't live. (387)

The changes in Pilar have to do with the ability to express herself verbally. When the life of the man she loves is endangered, Pilar, whose voice is rarely heard, shouts in public. Nicolás has been taken to prison, and she immediately demands his liberty. Her love for him is so great that she jeopardizes her honor. She reveals her sentiments by shouting at the sergeant on duty that she was prepared to give her life in exchange for Nicolás's freedom. Nicolás hears her words and realizes that

> there was an angel who protected him and however much [he] supposed that Pilar was an obscure, weak, and timid child without powerful connections, he could feel that this child, inspired by love, had become a strong, daring woman with abundant resources. (319)

It goes without saying that the novel privileges the love between Pilar and Nicolás. Society's overdetermination of love—the sanctioning of this particular type of love—emphasizes the epoch's underlying ideology. In other words, to receive society's rewards one must love in a certain way and also be like Pilar: "beautiful, good, fragile, and modest." Under this value system, one certainly expects Manuela, who abandons everything—"mother, home, honor, all that is respectable and sacred"—for her lover, to receive the scorn of the village. In contrast, Pilar, who goes against her role by speaking out, loses neither her honor nor the respect of the village because her action owes itself to a noble cause: "to save him was her only object, and little else was important to her" (364). The importance of her deed is shown by the fact that she is prepared to die and to lose everything for a good citizen of the village. Her action is exemplary and it merits every kind of ceremonious decoration.

It is not totally clear, however, that little else concerns her. In reality Pilar has nothing to fear because she has always known how to submit herself to society's mandates: she shows her passivity and femininity by waiting for just the right moment to act, and besides, she has always desired to marry "according to God's will." Manuela, on the other hand, is impulsive and disobedient: she flees prematurely with *el Zarco*, and she never wanted to be more than his lover. Manuela's fall is due to her defiance of all social rules; Pilar's success to her acceptance of them.

The difference between the two manners of being and thinking is marked by the flowers they each prefer: up to the last minute of her life Manuela insists that her favorite flowers are roses (symbols of love, passion, and evanescence), while Pilar always opts for orange blossoms (indicative of purity, and therefore carried by both newlyweds and dead virgins). Ultimately, though, what ruins Manuela is not that she has been a man's lover and has denounced the symbols reserved for women, but rather that she has fallen in love with a bandit. Society refuses to accept him over Nicolás, one of its most respectable citizens, even though Nicolás is an "ugly Indian."[10]

At the end, the good are rewarded and the bad are punished. Pilar, having worked within the confines of the law, can wear with happiness and pride her crown of orange blossoms and enjoy at her husband's side the "happy destiny" that "a good and protecting spirit had augured for her" (415). These last words suggest that obeying society's rules equals obeying God and that whoever conforms to the earthly commandments is guaranteed a divine protector. For her part, Manuela receives her deserved punishment: she witnesses her lover's execution and moments later she faces her own death.

In terms of adventure and intrigue, the romantic thread of *Gil Gómez, el insurgente* does not compare to that of *El Zarco,* but one does find again the dichotomy angel/demon. The novel weaves together two elements, a love story and a historical event. The principal characters in the love story are Fernando, Clemencia, and Regina; Gil Gómez dominates the historical aspect of the novel. For the purposes of this essay, we will concern ourselves with the love story.

As in all the works discussed thus far, this novel too privileges the woman whose qualities are similar to those of an angel. Clemencia represents this work's angelical figure; Regina is the antagonist. Besides the physical descriptions, which do not vary much from those already mentioned in the discussion of other exemplary characters, the novel marks the difference between the two women by means of the use of the voice. Clemencia, who lives only for Fernando, has no voice; what little she says always concerns him. Her existence revolves completely around his. Before Fernando's departure for the big city, Clemencia promises him: "I will wait in silence; I will suffer your separation with resignation. But if it should last too long, then, don't doubt it, Fernando, then I will die" (190).

Conforming to the romantic tradition, Clemencia's chores consist of playing the piano, caring for her garden, and praying to God. Her inane role is emphasized by the way she is considered an object by and for others. When Fernando is preparing to leave, his father consoles him, assuring Fernando that for his return he will receive a "prize." Fernando guesses, "Clemencia!" and his father concurs (194).[11]

In contrast to the submissive and docile Clemencia, Regina is presented as the sagacious and worldly woman. Unlike Clemencia, Regina imposes her voice and presence by being actively involved in the society and its politics. With regards to love, instead of living for men, she manipulates them, and it is they who struggle to be by her side. Regina does not wait; rather she makes others wait. While Clemencia remains in the village awaiting Fernando's return, in the city he meets Regina, the "angel-demon . . . who only two years before had appeared at the Mexican court, driving wild all those who saw her regal beauty, amazing them with her scandalous luxury, dazzling them with her exquisite taste in dress" (280).

Regina traps Fernando not only with her beauty, but also with the power of the word. Tired of her former lover, she invents a long and sad story in which he plays the role of a cruel villain. The purpose of her story is to incite Fernando; she believes that, given the love he feels for her, he will be disposed to kill her lover. Fortunately, the lover—albeit for selfish reasons—tries to make Fernando discern Regina's true intentions. As spectator and subject of the conversation between Regina and Fernando, the lover explains:

> It was a comedy in which Regina played the role of victim, I that of the executioner who never comes on the scene, you that of the vengeful lover . . . everything that you just heard from the mouth of that woman . . . is an invented story in order to arm you against me. (288–289)

As Fernando refuses to believe him, he continues:

> Don't you understand, you foolish, blind man, . . . that I—former lover of that infernal woman, witness to her misconduct and her crimes, eternal reclaimer of caresses that belong to me because they have been bought with blood—am for her a powerful obstacle that keeps her from sharing her bed with inexperienced and pretty youths like you whom she devours? (289)

Once convinced of the sincerity of the disdained lover's words, Fernando descends "from the heaven of illusion to the hell of deception" (290), and only then does he once again remember the woman who waits for him back home. He imagines her "innocent, pure, crying and waiting during his absence." On the other hand, Regina now seems to him an "impure and bloody courtier" who simply used him as a "blind instrument for a vile revenge" (291).

Repentant and disenchanted, Fernando renounces the new life he had adopted and decides to return to the village in search of his first love. Unfortunately, the two years of his absence have taken their toll on Clemencia's health; when he arrives to reunite with her forever, he finds her in agony. Death does not wait long, and Clemencia dies a little later in the arms of her beloved.

In spite of all her virtues, Clemencia does not receive the earthly recompenses that were granted to Pilar in *El Zarco*, but she can rest assured that her devotion to her beloved and her resigned patience have earned her a place in heaven. Nevertheless, everything has its price and, in order to gain heaven, Clemencia has had to renounce the pleasures of the body. A society—governed by the teachings of Christianity—that wants to inculcate certain ideas in the village cannot accept a stained young woman; thus, within the ideology of the novel, there exist only two possibilities: marry her or kill her. Díaz Covarrubias decides that his character should die, and in concordance with the social and religious laws Clemencia dies a virgin.

It is worth noting that in these two novels, as in various short stories, the bad women also have angelical characteristics, but only on a superficial level. Manuela seems a "Virgin" but only for her beauty and for being well dressed. Regina is considered an angel for exactly the same reasons: she has the "beauty of a queen," and she dazzles because of the "exquisite taste in her attire."

The characteristics attributed to women during the romantic epoch exhibit little diversity. With the objective of exalting a certain feminine figure, romantic literature normally juxtaposes two types of women: the angelical and the diabolical. Without exception, the good woman is willing to lose everything, including her life, for the man she loves or to await faithfully his return. The women who make their own decisions are excluded from the community and receive neither earthly nor celestial recompense.

THE POETRY

Critics and literary historians generally accept Ignacio Manuel Altamirano's poetic divisions in order to situate the various romantic poets inside of a historical-literary context. There are three groups: the Independencia, the Academia de Letrán, and the Liceo Hidalgo (Millán, 10). Some of the poets who composed the Independencia group are Francisco Manuel Sánchez de Tagle (1782–1849), Andrés Quintana Roo (1787–1851), and Francisco Ortega (1793–1849). They are considered poets of the independence period not only because their careers coincide with the historical event, but also because it becomes one of their principal themes.

The Academia de Letrán was established by José María Lacunza, Manuel Tosiat Ferrer, and Guillermo Prieto in 1836. Its objective was to provide writers with a forum where they could present readings of their works, talk about literature, and study foreign literatures. Quintana Roo presided over meetings attended by such writers as Manuel Carpio (1791–1860), José Joaquín Pesado, Eulalio Ortega, Ignacio Rodríguez Galván (1816–1842), Ignacio Ramírez, Fernando Calderón (1809–1845), and Manuel Payno. To Guillermo Prieto, "the great and transcendental thing about the Academia was its decided tendency to Mexicanize the literature, emancipating it from all other literatures and giving it a peculiar character." Prieto insinuates that this was a conscious and deliberate function of the group, unlike earlier writers who only "gave the first impulse to that tendency which appeared merely as an intermittent alleviation from a way of being" (Martínez, "Mexico," 1040). José Joaquín Blanco, more explicitly than Prieto, assures that in the Independencia group "a nationalist desire is *in no way* apparent; they have as cultural and poetic space a conjunction of pleiads, muses, oracles, orders from Saturn, the presence of Mars and Minerva, inspirations from Clio, hells and empyreals, heroes, nymphs, fates, manes, frugals, atlases, laurels, etc." (Millán, 24).

María del Carmen Millán agrees with Prieto in that the Academia gives "to Mexican letters its own character" (Millán, 15), but she puts greater emphasis on its professional role. She insists that there is a preoccupation for correcting the style, for having a critical orientation, and for accepting everyone who writes (11). Millán makes clear that the members of the Academia de Letrán imitated too faithfully the Spanish romantics and added little to the movement. She concedes, however, that they developed "precise characteristics in their attitude toward the world" and that by translating and imitating contemporary poets, they introduced "a series of readings that enriched traditional classical knowledge and expanded the literary horizons" (15).

Old members of the Academia de Letrán and writers of the next generation formed the Liceo Hidalgo in 1849. The journalist Francisco Zarco (1829–1869) directed it, and Francisco Granados Maldonado held the office of president. Some of its members included Mariano María Morali, José T. Cuéllar (1830–1894), Francisco González Bocanegra (1824–1861), Marcos Arróniz (?–1859?), Emilio Rey, Juan Suárez Navarro, Florencio M. del Castillo, Luis G. Ortiz (1832–1894), and Domingo Villaverde. Of all of them, only Zarco, Cuéllar, and Castillo have stood the test of time. Because of internal quarrelling, the literary activity was interrupted, and it was not until 1870, under the guidance of Altamirano, that the Liceo experienced its apogee. Numerous writers belonged to the Liceo; among them were José María Vigil (1829–1909), Alfredo Chavero, Vicente Riva Palacio, Francisco Pimentel (1832–1893), Ignacio Ramírez, José Peón Contreras (1843–1907), Cuéllar, Prieto, Manuel Peredo (1830–1890), Juan de Dios Peza (1852–1910), Roa Bárcena, Agustín F. Cuenca (1850–1884), Francisco Sosa (1848–1925), Manuel M.

Flores (1840–1885), and Manuel Acuña (1849–1873). From this second romanticism, the last two poets stand out (Millán, 15).

Mexican romantic poetry also exhibits the underlying ideology that surfaces in the prose, but neither as frequently nor as insistently. In the poetry, more than in the stories and novels, there is a greater insistence on repeating European ideas and themes. Nevertheless, it is possible to cite various examples that manifest some of the characteristics that make up the ideal model of woman. As is the case in narrative, the qualities appropriated to women are beauty, youth, and virtue—qualities normally ascribed with ethereal terms. The following analyzes poems focusing on those images that romantic ideology emphasized.

The poem "A una rosa marchita" (To a Withered Rose) by Fernando Calderón uses the image of a withered rose as a metaphor for a woman whose honor has been stained. A woman's loss of honor is parallel to a flower's decay: both forfeit beauty, youth, and happiness. With the intention of highlighting the contrast between honor and dishonor, the speaker juxtaposes images previous and subsequent to the offense. As one would suppose, the former images are positive and flattering: "Yesterday," as the speaker says to the rose, you were "the queen of the shaded forest" who inspired poets, but "today sad and disconsolate / you find yourself stripped of your charms." The consequences of her mistake are that "no one respects you; / . . . nothing remains of you, / . . . of your brilliant past and of your colors." The verses indicate that upon losing her most precious adornments, woman is unable to aspire to anything more than disdain and solitude.

However, the speaker comes to her rescue by offering to release her from the condemnation of "eternal solitude and bitter tears." He suggests that, because they are both in similar situations, she should consider him a good companion. He describes himself as "an unhappy young man, desperate, / whom horrible luck has condemned to / a perpetual wailing" and invites her to share his misfortune, presupposing that she has no other alternative. He generously offers her all his "caresses" and promises to be content with her "last fragrance."

The message could not be clearer: if a woman wants to retain her privileged place—as the inspiration of poets or as the companion of a good man—she must preserve her honor. If she is not careful, she will end up with someone equal to her or worse off than she, with a man of "sad fortunes" whose "hopes were snatched away, one by one / by an unfortunate destiny, like the enraged hurricane / snatched away your petals!"

To present his vision of woman, Ignacio Rodríguez Galván also makes use of the symbolic value of the flower, referring to it as "emblem of the beauty / of my adored virgin." Once again the ideal qualities mentioned above reappear: beauty, youth, purity, and the privileged place which every virtuous woman enjoys. Rodríguez Galván emphasizes the role of woman as a beautiful and fragile decoration whose obligation is to please man. Like the flower, a young and beautiful woman embellishes everything that surrounds her, and she occupies in her environment the place of the grand "dame." But, according to the speaker, to maintain her position not only must she be beautiful, young, and pure, but also she ought to be "melancholy" and to emanate "pleasing odors."

Although he recognizes the importance of appearance, the speaker remains aware that the passage of time "distorts" beauty. Therefore, he suggests that women should have two other qualities: virtue and discretion. The discrete woman who successfully defends her honor in spite of being surrounded by temptations—"in the venomous breast / of a grassy meadow"—is guaranteed that she will continue "illuminating" the heart of her beloved in her old age.

Curiously, even though the speaker appreciates the value of the flower for not having been contaminated by the "poison" of the meadow, he reveals his distrust and possessive nature upon deciding to uproot her stalk: "I prefer to see you / dead, . . . / than alive." He recognizes that the flower, removed from its environment, will suffer a premature death, but he prefers to enjoy it and to assure himself of its eternal fidelity rather than risk its possible contamination. His action demonstrates a certain egotism and an insecurity that in part parallels the reason why society desires to maintain women in an inferior position. Rosario Castellanos suggests that "to exalt a woman for her beauty" is to convert her into an "invalid," but the poem's speaker goes even further: he takes her life in order to be the only one to enjoy her ephemeral beauty.

To express similar ideas, Manuel M. Flores uses a technique opposite to that of Calderón and Rodríguez Galván. Instead of presenting a woman's good qualities, he presents her flaws. The beloved of "Hojas dispersas" (Dispersed Leaves) is not the perfect model readers should emulate, but rather the image of an ambitious and callous woman that everyone should avoid. The poem achieves her negative image through description as opposed to by means of representation of her actions: her beauty is considered false because it is only external; her soul is a "starless night," and her chest contains no heart. Besides the descriptive adjectives, the structure, which consists of alternate views, serves to undermine the woman's value. The first two stanzas present the woman's qualities in order to then sabotage them with her flaws, and the next two contrast her materialism with the speaker's idealism.

In the first stanza her dark soul obfuscates her physical beauty, and in the second her lack of heart extinguishes her "beauty," the "smile and happiness" of her lip, and her "sweet countenance." In the third, the juxtaposition of the speaker's and the beloved's respective values explain the obscurity of her soul and her lack of heart. While the idealistic speaker offers "a world" and "a sun" in exchange for her caresses and kisses, she demands money in return. It is ironic—though not inconceivable—that the speaker does not realize his mistake: he wants to exchange abstractions ("a world" and "a sun") for tangible things (caresses and kisses); and yet when the woman asks for remuneration, he is offended.

In the last two stanzas the speaker exposes his predicament: he feels weakened for loving "with such a crazy passion," and he considers that by leaving "a little of my life in every mouth, / a piece of my soul in every kiss" he has fulfilled his obligation. He does not, however, reflect on the implications of his demands. In a society that expects woman to be chaste and divine, her submission to caresses and kisses compromises her virtue. Therefore, he should realize that his petitions could only come to fruition with a professional, with one who receives money in exchange for the loss of her virtue.

Adhering to poetic conventions, the poems written by the romantics concentrate on the use of images, metaphors, and symbols to develop their themes. Instead of focusing on the duality angel/demon, the poets created a single image to present their vision of woman. In the case of the poems discussed above, the symbolic value of the flower is used to establish a model of conduct that all female readers should assume.

Perhaps owing to their brevity, the poems' message comes across almost too directly. In each of them, the mold constructed for all respectable women is clearly defined, and any attempt to deviate from it motivates serious consequences. Considering, once again, Castellanos, who asserts that "beauty is an ideal that men compose and impose," we can see that in poetry—just as in prose—the image of women has been created by men and that it is they who have invented the punishment for those women who do not follow the established precepts.

THEATER

In the theater, as Juan Miguel de Mora affirms, there was no author

> so brilliant as to be the foundation of a solid and true tradition: the collaborative pieces by Riva Palacio and Juan A. Mateos do not reach that quality; the best by Peón Contreras is *La hija del rey* [The King's Daughter]; the best writings by Manuel Eduardo de Gorostiza are mediocre and inspired by the European [genres]. (8)

A reading of the epoch's theater confirms Mora's remarks. Nevertheless, two popular plays, Fernando Calderón's *A ninguna de las tres* (Neither of the Three) and Manuel Eduardo de Gorostiza's *Contigo pan y cebolla* (Through Hell and High Water for You—literally, With You Bread and Onions), support the ideas presented in this essay.

Concerned with the hidden ideology of the time, Calderón's drama prescribes to the letter the role that all good women should adopt. In the play, the young Don Juan, whom Don Timoteo wants as a son-in-law, has the job of observing Timoteo's three daughters in order to choose a spouse from among them. The only problem is that neither one possesses the necessary qualities of a good wife. Each of them is obssessed by something foreign to the maintenance of home life: Mariquita "plays, sings, dances," and is "agile, alive, always joking and laughing"; Clara spends her time "reading literary and political magazines" (17); and Leonor, because of her "sensitive, inflamed, tender heart," cries about everything (18).

Given the qualities of Don Timoteo's daughters and because he not only approves of but has taken pride in their way of life, Don Juan decides that he is unable to marry any of them. Don Juan explains that he will not resign himself "to spend a life of torments, or at least of fastidiousness, with a wife of different temperament" than his (192). Don Antonio—Don Timoteo's friend— takes the liberty of interpreting Don Juan's words, and he advises Don Timoteo:

> You make a great mistake, taking for virtues what in your daughters are only shortcomings. Clara's lack of instruction, Mariquita's light temperament that takes nothing seriously, and Leonor's excessive sensibility are faults, Don Timoteo, grave faults, which you, a wise man, should have headed off. A man of good judgment will choose for a wife a woman who, fulfilling her duty, cares for the house; who cultivates her talent with energy; who, if she dedicates time to reading, does not want to pass herself off as knowledgeable; who is not always crying over fictitious characters; who does not occupy her head only with flowers, dances, and the theater; who wants to be instructed, without pretending to seem a *litteratus*. To use makeup and cleanliness without affectation, and to live always fulfilling the sweet obligations of her state and of her sex: here's a nice young woman for you! These, my friend, in my opinion, are the virtues of a wife. (195)

Don Antonio describes a woman who is self-effacing and dedicates herself to nothing other than the management of the house.

In his story "El abanico" (The Fan) Vicente Riva Palacio mentions the same list of faults that are attributed to women in Carlderón's play. This story warrants attention here because of its similarities to the play in question and because it reflects in detail the era's preoccupations.

Instead of a young man, the protagonist is a mature marquis "determined to marry" because he is "tired of playing the field." Also, we are told that, "as he was an intelligent and well-read man, he decided to settle down once and for all, looking for the woman *of his dreams*" (Huerta, 153, emphasis added). Just like the young Don Juan, the marquis finds similar objections in a variety of available women: one of them "occupies herself too much with her jewelry and her clothes"; another is too conscious of her beauty and goodness; another "only thinks about enjoying herself"; and the last "is too religious for what a husband needs" (Huerta, 154). As in Calderón's play, the faults are not bad in themselves, but they interfere with the ideal figure that men seek. In each case, what the marquis objects to is the fact that the women privilege their own interests and thus relegate him to an inferior position. At the story's conclusion he finds the perfect woman. She is young and extremely generous: the previous evening she had missed the opera because she was taking care of her sick nanny, and during a dance, when by accident a servant breaks her valuable fan, she does not even acknowledge the loss. To the marquis, these actions indicate a lack of egotism, and they assure that she will be disposed to give him her undivided attention.

In both the play and the short story the women say little or nothing; their futures depend on what men desire. The woman's only role is to wait and shelter the hope that her personality corresponds to the image of her beloved's dreams.

Contigo pan y cebolla is even more blunt in its sexism. The protagonist is Doña Matilde, a young woman of marriageable age whose life is in the hands of her father and her suitor. Don Pedro, her father, finds that Don Eduardo is an excellent companion for his daughter, and he does all that he can to facilitate Eduardo's success with his daughter. Don Pedro does not want to lose a good opportunity to marry off his daughter; therefore, he highly recommends Matilde to Don Eduardo. He says, "the girl is very docile and very well raised and very fearful of God"; and because she is "a very good daughter, . . . she will be a very good wife" and, of course, "a very good mother" (Gorostiza, 211–212).

Since Doña Matilde is not completely convinced she wants to marry, Don Eduardo makes himself responsible for inventing a situation that will persuade her. Even her servant sides against her as he is convinced that "nowadays girls don't know what they want" and that the problem takes root in the fact that "everyone [women, that is] reads the *Gaceta* and knows where Peking is . . . they spend time learning things of no importance . . . and they neither care about marrying, nor do they know how to cook" (216).

By making Doña Matilde an insipid character who has no business reading or becoming informed and, worst of all, has no valid reasons for refusing to marry, the play emphasizes the importance of male domination over women. Because women lack a male rhetoric, it is up to the men to speak for them and arrange their lives accordingly.

As expected, the male force wins, and Doña Matilde not only agrees to marry Don Eduardo, but also comes to realize that her ideals are meaningless. Ater a hard lesson, she has to admit that the men were right and that from now on she must abide by their rules. The play ends with a sarcastic and triumphant remark by her husband which corroborates the servant's words; he states that the problem with women is that they read too many novels. Thus, the implications of this play are that women should submit to male domination because "man knows best" and that the education of women should be severely limited if not cut out altogether.

The other theatrical works that were written during the same time period, such as those by José Peón Contreras or Ignacio Rodríguez Galván fit uneasily into a romantic paradigm because they are works that allude to the colonial period. This aspect of the works written during the same time that romanticism developed in Mexico requires a separate essay because they fall under the category of "cloak-and-dagger or historical-romantic dramas, based on legendary Roman conflicts, written in verse" (Magaña Esquivel, ix).

CONCLUSIONS

The works analyzed reveal several elements whose objective is the creation of the perfect woman. A review of Mexico's socioeconomic situation at that time makes it apparent that the models established for women manifested clearly defined political goals. As a consequence the new woman resembles a mannequin that conforms perfectly to the ideal dream of romantic men. This ideal figure is beautiful, religious, sincere, endearing, generous, and knows how to wait patiently.

To make this prodigious angel conspicuous, typically romantic authors resorted to generating an opposition between the angel and the demon. The tendentious nature of the model manifests itself in the preference given to the woman whose characteristics agree with those of the angel and in the way in which her opposite is ostracized from society. To convince readers to opt for the angelic image, a system of rewards and punishments is established. The angel-woman is guaranteed eternal life in heaven or fine earthly possessions; the devil-woman only receives society's deprecation.

It is true that the creation of a passive figure with neither ambiguities nor aspirations responds to the need for peace and well-being in a country suffering from political instability; however, it also represents the mechanism by which those who are in power and fear losing it repress women's voice and body. Because Arrom captures so well this attitude, I will end by reiterating her statement that "individual freedom, another tenet of liberalism, was not directly extended to women either, since liberals feared what women might do with too much freedom" (264).

NOTES

1. *Translator's note*: Unless otherwise noted all translations are my own. Page numbers refer to the original Spanish text.

2. The fact that our study centers on this particular ideological aspect of the romantic period does not disavow the possibility of others.

3. Cros, *Theory and Practice of Sociocriticism*. The page references following the citation refer to this English translation.

4. Ordóñez describes exactly the vision of the Malinche in her essay "Sexual Politics and the Theme of Sexuality in Chicana Poetry": "*Malinche, Malintzin Tenepal* (by her indigenous names), Doña Marina (by her Spanish name), has long—too long—been considered the Eve of Mexican history. As interpreter, guide, and mistress of the Spanish conqueror, Hernán Cortez, she symbolizes the mother of the mestizo people. But misogynistic historicism has also viewed her as the willing victim of violation, even

as a slut. Mexican poet Octavio Paz shapes her into a symbol of the violated native woman, 'la chingada' or the passive woman open to sexual violence. To another Mexican writer, Carlos Fuentes, *Malinche* generates betrayal and corruption in woman" (318 n.4).

5. According to John S. Brushwood, "*Jicotencal's* inclusion in Mexican literature is based on the setting, which is Mexico at the time of the conquest" (16 n.2).

6. Vicente Riva Palacio was general, jurist, and public official; José Joaquín Pesado was minister of the interior and of foreign affairs; and Manuel Payno worked as a senator in the government. Ignacio Rodríguez Galván also was involved in politics, but unfortunately he died in transit to South America where he was to occupy the position of diplomat. Guillermo Prieto became a representative to the Constitutional Congress and minister of finance. Ignacio Manuel Altamirano was a soldier, educator, bureaucrat, and ambassador in Spain, France, Italy, and Switzerland. Justo Sierra filled the position of undersecretary of public instruction and was a congressman and magistrate of the Supreme Court. (The information is to be found in *Cuentos románticos,* edited by David Huerta.)

7. In *Mujer que sabe latín*, Rosario Castellanos has a fitting explanation for the use of sculptural materials to describe these women. She notes: "Antithesis of Pygmalion, man does not aspire, through the beautiful, to turn a statue into a living being, but rather the opposite: to turn a living being into a statue.

"For what? To adore her, although only during a brief moment, according to what they tell us, to immobilize her, to make unattainable every project of action, to avoid risks" (12).

8. In addition, Dijkstra claims that "once a woman was dead she became a figure of heroic proportions" (50).

9. If this were a study exclusively of the novel, we would have to analyze Manuel Payno's *El fistol del diablo,* Díaz Covarrubias's *La clase media,* Inclán's *Astucia,* Cuéllar's *Los mariditos* or *Las jamonas,* and Altamirano's *Clemencia.*

10. It is Manuela who refers to Nicolás this way. But Pilar and the narrator see him in a different light. Pilar describes him as a very good man and a hard worker. "Besides, [she doesn't] find him ugly" (320). The narrator presents him as follows: "He was a dark-complexioned young man, with distinctly Indian features, but tall, slender, and herculean, well proportioned, and whose intelligent and benevolent physiognomy favored him. . . . Though it was apparent that he was Indian, he was not abject and servile, but rather a cultured man, ennobled by work and who was conscious of his strength and worth" (Altamirano, 321). It is not coincidental that both Pilar and the narrator have similiar opinions, given Altamirano's ideological bias. Altamirano's ideology, which privileges submissiveness, would naturally feel threatened by Manuela's opinion, an opinion that differs from society's values and reinscribes the role of the body and of passion into the woman's life.

11. In revising the translation, we noted that the ambiguity of the Spanish *su* (her, his, their[s]) makes this passage complex and important, for it reveals precisely the exclusion of women and of women's voices from all decision-making processes. In the passage, Fernando's father promises Clemencia to Fernando as a prize for the successful completion of his military training. What the passage excludes, then, is the relationship between Clemencia and her father; thus it highlights a relationship between fathers and sons that reflects exactly the ideologically determined decision-making process as a whole. As is evidenced in Silvia Arrom's discussion of the 1852 "Discourse on the

Influence of Public Instruction on the Happiness of Nations," which concerns "the
purpose of female schooling," decisions were made by fathers about their daughters *for*
their sons. This document makes clear that the fathers' interest is less the education of
their daughters than the maintenance of authority for their sons (see Arrom, *Women of*
Mexico City).

BIBLIOGRAPHY

Altamirano, Ignacio Manuel. "Atenea." In Huerta, 159–210.

———. *Clemencia*. Mexico City: Promexa Editores, 1979.

———. *El Zarco*. Mexico City: Promexa Editores, 1979.

Arrom, Silvia Marina. *The Women of Mexico City, 1790–1857*. Stanford: Stanford University Press, 1985. An excellent historical study of the education, legal, and labor
issues, class distinctions, and marital relations of women.

Azuela, Mariano. "Sobre El Zarco." In *Recopilación de textos sobre la novela romántica*
latinoamericana, ed. Mirta Yáñez, 495–501. Havana: Casa de las Américas, 1978. A
laudatory yet critical essay on Altamirano and his works. Other writers are mentioned cursorily in connection with romanticism.

Brushwood, John S. *The Romantic Novel in Mexico*. Columbia: University of Missouri
Press, 1954. The most complete study of the romantic novel available. It contains
useful and extensive plot summaries and discusses the origin of the Mexican novel
as well as the two different periods of romanticism. Its only pitfall is the insistence
on judging the novels from a stance within realism.

Calderón, Fernando. *A ninguna de las tres*. Mexico City: Universidad Nacional Autónoma de México, 1944.

———. "A una rosa marchita." In *Poesía mexicana,* ed. Francisco Montes de Oca,
79–80. Mexico City: Editorial Porrúa, 1968.

Castellanos, Rosario. *Mujer que sabe latín*. Mexico City: SepSetentas, 1973. A percep-
tive study of the role of women in general and in the works of Isak Dinesen, Virginia
Woolf, Doris Lessing, Flannery O'Connor, Clarice Lispector, María Luisa Bombal,
Silvina Ocampo, and María Luisa Mendoza.

Castera, Pedro. *Carmen*. Edition and prologue by Carlos González Peña. Mexico City:
Editorial Porrúa, 1950.

Castillo, Florencio M. del. "Botón de rosa." In Huerta, 139–150.

Cros, Edmond. *Théorie et practique sociocritiques*. Paris: Editions Sociales/Montpellier,
CERS, 1983. A comprehensive study of society from an ideological standpoint. Semantic, semiotic, anthropological, cultural, and methodological discussions of selected Peninsular and Mexican texts.

———. *Theory and Practice of Sociocriticism*. Minneapolis: University of Minnesota
Press, 1988.

Cuéllar, José. *Las jamonas*. In *La linterna mágica: Colección de novelas de costumbres*
mexicanas y poesía de Facundo. Barcelona: Tipo-lit. de Espasa y Compañía, 1889–
1892.

———. *Los mariditos*. Mexico City: Libro Mex Editores, 1955.

Díaz, Lilia. "El liberalismo militante." In *Historia general de México,* 818–896. Mexico
City: El Colegio de México, 1981. A discussion of Mexico's situation after 1848.
Among other topics, it deals with Santa Ana's dictatorship, the drawing of the 1857
Constitution, the War of Reform, the war with France, and the internal conflicts
between the liberals and the conservatives.

Díaz Covarrubias, Juan. *La clase media.* In his *Obras completas,* 327–397. Mexico City: Universidad Nacional Autónoma de México, 1959.

———. *Gil Gómez el insurgente, o La hija del médico.* In *Obras completas,* 145–326. Mexico City: Universidad Nacional Autónoma de México, 1959.

———. "La sensitiva." In Huerta, 211–229.

Díaz y de Ovando, Clementina. "Estudio preliminar." In Díaz Covarrubias, *Obras completas,* 5–187. A useful and extensive article which relates Díaz Covarrubias's personal life with the history of his time. It offers as well critical comments on each of his works.

Dijkstra, Bram. *Idols of Perversity: Fantasies of Feminine Evil in Fin-de-Siècle Culture.* New York: Oxford University Press, 1986. An excellent study of late nineteenth-century paintings which Dijkstra considers "a veritable iconography of misogyny." His purpose is to show how the intellectual conditions of the period contributed to our present way of thinking about sex, race, and class.

Fernández de Lizardi, José Joaquín. *La educación de las mujeres, o La Quijotita y su prima.* Mexico City: Feria del Libro, 1942.

Flores, Manuel M. "Hojas dispersas." In *Rosas caídas,* ed. Margarita Quijano. Mexico City: Imprenta Universitaria, 1954.

Franco, Jean. *Gender and Representation in Mexico.* New York: Columbia University Press, 1989. An insightful historical panorama of the representation of Mexican women in literature, historical records, film, and painting. Franco traces the female figure back to the seventeenth century with Sor Juana; she ends her study with an analysis of Elena Poniatowska's *Hasta no verte Jesús mío.* Her work is informed by feminist, cultural, and textual criticism.

Gómez, José Justo (Conde de la Cortina y Castro). "Euclea, o La griega de Trieste." In Huerta, 139–150.

González, Luis. "El liberalismo triunfante." In *Historia general de México,* 897–1015. Mexico City: El Colegio de México, 1981. González picks up where Lilia Díaz leaves off and covers the period between 1867 and 1910. He is primarily concerned with the socioeconomic development of the country and the political programs established by the government in control.

Gorostiza, Manuel Eduardo de. *Contigo pan y cebolla.* In *Los clásicos del teatro,* ed. Gerardo Luzuriaga and Richard Reeve, 204–250. Mexico City: Fondo de Cultura Económica, 1975.

Huerta, David. *Cuentos románticos.* Mexico City: Universidad Nacional Autónoma de México, 1973. To date the best collection of short stories available. It includes thirteen stories and biographical sketches of each of the authors.

James, Henry. *The Bostonians.* London: Macmillan, 1921. Originally appeared in *Century Magazine* from February 1885 to February 1886.

Leal, Luis. "Female Archetypes in Mexican Literature." In *Women in Hispanic Literature: Icons and Fallen Idols,* ed. Beth Miller, 227–242. Berkeley: University of California Press, 1983. Leal's essay traces the portrayal of women in Mexican literature from the early 1800s to the 1970s. He argues that even though women have been traditionally represented as either diabolical or angelical, recent literature proposes a new image which cannot so easily be divided.

Magaña Esquivel, Antonio. "Prólogo." In José Peón Contreras, *Teatro,* vii–xxvi. Mexico City: Editorial Porrúa, 1974. A biographical account of the life and works of Peón Contreras.

Martínez, José Luis. "México en busca de su expresión." In *Historia general de México,*

1017–1071. Mexico City: El Colegio de México, 1981. Establishes the origin of the romantic movement in Mexico and sets it in its sociocultural environment. He acknowledges all the major writers, mentions the impact of the literary journals, and provides an overall description of the intellectual atmosphere of the period.

———. "Prólogo." In *Poesía romántica,* ed. Alí Chumacero, ix–xxvi. Mexico City: Universidad Nacional Autónoma de México, 1941. Presents the general characteristics of romanticism in Mexico and discusses the role that each of the major poets played.

Martínez de Castro, Manuel. *Una hija i una madre.* Mexico City: Imprenta de I. Escalante, 1875.

Marx, Karl, and Friedrich Engels. *The German Ideology.* Ed. C. J. Arthur. New York: International Publishers, 1986.

Millán, María del Carmen, ed. "Prólogo." In *Antología, Poesía romántica mexicana,* 7–19. Mexico City: Libro Mex Editores, 1957. An informative prologue which delineates the historical development of the various groups that formed during the romantic period in Mexico.

Monsiváis, Carlos. "Clasismo y novela en México." *Latin American Perspectives* 11.2 (1975): 164–179.

Mora, Juan Miguel de. *Panorama del teatro en México.* Mexico City: Editora Latino Americana, 1970.

Ordoñez, Elizabeth. "Sexual Politics and the Theme of Sexuality in Chicana Poetry." In *Women in Hispanic Literature: Icons and Fallen Idols,* ed. Beth Miller, 316–339. Berkeley: University of California Press, 1983.

Payno, Manuel. *El fistol del diablo.* San Antonio, Tex.: Casa Editorial Lozano, 1927.

Pesado, José Joaquín. "El amor frustrado." In Huerta, 25–54.

Pizarro Suárez, Nicolás. *La coqueta.* Mexico City: Imprenta de Ana Echeverría de Pizarro e hijas, 1861.

Riva Palacio, Vicente. "El abanico." In Huerta, 151–157.

Roa Bárcena, José María. "Buondelmonti." In Huerta, 119–137.

Rodríguez Galván, Ignacio. *Poesías.* Mexico City: Librería La Ilustración, 1883.

Vázquez, Josefina Zoraida. "Los primeros tropiezos." In *Historia general de México,* 737–818. Mexico City: El Colegio de México, 1981. Predominantly an economic study of Mexico between 1821 and 1848. It also focuses on Mexico's international relations and the problems it faced trying to establish itself as an independent country.

Warner, Ralph E. *Historia de la novela mexicana en el siglo XIX.* Mexico City: Antigua Librería Robredo, 1953. A classical study of the period which provides background information on the writers it covers, the central themes of their works, and useful bibliographical data.

Williams, Raymond. *Keywords.* 1976. New York: Oxford University Press, 1983.

4

Nineteenth-Century Prose Fiction

MARIO MARTÍN-FLORES
Translated by David William Foster

I

Realism and naturalism in Mexico are framed temporally by the dictatorship of Porfirio Díaz (1876–1909). This sociopolitical phenomenon brings with it other factors like modernism and a late-blooming romanticism, each with its separate perspectives and different results. The political formula of Díaz's regime was "internal peace and external credit." In order to achieve the second goal, which was considered of prime importance for the reorganization of the country, foreign debts were renegotiated and progress was made in their payment, and important foreign loans were obtained for the renovation of the communications infrastructure, industry, and agriculture. An important investment of foreign capital takes place that reenforces and stimulates the economy. Relations of peace and cooperation are offered to all countries, and the new immigration policies are the result of this principle which involves opening the doors to foreigners unwelcome in their own countries for their progressive ideas; the goal is that they will serve as colonists and modernize Mexican agriculture. The failure of these strategies is analyzed by Federico Gamboa (1864–1939) in his novel *Santa* (1903).

The formula "little politics and much administration" served to neutralize struggles for power and at the same time to strengthen the exercise of an autocratic, authoritarian power, a strategy that can be perceived in *La parcela* (The Piece of Property; 1898), by José López Portillo y Rojas (1850–1923), and that Emilio O. Rabasa (1856–1930) criticizes in *La gran ciencia* (The Great Science; 1887). Public outlays are also reduced, with the goal of an orderly and efficient bureaucracy. Under the direction of Bernardo Reyes the army is reorganized and receives professionalized training, while a continuing supply of recruits is guaranteed by the diligent application of the law of conscription. That is, peace is ensured via the exercise of force and repression at the direct expense of the dispossessed.

Thus the immobilization of society allowed for "quiet and stability" as the necessary and favorable climate for transnational investors. In this way the economy achieved an annual growth rate of 8 percent during the last decade of the nineteenth century. But this prosperity only benefited the few. "Progress," except in the area of communications, was concentrated in the cities, which included no more than 25 percent of the total population. Commerce grew vigorously in the cities, and one out of every four citizens who formed part of the incipient and heterogenous middle class was involved in that sector, which José Tomás de Cuéllar (1830–1894) described in detail in his writings.

Seventy-five percent of all Mexicans lived in rural farming and ranching areas, generally as small landowners (the minority), sharecroppers, or contract laborers. The peasantry formed the large majority of the rural workers, and its members were exploited by the typical methods of the wealthy landowners, to such an extent that the owner had at his disposal his own jails, guards, and legal processes. These methods were denounced for the first time, if only timidly, in the short novel *Nieves* (1885) by José López Portillo y Rojas. The Law of Unused Land was promulgated in 1893, which allowed for the limited adjudication of available lands without the requirement that they be farmed or inhabited. The application of this law provoked conflicts over the possession of lands like the one involving Monte de los Pericos as described in the aforementioned *La parcela*. The law led to many independent peasants losing lands because they could not show titles and because they lacked the money necessary to defend themselves through the legal process; this topic is not dealt with in Mexican realism. By contrast, almost incredible latifundios were created consisting of millions and even hundreds of millions of hectares, like the Terrasas spread in Chihuahua, with more than one million hectares. A few years before the fall of Díaz, more than 80 percent of the national territory was concentrated in the hands of approximately twenty thousand latifundista families. There existed two strategies for the working of the land. The "feudal" landowners held the land as a backing for social prestige, as part of an aristocracy; these lands generally lay idle or were undercultivated. On the other hand, the capitalist landowners engaged in extensive cultivation, rotated their crops, and fertilized and irrigated their holdings. In *La parcela* López Portillo y Rojas contrasts these two models of landownership. In the rest of realist and naturalist literature, it is only the feudal landowner who is described, a propertied patriarch who administers people's lives and honor. The official attitude of the government toward the Indians is that of a capitalist landowner, and Porfirio Díaz himself affirmed: "We should not rest until we see every Indian behind his team of oxen, goad in hand, tilling the fields" (quoted in Gonzalez y Gonzalez, "El liberalismo," 964). This affirmation denotes a rigid social stratification based on racial and cultural prejudices proper to a positivist ideology.

Education is perhaps the most determining factor in the ideological and aesthetic configuration of the naturalist and realist texts. Porfirian society was still very far from the integration with written culture because, according to Francisco Larroyo in *Historia comparada de la educación en México* (Comparative History of Education in Mexico), "The official census of 1895 showed a population of 12,631,558 inhabitants, of which 10,445,520 did not know how to read or write and 329,007 read poorly" (287).

There is agreement in recent critical approaches to the novel at the end of the nineteenth century in Spanish America in questioning the authenticity of the term *realism*. Fernando Alegría asserts that the so-called realist current is only a fifth derivative of romanticism, a "romantic realism." John S. Brushwood, in *Genteel Barbarism,* supports Alegría's contention by concluding that there is no Spanish America that can without reservation be called realist. It is no longer valid to continue to measure the faithfulness of Latin American literary manifestation alongside the dominant European paradigm as a criterion of authority and validation. Rather, it is more important to determine how the new ideas in the novel were adapted to Latin American cultural development and in what ways they modified the world view of the writers, their ways for presenting it, and the ideological implications of the repeated attempts at mimesis.

In the novelists of the end of the nineteenth century there is the recurring avoidance of taking on the title of realists or, at least, of accepting it in its full European sense. There is, rather, an underscoring of the mimetic purpose of the work, such as one finds in the prologue by Rafael Delgado (1853–1914) to his *Los parientes ricos* (The Wealthy Relatives; 1902), where he explains that he means for his characters to be an "exact copy of Mexican reality." López Portillo, in the prologue to *La parcela,* understands writing novels as the conscious and precise reproduction of sociological phenomena, the social milieu, and the physical setting, and he claims that the text must be a "faithful mirror."

Rafael Delgado's and José Tomás de Cuéllar's novelistic production with variations can fall under the purview of Aristotle's definition of mimesis in the epic. In Emilio O. Rabasa a partially Platonic interpretation of mimesis predominates, while López Portillo wavers between the two ideological positions.

Aristotle situates the epic at a point of intersection, with history as factual and necessary reality, and philosophy as encompassing the essential and unchanging. Thus, he proposes an imitative reproduction of reality as an artistic activity that will pursue a middle course between truth and the impossible; this is the famous distinction between things as they are or were and things as they seem to or ought to be. It is here where we can discern the first trap into which Mexican realist writers fall. López Portillo and Rafael Delgado avoid mimesis in the attempt to present the desirable as necessarily factual. The fact that they may establish a concept of reality with these conventions is not a politically innocent act, and they are proposing semiurban societies that exist in conforming harmony with a stable order, impervious social classes based on a rigid hierarchy that are disrupted only by the isolated immoral acts of a few individuals. In this way they offered to readers an anesthesia of conformity deriving from the illusion of an easily perfectible world.

Cuéllar stands at the beginning of historical representation, and his photographic vision of untouched manners and customs is perhaps more authentic than Delgado's. Yet he lacks both the larger panoramic view of the social and the imagination for the adequately complex and structured narrative necessary to suggest a more permanent human backdrop than the one provided by a daguerreotype in his *Linterna mágica* (Magic Lantern; 1871–1892).

Rabasa is to be situated in the most balanced position of the Mexican real-ists. He attempts to provide flesh-and-blood representations for a scheme of already determined ideological concepts. Yet the intellectual scaffolding be-hind his types can still be perceived, as well as the settings and the plots to which they are artificially tied. Rabasa's is a sort of variation on the Platonic meaning of imitation, understood as one of the possible modes of the relation-ship to things in which one discovers the presence of ideas. Nevertheless, owing to the fact that the Mexican political system continues to be fundamen-tally the same, his works are still meaningful today.

These works are not sustained by an appeal to how things ought to be, but rather they fluctuate asystematically between the wishful thinking of moral philosophy and the social documentary involved in the representation of man-ners and customs. It is in this way that they betray their mimetic function by limiting themselves to a vague intermediary zone.

When Georg Lukács insists on defining the modern novel in formulaic terms as "the utopia of history," it is because he understands it as an imitative representation of reality that includes the portrayal of emotional and spiritual phenomena and not only the simple desire to conceal the factual reality of actual existence with the desire for an ideal perfection, as in the case of *La parcela* and other novels by López Portillo. *La parcela* belongs better to the normative ingenuousness of the epic than it does to the mature vigor of the novel, because there remains in López Portillo a strong presence of Divine Providence whereby human beings are not alone in the world. The plot of the novel turns on the theme of revenge between two landowners and their ser-vants, just like a medieval epic narrative. The landowners battle each other for their possessions, and their servants chivalrously take up arms in the defense of their masters' honor. In a medieval epic this would be equivalent to the ceremony that takes place between the feudal masters and their knights. The theme's epic physiognomy is more complete because in the conclusion of the plot there is not the failure of an ideal nor a vital break, but only a poetic denouement.

Beginning with the prologue to *La parcela* and throughout the development of the novel, the author insists on redefining national identity in terms of the motif of a childlike America and the noble savage of eighteenth-century ide-ology, and Gonzalo and Ramona love each other in a simple and natural way. The novel's clearly epic social conception of an naively incipient and only partially formed world demands a firm belief in youth, in force, in the primor-dial, and in the transformation of reality as an unfinished task in the face of European decadence, all of which positions *La parcela* on the margins of the modern novel in its lack of any problematizing of structures or of a vision of the personally and socially deficient.

All of Rafael Delgado's novels are bound to the same bucolic commonplace of the rejection of the city and praise for the countryside, which is turned into an archetype of stability and decency in the case of Pluviosilla or Villaverde, towns in his novels. The filter, whether renaissance or neoclassic, through which writers contemplated the rural world denied them a realist optic and the mimetic transposition of rustic life and its setting. The ideological effect is to consider the countryside as the extension of bourgeois pleasure whereby everything is beautiful and perfectible. The rural world could never be seen as the center for production or the exploitation of work, despite the fact that for the closing years of Díaz's regime more than 80 percent of the national territory was in the hands of only twenty thousand families.

By contrast, Rabasa is able to give his novels the stamp of what Lukács considers the mature vigor of the modern novel by imprinting them with a sense of the tragic and Lukács's leveling of the hierarchical order of the external world. Rabasa's tetralogy is nothing more than a tragedy in four acts with the archetypal denouement of the return of the "heroes," weary and embittered by defeat, to their homeland. Cabezudo and Quiñones at the end of *Moneda falsa* (Counterfeit Money; 1888) intuit their truth in the disillusionment and accumulation of blindly lived experiences. This ambiguity of novelistic irony more than anything else gives Rabasa's novels sustained interest.

The second mistake of a good share of Mexican realist novels lies with the adulteration of the basic goals of that movement, which was to serve as a mirror of social deficiencies. The efficacy of a text lies in its power of mimesis and the depth of its sociological knowledge. Realists in Mexico continued to make of the novel a rigorous aesthetic exercise for middle-class entertainment. In the prologue to *La parcela* the author goes to lengths to convince us of his serious intentions for social protest. Yet, such protests are not to be found in the text, and he says with certainty that his readers will find, instead of corrupt institutions, individuals who make mistakes but mend their ways. In totalitarian regimes like Díaz's, there is always the fear of falling into generalizations that interpret the national in allegorical terms. In the same prologue, López Portillo expresses the hope that his work will have the same social effect *Uncle Tom's Cabin* or Dickens's novels had in their own countries. A few years later in his inauguration speech before the Mexican Academy of Spanish, López Portillo refers to the social function of the novel, stating that it levels social classes by putting all readers in contact with good social customs and fine taste. Overwhelming the reading public with the spectacular riches of art in order to maintain the appearance of progress and power was part of the discourse of hegemonic domination used by many totalitarian governments in Mexico to ensure their stability from colonial times to the present. The political manipulation inherent in the social and artistic concepts of López Portillo in this speech is clear, and it is a long way from the image of "social reformer" that Roland Grass would have us accept. It is naive (if not perverse) to outline leisurely and sumptuous scenes of banquets and balls and to include them systematically in every novel for the purpose of social redemption and aesthetic purification, as Delgado and López Portillo did in theirs.

This bourgeois hedonism is also patent, even if in a different form, in Cuéllar and Rabasa, in that they insistently repeat caricatures, satires, and burlesques concerning the middle class's poor imitations and failed attempts at refinement and their tawdriness of efforts to attain good taste, which seems to have existed as a valid norm.

Realism in general rests on shaky ground that becomes the third trap in subscribing to a premise that reality is observable, rational and rationalizable, ordered, stable, inalterable, reducible to norms, and, moreover, describable. Lukács considers as impossible the total apprehension of the object via the method of knowledge called realism, to the degree that meaning cannot penetrate reality. The compulsive distraction of the narrators in the reproduction of the exterior nature of things is a barrier to intuition and, therefore, constitutes a lack of knowledge of the outline of what is real. In López Portillo, but especially in Delgado's fiction, descriptions are frequently the result of a highly skilled rhetoric. These works have caused some critics to engage in unrestrained praise, such as Ralph Warner, who considers Delgado to be the best stylist of the nineteenth century and also the country's first good psychologist. Nevertheless, *Los parientes ricos* and *Angelina* (1893) are filled with overblown poetic enumerations with no narrative or thematic function nor ideological purpose, which serves to confirm that someone who is good at descriptions is not a good realist per se.

An unrestrained descriptive impulse also undermines over and over again Cuéllar's goal of constructing a novelistic genre of manners and customs. Not only does this cause him to fall into the picturesque and caricature in order to sustain interest, but it also paralyzes the rhythm of reality and limits its perspectives and depth. Cuéllar thereby eschews a livelier and more permanent mimesis.

Ortega y Gasset in *Meditaciones del Quijote e Ideas sobre la novela* (1985; *Meditations on Quixote* and *Notes on the Novel*) asserts with respect to the novel: "Precisely because it is a realist genre par excellence, the novel is incompatible with exterior reality. In order to evoke its own inner reality, it must dislodge and abolish surrounding reality" (166). Thus the realists did not in fact provide us with a reality but with a referent, a mask without a face. The realists' opinion of an unchanging world subject to laws favored their political program, in consonance with that of Porfirio Díaz which was based on stability and social order (i.e., repression) in order to achieve progress, precepts that the large majority of the novelists of this regime accepted unquestioningly.

Another aspect that breaks with the concept of mimesis and undermines the verticality of the structure of Mexican realism is that the writers based their ideas on a scientific epistemology that has long since been discredited. Indeed, often what counted as fiction during the nineteenth century is today truth, and what then passed as science is today considered to be fantasy or imaginative speculation. Race, nature, and society are some of the commonplaces of the literature and science of the nineteenth century. López Portillo, perhaps out of Darwinian prejudice, establishes a hierarchy of the superiority of the races in favor of the white European, blessed with superior beauty, physical perfection, and the greatest potential, even though Europeans may on occasion be contaminated by social and moral vices, as in the case of *La parcela*'s Don

Miguel, because he is Frenchified, or the heroine in *Los precursores* (The Precursors; 1909). He places mestizos like *La parcela's* Gonzalo in a second category, and a third category corresponds to indigenous individuals like Don Pedro Ruiz, Gonzalo's father, whose physical presence is insignificant. Don Pedro is living proof of transcendence over the indigenous. The indigenous population is described by the author in his prologue in terms of the prevailing positivist prejudice that saw them as a sign of the barbarian. This willful and apparently scientific interpretation constituted in the realist novel an archetypal interpretation of society and of history, not to mention its stereotypic psychology of the characters. Thus, the narrative broke with a mimetic function, in the sense that it involved a deductive application of theses to the novels instead of an inductive observation of what was real.

Without a doubt the procedure by which the realists depart from mimesis to speak in a void is in the abuse of generalizations not only in the disingenuous application of scientific postulates, but also in the employment of a variety of formulas. One of these formulas that is obstinately repeated in Rabasa, Cuéllar, López Portillo, and Delgado is that of erasing, masking, and making over the specific traces of space, time, phenomena, and contemporary economic, political, and social events. This neutral atmosphere blurs the outlines and the nature of characters and, as a consequence, renders mimesis difficult for the modern reader confronted with a decontextualized realist narrative. The masking of context is not a politically innocent act, since it favors the permanence of the status quo. In order to conceal the gap at the heart of this evasion of contemporary reality, the novelists of the last quarter of the nineteenth century abound in details concerning setting and customs.

It is necessary to separate Rabasa from the rest because he does include a chronological sketch and places his novels in something like an imaginary geography: San Martín de la Piedra, the capital of the state, evokes point by point the political defects of the Díaz regime with such lucidity that they could even be applied to other autocratic governments that spring from the tradition of the strongman. However, although Rabasa engages in harsh social criticism, he was not as detailed or insistent in it as was Cuéllar.

The rest of the authors that have been mentioned are especially notable for a concept of time such as one finds in fairy tales, a "Once upon a time" and its complement "Far away in a place called [Pluviosilla or Villaverde or Citala or San Martín de la Piedra]." This hierarchization of the universe as both past and neutral serves to sever the reader of realist novels from supposed mimesis, leaving the real as a grimace of the abstract.

A determining factor in the constitution of mimesis is nature, a strategy and function of time as a structuring resource in realist novels. All types of identity become generic when the circumstances of time and space are altered. As a result, Mexican realist novelists sought to make the flow of narrative sequences conform to a chronological progression that was emphatic and punctual with regards to years, months, days, and hours, with the goal of involving the reader in a temporal experience that would substitute for the real as a historic event. The rigorous registry of time in realist narratives allows for the possibility of establishing the causes behind the conduct of certain characters, as well as justifying (almost always in a gratuitous form) the psychological evolution of a character by at times skimming over large periods of time in his life and portraying individuals in an already transformed state, as is the case of the protagonists in López Portillo's *Los precursores* or those of Rabasa's tetralogy composed of *La bola* (The Ball; 1887), *La gran ciencia, Cuarto poder* (Fourth Power; 1888), and *Moneda falsa,* not to mention in particular the transitions between each one of the novels in the tetralogy. In Delgado's *Angelina,* as well as in his *La calandria* (The Lark; 1891), and especially in *La parcela,* the temporal lapse in the story line is very brief. Delgado and López Portillo handle skillfully the procedure of advancing and temporally suspending with great precision various scenes at the same time, and they demonstrate an almost mechanical control over time in the service of narrative surprises. This temporal directionality as a basis of the narrative is not only felicitous, but also a masterful model of technical precision in Mexican literature, to the degree that at certain moments it matches the temporal reproduction by the reader.

The realist authors adhere to the Aristotelian precepts of the epic, with reference to the use of the unity of time, its proportions, integrity, and articulation. Their works assume the dimensions of modern novels in that they give the impression of developing a solid notion of time that captivates readers in a temporal mimesis, until the readers discern the fissure of the neutral dissonance between this atmosphere and temporal historical time, such that they distance themselves from the text.

One ideological implication lies in the use of the imperfect indicative and the preterit in order to recount events, as Gonzalo Navajas has pointed out in *Teoría y práctica de la novela española posmoderna* (Theory and Practice of the Postmodern Spanish Novel): "The past seems to be the most natural tense in which to narrate a story, and the past serves to establish an order and a hierarchy of values" (70). In *La parcela* as in the majority of the realist novels, this device serves to provide us with a past reality, an act already consummated by the omnipresent hand of the narrator as an authority that imposes his own laws. The discourse of a stable world, which is altered and returns to its earlier order in order to get better, finds its correspondence in the ideological discourse of the Díaz dictatorship that promoted a nostalgia for peaceful times gone by as a model, alongside the image of change as violence and barbarianism.

In *Los parientes ricos* a woman arrives in the capital with her two daughters in search of social betterment via marriage. Nevertheless, her faith is destroyed when she becomes the butt of jokes, and she ends up with one daughter humiliated and the other dishonored. The novel is a bitter Bildungsroman that warns us to restrain our social-climbing ambitions. No class is worse than any other, but pain and conflicts can be avoided if the classes remain stable and unchanging. This same mechanism is repeated point-by-point in *La parcela,* where male friends overlook grudges, provocations, and lawsuits in order to reestablish the old Edenic order which has been shattered.

Some writers believed that the simple fact of elaborating their narratives under the guise of realist propositions was enough to ensure their faithful rendition of the real, and this constitutes another one of the principal traps of the quest for mimesis. As we have already shown, the ideological presuppositions of realism are built on quicksand, a fact that extends both to structure and other features of the novel. The Spaniard Benito Pérez Galdós (1843–1920) was also in his day and age a paradigm for imitation of Hispanic realism. In his inaugural speech to the Spanish National Academy he offered some reflections on the task of the novelist, reflections that are questionable and that were poorly imitated: "Novels and the art involved in composing them lie in the reproduction of human characters, the passions, the weaknesses, the grandiose and the trivial, souls and physiognomies, the spiritual and the physical, which both constitute us and surround us" (Gullón, 64).

Although Pérez Galdós's rather primitive binarism can be questioned, it is important to point out the emphasis that he places on the depiction of characters as the main goal of the novel. It is a recommendation López Portillo did not adopt, to the detriment of *La parcela,* where the action serves as the driving force of the text in accord with the Aristotelian principle that it is the plot that speaks to the soul, with the characters being considered in second place to the supremacy of the story line. What happens in *La parcela* is that the characters, already viewed as stereotypes, are pulled along by the action and skip phases of psychological evolution, details that are necessary in order for readers to sympathize with and accept the inner nature of the characters so as to be persuaded of their verisimilitude and thus mimesis be achieved.

With respect to the relationship between plot and characters, there were three types of realist novels in Mexico in the nineteenth century. One type involved audacious studies of social types and characters articulated in terms of weak and diffuse plots with ambiguous endings, like those of Rabasa, Heriberto Frías (1870–1925), and López Portillo in *Nieves.*

Rabasa bases his four linked novels on the development of his characters. The political boss Cabezudo and Juan Quiñones, although they are antagonists, are moved by an ambition for wealth and power. Cabezudo rises via violence and maintains his ascendancy thanks to institutionalized government corruption, while Quiñones conceals his base material interests beneath an increasingly fragile idealism until he finally falls by exchanging his ideas for money. Although the bitter irony of the ending is based on a real human condition, which could lead the reader to identify with the conflict, the design of the plot development is so simple that it is predictable, even more so because of the constant foreshadowings by the omniscient narrator, who blurs the characters to such a point that the reader perceives them as only useful line drawings suggestive of the argument being pursued.

The second type of novel presents a plot that is fragmented into interdependent static vignettes. The plot line is sustained only through recurring characters and with the same tone and style as newspaper articles describing daily life, the *artículos de costumbres*. José Tomás de Cuéllar dissolves his characters and actions under the influence of a heavy-handed irony and lavish displays of the comical, which becomes almost mechanical and even gratuitous as far as the story is concerned. His narrative provides a flat photographic image, one that is frozen and artificially posed one frame at a time. Touches are added to the point of deforming the image in the interest of a sustained humorous exaggeration that distances the reader from what is genuinely real. This is in addition to the psychological mechanism of distancing that all spectators apply in order not to identify with a humorous attitude or development that is seen to be happening to someone else. If there were any reader identification involved, it would be to understand the text from the perspective of a tragedy.

The third type of realist novel, in terms of plot, are those whose architecture of action is more complex, with the intention of developing characters and a daring content that, because it depends on a precipitous conclusion, becomes disfigured and dispersed rather than resolved. One example is *La parcela,* where the two opposing landowners, after a series of deus-ex-machina civil and criminal suits, become reconciled with a couple of sentences, a few tears, and a warm embrace. In this fashion, two opposing personalities are blurred, personalities that had come to acquire the dimensions of psychological independence and through which social defects were being gradually revealed. The ending of the novel is precipitous because the plot loses all symmetry and especially because a former order is reestablished in terms of a return to the Díaz-era stability with a happy ending to satisfy bourgeois tastes. This unjustified conclusion, in which the criminal acts of Don Miguel and their repercussions in his servants are forgotten in the face of the preparations for the marriage of his daughter and her voyage to Europe, constitutes a rupture of mimesis in which the reader is displaced in the absence of a causal logic for what is now suddenly taking place in the novel.

If Mercedes Cabello de Carbonera (1845–1907), who was born in Chile, can be considered part of an essential Mexican reality, she and Rafael Delgado postulate sentimentalism as an integral part of reality and as the ethical complement of the Spanish American, to the extent that the average reader demanded sentimentalism from the novel and perhaps even expected it in order to identify with the text. If sentiment were to be accepted as a component of reality, the way in which it is treated would not be equivalent to the way in which it is manipulated in *La parcela* nor would it correspond to the effects of the action being depicted, to the extent that sentiment either outstrips the facts or remains submerged in them. We can observe how Gonzalo's love ends up ridiculous as a consequence of the author's insistence on refining this passion and giving it material form in the context of progress and civilization, in accord with the bourgeoisie of the period. And woman is no longer the mirror in which the lover constitutes himself as subject, but the pretext for the androgynous vanity of the hero. In the epilogue, Gonzalo's first words to his beloved after their fathers' reconciliation and permission for the pair to get married are: "See, Ramona? We can finally make our voyage." It is, of course, a voyage to Europe. These words contradict the narrator, who had insisted that the love of the two youths was profound, pure, and natural. Mimesis can never take place if characters are not true to themselves.

The protagonists of the Mexican realist novel are, in general, inconsistently characterized. They are flat and only serve to complement each other in a binary contrast that is elaborate but nevertheless ingenuous. They are moved along as vehicles for the action, they mimic the appearances of real people, and they act in silence, freezing when the voice of the narrator engages in lengthy descriptions. We know everything we need to know about them from their first appearance, and, therefore, they are fixed, rigid, fully formed, as though they were already dead.

Another one of the traps that Mexican realism falls into is visual objectivity as an incomplete substitute for the real. This creates a handicapped entity because hearing is missing, though needed in order to listen to the characters tell us about their inner world. Hearing is what allows for the text to attain reality and provides a place for the author, as Oscar Tacca has demonstrated in *Las voces de la novela* (The Voices of the Novel). *La parcela,* like all of the works of the period, abounds in precise descriptions that lack any narrative function. The novel is only able to provide us with an empty simulacrum of a distant and silent reality with which it is difficult to establish any mimetic relationship, even when the description strives to create the impression of reality.

In all of Mexican realism the presence of the author in his work (as most of the work was produced by men, with the exception of four novels by women writers) is almost that of a protagonist, and he intervenes gratuitously at any point: he presents, paraphrases, clarifies, repeats, belies, discusses, interrupts, interprets, judges, and condemns what the characters are thinking, saying, or doing. This continual and wordy authorial upstaging ends up by demonstrating to readers that what they are reading is fiction, destroying thereby in them any complicitous desire to identify themselves with either reality or fiction.

According to Lukács, irony is what provides the novel its natural objectivity. A large number of realist novels lose any chance of objective mimesis because they deal only in humor without any irony. Irony is an encounter with failure, and, as a consequence, it is the annihilation of subjectivity, the self-correction of weakness, according to Lukács. By contrast, humor in *La parcela* serves not to subvert any higher structure, but only to ridicule from the point of view of the bourgeoisie the upstarts of the middle class and their bad taste, their tawdriness, and their cheap imitation of what is refined; this can be seen in the case of the couple Estebanito and Chole (Estebanito is the ranch bookkeeper, and Chole is his fiancée). Humor as it appears in the novels of Cuéllar and Delgado punishes those who would seek to change static society. Only in

Rabasa and in some of Cuéllar's narratives and in López Portillo's own short stories do we find the ironic in the guise of a profound melancholy inclined toward reflection.

Heriberto Frías must be considered an extraordinary case in the Mexican novel of realism, since a large part of his literary production with a strong social content was written and published in exile and, therefore, on the margins of the determining political forces to which the rest of the novelists were subject.

Among all of the authors of Mexican realism, Rabasa stands out for the sure-handed incorporation of irony as a thematic and narrative recourse, and he is successful in distancing himself from the historical phenomena in order to provide us with a complete overview with all of the skepticism and ambiguity of the modern novel. His works are sufficient testimony to belie the still-prevalent view that the Díaz regime was an era of peace and progress. His solid political convictions are founded on the double optics of academic and journalistic sociology. Except for Rabasa, the realist novelists eschewed in their social and political criticisms anything that could lead to profound observations.

By way of concluding this discussion, we could assert that the ideological consequences of the novelists of Mexican realism derive from the hegemonic efforts of a totalitarian and dictatorial regime that led them to postulate a self-satisfied world of social conformity, with individuals who were ignorant or indifferent with regard to the true needs of the community. They denounced certain social and political defects, but these were shown as exceptions or individual, isolated cases: the exploitation of workers on a hacienda, company stores, torture, paternalistic and repressive authoritarianism. As far as politics was concerned, they focused on the purchase of power and the meddling of the Church in civil and penal matters. Concomitantly, these same writers who created a certain "consciousness" in society supported the official propaganda of social stability, a minimum of politics and a maximum of administration, material progress, and intellectual development in the guise of science, civilization, art, and refinement.

The ideological results of the realist novel in Mexico not only are the consequence of the orientation, convictions, and sociopolitical commitments of the novelists, but also derive from the maladjustments, displacements, and distractions that stemmed from the proposition of mimesis as the ultimate criterion, both as the imitative reproduction of reality in the text and as the fusion between reader and the dialectics of the world evoked by the text. The Mexican realists, in their quest for mimesis, fell again and again into various traps with their accompanying and inevitable ideological resonances such as a fragile and suspect convention with regard to truth and the presupposition that reality is rational, ordered, unchanging, and describable. They based themselves on a pseudoscientific and philosophical epistemology that must now be considered invalid. They engaged in gratuitous overgeneralizations. They adulterated the initial purpose of realism by frequently converting it into an aesthetic diversion. If sentiment is an ethical part of Mexican subjectivity, the realists mutilated it by transforming it into a social or aesthetic phenomenon. The past temporal perspective in the novel reenforces the condition of a stable world closed to change. Characters are resistant to reader identification because they have no independent status, owing to being treated as inconsistent, psychologically static, and untrue to their own nature. The narrator, as the result of authorial meddling, forces on the reader an awareness that what is being read is fiction, with an attendant destruction of mimesis. Due to the absence of irony, poetic subjectivity is never overcome.

II

It is probably difficult and perhaps futile to draw a definitive line of separation between realism and naturalism, owing to the presence in both of the same aesthetic and ideological codes. Moreover, both incorporate in their texts expressive formulas drawn from Spanish American modernism and even romanticism. There are evident throwbacks to romanticism in realism and naturalism, such as sentimental plots that underlie psychological tension and sustain narrative interest, along with characters defined in terms of physical, psychological, moral, ethnic, social, and political contexts. Also of romantic vintage are the staging of rather obvious conflicts that derive from the categorical division of the moral forces at issue, along with the tendency to melodrama and a disproportionate emotionality and the theatrical artificiality of plot organization. Another point of coincidence is the depiction of local color which in realism is presented as an artistic re-creation of a social act. In naturalism it appears with the same function, although it is more frequent to find local color writing as the demonstration of a certain cultural atavism opposed to progress and civilization.

There is no doubt that the naturalism that presents the most independent aspect and the greatest expressive vigor is the one that proposes sexuality as a code reduced by repression to being clandestine and that therefore systematically subverts the foundations of the socially and politically asexual patriarchal structure. This ideological posture was expressed for the first time by Amado Nervo (1870–1919) in two novels, *El bachiller* (The Seminarian; 1895) and *Pascual Aguilera* (1892–1896), novels that foreshadowed Federico Gamboa's *Santa,* which is by far the masterpiece of Mexican naturalism.

Pascual Aguilera is the first time that the body is privileged as an organic impulse between pleasure and the repression of sexuality. The sexual appears in this same work as an instrument of power and domination, with the body as an axiom that parallels the rural Mexican social body.

The novel opens with a scene in which Refugio comes down out of a tree with a bouquet of orange blossoms and asks Pascual to look away so he will not see her legs. The symbolism being proposed here is that of a tree (axis mundi) which is at the same time the axis of desire and the purity of a sexuality that has not yet been touched. It is in Refugio's sexuality, under the "tree of knowledge, of good and evil," where two orphans meet like Adam and Eve and discover their bodies and their desire. Pascual does not receive the blossoms as a sacramental symbol but as an erotic vehicle, which is in itself a transgression that anticipates those that will take place in the course of the novel. In due course, Pascual, in exchange for not proposing matrimony to her because of their social differences, suggests to Refugio that they could be lovers even if she were to marry Santiago. Refugio is the desire that descends from the tree of transgression, and she is silenced sexuality, locked away in the master's house by order of the priest Don Jacinto because he was afraid she "would jump the fence with her fiancé Santiago." The outlines of modernity are there in the ironic interplay in which Refugio is converted into a destabilizing factor of the feudal order in the very heart of the patriarch, thereby subverting the social paradigm of the master as a guardian of honor.

Pascual represents the feudal landowner and the exercise of power in order to obtain sexual control. He is insistently described as a satyr, libido itself in the pursuit of pleasure. Pascual emerges as the official ravisher of maidenheads of the district and at the same time the matchmaker who promises land to the young men who will agree to marry the maidens he has dishonored. Pascual shows up to spy through a crack in Refugio's door while she is slowly removing each one of her garments, and the scene is crucial because it constitutes the first total nudity in Mexican literature, as well as being a transgression of the linguistic codes of sacred liturgy in its privileging of the incarnation of the body as it is restored in its nudity, in a veritable act of almost religious liberty and eroticism. Another scene repeats the disrobing, but now Pascual is hidden in a corner of the room from which he emerges in order to rape Refugio. She is able to reject him, but she is left alone to confirm herself as a paradigm of repressed desire. Nudity is presented here as a way of recovering the image of the body, with eroticism as a confirmation of the body as narcissistic pleasure with the possibility of reconstituting oneself sexually.

The enraged Pascual, in order to avenge his rival Santiago, withdraws Santiago's salary and on other occasions pays him just in corn. The denunciation of the text exposes not only the injustices of the masters, but also what the narrator calls the traditional "atavistic" respect of the peasants for their lords. The narrative voice criticizes this reverence of the peasant class toward the patriarchal system.

At one point there is a description of the wedding night of Refugio and Santiago. Pascual is spying on them, and he is so excited that he is overcome by something like an attack of hysteria. He is found in this state by his stepmother, Doña Francisca. Pascual in a single bound carries her off to the very bed that had belonged to his father and to the ancestors of his stepmother. This event possesses an intricate ideological meaning because, as the narrative voice has stated, Doña Francisca is a women with exemplary endowments for procreation, but Pascual's father suffered from a form of sterility owing to excessive sexual activity, such that Francisca is a sign of a frustrated womb in search of a lost phallus and a repressed maternity. Nevertheless this woman assumes socially the burden of directing the pious acts of the women of the town, and she governs, along with the priest, the norms that staunch the discourse of sexuality. And in one pathetic monologue she recognizes that her pious stance is a false posture. She goes on to insist on describing her resistance to the sexual act as a "simulacrum" and as "one hour of love," which must be understood in terms of pure pleasure.

There is another subversion of the sacramental codes when, after she has made her confession and is engaged in carrying out her penance, she undertakes instead an intense erotic re-creation of what has happened by insisting on the audacity, force, quantity, and intensity of Pascual's caresses which made her blood boil and caused her to wander half-naked through the hallways of her house. The priest silences her and forgives her sin by maintaining that her sexual transgressions never took place. The same priest observes that if pregnancy occurs, society will undertake to turn her into a martyr and cast her out via "sarcasm, scandal, and shame," which gives the impression that if God forgives, society does not. The final paragraph of the novel subverts any hope for reconciliation with the divinity, since we see her kneeling before another Virgin Mother of Solitude, which is just like her in their shared isolation and subjugation. It is interesting to note how the novel deconstructs the figure of the Virgin Mother, who is suddenly transformed into a "terrible mother," into a mysterious force of repression, a quite unorthodox figure in Catholic tradition but one that is rich in meaning in an archetypal mythological interpretation.

As far as marriage, an essential institution of Western patriarchal society, is concerned, there are various violations in the novel of its social or religious normativeness. For Refugio it is the social and ecclesiastical legitimation of desire and a way to achieve her independence from the authority of the master. And for Francisca, matrimony, in a canonical religious sense, had not been consummated because it had not fulfilled the goal of procreation. It was simply a social convention that served to silence and to conceal the sexual excesses and the sexual incapacity of her husband. If this act is to be considered incestuous, what is being questioned are the bases of the universal patriarchal system via the transgression of the forbidden threshold of Western culture. In order to underscore the archetypal function of Pascual Aguilera as a transgressor, the narrative voice informs us that the act was consummated in his parents' and stepmother's forefathers' own bed. It is profoundly significant that Nervo provides as the concluding image of his two novels the death throes of one protagonist (the seminarian) and the actual death of the other (Pascual Aguilera), with an enigmatic smile that provides the text with an extraordinary ambiguity. In Pascual Aguilera it would seem to be the finally satisfied pleasure that is exchanged for life itself, a biologically degenerate life that ends up in natural organic decomposition. The fact that a separate narrative voice explains that Pascual's conduct was owing to hereditary factors diminishes his moral and social culpability and places him in the role of victim without any talk of remorse or eternal damnation. Nevertheless, Francisca may expect condemnation and social margination, a strong attitude of penitence and an internal struggle against remorse.

Nervo's enthusiasm toward the subversion of dominant ideologies is evident, especially in his prologue to the 1896 Barcelona edition of the two novels. But what is surprising is the profound and systematic systematizing of Mexican reality, which is difficult to accept as a youthful intellectual game. Thus, *El bachiller* takes up the conflict of a seminarian in the face of his repressed sexuality as the consequence of a sickly temperament and a religious code that is violently coercive and doctrinarily ambiguous and dangerous.

As is the case in *Pascual Aguilera*, there are various narrative voices in *El bachiller*. One of them conveys information, providing objective facts in the first and last paragraphs of the work, which are no less highly suggestive for the laconism. In both novels it is the narrative voice that establishes the familial and psychopathologic antecedents of the protagonists Pascual and Felipe. This premise of the omniscient narrator forewarns the reader as regards the reliability he or she ought to accord to Felipe, who is emotionally unbalanced for immutable genetic reasons.

The omniscient narration contradicts the sincerity of Felipe's mystic aspirations, while there is another voice that situates itself in an intermediary zone of direct impersonal narration. This voice reveals the intentions, aspirations, and fears of Felipe without any intervention on his part. Frequently in the narrative discourse there is a segment of the text that deconstructs what has been described, proposing an ambiguity and an irony that belongs more to the modern novel. This polyvalent and fluid voice is the underlying support for dramatic tension when it announces an epiphanic mystical state that turns out to be an erotic hallucination. This supposed ecstasy is a subtle irony that becomes evident when the luminous image is not that of Christ but rather that of a voluptuous and virginal woman whose lips draw close to his. Recognition of these voices makes possible the identification of the tonal registries of the text that are not those of a spiritual martyrdom. Felipe is not an epic hero, but rather he denies himself in a suicidal act. His castration is the final act of the negation and repressive violence of sexuality. Felipe is a novelistic character who fails in his attempt to attain his spiritual aspirations. He is given a harsh warning by an interior voice that adduces convincing ontological reasons for him to return to the life of love and work at the side of his wife and society, opinions that support those of Asunción, his wife.

The novel problematizes the nature of the Church as the mystic Body of Christ and provides evidence for the corporeal sexuality of those who are a part of it, individuals who are far from being asexual. The aesthetic efficacy of violence against the body is questioned, and mysticism is postulated as a labyrinth in which the individuals lose their ways among the images, overwrought emotions, and repressed eroticism.

Nervo's novel contains a vigorous criticism of the Church as a repressive structure whose patriarchal image serves the escapism of certain individuals. Such psychopathological cases were and are still frequent in Hispanic society, and it is sufficient to mention the elaboration of this conflict in *El hermano asno* (Brother Ass; 1924), by the Chilean Eduardo Barrios, and the figure of Luis Gonzaga in *Al filo del agua* (*The Edge of the Storm*; 1947), by the Mexican Agustín Yáñez (see below, Chapter 8).

III

Federico Gamboa published *Santa* a decade after the novels of Amado Nervo; *Santa* is without a doubt the most emblematic novel of Mexican naturalism. If Nervo underscored the transgression of sexuality in the guise of certain forms of patriarchal discourse, *Santa* is a discourse of prostitution, the voice of clandestinity, and as such it problematizes the social and ideological structures of the Díaz patriarchy. Gamboa, as though engaging in a dialectic of the clandestine, has provided in his text systematic traces, signs, ciphers, and symmetries on different levels of the narrative. This essay can only refer to the correspondences between what is explicit and what is avoided in the text by pointing out the ideological implications of desire, pleasure, and power.

Santa is the first Mexican novel to deal with the problem of prostitution as a phenomenon brought about by the exercise of multiple determining forces, two of which stand out consistently as dialectic principles: the discourse of sexuality (desire-pleasure) versus the discourse of power (phallocentric repression). The work could not have appeared at a more propitious time. It was published during the third decade of the Díaz dictatorship, which it problematizes from differing points of view, always indirectly and by making use of coded messages or incomplete but very suggestive metaphors. These are all, on the one hand, characteristically expressive formulas of clandestine discourse while, on the other, they are part of the stock and trade of a professional novelist. The repression of explicit speech was an established fact during the regime of Porfirio Díaz, and it is enough to recall the military persecution of Heriberto Frías for having written the novel *Tomóchic* (1892). The treatment of a marginal theme like that of the prostitute during the totalitarian regime of Porfirio Díaz was a deliberate act of transgression. As Michel Foucault emphasizes in his *The History of Sexuality*, giving voice to silenced sexuality possesses an enormous relevancy because of the extralegality it represents. Santa is insistently presented as the encodement of the subreptitious, as the ciphered protagonist of the Mexican who, after having been asphyxiated by rural morality, arrives in the big city—the sign of progress, order, and refinement—only to find herself even more exploited, alienated, and cast aside as so much human trash. The Foucaultian relationship between the sexual and the social refers to how the masculine, social-patriarchal, and repressive regimes assume the roles of the masters, superiors, victors, with the marginal, whether sexual, social, or political, belonging to opposing positions. One of the great accomplishments of *Santa* is that it traces these dialectical and antithetical oppositions not in a static and obvious form, but by articulating them within the efficient rhythm of narrative language. This change establishes the structure of Santa (as the central actor) and her transformation in the face of the different social structures she confronts, and even though the first space that the novel refers to is the Mexican capital, it is necessary to begin with her life in her mother's house in order to understand her evolution in a logical, temporal, and causal order.

Chimalistac is a real place which used to be on the periphery of Mexico City, and that is where Santa is born and raised. Two types of spaces are distinguished. First there are the exterior ones that are under masculine domination, the work place, daily life, courtship, and sexual pursuit. By contrast there is the isolated, closed world of *oikos* (the abode, or by synecdoche, the hearth), which according to Foucault designates the feminine world of reclusion under the control of the husband and father and where the woman administers the patrimony and religion. Santa's mother, although she is a widow, establishes a patriarchal organization with the help of her two sons, Esteban and Fabián. The tutelary protection of the home is in the hands of the Virgin of Guadalupe and the Virgin of Solitude, and the teaching of sexuality has served to declare it nonexistent. Thus, when Santa has her first menstrual period, she believes she is seriously ill. When her mother finds out, she tells Santa that she has ceased to be "sexless" because she is now potentially a mother—that is, she now exists as a sexual subject. This is the first time in Mexican literature that the biological cycle of feminine sexuality is referred to. In the oikos, sexuality exists only in the marriage chamber, and this is a daily torture for Santa. When Marcelino Beltrán, a subaltern stationed at the local military garrison, appears, sex assumes the dimensions of something pleasurable that is in conflict with the wedding band. When he courts and then deflowers her, Santa is initiated in desire and takes her place in the conflict between pleasure and guilt. Simultaneously, Santa seeks to legalize her sexual activity through matrimony and to remain within the realm of pure sexuality. The narrative voice insists that what animates Marcelino is his "little bit of authority," his sword and his stripes. It is appropriate here to point out the awareness of the narrative voice of the dialectic relation between the masculine as force and the feminine as submission. If the text demonstrates one voice that distances itself from the characters in order to categorize them socially, there is a second narrative voice that enjoys an intimacy with the protagonists, translating their experience into a rhetorical code. In this way we know that Santa was initiated simultaneously in terms of sex and in terms of pleasure. These two narrative voices which contradict each other, cancel each other out, or question each other are what provide the work with its irony, ambiguity, and plurality of meaning as in the case of the code of clandestinity and heteroglossia in the modern novel.

Santa suffers a miscarriage, and her family finds out about her double corporal transgression, and, in a highly suggestive scene, her mother and two guardian brothers choose to cast her out rather than to seek revenge. This failure to restore honor reaffirms the work in its dimension as a modern novel.

The decision to seek revenge, rather than expel the transgressor, would be the case in the epic. Santa is cast out of paradise in order to avoid gossip, and she departs because there is no longer any place for her in the home. "In order to be done with it," as she says, she crosses the ring of fire of the patriarchal in order to deny the oikos and all that the wedding ring symbolizes, which is sexuality restricted to matrimony and maternity.

The second important space of the novel is opened up when Santa arrives in Mexico City and obtains work in Elvira's brothel. But in this place, which should theoretically be a house of desire and pleasure and the negation of oikos, she begins to discover an exploitative commercial enterprise operated by two Spanish women, Elvira and Pepa, who keep their employees under lock and key with a military regime that is more oppressive and phallocentric than the patriarchal oikos. The manly Elvira smokes cigars (a suggestive phallic symbol) and uses words like a whip against the women under her. The relationship is typically that of the master who will be obeyed at any cost and the exploited slave.

Elvira's place is next door to a butcher shop, and this proximity serves the narrator to establish all sorts of linguistic correlations of a pathetic meaning based on the bestialization of the traffic in human flesh. The women are presented in a fragmentary fashion to be subsequently reified as sumptuous objects of pleasure, described only in terms of their clothes and accessories. Santa, in addition to undergoing the ritual of being exploited physically and then registered in a public hospital and with the police, suffers the trimming of her hair, a symbol of castration. As a consequence, Santa has been mutilated and incapacitated as far as desire and sexual pleasure are concerned, as these have been converted into an exercise of pretense and forced routine. She is merchandise on display with no rights to her own self. This alienation goes hand in hand with collusion between the madames and the civil authorities of the dictatorship. If Santa was initiated sexually by an agent of the established order, she is initiated into the profession of prostitute by a Mexican state governor. The text caricaturizes his official authority when he orders the brothel placed at the exclusive disposal of him and his associates, and his splashy economic prowess is ridiculed by comparing it with his pitiful sexual performance.

The critique of phallocentrism is systematic, especially with reference to the men who frequent the brothel. The narrative describes them as "loyal husbands," "model fathers," "elegant gentlemen," while Pepa sees them as "human bulls" and "a band of pigs." Pepa herself explains to Santa the social function of prostitutes vis-à-vis "respectable" women. When Santa hides the scapulary of the Virgin of Guadalupe who has failed to preserve her virtue, the novel becomes a "godless world," and Santa is left alone with the demand that she be nothing more than a useful sexual object, no longer a woman, but a ———.
One additional fact that confirms the isomorphic relationship between sex and power is the multiple irony of establishing a coincidence between Santa's apotheosis and professional prestige and the country's solemn celebrations of in-

dependence. While in the brothel Santa, in the midst of an orgiastic and sumptuous banquet, is stripped and bathed in champagne for the exclusive use of the dandies of the city, outside in the street the multitude is celebrating.

Both scenes have a reciprocal carnivalizing value. The bacchanal subverts the celebration of a national independence that was threatened by Mexicans committed to the French and to foreign economic control as exemplified by Elvira. The parody of the independence celebration becomes more obvious when they explain to Jarameño, an Andalusian bullfighter, why the independence cry is directed against the Spaniards; Spaniards were prominent among the hoards of immigrants Porfirio Díaz brought in to "renovate" the country at the turn of the century.

What had up until this point been an implicit clandestine discourse becomes explicit at the end of the second chapter in the sense that the symmetry between Santa's alienation and prostitution and foreign control of the country becomes more evident. The call for the restoration of the oikos goes unheeded by Santa when her brothers bring the news of the death of her mother and order her to return home with them. Santa, pursued by her guilt over not having been present for her mother's final suffering and death, takes refuge in the bosom of the Holy Mother the Church in order to redeem herself. She wishes also to reconcile herself with the maternal image in terms of which she was at least the "sexless other," the member of oikos who was not yet a woman. In the Church of Santa Clara, where as in every holy place the human body appears not to exist, Santa is discovered by the sacristan as a sign of pleasure or sin and is expelled, along with the ironic threat of calling the police in case she resists. The text implies that Díaz's lay government provided the Church with the force of the police, when in fact the Constitution prohibited any external display of religion, and religious buildings were the property of the state. From this moment on, Santa is a bruised body and mutilated in spirit.

Hipólito, the blind pianist at Elvira's, has important functions within the general code of sexuality in the text such as that of representing an always-deferred sexual desire. He loves Santa, but his grotesque physical image provokes repugnance rather than sexual appetite. He lives deformed erotic fantasies, elaborating them on the basis of visual descriptions that his young guide tells him. He considers himself prostituted as simply one more of the whores among the frequent "we" that is used to refer to the inhabitants of the brothel. In addition to suffering the pangs of Tantalus because of his unsatisfied desire, he represents the image of Orpheus, the musician in the house that burns in flames during the nighttime, who is able to provide Santa's repeatedly deferred salvation only moments before her death. Hipólito is the repression of the omnipresent desire in every relationship Santa establishes. Hipólito subverts Santa's sexual relations because he plays a role in them as a witness, counselor, and proxy.

When Santa is taken away to the hospital by the health inspectors, the exercise of her sexuality is thus openly declared to be dangerous for the public stability and well being (of the men). At this point the discourse of sex serves to exhibit ancestral vices along with administrative corruption, such as when the police commissioner is bribed with two tickets to go see Jarameño in exchange for information about how to circumvent the weighty bureaucracy of the dictatorship. As a consequence, Santa is legally turned over to Jarameño as a hostage for his exclusive sexual use while she is kept in hiding against her will. It is interesting to note in this relationship of sexuality and power how Gaditana, another one of the prostitutes, is attracted to Santa, a lesbian proposition that Hipólito identifies as a complete form of love. Gaditana is the active subject while at the same time being a total enslaved will. This lesbian relationship suggests the possibility of a consciousness on the margins of Elvira's power and a dynamic of pleasure foreign to the sexual exploitation by the masculine. It is a relationship postulated as existing among the vanquished, which Santa neither understands nor accepts. Santa is taken away by Jarameño to a guesthouse, a place where lives Feliciano, a member of the middle class who has fallen on hard times and who is the kept lover of the woman who runs the house. The various regions of Spain are represented by the guests, a Basque revolutionary priest and a Galician comedy actor who is being financed by a Catalan scientist involved in trying to interest the Mexican military in a submarine project; both are experiments in scale models. Gamboa ironizes this putative respectable oikos by displaying it to us as a court of pariah-like immigrants who are happy that a bullfighter's money and his concubine will improve the food and service of the house. Jarameño demands exclusive rights over Santa, threatening to kill her if she does not comply. Santa grows bored with being shut in, with the middle-class life and Jarameño's absences, and she decides to have sexual relations with the scientist. The bullfighter catches them, and he tries to kill Santa with the backdrop of explanations concerning the hatred separating the sexes as articulated by one of the narrative voices.

There is a systematic criticism of the dictatorship when the prostitutes appear before the Supreme Court as witnesses to a killing during a fight at Elvira's house. The women are subjected to insinuations and abuses at the hands of the authorities, and threats are made against them at the same time as they are left confused by the judicial proceedings. The law does not exist to serve the weak and innocent but, rather, makes use of them to stage a spectacle of despotism.

Rubio, a Porfirian bourgeois stereotype, represents for Santa the alternative of a refined and sensitive lover who, in addition to economic stability, offers her independence from Elvira, and she goes to live with him. Rubio soon makes known his opinions about matrimony and women by asserting that he respects his wife and esteems the flesh of his lover and that the two feelings are compatible. The sententious narrative voice, going against the grain of what other writers of the period would have affirmed, takes the opportunity to inveigh against the hypocrisy prevalent in respectable marriages, going on to point out that the cause lies with a social structure based on concealing and silencing the truth of this hypocrisy and its attendant false bourgeois morality.

Santa for Rubio is a mirror in which a subject capable of loving has been constituted.

Santa returns to Elvira's establishment, from which she is expelled for her alcoholism and her progressive illness: she is, in effect, discarded as a consumable object of pleasure, and she is considered a social risk while no longer being a part in the public-health machine. A young student rescues her from the street and takes her back to his garret. Santa is now in appearance free since she is no longer Elvira's property nor the concubine of any man, and she attempts to establish an alliance that will allow her to recover herself as an active subject of desire. In order to do this, it is she who supports the student economically in exchange for a certain amount of exclusivity. Santa fails because what she does is reproduce a masculine model of the exploitation of sexuality, and the problem is that she is impelled in her relationship with the sixteen-year-old not out of desire and pleasure but rather out of the ontological necessity to constitute herself as a subject with little actual reference to the student. As a result, she is exploited economically by the boy, and when her money ends, the relationship does also. Thus the text breaks with the social prejudice that establishes children as sexually neutral, since this boy manipulates a situation of phallocentric domination.

Santa moves on to the next stage, where she is now denounced and pursued by the health authorities while operating independently in low-class hotels with clients picked up in the street. Hipólito answers her call and serves as a deforming mirror that gives back to her the image of what she was when she was still a prestigious and sumptuous object.

Hipólito has a greater interest in Santa than merely possessing her, and he waits for the end of each tryst, rescuing her from the grimy hotels and taking care of her without ever pimping for her or exploiting her out of economic interest. But there comes a time when Hipólito deviates from the pact between the two of them and attempts to possess her. She pulls away from him for a time, during which, ruined and dying, she is thrown out of a brothel on the outskirts of town. Santa asks Hipólito for help, and he takes her to his broken-down hovel. Santa, first out of repugnance and then in order not to betray her fantasy of him, rejects Hipólito until he ceases to consider her an object of pleasure. Desire is replaced by nostalgia for what she once was, for her Other. Santa is reflected in her imagination in the mirror of her widowed mother, which excludes any association with sexual desire. By the same token, she takes refuge in her childhood and adolescence prior to her first sexual experience, which also involves another asexual ego. Hipólito denies his real desire and behaves generously and kindly in silence, perhaps without understanding but nevertheless recognizing in Santa her subjective fantasy. The blind man begins to inhabit the same fantasy and imagines himself to have made a home with her.

Some critics have attempted to see a sort of moral redemption for Santa, something like a Bildungsroman, in which she finally comes to learn the lesson of life, to stand morally disposed to find her place in the moral structures of society; in this view, Hipólito's love is her salvation. This reading is similar to that of readers of the original 1903 edition, and it was also the interpretation that was convenient for the regime and the bourgeois society of the day. But this position cannot be supported. The text is multiple in its meanings, and there cannot be only one way of decodifying it. If one postulates a redemption, then reference can be made to the one that takes place between Hipólito and Santa. These two members of the lumpenproletariat end up establishing an altruistic relationship of solidarity as equals, and neither attempts to exercise power in a master-slave equation. As for their correlation with sexuality, these two social outcasts are encapsulated in the transubjectivity of the fantastic as a form of subverting reality and seeking for themselves an alternative of freedom and personal being in the face of a phallocentric society in a country dominated by a patriarchal and repressive administrative and ideological structure.

IV

We may conclude by saying that the readings that have been traditionally offered of El bachiller, Pascual Aguilera, and Santa are questionable, as far as concerns works that correspond to the nineteenth-century Bildungsroman, to the extent that these works involve irony and function in terms of a certain dialectic mechanism in which naturalism problematizes reality and provides it with a polyvalent ideology. The discourse of sexuality, whether in terms of prostitution, castration, or incest, is presented as a phenomenon that questions the validity and the efficient functioning of phallocentric society and the patriarchal political structure.

Sexuality in the novels that have been analyzed is postulated as a continuum of attitudes in the quest for liberty and self-affirmation in the face of manipulation and repression on the part of authority. The forces of this authority are present in El bachiller under the guise of religion, while in Pascual Aguilera such forces are symbolized in the social and paradigmatic figures of the landowner and the priest. In Santa disruptive and alienating power is personified in the maternal oikos and in the conditions that "anachrocentrism" establishes in the economic, political, and social system in Mexico during the regime of Porfirio Díaz.

In naturalism, by contrast with realism, the problem of the proletariat, the marginal, and the clandestine is taken up. In Santa the broadest social spectrum to date in the Mexican novel is presented from a new perspective in which the underdog is emphasized and in which the false morality and the alleged education and urbanity of the other social classes are parodied.

In Nervo's novels, the peasant has already appeared as an individual (and not as a mass figure, as in realism). The individual is an object of manipulation at the hands of the dominant morality and of exploitation in the work place.

A closing remark might be that, if realism, although it does engage in a sort of criticism, ends up by basically supporting the androcentric political system, naturalism not only finds the moral conduct of individuals questionable, but also analyzes and denounces the bases, strategies, and consequences of the social, economic, and political structure by bringing this structure face to face with the discourse of sexuality. Sexuality, which is insistent in realism, is used in naturalism as a power that is transgressive of established norms of both criticism and satire, as well as parody and carnivalization.

BIBLIOGRAPHY

Alegría, Fernando. *Historia de la novela hispanoamericana*. Mexico City: Ediciones de Andrea, 1966. A fundamental text that provides a panoramic overview of the Latin American narrative from an ideological perspective.

Azuela, Mariano. *Cien años de novela mexicana*. Mexico City: Ediciones Botas, 1947. An excellent in-depth analysis of the development of the nineteenth-century Mexican novel.

Barrios, Eduardo. *El hermano asno*. Buenos Aires: Losada, 1946.

Brushwood, John S. *Genteel Barbarism*. Lincoln: University of Nebraska Press, 1981. Trans. by Lucía Garavito as *La barbarie elegante*. Mexico City: Fondo de Cultura Económica, 1988. Diverse theoretical models are brought to bear on representative nineteenth-century fictional texts, including various Mexican texts. This is a pioneering work on the nineteenth-century novel, despite the limitations of the various approaches as regards the ideological interpretation and assessment of the texts.

———. *Mexico in Its Novel*. Austin: University of Texas Press, 1966. Trans. by Brushwood as *México en su novela*. Mexico City: Fondo de Cultura Económica, 1987. This rigorous chronological registry of Mexican novels focuses on their sociohistoric context and content.

Castro Leal, Antonio. "Prólogo." In Rafael Delgado, *Los parientes ricos*. Mexico City: Colección "Escritores Mexicanos," 1944. This prologue is an important document in that it surveys the ideological and aesthetic position of Mexican novelists in the context of the European currents of the day.

Cuéllar, José Tomás de. *Baile y cochino*. Mexico City: Porrúa, 1946. Originally published as vol. 1 of *La Linterna mágica* (Barcelona: n.p., 1889–1892).

———. *Ensalada de pollos*. Mexico City: Porrúa, 1946. Originally published as vol. 2 of *La Linterna mágica* (Mexico City: n.p., 1871–1872).

Delgado, Rafael. *Angelina*. Mexico City: Porrúa, 1947.

———. *La calandria*. Mexico City: Ediciones de la Razón, Colección de clásicos agotados, 1931.

———. *Los parientes ricos*. Mexico City: Colección "Escritores Mexicanos," 1944.

Fernández-Arias Campoamor, J. *Novelistas de México: Esquema de la historia de la novela mejicana (de Lizardi al 1950)*. Madrid: Ediciones Cultura Hispánica, 1952. Despite numerous ideological and cultural imprecisions, this work provides a detailed synthesis of Mexican fictional production against the backdrop of Spanish works that are considered to be their models.

Foucault, Michel. *Historia de la sexualidad: La inquietud de sí*. Vol. 3. Mexico City: Siglo XXI, 1987.

Frías, Heriberto. *Tomóchic, novela historica mexicana*. Mexico City: Edinal, 1960.

Gamboa, Federico. *Santa*. Mexico City: Editorial Grijalbo, 1987.

Glantz, Margo. *Con la lengua en la mano*. Mexico City: Premiá Editora/La Red de Jonás, 1983. Contains an analysis of *Santa* as an allegory of woman as she is bestialized and sacrificed by the society of her day; written from a feminist point of view that is both audacious and inconsistent, although ultimately polemical.

Grass, Roland. *José López Portillo y Rojas: A Novelist of Social Reform in Mexico before the Revolution of 1910*. Macomb: Western Illinois Press, 1970. An extensive but careless essay that attempts to demonstrate the novelist's role as a social reformer as determined from his prologues, speeches, and critical notes which are examined uncritically with no attempt to contextualize them adequately or to contrast them with their place in the society of Porfirio Díaz.

Gullón, Agnes. *Teoría de la novela: Aproximaciones hispánicas*. Madrid: Taurus, 1974.

Larroyo, Francisco. *Historia comparada de la educación en México*. Mexico City: Editorial Porrúa, 1983.

López Portillo y Rojas, José. *Nieves*. In *Cuentos completos,* vol. 1, ed. Carballo. Guadalajara: Ediciones I.t.g., 1952.

———. *La parcela*. Mexico City: Editorial Porrúa, 1978.

———. *Los precursores*. Guadalajara: Ayuntamiento de Guadalajara, 1976–1978.

Lukács, George. *Teoría de la novela*. Buenos Aires: Ediciones Siglo XX, 1974.

Navajas, Gonzalo. *Teoría y práctica de la novela española posmoderna*. Barcelona: Ediciones del Mall, 1987.

Navarro, Joaquina. *La novela realista mexicana*. Mexico City: Compañía General de Ediciones, 1955. A complete and detailed panorama of Mexican realism with abundant biographical and historical information and a careful analysis of the works from a historicist point of view that fails to question the conventional knowledge on the production of the period. Nevertheless, this is the first academic analysis of Mexican realism.

Nervo, Amado. *El bachiller*. In *Obras completas,* vol. 1, 185–198. Madrid: Aguilar, 1962.

———. *Pascual Aguilera*. In *Obras completas,* vol. 1, 157–185. Madrid: Aguilar, 1962.

Ortega y Gasset, José. *Meditaciones del Quijote e Ideas sobre la novela*. Madrid: Espasa Calpe, 1985.

Rabasa, Emilio. *La bola y La gran ciencia*. Mexico City: Editorial Porrúa, 1948.

———. *Cuarto poder y Moneda falsa*. Mexico City: Editorial Porrúa, 1970.

Tacca, Oscar. *Las voces de la novela*. Madrid: Editorial Gredos, 1985.

Warner, Ralph E. *Historia de la novela mexicana en el siglo XIX*. Mexico City: Antigua Librería Robredo, 1953. Emphasizes the value of texts from the point of view of aesthetics, narrative style, and the representation of major characters in terms of their sentimental and moral nature. Unfortunately and despite various audacious statements, no systematic methodology is deployed.

Yáñez, Agustín. *Al filo del agua*. Mexico City: Editorial Porrúa, 1975.

5

Modernism

BART L. LEWIS

The artistic sensibility that seized Western culture in the middle years of the last century—anxious, introverted, disordering—is only now yielding to a successor. This modernism, a still unsettled name and chronology, is being replaced in critical discourse, even so, by firm asseverations on postmodernism. The Latin American case is troubled further by the presence of a style of writing, largely poetic and generally agreed to have prevailed from the 1880s to the 1920s, called *modernismo,* which purified romanticism and absorbed prevailing French influences. Thanks to efforts such as those realized by Evelyn Picón Garfield and Ivan A. Schulman in their recent book, "*Las entrañas del vacío*": *Ensayos sobre la modernidad hispanoamericana* (Inside the Void: Essays on Latin American Modernity[1]; 1984), the two modernisms are currently being examined as coincident and duplicative, with results that revolutionize the study of Latin American literature.[2] Just as decentering and revisionist theories are today relocating the points of emphasis of a world literary canon, so a reexamination of Latin American literary currents and their representative pieces, long held to be indisputable, reveals neglected, underestimated, or undiscovered works. The need for increased attention to Mexican modernism is particularly compelling because of that country's importance as an early center of modernist activity in Latin America. This study will thus highlight the works of five lesser-known modernist authors deserving of attention in light of present-day cultural broadenings, review contemporary scholarship on Mexico's consecrated modernists—Jesús Valenzuela (1856–1911), Manuel Gutiérrez Nájera (1859–1895), Manuel José Othón (1858–1906), Salvador Díaz Mirón (1853–1928), Amado Nervo (1870–1919), Efrén Rebolledo (1877–1929), José Juan Tablada (1871–1945), and Enrique González Martínez (1871–1952)—and reappraise the particular contributions of Gutiérrez Nájera, Díaz Mirón, and González Martínez. The underestimated artists Justo Sierra (1848–1912), Agustín F. Cuenca (1850–1884), Juan de Dios Peza (1852–1910), Laura Méndez de Cuenca (1853–1928), and María Enriqueta Camarillo (1872–1968), thought formerly to be minor or transitional figures, clearly contribute as well to the establishment of a new, "modern" aesthetic in Mexico, a regard for art as a muted exhibition of self. The vaunted Mexican modernists practice the art of an age and in so doing sculpt the monument that marks it. By their side are unrecognized writers of sensibility who form the intrahistoric weave that insured a free play of technical innovation, a disposition to the new, and the binding of a generation to successive ones. Mexican modernism was born into a world attuned to its resonant and studied rhythms.

In order to understand this new style that began to influence the cultivation of fine arts in the later years of the past century, we must confront an array of dates, signal events, and antecedent conditions, all of which attempt to depict an estrangement of artist from society. A working cover term for the period of art from approximately 1880 to the present is conceded to be *modernism,* while some cultural historians argue for a division around 1940 between modernism and postmodernism. If other labels such as *the new* and *vanguard* are also applied to the later years of the period, there appears to be an agreement that *the modern* and *modernism* describe an artistic turn that Western art took a hundred or so years ago as a result of social and cultural forces still largely present today. Modernism is thought to have accompanied the disillusionment of society with its increasingly technological and scientific base at the end of the nineteenth century, but since science builds on itself and only increases its momentum and critical mass, further separations and dehumanizations will inevitably occur. Thus modernism appears to be a piece of cultural baggage destined for humanity's voyage into an unending future. Art that seeks to tap wellsprings of the emotional and irrational will forever find itself at odds with the empirical and mechanistic. While an earlier cultural mode, romanticism, had also featured detached and brooding artists, they had ultimately reintegrated into society, bringing their oracular pronouncements back from the windswept crags. Romanticism had hoped to build society through art and literature; modernism's initial desire was to build an *alternate* reality through art. Thus the industrial revolution did not produce the alienation that positivism did later in the century. Solitude seemed to abide with the hum of the new industrialism. But as artists began to see the dysfunctions that scientific regulation could foster in society, realistic and naturalistic depictions began to inform Western art, revealing how human beings in a capitalist, positivistic milieu were overwhelmed by destiny and the machine. It was then modernism that provided the vehicle of escape from the colorless and painfully earthbound precisions of the industrial.

The components of modernism add up to a movement that separates the demonstrably rational from the sentiently irrational, with the latter in the hands of the lone artist, refined and agonizing. Yet the components may differ among themselves, both synchronically and diachronically.[3] For example, coexistent with Parnassianism and its notions of pure art were the French symbolists and their mystic transcendences. It mattered not that the art object was inaccessible to the common observer. The artist was responding to an injunction to preserve art's cultic appeal, its reception by initiates, whoever they might be. Still other of modernism's subordinate currents appear to consume themselves with linguistic frivolity or to plunge into a nihilism so meaningless that not even form can justify its coming into being. What is certain is that a new kind of art, dissociated from the naturally human and responding only to eccentric impulses toward arcane communication, had taken shape in the late nineteenth century and had given rise to the fragmentation of an earlier certainty in Western culture.

In the matter of a chronology for this modernist aesthetic, there is scarcely more agreement. Limits are proposed with an eye to certain key events or, as is often the case with literary history, in broad, encompassing terms.[4] The Nobel Prize–winning Spanish poet Juan Ramón Jiménez would bring modernism's terminus into a very recent past, speaking of a modernist century that began twenty years before the end of the nineteenth century (Schulman, 9). For Jiménez to speak of modernism's span in this way both affirms our understanding of its pervasive impact and demonstrates further the seeming impossibility of fixing its boundaries. Although determining a point of departure for modernism in the past century may threaten to collide with romanticism's full brilliance (the difference even now is plainly one of mending the rupture with society rather than refining it), there is wide agreement that modernism and its several permutations continue to the present. It is a cultural trend that endures largely because it cannot elude its name.

Do we fall victim here to presentism, the tendency to view the past in the narrowest way, as incomplete prelude to a more complete and comprehensible present? If so, we are only being "modern" and building as well on romanticism's idea of infinite perfectibility. If cultural development has brought us this far, we should be able to discern a swing of the pendulum, or a new parabola altogether. Do we view romanticism as separated from modernism by the enthronement of science and progress? Are we called upon to view as works of common genesis Justo Sierra's *Cuentos románticos* (Romantic Tales), Joyce's *Ulysses,* Faulkner's *The Sound and the Fury,* María Enriqueta Camarillo's *El secreto* (The Secret), and Juan Rulfo's *Pedro Páramo?* Certainly there are matters of national differences, endowment of talent and genius, self-appraisal, breadth of critical attention, and dissemination among a reading public to consider. But common to all these works, and those that have achieved some measure of acceptance by the literary establishment in the past one hundred years, is the presence, in varying degrees, of a self-conscious artist, exposed to an often-impassive world, spinning out tales or verses that match the visions glimpsed by, in Valle-Inclán's words, "the eyes of the imagination." It is significant that the modern age has given us the poet in an ivory tower, the *poète maudit,* the "stranger," the underground man, dangling and invisible, now a rhinoceros, now a cockroach. Condemning materialist, rationalist, and bourgeois society, modernist writers have directed their talents at showing contemporary life at its most venal and bloodless or eschewing present reality altogether in favor of a counterreality, immanent in a textual linguistic construct. The matter is not to mark the limits of the movement; it is to marvel at the astounding and numberless ways artists have contrived to perpetuate art in the absence of a reason for its existence, a self-sustaining *aleph* whose glistening facets power the next turn of the globe.

Despite the broad universal embrace of the modernist movement, it is only now that attempts are being made to understand Latin American modernism in this world context. And such efforts are not guaranteed a favorable reception. In a 1964 article Bernardo Gicovate disputes Jiménez's designation of a modernist century, warning that there are stylistic shadings and marked differences between then and now that such a designation plainly ignores (Gicovate, 220). The fact remains, however, that the world's modernism and that of Latin America share a remarkable number of traits, particularly if we view modernism in Latin America as the chastening, purifying stage of literary development between the largely derivative works of the early nineteenth century and the "new" literature beginning in the 1930s. With such an idea in mind we readily understand the alignment of the Latin American movement with Western literary renovation in that central to both is the fact of a redirecting of the cultural enterprise that was to last to our own day. The same inclination to reexamine that encourages this conclusion has led critics of Hispanic literature to set back the beginning point of modernism, previously agreed to be 1888 with the publication of Rubén Darío's *Azul* (*Azure*). Influential critics in the last twenty years have begun to see in the works of José Martí and Manuel Gutiérrez Nájera the real beginnings of Latin American modernism, fully a decade before the date traditionally associated with the movement's birth (Schulman, 9).

Not only does the present-day drive to decenter and displace the locus of an established literary tradition call for reinterpretation, but one reaches the conclusion as well that such a tradition may be based on a misreading of the supporting texts. Max Henríquez Ureña, for example, allows that the term *modernismo* was used by Darío as a general synonym for modernity (Henríquez Ureña, 156). Yet eager to concentrate on the movement in conventional terms, he hastens to specify that Darío by 1890 was speaking of a certain group of Latin American writers who were clearly guided by a "new spirit" in literature, a spirit motivated by *modernismo* (Henríquez Ureña, 156–157). This critic points out further that the word came to represent something that Darío had not intended, a synonym for "decadent," and that his term was only meant to indicate a modern spirit of renewal (Henríquez Ureña, 159). Looking at this original intent, we see that Darío's exaltation was of a freshening force exerted by artists who pursued color, lightness, vivacity, and loveliness. Such a burden of beauty could only redound to its creator, and the artist steps forward here as the guardian of the cultural treasure. In the life of the term *modernism* we see that the authoritative referential word, cultivated in its own medium, the printed text, yields itself up to misapplication and is condemned to meaning that is forever virtual. But the literary phenomenon it represents continues with its own life, described appropriately with language, the cultural commodity entrusted to the artist. Ricardo Gullón added his voice to those calling for a reappraisal of modernism as early as 1963. He recognizes the change in a world view that modernism brought about and reminds us once more that what is modern was prefigured by an earlier tendency, now destined for an undetermined conclusion: modernism's attitudes belonged to romanticism, but technical experimentation, ways to use language inventively, constituted the truly modern (Gullón, 15). The volume to be read and interpreted is the one written by the artist, in need of society but shaping his or her art in necessary isolation.

The case of Mexican modernism is particularly important because it is here by traditional lights that the literary movement gained an early foothold in Latin America. Due to the new critical attention focused on modernism, moreover, a Mexican modernist, Manuel Gutiérrez Nájera, long held as a precursor of the movement, is now regarded as a founder, along with the other three traditional "precursors," José Asunción Silva, José Martí, and Julián del Casal. Again, traditional criticism has placed the official beginning of modernism in Mexico at two dates, those of the foundings of two essential journals. In 1894 Gutiérrez Nájera and Carlos Díaz Dufóo founded the *Revista Azul,* which was published for two years. Lasting until 1911, the *Revista Moderna* began publication in 1898 under Jesús Valenzuela and Amado Nervo. Given the absolute allegiance to things French rendered by the early Mexican modernists, we are reminded that talk of "the modern" had begun in France as early as 1860. Considering the admiration of the Mexican naturalist Federico Gamboa for French writers, his flirtation with modernism in the salons of the day, and his ultimate surrender to clinical detail in the novel, we are once again assured that late nineteenth-century art was a dazzling spin of styles and ideas. In this regard we see the borrowings, graftings, and synthesizing that became modernism, a mixing that extends even to the masterpiece of modernist literature, Joyce's *Ulysses,* which José Emilio Pacheco takes to be a blend of naturalism and symbolism (xxiv). Then what was occurring in Mexico as early as the 1880s was a turning toward a European culture for inspiration, not unlike what the romantics had done in their time. The clear difference was that art, though universal, was available only to the initiate, that each artist who faced the abyss would in turn create a crystalline chorus to celebrate annihilation, or stare at it, lacking resolve.

The romanticism-modernism affinity, tentative and subject to qualification, does nevertheless permit a clearer understanding of how modernism grew naturally and at first unremarkably from mid-nineteenth-century Mexican literature. A key volume of stories by Justo Sierra is *Cuentos románticos,* taking from romanticism a gauzy sentimentality but converting it into an ornamented world of such *preciosité* that art itself is enthroned. Alfonso Reyes saw the similarity as very much in keeping with the progress of literary development and even qualified the poetry of the *Revista Moderna* as postromantic (Martínez Peñaloza, 25). The Latin American romantics had seen in their European counterparts models for nation building. The admiration that the Argentines Esteban Echeverría and Domingo Faustino Sarmiento had for Madame de

Staël, for example, was one based on her prescriptions that literature could model a better society. The artist was alone but only because he or she stood out front, leaderly and inspired. Modernism saw the artist attacking the same mainstream institutions and practices that the romantics had, but the modernist took a peculiar delight in separation. Moreover, by reminding us that we are considering the integration of a Third World, peripheral high culture into the dominant Western cultural discourse, the romantic/modernist axis helps us to understand Latin America's unique attempt to converge with world modernism. The rejection of industrialization, a bourgeois mentality, positivism, experimental science, and capitalism has only symbolic effect if the society has not progressed to a full practice of these societal pressures. But rejection in this case is a rejection of the worst elements that imperialist powers were attempting to impose, elements censured by dissidents within the more developed societies themselves. So the artistic elite, regardless of national origin, was united into a universal culture, having seen as the only purpose of life to cultivate beauty and dynamic structure as they interpreted it.

The viewing of the early Mexican modernists as late romantics provides a further insight into the history of Latin American letters in the nineteenth century. Because of their late appearance in Latin America realism and naturalism, prose fiction styles principally, are not intermediate developments in Mexico between romanticism and modernism. Rather, these styles coexist with other literary currents. We must not believe that there was an orderly progression from one movement to another in the nineteenth century. Then what conclusion have we reached? What is modernism but purified romanticism? There is a tendency to see all Latin American literature as romantic, and certainly modernism was no programmatic rejection of romanticism (Martínez Peñaloza, 29). Such views are faithful to the idea that Latin America is still becoming, is still seeking an identity within the community of nations, relying on romanticism's infinite perfectibility for some future glory. Because of our desire to relocate the origins of Mexican modernism and see in it a threshold to the modern age, evidenced today and practiced throughout the West, we welcome the interpretations of critics such as Carlos Ignacio González, who sees Juan de Dios Peza as a modernist, the romantic Manuel M. Flores as one who anticipates modernism, and Manuel Acuña as part romantic and part modernist (González, 22). The intent of this study is then not to abolish notions of modernism as a Latin American phenomenon in order to subordinate it to a more widely studied Western modernism. *Criollista,* vanguard, and boom literature would not have come into being in Latin America without the radical realizations of its modernist authors. But by finding practitioners of the new where none were suitably recognized as such before, we are able to embrace the modernist age with greater confidence and understanding. And in reviewing works by well-known Mexican modernists, those traditionally characterized as such, we understand what superb literary value lies in an age thought to be too mannered and formalistic.

We are drawn strongly to the beginning years of the artistic renovation, the origins of the Mexican modern, because the full development of the new style by the writers to be discussed so clearly assured its future cultivation. The sense of the modern, energetically at work by the 1890s, was to infuse the cultural enterprise without qualification from that point on, the global modernist take-over having also gained its ascendancy. With Gutiérrez Nájera now viewed as a founder, and romanticism and modernism admittedly less opposed than previously thought, our charge is to locate the first modernist purities amid romanticism's excesses, to identify a worldly spirit in an ingenuous song. Modernism as we have understood it in the present day, and in its most evolved form, is a surrender to art, and these writers chosen to expand the modernist canon are faithful to this tenet. In that the creation of transcendent art was a universal pursuit, the modernists chose to admire and absorb the beautiful in a global forum, and exoticism and cosmopolitanism came to characterize the movement. The Latin American, and particularly the Mexican, search for aesthetic perfection warrants special attention, again because of the peripheral position of these areas with regard to Europe and the fervent nationalism associated with them. Joan-Lluis Marfany in his 1982 article "Algunas consideraciones sobre el modernismo hispanoamericano" (Some Considerations regarding Latin American Modernism) takes the view that the "modernizing" of literature and culture was accompanied by the "modernizing" of society's economic base, with the desire not to reject the national but to give it parity with the imported. What was resisted and condemned was a *colonialist* imposition of the developed world's most objectionable systems onto Latin America, the reason for the artist's retreat in the first place. In the same way that modernism introduced a continental solidarity into Latin America, provincialism that had so fueled romanticism was now deemed narrow (97). While the romantic Altamirano called for and fostered a national identity for Mexican literature, the early modernists, well traveled and worldly, cultivated their talents in service to art, whatever its inspiration or place of contemplation.

The curious mystery of Justo Sierra is not how he will display his modernist credentials, but rather why his inclusion among Mexican modernists disappeared at all. In his own day he was conceded to be a prime cultural spokesman and the theoretician of a movement, one who felt the spirit of modern poetry and was the leader of the poetic generation from 1895 to 1910 (Estrada, vii). Estrada further places Sierra into the *Revista Azul* group, along with Gutiérrez Nájera, Díaz Mirón, and Luis Urbina (1864–1934), and lists his contributions to the *Revista Moderna* as well (Estrada, ix, 282). Sierra's utter immersion into the intellectual circles of the day and his involvement with notable figures of the innovative style put him at the heart and within the mind of the new aesthetic. His professional and personal associations with such modernists as Gutiérrez Nájera and Tablada were extensive. Telling evidence of his importance in the early years of this century is his appearance in a 1919 *Parnaso de México* anthology, edited by Fernández Granados. Four other authors included in the collection—Díaz Mirón, Gutiérrez Nájera,

Nervo, and Othón—are allowed one poem apiece, while Sierra's poems number thirteen and cover considerably more pages than those of his colleagues. Although Latin American intellectuals have always excelled in many areas of their countries' cultural and political lives, perhaps Sierra's accomplishments in Mexico's political and educational sectors eclipsed his literary achievements, particularly with excellence abundantly present in his colleagues' work. But there is forever the idea that from afar or nearby, avowedly or indirectly, poets and thinkers in Mexico from 1870 to 1910 owed something of their vision to Justo Sierra. Perhaps in his reluctance to publish his poems in *Revista Azul,* he could well have missed a stellar modernist position because of this hesitation to be so visible as a poet of the new style.

Sierra's poetry, full of the meter, rhyme, and form of the French Parnassians, is as exemplary of the modernist thematic as that of the most vaunted practitioner. He appropriately entitles one poem "Santuario del arte" (The Sanctuary of Art), echoing all modern sentiment that art is the sacred pursuit of devout initiates. He doubts science's ability to correct any ill and feels the weight of modernity's pessimism. In this way he becomes the modernist as man-in-conflict, discharging his official political and pedagogical functions under Porfirian positivism and retreating to artistic purity for solace as the aesthete.

Common to the poetry of the writers treated in this study is the finest and most subtle suggestion of a restrained hopelessness. Shored up by dazzling form—balanced, clearly measured, almost fatally correct—a remembrance of outrage expires into mere linguistic arrangement. Art survives as immanence. And this is why the new relocations of emphasis outside an established canon serve the Latin American, and Mexican, case so well. Traditional methods of dealing with Latin American modernism, not Western modernity, stress the formal innovations and the importance of epithet and musicality borrowed from the French. Newly discovered modernist exemplars, typical of the minority, peripheral, or oppressed artist, outdo canonical authors on several counts. Their formal brilliance is undeniable, but their ability to thread the most aching regret into the most controlled form stuns with its mastery. Taking as a world modernist example of this fusion of feeling and structure Yeats's "Sailing to Byzantium," we can understand something of what a poet like Sierra is capable of creating. Sierra shares with María Enriqueta Camarillo, among the other modernist discoveries, a penetration into the psychology of a child. There is something fitting here as well in our bringing these authors into a new light. The child and the marginal poet share a misunderstanding by elders, but the child grows and claims its portion of suffering, to be displayed and imposed.

Fanciful flight, a child's escapade but the poet's preferred mental disposition, informs Sierra's "Dios" (God), a modernist masterpiece. With suggestions of Sor Juana's *Primero sueño* (First Dream), the poem synthesizes a Latin American poetics of mysticism, experimentation, and estrangement. Sor Juana's cosmic longings are present, and modernist theoretician Nietzsche broods referentially within the poem's design. Challenging the limits set by mortal experience, the poet sees that what practical intelligence has accomplished has only moved humanity one step toward the vision that science proposed, one step away from "el mundo raquítico y vencido" (the rickety, conquered world; 57). Therefore, condor-like, he declares a flight into infinity "detrás dejando / de los planetas las opacas moles" (leaving behind / the opaque masses of the planets; 58). Earth-bound efforts at understanding and ennobling will continue, but such poor, tiny gestures they are. Propelled by his "loca y ardiente fantasía" (insane, burning fantasy; 58), the poet rises above this now-silent earth, "vieja gastada" (the old, exhausted one; 59), destined to rotate through space and mistakenly call the infinite power "padre" (father) instead of "verdugo" (henchman; 59). A world creaking with failure, where all we inherit comes to us deficient and tarnished, noiselessly rolls away from the poet, leaving him "en el umbral del templo" (at the threshold of the temple; 59). The modernist celebrant is now free, ascended to the post-Olympian aeries "con un sol eterno en la conciencia" (aware of an eternal sun; 60). The pure presence of thought and feeling, thankfully removed from known spheres, "la región maldita" (the cursed region; 60), may now seek God, but "¡tal vez has muerto!" (perhaps you have died; 60). Let there be a sign; a blinding flash comes: "Mi pensamiento audaz . . . / se comprendió por siempre quebrantado" (My daring thought . . . / now is forever broken; 61). The stars entone a hymn of thanks for all things, and for the poet. Seeing himself suspended in air, he asks forgiveness for his "infernal empeño" (infernal persistence), awakens, and rues his "terrible sueño" (terrifying dream; 62). The God who has retreated, or hurls thunderbolts and rehearses astral choruses in a remote, exclusive realm of eternity, is a modernist God, and the poet's encounter with Him is the desired one. Sierra's "Dios" takes a Western world of eroded faith and insensate mechanization into a twentieth century where only the artist can ask the meaningful, if doomed, questions.

So strongly felt in Sierra's poetry is modernist world-weariness. The sensorial adornment of Latin American modernism consistently associated with the poet's "Playeras" (Sea Songs) is much less a feature of his than his high regard for the perfection of form. Three of Sierra's sonnets particularly exemplify these previously undetected concerns: ennui and the replacement of meaning by form. In the poem "Spirita" (Spirit), only someone fleeing from a "siglo de agonía" (a century of suffering; 44) could find light in shadow and life in death. In this, Sierra's poetry anticipates art as vital experience, in which unmediated life is deconstructed into autonomous virtuality, reversed, refracted light. In fact, what is *contagio* (contagion) and *neurosis* to a world that believes the shadows on the cave wall was called "'amor' por el primer poeta" ("love" by the first poet; 44). Sierra's poem "A L . . ." (To L . . .) makes a further case for the autonomy of the poetic word that structures a world in which the only death to be feared is "tu olvido" (your forgetfulness; 45). Reading frees these imprisoned signs, and even if the poet is consigned to a lapidary death, "tu alma buena" (your uncorrupted soul) would provide a sustenance. Sierra's position as an early modernist writer is clearly in evidence in this poem in the suggestion of redeeming love, so dear to the still-lingering romanticism of the time. But these are no mimetic lovers; they have paused only to rest from "la existencia" (existence) and find themselves locked into a modernist poem seeking "una hora final pura y serena" (a serene and pure final hour; 45). For the perfect triumph of form, "Luis G. Ortiz" makes Sierra's most persuasive case. Favored by lush Petrarchan surroundings and made eternally youthful by Eros, Luis is nevertheless visited by death. Only the nightingales will continue his song, as posterity now says of him: "amó, fue amado y espiró entre flores" (he loved, he was loved, and he sighed 'midst flowers; 49). In a second section Sierra praises Luis's devotion to art, his successful cultivation of it, but counts his truest creation to be friendship, "mayor tesoro de pura poesía" (a greater treasure of pure poetry; 50). This Mexican modernist found art to be vital, a force to animate worlds, to give meaning to vague discontents, and to be productive of its own worth; art, says Sierra, gains superiority by transforming its impetus, ultimately exalting its own artifice.

If Justo Sierra, honored figure of Mexican letters, is to be inducted into a revised modernist canon for his world views and not his sheer endurance on the cultural scene, we are bound to do the same with Agustín Cuenca, disregarding, in his case, an early disappearance from his country's literary life. Cuenca is traditionally thought to have been denied his full potential. Counting modernist contemporaries as close friends, Cuenca is certainly disposed to profit from the stimulation of talented contemporaries, and to them we owe the few biographical facts on him that are available. One of the features of his poetry that most aligns him with the oncoming modernist view is a blending of the human and the environmental, the human and the circumstantial, André Breton's Nadja and the objective correlative in one early image. The need to reevaluate Cuenca's works is a pressing one and has been sensed by recent critics.[5] With his fine freight of distilled romanticism, a classical reverence for grace and perfection, and the diabolical sensibilities of the modernist, Cuenca creates a poetic world of pure form.

"Primera página" (First Page), as the title indicates, is a kind of literary manifesto in which the poet defines his relationship to the world. He invites an unnamed interlocutor to return to "tu fiesta orgiástica, y tranquila / déjame con mi mal y mis dolores" (your orgiastic, calm celebration/ leave me with my affliction and my sorrows; Castro Leal, *Cien mejores poesías*, 197). Implied here is a chaotic, lascivious, secular world, inhospitable and undesirable to a suffering poet whose own environment would not seem to induce torment. The poet's world is a place of Grecian beauty, complete with marvelous creatures and dreamy happiness (197). But the Arcadian land harbors threatening, unseen beings as well. If the poet shuns a realm of visceral pleasure in favor of his own solitary retreat, what unexpected attractions loom in this sanctuary? They are haunting, suggestive, signs of something beyond, not erotic or ostentatious. For the poet's silent interlocutor caught in his gush of sensuality, all is unrefined matter. Then let the bedeviling dreams come; there is a purity in them, a purifying, here where the muse cries. With an *abab* rhyme scheme and the modernist eleven-syllable line, the poem seems about to conclude with a reprise of the first stanza, but the final lines are not an exact duplication of the first ones. The slight change is enough to insist on the poet's elegant separation, to assert its external presence, to exalt the solitude. The first page written is the sacred text of declaration. While wicked traffickings abound in venues of profligate pleasure, there is one apart who, visited by visions and dream-beings, will perceive and experience perfectly. Alone and hushed, the prototype modernist artist asks only not to be touched by the banality of the unexamined.

The fact that Cuenca has been taken formerly without dispute as a romantic poet lies surely in what he appears to promote as a nostalgia at being left apart or behind. But there is no clearer statement of the modernist poet's *need* to cultivate a solitude in order to glimpse the pure, absolute truth of art than in his poetry, and specifically in such a poem as "A orillas del Atoyac" (On the Banks of the Atoyac). What gives Cuenca such a privileged position in a revised modernist canon is the utter ease and deception with which he seems to celebrate nature and yearn for an integration into its ebullient forgetfulness. He has succeeded in threading into his poetry the signs of negation that point to the new poetic sensibility. Of a crepuscular, nostalgic façade, his compositions masterfully lift the poet beyond regret to the superiority that living with the perfectly crafted poem brings. Subtitled appropriately "A una onda" (To a Wave), "A orillas del Atoyac" is a landmark work that clearly brings Mexican poetry to a perfect communication between poet and subject. The peripatetic *onda* (wave), like other carriers of animated matter in Cuenca's poems, bears "luces refulgentes" (bright lights) and "rosas deshojadas" (roses without petals) (*La lira mexicana,* 73). The romantic sigh is heard as the poet moans. The speaker marvels at the seeming indestructibility of the *onda,* given impetus by a sheer plangent life force that does not distinguish between feeling and instinct. The rushing wave, like the "fiesta orgiástica" of Cuenca's "Primera página" carries a brutal eroticism, a howling surrender to the visceral. But like all other drives that uproot and consume, in the coming modernist age there is an insidious delicacy, *memento mori,* or seductive deceit, termed here "la fragilidad de tus cristales" (the fragile nature of your glassy shimmering; 74). Then comes the moment of identification between the longing poet and the rushing current, whose movement is an oneiric image. The river races on to inevitable topographies, and the poet strengthens the ties to his reflected being in the river—all very romantic and bristling with the pathetic fallacy. Cuenca's poet, however, is wickedly central to his poem. Not only does he note the passing of crystalline water and see in it his own suffering, themes of romantic note, but also he alone remains as the current leads on. As the poem concludes, there is only a maniacal fixity of attention, the poet's baleful gaze, disembodied, vengeful. What lingers is *perception,* not regret. What is foretold is exalted presence—the modernist author will survive the ravages of the modern age. After Verdun, after Guernica, after Nagasaki, the nuclear priesthood, all eyes will scan the scarred earth and tell of what remains.

Having discovered a clear modernist world view and style in Mexican literature where only suggestions were allowed before and in advance of passing on
to figures who in their time were immensely popular but misinterpreted, we
are bound to present at this point a poet-novelist whose mind and literary
production astound for their breadth and mastery. The formidable María
Enriqueta Camarillo, whose life spanned almost an entire century, is the very
model of the neglected modernist. Because she spent so much time outside of
Mexico (a mobility befitting a modernist but removing her from the local
critical establishment) and because she was a forgotten, embattled old woman
at the end of her life, her modernist contributions are unclear.[6] A truly revolutionary and revealing approach to her works, anticipating a rise to higher
status among modernist authors, is the 1943 work by Angel Dotor, *María
Enriqueta y su obra* (María Enriqueta and Her Work). This critic senses what
is to give her commonality with the other freshly defined Mexican modernists
of her day—clairvoyance and transcendental insight. What Dotor's work really
points to is the discovery of a modernist sensibility where none was seen
before. Especially as a woman does María Enriqueta Camarillo offer valuable
additions to the expanding modernist canon, whose female contributors have
been limited to Juana de Ibarbourou, Delmira Agustini, Alfonsina Storni, and
Gabriela Mistral. To be sure, as in all modernist works, there is the romantic's
melancholy, but in Camarillo's case, the soulful wistfulness doesn't smother.
Her talent, and success, lie in her modernist ability to leave the trace. In her
poems, there are murmurs: a door is left open to the beyond; someone now
unseen has just opened it, and the disturbed air is still in motion.

In a production that includes various volumes of poetry and several novels,
we see the persistent theme of the artistic sensibility that, alone, understands,
fashions, recalls, and refines the surrounding environment. If there is a hope
in the modernist age, it is that a functioning brain will continue to interpret
and, in the face of grave disappointment, create reality. María Enriqueta Camarillo's works also carry her own illustrations, which are suggestive: slender
and delicate scenes of gardens, fountains, and unpeopled landscapes. In this
way there is something very traditionally modernistic in her work, in the manner of Darío, swans, and aristocratic elegance. But the stylishness that accompanies these drawings only partially conceals a bizarre vacancy, a threatening
abyss whose silence is an invitation to tumble through the symmetrical stalks
into true knowledge. Like the exquisite, enigmatic forms of Justo Sierra and
Agustín Cuenca, this formal skill associated with her, acknowledged in the
peak years of her artistic production, is the particular hallmark of these Mexican modernists, who had in mind the correspondences that give substance to
the otherwise vacuous shapes. Camarillo is viewed as a curiously pure poet,
free of the contemporary vices that were thought to accompany the cultivation
of *decadent* poetry and other experimental art of the present century. Perhaps
not an extravagant, excessive modernist, she is appealing because of the *suggestion* in her work of a world beyond the visible one. We are consistently

reminded by her work and her commentators that the retreat to *art* characterizes the modern age, art as product and art as process.

Her 1926 collection of poems, *Album sentimental,* is especially representative of her style and theme and links her closely with Justo Sierra and Agustín
Cuenca as the new modernist devotées who best explain Mexico's connection
to a world modernist movement. The "sentimental" is also most appropriate
in that it almost appears to be a knowing mockery of the fluttering emotions
of romanticism that she knew her gender to be associated with. There are no
such sweetness and restrained tears here, however. In her poems, words like
romantic and *sentimental* only establish a crepuscular or nocturnal setting;
present is an intricate web of the night that corresponds to feelings. In this,
she approaches the cosmic threshold of knowledge that Sierra achieves in
"Dios." As we view the poems of *Album* as a whole, we are fully persuaded that
a brooding, occult compulsion to assault the apparent informs essentially all
of María Enriqueta Camarillo's poetry. A poem like "Optica" (Perspective), for
example, makes clear that at every turn the poet will seek the perfect realm of
art, which is like its counterpart, life, but more comforting and welcoming,
inviting the poet herself, alone, to set the limits of experience: "Mas para ver
disminuir / mi dolor, me doy al sueño / que el soñar / es lo mismo que copiar
en un espejo pequeño / la vida y su batallar" (But to see my pain diminish / I
surrender to dreaming / because dreaming / is akin to copying life and its
struggles in a small mirror; 96). Once the mirror is in place, it captures
memory. Continuing the memory theme, her poem "Lejos recuerdo" (Far
Away Do I Recall) emphasizes that the poet's dearest possession, in the face of
the unfeeling throng, is sharpness of memory, presence of mind.

Nebulous landscapes and cloudy indecision are present in this Mexican poet
as well. In her work she uses the garden, the wood, the grove, and the path as
retreats, but these same features can also be passageways to a dark knowledge
that may destroy. Silence takes up a requested dwelling in the poet's private
precinct; melancholy tarnishes a brightened room. The garden offers quiet
repose but also a cessation of life. In this devotion to art, the poet offers images
of death, melancholy, the surprise of an unexpected presence, a sudden departure. These mortal acts are done up in a gentle, inviting way. As suggested by
the muted water colors of her book illustrations, María Enriqueta Camarillo
seeks the way hidden to the brute, listens for the rhythm out of range of the
insensate. Only the poet knows that the door left ajar is not to be closed.

The same sense of a hidden knowledge, a private suffering as anticipatory
of metamorphosis, is present in her novel *El secreto.* Her first-person narrator
is the adolescent-male Pablo, recalling the narrator of an early modernist
novel, Eduardo Barrios's *El niño que enloqueció de amor* (The Boy Driven Mad
by Love). The youngster is given to crafting objects with his hands but suffers
the hypersensitivity of a modernist hero. His family has recently undergone a
reversal of fortune, and the wealth of previous days is now being sold off.
Domestic uncertainty leads the boy to pyromaniacal experimentation. A fur-

ther twisted turn of mind leads him almost to drop his sister down a well. Forever exercising a great imagination, the adolescent is encouraged by his grandmother to be a sculptor and finds himself guided in his work by a "misteriosa luz; una voz ya lejana . . ." (mysterious light; a voice now distant . . . ; 226). Clearly he is rescued from destruction by the practice of creative art, but an illness brings him to another kind of delirious excess. Simultaneously, the father has left his loved ones in Spain and moved to a job in Buenos Aires in order to provide for the now-penurious family. Letters under his name cease, but an uncle continues to send news, and there is no hint of misfortune. The father returns to his family in Spain, and the "secreto" is revealed. Both of his arms were torn from him in an industrial accident in Buenos Aires. The threat, evil, and destruction of the machine age are clear. The son had been subject to irrational extremes and mad aggressions until his discovery of art. The fact that his arms can now replace his father's in the creation of beauty makes the perpetuation of art a necessity for life. The youngster (an emotional ingenue, a female temperament in a male society) passes through his period of torment, just as Sierra's poet had to be free of Earth in "Dios" and Cuenca's narrator had to surrender his attraction to the "fiesta orgiástica" in "Primera página." Common to these Mexican modernists is a coming of age into the cleansing realm of art, a shedding of mundane attractions in a painful whirl toward the absolute of beauty.

In this new modernist generation found to be eagerly producing alongside Gutiérrez Nájera and Enrique González Martínez in late nineteenth-century Mexico, the poet least secure in the role of innovator and undiscovered patriarch is Juan de Dios Peza. Although often treated as a poet of minor importance, in a 1967 anthology of Mexican poetry, *La lira mexicana*, Peza rates fifty-three pages to his nearest competitor, Gutiérrez Nájera, at twenty-three. A certain Fascistol takes the critic Puga y Acal to task for his harsh criticism of Peza in an 1888 article and admits that he too had been severe with this popular poet on the occasion of Peza's reading verses at the tomb of Benito Juárez (*Los poetas mexicanos contemporáneos*). The criticism that Fascistol examines is strangely out of place for a time in which poetry was aiming for an autonomous terrain. It would befit more the classical-romantic debates of some decades earlier but indicates the kind of misdirected critical discourse to which Peza's works have always been subject. Gutiérrez Nájera had praised Peza's verses in an 1885 article, comparing his work with the best of Hugo. The poems, *Algunos versos* (Scattered Verses), are dedicated to children, and it is on this basis that El Duque Job (Duke Job), as Gutiérrez Nájera was known, sees their tenderness. This delicacy and sweet affection for home have been the primary focus of criticism on the poetry of Juan de Dios Peza and have prevented the true modernist gleam in his work to shine through. He has traditionally been thought to be a prosaic poet, full of cheerful aphorisms and quiet reassurances. Two factors point to a need to seek in Peza's poems a new quality and direction: Gutiérrez Nájera's taste was unerring, and Peza's popularity meant that he had captured something that his time honored or marveled at. This is the case of a modernist who, while retreating to isolated towers, reeducates the tastes of his day.

Like his modernist colleagues Sierra, Cuenca, and María Enriqueta Camarillo, Peza studies the structure of abandonment. The wilted petals and eroded column are evidence that eternal time removes affection. Love can be preserved, but the poet still sees the eventuality of death. Transcendence, however, is possible in the survival of a flower, which for Peza is the soul of the poet living where once there was certain ruin. Blended with the suggestion of such Hispanic forebears as Martí and Quevedo and their butterflies and flames is also a romantic resignation that does not seem to uphold the modernist poet's superior courage. In a second poem, "Desolación" (Desolation), a respect for death as the only bringer of peace sets a romantic tone. But he echoes Gutiérrez Nájera in specifying the most carefully chosen site for expiration, a Wagnerian glory that hints at a passage to the afterlife of the accomplished. Already death issues a desirable call, an allure that is more than a reunion with a soul mate. With these first verses, there appears to be just a slight purifying of romantic excess. The popular poet has given only an egotistical moan to free the sentimental impulses of his audience. But the lengthy "Horas de pasión" (Hours of Passion) awaits to synchronize us to the beat of the poet as he too thrusts to the outward reaches of earthly hours to find the appropriate place for the mystic initiate.

The sixty-five cantos of "Horas de pasión," like Sierra's "Dios," are a modernist voyage of discovery. The appeal to the loved one is here, perhaps with a stouter sentimentality than among the other new modernists, but taking a collegial celebrant into the aery realm is to flee dull Earth with the hope of selective procreation. The cosmic joy at fixing an admiring gaze on the love object is present here: "Eres tú el ángel, exclamo, / Que en sueño miraba yo, / Tú tienes un sol y un cielo" (You are the angel, I exclaim / At whom I gazed while dreaming, / You have both sun and sky; *Lira mexicana,* 185). Such gratifications nonetheless do not remove the urge to know; what characterizes this poem and gives it a modernist distinction is its dialectical dynamic. Unlike certain romantic poems that display saddened lovers to be united at a point beyond mortality, this poem by Peza records the inertia of stasis, the entropy of loss, the impetus of inspiration; in short the world of "Horas de pasión" is the modern world, where closure is uncertain and appearances are only the latest suspicion. The shifting roles of benefactor and recipient, poet and addressee remind us that former certainties are questionable in the modern world. We are hard-pressed to understand who is the fortress and who the seeker of refuge.

The poet's uncertainty continues as, romantically, he continues to wonder whether, like the prized flowers of his love, his sacred union with the loved one will decline. Each canto, like each turn of perfidious Earth, seems to signal a change in the poet's attitude toward the beloved. He begins by vowing complete allegiance to her. And to arrive at some understanding of depth of union or definition of integration, the lovers in canto 17 engage in a dialogue. In true modernist fashion, truth and certainty are posited then withdrawn at every turn. What began as a gentle, detached exploration of two lovers' determining the nature of their interdependence becomes a parodic adventure in ontology. Such a challenging, decidedly unromantic and cerebral question now prompts another of the poet's unrestrained celebrations of the loved one, yet we wonder if the poet can be speaking with innocent delight. To intensify the bond, to insure that this problematic love has a chance for sincere survival, the poet moves the scene of revealing encounter to the decline of day in the West. Once again in this world of magic and delight, the hope of eternal love is rekindled. But the lover's presence is only a memory. His preoccupation is that she will pay homage to his tomb; he now fears that mortality may spoil a final separation. His concern, his wild discontent—he discovers after admitting that all things approaching this divine origin cause the pain of jealousy—came from a love born not of this world.

The poet's torment passes; the new dialectic has helped him to transcend the crepuscular discovery. He now perceives a rural abode where love flourished, but the beloved survives as a forceful memory. Through a night of insane love, the poet awakens to a resplendent morning in which the loved one is now clearly identified with light, nature, celestial bodies, animistic forces. The soul has met God in the presence of the radiant beloved, but the ensuing canto brings further ravings. The extremes of reaction that the loved one inspires, now glorious light, now distant memory, now madness, are at this point in the poem revealed to be varying and related measures of intensity that his devotion to her, as the only object of his worship, provokes. She is the unswerving object of his attention, and all attraction and defeat are tied to his absolute fixity on her as the one who commands his love, guides his steps, torments his dreams, and promises him a lodging in heaven. But true to the ludic nature of the work, he concludes the "Horas de pasión" with a sly erasure of all the aching and exalting that went before. The poet concedes that he is total illusion, dealing in lies and living by artful deceit. This is the true spiritual search of our age, expressed in the rhetoric of romanticism and infused with the psychology of ambivalence. Peza has brought romanticism to the late nineteenth century, allowed it full reign as a device to define the object of one's heavenly longing, then, with the insouciance that the age of relativism can playfully bring, admits that the search, the treasure, and the intensity are at best illusion which we choose to uphold, if only to perpetuate the dynamism of quest.

Completing the list of five Mexican modernists whose literary production is worthy of revival and redefinition is Laura Méndez de Cuenca. Wife of the poet whose work has also been studied here, Agustín Cuenca, her efforts on behalf of improving education for women in Mexico took her to Europe and the United States and led to her occupying a professorship to train female teachers in Mexico City. What is most prominent in her case and that of her colleague María Enriqueta Camarillo is that as accomplished women, world travelers, cultural ambassadors, and minority group members, their charge was to gain a measure of respect for themselves not only as cultivators of the new sensibility but also as female writers. It is appropriate to find among neglected modernists two women whose struggle for recognition coincided with what the male Latin American writer of the day was facing. As mechanization and mass production put ordinary citizens farther away from art and its sources of production, so intellectualism, to have any value in a consumer society, took on the definition of a commodity. Just as accumulation of wealth fueled the capitalist-technological machine, amassed knowledge came to be prized as raw material for culture.[7] Such economic/literary speculations are not lost on Laura Méndez de Cuenca, whose attention to the educational establishment and attachment to a literary husband would place her in a position of cultural dominance but social subordination. In her works, the modernist disillusionment of escape is clearly marked, and the return to the worldly hubbub is the return to reality that dehumanizes all beings and further subjugates women.

Her story "Rosas muertas" (Dead Roses) illustrates quite well the destructive clash between the world of the daily and the exhilaration of the elevated. One is reminded constantly in these modernist pieces that the poet, all superciliousness and flight, eludes reality not as an exercise in capricious disdain, but as necessity impelled by the will to survive. The removed and beautiful is, after all, sustaining. Equally, we have seen the inevitability of having to rejoin blighted dailiness, if only because the enlightened realm is evanescent. Herein lies the stereotypic world-weariness of modernism. Unlike the romantic, the poet cares not to invite the masses to visit the land of retreat; she exults in being there and casts baleful barbs at all who would recognize her fall. "Rosas muertas" recounts the arrival of several people at a place of quiet repose in the mountains after surmounting numerous obstacles. Typically, the narrator, seeking to put the common behind her, softens to think that, being away, the masses are tolerable.

The secret spot of repose must be gained at some expense, however. A bay is crossed, then the party reaches the foot of the mountain, and once they have found the path of ascension, the sanctified realm comes into view, so removed from the world as to be noiseless. Their retreat is one where only flight is real, where nothing grows or sits; birds dominate this realm. Like other modernist works studied, such as Peza's "Horas de pasión," a dialectical dynamic makes the narrator see the antithesis in the structure of paradise; it was gained because of flight from a place of danger. However, this seeming peril (not unlike the pleasing fauvist images that stun but invite) leads to a higher reality; tenderness grows from savagery. The faith that is overshadowed by humanity's cathedrals returns where God is the high priest. Yet the pure pleasure of solace and contemplation from a high point must yield again to the daily workings of society. A return to the public places of daily discourse is tasteless and offensive, reminding the narrator of the "rosas muertas" of the title. There is more authority in Méndez de Cuenca's work than in María Enriqueta Camarillo; her excellence centers on the definitive, refined statement, not the fiendish and surprising excesses of Camarillo. As with her modernist colleagues, there is the lingering suggestion of romanticism in the title of the work. Such amply demonstrated contacts between romanticism and modernism, however, now persuade us firmly that the central difference is one of ultimate intent. Where do these disaffected poets end up? Jitrik in his reappraisal of modernism aids us once more in finding a reason for the persistent connection between the two as a desire to be original on the part of Latin American authors, a desire born with romanticism and lived continually as a cultural reality (7).

Méndez de Cuenca's poetry leaves us with the same sense of regretted return to the life of ordinary experience. Representative of her style is "Invierno" (Winter). This modernist poet who so inspired Gutiérrez Nájera imparts the same tone of deep melancholy turned out in a dazzling formal display. The descriptions of the ravages of killing winter are done up in the best of modernist language, in alternating lines of eleven and seven syllables, with regular consonant rhyme. The return of spring signals new life and sounds, lacy skies and tuneful woods. Up to this point, the customary replacing of death with life is present, a skillfully constructed poem that catalogues the parts of nature where dormant life is temporarily at the mercy of imminent winter. But romantic optimism does not shed light into every shivering corner. Hearts themselves may never recover from the freeze; a troubled soul may so lament its loss, may so refine its suffering, that redemption is impossible. This manner of unrelieved suffering provides the nihilistic tone of which modernism is also capable.

Méndez de Cuenca shares with her modernist colleagues a high regard for the landscape. In her best-known poems, the idealized terrain, where the beloved is sought, where the first steps toward cosmic transcendence are taken, seems a most appropriate reminder of romanticism. One recalls well that the telluric appeal has been part of Latin American literature since the first chronicles recorded the American reality. We reasonably conclude that Mexican modernism does evolve naturally from previous literary styles there. What is so striking about these five rediscovered Mexican modernists is how much they revive a classical environment with sculpted greenery and a quiet and graceful balance, introduce into it a delirious romantic, and displace the arena of conflict finally into the apparatus of human perception in its purest form. Méndez de Cuenca and her colleagues truly do give such an autonomy to art that the reality of the work is transcendence itself. The referent is self-contained; connections to life are vestigial and fruitless.

How distant from the posed modernists of canonical fame seem Justo Sierra, Agustín Cuenca, María Enriqueta Camarillo, Juan de Dios Peza, and Laura Méndez de Cuenca. Their connections to the literary establishment of the day are clear; each was highly regarded and considered a mainstream author. Why did they not achieve the consecrated status of Díaz Mirón, Gutiérrez Nájera, González Martínez, Urbina, or Tablada? Sierra's renown came to him as essayist and educator, yet no poem so picks up the spiritualism of Mexican poetry or anticipates the great silent search to come as his "Dios." Perhaps Juan de

Dios Peza's enormous popularity gave him too much commerce in the marketplace of unexamined consumption to attract thoughtful criticism. Agustín Cuenca's brief life seems to have brought him only promise and not understanding. The curious cases of María Enriqueta Camarillo and Laura Méndez de Cuenca are particularly inexplicable in view of their high visibility as public servants, yet their prose infused into Mexican literature a studied, cerebral lyricism that Amado Nervo or Gutiérrez Nájera could not match. To the ironic frivolity of such consecrated figures, these two women authors opposed the transport of creative separation. Assuredly the final work on modernism as a Western phenomenon has yet to be delivered, but there is no doubt that the inclusion of Latin American *modernismo* into this epochal style is a matter of necessity. The detachment of artist from society and the accompanying defamiliarization of the art object that began in the late nineteenth century occurred in Mexico but was seen traditionally as a flight into excessive adornment or mysticism. What is most astounding about these Mexican modernists is how they continue the subjectivity of romanticism, a tradition of long standing in Latin American literature, and, quite without a parricidal thrust, refine it to pure solipsism. The new age began a century ago, and these five heralded its advent with aesthetic perfection and enduring prophecies.

With the understanding that these figures were skillfully picking up the spirit and practice of Mexican modernism, we now turn to the writers credited with broadly popularizing the new art. Because the cultural sensibility that arose in the middle years of the nineteenth century and continues today—Western modernism—is now seen to incorporate styles as diverse as Parnassianism and surrealism, it is obvious that the literature of Mexico during the same period is as varied. Precursors, cultivators of the high style, reactionaries, second-generation experimentalists—all previously assigned to separate periods—are coreligionists, believers in the art of fragmentation. Gutiérrez Nájera and Alfonso Reyes, María Enriqueta Camarillo and Octavio Paz: common to these Mexican writers is the retreat to the essence of art, the search for the structure of order. It is altogether fitting that the old designations are falling away. Gutiérrez Nájera as anticipatory of Rubén Darío, who then takes the condemning lash of González Martínez, is a false division. Certainly there are considerations of chronology, influence, intensity, and intent, but modern art, once released from its postromantic moorings, seized the cultural establishment and went its elitist way. The question is not when did modernism become vanguardism, but rather when did serious art detach itself from the mainstream of society and take its distant perch. Therefore, in seeking to understand Mexican modernism, we recognize a need to examine the nature of print culture in Mexico in the late nineteenth century (how a reading public received the written word), the thematic content of modernist works (as a rejection of a previous world view), and the place of the artist in the creation of art, both his or her role and angle of vision. In this way we achieve a full understanding of how art broke with its past and called attention to its new relationship with human perception.

Mexican writers in the last decades of the previous century, despite their philosophical aloofness, were in touch with society through their journalistic activities and public posts. With certain exceptions, Latin American writers contribute in visible ways to the public life of their countries, as befits the inheritors of the renaissance humanist tradition. Gutiérrez Nájera is famous for his stylish chronicles, Nervo for his contributions as a newspaper correspondent and diplomat, Díaz Mirón for his political activities, González Martínez for diplomatic service, Urbina for editorships: modernism did not flourish as a literary counterculture. Instead, it shaped a new culture that the public could accept or not, a high culture with a cosmopolitan base and exotic, international airs. Notions of elitism and conservatism in fact accompany traditional views of Mexican modernism, so in this way mainstream society (the masses who would follow a culture hero) was being left behind as art became a quiet music to be heard only by the select. For example, the all-important literary journals of the day were founded and financed by a wealthy arts establishment. The influential *Revista Moderna,* begun by Amado Nervo and Jesús Valenzuela, is just such a case. After a first issue published by Bernardo Couto Castillo, Valenzuela was a principal financier of the magazine, along with the wealthy Jesús Luján (Pacheco, xlv). Because of the journal's relatively lengthy duration, from July 1898 to June 1911, the modernist movement was fueled by its cultural edicts and, significantly, its economic example. This extended visibility of modernist writers made it a simple matter for them to develop and maintain a position as arbiters of taste. Together with their oligarchic influence came for many of them a rightist, conservative view in politics, reflective of the wider modernist trend. The presence of the well-heeled Luján as financial sponsor upholds this leaning as does the fact that the Mexican modernists generally supported Porfirian politics and Victoriano Huerta's attempt to reinstate that ideology. Politically, modernism was then tied to a conservative mentality, and the signal event of twentieth-century Mexico, its revolution, was not to be dealt with until a later generation of modernists, represented by Ramón López Velarde, confronted this social reality.

Growing from this conservative fixity and elitist detachment that characterized Mexican modernism is the vaunted spiritualism associated with such writers as Amado Nervo and Manuel José Othón. In these two writers abounds a religious or transcendental spirit, and we see in their poems the refined and purified incantations of celebrants at the altar of divine communication. Certain revisionist critics are recognizing in these artful spiritualists a reactionary stance that reassured the middle class of the survival of its way of life in spite of the revolution and of its still-intact and comfortable position above the revolutionary rabble (Blanco, 98). This same critic even considers Othón to be an antimodernist (Blanco, 164–165). Because of such extreme revision of previously held beliefs, one wonders if historical circumstances and personal associations have not won out over quality. For example, Amado Nervo falls so squarely and influentially within the cultural activity of his time that his modernist designation is all but inevitable. His guiding presence with *Revista Moderna* and his close association with Darío, Verlaine, Wilde, and Leopoldo Lugones in Paris grant him fine modernist credentials. Like other modernist innovators, he is thought to have understood and disseminated so effectively among his Latin American colleagues the European styles of the day (Jiménez Rueda, 176). In this way we understand once more how Mexican modernism is part of the entire Western reexamination of its culture. Both Othón and Nervo address in their works a widespread concern of the contemporary West: a crisis of the spirit, the malaise of the soul. Western Christianity and its doctrines and practices were weakened by biological and mechanistic assaults of the positivist age. To counter the onslaught of materialism, Othón and Nervo sought to interpret the serene mysteries of a supernatural world, one beyond rational perception. Art became an instrument of divination, and modernism had found a mystical transport. This spiritual reach into the unknown has been called one of modernism's chief characteristics, under the heading "religiosity" (González, 91). What Nervo succeeded so impressively in doing was to anticipate the existentialist search for meaning and being by his susurrous questioning of the nature of God. It must be said that Nervo's exquisitely wrought poems, so full of elegance, balance, and sculpted beauty, are formally removed from the howl of later modernism's most extreme poems, all shattered and free verse. But, reserved and tormented, or loose and shrieking, the anguish of doubt and searching are present in the new artistic age. The formal perfection of Mexican modernism is one more rebellion against a chaotic world. This graceful order, its controlled lines ringing with lyrical sonority, is aimed heavenward, to direct thoughtful people to the alternate reality of spiritualism.

Another discernable link between Mexican and Latin American modernism and the aesthetic that informs all modern art is the erotic-exotic one. Picasso's African masks, for example, find their counterparts in Eastern art forms used by Mexican modernists. The erotic as escape from a world of decline and disorder begins with certain Mexican poets of the period and continues through Pablo Neruda. The poet of fin-de-siècle weariness and sinister urgings is embodied in Efrén Rebolledo and José Juan Tablada, the latter considered the equal of Darío and Gutiérrez Nájera in bringing the French style to Mexican poetry (Estrada, 289). Tablada is further remembered as the importer of things Japanese into Mexican poetry, notably *haikai* (haiku), true modernist exoticism, while working directly with French models and eschewing Hispanic poetry altogether. There is a further comparison to be derived from this rejection in that the Argentine romantics denounced Hispanic literary works as retrograde and deficient, while seeking inspiration in French models. Rebolledo, like Tablada, treasured and imitated Japanese culture and like Tablada as well was given to the erotic in his poetry. The *decadent* is a further point of union between these two exoticists, having refined feeling and evasion to a heightened state of experience. They are viewed as renegade sensualists, dancing smartly to the swirl of geishas. Somewhere in the rustle of satin, the sighs of passion, and the whispers of seduction, Mexican modernism found another beat to join it to the rhythm of the modern.

Between the modernists whose works had escaped the canon altogether and those consecrated modernists whose spiritualism or exoticism put them at peripheral junctures in the development of the new style lie three well-known Mexican authors who assured the imposition, establishing, and continuation of modernism in Mexico: Salvador Díaz Mirón, Manuel Gutiérrez Nájera, and Enrique González Martínez. To their works we now turn in attempting to explore and appreciate the seismic impact that their modern view had on the Mexican understanding of art and literature. These three writers are particularly appropriate because each one has traditionally represented a stage in Mexican modernism: Díaz Mirón and the first leanings toward a new poetry, Gutiérrez Nájera and the arrival of a modernist style, and González Martínez and the death knell to this exquisite frivolity. But it detracts from all three to have been studied sequentially and not synchronically, as modernists of opposing, not differing, styles. Divisions among them are artificial ones. Díaz Mirón is cited as often as or more frequently than Gutiérrez Nájera as an influence on later poets. His influence reached Spain before Darío's. Gutiérrez Nájera himself is so completely a modernist that his long-standing "precursor" title is all but meaningless. And González Martínez's so-called rejection of modernist vacuity is nothing more than a change of direction; the swan's twisted neck after all still produces a swan song. We shall see, rather, that the three taken together make up a full portrait of Mexican modernism, complete with its postromantic shadings and enigmatic extensions.

Curiously, of these three major figures to be treated, Díaz Mirón is the only one who made no effort to write fictional narrative. Appearing in the newspapers for which he wrote, his prose works are generally short articles dealing with political or economic matters. In fact most of the prose pieces are his editorials written as director of *El Imparcial* (The Objective Observer) in 1913 and 1914. Even attempts at literary criticism are lacking, except in response to attacks. Because of his service as an elected representative, he seems much more interested in politics and foreign affairs than experimenting with fiction. His behavior toward others who appear to have offended good taste or honor required greater care and cultivation than anything but his poetry. He is very much the poet as outraged avenger, striking the romantic pose, defending his city and country against all enemies. His appetite for the controversial led him to polemics with the literary critic Puga y Acal. Like other modernists, Díaz Mirón wrote prose because the circumstances demanded it, and the tone varies markedly from that which he used in his poetry. He was a reluctant prose writer, caring more about issues than style. It is significant that one of the few examples of Díaz Mirón's theorizing about literature is a short defense of language that he put at the end of his major volume of poetry, *Lascas* (Bits of Stone; 1901). As a modernist, his concentration on language was fundamental to his writing, and in this brief note he defends his use of archaisms and neologisms by saying that his "reverence" for language has dictated this explanation. Even though his journalistic prose demonstrates a modernist purity of expression, it is to his poetry that we must turn in order to measure the full reach of his literary accomplishment.

Díaz Mirón's part in the integrated picture of Mexican modernism is to distill common themes into the new modernist potion, heady and costly, and to exhibit the artistic freedom that would lead to other modernist permutations in the twentieth century. There is a Cubist anticipation in his poems (González, 56), and his cultivation of every verse, each poetic stanza, as an autonomous unit is praised as unprecedented experimentation. As for his modernist themes, they belong to this poet born in 1853, and to all poets of the modern age: maddening beauty, nature's indifference to death, and the impossibility of complete communication, among others. His poetry dazzled his contemporaries with ringing new sounds and sensuous images of deep, suggestive color. True to modernist form, some of his works were deemed incomprehensible (the gap between public and poet was growing), and his colleague Amado Nervo took to a journalistic forum to defend both Díaz Mirón and the Argentine Leopoldo Lugones against such charges (Castro Leal, *Díaz Mirón,* 182). If the reading public was not yet ready for his metaphysical speculations, this too foretells modernism's future. The poet looks to his own dreams and fantasies and is allowed this eccentricity by the literary establishment: patrons, publishers, colleagues, and critics. Popular culture and serious art diverge sharply at this point, bringing once more the accusation that modern art is elitist. Certainly in the case of Díaz Mirón, his poems respond to a private call that his public demeanor did not allow.

This private response to the modern world whirring past him is brilliantly rendered in his poem "Ejemplo" (Example), published in *Lascas.* It is everything that a revolutionary work saturated with modern themes and styled to perfection should be. A fourteen-syllable sonnet, complete with classical references, a strong appeal to the senses, and sense-enforcing rhythms, "Ejemplo" unmistakably recalls certain poems by Baudelaire, a colleague in the new style. A putrid cadaver, suspended from a tree, rocks in the wind, its grotesque appearance laughable to the ragged crowd gathered to watch it. Its movements are like those of a censer, and as it sways, reeking, the sun climbs across a blue sky in a natural setting worthy of a Roman poet—so perfectly composed the poem, so repellent the image. It is in this that Díaz Mirón demonstrates his modernist credentials. There is order in the world: seasonal change, the regular passage of day into night, growth of plants, birth, and its beckoning negation, death. The world view that modernism brought is to mock this order (that science so efficiently presents to us) by exposing its uselessness and touting alternative systems. In "Ejemplo," we immediately react in horror to the decomposing cadaver (a vestige of the reader's relation to mimetic art), but the distance between it and a sympathetic world is so great that it appears to be one more element of a landscape set in motion, then allowed to perpetuate itself. Díaz Mirón's poetry tempts the senses only to leave us regretting that we can grasp so much meaninglessness.

Just as Díaz Mirón was the poet of private elegance and public controversy, Manuel Gutiérrez Nájera was the professional modernist roué. His undeniable importance in the formation of a modernist aesthetic points now in revisionist terms to his position as critic and organizing focus. With poems dating from 1877, he is central for having poeticized and interiorized the world around him, for having confessed to the bliss of false inspirations, and for celebrating blindingly perfect beauty. His work with *Revista Azul* gave him the opportunity to promote a desirable blending of literary currents and to tout his journal as "modern." He wore his Duque Job sobriquet well, living the role of dandified aesthete. It is this seeming disregard for matters of substance, and the modernists' support of Porfirian politics, that have led some critics to see his generation as romantic dabblers mindlessly upholding the status quo (Blanco, 54) or as little more than promoters of French culture in a now stable and peaceful Mexico. There has been, nonetheless, a constant recognition that Gutiérrez Nájera orchestrated a rejection of previous poetic styles and signaled something new (Castro Leal, *Poesías mexicanas*, v).

It is equally important to realize that Gutiérrez Nájera's work as a critic gave him an important role in promoting and defining Mexican modernism. In seeing him as a focal point of the new art, we must remember that just as he exalted musicality and Gallic grace in his poems, so he prized the pure, innovative verses of others. The praise he brings to a volume by Juan de Dios Peza is itself a striking example of the modern in criticism: his call was for eclecticism. He compares these poems by Peza to poems written for children by the venerable Victor Hugo. We recall at once that it was Hugo, the French romantic, whose phrase "L'art c'est l'azur" (Art is azure) served as the inspiration for Darío's landmark work *Azul* (Henríquez Ureña, 91). Romantic sentiment feeding the modernist current: again we see the affinity between the two sensibilities and wonder if modernism is not perhaps romanticism grown hopelessly sullen and dreamy. We understand in his criticism, finally, that this Mexican high priest of culture is balanced between the social solidarity of romanticism and the arrogant disdains of modernism. His most famous critical piece is "El arte y el materialismo" (Art and Materialism) that appeared in the August-September 1876 issues of *El Correo Germánico*. This essay makes a passionate appeal for a rejection of positivism in literature, represented to him by the materialization of art that he saw taking place in his day. The noble purpose of art—to uplift and provide glimpses of the divine—must not be lost in a world of objective clinical inquiry.

Gutiérrez Nájera's love of the spiritual as a retreat from materialism and of the exaltation of the senses, as well as his "neomysticism," are unavoidably romantic traits, and critical appraisals still maintain that his poetry is just that. His use of Greek classicism to structure his poems and to write of erotic love reminds us that the earliest European romantics, the Germans, believed that the Greek way was superior to its imitation, Roman art. Purity of form and grace in expression are the common bonds here, and no poet exceeds Gutié-rrez Nájera in respect for these poetic elements. The truly innovative aspect of his poetry is the reading of a world that is already poeticized; the poet only sees past the visible façade, distinguishes the verses, and reads the code. His "Nada es mío" (Nothing Is Mine) is an *ars poetica* of this view of the poet, on wings, commanding a universe. But just as the artist has the private knowledge to interpret, he is often compelled to conceal his secrets. In "Del libro azul" (From the Azure Book) the poet reacts to the physiology of love, the parts of passion, as he would to any puzzle that lured him, but these are not scientific dissections. It is the solitary search common to all the Mexican modernists, who arm themselves with feeling, pass into the mysterious region, and claim their arcane truth. Even in the poems that gleam with color and vibrate with movement, such as "El hada verde" (The Green Sprite) and "Mariposas" (But-terflies), there is a second reality. Things are not what they seem to be. Initial appearances are a trompe l'oeil, a vacant simulacrum that deceives the viewer with its brightness and animation. In "Mariposas" the night drives away the darting butterflies, their goodness, revealing them to be only illusions. The inspiration conjured up in "El hada verde" is false, induced. Modernism's fri-volity was never pointless. It is the last and finest creation of a single human mind, making use of all real objects, a bricolage, before the concrete slips away to reveal the eternal.

Gutiérrez Nájera's supposed preoccupation with death and grief, so often cited by critics, is then nothing more than an admission of limitations. As we have seen in other modernist poems, the poet can only go so far in laying claim to the sacred knowledge. She or he must either descend to the daily arena once more or surrender to the treasure. Let us consider the poems com-monly thought to illustrate Gutiérrez Nájera's morbidity. "Mis enlutadas" (My Companions in Mourning) represents the poet restrained in his flight of dis-covery. In other poems he initiates journeys and tests his power to explore. Here the reach toward infinity is thwarted by his own painful recognition of frailty. His ability to imagine, which usually insures pursuit of an ideal, now turns destructively inward, and he gives form to his *indecision* rather than to the customary resolve. In "Non omnis moriar," mortal life is simply used in a comparison with poetry, the latter of greater duration and worth. "Tristíssima nox" pictures the activities of night, sounds and noises; night is a perverse parody of day. With the coming of light, evil concludes, souls ascend, and peace settles. Modernist poetry is the poetry of passage, and here it is truly modern: flux and relativity are assured in our time, and the poet means to discover where all the energy is channeled. "Para entonces" (By Then), in which the poet specifies the conditions of his death, is really a kind of ac-knowledgment of the rules of the game, and in this we note an early existen-tialism. Our mortality will always defeat us, but we proceed as if we were indomitable. The creation of an alternate reality and the search for the absolute validate this poet's life.

Although prose was less cultivated than poetry among the modernists, Gutiérrez Nájera was one of the most prolific of the ones who did write narrative. He is credited with the creation of a new prose genre, the chronicle, that combined modernist lyricism with descriptions of current events. His stories are of the most diverse tones and themes, now playful, now grave, philosophical, and merely amusing. As a journalist he was an alert observer of the contemporary scene, and his eye was constantly trained on the people, events, and attitudes of his day. His prose pieces have as well a *decadent,* Poe-like quality in that, just as in his poems, an alluring appearance conceals an enigmatic second reality. In the case of "Felipe Vértiz" and "Una escena de Noche Buena" (A Christmas Eve Vignette) the hidden truth is death that comes suddenly, preceded by gaiety and pleasure. Gutiérrez Nájera's chronicles also include character sketches in which he depicts eccentric, colorful human types. "Dos y uno" (Two and One) tells of two friends exactly alike in tastes but opposite in temperament. The narrator happens upon verses written by his friend in which the narrator finds himself ridiculed and condemned. The surprise or inconclusive ending is often a feature of his stories, as is the case also with "Las extravagancias de Luna" (Luna's Eccentricities). The miserly title character is in Paris preparing a book about the end of the world but finds himself at a later point in the story in Mexico discovering snuff gathered from discarded cigarette butts. In the metafictional "En secreto" (In Secret), the newspaperman narrator invites readers to submit solutions to another reader's problem, which he revealed in a letter. Because the letter was published in a newspaper, no one would doubt that it is absolutely imaginary, but readers are asked to help nonetheless. There is a ludic auto-referentiality here that bespeaks a desire to test the limits of fiction. The whimsical "En horas de calor" (At Warm Times) represents modernist fiction as magical fantasy. The narrator of the story observes a friend packing for a trip, so he shrinks himself in order to fit into her luggage. The confused woman frantically seeks the tiny voice but has no luck. There are suggestions of Altamirano in "La fiesta de la virgen" (The Virgin's Feast) and Cortázar in "Una cita" (An Assignation). The release of the imagination in these stories anticipates the boom of new fiction that was to come after 1940.

In the matter of Gutiérrez Nájera's prose fiction, it is significant to note further that in his lifetime he began three novels and published chapters of each in journals. Not one was completed, but there is a fitting tribute here to modernism's accomplishments in establishing a different world view. The trace, the suggestion, the project are left for later modernists to develop. Also, one journal—the modernist's lifeline—for which Gutiérrez Nájera was writing a serialized novel folded, leaving this particular work without a forum. Such were the practical concerns these writers confronted. The Mexican modernists of the nineteenth century found their full stylistic liberation in poetry, but world modernist themes—the new mentality—are present in these novelistic fragments. One novel, to be called *Un drama en la sombra* (A Play in Shadows), is quite similar to Eduardo Barrios's *El niño que enloqueció de amor* in that the author intends to portray a wounded, marginal sensibility. In fact, his characters are usually women or children with a more challenging psychology to explore. He desires further to give voice to the voiceless by bringing these dramas out of "the shadow." A very poetic description of one Laura, beautiful in body and spirit, ends abruptly. Just as in other modernist prose that we have seen, the second novel fragment, *La mancha de Lady Macbeth* (Lady Macbeth's Spot), deals with a family that suffers financial ruin. The daughter and her younger brother are taken in by wealthy newlywed friends, suggested to be relatives as well. Paz, the daughter, wonders if she will be treated as a domestic or intruder. This narrative promises the most of all three in that, first, it is the lengthiest, with greater development of character, and additionally, because there is effective use of prose devices: an exchange of letters and a reportorially described setting. *Monólogo de Magda* (Magda's Soliloquy), again a psychological portrait of a troubled woman, is a study in the nature of love. Magda is a kept woman but preserves a virginal spot in her heart for love. Raúl, whose love she seeks, would be unable to understand her, and she wonders if her missing father ever could. To complete her despair, she doubts God's presence. Mental voices set up their conflicting views within her concerning the possibility of Raúl's love. Romanticism's torments come into view in these novelistic attempts, but there is too much modernist deliberation in them not to see the onset of a new way to understand human experience.

To Díaz Mirón's perfectly constructed surfaces and Gutiérrez Nájera's invitations to pass into discovery, we now add the equally refined divinations of Enrique González Martínez. Commonly regarded as a postmodernist, this Mexican poet is rather another voice in the stylized chorus of modernist seekers. Traditional criticism has seen in his poems a rejection of the art-for-art's-sake aesthetic and the so-called frivolity of modernism. Meaningless adornment never dominated the movement. Its initial decree was that questions be asked about a structure to things obscured by a pleasing but deceptive façade. Emphasis fell variously on structure and appearance, but the intent was the same. González Martínez's spiritual retreats have been called by one revisionist critic endless repetitions of the same banal idea (Blanco, 96) meant to reassure a besieged middle class. Perfection of form and precision of expression do consistently characterize his poetry, and in this he conforms to customary definitions of Latin American modernism. But above all González Martínez is the poet who, like Gutiérrez Nájera and to a lesser extent Justo Sierra, scrutinizes the bonds between the visible and invisible worlds, Baudelaire's *correspondances*. He enthrones vigilance and, continuing the influences of earlier modernists, points to a surrealist sensibility.

Art, poetry, as the proper medium of transport into the hidden realm is a repeated theme in González Martínez. His poem "Consonante" (Consonant), for example, examines consonants as impediments to poetic purity, but the verse will in some way be able to transcend the obstacle. The art work here is an act of conjuring: the word is the deed. Equally the poet steals away in "Fuente oculta" (Hidden Spring) to an essential source of poetry, removing himself from earthly distractions. Likewise in "Alas" (Wings) we are reminded to eschew the instability of life in order to behold the divine face. Something binds us to earth that we must overcome. Accompanying this desire to find the immaculate thought is the horrible burden of consciousness, a link to another modernist variation, existentialism. In "Al cruzar los caminos" (While Crossing Roads), the poet knows something remains to be learned, but there is agony in seeking. And finally, once impediments to knowledge are removed and the torture of awareness is assuaged, the poet ranges serenely about his mystical kingdom. Poems that display this idea are the ones most often associated with González Martínez and have brought charges of elitism. But within the larger context of Mexican modernism, this theme is understandable if the poet is to be the bearer of privileged wisdom. One of his most famous poems, "Irás sobre la vida de las cosas" (You Will Travel above Earthly Things), shows the refined artist listening to the silence and watching the shadow, ascending, containing in himself a microcosmic universe, in search of an occult truth. Present in the poem as well is the classical idea of knowing oneself, and again we see, as in Gutiérrez Nájera, a return to Greek principles of beauty and philosophy. Even his epochal "Tuércele el cuello al cisne" (Wring the Swan's Neck) merely refocuses the center of inquiry within the poet, not exclusively on the material signs of the world he seeks. "Silenter" (Silently) is perhaps this poet's clearest call to his fellow modernists: draw away, cloak yourself in dream, and cultivate your art. No more obvious rallying cry to the modern artist can be issued.

Like most modernists, González Martínez wrote very little prose fiction. In fact the 1971 volume of his complete works contains only three short stories. They are worth critical attention, however, because they offer a style not seen in prose works by other Mexican modernists treated here. They are quite close to the naturalistic manner of the day—realistic detail, a desperate social condition—but curiously lacking in psychological penetration or a fullness of treatment. They appear to be animated proverbs, and in this way form wins out over content. "Una hembra" (A Female) is the best example of this studied formalism. A woman, unloved by her father and mate, bears a child who is gradually rejected by its father. She decides to leave the familiar neighborhood to bring up the child on her own: the poem incorporates mistreatment and a harsh environment but is strangely distant and unengaging. "La chiquilla" (The Little Girl) leaves the same impression. The nineteenth-century omniscient narrator is missing, but there is no narratorial experimentation either. The story is so encrusted with language that no life comes through. This language is competently pictorial, not overwrought, but it appears static and composed. Further, it is modern in its lack of a sustained plot; there is story telling, but it concentrates on different scenes that are only related to each other, not parts of a coherent whole. The best of the three is "A vuelo" (In Flight), which deals with the child Pedrillo. Too ill to ring his beloved bells in the church tower, he makes a final attempt. In so doing he collapses and dies. In the surprise ending and the use of a child as protagonist, the story is reminiscent of Gutiérrez Nájera. The stories were published in Mexican news-papers in 1895, 1907, and 1908, so such erratic publication cannot offer a clue in seeing an evolution. Because his poetic production is vast and the prose pieces so few, it is more likely that these brief excursions into narrative did not suit him. He does contribute here, however, to the further application of the modernist view—language as tool of revelation, truth concealed to be liberated by the poet.

In the last years of the twentieth century, as we register the successes of the Latin American narrative—heir to Joyce, Proust, and Faulkner (modernists all) and bristling with native touches ("magical realism" to be precise)—we attempt to understand how a literature could have gained such excellence. The usual answers—energetic publicity campaigns, increased communications—are insufficient. Latin America was laying the groundwork for a "modern" art as early as the mid-nineteenth century in countries like Mexico, where roman-tic freedom and a sacred regard for art had begun to suffuse the cultural estab-lishment. So complete was the domination of this world view that all artists producing in Mexico from the 1870s on, recognized in their time or not, were in allegiance to its principles. The modernists that tradition has popularized, such as Gutiérrez Nájera, and those of equal quality but of less extensive treat-ment, such as María Enriqueta Camarillo, are creators of a style of art that continues, with only slight variation, to our own day.

NOTES

1. All translations are the author's.

2. A crucial fact revealed by comparing these two cultural movements is that tradi-tionally the *modernismo* of Latin America has been studied apart from any world-wide trends growing out of late nineteenth-century France, testimony to the neglect ac-corded to Latin American literature in general. The excellence and virtuosity now found in the contemporary novel of Latin America, for example, can be understood more profitably by setting back the cultural coming-of-age of that continent precisely to the *modernista* revolution.

3. For at least one modernist group, the new science biology held an artistic appeal, not an aversion: "There had already set in a reaction against the sentimentality and looseness of Romanticism . . . characterized by a kind of scientific observation which closely corresponded to that of biological science . . . The Parnassian group . . . seemed to have taken it for their aim merely to picture . . . natural phenomena as objectively and accurately as possible in impassive perfect verse" (Edmund Wilson, *Axel's Castle: A Study in the Imaginative Literature of 1870–1930* [New York: Charles Scribner's Sons, 1932], 6–7).

4. Frederick R. Karl in his book *Modern and Modernism: The Sovereignty of the Artist, 1885–1925* (New York: Atheneum, 1985), in spite of the titular span, suggests that modernism began with Baudelaire's obscenity trial for *Les Fleurs du mal* in 1857 and ended with Arnold Schoenberg's failure to receive a Guggenheim grant in 1945 (xiv).

5. Carlos Ignacio González laments Cuenca's fate in a 1972 book: "Antes ya del modernismo, y como un preludio y presentimiento de lo que iba a llegar a ser en

México pleno día, alboraba en un autor que ha pasado en las antologías a ocupar un sitio secundario, Agustín Cuenca" (Already before modernism, and as a prelude to and foreshadowing of what was to be in Mexico the full light of day, [modernism] was dawning in an author who has been relegated to a secondary position in anthologies, Agustín Cuenca; 97).

6. Typical of prior evaluations of her work is a 1939 appraisal: "María Enriqueta Camarillo que, al lado de las ardientes poetisas de hoy, parece dar voz, con más brevedad y finura, a todas aquellas dulces expresiones femeninas del discreto siglo XIX" (María Enriqueta Camarillo, beside today's ardent women poets, seems to articulate, with greater brevity and refinement, all those sweet feminine sentiments of the well-mannered nineteenth century; Castro Leal, *Cien mejores poesías*, xiii). Frank Dauster is more hard-pressed to characterize her work, noting "técnica y la forma modernista de sus versos; si es que hemos de considerarla como perteneciente a alguna escuela" (the technique and modernist form of her work, if we are compelled to associate her with some literary school; 131).

7. Noé Jitrik treats the relationship between art and economic factors during the modernist period at length in his book *Las contradicciones del modernismo* (The Contradictions of Modernism).

BIBLIOGRAPHY

Barrios, Eduardo. *El niño que enloqueció de amor. Pobre feo. Papá y mamá.* Buenos Aires: Editorial Losada, 1954.

Blanco, José Joaquín. *Crónica de la poesía mexicana.* 3d ed. Mexico City: Editorial Katún, 1981. Required reading for those who seek a revisionist view of Mexican modernism; a superb critical work.

Camarillo de Pereyra, María Enriqueta. *Album sentimental.* Ed. Angel Dotor. Madrid: Espasa-Calpe, 1926.

————. *El secreto.* Madrid: Editorial América, 1922.

Castro Leal, Antonio. *Díaz Mirón: Su vida y su obra.* Mexico City: Editorial Porrúa, 1970. A well-researched and thorough study of Díaz Mirón's career and personal crises.

————, ed. *Las cien mejores poesías mexicanas modernas.* Mexico City: Editorial Porrúa, 1939. A good measure of critical approval for its time.

Darío, Rubén. *Azul.* Ed. Juan Loveluck. Santiago de Chile: Zig-Zag, 1954.

Dauster, Frank. *Breve historia de la poesía mexicana.* Mexico City: Ediciones de Andrea, 1956. A useful survey of Mexican poetry.

Davison, Ned. *The Concept of Modernism in Hispanic Criticism.* Boulder, Colo.: Pruett Press, 1966. A respected and authoritative view of modernism as a reorientation of sensibility.

Díaz Mirón, Salvador. *Antología.* Ed. Francisco Monterde. Mexico City: Fondo de Cultura Económica, 1979. Good critical introduction to accompany some of the author's best texts.

———— *Lascas.* Ed. Manuel Sol T. Jalapa: Universidad Veracruzana, 1987.

Dotor, Angel. *María Enriqueta y su obra.* Madrid: M. Aguilar, 1943. A work-by-work study of the author's production.

Estrada, Genaro, ed. *Poetas nuevos de México.* Mexico City: Editorial Porrúa, 1916. An informative guide to the authors of the advanced modernist period in Mexico.

Fernández Granados, Enrique, ed. *Parnaso de México: Antología general.* Vol. 3, September. Mexico City: Editorial Porrúa, 1919. A surprising view of Sierra's high esteem as a modernist in his own time.

Gamboa, Federico. *Impresiones y recuerdos.* Mexico City: E. Gómez de la Puente, 1922. Mexico's outstanding naturalist author views the political, social, and literary scene of his day.

Garfield, Evelyn Picón, and Ivan A. Schulman. *"Las entrañas del vacío": Ensayos sobre la modernidad hispanoamericana.* Mexico City: Cuadernos Americanos, 1984. The best effort yet at bringing Latin American modernism onto a world stage.

Gicovate, Bernardo. "El modernismo y su historia." *Hispanic Review* 323 (1964): 216–226. An early call for further interpretation of the movement.

Gimferrer, Pere, ed. *Antología de la poesía modernista.* Barcelona: Ediciones Península, 1981. Modernist poets from Spain and Latin America are represented.

González, Carlos Ignacio. *Viñetas del cisne.* Oaxaca: Universidad Autónoma Benito Juárez, 1972. A fond look at the well-known Mexican modernists with an attempt to broaden the canon.

González Martínez, Enrique. *Obras completas.* Ed. Antonio Castro Leal. Mexico City: El Colegio Nacional, 1971.

Gullón, Ricardo. *Direcciones del modernismo.* Madrid: Editorial Gredos, 1963. A valuable source of theory and information on the Spanish modernists.

———, ed. *El modernismo visto por los modernistas.* Barcelona: Guadarrama/Punto Omega, 1980. Revealing appraisals of their contemporaries by the great modernists themselves.

Gutiérrez Nájera, Manuel. *Cuentos completos y otras narraciones.* Ed. Francisco González Guerrero. Mexico City: Fondo de Cultura Económica, 1983. González Guerrero's critical introduction stimulates new debate on the prose of Gutiérrez Nájera, including parts of his never-completed novels.

——— *Obras: Crítica literaria.* Mexico City: Universidad Nacional Autónoma de México, 1959.

———. *Poesías completas.* Ed. Francisco Gonzáles Guerrero. Mexico City: Editorial Porrúa, 1953.

Hamilton, Carlos. "La voz profunda y sencilla del modernismo: Darío–Nervo–Machado–González Martínez." *Cuadernos Americanos* 233 (1980): 239–255. A broadening of the concept of modernism to include later trends.

Henríquez Ureña, Max. *Breve historia del modernismo.* Mexico City: Fondo de Cultura Económica, 1954. The classic study, historical detail amply provided.

Jiménez Rueda, Julio. *Letras mexicanas en el siglo XIX.* Mexico City: Fondo de Cultura Económica, 1944. A useful historical study.

Jitrik, Noé. *Las contradicciones del modernismo.* Mexico City: El Colegio de México, 1978. A completely original interpretation of modernism from a socioeconomic point of view.

Karl, Frederick R. *Modern and Modernism: The Sovereignty of the Artist, 1885–1925.* New York: Atheneum, 1985.

La lira mexicana: Antología de las mejores poesías de los mejores poetas. Mexico City: Editorial Pax-México, 1967.

Marfany, Joan-Lluis. "Algunas consideraciones sobre el modernismo hispanoamericano." *Cuadernos Hispanoamericanos* 382 (1982): 82–124. Examines modernism within a nationalistic, Americanist perspective.

Martínez Peñaloza, Porfirio. *Algunos epígonos del modernismo y otras notas.* Mexico City: Edición Camelina, 1966. A work that essentially reviews existing opinions and theories of modernism.

Méndez de Cuenca, Laura. "Invierno." In *Las cien mejores poesías líricas mexicanas.* Mexico City: Editorial Porrúa, 1953.

———. *Mariposas fugitivas.* Ed. Servín Méndez and Rodolfo García G. Toluca, Mexico: Talleres Gráficos de la Escuela de Artes y Oficios, 1953. One of the few sources on the life and works of Méndez de Cuenca, together with an anthology of her poems.

———. "Rosas muertas." *Simplezas.* Paris: Librería Ollendorff, n.d.

Méndez Plancarte, Alfonso, ed. *Obras completas de Sor Juana Inés de la Cruz.* Vol. 1. Mexico City: Fondo de Cultura Económica, 1951.

Monterde, Francisco. *Agustín Cuenca: El prosista, el poeta de transición.* Mexico City, 1942. An attempt by a highly respected Mexican critic to give a talented poet his due.

Nervo, Amado. *Primavera y flor de su lírica.* Ed. Alfonso Méndez Plancarte. Madrid: M. Aguilar, 1971. Valuable introductory material to selected poems by Nervo.

Pacheco, José Emilio, ed. *Antología del modernismo (1884–1921).* Mexico City: Universidad Nacional Autónoma de México, 1970. A brilliant critical introduction that respects the movement to broaden the definition of Latin American modernism.

Pearsall, Priscilla. *An Art Alienated from Itself: Studies in Spanish American Modernism.* University, Miss.: Romance Monographs, 1984. A discussion of modernism's break with romanticism and its anticipation of current trends.

Puga y Acal, Manuel. *Los poetas mexicanos contemporáneos: Ensayos críticos de Brummel.* Mexico City: Imprenta, Litografía y Encuandernación de I. Paz, 1888.

Rela, Walter. *El modernismo: Caracterización de su estética.* Montevideo: Librería Editorial Ciencias, 1979. Further analysis of modernism as the adoration of form and imagination.

Ruiz, Ariel. "Reparo a la bondad de las crónicas periodísticas de don Manuel Gutiérrez Nájera." *Revista Iberoamericana* 52 (1986): 931–936. Display of evidence that Gutiérrez Nájera was racist and elitist in his journalistic writings.

Schulman, Ivan. *Génesis del modernismo.* 2d ed. Mexico City: El Colegio de México/ Washington University Press, 1968. A classic text for the study of Latin American modernism.

Sierra, Justo. *Cuentos románticos.* Edition and prologue by Antonio Castro Leal. 1st ed. Mexico City: Editorial Porrúa, 1946.

———. *Obras completas.* Mexico City: Universidad Nacional Autónoma de México, 1948.

———. *Poesías.* Ed. Dorothy Margaret Kress. Mexico City: Ediciones de la Universidad Nacional, 1937. A sound, helpful study of Sierra's poetry.

Yahni, Roberto, ed. *Prosa modernista hispanoamericana.* Madrid: Alianza Editorial, 1974. An anthology of the best of modernist prose with a preface that seeks modernism's roots in Latin America as well as France.

6

Twentieth-Century Poetry

ADRIANA GARCÍA

Contradictory opinions have been expressed regarding the elements that contributed to the development and flourishing of Mexican poetry in the twentieth century. Some speak about the importance of the political climate in the country at the end of the previous century while others reiterate the creation and publication of literary journals and the influence of literary societies.

In Mexico, a long political stability at the end of the nineteenth century enabled the establishment and proliferation of literary associations that stimulated the cultivation of the arts. The custom that writers grouped around the publication of particular literary journals and attended and exchanged ideas in literary societies became an entrenched tradition in the twentieth century. Although each generation of writers, who would be labeled according to the main literary journal to which they affiliated, developed its own criteria as to the importance of politics and sociohistorical events and their inclusion in their verses, those considered today to be the outstanding poets in Mexican literature have one element in common. These were all familiar with the teachings of esoteric religious groups that were popular in Europe during the last fifty years of the nineteenth century and had read and understood the major world literary figures that echoed these ideas.

Parallel to the poetic production of a metaphysical nature, some wrote poetry that was associated mainly with politics while others concerned themselves with social issues. In spite of the tendency to place these poets mainly within the previously mentioned categories, the majority did write at different epochs of their lives works that would reflect a political stance or a preoccupation with evils affecting society. However, all of them reflected upon individual human beings and their principal obsessions. Love, for example, was a forbidden and obsessive topic for those individuals who were homosexual. One group of poets, the Contemporáneos (Contemporaries; 1928–1931) in most instances veiled their homosexual preferences when speaking of love. Those writers who followed, and were heterosexual, chose to express love in highly erotic terms. This drastic change in the representation of passion led

Translations are my own unless otherwise indicated.

some to believe that it came as a reaction to the homoeroticism implied in the work of previous writers. However, the argument cannot be accepted categorically, for the expression of passion and love for both, homosexuals and heterosexuals, in some instances veiled a theosophical argument.

In 1867 Mexico entered an era of peace that lasted until 1910. The thirty-year dictatorship of Porfirio Díaz (1876–1911) brought "progress" to the country, and a consequence of these years of relative tranquility was the resurgence of all literary writing, as those previously involved in politics turned to the arts. Literary journals were founded, literary societies organized, academies and lyceums established. Institutions were founded such as the Mexican Academy in 1875, linked to the Royal Spanish Academy. The Hidalgo Lyceum was revived by Ignacio Manuel Altamirano (1834–1893), and the Mexican Lyceum for young writers came into being. These organizations, together with the support and stimuli of older established authors, provided an intellectual milieu conducive to literary production. Furthermore, Altamirano had also founded the literary journal *Renacimiento* (Renaissance; 1869) which published works in all literary genres, criticism, and translations of works by foreign authors. The active encouragement of Altamirano to stimulate interest in authors from Europe and North America was continued by Justo Sierra (1849–1912). The tradition of translating and publishing the works of world literary figures and of encouraging literary production through journals would continue throughout the twentieth century. Although both Altamirano and Sierra wrote poetry, they are not recognized today for their verses. Altamirano is remembered for his prose and his desire to create a national poetry conceived as one that portrayed the landscape, and Sierra for the support he provided to culture in general while holding various political posts, particularly as minister of education.

By the end of the nineteenth century all genres flourished. However, poetry became the most important form to be cultivated. The lyric poets of this time belonged to four groups: those that followed Altamirano; the romantics under the leadership of Manuel Acuña (1849–1873); the classicists in the Greco-Latin tradition; and the modernists. Of these four groups, modernism was the literary movement which formed the poets contributing the most to the evolution of lyricism in Mexico in the twentieth century: Ramón López Velarde (1888–1921), José Juan Tablada (1871–1945), and Enrique González Martínez (1871–1952). Modernism is the first literary movement (1880–1915) considered to be a Spanish American phenomenon. By 1880, many Spanish American writers had turned away from the excesses of romanticism and began to incorporate aesthetic ideas from the French Parnassians and symbolists as well as the Pre-Raphaelites and impressionists.

In search of new ways of expression, Spanish American writers read widely and shared ideas at literary gatherings and through the journals to which they contributed. These activities would be particularly significant in Mexico, not only at this time, but also throughout the twentieth century. Thus, if one attempted to list those writers read and discussed who had the greatest impact in the development of the writing of the Modernists, one would find their taste ranging from the Spanish *romancero* (ballad) tradition, the mystics, Luis de Góngora y Argote (1561–1627), and Gustavo Adolfo Bécquer (1836–1870) to almost all the major and minor figures of French romanticism, subsequent French literary movements, as well as other writers from North America and Europe (Faurie, 6). However, the individual that perhaps had the greatest impact on future generations, in Spanish America as well as Europe, was the French symbolist Stéphane Mallarmé in his anti-symbolist phase.

Poetry in Spanish America, particularly in Mexico, followed the same evolutionary path as in Europe. The modernists, like the French symbolists and later the surrealists, did not reject the philosophical tenets of romanticism. Writers from the three literary movements were attracted by illuminists and hermetics. In the nineteenth century, the ideas of Emanuel Swedenborg (1668–1772) provided a basis for their mysticism. Swedenborg's popularity stemmed from his ability to syncretize ideas originating in the Cabbala, hermetic cults, and occult philosophies. However, during this time, his esoteric ideas were not the only ones in vogue: "Christian Gnosticism and Rosicrucianism, Jewish Cabbalism and Hellenistic Neoplatonism" (Strelka, 20) were also popular. Proselytes of each group compared their concepts with those present in religions from other cultures in order to confirm and deepen their beliefs, and thus they developed a conceptual amalgam described by some as religious syncretism. Religious syncretism is the combination of beliefs from different groups and/or sects from Eastern and Western tradition. Basically this tendency to amalgam religious beliefs and even superstitions that coincide in the explanation of creation and the creative process, on the origin of humanity and the universe, is common among poets. This phenomenon takes place because it provides "metaphors for poetry" (Frye, 125).

Whether the underlying philosophy in the works of the modernists stems from Swedenborg, religious syncretism, hermetic Neoplatonism, or the symbolist–anti-symbolist literary models Rimbaud and Mallarmé is a topic still debated. However, it is undeniable that the poetic creations of the Mexicans are not as empty of ideological content as we have been led to believe. Octavio Paz (1914–) asserts in *Los hijos del limo* (*Children of the Mire;* 1974) that

The influence of the occultist tradition among Spanish American modernistas was no less profound than among European Romantics and Symbolists. Our critics, although aware of this fact, seem to avoid it, as though it were shameful. Although scandalous, it is true: from Blake to Yeats and Pessoa, the history of modern poetry in the West is bound to the history of hermetic and occult doctrines, from Sweedenborg to Madame Blavatsky. The influence of the Abbé Constant, alias Eliphas Levi, was decisive not only on Hugo but on Rimbaud. The remarkable affinities between Fourier and Levi, according to André Breton, are to be explained because both "place themselves in a vast current of thought which we can trace back to the Zohar and which disperses itself in the Illuminist schools of the eighteenth and nineteenth centuries. It is a trend of thought found in the idealist systems, in Goethe and, in general, in all who refuse to posit mathematical identity as the unifying ideal of the world" (*Arcane* 17). We know that the Spanish American modernistas—Darío, Lugones, Nervo, Tablada—were interested in occultist writings. Why has our criticism never pointed out the relation between Illuminism and the analogical vision, and between the latter and metrical reform? Rationalist scruples, or Christian scruples? In any case the relation is obvious. Modernismo began as a search for verbal rhythm and ended in a vision of the universe as rhythm.

Children, (94–95)

Paz maintains that one of the greatest concerns of Darío and most of the modernist poets was "the search for a belief . . . amid a landscape laid waste by critical reason and positivism . . . [which] opposes positivistic and scientific materialism as much as it does Christian spirituality" (*Children,* 95). The poet's search for a place in the universe and his or her desire to penetrate its mysteries, as perceived by the theosophists, is not evident in the works of many of the initiators of Spanish American modernism. A deeper understanding of the task of the poet in the act of creation within the context of religious syncretism did not appear until the early twentieth century with Amado Nervo (1870–1919). But, in his early works, like in those of his predecessors Salvador Díaz Mirón (1853–1928) and Manuel Gutiérrez Nájera (1859–1895), considered as initiators or precursors of modernism in Spanish America, Nervo reflected the characteristics of the embryonic stages of this movement. Their poetry lacked a metaphysical discourse.

Díaz Mirón, who began his career under the tutelage of Sierra and produced the poetry of *Lascas* (Chips of Stone; 1901) during the modernist period, continued with the same preoccupation for the poor and the oppressed. He also expressed an interest in religion, but it is not one that belongs in the theosophist tradition. He saw the role of the poet as one who deciphers the enigma of life, which might suggest an affinity with Baudelaire. However, Baudelaire's idea that the poet is a translator of the universe is not developed in Díaz Mirón's work. Baudelaire's conclusions derive from the concept that language reflects the universe and poetry connects that which is transmitted by the universe and language. The broader implications of the function of poetry, as seen by Baudelaire, is missing in Díaz Mirón.

A Mexican who wrote under the influence of modernism and received national and international recognition during his lifetime was Nervo. Of his poetic production there seems to be a consensus suggesting that his most important works are *Serenidad* (Serenity; 1914), *La amada inmóvil* (The Unmoving Beloved; 1915, published posthumously), *Elevación* (Elevation; 1917), and *El arquero divino* (The Divine Archer; 1922, published posthumously). The fame Nervo received during his lifetime has been gradually diminishing perhaps, because to this date his work has not been studied from the perspective of the theosophical discourse that was prevalent in Europe in the nineteenth century.

Concomitant with the culmination of modernism, which separated the artist from bourgeois society, the Mexican Revolution (1910–1919) put an end to the years of "peace" that the country had experienced during the dictatorship of Porfirio Díaz. A turbulent political decade followed, and there was little cultural activity (Monsiváis, "No con un sollozo," 716). However, the revolutionary events that were taking place had some impact on literature and the plastic arts. Although Nervo had served as a diplomat during these troubled years, his poetry remained in an ivory tower, and the conflicts never appeared in his verses. However, that was not true in the case of Tablada, González Martínez, and López Velarde. These poets who produced during the transition period between modernism and the *vanguardia* (avant-garde) movement have been credited, by outstanding poets of Mexico this century, as being the major figures contributing to the development of twentieth-century poetry in that country. They separated themselves from the existing aesthetic canon and initiated "la tradición de la ruptura" (the tradition of rupture) (Paz et al., *Poesía,* 426). This break with the established order brought about discussions among intellectuals on social problems at home and what it meant to be Mexican (Vázquez, 699).

In *Los senderos ocultos* (The Hidden Paths; 1911), González Martínez published the famous "Tuércele el cuello al cisne" (Wring the Neck of the Swan), written the previous year, calling for a change to new images and a new language. He rejected particularly the commonplace swan, which had become synonymous with the concept of "ivory tower" and escapism, and offered the owl as an alternative symbol. He defended his choice because it would convey better the hidden mysteries of nocturnal silence. Verlaine had made a similar pronouncement. Therefore, the idea did not originate with González Martínez. However, he did synthesize in his sonnet the changes that had been occurring among the leading modernists. This new tendency had appeared in Darío's *Cantos de vida y esperanza* (Songs of Life and Hope; 1905), where, without breaking with the past, the poet returned to society and expressed his concern with political events.

With "Tuércele el cuello," González Martínez, although not the originator of the call to a change in aesthetics, summarized the feelings of most of the poets of the time and brought about an end to an excessively aestheticized modernism in Mexico. Now, a literary period between modernism and the avant-garde ensues. Whether it can be called an interregnum or postmodernism is an issue that remains unresolved. Paz has rejected the label of postmodernism for chronological and ideological reasons, arguing the impossibility of speaking about a literary movement that lasted for only a few years, for by 1918 the avant-garde had initiated a new style. He calls this the second modernist revolution: "Symbolism in its anti-Symbolist moment" (*Children,* 96). This second modernist revolution was characterized by a change in attitude: "the new poets traveled on commercial ships and landed in Liverpool, not in Cytherea; their poems were no longer songs to old or new Romes but descriptions, rather bitter and reticent, of middle-class districts; nature was not the jungle or desert but the village with its orchards, its priest and his 'niece,' its girls 'fresh and humble like humble cabbages.' Irony and prosiness: the conquest of the poetry of daily life" (*Children,* 97). For Paz, it was the Argentine Leopoldo Lugones with *Crepúsculos del jardín* (*Twilights in the Garden;* 1905) and *Lunario sentimental* (*Sentimental Lunar Calendar;* 1909) and not Darío who introduced the change that González Martínez reflected in his sonnet "Tuércele el cuello."

In spite of González Martínez's voluminous poetic production, his very publicized sonnet, and claims by members of the Contemporáneos, as well as other critics, that say he is one of the three major Mexican poets in the twentieth century who molded future generations of poets in that country, the importance of his contribution is questionable. For Leiva, González Martínez's importance stems from his preference for "la sobria poesía interna" (a sober internal poetry) (Leiva, 10). The poet Jorge Cuesta (1903–1942) considered that González Martínez had initiated "an aesthetic liberation" and "a thematic renewal directed more toward valuing emotions from the past, purifying and deepening them." However, Cuesta added that he did not bring about a new sensibility (Cuesta, 99). Still, in spite of these assertions, Cuesta considered González Martínez (along with López Velarde and Tablada) one of the teachers of the Contemporáneos. For Xavier Villaurrutia (1903–1950), one of the most important aspects of González Martínez's work was his contained passion as evidenced in the manner in which he kept his pain and anguish a very private act, in "typical Mexican fashion" (*Obras,* 878). The influence of González Martínez claimed by these members of the Contemporáneos is questionable, for Cuesta and Villaurrutia were praising him exactly for what they rejected in their works: contained passion. There exists the possibility, of course, that for the Contemporáneos the term "contained passion" meant a technique of writing that veiled homosexual preference.

It is very difficult to speak of the homosexual preference of the Contemporáneos. We know that some of the poets that belonged to this group were homosexuals, and that some were bisexual, but cannot with absolute certainty say whether they all felt this attraction for men. This topic has not been debated nor mentioned in the past by individuals that have written on the Contemporáneos. Salvador Novo (1904–1974) is the only one that I know who speaks openly about homoerotic desire (see *Now*). The subject matter and themes of most of González Martínez's poetry was his own spiritual development tinged with "pantheistic" elements, and the poetic production of later years revealed a religious orientation bordering on the metaphysical (Dauster, *Breve,* 119–121). The emphasis on the religious element came about after the deaths of his wife and son, the poet Enrique González Rojo (1899–1939).

When González Martínez arrived in Mexico City from his native Guadalajara in 1911, he immediately became part of the capital's cultural life. The four volumes of previously published poetry had won him recognition among the writers of the time, both young and old. He joined the young writers who in 1907 founded the Sociedad de Conferencias (Lecture Society; 1907–

1908) which ultimately became the Ateneo de México (Mexican Athenaeum; 1909–1914) of which he served as president. Before the formation of the Sociedad, a literary journal entitled *Savia Moderna: Revista Mensual de Arte* (Modern Sap: Monthly Journal of Art; March–July 1906), similar to *Revista Moderna* (Modern Review; 1897–1911), was launched in 1906 and, in spite of its short life, gave cohesion to the group that belonged to the Sociedad (de Beer, 740). Ateneo de la Juventud (Athenaeum of Youth) was the name the Sociedad adopted before changing to Ateneo de México. Some members of the Ateneo were the following prominent individuals: Alfonso Reyes (1889–1959), Pedro Henríquez Ureña (1884–1946), Carlos González Peña (1885–1955), Alfonso Cravioto (1883–1955), José Vasconcelos (1882–1959), Rafael López (1875–1944), and López Velarde. In addition to establishing these organizations, the group was also responsible for the opening of the first Universidad Popular (University of the People; 1912–1920).

Ramón López Velarde, the second member of the trio of poets credited to have had the greatest influence on twentieth-century Mexican poetry, published during his lifetime only *La sangre devota* (Devout Blood; 1916) and *Zozobra* (Anguish; 1919). Three volumes of his works were edited posthumously: *El son del corazón* (The Tune of the Heart; 1932, poetry), *El minutero* (The Minute Hand; 1923, prose), and *El don de febrero* (The Charm of February; 1952, prose). This sparse production contrasts sharply with the voluminous work of González Martínez, but in spite of this slim bibliography, the importance of López Velarde in Mexican poetry is vast. His poetry has been described by Villaurrutia as one that elicits the simultaneous contradictory reactions of pleasure and disgust, a judgement with which Paz agrees. However, Villaurrutia concludes, it is poetry that ultimately seduces (*Obras,* 645). It can be said that, superficially, his poetry is set in a Catholic and orthodox provincial atmosphere, with the Bible and catechism as his main texts, and reflects a love which appears to be clothed by romanticism (Villaurrutia, *Obras,* 645).

Villaurrutia points out three main themes in López Velarde's poetry: different aspects of everyday life in the provinces, religion, and love. In his early work, love is romantic, but later on it acquires an erotic quality more akin to that of the tradition of the troubadours. This love had its origin in the Manichaeism of the Cathars of the Middle Ages and was described as a "passion of love (or, the French way: love-passion, something which is not identical either to passionate love or erotic passion)" (Paz, *Cuadrivio,* 116). This "passion of love" in López Velarde's poetry is also related to the underlying philosophy of his work. Paz has associated this love with the occult sciences, and he has also noticed the significance of symbols from the cabbala, astrology, and alchemy in López Velarde (Paz, *Cuadrivio,* 110). The poem "El candil" (The Oil Lamp) from *Zozobra* presents symbols associated with theosophist beliefs and develops an entire conceptual metaphysical framework based upon them.

The dualism present in "La derrota de la palabra" (Defeat of the Word), as shown by Paz, can only be explained through the teachings of religious syncretism. In a thorough exegesis of this work, Paz further explains some of the ideas espoused by the theosophists. However, he chooses to limit the discussion to a few aspects of their teachings. We must remember that for the theosophist the ego (soul) was bisexual and composed of will and imagination. The imagination (female) and the will (male), which translate thought in an act of passion, produce the poem. Therefore, as Paz explains, the poet's soul is his or her feminine half and also immortal side: "she, *the matchless Sybil,* is his own soul, his real identity" (*Cuadrivio,* 119). For López Velarde, then, his real identity is that of an artist.

As the poet of the "everyday life of the provinces," his composition "La suave patria" (The Gentle Homeland; in *Poesías completas*), published posthumously, comprises an appreciation of trivial daily occurrences and achieves what some individuals might consider the nationalistic poetry advocated by his predecessor, Altamirano. Although López Velarde became involved in the Mexican Revolution the day after it started, his discovery of "the novelty of the homeland" and nationalism was a product of "his aesthetics" and not the other way around (Paz et al., *Poesía,* 426). The value of his work lies in the contemplation of his province, country, universe, himself, but it is achieved through the utilization of the same prism used by the European troubadours from the Middle Ages. It is for this reason that Villaurrutia thought that prior to López Velarde there had not been a more intense and daring attempt to reveal "the hidden soul of a man; to bring out the deepest and most intangible anguish, to express the most vivid torment and the hidden anxieties of the spirit before the calls of eroticism, religion, and death" (*Obras,* 659). The nineteenth-century French writers Jules Laforgue (1860–1887) and Baudelaire influenced López Velarde. In both Baudelaire's and López Velarde's works one finds "the same continuous oscillation between sordid reality and the ideal life . . . idolatry for the body and horror of the body; the systematic and voluntary confusion between religious and erotic language" (Paz, *Cuadrivio,* 73). In order to judge appropriately the high regard many poets have for López Velarde's work, one need only see the evaluation done by Paz. For Paz, the poets that may be compared to López Velarde can be found only in English, specifically Ezra Pound and an early T. S. Eliot. Paz asserts that the only possible way to measure López Velarde's contribution to lyricism is by studying him from an international perspective (*Cuadrivio,* 79–80).

Tablada, the third poet credited to have had a major impact on twentieth-century Mexican poetry, is still considered "the youngest poet" of that country. Poetry written by him in 1920 was still influencing his compatriots in the decade of the sixties. Paz's poem *Blanco* (White; 1967), which may be read in at least six different ways, has as one source of inspiration Tablada's "Nocturno alterno" (Alternate Nocturne). Tablada began writing during the transition between romanticism and modernism; he shows influences from romanticism. However, almost immediately after the publication of his first works, he turned to modernism, and his importance in Mexican letters is based on his introduction of the haiku and ideographic verses that brought the avant-garde to his country. The publication of *Un día . . . : Poemas sintéticos* (One Day. . . : Synthetic Poems; 1919) and *Li Po y otros poemas ideográficos* (Li Po and Other Ideographic Poems; 1920, includes "Nocturno alterno") marked a definite rupture with traditional versification forms in Mexican letters. This change went beyond superficial innovation, for it was tied to an ideology that involved the connection between appearances and hidden meanings as set forth by Mallarmé in his "Un coup de dés jamais n'abolira le hasard" (Dice Thrown Will Never Annul Chance; 1895).

As early as 1893, Tablada began scandalizing the nation when he published an erotic poem entitled "Misa negra" (Black Mass), allegedly inspired by Baudelaire. This caused him (according to his autobiography) to promote the creation of a literary journal in which aesthetic ideas would not be compromised: as a consequence of the scandal around "Misa negra," the journal *Revista Moderna* was born. Tablada's devotion to Asia became manifest in his 1904 edition of *El florilegio* (The Floral Wreath), which included poems inspired by Japanese culture. This interest in Asia predates a trip in 1900 to Japan. The publication of *Al sol y bajo la luna* (In the Sun and under the Moon; 1918) showed that his fascination with Asia continued unabated. The most significant poem in this collection is "El poema de Okusai" (The Poem of Hokusai) extolling the genius of the Japanese painter (1760–1849) in his depiction of nature. This work is important because here Tablada moved from modernism to the avant-garde. It also contains some compositions that allude to theosophist beliefs, but these are not elaborated in a systematic manner. More poems depicting these theosophist beliefs were to appear in a book which he wanted to call "Intersecciones" (Intersections; 1924).

Since childhood, Tablada's dream was to become a painter, but the early death of his father left the family in financial difficulties making it impossible for him to pursue that career. However, he wrote extensively about Japanese art and painters and about Mexican culture and art. From 1920 to 1924, Tablada was dedicated to propagating Mexican culture and art in the United States and published some articles in 1923 in the American journals *International Studio* (1897–1931) and *Survey Graphic* (1924), a difficult task at the time, for Mexico had then a very unfavorable image as a consequence of the recent revolution. In 1927 his *Historia del arte en México* (History of Art in Mexico) appeared. He also edited an English-language journal on the plastic arts, *Mexican Art and Life* (1938–1939), printed in Mexico City, and wrote a political play entitled *Madero-Chantecler* (1910). Although he wrote many political pieces in both verse and prose (apparently to curry favor with individuals in power), a clear doctrine as to his political convictions is not discernible, except for the fact that he professed democratic ideals.

Mallarmé and Apollinaire are the obvious predecessors of Tablada in writing ideographic verses. However, it is well known that in the nineteenth century there was a widespread interest in France for both China and Japan. Tablada believed that the Chinese ideogram had the power to convey simultaneously lyricism, imagery, and sound and that by using it he would be able to express the multiplicity and dynamism of life. Although Chinese scholars disagree that the Chinese ideogram conveys these multiple meanings, the impression among many Western writers coincides with Tablada's interpretations. For Paz, "the ideogram and colored calligraphy are true perceptive representations of the image of the world" (*Signos,* 334). He explains further: "Typography aspires to be a sort of musical order, not in the sense of written music, but as a visual correspondence with the movement of the poem and the unity and separations of the image. At the same time, the page conjures the cloth of a painting or the leaf of a sketching album, and the writing presents itself as a figure that alludes to the rhythm of the poem and in a certain way evokes the object that the text designates" (*Signos,* 335–336).

With the publication of *Un día* the year before the ideographic verses appeared, Tablada had begun to liberate poetry from rhetoric. In the same year, which also marked the end of the Mexican Revolution, Tablada introduced a new versification form, a stanza of three verses consisting of seven, five, and seven syllables respectively: the Japanese haiku. He did not, however, limit himself to the Japanese model and used other stanza variations, of two and four, as well as three, verses, but all his haikai-hokku (haiku)—he vacillated on the nomenclature—shared the same common trait of brevity. The metrical form forced descriptive conciseness, while nature provided the subject matter, for example trees or animals. The haiku was "una crítica de la explicación y la reiteración" (criticism of explanation and reiteration) (Paz, *Signos,* 122). It possessed "verbal economy, humor, colloquial language, love for the exact and unusual image" (Paz, *Signos,* 122). This Japanese poetic form does not exist in a metaphysical vacuum; it has roots in its own religious traditions. There is no doubt that Tablada had a deep understanding of Japanese culture, traditions, and myths, and this knowledge is evident in his compositions. For example, the Mexican poet Efrén Rebolledo (1877–1929), who also visited Japan, wrote "Japanese" poetry but was unable to grasp the essence of the form. Thus, Rebolledo's poetry remained at the initial modernist stage (Paz, *Signos,* 122). Tablada seems to have had a real knowledge of Buddhism as opposed to what has been described as his semiliteracy with respect to standard Christian religious beliefs and traditional Western culture. Although his knowledge of occultism has been described as "unreal" (Paz, *Signos,* 126), in his novel, *La resurrección de los ídolos* (The Resurrection of the Idols; 1924), published in serial form in *El Universal Ilustrado* (The Illustrated Universal), Tablada presents his views about life, art, and the universe. These views stem from the same religious-syncretism background that nurtured his French literary predecessors. In true syncretist fashion, he points out similarities between Western, Eastern, and Aztec myths (in addition to those of Indian civilizations of Mesoamerica) in relation to the interpretation of the mysteries of the universe.

In *La resurrección* Tablada defines art, particularly cubism (1906). In order to do this, he utilizes the fictional character of the painter Amadeo, who attempted to paint the Aztec idols disinterred in archeological excavations at Xitepetec and to express his views on the combination of art and metaphysics:

"Amadeo had painted a colored poster, an essay of synthesis of the cosmic and spiritual forces that the idols represented" (*La resurrección,* 169). Another character complained that in "that Cubist poster" the idols could not be seen exactly as he saw them. The artist's response to the criticism was that what the individual desired to see could be captured in a photograph: "My picture, like all true paintings, is a distortion" (*La resurrección,* 171–172). The reference to cubism and to its significance is not fortuitous, for there is an allusion to his contemporary Carlos Pellicer (1899–1977) who would change to another aesthetic mode. Pellicer's poem "Exágonos" (Hexagons), mentioned in the novel, is remembered by a character listening to the music of the Mexican composor Chávez Ramírez (1899–1978). The reference indicates that the music of Chávez had been inspired by "Exágonos" (*La resurrección,* 274). Tablada's mention of the poem at this point in time is important in the history of the development of Mexican poetry and in determining Pellicer's aesthetic evolution.

Although "Exágonos" appears in Pellicer's *Material poético, 1918–1961* (Poetic Material, 1918–1961) with a publication date of 1941, it was composed before 1924, probably in 1923 when Tablada was writing *La resurrección,* and was dedicated to Tablada. The only book of poetry published by Pellicer prior to this date had been *Colores en el mar y otros poemas* (Colors in the Sea and Other Poems; 1921), dedicated to the memory of López Velarde. The volume that followed was *Piedra de sacrificios: Poema iberoamericano* (Sacrificial Stone: Iberoamerican Poem; 1924) with a prologue written by Vasconcelos and an epigraph from Darío's *Cantos de vida y esperanza.*

Chronologically, cubism was the first of the literary movements associated with the avant-garde, but it was not until Paz's *Blanco* that the tenets of the movement were fully incorporated into a poetic composition. The avant-garde encompassed in Spanish America an amalgam of different isms that arose in Europe in the first two decades of the twentieth century. The avant-garde movement, which was limited by Paz to the years 1918 to 1930 (*Sombras,* 206), included cubism, futurism, dadaism (begun 1916), imaginism (1912), ultraism (1917), *estridentismo* (stridentism; 1921), and surrealism (1924).

At the start of the twentieth century, the industrial revolution had brought about technological developments that affected every aspect of life. In the world of art, the first to respond to these changes in society were the painters, who in turn influenced the literary world. Those poets that emulated the painters developed such extreme aesthetic canons that they failed to attract many followers. Today, their poetry is read only within the context of literary history. This was the fate suffered by the works of E. F. T. Marinetti (1876–1944), the father of futurism; of Tristam Tzara (1896–1963) of dadaism; and of Manuel Maples Arce (1898–1981) of Mexican *estridentismo.*

In Mexico, the artistic upheavals brought about by futurism, dadaism, and ultraism gave rise to the *estridentista* movement. Opinions differ as to whether the major influence in the creation of *estridentismo* came from a combination of the postulates issued by the futurists, the dadaists, the creationists, and the ultraists or whether it basically reflected the tenets of futurism. There is playful use of language in the dadaist style in some Mexican poets. Tablada had incorporated some dadaist experiments in the volume *Al sol*. Thus, it is not strange to find his signature (one of only twelve Mexicans among two hundred signatories) in a manifesto dated December 1, 1921 (*Actual*, no. 1), drawn and signed by Maples Arce, the *estridentista* who gave birth to the movement. This manifesto was followed by other proclamations published in *Ser* (Being; 1922), *Irradiador* (Radiator; 1923), and *Horizonte* (Horizon; 1926–1927). The *estridentistas* under the leadership of Maples Arce remained together until 1927. New, minor movements inspired by them arose in other parts of Mexico, but they were short lived (Verani, 14).

Maples Arce began his poetic career with *Rag, Tintas de abanico* (Rag, Fan Inks; 1920), but introduced the new aesthetics in *Andamios interiores* (Internal Platforms; 1922) and in *Urbe* (City; 1924), a song to the masses and the industrial progress of the city. *Andamios interiores* bore the seal of the futurists with language that reflected an obsession with geometrical configurations and technical images attempting to depict the city. Yet, it was definitely not Mexico City. This metropolis had not reached the stage of mechanized development that Maples Arce depicts.

In his long Bolshevik poem *Urbe*, Maples Arce embraced the political tone evident in the works of the European futurists. He extolled Russia and welcomed the socialist ideas he predicted would come to Mexico. Poetry became denunciatory. It attacked the evils of the ruling middle class. But since the *estridentistas* failed to comprehend the basic structure of society responsible for the oppression of the workers, their accusations sounded superficial. Maples's *Poemas interdictos* (Forbidden Poems; 1927) received moderate praise, and in them he occasionally abandoned the language used previously. Some of his best verses are reminiscent of Tablada's innovations introduced in the haiku and of Pellicer's poetry. *Memorial de la sangre* (Memorial of Blood; 1947) is considered to be one of his best. Although one finds reminiscences of the dadaists and futurists, it definitely shows the influence of Pellicer.

Political events taking place internationally together with the tenets of the *estridentista* movement brought about a schism among Mexicans and other Spanish American writers. There would be those who embraced "social causes," singing to the Soviet Union, and those who continued laboring in "ivory towers." During the first five years of the 1920s, the important years for the *estridentista* movement, political peace had returned to Mexico. These were also years of great literary activity and intellectual stimulation. Through the influence of Alfonso Reyes, best remembered as a critic and thinker, both English and North American literature were introduced into Mexico. A diplomat for many years, occupying posts in Spain, Argentina, France, and Brazil, Reyes returned to Mexico in 1939, where he became instrumental in the foundation of El Colegio de México (The College of Mexico). Although he wrote poetry, that work has been eclipsed by his prose. It has been said that as a poet in Mexico, he "did not have any predecessors nor followers" (Paz et al., *Poesía*, 412). Perhaps his most important contribution to the development of poetry in Mexico was his idea of avoiding provincialism and keeping communication open to all cultures, since Reyes felt that Spanish American writers should concern themselves with themes that were of general human interest. José Gorostiza (1901–1973) would express the very same idea when he defended the aesthetics espoused by the Contemporáneos.

There were other Mexican writers at this time who did not belong to any particular movement and did not leave any memorable poetic works but who inspired and stimulated some of the Contemporáneos. One of them was Genaro Estrada (1887–1936) who did not belong to either the Ateneo or the Contemporáneos. He wrote four volumes of poetry, all in the avant-garde style. The imagery and subject matter of his work earned him the title of poet of "verde mar y luna desnuda" (green sea and naked moon), who in his last book was able to capture the popular vein (Dauster, *Breve,* 164). Vasconcelos was another active writer and thinker who during this time supported the younger writers, particularly those affiliated with the literary journal *Contemporáneos* (Contemporaries; 1928–1931). The poets that were associated with this journal were the ones that refused to become involved in politics. The Contemporáneos was a group that became cohesive through friendship. Merlin H. Forster considers that these individuals with dissimilar lyrical voices can best be described by separating them into subgroups using as criteria date of birth, early collaboration in school, and joint editorial efforts. Thus, the first group is composed of those born between 1899 and 1902; the second those born between 1903 and 1904; and the third those that fit within the same age category yet lacked the early school ties, while sharing in the editorial work of the journal (Forster, 7). Some lived openly as gays, while others chose discretion in order to further their careers in government. It is difficult to say whether all the members of the group were gay, but what we know for certain is what one of them has written on the subject (Novo). The first group included Jaime Torres Bodet (1902–1974), Bernardo Ortiz de Montellano (1889–1949), González Rojo, and Gorostiza; the second, Novo and Villaurrutia; and the third Cuesta and Gilberto Owen (1905–1952). Although in the periphery, Pellicer was also considered to belong in the group.

The Contemporáneos started working together in 1920, and their collaboration lasted until 1932, by which time several members had left the country and the journal had ceased to publish. Before the journal *Contemporáneos* was founded by Torres Bodet in 1928, some had worked together as early as 1918 in the journal *San-Ev-Ank* and then in *La Falange* (The Phalanx; 1922–1923). By 1927, Villaurrutia and Novo had founded and were coediting the journal *Ulises* (Ulysses; 1927–1928). They were being helped by two other poets: Cuesta and Owen (Forster, 14). *Ulises* published literary criticism and some nonliterary articles, as well as contributions from North American, Irish, and French writers, and dedicated extensive space to literary prose. Two projects were born from the activities of the journal: the creation of the "antinational" theater Ulises and the publication of a poetry anthology, *Antología de la poesía mexicana moderna* (Anthology of Modern Mexican Poetry; 1928), edited by

Cuesta. The volume was supposedly a collective effort, but the prologue bore only Cuesta's signature. The journal *Contemporáneos* was created when *Ulises* ceased to publish. Although changes occurred in the journal during its years of publication, the members had declared that their only goal was to "point out new trends in Mexican literature and culture" and reaffirmed this purpose at a later time (Forster, 19). The journal folded in 1931, and two reasons are given for its demise: the illness of its editor Ortiz de Montellano and the resignation of Estrada from a powerful political post that had served to protect the publication. After *Contemporáneos, Examen* (Examination; 1932) was organized under the direction of Cuesta, but a scandal brought about by the publication of a literary work containing crude language forced it to close down (Forster, 20).

The Contemporáneos was a group that declared its cohesiveness as a community and at the same time respected the individuality of each member. For this reason they said of themselves that they were a "grupo de soledades" (group of loners—Torres Bodet), "grupo sin grupo" (group without a group—Villaurrutia), and "grupo de foragidos" (group of outlaws—Cuesta) (Forster, 21). They have been accused of being concerned only with literature and the "limits they imposed on their cultural formation" (Martínez, 30). Gorostiza summarized their view of poetry as "an investigation of certain essences—love, life, death, God,— . . . where the poet claims ownership of the hidden powers of man and establishes contact with the one or that which is far beyond" (Gorostiza, *Poesía,* 10–11). Charges were leveled against a poetry that could not be understood by everyone, and Gorostiza responded that poetry was a discipline just like any other artistic and scientific discipline and that it could only be comprehended by those few individuals who possessed the knowledge to appreciate it. As a discipline "it becomes the object of labor of a minority that creates it or that simply possesses the background to enjoy its pleasure" (Gorostiza, *Poesía,* 13). A similar pronouncement on the nature of poetry was made by Octavio Paz in *La búsqueda del comienzo* (The Search for the Beginning; 1974). For Paz, "poetry does not exist for the bourgeoisie nor for the contemporary masses" (Paz, *Búsqueda,* 70). Although the poetry of the Contemporáneos does not, in general, reflect a concern for social issues, for which they have been criticized, Forster has summarized the positive contribution of the Contemporáneos to the nation: "Instead of rejecting their Mexican heritage, they demonstrated a serious desire to improve Mexican culture, literature and art" (22).

Pellicer, the oldest member of the group, had begun to publish poetry by 1914, and he is considered the one to have the least in common with the other members of the Contemporáneos. He was the direct heir of López Velarde's nationalism but chose to include all of America in his poetry. Tablada influenced his form, vocabulary, and imagery. Pellicer was the natural continuation of these two compatriots. In his book *Colores,* in which he dedicated the introductory poem to López Velarde and "Exágonos" to Tablada, he renders tribute to both. The debt of Pellicer to Tablada has been amply demonstrated by the younger Mexican poet Gabriel Zaid (1937–) in a study of Pellicer's work (Zaid, "Siete," 1099–1118).

There is a strong nationalism encompassing all of Latin America in Pellicer's poetry, and it follows in the tradition of Darío's *Cantos*. But this autochthonous element is tied to the imagery and some of the ideological tenets professed by the *estridentistas*. Pellicer did not ally himself with the socialist revolution of the Soviet Union but with the Spanish American tradition of the Uruguayan thinker José Enrique Rodó (1872–1917) in the essay *Ariel* (1900), in which he warns Spanish America to be wary of its North American neighbor. Later Pellicer used his poetry to denounce United States interventions in Latin American countries. Although he had proclaimed in "Exágonos" that he would not succumb to the materialistic-technological age controlled by science and would continue to enjoy menial things, Pellicer successfully incorporates in some of his poems the same technological language he had rejected. Instead of allowing technology to dominate his poetry, he uses it for the purpose of revealing other facets of the universe. The best poetry that Pellicer produced is that in which he describes objects and nature in the style of the French impressionist painter Claude Monet (1840–1926) (see "Estudio," in *Material poético,* 168). José Luis Martínez calls his poetry a mixture of sensuality and joy. The combination of these elements with nature and great American themes—description of the land, heros like Bolivar, patriotism, praise of Indian cultures—has led to his being called the poet of the "tropics." The later works of Pellicer show a preoccupation with death, which had been a main theme in the work of the Contemporáneos, and a search for God. Since his very early work, Pellicer used in his poetry many images that could be interpreted to belong to the hermetic-occult tradition. Both López Velarde and Tablada were familiar with theosophist works and had a knowledge of occult teachings. Thus, it is not strange to discover that Pellicer, a disciple and poetic equal of his compatriots, was familiar with some literature on the subject. His affirmation of his belief in Christ and Christianity, found in a prologue to a series of poems (inspired by the Nativity scene organized every year by his mother in their house), does not invalidate the possibility of finding a Rosicrucian connection to the evolution of his aesthetics.

Gorostiza has been called the least avant-garde of the Contemporáneos (Dauster, *Breve,* 153) and the one closest to the Spanish literary tradition. A slim volume of poetry entitled *Poesía* (Poems), first published in 1964, contains what appears to be his entire poetic production to that date: *Canciones para cantar en las barcas* (Songs to Be Sung in Boats; 1925), *Del poema frustrado* (Of the Frustrated Poem), and *Muerte sin fin* (Death without End; 1939). He left incomplete another extensive poem, "El semejante a sí mismo" (The One Similar to Himself). In his first book, *Canciones,* Gorostiza is closest to the ballads and songs of the Spanish seventeenth-century poet Luis de Góngora. Like Pellicer, his contemporary, Gorostiza was attracted to the sea; yet Gorostiza's sea is the key to his poetic world. The sea replaced the moon of the symbolists and assumed the attributes of the moon of esoteric tradition.

In *Canciones* and his following work, *Del poema frustrado,* Gorostiza continued to develop his own system of symbols that expressed his aspiration to attain knowledge. In this last work, one may find a series of metaphors that are understandable within the context of the esoteric tradition and that express the mysteries of the universe.

Gorostiza's *Muerte sin fin* has been placed within the tradition of Góngora's *Soledades* (Solitudes; 1636) and *Primero sueño* (First Dream; 1690) by Sor Juana Inés de la Cruz. Later, his models were "Nervo, González Martínez, López Velarde" (Gorostiza, *Poesía,* 14). In his prologue to *Poesía,* Gorostiza does not include Tablada, but his poem "Luciérnagas" (Fireflies) pays tribute to his compatriot by reelaborating some of the imagery and ideology of Tablada's *Li Po.* When Nervo published his *Juana de Asbaje* (1910), he rekindled among the Contemporáneos interest in the work of this seventeenth-century poet. Villaurrutia edited Sor Juana's *Sonetos* (Sonnets) in 1931 and in 1940 *Las endechas* (Doleful Songs) (Paz, *Sor Juana,* 365). Her influence is evident in Cuesta's conceit-driven sonnets and in Villaurrutia's "Décimas" (Ten-line Stanzas; 1941, in *Obras,* 79–82). The influence on Gorostiza was even more important, for he shared with Sor Juana the same interest in writers associated with esoteric traditions. The work of Sor Juana has shown that she had a knowledge of the cabbala, alchemy, and hermetic Neoplatonism that came from reading the work of the German Jesuit priest Athanasius Kircher. In Kircher one finds three opposite strains of thought: "the syncretistic Catholicism exactly as represented in the seventeenth century by the Jesuits, the 'Egyptian' Hermetic Neoplatonism inherited from the Renaissance, and the new astronomical and physical concepts and discoveries" (Paz, *Sor Juana,* 238). It is not superfluous to reiterate that Gorostiza probably had a model in his compatriot Sor Juana when he wrote *Muerte sin fin.* By the time Gorostiza arrived in London to occupy a post at the Mexican Embassy (1927–1928) he had knowledge of theosophist and occult writers. While in London, he became more familiarized with occult traditions through the Society of the Golden Dawn and the work of William Butler Yeats, a writer who had also developed within occult tradition his own system for explaining the cosmos (Mansour 141–156). The importance of the cabbala and of the cabbala in esoteric tradition, as well as in *Muerte sin fin,* has already been studied by numerous critics. In "José Gorostiza y la Cábala" (José Gorostiza and the Cabbala) Mónica Mansour traces the history of *The Zohar* (the key text for cabbalistic studies) from the thirteenth century and its importance among different esoteric groups, such as Masons and Rosicrucians, and in the works of William Blake and Yeats. She also indicates how *The Zohar* becomes one of the sources for Gorostiza's conception of the cosmos.

For José Joaquín Blanco, *Muerte* attempts to "crystallize an organic vision of the world" in the same manner as Yeats, Pound, and Eliot had done. *Muerte* is open to multiple and simultaneous readings as a religious text, as a philosophical text, as a biographical text of the poet's idea on poetry, and as a musical text in which a symphonic movement of perceptions takes place

(Blanco, 154). There is no doubt whatsoever that *Muerte* is the best example of a poetic tradition in Mexico that is firmly rooted in the same religious-syncretism tradition that molded the troubadours. In Mexico, as in Europe, writers, particularly poets, joined beliefs from Christian Gnosticism and Rosicrucianism, the Jewish cabbala and Neoplatonism. To this they added elements from Eastern religions. The religion of the troubadours was an amalgam of European and Eastern beliefs, whereas the Mexicans went one step further by also including some of the beliefs of the Indian cultures of Mexico. Tablada will do this and so will Paz.

Gorostiza left a limited poetic production, but it secured him a distinguished place in Mexican literature and Mexican poetry. He has been placed in the same category as T. S. Eliot, Yeats, Pound, Paul Valéry—a deserved honor. He never wrote narrative prose, and his critical essays are sparse. His most important essays were on what became a very acrimonious polemic on the subject of the value of literature and whether "nationalistic art" was of greater merit than one that concerned itself with human nature. The same subject matter would be the topic of his other reviews and articles. Gorostiza's opinions on the matter of aesthetics are important, for they reveal the new trends in Mexican literature, particularly poetry.

Villaurrutia was another member of the Contemporáneos who left a very limited poetic production, but he did write plays and a considerable number of critical essays and reviews (more than Gorostiza, but not as many as Torres Bodet). Forster has provided a concise summary of Dauster's division of Villaurrutia's major poetic works. One may separate his production into three distinct categories, each corresponding to one of his major collections: *Reflejos* (Reflections; 1928)—an objective picture of the world; *Nostalgia de la muerte* (Nostalgia for Death; 1938)—such objectivity left for solipsism; and *Canto a la primavera* (Song to Spring; 1948)—an anguish of death replaced by anguish of the unsuccessful lover (Forster, 83). The salient characteristic of his poetic work may be summarized by Villaurrutia's own description of poetry: "Difficult game, of irony and intelligence" (Villaurrutia, *Obras,* xi). The poetic compositions of *Reflejos* continue themes and imagery present in the early works that appeared in *Ocho poetas* (Eight Poets; 1923). His most important work, *Nostalgia,* contains all the major themes of his poetry: melancholy, nostalgia, loneliness, anguish to understand the contradictory nature of being (humanity is only a dream of someone else), existence, and the contradiction between life and death, with the realization that death only reaffirms life and that one cannot exist without the other (Rodríguez, "Fondo," 1119–1128). Villaurrutia says that death is "a country to which one returns," and in *Nostalgia* death is seen in this manner as something already known (*Obras,* 771). In a discussion of López Velarde's work, Villaurrutia indicates that Mexican poetry is characterized by "melancholy, . . . sadness, . . . circumspect and powerful weeping," as well as death (*Obras,* 771). The theme of death, although a constant topic in literature, reappeared in Mexican poetry during his time "perhaps because at times like the ones in which we are currently living, death is the only thing that cannot be taken away from humanity; you can take away fortune, life, illusions, but death, who is going to take it away?" (*Obras,* 771).

The three main themes in his work—love, night, and death—"are born from the testimony of the senses, but they become anguished and tragic when intelligence has bared them" (Martínez, 35). His love for other men and anguish for the need to keep it hidden is clearly expressed in his "Nocturnos" (Nocturnes), particularly "Nocturno de los ángeles" (Nocturne of the Angels). In an essay entitled "Memoir" that circulated in Spanish in Mexico but has only been published in English translation in the collection *Now the Volcano: An Anthology of Latin American Gay Literature* (1979), Novo reveals that the individual to whom "Nocturno de los ángeles" is dedicated, Agustín Fink, was a particular favorite among gays because of his physical attributes (25). Love and night were themes that became intertwined in the poetry, thus reflecting the lifestyle that had to be kept hidden for fear of the condemnation of society. Of these three themes, death became for Villaurrutia his primary obsession, for he considered it to be tied to life (Villaurrutia, *Obras,* xv). Although not a "Great Poet" (Blanco, 174), Villaurrutia left to younger poets an invaluable legacy on the importance of the "rigour of the word" (Martínez, 36).

It has been said that Juan Ramón Jiménez (1881–1958) was a major influence on many of the members of the Contemporáneos, particularly "Villaurrutia, Gorostiza and Gilberto Owen" (Cuesta, 19). Yet, Gorostiza's work does not reflect the presence of the Spaniard's influence. The source of his questioning of the origin and nature of God, the cosmos, and poetic inspiration is rooted in the ancient tradition of religious syncretism that dates back to the Middle Ages. Villaurrutia's poetry, however, definitely bears the stamp of Jiménez, as well as that of Sor Juana Inés de la Cruz. He was attracted also by López Velarde, whom he described as a "nocturnal" poet. With López Velarde, "the moment begins when Mexican poetry becomes filled with shadows, darkness and gloom. And López Velarde starts becoming a nocturnal poet. The feeling of the evening makes its appearance" (Villaurrutia, *Obras,* 771). Villaurrutia was also familiar with the works of such French writers as Jean Cocteau (1889–1963), Jules Supervielle (1884–1960), and Jean Giraudoux (1882–1944). He went as far as to paraphrase one of Supervielle's poems in his own composition "Nocturno de la estatua" (Nocturne of the statue).

Torres Bodet, a classmate of Villaurrutia and a member of the Contemporáneos, was a prolific writer, educator, and diplomat. He wrote poetry, narrative prose, critical essays, speeches, travel notes, and a book of remembrances. His literary production includes "fourteen books of poetry, seven of novels and short stories, nine of essays and criticism" (Carballo, 7). Sonja Karsen has separated Torres Bodet's poetic production into three separate periods. The first includes his works *Fervor* (1918), *Canciones* (Songs; 1922), *El corazón delirante* (The Impassioned Heart; 1922), *Los días* (The Days; 1923), *Nuevas canciones* (New Songs; 1923), *Poemas* (Poems; 1924), and *Biombo* (Folding Screen; 1925). The second period is composed of what has been called his mature poetry: *Destierro* (Exile; 1930) and *Cripta* (Crypt; 1937). The last one encompasses *Sonetos* (Sonnets; 1949), *Fronteras* (Frontiers; 1954), *Sin tregua* (No Truce; 1957), and *Trébol de cuatro hojas* (Four-Leaf Clover; 1958) (in Torres Bodet, *Versos y prosas,* 32–42).

The most recurrent themes in Torres Bodet's poetic works are the search for identity and the desire to communicate with others, loneliness, death tied to a preoccupation with the passage of time, and love. In work previous to 1932, a nationalistic theme appeared with a description of the essence of Mexico City as well as an occasional yearning for rustic life. In *Canciones* and *Nuevas canciones* the love theme was continued, with the Mexican landscape still present. *Destierro* brings a total separation from the Mexican atmosphere, and in *Biombo* an Asian theme predominates. In this collection Torres Bodet utilizes the synthetic poetry and haiku introduced by Tablada to create what are considered excellent examples of the form, especially when one takes into account that this style was in vogue at the time. Torres Bodet's poetic publications after his marriage in 1929 became particularly hermetic. The important theme in *Sin tregua* is the anguish and despair of an individual that chose to live a lie. Ultimately, Torres Bodet committed suicide. Novo suggested in his "Memoir" that an intimate relationship existed between Torres Bodet and Ortiz de Montellano, as well as others. However, Novo tells us that by the time Torres Bodet became secretary to Vasconcelos during the latter's tenure as chancellor of the National Autonomous University of Mexico, Torres Bodet busied himself "inventing and developing his persona" (37).

Torres Bodet's distinguished career as an educator began when he became secretary to Vasconcelos in 1921. He subsequently occupied diverse posts: for example, he was placed in charge of the Department of Libraries and served as professor of French literature for four years. By 1928 he conceived the idea of publishing a journal that would disseminate current literary ideas throughout the country. His former classmates González Rojo and Ortiz de Montellano, among others, offered their services as editors, and *Contemporáneos* was created (Torres Bodet, *Versos y prosas,* 20–21). That same year, Torres Bodet published a volume of literary criticism that included essays that had been written for the journal. The collection bore the name of the journal and demonstrated Torres Bodet's vast knowledge of literature, both ancient and modern (Martínez, 35).

Ortiz de Montellano assumed responsibility for *Contemporáneos* after the ninth issue, becoming its sole editor. Aside from this work, he had previously collaborated with Torres Bodet in *La Falange* and later in the creation of *Cuadernos Americanos* (American Notebooks; 1942–). In 1941 he edited *Letras de México* (Mexican Letters; 1937–1947). His poetic production consisted of four books: *Avidez* (Covetousness; 1921), *El trompo de siete colores* (The Spinning Top of Seven Colors; 1925), *Red* (Net; 1928), and, posthumously, *Sueño y poesía* (Dream and Poetry; 1952) (Forster, 124). Love and religion were the themes of his first compositions. However, in poems published in *La Falange,* he added Mexican subject matter as well as politics and topics of interest to children. In *El trompo* the love theme continues, but there are a number of poems that capture the Mexican atmosphere, in a symbolic description of Guadalajara or scenes and landscapes of the country. There are also poems that reminisce about Ortiz de Montellano's youth, as well as an occasional composition in which he speaks about his ideas on poetry (58). The language and imagery employed in this poem recall those used by the Cuban poet José Martí (1853–1895) in *Versos sencillos* (Simple Verses; 1891). The compositions of *El trompo* have many elements in common with the works published in 1925 by his friends Pellicer, Gorostiza, and Villaurrutia.

Ortiz de Montellano turned in *Red* to prose poetry, and along with these experiments he developed the themes that would be of greatest significance for him: the individual's constant dialogue with life and death and the world of dreams. His sonnet "Muerte de cielo azul" (Death of Blue Sky; 1937), collected in his posthumous work, *Sueño,* is considered his most perfect work. Although death is the main theme of this book, in his poem "Himno a Hipnos" (Hymn to Hypnos), to the god of dreams, he introduces the theme of dreams that would reappear in his other poems and narrative. Some of Ortiz de Montellano's prose narrations were collected also in *Cinco horas sin corazón* (Five Hours without a Heart; 1940). He also adapted Indian poems and composed dramatic fantasies based on Maya themes that were included in *El sombrerón* (The Top Hat; 1946). He completed a study on Nervo and a history of Indian and colonial literature (Martínez, 32–33).

Novo is another member of the Contemporáneos who cultivated every genre—drama, short story, novel, essay, chronicle, poetry—and he also contributed articles to the newspapers. His interest in the theatre can be traced back to his early twenties when he was cofounder of the theatre Ulises (1927) with Villaurrutia, as well as of the journal *Ulises*. Although he started his literary career with "Poemas de adolescencia" (Poems of Youth; 1918–1923) and published the volume *XX Poemas* (Twenty Poems; 1925) (both in *Nuevo Amor*) in his mature years, he concentrated on the theatre: directing, adapting, and translating plays. Novo's relationship with the different political figures in power had an impact on the subject matter that he chose for his poetry, for he was willing to use his pen for favors. He was not treated well by the Calles and Cárdenas regimes. However, he submissively accepted their shabby treatment. Under the rule of Díaz Ordaz, his tacit approval in the repression of a student movement confirmed his image "of being the reactionary and mercenary writer, capable of demanding payment for his brilliant service for the worst causes" (Blanco, 166). However, in some of his later poems, for example "Seamen Rhymes" (in *Nuevo amor*), written partially in English, he rebelled against a nationalistic trend current at the time. Aside from writing "hypocritically" about his country, he also spoke about "good manners, family morality." For this, society remunerated him with money and by accepting his life-style (Blanco, 168–169). This life-style, euphemistically described as flamboyant, was Novo's open homosexuality. In his "Memoir," Novo talks about his amorous experiences as a gay in Mexico City from 1920 to approximately 1940. In this autobiographical sketch, Novo speaks also about other important personalities of the time: Xavier Villaurrutia—with whom he shared a dwelling where both could take their paramours—Genaro Estrada, and Pedro Henríquez Ureña. According to Novo, Henríquez Ureña refused to accept his own personal homosexuality. When Henríquez Ureña married, Novo tells us, a rumor was attibuted to him, Novo, of having "prayed aloud: 'Lord, take care of him for me; protect him, Lord, for what on earth is he going to do with a woman?'" (*Now*, 42–43).

In spite of Novo's willingness to accommodate the wishes of those in power by writing for special causes (thus compromising his pen), his poetry, particularly *Nuevo amor* (New Love; 1933), received positive reviews. Of the Contemporáneos poets, Novo is considered one of the most interesting, with true poetic insights, and his love poems are thought to be of the highest quality. However, it has been said that in general he chose to hide behind humor and irony, marring the lyricism of his compositions. José Luis Martínez has synthesized the value of Novo's work: "If as a poet he renounced sentimental confession, as a writer of prose he has discarded all those rhetorical embellishments, conquering instead one of the styles with greatest verbal economy, of more universal effectiveness" (Martínez, 37).

Gilberto Owen is the member of the Contemporáneos who has been characterized as the anti-intellectual of the group. However, cultural allusions in his poetry reveal that the epithet does not fit him well. He published two books in editorial houses outside the country: *Línea* (Line; 1930) and *Perseo vencido* (Perseus Defeated; 1948). Jaime García Terrés in *Poesía y alquimía: Los tres mundos de Gilberto Owen* (Poetry and Alchemy: The Three Worlds of Gilberto Owen; 1980) analyzes in detail the long poem "Sinbad el varado" (Sinbad Aground) from *Perseo vencido* and shows the vast knowledge Owen possessed about hermetic and occult philosophies, which places him within the same tradition of religious syncretism of many of his compatriots.

Owen's poetry has been called an aspect of Villaurrutia's work: "the loneliness of an exacerbated and clandestine love at night in the streets of an enemy city. Villaurrutia fused this theme in a more audacious totality: Owen took the parcel of desolation and carried it further within himself, obsessively to its more bitter consequences" (Blanco, 191). For Owen, homosexual love is permeated with a sense of guilt, a legacy of his Catholic upbringing, and this is what distinguishes him from Villaurrutia, who never cared about theology: "For Owen, clandestine love was not paradise; it was outside God" (Blanco, 192). Since Owen lived part of his life outside Mexico, his work did not have wide circulation there. During his lifetime, he was known in Mexico only through the sporadic publication of his poems in journals and newspapers.

Cuesta, the poet who became the spokesman for the Contemporáneos, is best remembered for the previously mentioned *Antología de la poesía mexicana moderna*. When it appeared, it was not positively received and was particularly criticized for excluding poets like Gutiérrez Nájera, who were sacred at the time. A polemic ensued, and a phrase was coined to describe the book, using a play of words on Cuesta's name (costs): "La *Antología* vale lo que Cuesta," or the *Anthology* is worth what it Costs (Cuesta, 21). Cuesta's comments on the works of the members of his own group reflect his value as a critic for his own generation and those that followed. Ironically, he said: "The Mexican reality of this group of young writers has been its abandonment, and they have not complained, nor have they pretended to falsify it: it has allowed them to be the way they are. It is marvelous how Pellicer *deceives our landscape;* how Ortiz de Montellano *deceives our folklore;* how Salvador Novo *deceives our customs;* how Xavier Villaurrutia *deceives his admirable and dangerous anxiety toward everything that surrounds him;* how José Gorostiza *deceives himself;* how Gilberto Owen *deceives his best friend*" (Monsiváis, *Poesía,* 32).

Cuesta's entire poetic production (twenty-eight poems) appeared posthumously in the collection *Poesía* (Poetry; 1958). Although a "good writer" because of his culture, intelligence, and style, his poetry has received negative reviews for his use of improper grammatical constructions and his inability to handle metrical forms. These flaws contributed to the obscurity of his verses. Even though he treated the same themes that had preoccupied his friends, he was unable to communicate his ideas. Thus, "one cannot really tell what it was that he investigated in his poems" (Blanco, 194).

The Contemporáneos left an important legacy to Mexican letters in general and in particular to Mexican poetry. They definitely established the tradition of literary journals that began at the end of the nineteenth century, introduced North American and English literature to Mexico by publishing translations of works by T. S. Eliot and St. John Perse (although a review of the journal does not reveal an excessive number of such translations), adopted and adapted themes and language internationally current, while at the same time they maintained and promoted a tradition of philosophical inquiry dating back to their compatriot Sor Juana Inés de la Cruz. In their poetry, the metaphysical would proceed from varied sources: from religious syncretism (already present in some of their predecessors) and from the ideology they perceived to be latent in world writers (for example, Juan Ramón Jiménez). Some would cultivate the nationalistic theme, either in concrete terms (with allusions to the revolution, heroes, or a specific national atmosphere, in the tradition of López Velarde), while at the same time others portrayed lyrically a particular landscape. They moved toward eliminating the distinction between prose and verse, cultivating prose as poetry, a lesson they learned from the avant-garde. Although Tablada had an impact on the development of their language, imagery, and conciseness of expression, they did not experiment widely with structural forms, preferring established metrical patterns, especially the sonnet form, for their compositions. It would not be until the next generation of poets, gathered around the journal *Taller* (Workshop; 1938–1941), that the lessons learned in Tablada, as well as other Mexican authors, would be felt.

Taller provided cohesion to the generation of poets that succeeded the Contemporáneos. This group included Paz, Efraín Huerta (1914–), Alberto Quintero Alvarez (1914–1944), Neftalí Beltrán (1916–), Rafael Solana (1915–), and others born around 1914. Prior to collaboration in *Taller,* these poets had contributed to the literary journals *Barandal* (Balustrade; 1931–1932) and *Cuadernos del Valle de México* (Notebooks of the Valley of Mexico; 1933–1934), which Paz had founded and edited. Although *Taller* was originally conceived and sponsored by Solana, Paz assumed the task of editing it after the fourth issue.

The most important member of the group was Paz. He has stated that, in a nebulous manner, the group identified history and poetry as their main concerns. Like their predecessors the Contemporáneos, they met in coffee houses, attended art exhibits, concerts, conferences, and experimental theatre productions (Paz, *Sombras,* 95). They inherited from the Contemporáneos a sense of the term "modernity," which they soon modified, and they shared with them some aesthetic values and the feeling of being isolated from society. The one element that distinguished these individuals from the previous group was their interest in politics. As a consequence of this concern, they participated actively in rallies devoted to leftist ideologies.

Initially, the members were attracted by Marxist thought and related offshoots originating in Russia, but the alliance between Joseph Stalin and Adolf Hitler eventually led some to abandon Marxism. The Spanish Civil War (1936–1939) and the beginning of World War II (1939) were international events that made them redefine their aesthetic canon. Some of the early poems of the Taller group echoed the nationalism and social realism that were in vogue. A few members refused to use poetry as a political weapon. Still, although the Taller poets felt close to the Contemporáneos, the futurists who were still active were promoting the marriage of politics and art, with Russia serving as the model of a progressive society. The two individuals recognized as the outstanding poets of the time were Paz and Huerta. The subject matter of their poems provides the best illustration of the ideological split that occurred within the group, with Huerta choosing to write primarily compositions of a sociopolitical nature. The issue of the marriage of politics and art and whether the choice of subject matter determines the quality of a poetic composition is an issue still debated in Mexico.

Klaus Müller-Bergh summarized the aesthetic tenets of the *Taller* writers, formulated by Paz, as being: (1) poetry preoccupied with language, which meant searching for the word that could not be limited to any method of expression; (2) poetry seen as a vital activity, with love and poetry appearing as the two faces of the same reality, driving the individual both to recover the Edenic self prior to the Fall and to reach the Other side; (3) poetry with the dual task of changing humanity and society and achieving this through the simple act of creation, the poem considered to be by its very nature a revolutionary act—for most of these poets love, poetry, and revolution were synonymous—; and (4) the affinity with the Spanish mystics, the surrealists, D. H. Lawrence, and some German and English romantics, as well as other contemporary poets writing in Spanish whose ideas coincided with theirs (in Roggiano, ed., 56–57).

From the group, Huerta chose to write mainly sociopolitical and erotic poetry. His most important production was that which concerned itself with injustice, inequality in the distribution of wealth, exploitation of the masses, the dark side of the inhabitants of the city, racism as experienced in the United States, and wars and destruction carried on in the name of liberation and democracy. Of his entire production, his book *Los hombres del alba* (Men from Dawn; 1944) is considered to be his best. It contains many of the ideas already indicated above, as well as his preoccupation with the pollution of the city. In his "Declaración de odio" (Declaration of Hate; 1937; in *Poesía completa,* 102–105), Huerta ennumerates all those elements that are contributing to the destruction of his city. The contamination of the atmosphere, which in the 1980s becomes a major concern for some Mexican poets, is already present in this composition. He also condemns all those individuals he blamed for the decay of the city, including prostitutes and homosexuals, as well as all who sell their beliefs for some material comfort. In spite of this apparently negative diatribe against his native city, Huerta does see hope in the masses and in those who struggle to remedy its misery. His *Poesía completa* (Complete Poetic Works; 1988) reveals that his faith in communism remained constant throughout his life. The love expressed in his earlier poetry, however, does change, increasingly becoming highly erotic. Gradually these compositions transmit also an almost misogynist message. In the collection *Circuito interior* (Internal Circuit; 1988), in the poem "De los desnudos será" (It Must Belong to the Naked; 1974?), Huerta openly attacks women poets.

Another theme in Huerta's poetry is Mexico's indigenous past, but viewed in terms of its destruction and how the same fate awaits the present country (see for example *El Tajín;* 1963). Huerta is concerned with universal destruction, and thus Hiroshima and Nagasaki appear in his compositions. Younger poets will echo this same concern, particularly when they evaluate the twentieth century and how future generations will characterize it. Although Huerta and Paz parted company over the value and function of poetry, today we see that both left an indelible mark on the generations of poets that followed.

The general consensus is that the previous group, the Contemporáneos, could not be described as a unit; the same can be said of the Taller group. Neftalí Beltrán, for example, is the perfect heir of the Contemporáneos tradition. His *Poesía; 1936–1977* (Poetry; 1936–1977; 1978) may be read exactly as one would read Villaurrutia's work. His poetic production shows the same preoccupations as that of his predecessors, and its interpretation may fit within a gay discourse.

During the decade of the thirties, some of the Contemporáneos had begun to incorporate elements of European surrealism. However, the Mexicans adopted only the technical aspects of the movement. The relationship between form and ideology which was an important element in the conceptual framework of European surrealists was lacking in Mexican surrealism. They had not understood the goals of the surrealists in employing automatic writing, which was used originally in order "to destroy the language stereotype, to emancipate the Word so that it could unleash a greater measure of its potential energies"

(Balakian, 2). Automatic writing became a temporary fad in Mexico, and Paz was the first Mexican author to write a surrealist composition. As a continuum of their vision of the function of form, the European surrealists adopted the hermeneutic procedures of the science of interpreting scriptures, in order to "retrieve from a seemingly static text its capacity for polyvalence." In their relationship with society they left "the ivory towers of the symbolist writers and descended into the streets, there to cull experience, reshape it and return it to humans in whatever stations of life . . . who needed to have their faculties sharpened not by subtle abstractions but by the concrete forms of existence they encountered daily and took too much for granted" (Balakian, 2). Paz did not become familiarized with surrealism until 1937, when he and Pellicer traveled to Europe to attend the Second International Congress of Antifacist Writers in Republican Spain. During this trip, Paz visited France, where he met individuals that were members of the surrealist movement. Although Paz did not fully understand at this time the surrealists' aesthetic canon, he has indicated that he did sympathize with their attitude toward politics (which was Marxist oriented) and comprehended vaguely their ideas on art.

Paz's work shows typical surrealist preoccupations with technique and content, use of symbols, and view of the creative process. For his poem *Piedra de sol* (*Sun Stone;* 1957) he was called the "sturdiest heir" of surrealism. In support of this argument, Anna Balakian has pointed out a statement made by Paz that reflects a surrealist tenet: "Liberty of the Word that gives you its liberty" (7). In *Piedra de sol* "images of fire, earth, air, and water convey the same inviolate sense of the totality of life and solidarity of all natural phenomena as in [André] Breton's work. Like his predecessor, Paz forges ahead in the labyrinth in search of phosphorescence. He looks for the sacred in signs and numbers. He shares Breton's need to create exaltation and to provoke vision and vertigo" (7–8). In spite of this accurate description of the surrealist element in this volume, a review of the evolution of Paz's poetry bears out his claim that surrealism did not initially mold him but that, rather, his own vision of the world and of poetry coincided with surrealist ideology.

Prior to embracing the surrealists, Paz's poetry of the forties already included symbols that have always been linked to the tradition of religious syncretism. During this decade, in 1943, Paz left Mexico for a period of ten years that took him to the United States, where he studied and held various employments. He then moved to Europe in 1945 to occupy a minor diplomatic post in Paris. After Tablada's death in 1945, Paz wrote an essay to his memory that brought about a revival of Tablada's work. A retrospective review of Paz's poetry demonstrates that Tablada was perhaps the single most important Mexican poet to have influenced him. Paz was attracted to Tablada, for he realized that Tablada's introduction and utilization of new modes of poetical expression came from his knowledge of a literary tradition that was constantly experimenting with artistic forms closely tied to metaphysics that aided the artist in unveiling and recreating the secrets of the cosmos.

Paz possesses an extensive bibliography that encompasses poetry, art and literary criticism, and drama. It includes twenty-four volumes of poetry, two of poetical prose, and a play. He also published some twenty-nine books of essays and literary criticism and edited and coedited numerous anthologies, most of them on Mexican poetry, and collections of poetry translated from various languages. Although by volume and diversity alone his bibliography would be impossible to characterize with one sweeping statement, one can say that it is the diversity in subject matter that allows one to place his work within the literary tradition of the religious syncretists. As a follower of religious syncretism he has studied and compared universal cultures and myths, delved into his own culture's myths, analyzed and written about world literary figures, reflected upon the plastic arts and music, and commented on the relationship between form and technique and ideas. This wide range of interests corresponds to his intellectual necessity to understand, grasp, and transmit the essence of the cosmos. In this sense, he belongs in the same category of writers with whom Breton (1896–1966) allied himself and in the poetic tradition of his compatriots Sor Juana Inés de la Cruz, López Velarde, Tablada, and Gorostiza.

Paz prefers to forget *Luna silvestre* (Savage Moon; 1933), his first collection of poems (Roggiano, ed., 9). *Raíz del hombre* (The Root of Man; 1937) and almost all of the poetic production prior to *Libertad bajo palabra* (Freedom on Parole; 1949) have suffered the same rejection (Paz, *Poemas,* 11). In spite of his condemnation, it is useful to refer to them in that they present the themes that became constants in his work: poetry, love, eroticism, and woman. With time, these symbols gradually grew in complexity as he tried to convey multiple meanings. Imagination, inspiration, wisdom, and revelation became joined to "the woman." The "love-passion" theme, which is neither passionate love nor erotic passion and which Paz himself indicates is present in López Velarde's work—the one that comes from the troubadours of the Middle Ages and is anchored in a religious tradition—is the one that he further develops.

Although there appear to be echoes of Jiménez and Rainer Maria Rilke in *Luna silvestre,* Paz had not yet read the work of Jiménez when he wrote these poems (Roggiano, ed., 57–59). If there is an influence from Jiménez, it is one that could have been filtered through the Contemporáneos, who were admirers of this Spanish poet. Subsequent to *Luna* many poetic compositions express the same desire that Jiménez had of finding the exact word that would unveil the mysteries of the world. However, the discourse used by Paz stems from the religious syncretists. Although Paz has written frequently on the subject of religion in relation to the works of Mexican and European writers, he has never declared an affiliation to any particular individual or group.

At the end of the 1930s, the civil war in Spain and Paz's personal experiences with the Mayan peasants of Yucatán, where he went to found a school for the Indians, led Paz to write two poems of a sociopolitical nature: *¡No pasarán!* (They Shall Not Pass; 1936) and *Entre la piedra y la flor* (Between Stone and Flower; 1941). Paz returned to sociopolitical verse in *Ladera este (1962–1968)* (Eastern Slope; 1969) as a reaction to political events that occurred in Mexico City in 1968 when a repressive government massacred students that were protesting at the Tlatelolco square. The poem on this tragic event bore the title "Intermitencias del oeste (3)" (Interruptions from the West [3]) and the subtitle "México: Olimpiada de 1968" (Mexico City: The 1968 Olympics).

At the end of the forties, Paz published two important volumes of poetry, one in verse, the second in poetic prose: *Libertad bajo palabra* and *¿Aguila o sol?* (Eagle or Sun?; 1951). Of the two, *¿Aguila o sol?* definitely marks his aesthetic affiliation with surrealism. The poetic composition "Mariposa de obsidiana" (Obsidian Butterfly), which had been included in Breton's *Almanach surréaliste du demi-siècle* (Mid-Century Surrealist Almanac) published in 1950, appears in this collection. In this poem, Paz utilizes Aztec myths in the same manner as the religious syncretists in Mexico and Europe had previously done in their desire to reaffirm their interpretation of the creative process. The goddess Itzpapalotl functions in this composition as an equivalent to Venus, the symbol of poetic inspiration for the syncretists. In explanatory notes to *Piedra de sol,* Paz speaks about a parallel between Venus and Quetzalcoatl and all of Venus's multiple manifestations as envisioned by the ancient people of the Mediterranean. He employs the same process when talking about Quetzalcoatl and shows how both are symbols of the "essential ambiguity of the Universe" (Paz, *Poemas,* 675). "Hacia el poema" (Toward the Poem), the prose-poem that concludes *Aguila,* summarizes a similar religious syncretists' view about the significance of the poem. In this work, the poem is the child of the love affair that takes place between one man-sun and one woman-moon or the result of a successful coupling within the bisexual ego (composed of will-male and imagination-female) that has enabled the poet to create (Paz, *Aguila,* 117).

In the collection *Salamandra 1958–1961* (Salamander 1958–1961; 1962), the poem that bears the title is a composition that melds Japanese, Aztec, and European symbols and beliefs in typical syncretist tradition. In *Ladera este,* Paz adds myths from India, which he later develops extensively in his book of prose-poems *El mono gramático* (The Monkey Grammarian; 1974), which delves into the origin of language, its importance in the artistic process, and religion.

Topoemas (Topoems; 1971), *Discos visuales* (Visual Disks; 1968), and *Blanco* are what Paz has labeled "space" poetry, and all bear the influence of Tablada's haikus and ideographic poetry. *Blanco,* especially, was inspired by Tablada's "Nocturno alterno" in *Li Po.* Of course, there are other models for these compositions, such as Mallarmé's "Un coup de dés" and cubism. Apollinaire had seen in cubist paintings a "fourth dimension of reality, which he deemed not only a proof of creativeness but of divinity. This new dimension was conveyed by simultaneous representations in various perspectives, giving the impression of the immensity of space which overflowed in all directions at the same time and suggested the infinite" (Balakian, 87). He had also seen in the cubists "a fusion of science and metaphysics" (Balakian, 87).

Renga (1972), written with the collaboration of Jacques Roubaud (French section), Edoardo Sanguinetti (Italian section), and Charles Tomlinson (English section) and dedicated to André Breton, was inspired by the Japanese form of collective poetry. The renga had an extraordinary vogue during two epochs in Japanese history: the Heian (794–1192) and the Muromachi in the fifteenth century. Here again, Paz is attracted by Asia, but in the Tablada tradition, in which there is a correspondence between form and religious discourse. Paz envisions *Renga* as an idea that brings back "universal correspondences" (*Renga*'s pages are not numbered, but they would be the equivalent of thirteen). His image and description of the cosmos correspond to the universe of the theosophists. He tells us: "We no longer see the macrocosm and microcosm as the two halves of a sphere, but we conceive the entire universe as a plurality of systems in movement; those systems reflect upon each other and, upon the reflection, they combine in the same manner as the rhymes in a poem. In this way they transform themselves into other systems, each time more transparent and abstract, systems of systems, true geometrical formations of symbols, until, imperceptible to our organs of observation, they end up evaporating—again in the same manner as rhymes that end in silence and of writing that resolves into a void" (*Renga*, 13–14).

Paracelsus, one of the most important individuals claimed by the Rosicrucians in the development of the ideology that constitutes the basis for their beliefs, explains: "Nature being the Universe, is *one*, a *unit*, with many parts, and its origin can only be one eternal Unit. It is an organism in which all natural things harmonize and sympathize with each other. The world is Nature, it is the Macrocosm. Everything is the product of one universal creative effort; the Macrocosm (great world) and the Microcosm (man) are one, though individual units. They are one constellation, one influence, one breath, one (have the possibility of) harmony" (Clymer, 118). Paracelsus described creation as an act of the imagination of the "universal" or "cosmic" mind, thus it follows that "if man's imagination is sufficiently strong . . . it will be able to create things" (Clymer, 125). Evidently, the conceptual premise for the composition of *Renga,* the idea of a collective mind for the universe, has its source in the Platonists and their followers. An essay by Jacques Roubaud introducing *Renga* explains the relationship between form and content as envisioned by one of its greatest Japanese cultivators: art designed "to penetrate the talent and vision of another," for all the arts come from "a translation of what lies in the heart of things and is understood by the artist's own heart." This collective effort also wishes "to apprehend the undecipherable mystery of the other" (*Renga,* 31). The utilization of the Japanese form, with a full understanding of the basis for its creation, is for Paz only one more excursion into the world of the religious syncretists.

In a prologue to *Renga,* entitled "Centro móvil" (Movable Center), Paz explains the strict versification rules required by this type of composition and his idea that their collective poem revolves around two contradictory yet complementary elements: "the diversity of languages and the community of the poetic language" (*Renga,* 20–21). What evidently attracted Paz to experiment with this form, abandoning the lineal succession of composition practiced by the Japanese and adopting instead a zig-zag pattern, is that in itself it conveys "opposition and reconciliation of terms: the poem turns on itself and its way of elapsing is the dialectic negation" (*Renga,* 21).

Attempts have been made to classify and describe Paz's poetry through the evolution of stylistic variations in his verses (imagery, punctuation), by ideology and subject matter, by the references to different religious beliefs, or by his personal experiences. Almost 90 percent of his poetic production reflects an obsessive need to re-create the cosmos; to find the Word, the expression that will capture the ever-changing yet permanent face of nature; to understand why the essence of the universe can only be achieved by translating the intangible that lies within the context of opposites: life/death, silence/noise. He did write poetry of a sociopolitical nature, but within the totality of his poetic production there are few such compositions, for, as mentioned earlier, he had opted to write his political commentaries in prose. Paz's prose production, about thirty-two volumes of essays, is almost as important as his poetry. His classic *El laberinto de la soledad* (*The Labyrinth of Solitude;* 1950), on the nature of the Mexican, won him immediate international recognition, and his volumes on literary criticism on his own compatriots and world literary figures make him one of the best critics in Mexico.

It is impossible to do justice to Paz's contribution to his country and to Spanish literature in general. In his continued participation in founding literary journals, editing and coediting them, he has attempted to maintain the Mexican traditions of keeping art free from governmental dictates and disseminating the works of young Mexican writers, as well as keeping his compatriots abreast of recent literary trends. He has written on Mexican art and has served his nation by occupying different diplomatic positions.

By 1972, Paz was considered "undoubtedly one of the giants of today's literary world" (Phillips, 1), and in 1973 he was called "the leading, exemplary intellectual of Latin America whose pronouncements are awaited with excited anticipation all over the literary world" (Ivask, vii). However, in his own country, his compatriot Blanco, after an impartial and in general positive review of Paz's work, objected to Paz in personal terms, because Paz to him had become accustomed by the 1970s "to being irrefutable and [did] not propitiate criticism, but servile devotion. . . . There is nothing more tragic than having a great writer alone, without competition, without refutation, without enemies that will truly challenge him: he becomes petrified like a cathedral, into which one could enter only to say mysterious prayers with devotion or for the purpose of breaking all its windows with stones" (223–224). Blanco does conclude that the country owes him a debt of gratitude, for Paz has enriched it, but it is exactly for this reason that more is demanded and expected from him (224). Paz has not disappointed his country. His work has consistently received the highest accolades from critics at home and abroad. After receiving numerous international prizes, he was finally awarded the Nobel Prize in 1990.

After the Taller generation, another group of Mexican poets joined ranks around the literary journal *Tierra Nueva* (New Land; 1940–1942). These included Manuel Calvillo (1918–), Wilberto Cantón (1923–1979), Alí Chumacero (1918–), and Jorge González Durán (1918–). Unlike their immediate predecessors who met in bars and coffee houses, they gathered at the National Autonomous University and appeared to be less concerned about social and political problems (Paz, *Sombras,* 97). It is perhaps for this reason that the aesthetic ideology of these writers is considered to be closer to that of the Contemporáneos than to the Taller group.

Of the Tierra Nueva writers, Chumacero, who was codirector of the journal, is considered to have been its most valuable contributor and almost the direct heir of his compatriots Villaurrutia and Gorostiza. Until the fifties, the most frequent themes of his poetry, particularly in his collection *Palabras en reposo* (Words in Repose; 1956), were "anguish in the presence of the enigma of death, desire, love, and solitude" (González Peña, 427). In his first book, *Páramo de sueños* (Desert of Dreams; 1944), the preoccupation with death, love, solitude—themes that characterized the Contemporáneos—appeared as his main concerns. Although it has been indicated that Chumacero ultimately finds hope and salvation in a woman's body, his poetic corpus does not sustain this conclusion (*Poesía completa,* 8). *Poesía completa* (Complete Poetic Works; 1980), a slim volume of poetry, brought about a renewed interest in his work and the "rediscovery that it possesses considerable originality and extraordinary lyrical power, if [sic] so dense as to be sometimes almost incomprehensible" (Dauster, *Double Strand,* 27). Indeed, Chumacero's poetry, with the exception of a couple of poems, is hermetic.

After Taller and Tierra Nueva, a new group of poets, classified by Dauster as the generation of 1954, emerges. It is now that with Rosario Castellanos (1925–1974) "women poets enter fully into the reviews and groupings that are a dominant factor of Mexican literary life" (Dauster, *Double Strand,* 29). Primarily known as a novelist for *Balún-Canán* (*The Nine Guardians*; 1957) and *Oficio de tinieblas* (Labor of Gloom; 1962), Castellanos also wrote short stories, drama, and books of essays. In the essays that make up *Mujer que sabe latín* (A Woman Who Knows Latin; 1973), she discusses the role of women in society and the broader issue of feminism. As a poet, Castellanos's early compositions, *Trayectoria del polvo* (Trajectory of Dust; 1948), *Apuntes para una declaración de fe* (Annotations for a Declaration of Faith; 1948), and *De la vigilia estéril* (Of Sterile Vigil; 1950), do not reflect feminist themes but rather the anguish and loneliness of an individual. Her expression of the pains suffered by love unrequited, betrayal, and anguish, as well as her compositions that speak of the pre-Columbian past, have been judged by some as sentimental.

In *Poemas (1953–1955)* (Poems [1953–1955]; 1957), "Lamentación de Dido" (Dido's Lament), Castellanos retells the story of Dido in order to show the ultimate fate of a woman spurned. Although Castellanos had an unhappy marriage that ended in divorce, she claimed throughout her life that her love poems were not autobiographical. However, before her death she did admit to the possibility of unconsciously projecting some of her experiences into her poems. After *Poemas* her works have more of a feminist orientation. She also begins to write about social and political injustice. Her last compositions also speak about her love for her son, Gabriel. The work *Poesía no eres tú: Obra poética, 1948–1971* (You Are Not Poetry: Poetic Works, 1948–1971; 1972), a compilation of previously published and new compositions, includes also Castellanos's versions of works by Emily Dickinson, St. John Perse, and Paul Claudel. According to Elena Poniatowska in a prologue to *Meditación en el umbral* (Meditation at the Threshold; 1985), one of the strongest influences on Castellanos was the North American poet Dickinson (11). In Castellanos's feminist compositions after 1957, one encounters poems that recall the works of the Argentine Alfonsina Storni (1892–1938) and the Puerto Rican Julia de Burgos (1916–1953). In true Mexican tradition, Castellanos also occupied a diplomatic post. She served as ambassador to Israel, and it was there that she accidentally electrocuted herself.

Two other Mexican women poets prior to Castellanos merit critical attention: María Enriqueta Camarillo y Roa de Pereyra (1872–1968) and Concha Urquiza (1910–1945). María Enriqueta wrote under the influence of romanticism, while Urquiza's compositions are for the most part religious. However, some of her poems also reflect the theme of carnal love. During the forties, a few women writers founded and contributed to the journal *Rueca* (Spinning Wheel; 1941–1948). Apparently, however, *Rueca* never became a feminist periodical. During this decade, other feminine voices were heard. The group includes Guadalupe Amor (1920–), Dolores Castro (1923–), Emma Godoy (1918–), Margarita Michelena (1917–), Margarita Paz Paredes (1922–), and Aurora Reyes (1910–) (Valdés, viii). Of these, Paz Paredes in *Litoral del tiempo* (Littoral of Time; 1978) and Reyes reflect political concerns in their poetry. But the rest will follow for the most part traditional expression and write on religious or personal questions.

Some of the other poets included in the group are Jaime Sabines (1926–) and Marco Antonio Montes de Oca (1932–), as well as two individuals born in Spain but associated with Mexico; Tomás Segovia (1927–) and Manuel Durán (1925–). At the same time, the names of other women writers become known. The elements that characterized the writing of the previous group of women writers, "the acceptance in general of certain readings, especially the Bible, the affinity in language, themes and images, in the possibility of mutual influences" (Valdés, viii), will be abandoned. Of these newer writers, Thelma Nava (1931–) was recognized as an innovator.

Of the male poets, Sabines's work is considered to be close to that of Efraín Huerta, and as a consequence he has been called a social poet, a label reaffirmed by his use of everyday language to express daily occurrences. Others consider him to be an heir to López Velarde. The theme of death, so important in Mexican literature, becomes obsessive in Sabines's work. For him, death is "a constant menace slowly corroding us and ever undoing us" (Dauster,

Double Strand, 88). He expresses anger when facing the death of a loved one and at "the indifference or absence of a caring God" (Dauster, *Double Strand,* 89). Women in Sabines's poetry have been associated with the Virgin Mary; thus, through her, the poet strives for a liberation from his Christian upbringing that reminds him of personal guilt and the recognition of his own mortality (Dauster, *Double Strand,* 100). *Nuevo recuento de poemas* (New Recounting of Poems; 1977, augmented in 1983) includes poetry previously published, such as *Horal* (1950), *Tarumba* (1956), and *Yuria* (1967). *Nuevo recuento* does not reveal any variation on the themes already mentioned.

There is a general agreement that Montes de Oca is an excellent poet but that "his poems lack a cohesive unity" (Poniatowska, 34). Many echo the view that he is a great creator of images. In *Poesía reunida, 1953–1970* (Gathered Poetry, 1953–1970; 1971), an autobiographical prologue reveals the enormous scope of the international poets he most admires, while Paz among the Mexican towers in his estimation. Montes de Oca promoted a literary movement called poeticism, founded by Enrique González Rojo (1928–) (a younger relation to the aforementioned González Rojo) and Eduardo Lizalde (1929–). Their goal was to "rationalize different techniques to create images in poetry and assign to them a value in the poem according to its complexity, originality, and clarity" (Montes de Oca, 23–24). They believed that traditional poetry was too linked to irrationality and emotions and thus lacked adequate creative apparatus. Only a thorough study of all possible images and metaphors would provide them with the key to the "laws that govern and produce them" (Montes de Oca, 24). Montes de Oca confesses that he later realized that all the postulates of the group were basically false, except for one: the need for clarity. He also expresses a preference for images that are logical. It is perhaps Montes de Oca's obsession with technique that has led others to feel that his works lack a cohesive unity, while continuing to acknowledge that he is a great creator of images.

The most recent generation of poets is molded by the urban center of Mexico City. An increasing pollution problem, a stagnant governmental bureaucracy serving a population that has grown from two to twenty million since 1940, and insufficient housing and public services for the masses have brought about a renewed interest in cultivating poetry of a sociopolitical nature. These poets would follow Efraín Huerta's view that poetry needed to be used for social purposes. However, they do not like Huerta's poetry, seeing in it service to one political trend that lacks transcendence. They also reject Paz's poetry, considering it the "rear guard of European poetry" and Paz himself a thinker "who endorses irrationality" (Poniatowska, 35). Five poets, known for the name of the work they published together, *La espiga amotinada* (The Mutinous Spike; 1960), are identified as having been the successors of Huerta. They are Juan Bañuelos (1932–), Eraclio Zepeda (1937–), Oscar Oliva (1937–), Jaime Augusto Shelley (1937–), and Jaime Labastida (1939–) (Dauster, *Double Strand,* 33). In an interview with Elena Poniatowska, the members of this group declared that among the ideas that united them there was a commonality in "thinking that poetry is a product of an individual directed toward another individual" (Poniatowska, 28) and also in the same lyrical goals. Two members of the group, Labastida and Bañuelos, have participated actively in politics and joined in demonstrations protesting injustices against workers. They confess a lack of pride in their involvement in these activities, for their presence merely shows the lack of revolutionary organization among the working class.

In *Espejo humeante* (Smoking Mirror; 1968), Bañuelos continues to express themes that are a mainstay of Mexican literature—the passage of time and loneliness—but he also denounces racism in the United States, war, and the bombing of Hiroshima. He speaks about political prisoners and the inequalities in the distribution of wealth. He is particularly ironic when he discusses individuals who are dead and are mourned for having been great benefactors, when in reality the money they distributed had been acquired by exploiting those same persons they appeared to protect. Most of these issues have been of primary importance in the poetic works of all those writing during the last thirty years, with the added concern of the pollution that is destroying Mexico City.

In the early decade of the sixties, Mexico saw in its oil production and the rising cost of this product the solution to its economic problems. The "flower-child culture" of the United States, coupled with an optimistic view of Mexico's future, brought about what Dauster has labeled a "go-go" atmosphere. Rock music and the protest movements imported from the United States also contributed to the creation of an almost unreal life-style. These "happy" years came to an abrupt end in 1968 "when right-wing paramilitary and official forces attacked a demonstration of students" (*Double Strand,* 31). This episode, remembered as the Night of Tlatelolco, made intellectuals realize that they were still living under autocratic rule. A wave of repression followed in which independent newspapers were purged. For Mexican artists, who by tradition had always supplemented their incomes through "teaching, journalism or editorial work, all of which are subject to considerable public and private pressure," this action against the press brought insecurity. The poetry written after 1968 reflects the fears of the times and the pessimism that they, as Mexican writers, would be unable to solve their problems. Dauster has noticed that in spite of this negative note, the poetry was one "of great vigor" (*Double Strand,* 31).

The representative poets of the group are Isabel Fraire (1934–), Gabriel Zaid, José Carlos Becerra (1937–1970), Homero Aridjis (1940–), and José Emilio Pacheco (1939–). Of these, the work of Fraire has received particular attention. Unfortunately, one does not know whether this has happened because she deserves to rank among the best writers in Mexico today or because she happens to be a woman poet and the feminist movement has become an important contemporary issue. Her books *Sólo esta luz* (Only This Light; 1969) and *Poemas en el regazo de la muerte/Poems in the Lap of Death* (1977) reveal an ability to voice that which cannot speak, as Castellanos defined the task of a poet. In *Sólo esta luz,* Fraire is able to capture the beauty of nature and the urban setting and to relate them to a psychological frame of mind. Usually her reflections are tied to various aspects of love. In *Poemas en el regazo de la muerte,* winner of the 1978 Villaurrutia Prize for poetry, she recounts her impressions of the beauty captured in different paintings, thereby recalling Keats's "Ode to a Grecian Urn," a poem to which she will refer in one of her compositions. She portrays herself in other poems as "suffering the indignity of writing her poems in the lap of this world's moribund cultural and social values" (*Poemas,* n.p.). The destruction of the world and the misery and poverty found in it are constant themes in this volume. The title of the work conveys the poet's view that "all creativity is conditioned by the certainty of death" (*Poemas,* n.p.).

By the time of his death at the age of thirty-three, Becerra was already recognized as a promising young poet. His entire production was published posthumously by Pacheco and Zaid as *El otoño recorre las islas: Obra poética 1961–1970* (Autumn Traverses the Islands: Poetic Work 1961–1970; 1973). The tone that permeates his early works is one of sadness and loneliness, and there is the constant expectancy for something or someone who never arrives. Thus, the mood created suggests autumn, while autumn's desolation accentuates this melancholic state. The city is inhospitable and empty, and its inhabitants are concerned with pomp and circumstance while they hide behind masks. The city is compared to a swamp where individuals drown. Becerra also condemns aggression against other countries and other individuals, as well as the Tlatelolco massacre of 1968, and he decries the use of napalm and bemoans the lack of communication between the United States and other countries. In "Días dispuestos alrededor" (Days Arranged Around), he seems prophetic about his own death, which occurs in an automobile accident. A first reading of his writing reminds one of the work of Bañuelos. Becerra also writes about love, in some cases in highly erotic terms. Yet the figure of woman, although graphically described, suggests that she is a symbol for other things.

Many of Becerra's poems tend to resist interpretation and could at best be described as hermetic. Perhaps he, like his admired Cuban colleague José Lezama Lima (1910–1976), had begun to question human problems from a metaphysical and philosophical point of view. In his correspondence with Lezama Lima, we find an interest in the discourse of one of Lezama Lima's characters on the topic of homosexuality, on how it fits into the concept of the *one* and how it relates to Saint Thomas Aquinas's teachings and Plato's concept of split beings (Becerra, 304).

Aridjis, Pacheco, and Zaid have written widely in prose, with Pacheco and Aridjis publishing prose fiction. Both Pacheco and Zaid are recognized literary critics, and Zaid has also delved into economics and politics (Dauster, *Double Strand,* 32–33). Montes de Oca (from the previous generation), Aridjis, and Pacheco have established reputations as poets. However, after Paz, Pacheco is today perhaps the best-known poet of Mexico.

Dauster considers the constant theme in Pacheco's poetry to be "the uncertainty and impermanence of a decaying world," and time is treated as if it were in "constant change within which we are trapped without anchor" (*Double Strand,* 32). With the volume of poems *No me preguntes cómo pasa el tiempo* (Don't Ask Me How the Time Goes By; 1969), which earned him first prize in the Second National Poetry Contest at Aguascalientes that same year, Pacheco won recognition and a place among Spanish American poets. Prior to this work, Pacheco had published two volumes of poetry: *Los elementos de la noche* (The Elements of Night; 1963) and *El reposo del fuego* (The Repose of Fire; 1966). He has also compiled anthologies on Spanish American Modernism and twentieth-century Mexican poetry, in collaboration with Paz, Aridjis, and Chumacero, and one on nineteenth-century Mexican poetry, *La poesía mexicana del siglo XIX* (Mexican Poetry of the Nineteenth Century; 1965).

He has translated the works of foreign poets and incorporated these translations into his own creative world, because he does not believe that anyone writes poetry but rather that poetry is made by everyone. Pacheco's encyclopedic knowledge of world writers, composers, artists, and philosophers makes a brief summary of his main themes an impossible task. Although, like Paz, he possesses a discourse firmly based in philosophy and is preoccupied by his inability to find the exact word as expressed in "Goethe: Gedichte," he is obsessed by his country and his compatriots, for, as he says, "I belong to a transitory time, to a world which crumbles before my eyes" (*No me preguntes,* 23).

In spite of Pacheco's constant pessimistic view of the world, his composition "Homenaje" (Homage) is a poem offered by Paz as an example of Pacheco's affirmation of life and poetry through nature. In this poem, Pacheco sees how the rain-poetry penetrates "en los desiertos de concreto" (in the deserts of concrete) and is the "única eternidad que sobrevive" (the only eternity that survives) (*Alta traición,* 81). Pacheco finds a refuge in poetry, which is his defense against time and the weapon that defies death. It is the key that enables humanity to take possession of the world (Vargas Llosa, in Verani, 17). In some of his most recent poetic compositions, he is concerned with the pollution that is destroying his country. This is one of the most important themes in a 1980s poem "Malpaís" (Badcountry), a term which he defines as "arid land, desert like and disagreeable; without water or vegetation, commonly covered with lava" (*Alta traición,* 110).

In *Irás y no volverás* (You Will Leave and Not Return; 1973), Pacheco also writes about the destruction of Vietnam, the pollution of Mexico City, and his recollections about different cities where he has lived. Pacheco reflects on the role of poetry as an instrument of change in the world and seems to accept that this is a genre that usually ends in libraries gathering dust. One finds in almost every one of his books poems that may be labeled zoological. In two of them, the crab and the scorpion are described as they appear in their environment while also tied to their astrological meanings. Pacheco seems determined to write about all the animals in the world and has already written sufficient compositions on the topic to merit publication under one comprehensive title.

Guadalupe Amor has attempted to work on the same matter in *Breve zoológico prehistórico e histórico* (Brief Prehistoric and Historic Zoo; 1975), but her poems lack the depth and lyricism of Pacheco's compositions.

Los trabajos del mar (The Works of the Sea; 1983) and *Ciudad de la memoria* (City of Memory; 1989), Pacheco's latest works, reflect his constant preoccupation with the oppressed, environmental contamination, and the wars and destruction with which this twentieth century will be identified. In "El cuchillo" (The Knife), from *Ciudad de la memoria,* Pacheco labels this century the one that is bleeding (52). This last collection of poems appears to contain Pacheco's most anguished poems on the situation of the universe.

In a presentation that Pacheco made of the poetry of Huerta, he affirmed that "a poem is not a political act and its worth is only measured in artistic terms." He added that poetry had always been compromised until some sorcerers in the previous century compromised it only with poetry (Klahn and Fernández, 29). A poem is not good or bad because of its theme, be it politics or love; rather, its value lies in its ability to transcend to the universal (Klahn and Fernández, 30). In the Pachecho generation one does not find a rupture between art and politics. Although there is a classical philosophical base for the generation's interpretation of the essence of the universe and the creative process, a clear ideology within the tradition of the religious syncretists, which molded the discourse of previous Mexican writers, is not evident.

The concern with the destruction of the environment has become the main obssession of Aridjis also. The disastrous changes occurring in the city as a consequence of air pollution have made him assume a personal responsibility to fight against this problem. Of his last collections of poems, *Imágenes para el fin del milenio* (Images for the End of the Millennium; 1986) and *Nueva expulsión del paraíso* (New Expulsion from Paradise; 1990), published together as one volume in 1990, the poetry of *Imágenes* concerns itself almost entirely with pollution. His last volume reflects his despair before this destruction caused by humanity.

Among a younger group of poets, Elsa Cross (1946–) seems to be choosing the religious-syncretist path. She is creating "hard-edged poetic visions that reflect a more modern anguish" (Dauster, *Double Strand,* 33) and at the same time, like Paz, has shown interest in "the Provencal or early Italian poets and [in] their spiritual brethren the Cathars" (Dauster, *Double Strand,* 33).

The publication of *La dama de la torre* (The Lady of the Tower; 1972) brought Cross immediate recognition. Her poem "Montsegur," which alludes to one of the most famous places in Europe that suffered persecution due to its connections to the Cathars, establishes her ideological foundations. Within this framework Cross will re-create nature and her experiences of love. In *El diván de Antar* (The Poems of Anterus; 1989), it is explained that in Arabic the word "divan" meant a book of poems. Although the work was submitted to the 1989 Aguascalientes Literary Contest, where it won a prize under the title "Book of Poems," Cross preferred to publish it with the original Arabic word (*Diván,* 6). The work appears to narrate the feelings of a woman as she contemplates her sleeping lover. She allows her imagination to wander and to re-create spaces with the desire of communicating with him. Although basically this is a hermetic text, one could venture to guess that this is Cross's vision of the poetic process and its inspiration.

Sandro Cohen has published an anthology of works by poets born after 1940 in which he shows that poetry in Mexico is a genre very much alive and supported by the production of young poets with great talent. In *Palabra nueva: Dos décadas de poesía en México* (New Word: Two Decades of Poetry in Mexico; 1981), Cohen includes poets already discussed above, as well as others that are not even alluded to in this brief survey. There are many individuals writing in Mexico whose works merit an extensive commentary, and the same holds true for poets that have only been mentioned in passing in these pages.

This survey of the ideological trends in twentieth-century Mexican poetry has basically to conclude here. It is indeed difficult to speak on the production of the younger writers since they are still in the process of publishing with a developing and adjusting view of their contemporary reality. We can conclude by saying that Mexican poetry continues adapting to its autochthonous tradi-tion European themes and topics and literary devices and forms of experi-mentation and that, as in the past, the tradition of the publication of literary journals continues. Some are returning to religious syncretism, while others cultivate a sociopolitical vein that attempts to divorce itself from one particular political group. Now, in general, there seems to be a retrospective examination of the century and a concern about armed conflict, the impact of environmen-tal pollution, and the future of the disenfranchised. As poets, they question the value of their artistic production in an attempt to change the human con-dition. Yet a note of hope remains that perhaps they are able to speak for those who are unable to do so for themselves.

BIBLIOGRAPHY

Amor, Guadalupe. *Breve zoológico prehistórico e histórico*. Mexico City: Editorial V Siglos, 1975.

Aridjis, Homero. *Imágenes para el fin del milenio* and *Nueva expulsión del paraíso*. Mex-ico City: Editorial Joaquín Mortiz, 1990.

Balakian, Anna. *The Road to the Absolute*. Chicago: University of Chicago Press, 1986.

Bañuelos, Juan. *Espejo humeante*. 6th ed. Mexico City: Editorial Joaquín Mortiz, 1986.

Bañuelos, Juan, Eraclio Zepeda, Oscar Oliva, Jaime Augusto Shelley, and Jaime Labas-tida. *La espiga amotinada*. Mexico City: Fondo de Cultura Económica, 1960.

Becerra, José Carlos. *El otoño recorre las islas (Obra poética 1961–1970)*. Ed. José Emi-lio Pacheco and Gabriel Zaid. Prologue by Octavio Paz. Mexico City: Ediciones Era, 1973.

Beltrán, Neftalí. *Poesía (1936–1977)*. Mexico City: Fondo de Cultura Económica, 1966.

Blanco, José Joaquín. *Crónica de la poesía mexicana*. 4th ed. Mexico City: Editorial Katún, 1983.

Breton, André, with Benjamin Péret. *Almanach surréaliste du demi-siècle*. Paris: Sagittaire, 1950.

Carballo, Emmanuel. *Un mexicano y su obra: Jaime Torres Bodet*. Mexico City: Empresas Editoriales, 1968.

Castellanos, Rosario. *Apuntes para una declaración de la fe*. Mexico City: Ediciones de América, 1948.

———. *Balún Canán*. Mexico City: Fondo de Cultura Económica, 1957.

———. *Meditación en el umbral: Antología poética*. Ed. Julian Palley. Prologue by Elena Poniatowska. Mexico City: Fondo de Cultura Económica, 1985.

———. *Mujer que sabe latín*. Mexico City: Fondo de Cultura Económica, 1984.

———. *Oficio de tinieblas*. Mexico City: Editorial Joaquín Mortiz, 1962.

———. *Poemas (1953–1955)*. Mexico City: Colección Metáfora, 1957.

———. *Poesía no eres tú (Obra poética: 1948–1971)*. Mexico City: Fondo de Cultura Económica, 1972.

———. *De la vigilia estéril*. Mexico City: Ediciones de América, 1950.

———. *Trayectoria del polvo*. Mexico City: Colección El Cristal Fugitivo, 1948.

Chumacero, Alí. *Alí Chumacero de bolsillo*. Prologue by Felipe Garrido. Guadalajara: Universidad de Guadalajara/Xalli, 1990.

———. *Palabras en reposo*. 2d ed. Mexico City: Fondo de Cultura Económica, 1965.

———. *Páramo de sueños*. Mexico City: Universidad Nacional Autónoma de México, 1960.

———. *Poesía completa*. Prologue by Marco Antonio Campos. Mexico City: Premiá Editora, 1980.

Clymer, R. Swinburne. *The Book of Rosicruciae*. Quakertown, Penn.: The Philosophical Publishing Company, 1947.

Cohen, Sandro, ed. *Palabra nueva: Dos décadas de poesía en México*. Mexico City: Premiá Editora, 1981.

Cross, Elsa. *La dama de la torre*. Mexico City: Editorial Joaquín Mortiz, 1972.

———. *El diván de Antar*. Mexico City: Editorial Joaquín Mortiz, 1990.

Cruz, Sor Juana Inés de la. *Endechas*. Ed. Xavier Villaurrutia. Mexico City: Taller, 1940.

———. *Primero sueño*. Prologue and notes by Natalicio González. Mexico City: Editorial Guaranía, 1951.

———. *Sonetos*. Ed. Xavier Villaurrutia. Mexico City: Ediciones de "La Razón," 1931.

Cuesta, Jorge. *Antología de la poesía mexicana moderna*. Mexico City: Fondo de Cultura Económica, 1985.

———. *Poesía*. Mexico City: Editorial Estaciones, 1958.

Darío, Rubén. *Cantos de vida y esperanza*. In his *Obras poéticas completas,* ed. Alberto Ghiraldo. Madrid: M. Aguilar, 1932.

Dauster, Frank. *Breve historia de la poesía mexicana*. Mexico City: Studium, 1956.

———. *The Double Strand: Five Contemporary Mexican Poets*. Lexington: The University Press of Kentucky, 1987.

de Beer, Gabriella. "El Ateneo y los ateneístas: Un examen retrospectivo." *Revista Iberoamericana* 148–149 (1989): 737–749.

Díaz Mirón, Salvador. *Lascas*. Jalapa: Tipografía del Gobierno del Estado, 1901.

Faurie, Marie-Josephe. *Le Modernisme hispano-américain et ses sources françaises*. Paris: Centre de Recherches de L'Institut d'Etudes Hispaniques, 1966.

Forster, Merlin H. *Los contemporáneos: 1920–1933*. Mexico City: Ediciones de Andrea, 1964.

Fraire, Isabel. *Poemas en el regazo de la muerte / Poems in the Lap of Death*. English and Spanish, trans. Thomas Hoeksema. Pittsburgh: Latin American Literary Review Press, 1981.

———. *Sólo esta luz*. Mexico City: Ediciones Era, 1969.

Frye, Northrop. *Anatomy of Criticism: Four Essays*. Princeton: Princeton University Press, 1971.

García Terrés, Jaime. *Poesía y alquimia: Los tres mundos de Gilberto Owen*. Mexico City: Ediciones Era, 1980.

Góngora y Argote, Luis de. *Soledades*. Commentary by D. García de Salzedo Coronel. Madrid: Imprenta Real, 1636.

González Martínez, Enrique. "Tuércele el cuello al cisne." In his *Los senderos ocultos*. Mocorito: Imprenta de la "Voz del Norte," 1911.

González Peña, Carlos. *History of Mexican Literature*. Trans. Gusta Barfield Nance and Florence Johnson Dunstan. Dallas: Southern Methodist Press, 1968.

Gorostiza, José. *Canciones para cantar en las barcas, Del poema frustrado, Muerte sin fin*. In his *Poesía*. Mexico City: Fondo de Cultura Económica, 1964.

Huerta, Efraín. *Circuito interior*. Mexico City: Editorial Joaquín Mortiz, 1977.

———. *Los hombres del alba*. Mexico City: Géminis, 1944.

———. *Poesía completa*. Ed. Martí Soler. Prologue by David Huerta. Mexico City: Fondo de Cultura Económica, 1988.

———. *El Tajín*. Mexico City: Pájaro Cascabel, 1963.

Ivask, Ivar, ed. *The Perpetual Present: The Poetry and Prose of Octavio Paz*. Norman: University of Oklahoma Press, 1973.

Klahn, Norma, and Jesse Fernández. *Lugar de encuentro: Ensayos críticos sobre poesía mexicana actual*. Mexico City: Editorial Katún, 1987.

Labastida, Jaime. *La espiga amotinada*. See entry for Bañuelos.

Leiva, Raúl. *Imagen de la poesía mexicana contemporánea*. Mexico City: Imprenta Universitaria, 1959.

López Velarde, Ramón. "La derrota de la palabra." In his *Obras completas*. Mexico City: Editorial Nueva España, 1944.

———. *El don de febrero y otras prosas*. Edition and prologue by Elena Molina Ortega. Mexico City: Imprenta Universitaria, 1952.

———. *Poesías completas y El minutero*. 6th ed. Edition and prologue by Antonio Castro Leal. Mexico City: Editorial Porrúa, 1971. Includes *El son del corazón* (1932), *La sangre devota* (1916), and *Zozobra* (1919).

Lugones, Leopoldo. *Los crepúsculos del jardín: Poesía*. Buenos Aires: A. Moen, 1905.

———. *Lunario sentimental*. Buenos Aires: A. Moen, 1909.

Mallarmé, Stéphane. "Un coup de dés jamais n'abolira le hasard." In *Stéphane Mallarmé: Selected Poetry and Prose,* ed. Mary Ann Caws. New York: New Directions, 1982.

Mansour, Mónica. "José Gorostiza y la Cábala." *Nuevo Texto Crítico* 2.3 (1989): 141–156.

Maples Arce, Manuel. *Andamios interiores*. Mexico City: Editorial Cultura, 1922.

———. *Memorial de la sangre*. Mexico City, 1947.

———. *Poemas interdictos*. Jalapa: Ediciones de Horizonte, 1927.

———. *Rag, Tintas de abanico*. Veracruz: Catalán Hermanos, 1920.

———. *Urbe. (Super-poema bolchevique en 5 cantos.)* Mexico City: Andrés Botas e Hijo, 1924.

Martí, José. *Versos*. Ed. Eugenio Florit. New York: Las Americas Publishing Co., 1962.

———. *Versos sencillos*. New York: Louis Weiss & Co., 1891.

Martínez, José Luis. *Literatura mexicana siglo XX: 1919–1949*. Mexico City: Antigua Librería Robredo, 1949.

Monsiváis, Carlos. "No con un sollozo, sino entre disparos (notas sobre cultura mexicana 1910–1968)." *Revista Iberoamericana* 148–149 (1989): 715–735.

———. *La poesía mexicana del siglo XX*. Mexico City: Empresas Editoriales, 1965.

Montes de Oca, Marco Antonio. *Poesía reunida: 1953–1970*. Mexico City: Fondo de Cultura Económica, 1971.

Müller-Bergh, Klaus. "La poesía de Octavio Paz en los años treinta." In Roggiano, ed., 53–72.

Nervo, Amado. *Juana de Asbaje*. Madrid: Imprenta de los hijos de M. G. Hernández, 1910.

———. *Obras completas*. 2 vols. Ed. Francisco González Guerrero and Alfonso Méndez Plancarte. Madrid: M. Aguillar, 1962.

Novo, Salvador. *Antología 1925–1965*. Mexico City: Editorial Porrúa, 1966.

———. "Memoir." In *Now the Volcano: An Anthology of Latin American Gay Literature,* ed. Winston Leyland, 11–47. San Francisco: Gay Sunshine Press, 1979.

———. *Nuevo amor y otras poesías*. Mexico City: Fondo de Cultura Económica, 1961.

Ortiz de Montellano, Bernardo. *Avidez*. Mexico City: Librería de la Cultura, 1921.

———. *Cinco horas sin corazón*. Mexico City: Letras de México, 1940.

———. *Red*. Mexico City: Contemporáneos, 1928.

———. *El sombrerón*. Mexico City: Editorial de la Estampa Mexicana, 1946.

———. *Sueño y poesía*. Prologue by Wilberto Cantón. Mexico City: Imprenta Universitaria, 1952.

———. *El trompo de siete colores*. Mexico City: Editorial Cultura, 1925.

———, ed. *Letras de México (1937–1947)*. Mexico City: n.p., 1937–1947.

Owen, Gilberto. *Libro de Ruth*. Mexico City: Ediciones Firmamento, 1944.

———. *Línea*. Buenos Aires: Editorial Pora, Cuadernos del Mar de la Plata, 1930.

———. *Obras*. 2d ed. Ed. Josefina Procopio. Prologue by Alí Chumacero. Compilation by Josefina Procopio, Miguel Capistrán, Luis Mario Schneider, and Inés Arredondo. Mexico City: Fondo de Cultura Económica, 1953.

———. *Perseo vencido*. Supplement to *Revista de San Marcos*. Lima: Universidad de San Marcos, 1948.

Pacheco, José Emilio. *Alta traición: Antología poética*. Madrid: Alianza Editorial, 1985.

———. *Ciudad de la memoria: Poemas 1986–1989*. Mexico City: Ediciones Era, 1989.

———. *Los elementos de la noche*. Mexico City: Universidad Nacional Autónoma de México, 1963.

———. *Irás y no volverás*. Mexico City: Fondo de Cultura Económica, 1973.

———. *No me preguntes cómo pasa el tiempo*. Mexico City: Editorial Joaquín Mortiz, 1969.

———. *La poesía mexicana del siglo XIX*. Mexico City: Empresas Editoriales, 1965.

———. *El reposo del fuego*. Mexico City: Fondo de Cultura Económica, 1966.

———. *Los trabajos del mar*. Mexico City: Ediciones Era, 1983.

Paz, Octavio. *¿Aguila o sol?* Mexico City: Tezontle, 1951.

———. *Blanco*. Mexico City: Editorial Joaquín Mortiz, 1967.

———. *La búsqueda del comienzo*. Caracas and Madrid: Editorial Fundamentos, 1974.

———. *Children of the Mire: Modern Poetry from Romanticism to the Avant-Garde*. Trans. Rachel Phillips. Cambridge, Mass.: Harvard University Press, 1974.

————. *Cuadrivio*. Mexico City: Editorial Joaquín Mortiz, 1969.

————. *Discos visuales*. Four poems printed in four paper disks. Art by Vicente Rojo. Mexico City: Ediciones Era, 1968.

————. *Entre la piedra y la flor*. Mexico City: Nueva Voz, 1941.

————. *El laberinto de la soledad*. Mexico City: Fondo de Cultura Económica, 1950.

————. *Ladera este, 1962–1968*. Mexico City: Editorial Joaquín Mortiz, 1969.

————. *Libertad bajo palabra*. Mexico City: Tezontle, 1949.

————. *Luna silvestre*. Mexico City: [Miguel N. Lira y el maestro don Fidel Guerrero imprimieron esta fábula], 1933.

————. *El mono gramático*. Barcelona: Seix Barral, 1974.

————. *No pasarán*. Mexico City: Simbad, 1937.

————. *Las peras del olmo*. Mexico City: Universidad Nacional Autónoma de México, 1957.

————. *Piedra de sol*. Mexico City: Tezontle, 1957.

————. *Poemas (1935–1975)*. Barcelona: Seix Barral, 1979.

————. *Raíz del hombre*. Mexico City: Simbad, 1937.

————. *Salamandra 1958–1961*. Mexico City: Editorial Joaquín Mortiz, 1962.

————. *Los signos en rotación y otros ensayos*. Madrid: Alianza Editorial, 1971.

————. *Sombras de obras*. 2d ed. Barcelona: Seix Barral, 1986.

————. *Sor Juana Inés de la Cruz, o Las trampas de la fe*. Barcelona: Seix Barral, 1982.

————. *Topoemas*. 6 leaves. Mexico City: [Imprenta Madero?] 1968?.

Paz, Octavio, Alí Chumacero, José Emilio Pacheco, and Homero Aridjis. *Poesía en movimiento: México, 1915–1966*. Mexico City: Siglo XXI Editores, 1966.

Paz, Octavio, Jacques Roubaud, Edoardo Sanguinetti, and Charles Tomlinson. *Renga*. Mexico City: Editorial Joaquín Mortiz, 1971.

Paz Paredes, Margarita. *Litoral del tiempo*. Presentation by Efraín Huerta. Prologue by Roberto Oropeza Martínez. Mexico City: Ediciones del Gobierno del Estado de Guanajuato, 1978.

Pellicer, Carlos. *Colores en el mar y otros poemas*. Mexico City: Librería "Cultura," 1921.

————. *Material poético: 1918–1961*. Mexico City: Universidad Nacional Autónoma de México, 1962.

————. *Piedra de sacrificios: Poema iberoamericano*. Prologue by José Vasconcelos. Mexico City: Editorial Nayarit, 1924.

Phillips, Rachel. *Poetic Modes of Octavio Paz*. London: Oxford University Press, 1972.

Poniatowska, Elena. "La espiga amotinada." *El Rehilete* 2 (August 1961): 27–39.

Rodó, José Enrique. *Ariel*. Barcelona: Editorial Cervantes, 1930.

Rodríguez, Manuel Martín. "El fondo angustiado de los 'Nocturnos' de Xavier Villaurrutia." *Revista Iberoamericana* 148–149 (1989): 1119–1128.

Roggiano, Alfredo, ed. *Octavio Paz*. Madrid: Editorial Fundamentos, 1979.

Sabines, Jaime. *Horal*. Tuxtla Gutiérrez, Chiapas: Departamento de Prensa y Turismo, 1950.

————. *Nuevo recuento de poemas*. Mexico City: Editorial Joaquín Mortiz, 1977.

————. *Tarumba*. Mexico City: Colección Metáfora, 1956.

————. *Yuria*. Mexico City: Editorial Joaquín Mortiz, 1967.

Strelka, Joseph. "Comparative Criticism and Literary Symbolism." In *Perspectives in Literary Symbolism: Yearbook of Comparative Criticism*, 1–28. University Park: Pennsylvania State University Press, 1968.

Tablada, José Juan. *Al sol y bajo la luna*. Mexico City: Librería de la Viuda de C. Bouret, 1918.

————. *Un día . . . : Poemas sintéticos.* Caracas, Venezuela: Imprenta Bolivar, 1919.

————. *El florilegio.* Mexico City: Imprenta de I. Escalante, 1899.

————. *Historia del arte en México.* Mexico City: Compañía Nacional Editora "Aguilas," 1927.

————. *Li Po y otros poemas ideográficos.* Caracas, 1920. "Nocturno alterno" appears in this collection.

————. *Madero-Chantecler.* Published under the pseudonym Pinahete Alcornoque y Astrágalo. Mexico City: Compañía Aserradora de Maderos, 1910.

————. "Misa negra." Originally in newspaper *El País,* January 1893. See *Obras: Poesía, I,* ed. Hector Valdés, 269–270. Mexico City: Universidad Nacional Autónoma de México, 1971.

————. *La resurrección de los ídolos.* Mexico City: El Universal Ilustrado, 1924.

Torres Bodet, Jaime. *Biombo.* Mexico City: Herrero Hermanos, 1925.

————. *Canciones.* Mexico City: Editorial Cultura, 1922.

————. *El corazón delirante.* Mexico City: Editorial Porrúa, 1922.

————. *Cripta.* Mexico City: Loera y Chávez, 1937.

————. *Destierro.* Madrid: Espasa-Calpe, 1930.

————. *Los días.* Mexico City: Herrero Hermanos, 1923.

————. *Fervor.* Prologue by Enrique González Martínez. Mexico City, 1918.

————. *Fronteras.* Mexico City: Tezontle, 1954.

————. *Nuevas canciones.* n.p. [Madrid]: Saturnino Callejas, 1923.

————. *Poemas.* Mexico City: Herrero Hermanos, 1924.

————. *Sin tregua.* Mexico City: Tezontle, 1957.

————. *Sonetos.* Mexico City, 1949.

————. *Trébol de cuatro hojas.* Paris: Imprimerie nationale de París, 1958.

————. *Versos y prosas.* Ed. Sonja Karsen. Madrid: Ediciones Iberoamericanas, 1966.

Valdés, Héctor, ed. *Poetisas mexicanas: Siglo XX.* Mexico City: Universidad Nacional Autónoma de México, 1976.

Vázquez, Josefina Zoraida. "Antes y después de la revolución mexicana." *Revista Iberoamericana* 148–149 (1989): 693–713.

Verani, Hugo. *Las vanguardias literarias en Hispanoamérica (manifiestos, proclamas y otros escritos).* Roma: Bulzoni, 1986.

Villaurrutia, Xavier. *Canto a la primavera y otros poemas.* Mexico City: Editorial Stylo, 1948.

————. *Décima muerte y otros poemas no coleccionados.* Mexico City: Nueva Voz, 1941.

————. *Nocturno de los ángeles.* Mexico City: Hipocampo, 1936.

————. *Nocturnos.* Mexico City: Fábula, 1931.

————. *Nostalgia de la muerte.* Buenos Aires: Sur, 1938.

————. *Obras.* Compilation by Miguel Capistrán, Alí Chumacero, and Luis Mario Schneider. Prologue by Alí Chumacero. Bibliography by Luis Mario Schneider. Mexico City: Fondo de Cultura Económica, 1966.

————. *Ocho poetas.* Mexico City: Editorial Porrúa, 1923. With poems from Francisco Arellano Belloc, Ignacio Barajas Lozano, José María Benítez, Rafael Lozano, Miguel D. Martínez Rendón, Bernardo Ortiz de Montellano, and Jaime Torres Bodet.

————. *Reflejos.* Mexico City: Editorial Cultura, 1926.

Zaid, Gabriel. "Siete poemas de Carlos Pellicer." *Revista Iberoamericana* 148–149 (1989): 1099–1118.

7

Twentieth-Century Theater

KIRSTEN F. NIGRO

ON ESTABLISHING THE CANON

In order to rethink the canon of modern Mexican drama, it seems logical to first look backward to see how that canon came to be in the first place. A brief outline history of Mexico's dramatic heritage, one that condenses but follows the more expanded and official ones, would necessarily look as far back as pre-Columbian Mexico, to the rich and varied theatrical presentations of the Aztec and other Indian peoples, presentations that combined ritual, religion, and entertainment in ways not altogether different from those of other native American populations (Arrom; Arroniz; Potter). The allegorical and didactic nature of much of this theater seemed almost tailor-made for the purposes of the evangelizing priests who soon followed the conquistadores, priests who were themselves steeped in the tradition of another kind of allegorical and didactic theater—the Spanish medieval and early Renaissance *autos,* short religious plays about saints and other figures of the Holy Church. The two theatrical traditions were soon blended into a new "missionary theater" that retained many of the presentational aspects of indigenous theater, with a wholly Catholic and apostolic content and purpose. This blending of two cultures and of two art forms produced what can be considered the first uniquely Mexican drama.

However, this theater represents a very short-lived chapter in the historical accounts of Mexican theater, which consider the subsequent three hundred years as pretty much a blank or cultural vacuum. In accounts of the theater in colonial Mexico, only three names are usually singled out—those of Sor Juana Inés de la Cruz, who wrote significant *autos* and *comedias* (full-length plays) in the tradition of Calderón de la Barca; Fernán González de Eslava, the Spanish-born master of comical *entremeses* (interludes); and Juan Ruiz de Alarcón, the dramatist of social manners who was born in Mexico but wrote so much of his work in the mother country that Spain quite legitimately can claim him as her own. Theater historians attribute this dearth of autochthonous playwrights to the fact that almost all significant theater activity was brought to, rather than produced in, Mexico. Because plays, actors, scenographers, and just about anyone else involved in playmaking were imported almost exclusively from Spain, there was little opportunity for local talents to gain theatrical experience, and if they did write, there was no venue for testing their works. In addition, being of the Old World, the imported plays reflected little if anything of the social reality then taking shape in Mexico. Consequently, theater at this time was colonial in two senses—first, because of the historical period labeled "colonial" to which it belongs, and second, as a consequence of being a colonized theater, made by and for the outsider.

As with most other art forms in Spanish-speaking America, the wars of independence did not bring with them total independence for the stage. According to theater historians, much theater activity continued to be imported and therefore reflective of European tastes and artistic paradigms (Dauster, *Historia del teatro;* History of the Theater). Romanticism was the major influence of the time, and although it brought with it an interest in local color and the picturesque, the major playwrights staged were the likes of Victor Hugo (1802–1885), Alexandre Dumas (1802–1870), and the Duque de Rivas (1791–1865). Although historians of the period list the names of homegrown playwrights, only one—Manuel Eduardo de Gorostiza (1789–1851)—is considered first-rate, particularly for his gentle satire of romantic and love-struck youth, *Contigo, pan y cebolla* (With You, Bread and Onions; 1832).

It is with the late nineteenth century and early part of ours that theater historians begin to make claims for uncovering the first real foundation stones of modern Mexican drama (Magaña Esquivel; Nomland; Reyes de la Maza). They see it not so much in any outstanding individual or particular group, but rather in a growing presence of Mexico herself on the stage. As a consequence of the romantic emphasis on the picturesque and of the continued focus on the local in realism and regionalism (both of them imported from abroad), more and more plays, whatever their quality, were written by native-born Mexicans who concentrated on their own national reality. Few historians indicate that these plays ever became current theatrical fare, for this was, according to them, still dominated by foreign, especially Spanish, impresarios, so much so that it is not until the late 1920s that Mexican actors on stage, playing the parts of Mexicans, were allowed to use the Spanish typical of Mexico and not of the mother country.

With its decidedly European tastes, the long period of Porfirio Díaz's reign (1876–1910) certainly was not the most fertile time for local talent to grow and prosper. The advent of the 1910 Mexican Revolution, not surprisingly, had an initially quite disruptive effect on theater activity. By the early 1920s, however, the gunpowder and dust had settled down sufficiently for the theater to start up again, and the revolution itself became a central theme in many plays of that period, especially in the then popular *teatro de carpa,* or *teatro de revista,* a vaudeville-like review with musical and melodramatic routines, many of them satirical of political figures of the times. It is from about 1925 on that all histories of Mexican theater begin to talk about renovators and experimenters, of the individuals and groups who worked hard to make of their country's playwriting and play production a legitimate and critically acclaimed enterprise (Mendoza López; Schmidhuber, *El teatro mexicano*). However, they did not all approach this goal from the same direction. Some, like the Teatro de Murciélago and the Teatro de Ahora, rather in the line of the Mexican muralists, wanted a serious national theater that would deal with the sociopolitical realities of Mexico's past and present. For these groups, then, a national theater meant one that was rooted in the particular, whereas for other renovators the particular had no meaning without the universal. For example, El Grupo de los 7 Autores, which was formed in 1925, and the Teatro Ulises, which came together three years later, were much more cosmopolitan in their outlook and wanted to make world theater known to Mexican audiences, although they did at the same time actively champion some Mexican playwrights and were instrumental in putting together a few brief seasons dedicated partially or wholly to their work.

Although most histories give a critical nod to experimental efforts like that of Ulises over the social-reformist ones of others like the Grupo de Ahora, it is in fact the more realistic vein of theater that actually came to take hold of the Mexican stage in the 1940s and 1950s, a triumph which is attributed almost unanimously to one playwright—Rodolfo Usigli (1905–1979). His play, *El gesticulador* (The Gesticulator; written 1938, staged 1947) is an exploration of the ethos and psyche of the Mexican nation, as well as a study in the posturing and role-playing that define its political structures and behavior. Although *El gesticulador* deals with almost Pirandellian issues about reality and fiction, it is written for a proscenium stage, to be mounted behind an invisible fourth wall. Usigli long championed this realistic method, and as a professor of dramatic literature at the National Autonomous University of Mexico, he was a great influence on younger playwrights during that period, who through him came to know the works of George Bernard Shaw (1856–1950), Eugene O'Neill (1888–1953), Arthur Miller (1915–), and Tennessee Williams (1911–1983).

Usigli's influence at the time was such that many histories see him as the pivotal figure in the creation of modern Mexican drama, as a kind of equator between what was a centuries-long preface to the main act of Mexican drama. It is only with and after Usigli that theater histories begin to talk of first-rate *playwrights* (as opposed to the occasional and often mediocre writer of plays), such as Salvador Novo (1904–1974), Emilio Carballido (1925–), Hugo Argüelles (1932–), Luisa Josefina Hernández (1928–), Celestino Gorostiza (1904–1967), Sergio Magaña (1924–1990). Terms like *pioneers* and *precursors* give way to ones such as *founders* and *classics*.

However, during the next chapter in the history of Mexican theater, the realistic movement lost much of its impetus. Its first organized opposition was the group known as Poesía en Voz Alta, whose very name—Poetry Out Loud—makes clear their mission to bring poetry back onto the stage (Unger). But it is the so-called new theater of the 1960s that mounts the most successful attack against traditional proscenium theater. Like the decade that gave it birth, this theater is fragmented, rebellious, often frontal and aggressive. The

names of international figures like Bertolt Brecht (1898–1956), Erwin Piscator (1895–1966), Antonin Artaud (1896–1948), and Peter Weiss (1916–
1982) begin to creep into histories and criticism, as so-called epic and documentary theater and the theater of cruelty find their way onto Mexican stages.
New names like those of Vicente Leñero (1933–) and Maruxa Vilalta (1932–)
begin to be more prominent, while the Beatles and all the other emblems of
1960s pop culture become critical tools for understanding fringe theater like
that of the Onda (roughly translated the Wave), written by youths alienated
in and by the megalopolis of Mexico City. In the 1970s there is the so-called
Nueva Dramaturgia, New Dramaturgy, written by young playwrights like Víctor Hugo Rascón Banda (1948–), who build a logical bridge into the 1980s with
a theater that, although firmly committed to Mexican reality, is wholly iconoclastic in its technique (Burgess, *New Dramatists;* Burgess, "Nuevo teatro").

ON QUESTIONING THE CANON

Although this is the raw data of the development of Mexican drama, these
facts do not speak for themselves or tell the whole truth. For this or any other
history can be as significant and as revealing for what it does not include,
emphasize, or value, as for what it does. While no historical account can be
totally complete, the very fact of its inevitable incompleteness should be accounted for in a discussion of artistic canons, whose purpose, after all, is to
single out certain works and exclude others. Therefore, while one may not
want to argue whether the history broadly outlined above is technically—that
is, factually—correct, there is still much to be questioned about how and why
certain texts are selected and valorized over others.

If for years the canon has been seen as something stable and enduring,
embracing the forever-great works of art, in recent years its sanctity has been
seriously questioned. Reader-response critics, for example, have attacked it
with perceptual arms, as it were, for as they began to analyze the way that we
read and respond to literature, they had to deal with the inescapable fact that
not all of us read or respond to art in a like fashion (Fish; Tompkins; Suleiman
and Crosman). There also has been a growing realization of the importance
not only of individual but also of cultural and historical differences in these
processes, what Hans Robert Jauss has called "horizons of expectations and
experience." Yet, within these differences there seem to be enough coinci-
dences to allow for understanding between the artist and his or her public. As
Jonathan Culler has noted, "It is his experience of reading, his notions of what
readers can and will do, that enables the author to write, for to intend meanings is to assume a system of conventions and create signs within the perspective of that system" (50). If meaning is largely conventional, it therefore cannot
be something locked up in a work forever, but rather, it changes and shifts
with differing conventions of reading and artistic creation. And if meaning is
a shifting sand, so then is the concomitant process of evaluation that always
accompanies the act of interpretation. To quote Kenneth E. Boulding, "The

subjective knowledge structure or image of any individual or organization consists not only of images of 'fact' but also images of 'value' " (11). That is to say, when we read or view a work of art, we not only try to make meaning but also pass judgment, and this of course is what ultimately establishes the canon. Like sense-making, however, valuations are the products of conventions, which by their very nature and definition are transitory; consequently, the canon, far from consisting of holy tablets, is actually a list of works that for whatever reasons have been judged to be better than others.

Not surprisingly, there is some theoretical disagreement as to what these "for whatever reasons" might be. Some see convention making and convention following as an ideological process and not just a self-generating artistic one closed upon itself. As Juan Villegas has noted,

> The perception that all critical discourse is a discursive practice, and as such, is an ideological practice, should lead to an acceptance that all "readings" of texts . . . are "ideologized" readings from the perspective of the emitter of critical discourse. . . .
> From this vantage point, then, the predominance or hegemony of an aesthetic system consequently is a phenomenon whose roots are historical and contextual, whose validity is historical and not "universal" or "eternal." (17–18)[1]

Ideology in this context, however, goes well beyond its more common usage as formalized political beliefs to encompass the very structures that define and are defined by all aspects of a given culture, culture being understood along the lines of Peter Berger's definition of it as "the totality of man's products" (6). When seen in this light, ideology is not something certain writers or readers have more or less of than others, but something they all share, although it may be of a different variety.

The valuation of one text above another, therefore, can be considered an ideological act, one that displaces or totally excludes another text from a position of influence. And because of this, texts are not just innocent aesthetic objects: they can be centers of considerable power or, alternately, pose a threat to those same centers. The struggle of minority, Third World, and women's art to find a place for itself within dominant artistic, economic, and academic structures or to create a space of its own offers testimony to how unwillingly these spaces are shared or relinquished. This is not to turn art and its production and reception into a battlefield of competing interests only, but rather to admit, along with Edward Said, that texts (be they creative or critical) are worldly and, therefore, are "an act of will with ascertainable political and intellectual consequences" (220).

This essay will explore various consequences of that worldiness on the so-called canon of Mexican drama. But from the outset it should be noted that the very existence of such a canon is not necessarily a given within larger notions of the canon of world drama. For, as with most Latin American drama, that of Mexico has not been given much if any attention by the critical arbiters who establish the larger canon. This is surely due in part to ignorance, to not being familiar with the drama of Spanish-speaking America. But it is also in no small measure due to standards of supposed universal and enduring values that are set by those same arbiters, values that have the effect of shunting aside theater that is overtly culture- and period-specific, as is much of the drama of Latin America. Under closer scrutiny, these standards prove illusory, or at least they can be shown up for their ideological biases. Nonetheless, they are among the most compelling and entrenched in the process of canonizing world art, with the effect that the vast majority of non-European or non–North American drama does not even enter into the running.

Unfortunately, these same notions often play a very powerful role in how a nation canonizes its own drama. This has been particularly true in Mexico, which as a colonized nation has struggled to come to terms with its hybrid, mestizo identity. In the brief history of its drama outlined above there is a thread that runs throughout: the conflict between a theater that is national in its form and content and one that is European or foreign in origin. The latter is most often considered the really quality theater, while the former is labeled parochial and clumsy and therefore of lesser artistic value. For some of its historians, Mexican theater only becomes consequential when it resolves this conflict in plays that are "so Mexican that they are universal," meaning that since Mexico is part of the larger world community, whatever is particularly Mexican must also be shared throughout the globe. This does not really solve the problem and begs the question of who and what defines the supposedly "universal" and why a national art would aspire to it in the first place.

Nonetheless, this is a mighty issue in the establishment of a canon for Mexican drama. Because universality is seen as such a sine qua non for quality, it has had the effect of making many Mexicans themselves underappreciate, if not totally ignore, their own dramatists. On the one hand, this manifests itself in the way the history of Mexican literature is written, where plays and playwrights, with very few exceptions, are given little or no space. On the other hand, those who do compile histories and critiques of Mexican drama tend also to be guided by these same notions of excellence, with an added one that has a profound effect on how the canon is established: their literary bias at the expense of performance. Thus, the canon as established by most histories does two things: it singles out for special praise those plays that supposedly transcend the purely Mexican and those that are considered to have enduring value as playscripts—that is, as works of literature. Consequently, plays that have never or only rarely been performed are sometimes rated over those that have had a successful stage life but are judged to not read as well (if they are textual at all, for scriptless plays have a nearly zero chance of ever being given serious consideration for the canon). This also means that the canon according to these criteria excludes most if not all popular manifestations of theater—variety shows and vaudeville, as well as so-called lowbrow comedy and melodrama.

There is another equally important aspect of this traditional drama versus theater, of the written text versus performance dichotomy. For if the literary bias often reflects essentialist values about quality and worth, the performance one is often defined by notions of worth that have more to do with budgets than with aesthetics, given that a major dimension of the theater's worldliness is that it is most often an economic venture, that it languishes or thrives at the box office. In Mexico this has the effect that many national playwrights struggle to get their works commercially produced, and when they are produced, there is often the added struggle of getting a public to view them. This problem is so serious and so long-standing that the playwright Emilio Carballido has felt compelled to make it an issue in some of his plays. For example, in *Tiempo de ladrones* (Thieves' Time; 1983), a nineteenth-century theater impresario scoffs at his actors' suggestion that they create a national theater: "And just what do you want me to do? Mexican plays are of the most detestable kind. And I'm not going to force the public to see them, just because the government is going to subsidize the season. . . . What Mexican writers are there? I've worn my eyes out reading them all, dead and alive. There is no one!" (51, 54).

These difficulties in creating an appreciation of national playwrights means that in terms of performance, the theater in Mexico as a socioeconomic and entertainment enterprise will not wholly coincide with the canon as established by academics and critics, with a double-edged consequence: some of the canonized plays are not given a fair chance for production if commercial ventures see them as economically risky, and the plays that are successfully produced may be less literary and more popular or theatrical than the academic canon permits.

These kinds of contradictions make clear that there is not just one canon but various, and who establishes them is as important as what is established. And as none of them is sacred, each can be questioned, scrutinized, and when necessary even rewritten. However, that is an enterprise that goes well beyond the scope of this essay, as well as the abilities of this reseacher. Indeed, here I will talk about the one canon I know best—the one established by North American scholars. In many ways it conforms to the canon as written by Mexican theater academics, as we borrow a great deal from their work. Unquestionably, our geographical distance from the day-to-day theater world in Mexico sometimes results in unique valuations or omissions. By the same token, this distance can sometimes allow for more perspective, a better opportunity to see where there are gaps to be filled and reevaluations to be made.

RETHINKING THE PRELUDE

As noted above, there is rather a consensus among North American scholars, at least, that Mexican drama has its first full-fledged practitioner in Rodolfo Usigli and that his *El gesticulador* is the play that really sets the stage for twentieth-century Mexican drama. Certainly it is the one work that is included in most everyone's canon, and with good reason. For with *El gesticulador,* Usigli successfully joins together two dramatic currents that were then struggling to gain legitimacy in Mexico: playwriting in a serious realistic manner (à la Ibsen and Shaw) and playwriting with a national focus and concern. With its keen depiction of the posturing and role-playing endemic to the Mexican political scene, *El gesticulador* continues to be relevant if not prophetic forty years after its premiere and is still periodically revived by major theater groups. And for a very long time, it was the only Mexican play to have successfully traveled abroad.

Because of its critical success and influence on subsequent playwrights, *El gesticulador* is seen as the one play that breaks with a theatrical past that for the most part is best forgotten. Certainly theater historians recognize Usigli's debt to his immediate predecessors, for example, the Teatro de Ahora, which was committed to staging plays politically and spiritually allied to Mexican reality. But the debt is seen as a practical and not an artistic one, in that the Teatro de Ahora is given credit for championing a national theater but of doing so with a limited talent. Thus, the following evaluation of the Teatro de Ahora is not atypical: "It is a political theater with an almost exclusively revolutionary purpose, and this pamphleteering quality resulted in an excessively crude didactic social realism" (Dauster, *Historia del teatro,* 64). Consequently, the group's work is mostly relegated to the realm of historical curiosities, when it is given consideration at all. This devaluation of the Teatro de Ahora needs serious reconsideration, in part because it carries with it implicitly the notion that overtly political theater is necessarily flawed (in itself an extraordinarily loaded value judgment) and also because one of the Ahora plays, *San Miguel de las Espinas: Trilogía dramática de un pedazo de tierra mexicana* (San Miguel of the Spines: A Dramatic Trilogy about a Parcel of Mexican Land; 1933), by Juan Bustillo Oro (1904–1989), rivals if not excels *El gesticulador* in theatrical merits.

The San Miguel of the play's title is a dry and hot desert ranch somewhere in northern Mexico. The spines of the cactus in this part of Mexico draw real blood, but to live in San Miguel is also to bleed from the crown of spines worn by the poor campesinos who struggle to squeeze a drop of water from the barren land that they farm. Unfortunately for them, more blood than water flows during the play's three acts, which cover a time span from the eve of the Mexican Revolution to the early 1930s. Each act is like one in a bleak and somber opera, in which the recurring theme or leitmotif is the dam that is supposed to bring relief and prosperity to the peasants. Of course, it never does; quite the opposite, as it is the cause of violent death and much bloodshed.

San Miguel de las Espinas recounts a tale very much like the one in *El gesticulador,* in which political intrigue, chicanery, and assassination are equally standard fare. But technically the plays are worlds apart, and it is in the telling of his story that Bustillo Oro has created a work quite extraordinary for its time in Mexico. To speak in terms of the operatic when describing it is not mere hyperbole, for this is a play grand in scope, tone, and theatricality. Although the subject matter is absolutely social-realist and the play's purpose is unquestionably didactic and reformist, Bustillo Oro's theatrical ideolect has more in common with Guiseppi Verdi (1813–1901) than with André Antoine (1853–1943) or Henrik Ibsen (1828–1906). But there is also a lot of the artistry of Erwin Piscator, as well. The allusion to Verdi and to Piscator in a single breath may seem odd, to say the least, but in *San Miguel de las Espinas,* the use of choral elements contrapuntally on and off stage, the highly theatrical use of sets, as well as the pictorial quality and composition of some of the dramatic frames are certainly evocative of grand opera, whereas the episodic structure, the experimental use of spotlights, and other anti-illusionistic techniques reflect Bustillo Oro's early knowledge of the staging experiments engaged in by Piscator and other European theater mavericks during the 1920s and 1930s (Cucuel; Schmidhuber, *El teatro mexicano*).

From the moment the curtain rises on the play, its creatively hybrid quality is obvious. The fixed-feature space of the setting itself is very representational or iconic and stands for the façade of the rundown ranch house of San Miguel. A fence backstage with an entrance arch opens onto the bleak desert beyond, with its variety of cactus. A great many building materials are stacked up against the ranch house and fence; upstage right there is an improvised workspace (chairs and a table under a canvas canopy) and rolls of engineer's drawings and plans. However, the realism of the setting as visual sign is undercut by the frankly operatic manner in which the play's action opens. The stage is gradually engulfed by the light of dawn, first the background of desert landscape and then stage front. Simultaneously and offstage, a chorus of men and one of women recite alternately and then in unison what functions as a kind of lament and hopeful prayer, as well as an introduction to the play's situation and theme. The use of a chorus in the midst of a largely representational play has a decisive function in and effect on *San Miguel de las Espinas.* Harkening back to the Greek chorus while anticipating the Brechtian commentator/narrator, the chorus here has an alienating or distancing effect; that is to say, it breaks the dramatic illusion, thereby framing and pointing to the play's theatricality. Unexpected within the play's realistic framework, the lyrical quality and commentative aspect of the chorus's words stand out for the audience, who will focus special attention on what they have to say and accept the chorus as a kind of intermediary between the worlds on and off stage.

The operatic quality of the chorus, of course, also evokes the grandeur, the epic, of the revolution, but more important, it embodies the collective nature of that dramatic historic event. The chorus represents and speaks for the people, the major protagonists in the revolution; indeed, *San Miguel de las Espinas* is the theatrical equivalent of *Los de abajo* (*The Underdogs,* 1915), by Mariano Azuela (1873–1952), where the sense of a mass sociohistorical movement was the principal motif. And, as in Azuela's novel, there is in Bustillo Oro's play also a sense that the revolution is a violent whirlwind that destroys all that it sucks in. This is expressed theatrically by the fast-moving and rather episodic nature of the plot, as well as by the explosive confusion of violence that closes each act, as for example, at the end of act 2:

A round of gunfire startles the women and children, making them huddle together at the side of the hut. Screams and more gunshots are heard offstage, center. A few seconds later, Secundino el Chivo and two other men enter hurriedly, trying to defend themselves with their rifles. But the soldiers are too close behind them; they are surrounded and taken prisoner. (72)

As noted earlier, Bustillo Oro has a keen sense of the visual in this play, as evidenced not only in the stage settings he asks for, but also in his composition of specific stage frames, many of which are highly evocative of frames in the now-famous murals that were being painted at about the same time that he wrote *San Miguel de las Espinas*. In these murals, episodes from or aspects of Indian life were given prominence, and certain poses or actions seem now almost to have been mythified by many of the muralists, in particular by Diego Rivera: poses of women grinding corn, of arms raised in defiance, of children held high, in supplication to God. Given that theater is also a visual art, it is not surprising that Bustillo Oro sought to present these same kinds of images on the stage; for example: "At this moment two women come out of the hut upstage, carrying their traditional cooking utensils. They place them on the ground and squat down quietly. One of them grinds corn while the voices [the chorus] inside keep on talking" (50); or "Lights out. A spot focuses only on the women and children huddled together. Some mothers lift their children up toward the sky" (72).

It is rather surprising, therefore, that the Mexican artistic canon in general includes hardly any theater, much less *San Miguel de las Espinas* in the space allotted to "revolutionary" works, in both form and content. Yet as one looks back, it is remarkable to see how ahead of the times Bustillo Oro actually was, to realize just what he was hoping to do with the stage and his awareness of theatrical innovation. Like Piscator and Brecht, he saw the stage as the space where the collective struggle of the oppressed could be enacted, but unlike them, Bustillo Oro had in his own country the raw historical subject matter from which to fashion revolutionary theater. Throughout *San Miguel de las Espinas* there are obvious elements of what we now associate with Brechtian theater: the episodic form, the use of spotlights, a chorus/narrator, an emphasis on collective action rather than individual psychology. And yet, Piscator and Brecht are not mentioned as influences in Mexican theater until the 1960s, with plays like Emilio Carballido's *Un pequeño día de ira* (A Little Day of Anger; 1962), which so clearly emulates the epic paradigm.

The failure to remember or appreciate a play like *San Miguel de las Espinas* not only gives a false sense of the development of Mexican theater in general, but also has meant that traditionally Usigli's *El gesticulador* has been considered both the first modern play and the only play of worth about the Mexican Revolution. And interestingly enough, as Usigli presents it, the revolution is more a psychological and personality problem than a sociopolitical one. Indeed, one could argue that it is precisely this quality that makes *El gesticulador* such a popular play with many North American critics and canon-setters, for it follows the theatrical paradigm that most often satisfies our requirements for so-called good drama—that is, it creates well-rounded and psychologically interesting characters who, while very much caught up in a particular (Mexican) situation, can also be seen more abstractly as universal symbols (e.g., of our need to play-act, to be other than what we are, or of our need to believe what we know is not true). Bustillo Oro's play does not allow as easily for this kind of abstraction, although its technical innovations certainly give it an almost "larger-than-life" resonance.

Whatever the case, a reconsideration of *San Miguel de las Espinas* and other plays, and not only of the Teatro de Ahora, would most probably force critics and theater historians to rethink when and how the modern stage of Mexican drama was really set.[2] As a result, Usigli would certainly have to share his special place with Bustillo Oro, but then it would be convincingly shown that the innovators of the 1960s and 1970s had a pivotal precursor in the history of their own national theater. Indeed, the critic Frank Dauster, initially so harsh in his evaluation of the Teatro de Ahora, has come to see it in another light by underscoring the innovative changes that Juan Bustillo Oro worked on the realistic paradigm. As Dauster notes, "It is curious that the playwright who is most in tune with the New Theater [of today], and unquestionably with a theater future to his, should be a writer who worked separately from the experimenters of his time and who is almost forgotten today" ("La generación de 1924," 22).

TOWARD A FUTURE CANON

Looking back of course is always easier than projecting into the future, and so it is certainly risky to speculate on the canonical or noncanonical fate of very contemporary texts; some that are out of favor today may well be in favor tomorrow. However, there are patterns of evaluation that would indicate that certain kinds of works will be passed by. If the work of the Teatro de Ahora, back in the 1930s, has been dismissed as too political, as historical relics of little artistic worth, then much of what has been written and produced these past twenty years in Mexico may suffer a similar critical snub, largely because with the 1960s playwriting became far more concerned with the theatrical and performance potential of a written text. Thus, if mostly literary yardsticks are used to measure the worth of this drama, then much of it may well be cast into oblivion. Some probably deserves it (a statement revealing of my own ideological biases, to be sure), but some of it may not. I put forth as a brief example *El extensionista* (The Government Man; first performed 1979), by Felipe Santander (1935–), in which a newly graduated agronomist, Cruz López, is sent by the federal government to teach the campesinos how it is they really should be doing their farming. In the course of his stay there, he is transformed from a rather snobby city boy into a compassionate and caring member of a rural community that has been abused by its own local officials with the blessing of their even more corrupt counterparts in Mexico City.

Poised on the verge of insurgency, the townsfolk are interrupted by the Cancionero (a kind of singing narrator) who has weaved in and out of the action throughout, offering commentary, summarizing events, singing Mexican *corridos,* or ballads. He interrupts the stage action in order to open it up into a public forum, giving audience members a chance to write the play's ending: Will there be an armed or peaceful revolution? Will there be change? How can there be change in the face of such corruption? As the Cancionero says: "Therefore we ask that you please give us suggestions about how, in your opinion, what's happened here should end. We'll take some of these suggestions, we'll discuss them, and finally, you will decide by popular vote which ending we'll give the play" (112).

Even so brief a plot summary gives an idea of the Brechtian-cum-1960s participatory theater flavor of *El extensionista,* with its singing narrator and anti-illusionistic framework. In addition, it is highly episodic, with a largish cast and very little psychological development of characters. In a word, it is representative par excellence of so much of recent alternative, openly political, anticommercial, antiliterary theater. Consequently, a mostly academic reading of the text could easily lead one to agree with the conclusion that it is "a text that might well not reach the status of a classic work" (Woodyard, 12; quoted by Schmidhuber, "La dramaturgia mexicana," 129). However, *El extensionista* proved to be one of Mexico City's longest-running plays with well over 2,000 performances. It has been performed in the United States and Europe and won the Cuban Premio Casa de las Américas in 1980. Its English translator Joe Rosenberg, who read the text with an eye to the stage (and not the page), reacted to it in a very different way: "When I sat down to the task, it didn't prove to be as difficult as I had thought. The script is extremely well put-together. I found the flavor of the campesino way of life practically falling out of the words. More important, this was a playscript in which the characters transcended their locality. It dealt with the psychological warfare of he who needs to be trusted and he who has too often been betrayed. It was more than regional dialogue I found myself translating; I was involved in the international language of life everywhere" (n.p.). By this evaluation, then, *El extensionista* would be ripe for canonization. However, because it is largely the academic, text-bound criteria that tend to establish the canon, Santander and other similar playwrights may well find that their work will merit only passing reference or footnotes in future histories of Mexican drama. This is not so much to make an apology for *El extensionista* as to underscore what is a major problem here—that the guidelines for canonization, as presently defined, have little to do with the reality of much playwriting and playmaking during the 1960s and 1970s. And if those guidelines are not modified or rewritten, then a major chunk of important work may well be excluded from critical consideration. Happily, the recent publication of Frischmann's *El nuevo teatro popular* has established the importance of this theater and offers a paradigm for its study.

POLITICAL CENSORSHIP AND THE CANON

El extensionista also exemplifies another way that plays can sometimes never even get into the running for canonization—they are denied a stage space to bring them to life. With *El extensionista* this was almost the case, for commercial and government-owned theaters refused their facilities to Santander, sometimes with an outright no, others by more devious means. In the end he was helped by young, alternative theater people, who offered him their less-than-luxurious stage in the Teatro de la Juventud. Powerful theater critics refused to review the play, and its popular success owed more to word of mouth than to press releases. Santander managed to overcome all the official and monetary obstacles that were put in his way, obstacles that were clearly meant to keep dead on the page a play that makes a powerful critique of offical corruption and greed in Mexico.

For Vicente Leñero this kind of blacklisting has been a continuous problem since he began his playwriting career in 1964. In his theatrical autobiographies, *Vivir del teatro* (Living from the Theater; 1982 and 1990), Leñero recounts how on numerous occasions producers have been reluctant to back his work because of its critical look at Mexican history and its current politics. Sometimes the situation has been slightly different, in that Leñero has managed to find both a first-class producer and director but no available theater, or rather, no government-subsidized theater space (which is the major kind at the disposal of Mexican playwrights like Leñero, whose work will not command the audience that imported Broadway plays do and therefore cannot take the risk of renting more expensive, commercial theaters).

Readers at all familiar with Mexican literature will know that Vicente Leñero is a renowned writer both within and without that country. Thus mention of him in relationship to noncanonical works may seem rather odd; however, Leñero's travails with direct and indirect censorship in Mexico show to what degree even established writers there run the risk of being silenced. The two most celebrated cases for Leñero were in 1983, with his play *Martirio de Morelos* (The Martyrdom of Morelos), and in 1988, with *Nadie sabe nada* (Nobody Knows Anything). Both are works of extraordinary artistic merit but ran afoul of the authorities because of their questioning of Mexican official history and of the forces that write, or perhaps invent, it. In other words, these are plays concerned with censorship that ironically, or better yet, metatheatrically, experienced their own subject matter.

Martirio de Morelos deals with the last days in the life of the priest José María Morelos, a figure revered in Mexican history for his key role in the nineteenth-century wars of independence. Morelos was taken prisoner, tortured, condemned in civil, military, and ecclesiatical trials, and was then executed in November of 1815. Like most revolutionary heroes anywhere, the Mexican Morelos has over the years been portrayed as a brave and noble man, who endured great suffering but died a martyr to his cause. However, in reading some little-known texts, Leñero found references to a different Morelos, to one who actually broke when tortured, giving the Spanish important names and secret plans of the independence forces. As Leñero explains it, this did not diminish Morelos in his eyes. Rather, it cast him down to human scale, making him more accessible to real people who undoubtedly would have done as Morelos did.

Reading these texts also made Leñero wonder about written history itself and question its suppposed truthfulness. In the play Leñero introduces a character named El Lector (The Reader), who reads from an enormous volume of Mexican history as Morelos listens in disbelief at the version it gives of who he was. This sets up the basic dramatic situation, in which Morelos retells history as he himself experienced and shaped it, at least according to the alternate version that Leñero had discovered. Simultaneously, as Morelos tells it, this history is acted out on stage for the contemporary Mexican audience. Unfortunately for Leñero and his director, Luis de Tavira, there were many in this audience who took extreme offense to the play, even before it opened; based on hearsay, they labeled *Martirio de Morelos* sacrilegious and insulting to a national hero. Patriotic groups protested and, worse yet, the new president, Miguel de la Madrid, turned out also to be a fervent "Morelista."

Soon before the play was scheduled to premiere at one of the theaters of the National Autonomous University of Mexico, word came that it was being cancelled, although it was not clear who made the decision, whether the University or some even higher authority. Once the word spread, there was a general outcry among the artistic community, and a compromise was reached. The play's actual opening would be postponed by a few days, allowing for private previews in which University-invited guests would decide whether the play was indeed offensive. As Leñero has said, it was understood that these previews were really a way for the powers-that-be to get out of an uncomfortable situation: to be able to say that the play had been reviewed by censors, but those so chosen that the play would suffer no delay in its run. Although Ignacio Retes, a director, protested that this too was a kind of insidious censorship, Leñero and the others involved with the play signed a document agreeing to these terms. However, when the agreement was made public in the newspapers, the names of the University rector and other important University officials were not there, just those of the minor bureaucrats involved, thereby erasing from the record any connection with higher authorities in this episode of attempted censorship.[3]

Martirio de Morelos was mounted as scheduled, but in 1988 Leñero and de Tavira found themselves fighting censors again; this time, however, their opening night was cancelled. With *Nadie sabe nada,* Leñero tackles not Mexico's past, but rather her very corrupt present, in which collusion between powerful members of government and the press work to silence what one of the characters in the play calls "Mexico's Watergate." Subtitled a "Thriller in Two Acts and Thirteen Scenes," *Nadie sabe nada* is a theatrical tour de force, both for its staging demands (seven simultaneous sets and over two dozen characters) and for the riveting story it tells—one of intrigue, corruption, rape, drug-dealing, and murder. However, the story hit too close to home, with its direct and indirect allusions to present-day labor leaders, politicians, government officials, and newspaper czars. Citing "orders from above," officials of the Fine Arts Institute delayed the production's opening; meanwhile, censors demanded that certain parts of the play be deleted or changed (such as references to President Carlos Salinas de Gortari and the playing of the National Anthem at the end of the play, an obvious irony given that it comes on the heels of a gruesome political murder and other unsavory events). For Leñero these were not compromising changes, although again, this episode shows that, the official version notwithstanding, all too often playwrights in Mexico must fight a hostile government bureaucracy in order to get their work staged.

REGIONAL CENSORSHIP AND THE CANON

There is another kind of censorship in Mexico that can deny a playing space to playwrights; more specifically, a censorship that silences them because of their geographic destiny. The problem of geographic destiny is a major one in Mexico, where the capital city dominates everything cultural and economic. For the theater, this has damning consequences, as playwrights are forced to migrate to Mexico City if they want a successful career. As a consequence, the development of a meaningful regional theater (which has helped somewhat to break the total monopoly New York City has held in this country) just has not been possible in Mexico. As the playwright Guillermo Schmidhuber de la Mora has noted:

> The Province, according to its Latin etymology, means a barbaric land that is still to be conquered: *pro vinci.* For many Mexico City theater people this is the only definition that seems true, since it is in the capital city that official theater work is planned and done, helped along by the fact that the majority of playwrights, directors, and professional actors are inhabitants of that metropolis. Every now and again they go out on tour, hoping to "do the provinces," with the same adventuresome spirit of the Spanish companies who during the nineteenth century dreamed of "doing America," and ventured forth into barbaric lands, casting their fate to the winds. The province for these theater artists represents a cultural backwater.

> ("El teatro mexicano," 23)

Although marginalized, this regional theater is nonetheless very much alive, and its exclusion from the canon gives a quite blinkered vision of theatrical life in Mexico as a whole. For example, the peninsula of Yucatán has a long and rich theatrical history dating from pre-Columbian times, its real flourish beginning with the 1910 Revolution when many theater artists fled the capital for safety in Yucatán. While there, these exiles staged plays by homegrown Yucatecan playwrights who had begun writing as early as the 1800s. As Fernando Muñoz has noted, "Yucatán is the only state in the country with a regional theater that has developed various genres: tragedy, opera, comedy, vaudeville, which is today what one understands for regional theater in Yucatán, and which . . . is similar to the vaudeville and political review in Mexico City and to the Cuban *bufo*" (11).

There is, however, a younger regional theater that should be of considerable interest, particularly to U.S. scholars: the border theater. Not surprisingly, the borderlands, like Yucatán, are seen from Mexico City as either a cultural backwater or a place unconnected to the capital-city reality. Indeed, the prejudice against the *fronterizo* (Mexican who lives in the border zone), who rubs elbows with the U.S. and whose culture is another kind of *mestizaje,* may well have something to do with the marginalization of this particular regional theater. Whatever the case, *fronterizo* plays are very much connected to our north-of-the-border experience or visions of Mexican reality, and consequently, we, at least, should make some space for them in our consideration of Mexican drama.

As might be expected, the Northern borderlands theater has much in common with Chicano theater, which is also concerned with the interface of two often conflictive cultures; in addition, *fronterizo* playwrights explore and express what is and is not rich and wonderful about their particular Mexican experiences. For example, in the collection of prizewinning plays *Tres de la frontera tres* (Three from the Border, Three; 1986) one play, Francisco Ortega Rodríguez's *La frontera* (The Border), deals with corruption in the newspaper world, through a combination of conventional realism and rapid, episodic frames; the second, *De acá, de este lado* (Over Here, On This Side) by Guillermo Sergio Alanís O., is a black, almost absurdist satire of the greed of those who think that crossing the border brings with it instant wealth; and the third play, *Cupido hizo casa en Bravo* (Cupid Set Up House in Bravo) by Irma Guadalupe Olivares Avila, is a delightful comedy of errors involving mismatched lovers, mistaken identities, and a cow named Clariza. However different these plays may be, they do have a distinctively regional flavor, in their theme, locale, and idiomatic turns.

Still, these plays are no more local than some by capital city dramatists whose work is not in turn banned from provincial stages. And while they are plays by perhaps less-experienced playwrights, one of them, *De acá, de este lado* is a very accomplished text indeed. Over here, on this side, is where a Mother, her Daughter and Son, and their Neighbor live, "in a town in an underdeveloped country that borders on a world power" (53). Although a one-acter, the play has three distinct temporal movements, each of them marked by an important holiday in Mexico: the Fiestas Patrias (September 15), the celebration honoring the Virgin of Guadalupe (December 12), and Mother's Day (May 10). These movements are subtly indicated by the Neighbor who in each instance comes to inquire about the Mother's other son, the eldest one who went across to the other side to make his fortune. The answer is always the same: that he has not written yet, but that soon, very soon, they will be millionaires. Indeed, the Mother's faith in her would-be Horatio Alger son is such that she refuses to let her other children work or to go even out of the house, because they must be there when the letter arrives; also, if they are soon to be rich, she does not want them mingling with all the poor people on their side of the border. She will not even let them eat "until we have the food that we deserve" (67). So, another way that the temporal transitions in the play are marked is by the characters' visibly progressive state of starvation. When her other two children come to realize that their Mother is slowly kill- ing them because of her own pride and stupidity, they strangle her and flee for their lives. At that point, the Neighbor arrives again, the Mother awakens from what has been a bad dream, and although she is perturbed by what she has just dreamed, she says that yes, she thinks she will send her eldest son across the border to see if he can make a little money to help them out. When the Neighbor wishes him good luck, the Mother answers, "No, it's us, the ones who stay here on this side, who God should help" (83).

In *De acá, de este lado,* the playwright Guillermo Sergio Alanís O. inverts what in many other plays is a focus on what happens to those who dare to cross over to the North, as in *Los ilegales* (The Illegals; 1980) by Víctor Hugo Rascón Banda. Here the emphasis is on why they go in the first place and what happens to those that they leave behind. Rather than presenting this in a con- ventional, that is realistic, fashion, the playwright metaphorizes it. The whole question of hunger, which is usually seen as a concrete, very real reason why Mexicans risk their lives to get to the other side, is seen also as a metaphorical hunger, a hunger for money, of course, but also a lack of spirit, of love of family and country. For it is no coincidence that the Neighbor's visits fall on cherished festive days in Mexican culture, festivities that the Mother deems beneath her and her family, the soon-to-be millionaires. Instead of joining the communal celebration of these days, the Mother keeps her children seques- tered at home, where they celebrate privately by play-acting scenes from their future when they will be filthy rich, from their past when their mother forced their father to leave, and from their present when the two siblings recognize their incestuous desire for each other. These sequences are at times funny (in a dark way) and at others pathetic and serve as reminders of what happens when a nation (ghosted by this family) turns its back on its larger, public reality and closes in egotistically and incestuously on itself.

Hunger in this play works also on another level. The Mother denies her children love and food, and so they end by turning on her in a fantasized act of vengeful matricide, not only against her as their biological mother, but also against her metaphorically as the Mother Country, which, in like fashion, is starving her own children through neglect, physical abuse, and self-centered greed. Thus the play works on two effective levels, for it points to the very real and at the same time metaphorical hunger that makes Mexicans flee their country, while also suggesting that perhaps the mother country deserves this abandonment, that it could end by killing her too. By making this a play within a dream, Alanís O. seems to suggest that this is not an inevitable denouement, although a very probable one, given that the Mother does decide to send her eldest to the other side anyway, where he will in all likelihood never be heard from again.

SEXUAL PREFERENCE AND THE CANON

De acá, de este lado is a dense little play that manages in a short space to make a complex statement about what it is to live on the southern side of the border. It is, however, a statement that because of geographical isolation and discrimination may well not be heard in Mexico's central valley or find a place in the academic canon of Mexican theater. There also is another new theatrical voice in Mexico that is now, and probably will remain, both culturally and politically disenfranchised, but for different reasons—the so-called teatro gey (gay theater).[4] The literature of the Onda of the 1960s, with its total iconoclasm and hippy rebelliousness, opened the literary floodgates to once-taboo subject matters, among them drugs and liberated sex, both hetero- and homosexual. Yet it is one thing to describe these life-styles in a narrative account and quite another to publicly put them on a stage. Not suprisingly, then, gay theater is more a matter of written than of represented texts. M. M.: Un mito (M. M.: A Myth; 1984) by Alberto Arteaga Olguín (1945–) is a very good example of why this gay theater will with great difficulty have access to the middle- and upper-middle class that constitutes most of Mexico's theatergoing audience. The play, which won first place in the Primer Concurso de Teatro Salvador Novo, is a bold and often shocking (by heterosexual standards at least) depiction of the violence and degradation to which male homosexuals can be submitted in a culture where machismo rules supreme. The play covers a few days in the life of Marilyn, a transvestite who dresses like Marilyn Monroe for his nightclub act but who looks every inch a man in his street clothes. Marilyn's world is a hallucinogenic one of cocaine sniffing (although he himself is addicted only to prescription drugs, as was his namesake), multiple sex partners (the play was written before AIDS had become a real public issue), pornography, and sadomasochism that reaches even the point of castration. There are moments in which oral sex is performed (or at least simulated) on stage. And this being a man's world, there are no female characters, although women and their bodies are very much a presence for the male characters, who are either the passive female in gay relationships or bisexual or, in the case of one character, on the verge of having a sex-change operation. Needless to say, this is a world in which sexuality, whatever its permutations, is the main life force.

On one level, the play's action is certainly of the Prince of the Night variety in its depiction of a dark subworld and, as such, could easily work against its

own purposes; that is, it could confirm rather than disprove popular heterosexual misconceptions and fears about homosexuality. Yet there are two aspects of *M. M.: Un mito* that would help obviate against this: the fact that
almost all the violence is done to and not by homosexuals and the impact of
the central character, Marilyn, who functions to place gay issues within the
context of the larger social ones that plague Mexico today. That the playwright
means for Marilyn to stand for something beyond her-himself is patent from
the very first stage direction:

> We see three pyramids like those at Teotihuacán; the ones on the left and the right
> are two-dimensional. The pyramid upstage, center . . . is usable. . . . On both sides
> of it, an ecclesiastical chest with a cross on top. To its sides, an enormous photo-
> graph of Marilyn Monroe, naked. Other moveable sets will represent the Transves-
> tite's room, and La Traidora's. . . . The Transvestite's apartment—the bedrooms,
> with a bed and a dressing table. . . . A replica of Quetzalcoatl's head on one side of
> the room, and what would be the back wall in the outline of a pyramid. (213–214)

The combination of the pre-Hispanic and twentieth-century North American
pop culture is an instant, visual shorthand for what is a major issue throughout the play: the problem of identity—one's personal sexual identity and a
nation's collective identity.

This is not to say that the playwright uses homosexuality as just an excuse
to talk about something else, or as some kind of negative metaphor for frac-
tured personas and emotional psychoses. At least such is not the case of this
Marilyn, who has no doubts about his sexual identity, unlike the men who
bash him or his secretary, La Traidora, who wants to be a transexual and
thereby, according to Marilyn, tamper with what nature made him: "What
you're going to do, in addition to being a physical castration, is a mental castration. Would you like to spend the rest of your life like a useless piece of
flesh?" (240).

It is not Marilyn's sexuality itself that is a problem here, but rather what he
considers a cultural betrayal: therefore, the importance of the fragmented stage
(as regards its cultural morphology), the confusion of the pre-Columbian and
the post–World War II, of the Mexican and the Gringo. As Marilyn explains,
his first big stage role was as La Malinche, who, at least in Marilyn's script,
lived to regret her treachery to her people, a treachery that Marilyn then went
on to repeat by assuming the identity of a foreign goddess, of someone who
ironically was herself a fragmented soul but who, unlike the transvestite, never
came to grips with her sexuality. So when the Marilyn in Arteaga's play dies
from an overdose of sleeping pills, it is not so much to escape his sexuality as
it is to put back together the pieces of a shattered cultural self. As he says, "I've
got this feeling that I'm an intruder in my own house. . . . And the most terrible
thing about this is that I lost my identity in some dark corner of my past, my
particular form of being" (271). Like the other Marilyn, this one also places a

phone call before dying, to a lover in the United States (his final cultural betrayal?), and as the voice at the other end calls out to Marilyn, it is heard against a background of pre-Hispanic music. Then this music

> fades away and someone recites patriotic poetry to the accompaniment of heavy metal or punk rock. The cyclorama divides into three; the part on the right is under a green-hued light, the center part under a white light, and the left part under a red one. There is a loud rifle shot, and suddenly, a white sheet comes falling down; it has etched on it an outline of the Mexican Republic, with a bloodstain in the middle. When the sheet has draped itself over Marilyn's lifeless body, large amounts of garbage begin to rain down, covering him as well. (278)

This ending itself is rather like Marilyn's life (and, by extension, his national, Mexican heritage): an exaltation and a profanation of cultural symbols, a nearly psychodelic fusion of the new and the old, the autochthonous and the imported, sight and sound, the pure and the impure, sacred flags stained with blood, and human lives wasted into garbage. In other words, this is a visual image of a cultural schizophrenia which, as Arteaga presents it, poses far more of a personal and a national threat than homosexuality ever could to a country like Mexico. So in this sense, the play is both a call for tolerance toward the gay community and an alert to the dangers of not recognizing who one's real enemies are.

ON BEING NONCANONICAL BY CHOICE

The coupling of homosexual with larger social issues in Arteaga's play follows what seems to be a very general trend in much alternative (and consequently, noncanonical) Mexican theater: its strong ties and commitment to local and national reality. It does not take too much imagination to see why these kinds of texts would make theater promoters nervous and, therefore, why their chances for staging are limited. But not all noncanonical Mexican theater is text-based, nor does it need conventional performance spaces. As such, it is not absolutely beholden to the theatrical power elite. As most everywhere else, in Mexico the 1960s and 1970s produced a rich and varied crop of experimental, independent, or fringe theater groups that performed in the street, in city squares, in schools, on rooftops, or wherever else that was available to them. Theirs was subsistence, literally poor, theater, and much was politically motivated (Frischmann, "El nuevo teatro popular" and *El nuevo teatro popular*). Some groups still survive, but most of them died an early death. Still, many of them left a legacy and a will to do theater as a group activity, creating communal texts and improvising performance spaces. So the very purpose of this theater is to be noncanonical, to be marginal, because the work is by nature against the dominant theatrical culture.

One expression of this kind of theater continues to be the *teatro de la calle* (street theater), ranging from street performers in parks and plazas on a Sunday afternoon to the clowns and fire-eaters who perform at busy city intersections as a way to earn a meager wage. But there is also another manifestation of street theater, one which takes "staged events" to poor neighborhoods called *vecindades* and integrates them into daily life there. These are areas of such extreme poverty that some people are forced to live in caves and of such extreme violence that actors have found themselves caught up in gang fights and other dangerous incidents. *Pareces un Otelo* (You're Like an Othello; 1988), by the new wave *teatristas* Arturo Ramírez and Martín López Cruz and presented by Roberto Javier Hernández's Teatro de Vecindades, is an excellent example of such performances. A paraphrase of Shakespeare's *Othello,* the presentation takes place during the mock wedding party for a young couple. The actors are dressed as would be the various people of a *vecindad,* and most of the play consists of their dancing and raucous merrymaking. There is some (make-believe) drinking and drug-taking, lots of sexy dancing and flirting. Indeed, watching this is very much like spying on someone else's party, although the expectation is that members of the audience will join in the fun, as has sometimes happened. The party sequence is long, and at a certain point, one can forget that this is a performance, which is exactly the group's purpose. The actors and their activities seem to blend into the environment, except that a contrived tragedy is in the making, as innuendo and a white handkerchief incite the jealousy of the groom, who ends by drowning his new bride. This is theater, of course, but it is so naturally woven into the rest of what has happened that a casual passerby or audience members who are not paying close attention might not realize that it is.[5] There is only one obviously theatrical dimension to *Pareces un Otelo,* and that is the presence of a dwarfish woman, dressed in white lace, a combination Posada *calaca* (a Day of the Dead Skull) and Llorona figure, who has sat on the sidelines throughout the party-play, putting on her makeup and primping, as if getting ready for some kind of important event. Only at the end does she rise and walk away into and with the crowd. She, of course, functions symbolically to signify the bride's marriage to Death.

An important aspect to note about *Pareces un Otelo* is that unlike much 1960s street theater, this is not an openly political piece. Its purpose is not to go to the *vecindades* and teach people there something they did not know before; rather, it is much more like environmental theater, in that it becomes a part of where it is performed. Of course, what it performs has some relationship to that world, in this case its depiction of destructive kinds of behavior that, egged on by machismo, drugs, and alcohol, explode into the uncontrolled violence which leads these already marginalized people to kill each other and to brutalize their women. At no time does anyone say this during the performance, for here the showing is the telling, and the expectation is that those who are watching (or joining in) will recognize how self-defeating this behavior is.

The *teatro de vecindad* is an answer to a very real crisis situation in Mexico, one in which the urban poor are more and more alienated from the economic and cultural mainstream and from themselves. This theater is a way of taking performance art to them, but on their own terms and in their own context. There also has been in Mexico an attempt to do the same with the rural and/ or indigenous population, to pick up the lost thread of what was once the rich tradition in autochthonous theater that was mentioned at the beginning of this essay. Such theater has been called by various names: *teatro indígena; teatro campesino; teatro antropológico*. The rubrics however are not as interchangeable as some might think them. The adjective *indigenous* is especially problematic, as it implies something native, something pre-Hispanic that still survives today in a relatively uncontaminated form. This is how Cayuqui Estage Noël, an expert from the National Autonomous University of Oaxaca defines it, and his own extensive studies have shown where and how pre-Columbian manifestations of this theater are still remembered and performed in Mexico. He notes that the word *theater* actually does not even exist in the Indian languages, because they do not recognize it as a separate phenomenon as we in modern Western cultures do. Rather, it is integral to the world of ritual and dance, and therefore, this performance art (which we call theater because of its structural similarity to our enacted drama) is not beholden to written texts. Also, its sole purpose is "to maintain the cosmic balance by means of methods that are both *catalytic* and *protective;* it is activist at the same time that it is an amulet" (Estage Noël, 5). Not surprisingly, then, these performances are highly symbolic and totally nonrepresentational in the Western sense. Indeed, according to Estage Noël, they are impenetrable to outsiders, who do not share and therefore cannot decipher their symbolic codes.

The question of outsiders is a highly controversial one, for in the past decades there has been a significant and official governmental effort to foster indigenous theater; this is why the question of terminology becomes pivotal. For if nonindigenous people work with this theater, and if they attribute to it a sociopolitical rather than a ritualistic purpose, it is then questionable whether the result can be labeled "indigenous." For Estage Noël it cannot and should not be, whereas for others, the key is who performs rather than who promotes it. For example, in the 1970s there were Brigadas Teatrales, sponsored by federal agencies, whose mission was to teach the rural population how to make a theater of its own (Meyer). The brigades were composed of local participants under the tutelage of a trained actor who coached them in the ways of making group theater based on their local language, beliefs, history, and present socioeconomic situation. The goals were to spark enthusiasm and self-pride in these rural communities and also to use the theater for consciousness-raising. Because of the presence of outsiders, who were salaried by the government, it is not hard to see why there were and still are concerns here about cultural manipulation and hidden agendas and, if not that, at least about some well-intentioned but misguided notions concerning the kind of performance methods that are best suited to a rural, indigenous people—for example, the imposition of a Stanislavskian acting technique on a tradition which, as Estage Noël indicates, is anything but psychological and realistic.

These joint efforts also have been called "peasant theater" (to underscore their rural nature) and "anthropological theater" (to underline the importance of research and discovery about native forms and subject matter). This is a theater that perhaps because of its marginality has reached a wider public in a single performance than most commercial, canonical theater could ever hope to. The Teatro Campesino de Tabasco is certainly the best-known and most critically acclaimed group, especially for its adaptation of *Bodas de sangre* (*Blood Wedding;* 1932) by Federico García Lorca (1898–1936). Directed by María Alicia Martínez Medrano, the performance takes place outside, in a rural setting (for example, on the hillside of a small town near Jalapa during the Seventh National Theater Competition in 1984). The story, reworked into a campesino setting and told in the Oxoloteca language, is enacted by a truly epic and impressive cast, as can be appreciated in this description of the Jalapa performance:

> Over the very ample and green natural stage more than one hundred and fifty actors on horseback, carts and two orchestras—a band of wind instruments and another of marimbas—, a chorus of dancers and singers, and a solitary horserider: Death, who rode around as a terrible and ineluctable omen, wearing a many-metered black train that wrapped itself around everything that was happening—all this left the spectators astonished by the way Lorca's text had been transcribed into the native culture of the area. (*VII Muestra Nacional,* 67)[6]

The Teatro Campesino de Tabasco is a fine example of how a trained practitioner has worked closely with local people, helping them to train each other, for at a certain point (at least theoretically) the outsider steps back and lets the pupils take over his or her role. In the case of *Bodas de sangre,* a canonical text-based play was adapted to a campesino situation, but for later productions local tales with pre-Hispanic roots, like the story of the Jaguar or of the god of the underworld, Xibalbá, have provided the subject matter. The work of Maricela Lara in Milpa Alta and in Veracruz is of this latter kind. She has worked with the rural populations there in performances of *La Llorona* (The Weeping Mother) and the *Mulata de Córdoba* (The Mulatta of Cordoba), both of them well-known and strongly felt legends that deal with the encounter between the Hispanic and pre-Hispanic worlds. Lara calls her theater anthropological because of the amount of joint research that she and her theater troupes, made up of workers and ordinary people, engage in—not so much formal, bookish research as the personal kind that delves into the inner resources and knowledge of her coworkers. For example, there were sessions in which participants gave their versions and interpretations of the Llorona legend; little by little these stories came together to form their particular version. And in the process of casting roles, important discoveries were made, as when the Indian playing Cortés could finally enter into the skin of the oppressor and finally begin to understand who this white man was: "And we couldn't understand why white men were so interested in our women, our land and our gods. So we had to dress ourselves as Spaniards in order to tell these stories" (Lara, 20). The first performance of *La Llorona* was scheduled according to when the signs of the moon would be auspicious in March of 1987, and like many other similar events its audience was large, numbering around 3,500 people. As Lara notes: "We were able to communicate something of our own. In our own way. A communication combined with a theatrical expression. Our roots, our internal world, which we made manifest in a theater production that everyone in the public appreciated" (21). This feeling of camaraderie, of group, is one of the most profound that is felt by the campesino or anthropological theater, and it is perhaps this self-sufficiency that makes it cherish rather than bemoan its existence on the fringes of legitimate, canonical theater.

SOME FINAL WORDS ON RECONSIDERING THE CANON

In January of 1989 the National Foundation for the Scenic Arts and Escenología A.C. organized a quite unusual meeting in Mexico City to talk about the state of Mexican theater, a meeting to which the "gods" of theater arts purposely were not invited, so that an open forum could be given to the noncanonized but equally important makers of Mexican drama. Important and varied, for there were representatives from the so-called *teatro al aire libre* (open-air theater), *teatro de la sierra* (theater of the mountains), *teatro regional* (regional theater), *teatro participativo* (participatory theater), *teatro estudiantil* (student theater), *el tercer teatro* (the third theater), *teatro de la calle* (street theater), and *teatro independiente* (independent theater), all of whom expressed no regrets about their peripheral situation, although they would certainly welcome a little help (economic and spiritual) to continue their work. The presence of these groups confirmed two very imporant things about Mexican theater that have been suggested in this essay: that the official canon is too biased toward the playwright, who figures quite large there but in a meeting like that one was only one presence (and a minor one, to be sure); and that to speak of the canon is not really productive, for in reality, there are many canons, each of them established according to very different criteria. And even with the varied representatives at this meeting, some were still left out; for example, those from children's theater and the circus. The research for and writing of an essay such as this one has forced me to go well beyond the limits of what I once thought was the canon of Mexican drama, and even so I too have not covered all the territory. There are periods in the past that need serious reconsideration, notably the nineteenth century, which has a bad reputation according to most theater historians but which in the words of the playwright Emilio Carballido was a veritable outpouring (a "catarata") of theatrical activity. Much more could and should have been said about the *teatro de revista,* or vaudeville, that for so long was the premier expression of Mexican popular theater (Luzuriaga; María y Campos). And finally, any reconsideration of the canon should look more closely at works that have earned entry into that dubious club, to see why they did, that is, what artistic and ideological values they confirmed in the eyes of canon-setters. Still, this overview does at least give some sense of the rich variety and texture of the modern stage in Mexico and, hopefully, offers some guidance to those readers who might want to further explore the many canons of Mexican drama.

NOTES

1. Translations from Spanish to English are mine throughout this essay.

2. In the interval between my writing this essay and its publication, other scholars, most notably the Mexican Guillermo Schmidhuber, have begun this process of serious rethinking, which confirms many of the premises of my efforts. I am gratified by this coincidence and thank Schmidhuber, especially for his labors in *El teatro mexicano en cierne, 1922–1938.*

3. I will note that this is the version of things provided by Leñero and his supporters. Some of these UNAM officials, who will remain unnamed, have quite another version, as has been pointed out to me personally. And so, is there real, true text here?

4. The exclusion of women's theater in this discussion of canons is not an oversight. However, given the space constraints, gay theater, which has had no access to legitimate stages, seemed a better choice for discussion. This does not mean, of course, that women have found all theater doors opened to them in Mexico, but playwrights like Luisa Josefina Hernández, Maruxa Vilalta, Elena Garro, and, more recently, Sabina Berman and Carmen Boullosa have had success with getting works staged.

5. My experience of *Pareces un Otelo* was not in a *vecindad;* rather, I saw it produced for the benefit of participants in a symposium on Mexican theater held in the Teatro Jorge Negrete in Mexico City. This viewing was unique, to be sure, but provided some interesting touches. The audience and performance space were out of context, in that we were outsiders to the play's action, and the Teatro Jorge Negrete is definitely nowhere near a *vecindad.* However, people unrelated to the event or to the audience ambled down the street, watched, some stayed, others left. A cleaning lady walked through the performance space, on her way to an office building. Elegant patrons of the Teatro Jorge Negrete arrived to see the performance of their choice: the very canonical *La Celestina.* And strangely enough, an ambulance just happened to be parked at the end of the street, an unwitting prop in a performance that ended with a "make-believe" death.

6. In August 1986 this production of *Bodas de sangre* was brought to the U.S. as part of the late Joseph Papp's Festival Latino. Gloria Waldman recorded the event, which was presented in "the natural amphitheater of the Catskill mountain town of Thompson Park with one hundred thirty-five actors, dancers, and musicians from the State of Tabasco in Mexico. First ten, then twenty Indian men, all dressed in white, on horseback, galloped towards the stage-plaza, approaching at every angle, from all parts of the forest. The women entered on foot, wearing colorful native skirts, dancing and laughing as they appeared from another part of the woods. Then more horses and more

children adding to the others who gracefully placed themselves in what would become a tableau, a living picture. . . . And through this striking natural 'set' parades Death, on a black horse, sober, terrifying, touching all corners of the green expanse and silently riding away" (102).

BIBLIOGRAPHY

Alanís O., Guillermo Sergio. *De acá, de este lado.* In *Tres de la frontera tres: Primer concurso de obras de teatro de la frontera norte,* 51–83. Mexico City: Secretaría de Educación Pública, 1986. A one-act play, of an absurdist variety, that deals with a Mexican mother who stays on her side of the border, waiting for her son, who has gone over to the other side, to send money that never comes.

Arrom, José Juan. *El teatro de Hispanoamérica en la época colonial.* Havana: Anuario Bibliográfico Cubano, 1956. The most thorough and now-classic study of colonial Latin American drama. It offers descriptions of basic types of theater during that period, as well as of representative plays.

Arroniz, Othón. *Teatro de evangelización en Nueva Espana.* Mexico City: Universidad Nacional Autónoma de México, 1979. An expert study of the evangelizing theater that Catholic priests used in New Spain to convert and baptize the indigenous population in the period subsequent to the conquest.

Arteaga Olguín, Alberto. *M. M.: Un mito.* In *1er Concurso Salvador Novo,* 211–278. Mexico City: Editores Mexicanos Unidos, 1984. A prize-winning play that deals with male homosexuality and cultural identity in Mexico.

Azuela, Mariano. *Los de abajo.* Mexico City: Fondo de Cultura Económica, 1960.

Berger, Peter. *The Sacred Canopy.* Garden City: Doubleday, 1967. A phenomenological study of culture, with existentialist overtones. The major premise is that we ourselves make order out of chaos, and therefore, we alone are responsible for our actions in this world.

Boulding, Kenneth. *The Image: Knowledge in Life and Society.* Ann Arbor: University of Michigan Press, 1969. A pioneering study of how the acts of perception and of meaning-assignment are simultaneous to and inextricable from the act of value-giving.

Burgess, Ron. *The New Dramatists of Mexico, 1967–1985.* Lexington: University of Kentucky Press, 1991. An analysis of plays by Mexican playwrights who began to write and stage their plays during the turbulent 1960s and the post-Tlatelolco ambience of the 1970s.

———. "El nuevo teatro mexicano y la generación perdida." *Latin American Theatre Review* 18.2 (Spring 1985): 89–92. An overview of Mexican playwrights of the late 1970s and early 1980s, with emphasis on their problems in getting published and produced in Mexico.

Bustillo Oro, Juan. *San Miguel de las Espinas: Trilogía dramática de un pedazo de tierra mexicana.* In *Teatro mexicano del siglo XX,* 2.25–148. Mexico City: Fondo de Cultura Económica, 1981. A three-act play about the exploitation of rural peasants in northern Mexico before, during, and after the Revolution of 1910.

Carballido, Emilio. *Un pequeño día de ira.* Havana: Casa de las Américas, 1961.

———. *Tiempo de ladrones: La historia de Chucho el Roto.* Mexico City: Editorial Grijalbo, 1983. A play about Chucho el Roto, a nineteenth-century Mexican Robin Hood, who robbed the rich in order to give to the poor.

Castellanos, Rosario. "La mujer y su imagen." *Mujer que sabe latín,* 7–21. Mexico City: Fondo de Cultura Económica, 1984.

Cucuel, Madeleine. "Les Recherches théâtrales au Mexique." In *Le Théâtre mexicain contemporain,* ed. Madeleine Cucuel. *Les Cahiers du CRIAR* 127.7 (1987): 5–57. Rouen: Université de Rouen. An overview of experimental theater groups and movements in the first part of the twentieth century in Mexico; special attention is given to Juan Bustillo Oro.

Culler, Jonathan. "Prologomena to a Theory of Reading." In *The Reader in the Text: Essays on Audience and Interpretation,* ed. Susan Suleiman and Inge Crosman, 46–66. Princeton: Princeton University Press, 1980. A discussion and analysis of the importance of writing and interpretive conventions in both the creation and understanding of literature.

Dauster, Frank. "La generación de 1924: El dilema del realismo." *Latin American Theatre Review* 18.2 (Spring 1985): 13–22. A review of Mexican playwrights belonging to the Generation of 1924 who searched for new theatrical forms that broke with the strictures of stage realism.

———. *Historia del teatro hispanoamericano, Siglos XIX y XX.* Mexico City: Ediciones de Andrea, 1973. An outline history of Latin American theater in the nineteenth and twentieth centuries, organized chronologically and by country.

Estage Noël, Cayuqui. "Teatro indígena: Lo que es, lo que no es, lo que parece ser, lo que puede ser y lo que debe ser." Unpublished manuscript. A study of indigenous theater that argues that it is of, by, and for the native Indian population, as opposed to a pseudo-popular theater made by outsiders, which merely pretends to be indigenous.

Fish, Stanley. *Is There a Text in This Class?* Cambridge, Mass.: Harvard University Press, 1980.

Frischmann, Donald. *El nuevo teatro popular en México.* Mexico City: Instituto Nacional de Bellas Artes, 1990. The first comprehensive study of popular, indigenous, and alternative theater in Mexico of the 1960s and after. Excellent discussion of *El extensionista.*

———. "El nuevo teatro popular en México: Posturas ideológicas y estéticas." *Latin American Theatre Review* 18.2 (Spring 1985): 29–37. An overview of popular theater in Mexico since the 1960s, with a discussion of the political and artistic pressures that have worked to define it.

García Lorca, Federico. *Bodas de sangre.* In *Federico García Lorca: Obras completas,* 1173–1272. Madrid: M. Aguilar, 1967.

Gorostiza, Manuel Eduardo. *Contigo, pan y cebolla.* In *Teatro,* 232–330. Mexico City: Editorial Porrúa, 1952.

Jauss, Hans Robert. "The Changing Horizon of Understanding." In *Identity of the Literary Text,* ed. Mario J. Valdés and Owen Miller, 146–174. Toronto: University of Toronto Press, 1985. A pivotal discussion that postulates that the response to art is conditioned by the perceiver's expectations, which in turn are conditioned by individual, collective, artistic, and historical contexts.

Lara, Maricela. "Calles y espacios al aire libre para las leyendas de México." *Repertorio* 9–11 (1989): 19–22. An overview of the author's work with anthropological theater in Milpa Alta and Veracruz, Mexico, with a description of the group dynamics and anthropological research involved in creating this kind of theater.

Leñero, Vicente. *Martirio de Morelos.* Mexico City: Editorial Océano, 1985. A three-act play about the last days of the nineteenth-century Mexican revolutionary priest José María Morelos y Pavón. Leñero questions the official historical record by depicting a Morelos who rather than a super-hero was a human being who broke under the pain of torture.

―――. *Nadie sabe nada: Tres de teatro*, 9–116. Mexico City: Cal y Arena 1989. A play in two acts and fourteen scenes, which takes place in at least eight different places represented realistically on stage and which tells the suspenseful tale of a "Mexican Watergate," full of deceit, corruption, power-brokering, and murder.

―――. *Vivir del teatro*. Mexico City: Editorial Joaquín Mortiz, 1982. A chatty, intimate autobiography in which Leñero tells the story of his development as a playwright, how he wrote his plays, and his adventures and misadventures in getting them staged.

―――. *Vivir del teatro II*. Mexico City: Editorial Joaquín Mortiz, 1990. Deals with plays written between 1982 and 1988.

Luzuriaga, Gerardo. "On the 'Revista política' during the Mexican Revolution." Unpublished manuscript. Written during a group research project at the University of California, Irvine (Humanities Research Institute 1990), this study addresses issues of marginality and the exclusion from the canon of this popular Mexican theatrical form.

Magaña Esquivel, Antonio. *Medio siglo de teatro mexicano, 1900–1961*. Mexico City: Instituto Nacional de Bellas Artes, 1964. A traditional outline history of Mexican theater from the turn of the century until the 1960s.

María y Campos, Armando de. *El teatro del género chico en la Revolución mexicana*. Mexico City: Biblioteca del Instituto Nacional de Bellas Artes, 1956. The most authoritative and complete compendium and study of political vaudeville during the 1910 Revolution.

Mendoza López, Margarita. *Primeros renovadores del teatro en Mexico, 1928–1941*. Mexico City: Instituto Mexicano de Seguro Social, 1985. A personal recollection of the various theater groups and playwrights who opened up the Mexican stage to the influence of European avant-gardists.

Meyer, Germán. "Caminando: Los senderos de una experiencia de promoción teatral en el campo." *Escénica: Revista de Teatro de la UNAM* 1.4–5 (September 1983): 56–61. A personal recounting of the author's work with government-sponsored theater brigades that collaborated with rural Indian and mestizo populations in the creation and production of original plays.

Muñoz, Fernando. *El teatro regional de Yucatán*. Mexico City: Grupo Editorial Gaceta, 1987. A thorough and informative history of regional theater in the Yucatán, with mention of its historical, cultural, and linguistic peculiarities.

Nomland, John B. *Teatro mexicano contemporáneo, 1900–1950*. Trans. Paloma Gorostiza de Zozaya and Luis Reyes de la Maza. Mexico City: Instituto Nacional de Bellas Artes, 1967. A descriptive and fact-filled history of Mexican theater in the first half of this century.

Olivares Avila, Irma Guadalupe. *Cupido hizo casa en Bravo*. In *Tres de la frontera tres: Primer concurso de obras de teatro de la frontera norte*, 85–139. Mexico City: Secretaría de Educación Pública, 1986. A prize-winning comedy set in the north of Mexico; a farce about mistaken identities, young love, and a cow named Clariza.

Ortega Rodríguez, Francisco. *La frontera*. In *Tres de la frontera tres: Primer concurso de obras de teatro de la frontera norte*, 11–50. Mexico City: Secretaría de Educación Pública, 1986. A prize-winning play set in Tijuana and which explores corruption in the newspaper world.

Potter, Robert. "Abraham and Human Sacrifice: The Exfoliation of Medieval Drama in Aztec Mexico." *New Theatre Quarterly* 2.8 (November 1986): 306–312. A study of the influence of medieval religious drama in the creation of so-called missionary theater in Mexico.

Ramírez, Arturo, and Martín López Cruz. "Pareces un Otelo." 1988. No text.

Rascón Banda, Víctor Hugo. *Los ilegales*. Mexico City: Universidad Autónoma Metropolitana, 1980. Episodic documentary-like play about the abuses and indignities Mexicans suffer at the border, as well as across it.

Reyes de la Maza, Luis. *Cien años de teatro en México, 1810–1910*. Mexico City: Sep-Setentas, 1972. A descriptive and anecdotal history of Mexican theater in the century between independence and the Revolution of 1910.

Rosenberg, Joe. "The Fame of Felipe Santander!" In *Prologue Magazine*. Milwaukee: Milwaukee Repertory Theater, n.d. A discussion of the author's experience as the English-language translator of Felipe Santander's *El extensionista*.

Said, Edward. "Criticism between Culture and System." *The World, the Text, and the Critic*, 178–225. Cambridge, Mass.: Harvard University Press, 1983. A discussion of the relationship between literature and the world from which it issues; a critique of literary theory that does not account for the worldliness of written texts and of their readers.

Santander, Felipe. *El extensionista*. Havana: Casa de las Américas, 1980. A prize-winning play in the Brechtian mode that deals with official corruption and the exploitation of the rural poor in Mexico.

Schmidhuber, Guillermo. "La dramaturgia mexicana actual." In *Le Théâtre mexicain contemporain*, ed. Madeleine Cucuel. *Les Cahiers du CRIAR* 127.7 (1987): 127–133. Rouen: Université de Rouen. An overview of Mexican theater in the past twenty or so years.

———. *El teatro mexicano en cierne, 1922–1938*. New York: Peter Lang, forthcoming. A thorough historical review of theater practitioners who have not been given due credit for establishing the foundations of modern Mexican drama. Excellent discussion of Juan Bustillo Oro and an important step in rewriting the canon.

———. "El teatro mexicano y la provincia." *Latin American Theatre Review* 18.2 (Spring 1985): 23–27. An overview of provincial theater in Mexico and its struggle to gain acceptance in and support from Mexico City; also a discussion of the province as subject matter in the works of major Mexican playwrights.

"VII Muestra Nacional de Teatro: Xalapa 1984." *Escénica: Revista de Teatro de la UNAM* 1.9 (September–December 1984): 59–72. A summary of this national theater festival, held in the summer of 1984, in Jalapa, Veracruz.

Suleiman, Susan R., and Inge Crosman, ed. *The Reader in the Text: Essays on Audience and Interpretation*. Princeton: Princeton University Press, 1980.

Tompkins, Jane P., ed. *Reader Response Criticism: From Formalism to Post-Structuralism*. Baltimore: Johns Hopkins University Press, 1980.

Unger, Roni. *Poesía en Voz Alta in the Theater of Mexico*. Columbia: University of Missouri Press, 1981. A well-documented study of the development of this experimental theater group in the 1950s, which included writers like Octavio Paz, Juan José Arreola, and Elena Garro, as well as painters like Leonora Carrington.

Usigli, Rodolfo. *El gesticulador*. Mexico City: Editorial Stylo, 1947. A classic play about a man who first pretends to be and then seems to believe himself to be a general from northern Mexico who disappeared in the early days of the revolution; an analysis and critique of the Mexican national character and of the Mexican penchant for social and political posturing.

Villegas, Juan. *Ideología y discurso crítico sobre el teatro de España y América Latina.* Minneapolis: The Primsa Institute, 1988. An insightful and polemical treatise on cultural imperialism in literary criticism and the consequent need to account for ideology—both the creator's and the receptor's—in the analysis of specifically Latin American and Spanish theater.

Waldman, Gloria. "Festival Latino Diary." *Latin American Theatre Review* 20.2 (Spring 1987): 99–105. A summary-review of the 1986 Festival Latino held annually in New York City and sponsored by the late Joseph Papp.

Woodyard, George. "El teatro mexicano del siglo XX: Desarrollo y periodización." Unpublished manuscript. A summary of twentieth-century Mexican drama using the generational format proposed by José Juan Arrom.

8

Twentieth-Century Fiction

LANIN A. GYURKO

The richness of the Mexican narrative in the twentieth century makes it difficult to encompass all major trends and ideologies in a single essay. To avoid the pattern of a general survey, the primary focus will be on narratives that directly or indirectly treat the theme of *la mexicanidad*, the quest for and the articulation of the components of the Mexican national identity. Such an intellectual and artistic quest in Mexico inevitably is multitemporal and multicultural in nature, involving the evocation of Mexican history from pre-Columbian times through the conquest and the three-hundred-year colonial period, the reform epoch in the nineteenth century under the liberal Benito Juárez (1858–1872), the French Intervention and the monarchy of Maximilian and Carlotta, the Porfirian dictatorship and the Revolution of 1910, culminating in the myriad social and political issues facing contemporary Mexico. *La mexicanidad* in literature finds much of its inspiration as the result of the cataclysmic revolution, a movement that gave Mexico a sense of its own identity and produced a creative explosion in literature, painting, and film. The great importance of *la mexicanidad* is evident in that it characterizes the work of three of Mexico's muralists who have gained world renown and in the 1920s and 1930s led the narrative artists in a brilliant evocation of a Mexican society reborn after centuries of foreign domination and internal oppression: José Clemente Orozco, Diego Rivera, and David Alfaro Siqueiros. Key works by several of Mexico's foremost essayists also sparked the aesthetic movement to contemplate and define the meaning of the Mexican national identity: *El perfil del hombre y la cultura en México* (*Profile of Man and Culture in Mexico;* 1934), by Samuel Ramos (1893–1959); *Hernán Cortés, creador de la nacionalidad* (Hernán Cortés, Creator of Our Nationality; 1941), by José Vasconcelos (1882–1959), philosopher and a candidate for the presidency; and the vastly influential *El laberinto de la soledad* (*The Labyrinth of Solitude;* 1950) and its sequel, *Posdata* (*The Other Mexico: Critique of the Pyramid;* 1970), by the Nobel Prize–winning poet and essayist Octavio Paz (1914–).

The orientation of this chapter is not to diminish the accomplishments of those novelists who in the early part of the century form part of Mexican *literatura de la vanguardia* (avant-garde literature) and who in the latter half of this century are typified by their concentration on the self-referential narrative, or *écriture*. Without delving into the polemic of *literatura comprometida* versus *arte por el arte* (engagé literature vs. art for art's sake), so important in the evolution of Latin American literature, this study will focus on the experimental and the metaphysical as they are fused with history and anthropology to form the *novela totalizante*, or all-encompassing novel. For a complementary vision, an extensive analysis of novelists who are either more personal or psychological in orientation or more self-consciously metaphysical and who place marked emphasis on innovations in narrative structure and style primarily for their own sake, the reader is referred to the studies on *écriture* writers listed in the annotated bibliography at the end of this study.

Rather than to movements or periods in the development of the novel, the term *novela totalizante* is best applied to the works of specific novelists, beginning with several members of the boom generation of the 1960s in Latin America. Carlos Fuentes (1928–) is generally considered to be the founder of the all-encompassing novel, with works such as *La región más transparente* (*Where the Air Is Clear;* 1958), *La muerte de Artemio Cruz* (*The Death of Artemio Cruz;* 1962), *Terra nostra* (*Terra Nostra;* 1978), and *Cristóbal nonato* (*Christopher Unborn;* 1987). Another proponent of this expansive and synthesizing vision, in which history and philosophy, religion and myth, linguistics and the visual arts, are all fused, is Fernando del Paso (1935–), in works such as *José Trigo* (1966) and *Palinuro de México* (1977). In the development of the Mexican novel in the twentieth century, the all-encompassing novel, which in general attracts fewer readers than shorter, more direct and incisive works, is the exception rather than the rule. In the eighties and nineties, even the fiction of Fuentes, with its emphasis on shorter works like *La campaña* (*The Campaign;* 1990) and on novellas and short stories, is in accord with this "less is more" trend.

The Mexican novel is most vibrant and most original when it responds— eloquently, emotionally, incisively—to the complex and captivating world that is modern Mexico. Mexican fiction that reflects, explores, and at times scathingly critiques Mexican reality can be divided into four major categories. The first, which spans almost the entire twentieth century, one of the most prolific, profound, and original currents in Mexican literature, is the novel of the Mexican Revolution. Among the nations that have experienced revolutions, none has a body of literature so complex, vital, and insistently questioning of the revolutionaries and their leaders, as well as of the revolutionary goals and the methods utilized to achieve them. The second category encompasses those narratives that focus on the aftermath of revolution, including the Cristero revolt during the late 1920s and the often-painful construction of a new society. Unlike the earlier novels of the revolution, sometimes autobiographical in nature, written during the very time of brutal national upheaval, these novels become increasingly cosmopolitan as they explore new linguistic structures and enter into the realms of surrealism, magical realism, the mythic, and at times even the supernatural. It is in this second phase that provides dense and fascinating works like Juan Rulfo's *Pedro Páramo* (1955), as well as the all-encompassing novel, including Fuentes's expansive and convoluted *La región más transparente* and the baroque synthesis of all epochs of Mexican history found in Fernando del Paso's *José Trigo.*

Historically, the tragic massacre in 1968 of the students in the Plaza of the Three Cultures (also known as Tlatelolco) marked the end of the illusion of Mexico as a democracy; it also changed substantially the course of the Mexican narrative, impelling it away from the experiments in time and space and point of view, so stunningly exemplified by Fuentes's *Cambio de piel* (*A Change of Skin;* 1968), toward a direct and penetrating examination of the political structure and the nature of power in Mexico and the repercussions of the student movement, which some have seen as a second Mexican revolution. The complex, extensive body of literature created in response to the crackdown, the Literature of Tlatelolco, is the third category that will be examined. The fourth division will focus on those works that treat contemporary political and socioeconomic problems through a combination of satire, irony, and expressionistic hyperbole. Some of these problems, like air and water pollution, urban violence, poverty, and disease, all evoked by Fuentes in his withering examination of the Mexico City of 1992 as a phantasmagoria in *Cristóbal nonato,* appear as virtually unsolvable. Fuentes posits but a faint hope, in the form of the fetal narrator Cristóbal, for positive change. An issue that has characterized Mexico for centuries, the struggle to maintain and assert an autonomous identity in the face of foreign powers from without and *malinchistas,* or betraying forces, from within, continues to preoccupy novelists in the last quarter of the century. In Mexico the present is ineluctably bound to the recent and remote pasts of the nation. Perhaps this explains the emergence of the new historical novel in the last decade of the century, a trend heightened by the quincentennial, the marking of the five-hundredth anniversary of Columbus's "discovery" of the "New World."

Throughout the twentieth century, from the 1895 publication by Heriberto Frías (1870–1925) of *Tomochic,* the fictionalized account of the destruction of a village by the government troops of Porfirio Díaz—a destruction that the author himself, as a federal soldier, was ordered to participate in—to the vast, convoluted epic novel *Noticias del imperio* (News of the Empire; 1987) by Fernando del Paso, in which the demented mind of the Empress Carlotta, virtually imprisoned in her castle at Bouchot in 1927, constitutes a bizarre "theater of memory," novelists provide penetrating perspectives on national problems. Del Paso's work is, on the one hand, rigorously documented, demonstrating his command of the historical record, and on the other inspired by the dramatic masterpiece *Corona de sombra* (*Crown of Shadows;* 1943) by Rodolfo Usigli (1905–1979), as Carlotta's mind alternates between the evocation of the tragic course of Maximilian's ill-fated venture as emperor of Mexico (1865–1867) and contemplation of the disintegration of the Hapsburg and other European empires as the result of the First World War.

Literature as fused with history achieves its most sustained, vivid, and significant expression in the novel of the 1910 Mexican Revolution. Begun in

1915 with the serial publication of *Los de abajo* (*The Underdogs*) by Mariano Azuela (1873–1952), the novel of the Mexican Revolution has continued throughout the century. Testimony not only to its continued viability but also to its seeming inexhaustibility are novels like *Hasta no verte, Jesús mío* (Until I See You, My Jesus; 1969) by Elena Poniatowska (1933), the first-person account of the bold, outspoken *soldadera* (both female soldier and male soldier's companion) Jesusa Palancares, and *Gringo viejo* (*The Old Gringo;* 1985) by Carlos Fuentes, which depicts the adventures and the presumed violent death in Mexico (1914?) of the North American short-story writer and acerbic journalist Ambrose Bierce, who in his seventies crosses the border at El Paso to join the army of Pancho Villa, preferring to die in battle rather than of old age.

Many of the novelists take either a decidedly negative or a markedly ambivalent perspective on the revolution, as they emphasize its excesses, its blood lust, and, many times, the betrayal of its initial ideals of land, labor, and educational reforms. The narrative vision, critical and pessimistic, is often at odds with the official historical record, which is far more Manichean, in contrasting the tyranny of the Díaz epoch with the reformist and egalitarian society that emerged as the result of the revolution.

The founder and major exponent of the novel of the Mexican Revolution is the aforementioned Mariano Azuela. Traces of Azuela's often ironic and cynical vision, his relentless examination and constant questioning of the motives and goals of both revolutionary leaders and their followers, and his undercutting of bombastic rhetoric and exposure of the rampant corruption and the incessant and destructive power struggles are found in subsequent works by Agustín Yáñez (1904–1980), Juan Rulfo (1918–1986), and Carlos Fuentes. In novel after novel, Azuela examines all phases of the revolution, from its representation by the despotic Andrade family in *Mala yerba* (*Marcela, a Mexican Love Story;* 1909), to the confused beginnings of the struggle in *Andrés Pérez, maderista* (Andrés Pérez, Supporter of Madero; 1911), to the apogee of Pancho Villa and his rapid defeat in *Los de abajo,* to the chaotic and devastating struggles among the numerous revolutionary factions, to the counterrevolutionary War of the Cristeros, which occurred during the Calles regime (1924–1928), in *El camarada Pantoja* (Comrade Pantoja; 1937), to the rapid rise to material wealth of the revolutionaries in *Nueva burguesía* (The New Middle Class; 1941). Maintaining his independence from all of the revolutionary regimes, Azuela staunchly becomes the gadfly, the conscience of the revolution, upholding its most idealistic phase, that of the government of Francisco Madero (1911–1913).

But the greatest narrative achievement of Azuela is his taut and powerful work *Los de abajo.* Azuela here provides a harsh but dynamic portrayal of the popular revolution. The original English translation was accompanied by sketches done by the great muralist José Clemente Orozco. The satiric vision of the followers of Porfirio Díaz and revolutionaries alike that characterizes Orozco's mordant vision with its slashing lines finds its parallel in Azuela's demythifying vision and his stark and trenchant style. The opportunism, greed, cruelty, even pathological sadism of the "underdogs" are revealed, as Azuela vividly creates a vision of fierce battles and equally furious sackings and burnings and executions. Like Orozco, Azuela pictures the revolution in all its savagery and orgiastic frenzy and cruel—not glorious—martyrdom. A master of characterization, Azuela creates a gallery of unforgettable characters, both major and minor. The sadistic Güero Margarito, whose destructive impulses are finally turned on himself as he commits suicide, enjoys torturing the federal soldier he has taken prisoner by playing a game of Russian roulette with him while at the same time starving him to death. The aggressive and taunting *soldadera* La Pintada, extremely jealous when the revolutionary commander Macías takes another woman as his mistress, knifes her rival, Camila, to death in a fit of rage. Revolutionaries like Venancio and Pancracio are animalized in their brutality, and the soldiers engage in endless conversations on their lust for killing. With macho arrogance they first recount exploits in battle and then the gratuitous and heinous killing of completely innocent persons who, for example, did not serve them rapidly enough or the person who happened always to be seated in the same place and at the same time everyday and thus became an intolerable irritation to the soldier who shot him.

Adding to the complexity of *Los de abajo* is the fact that at times the soldiers are evoked positively, as Azuela depicts the exuberance of the troops as they ride wildly through the sierra, free of the tyranny of the hacendado or the cacique, of the endless toil that leads only to new debts. But even this moment of jubilation is undercut as the revolutionaries in the distance are perceived as mere toys strung out against the skyline. And indeed, they are not in control of their destinies: Azuela portrays the revolution as an immense hurricane in which human beings are reduced to dry leaves hurled along, unable to determine the outcomes of their lives. The theme of a deterministic, cyclical time pervades the narrative. At the outset, it is the small farmer Demetrio Macías whose home is invaded and whose wife is threatened with rape. Yet at the end, the revolutionaries themselves become reduced to the predators, despised by the very populace that at the outset had joyously welcomed them as liberators. After all their many battles, Macías's band of revolutionaries at the end find themselves in the same place, the Cañón de Juchipila, where they were at the outset, when geographically they were *los de arriba,* the top dogs, and had ambushed and slaughtered the federal troops in the canyon below. Now they themselves are marching through the bottom of the canyon, and since Macías well knows the strategic advantage anyone at the top holds, his leading his men into the canyon seems almost to be a Thanatos march. He and his men becomes the victims of fellow revolutionaries, of the *carrancistas,* the followers of Victoriano Carranza. After the tumultuous and divisive Convention at Aguascalientes, which Azuela depicts with its streets littered with garbage that become symbolic of moral putrefaction, the revolution rapidly disintegrates into a struggle for power among opposing revolutionary factions now that their common enemy, the "usurper" Victoriano Huerta, has been vanquished.

Macías, the symbol both of the leader Julián Medina, under whose command Azuela himself served as a doctor, and of the charismatic and terrifying General Villa himself, is evoked ambivalently. He is portrayed as a valiant leader, loyal to the revolution and devoted to his men, and yet a pawn of the wily *curro,* or city slicker, Luis Cervantes, the opportunist who repeatedly spews forth a rhetoric of revolutionary idealism in order to animate an initially reluctant Macías to continue the "noble" struggle. Macías becomes a veritable killing machine, and his reckless tactics of charging straight at the enemy and lassoing machine guns parallel the temerarious charges of Villa and the Dorados, the "Golden Boys," Villa's special cavalry, attired in golden-colored uniforms, who were famous for their lightning attacks. But the fated Macías cannot stop fighting, even when he no longer has any idea of why he is fighting and indeed becomes increasingly puzzled at seeing his band joined by more and more former government soldiers fleeing the *carrancistas.* The absurdity of Macías's situation is articulated by the insane poet, Valderrama, who proclaims his love of the revolution not for any ideal nor for any particular leader but merely because it is revolution, violent and explosive. Yet even the madman is depicted as saner than Macías. Sensing the self-destructiveness that has come to characterize Macías and the inevitability of defeat, Valderrama deserts the band. Only the manipulator and exploiter of the revolution, Cervantes, survives, even prior to Valderrama's departure, as he leaves the bloodshed behind by fleeing to the United States to open a restaurant.

Azuela continues his scathing indictment of revolutionary excesses as he portrays the soldiers entering the lavish mansion of a *porfirista* (supporters of Porfirio Díaz) family in Zacatecas. Here he stunningly presents a clash of two cultures, as the revolutionaries ride their horses into the drawing room of the mansion, tear down the expensive drapes to use as sweat blankets for their horses, rip the paintings from the walls, and, seeing them of little value, destroy them while keeping only the gilt frames. Drunkenness, prostitution, torture, and killing of their prisoners combine to create the indelible impression of *los de abajo* as savage and mindless, devoted only to the satisfying of instinctual desires. Reductive symbolism, with emphasis on the futility of revolution, is continued in what is now regarded as a classic scene—one alluded to again and again by one of the primary continuers of the novel of the Mexican Revolution, Carlos Fuentes—when Macías after the death of his beloved Camila returns but briefly to his wife and to the child who does not recognize him. When asked by his wife why he must continue to fight, Macías hurls a stone over the rim of a canyon. This stone, launched on a predetermined trajectory and unable to stop its fall, symbolizes the heroic but pathetic Macías himself, compelled to continue the struggle.

The severe disillusionment of Azuela, who had begun as a staunch supporter of Madero's challenge to the Porfirio Díaz regime, finds its most cynical and bitter expression in the pronouncements of Solís, one of the officers of the revolutionary general Natera. Ironically, although Solís's lack of confidence in the course of the revolution has impelled him to withdraw from the fighting, he is as fated as all of the other revolutionaries on the battlefield, as he is suddenly killed by a stray bullet. Solís evokes a frightening vision of a people who have risked their lives to defeat one tyrant only to raise up in his place thousands of new despots.

Azuela's irony extends even to his portrayal of the Centaur of the North, Pancho Villa, whose appearance is excitedly, even wondrously anticipated but never realized. Azuela recites the many myths surrounding Villa, whom Cervantes elevates as "our Mexican Napoleon," including Villa as the generous and invincible Robin Hood. Yet he undercuts this legendary status by the fact that none of the persons who so embellish Villa and his Dorados has ever seen him.

A character in Azuela's short story "José María" (1929) remarks that in the absurd as in the abyss is found the sole and absolute truth. The revolution as a theater of the absurd is evoked by Azuela in his brief, satiric novel *Andrés Pérez, maderista*. The title is extremely ironic because Pérez, a forerunner of Luis Cervantes and a journalist who is secretly critical of the Díaz regime, is not a revolutionary, preferring amorous to political intrigue. Indeed, although he has left Mexico City for the countryside and a vacation, he finds himself rapidly and absurdly drawn into the revolution when he is mistaken for a political activist and even an incendiary. Responses of those he meets vary. Although the followers of Madero thrust money upon him to lead a major attack, other peasants are extremely wary of him and have taken precautions by constructing hiding places for themselves so as not to be drawn into the revolution.

As he will do again and again in his works, Azuela draws an effective contrast between the genuine idealist, in this case Antonio Reyes who has invited his friend Pérez to his estate, and the cynic and opportunist, here represented by Pérez who thinks only of taking the money and running, but who, before he can depart the town, is arrested as a revolutionary, his funds confiscated and, ironically, stolen from him by the local political boss. Reyes is cut down at the very outset of the fighting, as is the overseer Vicente. The latter is executed not by the government troops but by his own men at the orders of their commander, the self-appointed General Hernández. It is to regain the family lands which had been confiscated by Hernández, protected by the Díaz regime, that Vicente had joined the revolution, only to find that prominent among the Madero supporters now that Porfirio Díaz had departed the country was his archenemy Hernández.

As will occur so often in the works of Fuentes, the true idealist perishes while the opportunist triumphs. Depth is afforded to the character of Pérez as he at the end, deeply moved by the demise of his friend Reyes and influenced by Reyes's unremitting idealism, vacillates as to whether to return to Mexico City to take up the cause or remain where he is. Self-interest ultimately prevails, and Pérez betrays the memory of his friend when he remains to begin an affair with María, Reyes's widow who all along has been attracted to the rakish Pérez.

As a journalist, Pérez writes only to please his superiors at *The Globe*, a newspaper controlled by the *porfirista* regime. Thus, when a student protest is suddenly and violently quelled by the police, although his first impulse is to tell the story as one of brutalization of the student protestors by an oppressive authority, he quickly changes it to emphasize the victory of law and order over student rioters. Adding to the irony and to the absurdity of his situation is the fact that Pérez is denounced to the local authorities as a *maderista* by his superior on the newspaper, who has hated him because of his independence and has launched a personal vendetta. Ironic too is that even Pérez's attempts to inform the many who do welcome him as a revolutionary serve only to fortify his listeners' belief that he is a true revolutionary, needing to conceal his motives for the time being.

In another short novel, *Las moscas* (*The Flies;* 1918), Azuela lambastes the class of spineless bureaucrats whose loyalty is only to the government that employs them, including one family who is proud that a member served as doorman for every Mexican regime from Maximilian to Madero. The members of the shrewd Reyes Téllez family hedge their bets; two of the sisters follow the troops of Pancho Villa in case he should prove to be victorious, while their brother is assigned to remain with the forces of Alvaro Obregón.

The novel which in many aspects complements *Los de abajo,* so much so that it could very well have been entitled "Los de arriba," the upper crust, is *Las tribulaciones de una familia decente* (*The Trials of a Respectable Family;* 1918), which chronicles the tribulations of a *porfirista* family, the Vásquez Prados, who are forced to leave Zacatecas after the rebel victory and to emigrate to Mexico City, where they suffer intense alienation and constant humiliation as their privileged status is dissolved and they are at the mercy of the forces of Carranza, who has occupied the capital. In two other novels, *Mala yerba* and its continuation, *Esa sangre* (That Bad Blood; 1938), Azuela excoriates the landowners, focusing on the family of the arrogant Andrades, who are accustomed to making their own laws. But in *Las tribulaciones de una familia decente,* Azuela softens his stance toward the propertied class and in the figure of the sarcastic but idealistic Procopio evokes a manager who is genuinely concerned for the peasants and their welfare. Indeed, Procopio and his daughter Lulú are the only ones who for a time at least determine to adjust to the new revolutionary society, as they seek employment and even salvation through labor. But the stress of the sudden and constant change and the shock of realizing that Pascual, the sinuous husband of Procopio's daughter Berta, has betrayed the family by appropriating their properties which he then utilizes to ingratiate himself with the followers of Carranza, occasion Procopio's fatal heart attack. Throughout the novel, Azuela caricatures top dogs and underdogs alike. The effete poet Francisco José remains oblivious to the revolution and to the suffering of his family. Instead, he dedicates himself to an escapist art for art's sake as he writes poems praising the colonial ruins. The opportunistic La de Tabardillo, who seems to have stepped out of a picaresque novel, ingratiates herself into the favor of the flighty mother of the Vásquez Prado family, Agustinitas. The lies and flattery of La de Tabardillo lead first to her being loaned money by the increasingly impoverished family and finally to her stealing what little remains of their funds before she disappears forever.

The first part of *Las tribulaciones* is narrated by the ironically named César, who even as an adult is dressed in knee pants by his overprotective mother and who begins his account with an encomium of his ancestors—a thrust toward the glorious past by a family that has been suddenly and permanently stripped of its exalted social and economic standing. César emphasizes how by constantly changing its political allegiances the family has been able not only to survive but to prosper down through the centuries. Yet even this chameleonic strategy fails them in the turbulent and chaotic revolutionary world, where the groups of celebrating *carrancistas* are suddenly displaced by the hordes of *villistas* and *zapatistas,* and these representatives of the Indian Mexico, with whom the Vásquez Prado family now come into violent confrontation, are evoked as beings from another planet. How ideologically desperate the family has become is emphasized by the fact that Agustinitas, whose obsession is the rapid return of the family estates, places her hopes in the victory of Pancho Villa, fighting against the forces of Carranza, and she even celebrates Villa's entry into Mexico City, perceiving him as the redeemer of the *porfiristas.* In many aspects but most significantly in its self-defeating divisiveness, the family becomes symbolic of the course of the revolution itself. One member, Archibaldo, joins the supporters of the legendary Zapata; another element, led by Agustinitas and Francisco José, roots for the victory of the nephew of Don Porfirio, Félix Díaz; still another contingent, led by Pascual, joins forces with the *carrancistas.* Ironically, at the end even the astute Pascual, who has enriched himself enormously at the expense of the very family whom he so exalts, is devoured by the maelstrom of intrigue and violence which he has seemed to be able to control—killed by the political faction in which he had placed his confidence.

In many of Azuela's novels the revolutionary leaders, Villa, Carranza, Obregón, Calles, are in the background, shadowy figures whose impact on Azuela's character creations is great nonetheless. In *Las tribulaciones,* the basilisk glance of one of the revolutionary leaders is sufficient to kill the pusillanimous César. At the very end of *Las moscas* the highly touted Villa appears but only briefly. He is now evoked as a solitary figure, no longer, after his stunning defeat at Celaya, surrounded by enthusiastic throngs. He is juxtaposed with the dying sun, as Azuela thus signifies the waning of Villa as a national power—undercutting the wild and fervent prophecy of Moralitos's grandmother, another of Azuela's minor but unforgettable characters, that Mexico would be ruled by four Panchos, including Francisco Madero and Francisco Villa.

In the fascinating *El águila y la serpiente* (*The Eagle and the Serpent;* 1928), the revolutionary leaders are on center stage, and their personalities and programs, actions and motives, are closely and penetratingly examined by a master of style and a profound analyst of the complexity and the contradictoriness of human nature, Martín Luis Guzmán (1887–1976). This is a hybrid work, which can be considered a series of short stories, an autobiography of the young Guzmán's experiences in the revolution, a series of essays on the national identity, and a work considered by Guzmán himself as a novel. Over and over again Guzmán in highly dramatic terms depicts the confrontation of the intellectual, urbane and contemplative, with the rude and crude and sometimes even barbaric forces that nonetheless were seen as necessary to defeat the reactionary forces of the neo-Díaz supporters of Huerta. Many times Guzmán comes close to death, not on the battlefield, not against the federal forces, but against the very commander, Pancho Villa—whom Guzmán evokes in terms of a jaguar that has to be tamed—whom he supported and served after losing confidence in Carranza. At times Guzmán quietly records his triumphs at harnessing the barbaric impulse, as when he and Llorente intervene, at the risk of aggravating the volatile temper of Villa and being shot to death themselves, to calm an enraged and extremely vengeful Villa and to persuade him not to execute the 160 prisoners who had surrendered to him. The new decision of Villa to spare the lives of the prisoners must be communicated by telegraph, and Guzmán masterfully creates a mood of suspense by concentrating in a cinematic "close-up" on the tense and nervous fingers of the telegraph operator.

Rejecting a military career on the advice of his father, who himself was a military officer, Guzmán repeatedly uses psychology to influence and even to control Villa's behavior. In this instance Guzmán appeals to Villa's pride, to his sense of how a master general would treat men who had voluntarily put down their arms. Yet at other times, Guzmán cannot halt the harsh "revolutionary justice" that is applied instantly and cruelly, without trial or witnesses, jury or judge, to the supposed malefactors. Guzmán is unsuccessful at persuading Villa's general, José Robles, or even the president pro tem of Mexico, Eulalio Gutiérrez, to pardon five counterfeiters whom Villa has sentenced to be executed immediately—even though Villa himself has just given Guzmán thousands of freshly printed pesos that Villa himself has manufactured.

Much of the fascination and extremely tense dramatic atmosphere of El águila y la serpiente derives from the series of direct confrontations between Guzmán and Villa. Villa, evoked as the arrogant macho, time and again challenges Guzmán, the "tenderfoot," to prove himself—with the pistol, with the lariat—and Guzmán responds to these challenges and is even rewarded for his prowess by the extremely capricious, at times punitive and at other moments munificent, Villa. And indeed, the dominant personality of this work, which was tentatively entitled "A la hora de Pancho Villa" (The Hour of Pancho Villa), is the Centaur of the North, who is evoked with continued ambivalence, with admiration and terror, doubt and dedication, as a charismatic and deadly leader. When Guzmán encounters Villa for the first time in a darkened hovel in Ciudad Juárez, he depicts him as a wild animal in his lair, despite the unrestrained enthusiasm that fellow revolutionaries and intellectuals like Vasconcelos have evinced for Villa's leadership. At a subsequent point in the narrative, in the chapter with the ominous title "Pancho Villa's Pistol," Guzmán portrays him as the very incarnation of destruction, as a man fused with his pistol. And at still another point, in "A Perilous Sleep," Villa emerges not as sullen and hostile but as a loquacious and enigmatic raconteur, speculating on the nature of sleep and astutely enhancing his own legendary status by giving his rapt listeners the image of himself as a noble, valorous, and self-sacrificing leader. Here is the heroic Villa, whose devotion to his men is so great that he endangers his own life by deliberately slowing down his flight from the pursuing *federales* because he has failed to arouse from a deathlike sleep an exhausted companion, Urbina, yet refuses to abandon him.

The very title *El águila y la serpiente* is a reference to the emblem on the Mexican national flag and is a reflection of the quest by Guzmán not only for the just and enlightened revolutionary and national leader who will put aside personal ambition and striving for power, but also for the spiritual essence of the Mexican national identity. The young, enthusiastic, idealistic, and intrepid Guzmán plunges into the violent and chaotic military phase of the revolution. Yet, ironically, the end of the work depicts an increasingly disillusioned and apprehensive Guzmán, seeking to flee from the clutches of Villa. Here yet again Guzmán uses psychology to outwit his leader. Instead of openly deserting him and thus running the risk of being fanatically pursued and perhaps killed by Villa, Guzmán boldly enters the "lion's den" to confront an increasingly desperate Villa and requests permission to join his family. At the beginning of the work, it is the heinous act of Huerta—the assassinations of Francisco and Gustavo Madero and Vice President Pino Suárez—that is condemned by Guzmán. But at the end it is the capricious and ignominious execution of David Berlanga, a leader whom Guzmán evokes as the idealistic conscience of the revolution, that anguishes Guzmán—a murder perpetrated by Rodolfo Fierro, whom Guzmán views as one of the most sadistic and brutal of the Villista generals, on direct orders of Villa. Once again, as in the pessimistic vision of Azuela, the revolution is depicted as a monstrous force that devours its own young. Indeed, the opposition, the *federales,* are most often but a shadowy phenomenon, such as in the chapter in which Guzmán evokes the city of Culiacán after the revolutionary victory, the federal forces having fled. Time and again it is revolutionary blood-lust and despotism that Guzmán chronicles and condemns. Thus Guzmán evokes the draconian reprisals taken by Cosío Robelo against those who defy the decree against looting issued by Obregón—death by the firing squad. One of the most chilling episodes recounted by Guzmán, and later to influence Fuentes in his novel *Gringo viejo,* is the monstrous way in which Fierro executes three hundred prisoners by compelling them to perform a gruesome *danse macabre,* literally to run for their lives to attempt to escape his bullets by reaching and scaling a wall. When moans are heard issuing from one of the mounds of corpses, Fierro orders a soldier to give the coup de grâce to the victim who is disturbing his sleep.

Yet one of the basic compositional principles of *El águila y la serpiente* is balance. Contrasting with the Villa of darkness is a Villa of light. At times Villa is evoked as a person whose body blocks out all the light and, in one episode, as a somber figure from whose eyes emanates the shadow of death. Yet at another point, as the boisterous revolutionaries watch a documentary film at the Convention of Aguascalientes, Villa appears on the screen ringed with light. Physically this is the glaring light of the projector, but Guzmán endows it with a spiritual significance. He cannot restrain his awe and his admiration for Villa, who now appears as a supernatural being, bathed in a radiant and transcendental glow.

In recounting the viewing of this film by the trigger-happy revolutionaries, Guzmán seems to be updating the theme of illusion and reality developed by Cervantes in *Don Quijote*. The hidalgo, or gentleman, who in the sixteenth century becomes crazed after reading novels of chivalry and sallies forth to right the wrongs of the world, becomes so entranced on viewing a puppet play performed by Maese Pedro that he enters the fray and lops off the heads of the puppets whom he sees as adversaries. Similarly, the excited revolutionaries, upon seeing the image of Carranza mounted on his horse cross the screen, fire bullets at it, not realizing that Guzmán and others are in back of the screen, and if Carranza had been on foot rather than on horseback, they would have been killed.

In one of the most horrifying chapters, "The Military Hospital," Guzmán recounts his experience in a poorly equipped hospital in Culiacán. As he views the wounded, Guzmán is amazed at the myriad trajectories that the bullets have taken through the bodies of their victims, and he imbues the bullets with a weird, capricious life of their own. Countering the brutality of some of the revolutionary generals are the courage and idealism of others, like Iturbe, the victor of Culiacán, or Robles or Diéguez or the great *villista* general Felipe Angeles, whom Guzmán portrays in an unaccustomed way, not on the battle-field or planning strategy, but alone and meditative and even melancholy, as if he were a harbinger of the ultimate defeat of the revolutionary idealists. Guz-mán expresses continued reservations about the *villista* troops, even the re-splendent Dorados, whom he evokes as menacing and cruel. Yet Guzmán also manifests severe misgivings about Villa's adversary Obregón, whose inflated prose style Guzmán attacks as indicative of his masked, theatrical quality. The leadership of Venustiano Carranza is questioned as well, as Guzmán unequivo-cally delineates him not as the New Man of the revolution but, in his love of pomp and ceremony and in his desire to be surrounded by fawners and flat-terers, as a continuation of the past, as Guzmán sees the future government of Carranza as a continuation of the dictatorship of Porfirio Díaz.

In contrast with the enthusiasm expressed for Villa by the emotional Vas-concelos or by Alberto J. Pani, undersecretary for education in the government of Madero and whom Guzmán served as private secretary, the Pani who was later to become the Carranza government's minister to France and to serve Obregón as finance minister, Guzmán's constant restraint and measure made him hesitant to place his faith and his support in any one leader. Thus Guzmán rejects the blind cult of the macho, the valiant and heroic leader who by force of arms will redeem Mexico. Yet, ironically, in a later work, his mammoth biography of Villa, Guzmán modifies his position. In *Las memorias de Pancho Villa* (*Memories of Pancho Villa;* 1938), without the constant irony of Azuela, Guzmán re-creates Villa as idealist and savior. Perhaps because Guzmán failed in his continued quest for the responsible and noble and self-sacrificing leader so desperately needed during and after the military phase of the revolution, perhaps because Guzmán himself was not willing to accept the offers repeatedly tendered to him to become a military leader, thus placing himself in a position to become a leader of the nation, Guzmán is compelled to create through his literary vision and imagination the hero whom he did not find in his youth.

Unwilling to devote himself unstintingly to any of the leaders, who fail to measure up to his rigorous standards, Guzmán is even more apprehensive of the masses of revolutionary soldiers. In Azuela's *Los de abajo,* as we have seen, these revolutionaries are constantly caricatured and their coarseness and barbaric acts are emphasized, but they are at least individualized. For Guzmán, time after time *los de abajo* appear as an indistinguishable mass, anonymous beings engulfed in shadows or in night, portrayed in their drunkenness and mindlessness as a hydra-headed beast or as a gigantic reptile. In marked contrast, in Fuentes's *Gringo viejo,* *los de abajo* are finally given a face that is kindly and sensitive and human, one that coincides with the ennobling of the people, individualized and dignified, in the murals of Diego Rivera.

Many of the novelists of the Mexican Revolution have evoked the military phases of the conflict, as is done extensively by Gregorio López y Fuentes (1897–1966) in novels like *Campamento* (Encampment; 1931) and *Tierra* (Earth; 1932), the latter of which focuses on the supporters of Zapata, and by Rafael Muñoz (1899–1972) in adventure novels like the electrifying *¡Vámonos con Pancho Villa!* (Let's Go with Pancho Villa!; 1931), which traces the spellbinding effect that Villa exerts over Tiburcio Maya, and *Se llevaron el cañón para Bachimba* (They Took the Cannon Away to Bachimba; 1941), a portrayal of the Pascual Orozco revolt, and in his short stories included in volumes like *El feroz cabecilla y otros cuentos* (The Fierce Leader and Other Short Stories; 1928). Other novelists delve extensively into the socioeconomic and political aspects of the revolution, into the rivalries among the revolutionaries themselves for the presidency of Mexico, and into the turbulent years of revolutionary aftermath in the decade of the twenties, in which political power and violence were inextricable and in which a counterrevolution was fought by the populist Cristeros. Azuela's scathing novel *El camarada Pantoja,* which was not published until more than a decade after it was written, traces the rapid rise to power of the servile Catarino Pantoja, who at the end becomes governor-elect of the state of Zacatecas. Seeking to emulate his leaders in many aspects, he desires to shed his wife, Chata, for a younger mistress, who is subsequently killed by the jealous wife. The action of the novel takes place against the background of the Calles regime and the Catholic counterrevolutionary Cristero conflict.

In his bold and fascinating narrative of the labyrinthine world of Mexican politics in the twenties, *La sombra del caudillo* (The Shadow of the Tyrant; 1929), Guzmán concentrates on the somber world of an era of extreme instability, rampant opportunism, corruption, and explosive conflict. This novel is replete with shadows—shadowy political forces, shady dealings, shadow characters, shadow candidacies, and perhaps the greatest shadow of all, of the entire Mexican Revolution of 1910, the shadow of Pancho Villa, advocate of the oppressed, that contrasts with a polarized Mexico in which the masses are still dispossessed. Indeed, Guzmán, novelist, journalist, envoy of Pancho Villa, military adviser to General José Robles, colonel in Villa's revolutionary army, throughout his life was preoccupied with the revolution and its impact on Mexican society. *La sombra del caudillo* evokes a closed-in, even stifling, atmosphere that is obsessively political and politicized. It is a nebulous world of incessantly shifting allegiances and alliances that form and dissolve and coalesce again, a chronicle of the treacherous forces that engulf and finally destroy the protagonist, Ignacio Aguirre, evoked as a hero-victim from the very start of this highly fatalistic work. Here Guzmán captures in eloquent, classic prose the incendiary atmosphere of revolutionary aftermath, with former generals still lusting for battle and ready to throw their armies into the field at the slightest provocation.

In *La sombra del caudillo,* Guzmán writes both a political novel and a spy thriller. His narrative is carefully orchestrated toward a crescendo of intrigue, betrayal, violence, and mass murder. At the outset of the novel, the uproar and violence at the convention of the Partido Radical Progresista (Progressive Radical Party) at Toluca and the rapid degeneration of the initial atmosphere of superficial cordiality and unity adumbrate a horrendous cycle of violence begetting increased violence—the kidnapping and torturing almost to death of the innocent Axkaná by the agents of the Caudillo, the threat by Hilario Jiménez, the Caudillo's protege, to massacre the Aguirre supporters, and the murder of the deputy Canizares—until at the end there is a bloodbath that consumes Aguirre and his followers, with only Axkaná escaping alive.

Guzmán presents not only the reclusive Caudillo but also the whole of Mexico as a vast shadow land. The invisible Caudillo, who never makes public appearances because he is fearful of assassination, constantly operates behind the scenes. His machinations are reflected everywhere: in the duplicitous behavior of the generals who earnestly and repeatedly pledge their loyalty to Aguirre but who are in fact the minions of the Caudillo; in the pusillanimous doctor who treats Axkaná after he has been forced to imbibe an immense quantity of alcohol by his mysterious captors and yet who attempts to cover up the crime of attempted murder by dismissing it as a mere case of intoxication; in the politicians and deputies, including Hilario Jiménez, the handpicked successor of the Caudillo, who suddenly become the recipients of lavish gifts. Not only the Caudillo but so many of the other characters are derealized into mere shadows. The presidential candidacy of Ignacio Aguirre never really emerges from the inchoate, shadow stage. Ironically, Aguirre, who has been forced into defying the Caudillo and who now attempts to project himself as the candidate of the people, has for his entire political career functioned as but a shadow of the Shadow, as a subservient minister of war who has acted as merely the agent of the Caudillo, in order to exploit and betray and even to eradicate the enemies of his master. Thus Aguirre, despite his naive faith in the power of public opinion to elevate his candidacy, is never really perceived by the public as a viable alternative to the Caudillo. And, even though politically Aguirre breaks with his former mentor-protector, Aguirre remains psychologically dependent, if not on the Caudillo himself then on the type of stifling patronage system fostered by the Caudillo. We may surmise that Aguirre received his powerful position not because of any particular competence—indeed, in the time-span of Guzmán's narrative he displays little—but as a reward for loyal service to the Caudillo. To an overwhelming extent, Aguirre, like Hilario Jiménez, has been the Caudillo's creation.

The shadows, natural, political, and psychological, that proliferate in *La sombra del caudillo* underscore not only the menacing power of the Caudillo that creeps into every corner, but also the perpetual haziness, the inability in this fluctuating shadow land to distinguish between friend and foe, between loyal followers and spies. Although the weak and narcissistic Aguirre naively believes that he has many steadfast allies among the politicians and generals who pay court to him, feeding his ambitions for ultimate power, most of these, like the sycophantic Catarino Ibáñez, the governor of the state of Mexico, and later the ruthless general Julián Elizondo, are but shadowy adherents who secretly betray him.

Guzmán sees the electoral process in Mexico as degenerating into ineffectiveness because the middle classes refuse to take an active role, limiting themselves instead at the convention of the Partido Radical Progresista to the passive roles of aloof and disdainful spectators or, like the ancient Romans watching a combat between gladiators, egging on the combatants but never becoming involved themselves in the savage struggle between Aguirre and Jiménez, even though they secretly support Aguirre as a force of relative independence from the Caudillo, in contrast to Jiménez, who represents a continuation of the Díaz system. The cowardice and the apathy of the people directly or indirectly serve to perpetuate the dictatorship. The Indian masses are evoked as but pawns in the sinister political game, as they walk to the Toluca Convention, motivated by the promise of a free meal if they perform on cue, shouting out the name of the officially designated candidate. Yet the Indian masses do not even know for whom they are cheering. There are no representatives of these Indian peoples at the convention, no voting delegates. Compounding the atmosphere of confusion in the convention and at the same time symbolizing its inherent absurdity, since what ultimately matters is the will of the Caudillo, the masses garble and confuse the names of the candidates.

The same irresolution that Aguirre, who like Andrés Pérez is many times diverted from politics by his amorous entanglements, has all along manifested regarding his candidacy he also reveals in regard to entering into armed rebellion. One of the reasons why seasoned and crafty generals like Elizondo ultimately betray Aguirre is precisely this vacillation, this unpredictability. Discontent with the absolutism of the Caudillo, which deprives them of the power they feel they deserve, and having fought and won on the field of battle, Elizondo and others desire to break with the Caudillo but only for a sure thing—or at least for a powerful and decisive leader. For them to follow the moody and mercurial and easily distracted Aguirre places them in extreme danger. Unlike the increasingly desperate and vulnerable Aguirre, who has permanently broken with the Caudillo and who now has nothing to lose, Elizondo will fight only if he is confident he can win. The one advantage that Aguirre had over the Caudillo, that of surprise, is now irretrievably lost. Elizondo, who has secretly decided to remain loyal to the Caudillo, uses Aguirre's own weaknesses against him. Remaining in the Aguirre camp, where indecisiveness and panic prevail and where there is no danger to him, Elizondo seeks cleverly to mute the force of those generals who want to declare themselves immediately in armed rebellion—knowing that this is what his superior, the Caudillo, most dreads, since once again, as it did in the epoch of Francisco Madero, revolt could spread like a conflagration and topple the Caudillo as rapidly as it did Porfirio Díaz.

As in *Los de abajo,* a cyclical time process dominates *La sombra del caudillo,* which both begins and ends with an evocation of Aguirre's Cadillac, a paradoxical symbol of his machismo, of the power and wealth that he has acquired as the result of a revolution fought to benefit the poor and the oppressed, and also of his betrayal of revolutionary ideals. At the end of the narrative, the Cadillac again appears, but it is now in the possession of Aguirre's slayer, Segura. Its reappearance signifies that the cycle of bloodshed brings to the top only new oppressors.

Perhaps because for so long a time he has been forced to play the role of surrogate son to the seemingly benevolent and protective Caudillo, Aguirre cannot succeed in projecting the image of the father figure and protector of the people that is so desperately sought after, as is exemplified in the very moving episode in which Axkaná, who many times acts as the conscience of the corrupt and dissolute Aguirre and indeed who is the center of idealism in the narrative, awakens the deep-felt aspirations of the Indian people for social justice and national reform. Instead, in Guzmán as in Azuela and later in Fuentes, it is the mere mask of idealism that is over and over again raised up. With consummate cynicism, General Leyva and deputies Ricalde and López Nieto, after finalizing their plans to massacre Aguirre's supporters in the Chamber of Deputies, justify their actions in the name of the true idealists and martyrs of the revolution. Thus the initially legitimate and peaceful opposition to the Caudillo and Jiménez raised by Aguirre is countered with secret plans for his extermination—under the idealistic shadow of Emiliano Zapata.

Agustín Yáñez too has been preoccupied with the revolution of 1910, which one of the characters in his epic novel *Las vueltas del tiempo* (The Cycles of

Time; 1973) states is the most significant event in the entire history of Mexico. *Al filo del agua* (*The Edge of the Storm;* 1947) and *La creación* (Creation; 1959) are other works which concentrate respectively on the onset of the revolution and on the turbulent postrevolutionary period and the dramatic changes occurring in Mexican visual art and music as the result of a revolution that plunged Mexico into a quest for its national identity and toward an exuberant affirmation of that identity. In contrast to Azuela and Guzmán, who often narrate from the point of view of eyewitnesses to revolutionary events, Yáñez, while not a direct participant in the revolution, helped to mold the new society that emerged from the conflict, first as governor of Jalisco and then as minister of education in the government of Díaz Ordaz.

Al filo del agua is a novel of innerness in which the minds of many of the characters in the provincial town of Jalisco, where all of the action takes place, are explored through sophisticated stylistic and stream-of-consciousness techniques. Here it is not the event, the oncoming of revolution, nor the social institution, the authoritarian Church with its opposition to social reform and its control over almost every aspect of the parishioners' lives, but the inner reactions of the characters that become the chief object of narrative concern, as Yáñez reveals inner worlds of conflict, pent-up emotions, guilt, and repressed sexual desire. The suppression of natural instinct is predominant in this suffocating town where even couples joined in matrimony are looked upon with suspicion and the statues of the male saints are placed on the opposite side of the church from those of the females, a town which is bereft of the social center, the alameda, because the priests do not want the sexes to intermingle, a town where many keep their coffins in their living rooms to be able to meditate on death, and indeed where love itself is seen as a form of death. The severe limitations on personal freedom lead to explosive reactions—insanity, violence, murder, and rebellion.

Revolution thus becomes a striving for more than just political reform or for economic betterment, in a town where the political presence is marginal, subordinate to the clergy, and where there is very little poverty. Instead the emphasis is on moral and emotional emancipation. The narrative draws many contrasts among the three parish priests, the guilt-ridden Don Dionisio with his acute sense of the responsibility for all of those in his flock; the harsh, fanatic Padre Islas, whose name (Islands) symbolizes his isolation from everything human, to the extent that he finally suffers a severe nervous crisis, but whose authority over the village has increased at the end; and the reformist-minded Padre Reyes, whose initial attempts to open up the townspeople and to promote social interaction meet with failure. Indeed, augmenting the tension of the work is the constant contrast between the repressive control over the inhabitants exerted by the priests, which includes censorship of the mail and compulsive spiritual retreats that encourage the penitents to flagellate themselves, and the liberating forces from the external world, like the mysterious and enchanting woman, Victoria, who one day appears in the village, the students at home for the holidays with their stories of the outside world, the traveling musicians who with their melodies awaken long-suppressed desires among the townspeople, those who have gone to the United States to work and return with their heightened social and political awareness, and finally, the oncoming of the revolution.

And yet the atmosphere of apocalyptic change, of titanic devastation that destroys the old order to give birth to the new, which has been stressed throughout this narrative, is an ironic one, because revolution itself is an anticlimax, similar to a violent but brief desert shower that bursts forth and then passes on. At the end, the town is absorbed not with the revolutionaries, who have come and gone, joined by the rebellious niece of Don Dionisio, María, and by the widow of González, but with condemning their spiritual leader for apparent laxity in allowing this to happen. The most powerful force in the work thus is not the revolution at all but the willful and close-minded and unforgiving Islas, whose spirit dominates the sanctimonious and petty-minded people. Ironically, although there is a seemingly endless celebration of Lent in the town, Easter with its message of hope and joy and resurrection is hardly celebrated at all, as the dark-robed women and the sullen men eke out their existence, proud in their provincialism, seeing themselves as the religious center of the universe. Constant repression leads to bursts of violence, seen in the acts of Damián Limón, who murders his father and then kills his beloved Micaela when she refuses to depart from the town with him.

One of the most unique of the characters in this dense work, with its baroque style that effectively captures an atmosphere of spiritual heaviness and impenetrability, is Lucas Macías, who with no individual identity is a type of collective historical consciousness. Every time he is told of a current event, he immediately relates it to a similar occurrence in the past. It is significant that with the dramatic victory of Madero, Macías for the first time focuses directly on the present, a seeming indication that this event has broken forever the ties with the past. Yet, significantly, Madero's triumph also coincides with Macías's death. Another center of mystery and idealism is the town bellringer, Gabriel. Of unknown origin, Gabriel is taken in by Dionisio, and his ringing of the bells becomes a poetic phenomenon, as he is mythified as the emotional and spiritual center of the town. Gabriel will later become the anguished protagonist of La creación, as he struggles, under the patronage of Victoria and the guidance of María, to define both Mexico and himself through his music.

Las vueltas del tiempo provides another sequel to Al filo del agua. Written between 1948 and 1951, it was not published until 1973. It focuses in the narrative present on the funeral of Calles and traces the varying reactions of those attending the funeral to the career of the Mexican president who reacted violently against the Church. It is ironic that María, who in Al filo del agua is seen as a dreamer, one who secretly reads forbidden romantic novels and who longs to escape from the incarceration that is life in the pueblo, at the end running off with the revolutionaries, is here portrayed at a later stage in her life, where instead of being an Adelita or María Pistolas she is seen as allied with the most powerful interests in postrevolutionary society. Her stolid, industrious, and ambitious husband, Jacobo Ibarra, who in *Al filo del agua* is seen as a person whom the volatile María detests but whom she marries as a means of punishing her former suitors and defying social convention, here has become the force that cements her to the power elite. María emerges as one of the closest friends and confidants to Calles. Damián Limón stands in ironic contrast. He also appears in *Las vueltas del tiempo* but as a marginalized figure, embittered that others who did none of the fighting have now reaped lavish rewards and have rapidly amassed fortunes that exceed those of the very *porfiristas* whose corruption and unbridled wealth the revolution was fought to overthrow.

Like Azuela, Yáñez becomes cynical of the way that the revolutionary ideals have been betrayed. The Indian consciousness, still divorced from the mainstream of modern Mexico, is represented by the character significantly named Juárez, in reference to the Zapotec Indian Benito Juárez, president of Mexico and a liberal reformer. Addressed by his nickname Juaritos, he attends the funeral because he is in agreement with the fierce anticlericalism of Calles. Yet this Juárez is depicted by Yáñez as an extremist who seeks the return of the ancient Aztec god Huitzilopochtli as a powerful presence that will restore the ancient grandeur and might of Indian Mexico. Unlike D. H. Lawrence, who in *The Plumed Serpent* (1926) sees the return of the ancient gods Quetzalcoatl and Huitzilopochtli as a transcendental alternative to a desiccated and spiritually bankrupt modern society, Yáñez is very skeptical of this summoning up of the ancient spirits. Juaritos is depicted as a person beset with delusions of grandeur, impossible to actualize, which undercut him. In his megalomania, Juaritos even rejects his namesake, Benito Juárez, for being unfaithful to his Indian heritage and, instead of restoring an Indian empire, instead of becoming another Moctezuma, for having adopted the liberal ideology that Juaritos scorns because it is a product of Western culture. The narrative ends with a sharp focus on the anguished Heliodoro Camacho, whose family suffered persecution during the Calles regime but who as a funeral attendant is compelled to assist at the burial. To add to his troubles, at the end Heliodoro finds that his two daughters have been arrested for prostitution and he himself is arrested for the beating of his wife: he is unable to halt the downward spiral of his life.

The influence of both Yáñez, with his envisioning of rural Mexico in terms of classical Greek and Roman mythology and biblical characters and legends, and Azuela, with his wry and mordant humor and his capturing of the rough and spicy idiom of the street and the tavern, is found in the dark vision of Juan Rulfo. Rulfo's first major work is a volume of short stories that concentrate on rural Mexico, *El llano en llamas* (*The Burning Plain and Other Stories;* 1953). The title story portrays a band of former revolutionaries who after their defeat turn to banditry and dedicate themselves to cattle rustling and to burning fields of sugar cane. The sadistic pleasure that these outlaws take in torturing their prisoners, compelling them to play the role of bullfighters while they become bulls sporting makeshift horns tipped with razor blades, is reminiscent of the monstrous and sadistic actions of Güero Margarito in *Los de abajo*. Many of Rulfo's short stories focus emphatically on indigenous Mexico, like the poignant and exceedingly ironic story "Nos han dado la tierra" ("They Gave Us the Land"), in which a small group of peasants slowly cross a hot, desert wasteland, the land that they have been given by the new government but which is impossible to cultivate. Deprived of horses and rifles by the authorities who fear that the discontented peasants will once again resort to revolution, they vainly protest their victimization to the federal representative. A single drop of rain falls, symbolic of the desperation of their state and also of the impossibility of redemption.

"Es que somos muy pobres" ("We're Very Poor") focuses on the stunned and utterly passive reaction of impoverished Indian villagers to the roiling flood waters that carry off their animals and destroy their property. Intense repetition conveys the mesmerizing effect of the rapidly rising flood waters on the Indians, who do nothing to halt the destruction. The narrator, a young boy, watches the waters carry away the young cow that was to be the dowry of his sister Tacha and acknowledges the inevitability that she will be impelled on the same negative trajectory of poverty and prostitution as her two older sisters. Even her nickname, Tacha, on the literal level derived from Anastasia, also means "stain" and underscores the fatalism that enshrouds her existence.

"En la madrugada" ("At Daybreak"), a story wrapped in physical mist that symbolizes its ambiguity, details the imprisonment of a ranch hand who does not know whether he killed his master or not but who is so intimidated by the accusation that he accepts the blame. Once again, the abyss between the helpless *los de abajo* and the arrogant and contemptuous and tyrannical *los de arriba* is chronicled, as the boss of the town, ironically named Don Justo (Just), is evoked as so powerful that he is even the owner of the light. "Diles que no me maten" ("Tell Them Not to Kill Me") develops a repeated theme in Rulfo's work, that of the bitterly conflictive relationships between fathers and sons, seen also in stories like "Paso del Norte" ("Pass to the North") and "No oyes ladrar los perros" ("No Dogs Bark"). Although the anguished Juvencio Nava repeatedly begs his son to intervene with the authorities to save him from imminent execution, the son is extremely reluctant to do so, apprehensive that they will shoot him as well. This is a story of vengeance, finally taken by the son of Guadalupe Terreros, brutally murdered years before by Juvencio as the result of a quarrel between the two over watering rights. For the rest of his life the cowardly Juvencio remains a hunted man, pursued by the authorities but even more persecuted by his own self, by his inexpiable feelings of fear and guilt. Finally captured, Juvencio attempts to gain release through the intervention of a son who finds it impossible to feel any emotion, either love or tenderness or even sympathy, for the father who had deserted him.

"Luvina," the story that anticipates Rulfo's masterpiece, the novel *Pedro Páramo* (1955), is the story of a young man, seemingly a persona of the idealistic and socially committed Rulfo himself who worked for the Instituto Nacional Indigenista (National Indigenous Institute), who travels to the town of Luvina, devastated by the revolution, with its abandoned church and its ghostly in-habitants, in an attempt to convince them to leave the wasteland. But the grim inhabitants stubbornly refuse to leave, stating that this is the place where their ancestors have been buried. As occurs so often in the somber world created by Rulfo, the dead control the living. Although physically the narrator has left the town whose lyric name San Juan de Luvina (Saint John of Luvina) belies its nature as a purgatory of tormented souls, psychically he keeps reliving his traumatic experiences there, unable to purge himself of his past. He remains mired within himself and his drunkenness, oblivious to the life around him—mesmerized by the town of living death that is Luvina, and which fore-shadows the hell world of Comala in *Pedro Páramo*.

The protagonist of Rulfo's concentrated and extremely complex and am-biguous novel that fuses present and past, memory and oblivion, the living and the dead, and reality and the supernatural is the cacique Pedro Páramo, whose last name, "wasteland," signifies both the devastation that he brings to the lives of all around him and the spiritual barrenness of his own life, as he remains deprived of the only person whom he ever loved, the enigmatic and unattainable Susana San Juan. Exercising a despotic authority over the town of Comala, Páramo is evoked indirectly through the warped and tormented lives of his victims. Rulfo's novel contains elements that link it to the tradi-tional regionalist novel: the focus on the inhabitants of a small, isolated, rural Mexican town, the emphasis on popular speech and customs, the background of revolutionary struggles. But the regional novel, in general, offers a minute depiction of scene and setting with only occasional glimpses into the inner lives of the characters.

In *Pedro Páramo,* the opposite is true. Outer reality has vanished. The au-thor's aim is to find objective analogues for a state of mind or condition of the soul. Comala is at once a ghost town and a realm of lost spirits. It is populated by the remnants of characters physically shattered and morally degraded by Páramo. The destructive fury of the cacique, who seeks to avenge the acciden-tal shooting of his father, results in a hell world of suffering during his life. And after his death, the chaos and devastation that Páramo has wreaked are perpetuated. Dissociated psychic states—love, hate, guilt, terror—naked feel-ings that have lost the self that once incarnated them, float in eternal time and space. These scraps of consciousness which reflect the fragmentation of the narrative structure as a whole define the basic themes of the novel: disinte-gration of the universe, loss of an integral self, and the hopelessness of redemption.

The mind of the disoriented Juan Preciado, who narrates his descent to Comala in search of his father, Pedro Páramo, in order to reclaim his family inheritance, is depicted in the process of attempting to impose order and meaning upon an external nothingness. The nullity of Preciado's perceptions, comprised of images that reflect mirages of human beings, is reduced even further by the fact that these impressions are filtered through the mind of a narrator who himself has ceased to exist. Preciado becomes asphyxiated by the atmosphere of moral putrefaction which he, in sleeping with the woman who has formed part of an incestuous couple, participates in; he narrates from the tomb.

Shifting points of view that alternate among the first-person voice of Preciado, third-person omniscient author narration, and stream-of-consciousness soliloquies underscore the difference between image and essence, between the external manifestation of character and internal identity, concealed and impenetrable. Narrative technique defines the quality of experience: appearance and action are generally conveyed through the more objective third-person narration, emotionally charged experience through interior monologues. From an external point of view, Páramo is depicted as a ruthless dictator, but his soliloquies reveal his wistful, brooding, sensitive nature and his subordination to the illusion of love.

In adolescence as in senility, Páramo is mesmerized by an idyllic vision of Susana San Juan, a person who like the soaring kite in one of his reveries always escapes him. Ironically, the object of his romantic fantasies is revealed through her own interior monologues as a guilt-ridden and tormented sinner. She blasphemes against God for depriving her of her first husband, Florencio, and enters into an ambiguous, presumably incestuous relationship with her father, Bartolomé. In her estrangement from the external world and obsession with the past, Susana is strangely similar to the self-absorbed Páramo. Although both characters experience an all-consuming devotion, neither can understand or even communicate with the other. Susana spends the final years of her life as Páramo's wife in name only, taking refuge in memory, in insanity, and in erotic delirium. Rejecting the attempts of Padre Rentería to perform extreme unction, she dies unconfessed. The irony of her fate is that, like all of the characters in this phantasmagoric novel, she can find no relief from the anguish that has characterized her life. Her spirit continues to suffer in the grave, as she is haunted by an illusion of a paradise that she will never enter. Similarly, the isolated and extremely embittered and vindictive mother of Juan Preciado, Dolores, conjures up the vision of Comala as a verdant and breeze-filled paradise, a lyric vision that Juan takes with him to Comala and is shocked at how it contrasts with the hot, dry, deadly atmosphere, the miasma created and sustained by the malefic Páramo.

Susana, the ethereal woman whom Páramo in his febrile imagination conceives of as ascending to heaven, becomes a poetic abstraction of love. Of her external appearance, only brief mention is made. Even when she is obsessively evoked by Páramo, the only physical attribute described is her green eyes. The outer appearance of the cacique too is vague; he looms as a huge but undefined figure. More myth than man, he is a paradoxical symbol of intense love and pure hate, the latter being the way in which another illegitimate son, Abundio, depicts him sardonically at the very start. Only at the very end do we understand the reason for Abundio's enmity: Páramo had the opportunity to save Abundio's wife but did nothing to intervene.

The narrative of external action that traces Páramo's rapid ascent to power, as he rebuilds his father's estate through chicanery and terror, is counter-pointed by the awesome growth of his fantasies. The cacique's power, inde-structible from the outside, is eroded from within, like that of so many of the power figures in the Mexican narrative—the draconian General Francisco Ro-sas in Elena Garro's *Los recuerdos del porvenir* (*Memories of the Future;* 1963), Artemio Cruz in Fuentes's *La muerte de Artemio Cruz,* the *mater terribilis* Clau-dia Nervo in Fuentes's *Zona sagrada* (*Holy Place;* 1967). When El Tilcuate, one of Páramo's henchmen, returns to inform the now-listless cacique of the shifting power struggles of the revolution, the destructive consequences of which the cacique has astutely managed to avoid, he finds that his leader has lost all interest in the outcome. Paralleling the outwardly jovial but devious and conniving landowner Rosalío Mendoza in Fernando de Fuentes's classic film *El compadre Mendoza* (Best Friend Mendoza; 1933), who welcomes and lavishly entertains the forces of Zapata then later does the same with the op-posing Huerta troops, thus managing to keep his estates and his fortune in-tact, Páramo survives the revolution by suborning it. When the revolution-aries arrive at his estate ready to destroy it, Páramo welcomes them, joins them, and infiltrates their forces with his own men, thus neutralizing their destructiveness.

Toward the end of Páramo's tormented existence, which has alternated be-tween brooding and self-crippling absorption in the self and acts of murder, including even that of the father of Susana San Juan, the illusion of Susana that has always been part of Páramo's consciousness now becomes almost the whole of it. His grief and despair after the death of Susana are never mani-fested; he bears his suffering behind the macho's stoic façade. Ironically, Pá-ramo is defeated by the very mesmerizing and at the end overpowering illu-sions through which he has sought redemption. The vindictive Abundio merely gives the coup de grâce to a person who has perished long before. And the timid and vacillating Preciado who comes to Comala after the death of his father—the end of the novel is really the beginning—encounters only ruins.

The temperamental cacique as almost absolute power and as sole sustainer of Comala is indicated when Páramo, outraged that the town should dare to engage in a celebration on the day of Susana's funeral, instead of resorting to his characteristic vengeance by violence, simply folds his arms and refuses ever again to help anyone in the pueblo, a withdrawal that leads inevitably to the stagnation and finally the collapse of the town. Similar to Guzmán in *La sombra del caudillo,* Rulfo chronicles the passivity of the people: the truckling by Padre Rentería to Páramo's will again and again in exchange for the ca-cique's gold; the procuring by Damiana Cisneros of girls for the lascivious Miguel Páramo; and the willingness of Rentería's niece Ana to succumb to Miguel's amorous advances even though he has murdered her father. It is significant, however, that at the end Rentería breaks free of Páramo's control and joins the revolution. The fate of Rentería remains unclear, but he is the only one in the narrative to assert and sustain an independent self.

Like Rulfo and Yáñez, Elena Garro is a master at collective characterization.

Her fascinating novel *Los recuerdos del porvenir* like *Pedro Páramo* combines passages of haunting lyricism and beauty, as she describes the natural world of Ixtepec, a small rural Mexican town, with sharp, monstrous evocations of violence and death. Garro explores the anxieties, fears, preoccupations, and passivity of the reactionary townspeople, who despise the Indian populace and condemn Francisco Madero, whom they see as the source of all their woes. Yet some of the townspeople, who suffer from the occupation of their town by the government troops under the command of the brutal Francisco Rosas (sent to quash all dissent and close the church, forbidding Masses and expelling priests and even burning the statues of the saints and the Virgin), dream of the return of the *zapatistas* whom they idealize as social redeemers and associate with singing and with joy. Garro is deeply cynical concerning the actualization of the redemptive promise of the revolution, as she depicts a grim world where the popular leaders Villa, Zapata, and Felipe Angeles are all killed and where the revolutionary leaders quickly ally themselves with the old order, the aristocratic followers of Díaz, to continue their land grabbing at the expense of the people.

Like *Pedro Páramo, Los recuerdos del porvenir* is a dense and brooding novel of impossible love. Paralleling the all-consuming love of Rosas for his mistress Julia, who exercises the same fascination over the sterile town that the provocative Victoria does in *Al filo del agua,* is the desperate and insane love that Isabel bears for Rosas. The crushing weight of both past and future is starkly symbolized by having the consciousness of the town represented by a huge stone. Specifically, the stone signifies the immense burden of guilt, opprobrium, and suffering born by the imaginative and freedom-loving yet fated Isabel Moncada. Despite the fact that Rosas is responsible for the deaths of both of her brothers, Juan and Nicolás, because of their participation in a Cristero conspiracy, Isabel defiantly reiterates her love for the general. The ferocity of her passion is symbolized by her blood-red dress, in contrast with the pink dress worn by the ever-distant Julia. Garro masterfully blends the influence of Yáñez and Rulfo with that of classic Roman authors like Ovid. At the end of the novel, the unrepentant Isabel is suddenly transformed into a stone which is laboriously rolled up the hill by Gregoria to rest at the feet of the Virgin to whom Isabel has refused to confess. This supernatural transformation parallels many of the episodes of Ovid's *Metamorphosis* in which characters who defy the will or desires of the gods are punished by these deities, like the supercilious Arachne's transformation into a spider by Athena or Daphne's transformation into a tree by the pursuing god Apollo because she has refused to correspond to his love.

From the time of youth, characters in Garro's work have only memories of the future because they are tragically manqués; they have no genuine, expansive, spiritually fulfilling past or present on which to construct a complete and meaningful existence. They possess only the inescapability of the untimely death that comes to Isabel and her brothers, as well as to Rosas, who suffers a death-in-life. Ironically, even though Rosas, relenting to the pleas of his mistress Isabel, orders his men to let Nicolás escape and execute someone else in his place, the valiant and doomed Nicolás determines to die. In the hallucinatory and nightmarish world created by Garro, even childhood games, which usually are the quintessential expression of exuberance, joy, and freedom, are overshadowed by fate. The game of "Rome and Carthage" that Isabel and her brothers play as children has ominous overtones, as it alludes to the fanatic desire of imperial Rome to destroy its enemy Carthage. This adumbrates the final dissolution of the Moncada family and indeed the destruction of the town of Ixtepec by the military forces. Even occasions of ostensible conviviality and celebration like the fiesta hosted by Carmen Arrieta suddenly turn into instances of entrapment and oppression. In the middle of the festivities, Rosas is given information concerning the participants in the Cristero conspiracy, and he acts ruthlessly to punish all involved, issuing orders that lead to the arrest of the hostess and the execution of her husband.

Even the ending of *Los recuerdos del porvenir* is highly fatalistic and dominated by a cyclical time process. Although the internally devastated Rosas leaves the town, another general arrives, and the hangings of the townspeople continue, abetted by one of their own number, the avaricious Rodolfito Gordíbar, who denounces his enemies to the military authorities and then appropriates their lands.

As in *Al filo del agua,* only the outsider represents genuine freedom. Félix Hurtado, the stranger who arrives in Ixtepec, is an imaginative and poetic force. He is the only one who is able to awaken a genuine emotion from the stonelike Julia and the only one bold enough to take her away from the general. Hurtado states that what Ixtepec needs is illusion. He thus becomes a representative of the author herself, who with her lyric style again and again suffuses the town, its natural setting, its streets, and its buildings with a poetic grace, with a beauty and wonder and awe that the narrow-minded inhabitants of the town themselves are oblivious to. At times Garro's style is highly symbolic. For example, emphasis on the insects that are silently and relentlessly destroying each other symbolizes the way in which the vicious but ever sanctimonious townspeople prey upon one another and even pander to the military authorities, exploiting Rosas's insane jealousy concerning Julia and frequent bouts of depression to impel him toward acts of violence from which they immediately benefit.

After Julia disappears forever from the town with her lover Hurtado, Rosas in his fury executes many of the townspeople, not so much for their sympathy with the priests like Padre Beltrán or for posting Cristero signs and portraits or even for their killing of his own soldiers, but to take personal vengeance against the town that has protected Hurtado and facilitated his escape. The viciousness of Rosas contrasts with the pusillanimity of the townspeople. One of the few to defy his authority is the madman, Juan Cariño, who believes that he is the president of the republic. Once again, as in so many of the novels of Azuela, the eccentric and madman emerges as a conscience figure, as a voice of protest and of truth.

How closely Mexican literature is linked with historical reality is also evident in the profound and extensive literary response to the massacre of students in the Plaza of Nonoalco Tlatelolco. On October 2, 1968, there occurred a confrontation between armed soldiers and police and five thousand student demonstrators massed in Tlatelolco, also known as the Plaza de las Tres Culturas (Plaza of the Three Cultures) in Mexico City. The students and others who were witnessing the speeches were unarmed and were holding a peaceful protest rally. According to eyewitness testimonies, the students were trapped in the plaza, denied sanctuary in the historic church of Santiago Tlatelolco, and were mercilessly gunned down by the police and soldiers who engaged in relentless machine-gun fire. It has been estimated that four hundred students were massacred that night; thousands were imprisoned. This was at the time of the celebration of the Olympic Games in Mexico City, and several sources have related the government crackdown on the striking students to these games and the need to project an image of internal order to international visitors. Some accounts stress that the students, in order to attain their goals of educational and political reform, deliberately sought to embarrass the government by taking advantage of the presence of many foreign journalists in Mexico City and the focusing of worldwide attention on Mexico as proud host of the games and to utilize this moment as a publicity forum: disrupting the games would thus hold the hope of compelling the government to accede to the students' list of six demands. Other authorities assert that the Mexican government, which itself was promoting the Olympics in order to showcase a technologically advanced and commercially prosperous Mexico as part of an attempt to eradicate the image of Mexico both as an underdeveloped country and as a country plagued by violence, sought to suppress student dissent in order to perpetuate the postrevolutionary image of Mexico as a peaceful and stable democracy, an image that was shattered by the massacre.

Although historians have tended to minimize the impact of the student protest movement on Mexican society as a whole, Mexican novelists, dramatists, and poets have again and again underscored its key importance. Carlos Fuentes in an essay entitled "Disyuntiva mexicana" (Mexican Disjunctive), included in his *Tiempo mexicano* (Mexican Time; 1970), emphasizes its overwhelming significance, one fully attested to in the vast literature that surged forth as a creative protest to the violence and social injustice:

> The events of 1968 signified for Mexico a crisis of development, of transformation, and of conscience comparable only to those which the manuals of history and the public monuments consecrate as definitive epochs of our national existence: Independence, Reform, and Revolution. Everything that our country *is* came together, tacitly or explicitly, to make the movement of 1968 be what it was. (147)

Many of the creative authors who write about the massacre do so from a multitemporal perspective, not only examining the crucial events of August, September, and October 1968, but also fusing various epochs of Mexican his-

tory: the contemporary period, the ancient Aztec past, the conquest, the colonial period, thereby establishing a temporal simultaneity that makes past
epochs in Mexico not museum pieces or dusty archives but a living part of the
present. This intricate temporal synthesis is almost inevitable, since the very
site of the massacre constitutes one of the most striking examples of cultural
syncretism in all of Mexico. Here, side by side, are the ruins of the ancient
Aztec temples where blood sacrifices were rendered by the obsidian-knife-
wielding priests to propitiate their gods, a Spanish church built in the sixteenth century atop the Indian ruins, and a cluster of modern apartment
buildings. Tlatelolco was the site of the last brutal clashes between the conquistadors and the heroic resisters of Spanish invasion and domination. The
Tlatelolcans, led by the fanatic and intrepid youth Cuauhtémoc, the last of the
Aztec emperors, fought not only against the Spanish but also against the supporters of the cowardly Emperor Moctezuma, who surrendered his whole
kingdom to the invaders. In his intricate mythopoetic novel *José Trigo*, written
prior to the student massacre but viewed by some as a darkly prophetic work,
Fernando del Paso focuses on Nonoalco achronologically, covering centuries
of time, juxtaposing the fall of the ancient Aztec Empire in the early sixteenth
century with the violent repression by the government of a strike by railroad
workers in 1960. This strike took place in Tlatelolco, then the center of Mexico's railway system. Significantly, one of the major demands of the student
protestors in 1968 was the freedom of Demetrio Vallejo, the leader of the
strike who had been imprisoned under Article 145 of the Constitution, the
article the students sought to have repealed because it mandated incarceration
for those involved in the highly nebulous crime of "social dissolution." The
character Luciano, the union leader who is betrayed and assassinated in Del
Paso's novel, represents the aspirations of the workers for social justice.
Even the structure of Del Paso's novel coincides with its fatalistic theme. As
José Luis Martínez has pointed out, the numbers of the chapters first rise, one
through nine, to a center point, then reverse themselves to indicate a descent,
thereby duplicating the form of a pyramid. The structure evokes the ancient
pyramid that once stood in Nonoalco Tlatelolco, the pyramid of blood sacrifices. In Fuentes's powerful drama *Todos los gatos son pardos* (All Cats Are
Gray in the Night; 1968), the theme of the conquest of Mexico is juxtaposed
with the confrontation between students and police in the plaza, which Fuentes evokes pessimistically as the eternal site of crime. And in his vast totalizing
novel *Terra nostra,* Fuentes extends the fatalistic cyclical time of blood sacrifice rendered to appease the wrath of parasitic gods to encompass even the
remote future of Mexico. In his burlesque of the rampant indigenism that
characterized postrevolutionary Mexico, which placed an extraordinary emphasis on the ancient Aztec peoples while de-emphasizing the present indigenous populace and their overwhelming problems of hunger, disease, and illit-
eracy, Fuentes evokes a Mexico of the year 2000 that reopens the ancient
ceremonial and sacrificial pyramids of the Aztecs. In this vast epic and mythic
novel, Fuentes alludes to the students of Tlatelolco as he evokes twenty mys-

terious youths who signify the twenty months of the Aztec year. These young
people speak in Nahuatl (the classic language of the Aztecs) and symbolize
the forces of democracy and idealism.

María Luisa Mendoza (1931–), herself a resident of the Cuauhtémoc building adjacent to the plaza and an eyewitness to the massacre, writes what she
terms a *cronovela* (literally, docunovel, a combination of chronicle and fiction),
Con él, conmigo, con nosotros tres (With Him, with Myself, with Us Three;
1969), in which she expertly fuses several historical periods in Mexican history: the tragic events of 1968; the Decena Trágica, the violent ten days in
1913 that ended in the assassination of Francisco and Gustavo Madero; and
the reform period of Benito Juárez. In a dense baroque style that often erupts
into a cascade of powerful images, Mendoza captures the tumult of actions
and emotions and conflict and expresses her rage and her grief over the massacre. Adopting a stream of collective consciousness technique similar to that
utilized in *José Trigo,* Mendoza develops a vision that is both historical and
subjective, an eloquent expression of collective grief and personal sorrow.
Throughout the whole first chapter of Mendoza's novel there is an obsessive
concentration on blood, a reference to the bloodstained plaza after the shoot-
ings, the same plaza that in Aztec time ran with the rivulets of blood of the
victims of sacrifice. The blood itself becomes the protagonist, blood that is
weirdly personified, similar to the stream of blood animated by Gabriel García
Márquez in his epic and surrealistic novel of Latin America, *Cien años de soledad* (*One Hundred Years of Solitude;* 1967).

Like Mendoza both a novelist and a journalist, Elena Poniatowska is the
author of *La noche de Tlatelolco* (*Massacre in Mexico;* 1971), the most variegated and intricate response to the events of 1968. Dedicated to her brother
Jan, who had participated in the events of Nonoalco Tlatelolco and who died
later that same year, Poniatowska's work, like the cronovela of Mendoza, represents another of the new directions in Mexican literature developed in response to the urgent need to give voice to the collective tragedy. Like the work
of Carlos Monsiváis (1938–) in *Días de guardar* (Days to Cherish; 1970), it is
both documentary and creative, combining the verbal and the visual. Although the taking of photographs of the massacre was forbidden by the soldiers, photographs were secreted out, and many were included in Poniatowska's searing work. These shocking photographs of the dead bodies bear
witness to the youth of many of the victims and to their innocence. One of the
most haunting of the pictures is that of hundreds of pairs of women's bloodstained shoes littering the Plaza, testimony to the panic-stricken flight of their
owners and also to the deadly surprise of the attack. Basing her work, which
she characterizes as a "collage of voices bearing historical witness," on interviews with hundreds of persons in an effort to convey to the reader the multiple sides of the tragedy, Poniatowska presents excerpts from the declarations
of students and professors, soldiers and government officials, onlookers to the
demonstrations, peasants and tradespeople, parents and relatives, those un-
abashedly supportive of the students and those who are outspokenly critical

of their movement. Like Mendoza at times, Poniatowska employs a baroque style, lavish in its exuberant pyramiding of phrases and images, to convey dramatically the initial optimism and even exhilaration of the students marching to the Plaza de la Constitución (Constitution Plaza). Some of the testimonies are incessantly repeated, like the laconic and horrifying statement of one of the soldiers reporting to his superior, "They're dead bodies, sir," that constitute a type of fatalistic refrain.

Some of the voices recorded by Poniatowska are only a few phrases in length, while others run for pages. One after another they continue, without analysis or commentary, without interruption by the author herself, who confines her own interpretations to the very beginning of the two major divisions of the work. The first part focuses on the series of events leading up to October 2, beginning with the street battle between two gangs, the Ciudadelans and the Spiders, both of which frequented the Ciudadela district, and the subsequent skirmish of students from a vocational school with those of a preparatory school. The second part evokes the night of terror itself and the aftermath of Tlatelolco. Indeed, the fragmentary, pointillist technique deliberately adopted by Poniatowska not only succeeds in conveying the immediacy of the experience in a most compelling way, but also provides the narrative space or opening for the reader to become what Fuentes in *Cristóbal nonato* refers to as the Elector. Both of these texts, as well as other innovative works like Gustavo Sainz's *Gazapo* (1965), written before Tlatelolco but insightfully and cogently exploring the "generation gap" and the estranged and bewildering world of its adolescent protagonists, as well as the highly fragmented and chaotic narrative of *José Trigo,* which not only fuses multiple times but also combines prose with poetry and dramatic dialogue, posit an active reader who is transformed into a co-creator of the novel as the Elector enters the space of ambiguity and arrives at his or her own conclusions regarding the complex and problematic reality that is evoked.

Extending her work back into remote epochs, Poniatowska intercalates fragments of a poem from the ancient *Cantares mexicanos* (Aztec Songs), from one of the short stories of Juan Rulfo, and also a poem of one of Latin America's greatest fighters for freedom, the Cuban essayist, poet, soldier, and patriot José Martí (1853–1895). It is Martí's brief poem that encapsulates the goal and the essence of Poniatowska's own work as well as that of many of the novels of Tlatelolco, some written by former students who were directly involved in the protests. Martí quests for a literary expression that is not rarefied or convoluted, not designed for an elite intelligentsia, neither frivolous nor decorative nor arcane, but a literature that is open and direct and socially committed:

> In the Americas
> a new people has already begun to flower
> a people eager for prose that carries weight
> and noble verses

and asking for hard work and honesty
in politics
and in literature.   (*Massacre in Mexico,* 165–166)

Although most of the reactions recorded by Poniatowska reflect her own
great empathy for the student cause, some of the responses are distinctly unfavorable and demonstrate how controversial the student movement was
within Mexican society as a whole. The majority of the accounts express, directly and poignantly, support for the students or the outrage and shock of the
students' relatives, like that of the anguished mother who defies the authorities
in her quest to find her son's body. In contrast are unsympathetic commentaries like the one from a "mother of a family" who inveighs against the students,
expressing a viewpoint shared by some that the students enjoyed a highly
privileged status within Mexican society and were engaging in a luxury of
protest that most Mexican workers and professionals could not afford. Other
opinions recorded in Poniatowska's multifaceted work, equally indignant and
equally critical of the students, reflect the difficulty that many of the older
generation had in coming to grips with the long-haired males and the short-
skirted females of the new generation. This inability to accept differences in
dress and in hair style and in social mores led to the degrading act in which a
soldier publicly cut off the long hair of one of the student protestors with his
bayonet.

A promise of a new democratic Mexico, with emphasis on the expression of
youthful exuberance and joyousness, combined with a sense of the tragic, is
present at the beginning of *La noche de Tlatelolco* and also in the first part of a
series of poems on the student movement written by José Emilio Pacheco
(1939–) and entitled simply "1968, I, II, and III," from his collection *No me
preguntes cómo pasa el tiempo (Don't Ask Me How the Time Goes By;* 1969).
Here is emphasized an important characteristic of almost all of the literary
responses to Nonoalco Tlatelolco: they seem to form part of a single, immense,
extraordinary text. Many of them, like the works of Pacheco, Fuentes, Octavio
Paz in his sequel to *El laberinto de la soledad,* entitled *Posdata,* necessitated by
the events of 1968, and Luis Spota (1925–1985) in his novel *La Plaza* (The
Square; 1972) represent a skillful utilization of intertextuality. All of these
visions are at the same time personal and collective. A poem by Rosario Castellanos (1915–1974) is included in and indeed was written especially for the
volume by Poniatowska, which also includes part of a poem by Pacheco; portions of the Poniatowska work are in turn present in the novel of Tlatelolco
written by Spota. Paz writes a highly illuminating essay on Tlatelolco, which
he compares with the riots by the disadvantaged and oppressed in Mexico City
in 1692, riots also brutally crushed by the authorities. This essay on the viceregal epoch forms the prologue to the English translation of Poniatowska's
work, *Massacre in Mexico.* And in *Posdata,* Paz develops the idea of the irrup-
tion of the fatalistic, insatiable forces of blood sacrifice from the Aztec past

into contemporary Mexican society that Fuentes so brilliantly developed in his fiction during the fifties, in both short stories included in the volume *Los días enmascarados* (The Masked Days; 1954), like "Por boca de los dioses" (Through the Mouth of the Gods) and "Tlactocatzine, del jardín de Flandes" (Tlactocatzine, from Flanders' Garden), and in his epic novel of Mexico City in all epochs, from the pre-Columbian past to the era of Miguel Alemán, *La región más transparente,* in which the eloquent but ominous narrator Ixca Cienfuegos emerges as the twentieth-century incarnation of the ancient Aztec god of war and death, Huitzilopochtli. Ixca uses many tactics in his efforts to obtain victims of blood sacrifice to appease his mother, the isolated and relatively immobile, idol-like Teódula Moctezuma, who becomes a contemporary incarnation of the Aztec goddess Coatlicue, a *mater terribilis,* dread goddess of both life and death, womb and tomb, with her skirt of serpents and necklace composed of severed human hands and skulls. Thus not only *José Trigo* but also *La región más transparente* becomes eerily prophetic of the incidents of 1968, as Ixca intones pessimistically, in an idiom that conjures up the dread *xochiyaollotl,* or war of the flowers, in which human beings were captured alive for subsequent offerings to satiate the hunger of the gods:

And further it is decided that the anonymous river shall continue washing blood upon execution walls the length of the tropic flatland and the width of the high plateau, that bodies shall go on falling before the shells of Bazaine and Dupin, that the great Mexican blood lake shall never dry, the only eternal river, the only dampness flowering beneath the furious sun.

(*Where the Air is Clear,* 370)

In turn, Fuentes dramatizes Paz's concepts of the pyramid of power that still characterizes contemporary Mexico and the fusion of the figure of the Aztec *tlatoani,* the emperor with absolute power, with the modern Mexican president in his previously mentioned drama *Todos los gatos son pardos.* Fuentes has emphasized that history leaves out the emotions. In contrast, literature in its development of character and action, scene and setting, puts back these emotions. And in the extensive and powerful literary response to Tlatelolco is captured not only historical data but also the intense and often anguished psychological reality underneath the facts and statistics.

For many Mexican authors, including Fuentes, Sainz, and Poniatowska herself, Tlatelolco is a continuing preoccupation, as literature keeps alive what Fuentes has termed a modern culture that is based on oblivion and which seeks to relegate history to oblivion. In *Fuerte es el silencio* (Silence Is Strong; 1980), Poniatowska examines the whole portentous decade beginning with 1968. She again focuses on Tlatelolco as well as on other social problems like the hunger strikes of the mothers of disappeared political prisoners and the burgeoning number of those who come to Mexico City from the provinces and yet who cannot find work and are forced to live in abject poverty. In *Cristóbal nonato* Fuentes evokes a phantasmagoric Mexico City of 1992, where a black acid rain falls incessantly, where satellite cities comprised of *paracaidistas* (squatters) are larger than those of Paris or Rome and yet are nameless, and where the government dedicates itself to creating new symbols and national holidays and constructing what Fuentes ironically terms a vast Potemkin village, in reference to the idealized peasant villages that Potemkin created to impress the Empress Catherine that her subjects were living in abundance and happiness. The parents of the protagonist of the narrative, Angel Fagoaga, are scientists imbued with a deep social concern in their labors to alleviate Mexico's overwhelming problem of hunger; so dedicated are they to their investigations that they have decided not to have children. Yet the night of October 2, 1968, the night of death and destruction all around them, impels them to create new life as a response. Tlatelolco appears as a major theme also in *Manifestación de silencio* (*Shadows of Silence;* 1979), one of the novels by the grandson of Mariano Azuela, Arturo Azuela (1938–). And Gustavo Sainz (1940–) in *Compadre lobo* (Brother Wolf; 1978) pays homage to this immense silent demonstration by the students by evoking it at the very end of the novel.

It is significant that Poniatowska, who perhaps knows more about the specific details of the confrontation than anyone else, rather than emphasizing any single reason for the repression, underscores the indeterminacy of the motives:

> We shall probably never know what motive lay behind the Tlatelolco massacre. Terror? Insecurity? Anger? Fear of losing face? Ill-will toward youngsters who deliberately misbehave in front of visitors?

> (*Massacre in Mexico,* 207)

Because of the many ambiguities surrounding the events of Nonoalco Tlatelolco that to this day have not been resolved and because of the fragmentary historical record and the censorship of the press, the literary response to the massacre becomes extremely important. Extensive, detailed, and penetrating, the literature of Tlatelolco with its portrayal of multiple times and spaces and of myriad ever-changing points of view, with its incorporation of ambiguity and irony and paradox and its fusion of both the visible (the sociopolitical) and the invisible (the psychological and mythic Mexico) allows us to gain a deeper understanding of the complex world of Nonoalco Tlatelolco and of Mexico itself.

As ironic as the titles of many of Azuela's works is *La región más transparente,* the first novel by Carlos Fuentes, because there is very little that is transparent. The center of the narrative is the murky and enigmatic Ixca Cienfuegos, a sinuous and deceitful character who baffles the persons with whom he comes into contact. The sinister Ixca discounts the present and future of Mexico because for him the whole of the national identity is resident in its Aztec past, both Mexico's origin and its inalterable fate. Teódula Moctezuma, the mother of Ixca and the mother of the gods, also appears disguised—as an old Indian woman. She seems to be praying to the Catholic Virgin of Guadalupe, yet the emphasis in her devotions on the offering up of her heart and on the skirt of serpents worn by the deity indicates that she is really praying to the ancient Aztec goddess Coatlicue, the great earth goddess and the mother of Huitzilopochtli, god of war and god of the fiery sun. Like the stone idol of Coatlicue, now in the Museum of Anthropology in Mexico City, Teódula is immobile, suspended in a timeless, mythic, and cosmic time. The dread Coatlicue is represented as wearing a necklace of human skulls and severed hands. She thus symbolizes the earth not only as life-giving womb but as tomb. Coatlicue gives birth to death. Immediately after his birth, Huitzilopochtli puts to death her other children, who had been plotting to kill her. Like her patron goddess, Teódula too has given birth to death. She has lost all of her children but one—Ixca. She is fanatically engaged in a death cult, as she disinters and prays over the skeletons of her dead husband and children. Her last name, Moctezuma, indicates the human side of this ambivalent character creation, her link with the Aztec emperor who was defeated by Cortés. Teódula, as twentieth-century descendant of Moctezuma, incarnates the Aztec demand for retribution against the descendants of the conquerors. Ixca is compelled to become the instrument of that vengeance. Teódula insistently demands that he bring her a blood sacrifice; only by death can they be redeemed.

Yet, unlike the indigenists whose position is forcefully represented by Ixca, Fuentes himself sees the national identity as far more complex. Thus he develops several other characters who represent opposing points of view. Among these persons is Federico Robles, who, although he himself is an Indian, dismisses the ancient indigenous past as barbaric and irrelevant. Fuentes evokes modern Mexico as a country in flux, still groping for a national definition and for an effective way to assert itself. Thus it is that Fuentes chooses as his most explicit symbol of contemporary Mexican society not the brash, authoritative Robles but a person who in most every respect is his opposite. Rodrigo Pola is an introspective, self-doubting, constantly frustrated youth incapable of any sustained action. For most of the self-indulgent characters portrayed in *La región más transparente,* the mask of social distinction or intellectual and artistic superiority that they don is a means toward an end—fame, wealth, prestige, power. But for the hapless Rodrigo, the mask becomes an end in itself, a whole philosophy of life. Yet so often does Pola have recourse to mere posturings instead of sincere emotions and authentic convictions that he loses the ability to relate not only to the outside world but to himself as well, and as he contemplates himself in the mirror, his reflected image seems to possess greater substance than does the living Pola.

Pola subsequently betrays the idealized memory of his father, who died in the revolution, as he adopts a surrogate, materialistic father, Robles. This theme of betrayal resounds throughout the narrative, as it does throughout *La muerte de Artemio Cruz* and *La cabeza de la hidra (Hydra Head;* 1978). Fuentes evokes Mexican history in terms of the Cain motif as a recurring cycle of betrayal and blood sacrifice from the conquest to the War of Independence and the Mexican Revolution to the present. His bleak vision is influenced by that of Paz who in *El laberinto de la soledad* emphasizes that the first betrayal in Mexican history is that by the Aztec gods, who abandoned their people to the mercy of the conquistadors.

Four main types of determinism characterize *La región más transparente:* historical, socioeconomic, psychological, and mythic. Socioeconomic determinism is seen as operating most strongly on the lives of those at the bottom of the social hierarchy, many of whom cannot find a place in the new post-revolutionary Mexican society whose commercial and technological advancement is so arrogantly touted by Robles. Some, like the fated laborer Gabriel, are forced to abandon this society when they emigrate to the United States in search of work. Yet when Gabriel returns to his homeland it is only to find death, and he dies by violence in a tavern brawl. Others, like the victors of the famous División del Norte (Northern Division) of Pancho Villa, take pathetic refuge in celebrating the mere memory of glorious triumphs that proved ephemeral. Others, like the disheartened prostitute Gladys and her former boyfriend Beto, with whom she is reconciled for a brief time in the brothel, escape into mythic fantasy, into a collective unconsciousness of the Indian world as a pre-Columbian paradise, forever devastated by the coming of the conquistadors.

La región más transparente is a vast, kaleidoscopic work, one that provides a panorama of all social classes in modern Mexico, beginning with the haughty remnants of the Porfirian aristocracy like Doña Lorenza de Ovando, who escapes into the refuge of memories of past wealth and social distinction, and her niece Pimpinela, who unlike her ossified aunt is incessantly active as she struggles to regain her former economic power by intermingling with the new revolutionary elite and trading "class for cash," as she panders to the desires for social legitimacy on the part of garish nouveaux riches like Robles's wife, Norma Larragoiti. In their desperate need to gain acceptance into this new elite, many sacrifice talent, intellect, and integrity, like the weak and vacillating Rodrigo Pola, who begins as a dedicated poet but who finally sells out to the establishment, writing movie scripts to be made into potboiler but immensely profitable films that provide him with the wealth essential to cement his marriage with the grasping Pimpinela.

As in the works of Azuela, amidst an atmosphere of rampant commercialism and status-striving, Fuentes creates a center of idealism, in this case the Hamlet-like intellectual Manuel Zamacona, who like Félix Maldonado, the protagonist of *La cabeza de la hidra* (see below), futilely wrestles with the problem of the definition and assertion of both the Mexican national identity and of himself. In contrast with the fanatic and inalterable Ixca, Zamacona links the origins with originality born out of synthesis, just as he is the offspring of the Indian Robles and the Spanish-descended Mercedes Zamacona. Ironically, although he confronts Robles and challenges the latter's self-righteousness and pompous self-satisfaction, Zamacona never comes to the realization that Robles is his own father. Here is an indication of the abyss between father and son that is repeated throughout Fuentes's fiction: in *Las buenas conciencias* (*The Good Conscience;* 1959) seen in the estrangement between the young, idealistic Jaime Ceballos and the spineless father Rodolfo whom Jaime blames for his cowardly abandonment of Jaime's mother, Adelina, because of her socially inferior position; in the great and finally unbridgeable gap between the overly sensitive Guillermo Nervo and the weak father in *Zona sagrada* who unprotestingly allows his wife, the cinematic actress Claudia Nervo, to kidnap his son; in the refusal of Javier Ortega in *Cambio de piel* even to recognize his economically ruined and spiritually devastated father, Raúl.

The introspective and anguished Zamacona is one of the purest voices of idealism in *La región más transparente.* Yet with tragic irony, Zamacona, who has dared to challenge the fatalism of Ixca and has affirmed the necessity for Mexico to confront the terrors of the ancient past, reduce them to reason, and transcend them, himself becomes the victim of the ancient curse of blood sacrifice. Zamacona is senselessly shot and killed after he has entered a cantina on his way back from vacation at Acapulco. The murderer fires at him merely because he is offended by the way that Zamacona has looked at him. Yet this affront is only imaginary; the killer's real resentment is over the refined appearance of Zamacona, his middle-class status, that of the *catrín* (dandy), which the frustrated man, the *pelado* (down-and-outer), has been denied.

Zamacona challenges the conceited Robles, who avers that the goals of the revolution have been fulfilled, primarily because Robles himself has risen from poverty and obscurity to a pinnacle of financial success, as Robles prides himself on doing, not merely by dint of relentless energy, but because he has been protected by the strong generals who emerged victorious in the revolution. For the skeptical and constantly questioning Zamacona, the Revolution of 1910 is only a first step rather than a finished process. In order to be effective, the process of completing new social, economic, and intellectual structures must be a dynamic and a continual one. Yet the eloquent Zamacona, who here becomes a spokesman for Fuentes himself, emphasizes that just the opposite has occurred, that the revolution has become stagnated and its original goals diverted toward unbridled materialism and callous neglect of the impoverished and the oppressed, in whose name the revolution was originally fought. Zamacona blames not only the plutocrats but also his own class, the intelligentsia, whose paralysis and endless rounds of partying to become trinkets for the social elite contribute to the ossification of social reform. Ironically, Zamacona, who is first seen at the lavish fiesta given by the ostentatious Bobó, is one of the prime examples of the decadent and pusillanimous intellectuals whom he scorns. Zamacona finally admits his lack of courage to actualize his idealism, just before he is swept away, ironically, on September 15 during the celebration of independence from Spain.

At the time when *La región más transparente* opens, Robles is depicted at the very height of his power. He even exalts himself as a national hero, as a creator and sustainer of the revolution through his indefatigable labor to build a prosperous new society. Although Robles himself was one of the underdogs, he has sought to isolate himself from all contact with the disadvantaged, constructing a huge colonial-style mansion for himself. Yet he prefers to suppress the fact that in his rise to power he destroyed the careers of many of the original idealists, like the person whom he once regarded as a friend and even a soul mate, Librado Ibarra.

The course of the narrative traces the final awakening of Robles's sense of social responsibility and his symbolic assumption of the burden of guilt for the deaths of true revolutionary idealists like his cousin Froilán Reyero, individuals who had sacrificed their lives to give Robles the opportunity to rise in Mexican society.

The chameleon-like Ixca Cienfuegos, both a spokesman for the Indian people, for those like the disconsolate prostitute Gladys García and her boyfriend Beto who have no voice, and a voice of social conscience, prods Robles, who exalts himself as the architect and even savior of the nation, to review his past and his role as a valiant revolutionary fighter that Robles has all but forgotten. Ironically, although Robles has continually emphasized himself as a self-made man, he is a person who for most of his life has been carried along by the course of events. In his youth, he had been unaffected by the revolutionary idealism that motivated many of his friends to join Madero and Zapata. Ironically, he is for a time more influenced by the priest who rejoices in the triumph of the reactionary forces of Huerta. Neither the rape of his mother by the federal troops nor the impressment into service of his brother causes Robles outrage. Robles too is later captured by the government forces, an indication that he could have spent his military career fighting for Huerta and the preservation of the status quo. His strongest motive for siding with the opposing forces seems to be his rebellion against his childhood religious training and service.

From a complete negation of his indigenous past, Robles moves to an integration with and an expiation of it, symbolized by his marriage to his Indian mistress Hortensia Chacón, who is an Earth Mother in a benevolent sense, an incarnation of the ancient Aztec goddess Tonantzín, in contrast with the formidable and bloodthirsty Coatlicue. In contrast with his childless marriage with Norma, who loathes him, the union with Hortensia is a fertile one, and the son born of their union seems to promise a redemptive change, as Robles begins a new life, on the land, far from the corrupt power center that is Mexico City. Robles's superficial and supercilious wife Norma perishes by fire, trapped in her mansion, a death developed in terms of a sacrifice to appease Teódula/Coatlicue. Robles's financial empire has toppled because of the false rumors spread by Ixca Cienfuegos, the confidant who betrays him. Yet despite his spiritual reawakening, Robles, like the passive Zamacona, finally comes to symbolize but an abortive, or at best an ambiguous, idealism. Although Robles had previously vowed that if he were ever financially ruined he would immediately resume the struggle to rebuild his empire, Robles now renounces materialism and status-striving, withdraws altogether from the power center that is Mexico City, and lives quietly and anonymously on the land, thus returning to the agrarian way of life of his Indian ancestors. Robles has gone from one extreme to another, from a relentless desire for total domination to a complete disengagement. Of all the characters in *La región más transparente,* only Robles represents a hope for social change. Only the new Robles has the moral stature, vitalism, courage, and experience necessary to gain and wield power with ethical responsibility. He does gain a personal transcendence, as opposed to the initially idealistic Rodrigo Pola, who sells out in order to gain social acceptance, or to the defeated Zamacona, who realizes that he lacks both the courage and stamina to put his ideals into effect.

Robles does gain a personal transcendence, yet his moral victory does not imply a national redemption because he chooses to drop out of the system rather than struggle to reform it. And it must be remembered that Robles has not voluntarily renounced his empire but has been driven from it. Whether his newfound moralism would ever have surfaced if he had not first been stripped of his power is questionable. In addition, the power vacuum that Robles leaves is immediately filled by Roberto Régules, the shrewd financier who had directly brought about Robles's downfall and who will be even more ruthless than that titan whom he has demolished. The time of the narrative is thus not linear but cyclical, as in so many of Fuentes's deterministic works, not only sociohistorical visions like *Las buenas conciencias,* but also chilling works of the supernatural and of demonic possession, like *Aura* (1962), *Cumpleaños* (*Birthday;* 1970), and *Una familia lejana* (*Distant Relations;* 1980).

In *Las buenas conciencias* Jaime Ceballos, the protagonist, is seen as a youth who questions the materialism and the hypocrisy of his family, in particular that of his sanctimonious and ruthless uncle Balcárcel, and who shelters the runaway union leader pursued by the authorities, Ezequiel Zuno. But despite his adolescent rebellion, Jaime at the end acknowledges his weakness and succumbs to familial pressure, renouncing his independent self and reentering the stifling confines of the Balcárcel mansion. In *La región más transparente,* Ceballos appears at the very end, as the fiancé of the daughter of Régules, Bettina. The spineless Ceballos renounces his independent ambitions to become a lawyer and accepts the role as a cog in Régules's empire. And in *La muerte de Artemio Cruz,* the sellout of Jaime Ceballos is complete, as he appears as bold and scheming, attempting to become Cruz's successor and to supplant the memory of Cruz's son Lorenzo. At the end of *La región más transparente,* Ixca disappears, voicing deep pessimism and counseling resignation for the indigenous population as the only means of countering the oppressive system. The blood sacrifices that have been rendered of both young and old, rich and poor, of the braceros Gabriel and Manuel Zamacona, the taxicab driver Juan Morales, and the arriviste Norma Larragoiti, have proved futile. Blood sacrifices in ancient times as in the present lead only to an insatiable demand for new sacrifices. Instead of the restoration of the ancient indigenous power that Ixca had thought would be his reward, he finds that he is relegated to poverty and insignificance, and at the end of the work, in extreme depression and frustration, he inveighs against his mother for her false promises.

Just as Fuentes continues the saga of the hypocritical Jaime Ceballos in several narratives, so too does he focus again on the Robles family in *Cristóbal nonato*. As occurs in the lives of so many of Fuentes's characters, Robles Chacón, the son of Robles and Hortensia Chacón, first appears as an idealistic and concerned leader, when on the terrifying night in October 1985, when Mexico City was struck by a devastating earthquake, he leads a group of rescuers and saves many of the victims trapped underneath mounds of rubble in the collapsed buildings. But as in the case of his father, ambition and opportunism crush Chacón's initial spirit of idealism. Chacón rises in the political hierarchy to become a key minister in the government of José María y Paredes, and the people become Chacón's "plural enemy," to be duped with a "bread and circus" atmosphere. When a revolt led by the demagogue Matamoros and under the banner of the Virgin of Guadalupe breaks out, reminiscent of the people's rebellion in 1810 under Hidalgo, it is Chacón who orders the massacre of the rebels, but only after the mob has invaded the lavish mansion of Chacón's chief rival, Ulises López, and killed both López and his wife in revenge for their having burned the shanties of the squatters. The shrewd Chacón allows the revolt of the masses to proceed only long enough to eliminate his enemies. Then he quashes it and hands over its leader to be executed by General Inclán, whom Fuentes develops as a grotesque character, on the model of Tirano Banderas (Tyrant Banderas), the military despot who is the archetypal protagonist of the grisly novel by the same name (1926) by the Spanish writer Ramón del Valle Inclán. Inclán in *Cristóbal nonato* is finally killed in what Fuentes develops as a bold, heroic act by the uncle of the protagonist, Fernando Benítez. Benítez constitutes the center for idealism in the narrative and is an allusion to the great champion of indigenous Mexico, the anthropologist and novelist Fernando Benítez (1912–), mentor of Fuentes. Nonetheless in the end the power of the duplicitous Robles Chacón has been strengthened. Fuentes underscores the essential futility of rebellion, both the one in Mexico City and a previous one by the dispossessed in order to bring about the collapse of the independent power of the state authorities. Yet *Cristóbal nonato* overall is more optimistic than *La región más transparente*. At the end, Cristóbal's parents, named Angel and Angeles to emphasize the birth of Cristóbal as a Christ figure, resolve to remain in Mexico regardless of all of its problems, despite the lure of the ships that are about to sail for Pacifica, the Orient that Fuentes evokes as the new and genuine utopia. Told from the point of view of the fetus Cristóbal, whose development for nine months in the womb is traced, this narrative ends with an emphasis on new life and hope. This emphasis makes it in many senses a complementary vision to *La muerte de Artemio Cruz*, with its evocation of the protagonist's imminent death.

Like Federico Robles, who for most of his life has negated his Indian origins by donning cashmere suits and powdering his dark features white—exactly as did Porfirio Díaz, whose life Robles is subconsciously emulating—Artemio

Cruz, the protagonist of Fuentes's greatest novel, *La muerte de Artemio Cruz*, is also depicted as a *vendepatrias* (national traitor) as he publicly proclaims through his newspaper his adherence to the egalitarian ideals of the Mexican Revolution. He makes such proclamations while secretly dealing to exploit Mexico's natural resources with foreign investors, exactly as had occurred in the Díaz epoch, when Mexico was known as the mother of foreigners and the *madrastra,* the stepmother, of Mexicans.

Throughout his life and even on his deathbed, Cruz is portrayed as a conglomeration of warring selves. The split in his identity is underscored by the very structure of the novel. Instead of being portrayed as a coherent whole, Cruz's identity is fragmented into three native voices, first-, second-, and third-person segments, that keep alternating throughout the narrative. In an interview, Fuentes has stated that the symbol of Mexico is Coyolxauqui, the goddess of the moon, whose body is portrayed as dismembered in the gigantic disc that was discovered in 1978. The fragmented body represents Coyolxauqui's destruction by Huitzilopochtli, Aztec god of the sun. The fragmentation, the self-divisiveness of Mexico is also symbolized by Artemio Cruz.

The physical disintegration of the protagonist, as he lies on his deathbed after suffering from an attack from which he will not recover, as well as his spiritual dissolution, his incapacity to master himself by integrating self-serving ego and social conscience, self-deifying ambition and arrogance and a sense of social responsibility to carry out the ideals of the revolution in which he fought, are underscored in that throughout this lengthy narrative the three voices always remain separate. Each narrative voice reflects a different aspect of Cruz's self. His anguished, dying self is expressed through the extremely fragmented and chaotic style of the first-person monologue, which lapses into sterile repetition as Cruz's extreme pain and delirium increase. The second-person narrative is his conscience and collective consciousness, a voice the rapacious Cruz has suppressed throughout his life but which now suddenly gains in power and authority and imposes itself on the stricken magnate and expresses itself in a dense, baroque, authoritative style. Cruz's outer life and key episodes from his past are conveyed through the terse, more objective third-person accounts. These diverse, often contradictory aspects of self, which present Cruz as one of the most complex and ambivalent of all characters in Latin American literature, are fused only negatively, as at the end of the narrative all three voices condense and collapse, abolished by death.

There are several parallels between Azuela's Andrés Pérez and Artemio Cruz. Throughout Cruz's life, as in the career of the arch compromiser Pérez, the spiritual double is sacrificed, and in its place there remains only the mask of hypocrisy. After deserting his troops on the battlefield, Cruz returns to camp inwardly ashamed; yet his commanding officer, who does not know the true circumstances, believes him to be a hero. This facade of military heroism that Cruz accepts will later be cynically exploited by him as he uses it to gain election as regional deputy and to facilitate his rise to economic power. Cruz finds an uncanny reflection of the valiant, self-sacrificing person whom he has the potential to become in the soldier on the battlefield whose green eyes reflect his own and who stays to fight and die. And Cruz encounters yet another spiritual double, one whom he will also betray, in Gonzalo Bernal, an envoy of Carranza, whom Cruz finds as a cell mate in one of Villa's prisons. The two men are similar in age, in their bitterness, and in the fate they confront, imminent death by the firing squad. Bernal has lost his revolutionary idealism, similar to the cynical Solís in *Los de abajo*. Devastated after the death of the only woman he will ever love, the Indian girl Regina, who has been hanged by the federal forces, Cruz has lost his romantic idealism. Outwardly, Cruz and Bernal are opposites. Bernal is the son of a Porfirian aristocrat, Don Gamaliel. He turns revolutionary not only out of ideological conviction but as a means of defining himself by rebellion against his materialistic father and against the life of luxury that he both needs and yet condemns for being dependent upon. Cruz, on the other hand, is the illegitimate son of the hacendado Atanasio Menchaca and a mulatto slave, Isabel Cruz. The boy Cruz survives only because the father, who wanted to kill him at birth, was himself betrayed and murdered.

Cruz joins the revolution to fulfill the ideals set for him by the anticlerical teacher Sebastián, who has become a surrogate father figure whose approval Cruz wishes to receive. The sensitive and intellectual Bernal, who shudders at joining popular leaders like Villa who are uncompromising in their bloodthirstiness, questions the leaders of the revolution, in whom he has lost faith. Cruz, on the other hand, makes a declaration of blind loyalty to Obregón that indicates his lack of an ideological position. Indeed, Cruz's unthinking stance corroborates Bernal's assessment of the revolution as disintegrating into personalism. It is ironic that the death of Bernal serves only to provide a launching point for Cruz's career as latifundista, a point which again attests to Mexican history as a cyclical process by which those who overthrow the power brokers of the past become merely their successors in exploitation. It is a pattern that not only is followed by Cruz and Robles, but also would have become the destiny of the revolutionary leader Tomás Arroyo, one of the central characters of Fuentes's *Gringo viejo,* had he lived. Just as Robles is defined in terms of the despotism of Díaz, Cruz is developed in terms of a twentieth-century conquistador; and Arroyo, instead of identifying with Villa and the exploited peasants, seeks to become the heir of his father, Miranda, to become the new master and sole possessor of his father's vast estates, instead of dividing the land with his fellow revolutionaries. Cruz enters the home of Gamaliel Bernal on the pretext of sharing Bernal's last moments and bargains with the defeated oligarch, claiming his daughter Catalina as a prize of war. Ironically, in his fierce protecting of Gamaliel's estates, Cruz becomes the aggressive and ruthless son that Gamaliel had wanted his true son Gonzalo to become.

Although he succeeds in building an empire, Cruz is nevertheless plagued by feelings of guilt and inadequacy. With his only son, Lorenzo, Cruz attempts to expiate that guilt by instilling in his son an idealism and a thirst for adventure that ends with Lorenzo going off to Spain to fight courageously and to die as a martyr in the Spanish Civil War, a death through which Cruz feels himself redeemed for his past cowardice and betrayal in the Mexican Revolution. Ironically, although the plutocrat Cruz in reality is continuing to betray the ideals for which the revolution was fought, Lorenzo dies mistakenly believing that he is upholding his father's role as valiant hero.

Throughout his life, Cruz seeks a *cambio de piel,* a redemptive self-renewal in many forms: through a brief affair with Laura, which he terminates when she demands that he divorce Catalina and enter a genuine relationship with her; through Lorenzo; through the vision of a pastoral life; and finally, as an ironic compensation, through power and material wealth. It is ironic too that, although on his deathbed Cruz cannot summon up the image of his son's face, the images of his lavish material possessions and his innumerable antiques are all clear and precise. Although in his egomania he even dares to bargain with God, offering to believe in Him in exchange for terrestrial immortality, Cruz will gain immortality only in an ironic form through the thousands of proto-Cruzes that have been attracted to him, like Jaime Ceballos and the obsequious Padilla, men who will become his inheritors by perpetuating his avarice, hypocrisy, and ruthlessness. His newspaper will survive him, with the title that contrasts ironically both with his destiny and with his own spiritually dead life, *Vida Mexicana* (Mexican Life). It will continue to be published, testifying to the triumph of the elaborate mask of idealism and self-righteousness that Cruz as "revolutionary hero" has donned throughout his life. The spirit of true idealism, of rebellion to achieve social justice, remains in *La muerte de Artemio Cruz* as only a shadowy presence, as the second-person narrative at the end evokes a group of insubstantial figures who will one day rise up to destroy the legacy of opportunism and exploitation perpetuated by Cruz.

Fuentes's spy thriller *La cabeza de la hidra* in many respects, in particular in its concentration on the struggle to define and protect the Mexican national identity threatened by forces from without and insidious forces from within, is a continuation of *La región más transparente* in the seventies. Similarly, *Cristóbal nonato,* with its emphasis on political instability and the loss of Mexican territory and the occupation of Veracruz, extends this focus to concentrate on Mexico City in the eighties and nineties, a megalopolis toward which Fuentes expresses an ambivalent, love-hate relationship, burlesqued on the one hand by being referred to as Makesicko City and yet lauded for its tremendous capacity to survive and prevail over countless calamities. In *La cabeza de la hidra,* Fuentes creates a dark vision of espionage and petropolitics in the incessant struggle among rival factions for national political power that continues the preoccupation of Guzmán's *La sombra del caudillo.* Once again, the dominance of cyclical time is evident. Fuentes adds an epilogue to the novel that flashes back to the epoch of the conquest and depicts Mexico's oil-rich lands as "la tierra de la Malinche," the land of Malinche, the Indian woman who was guide, interpreter, and mistress of Hernán Cortés. Just as the Mexico of ancient Aztec times was betrayed from within, not only by Malinche who revealed many aspects of the indigenous culture to the invaders but also by the cowardly Emperor Moctezuma who surrendered his whole kingdom to the conquistadors, so Fuentes sees the possibility of Mexico once again being vulnerable to a pattern of internal subversion facilitating external control.

Like Guzmán, Fuentes is a master at creating and sustaining suspense. *La cabeza de la hidra* is a fast-paced narrative that traces the kidnapping and torturing of the idealistic Félix Maldonado. The dictatorial Director General plots to assassinate the president and to place the blame for the crime on Félix. When the latter refuses to cooperate, he is suddenly stripped of his identity and forced to assume that of Diego Velázquez. In this taut, rigorously constructed novel, even names have multiple significance. At the outset, Félix is facetiously evoked as the Mexican double of the Spanish court painter Diego Velázquez. But in this fatalistic narrative, humor always cedes to tragedy. The name Diego Velázquez, which will be forcibly imposed on Félix, also constitutes an allusion to the sixteenth-century governor of Cuba at the time of Cortés's expedition to and subsequent invasion and conquest of Mexico, which Fuentes uses as the archetype of attempts over the centuries to suppress the national autonomy. Ruthlessly victimized by the agents of the shadowy Director General, Félix in his plight parallels the essentially innocent Axkaná, the conscience figure in *La sombra del caudillo*. As in Guzmán's novel of incessant intrigue and brutality, a similar patterning of escalating violence occurs: the scarring of the face of Félix, who becomes the victim of compulsive plastic surgery and who is forced to assume the new name and new identity; the brutal slaying of Félix's ideal love, Sara Klein, whose throat is cut; the execution of her lover Jamil; the attempted slaying of Bernstein; the murder in cold blood of Captain Harding; the defenestration and death of Angélica, on the orders of her own brother, the treacherous Timón; the shooting in the head of Abby Benjamin; and, finally, the repeating at the novel's end of the presidential reception and the second attempt at assassination. The result is a narrative that like *La sombra del caudillo* and like Fuentes's own *La región más transparente* is saturated with violence from beginning to end.

Reproducing a feature of Guzmán's novel, much of *La cabeza de la hidra* also takes place in the shadows. The two dominant figures in the narrative, the Director General and his antagonist Timón, are never specifically identified, a circumstance that not only increases their mythic, at times even supernatural aura, but also emphasizes that their struggle for power is one not only characteristic of Mexico in the seventies but also imbued with a universal significance. The machinations of the Director General are constantly thwarted by the equally shadowy Timón, the head of a petrochemical empire and, ironically, the person who has bought the mansion formerly belonging to the mercenary and power-obsessed Artemio Cruz. Timón regards himself smugly as a "national preserver," but his actions in establishing and funding his own private espionage system indicate that he is interested primarily in conserving and expanding his vast fortune by keeping Mexican oil in Mexican—and his own—hands. Throughout their works, both Guzmán and Fuentes create characters who serve as a moral focus, as a center of idealism, in contrast to a prevailing atmosphere of political corruption or at best political expediency. In *La sombra del caudillo,* this center is the sensitive and eloquent Axkaná, who addresses the Indian masses and succeeds in communicating with them and receiving their approbation; in *La cabeza de la hidra,* the imaginative and idealistic center is Félix Maldonado, who is repeatedly linked with Lázaro Cárdenas, who for Fuentes is one of the greatest of Mexican leaders and a symbol of the actualization of the ideals of the revolution. It is significant that Félix is conceived on the very day in 1938 that Cárdenas nationalized the petroleum resources of Mexico, an act that created a new Mexico and a new climate of hope and that enabled Félix's father to advance economically and to support a larger family.

More than any other Mexican writers, Fuentes skillfully incorporates other arts into his narrative, masterfully blending painting and sculpture, architecture, music, and film into a dazzling totalizing novel that has remarkably expanded the boundaries of the narrative and affirmed its openness and imaginative exuberance. Many times in the works of Fuentes characters contemplate a painting that functions as a mirror of their present situation or future fate. In *La cabeza de la hidra,* a huge painting by Ricardo Martínez hangs prominently over the fireplace in the elegant home of the aristocrat Rossetti. Martínez in his masterful art evokes the Indian presence, as does Fuentes throughout his works, in mythic and even supernatural dimensions. The huge, somber, naked, idol-like forms wrapped in mists provide a reflection of Félix's inchoate and nebulous identity. In Martínez's haunting and paradoxical vision, the Indian appears as a mammoth, ponderous, brooding presence, one that is at the same time on the verge of vanishing—or on the threshold of being born. Similarly, the Indian presence in the twentieth-century Mexico evoked by Fuentes is still waiting to be reborn, to emerge from the state of suspended animation into which it had been cast since the epoch of the conquest when the Indian civilization—language, customs, political and religious and educational systems—were all destroyed. And the ease with which the mestizo Félix is deprived of an identity and a new identity forcibly imposed on him, that of Diego Velázquez, indicates Fuentes's concern that Mexico in the future could once again be deprived of its "face," of its autonomous identity.

Upon leaving the Rossetti mansion, Félix sees the Martínez painting suddenly come to life before him as he encounters the Indians, traveling on foot in the shadows as they did in the times of the conquest. Félix can find no basis of contact, to say nothing of rapport, with these silent and spectral forms. Indeed, he responds to them with much of the same astonishment and incomprehension as did the members of the Vásquez Prado family to the Indians who had suddenly stepped out of their familiar and submissive roles on the hacienda—as strange and frightening beings from another planet.

In *La región más transparente,* the decadent host and eternal party giver with the Frenchified name, Bobó, decorates his lavish home with Aztec chic, a small statue of Coatlicue on every step. But the hedonistic nouveaux riches display only disdain and contempt for the suffering Indian masses or at best a perfunctory noblesse oblige, as when Norma every week hands out through the iron gates of her mansion her cast-off clothing to the poor, to appease her conscience. In the twenties as well as in the seventies and eighties, the Indian is constantly evoked in Mexican literature as a force still suspended in time and space, unintegrated into the fast-paced, technological Mexico. An eloquent bridge between this computerized world and the Indian tribes that still dread the night and worship the sun is presented by Fuentes in *Cristóbal nonato,* as he portrays Fernando Benítez's journeys into the jungle in search of these lost Indian worlds.

In *La cabeza de la hidra,* the Indian presence as "dangling man" is symbolized by the Indian elevator operator, who must every day deal with the *ninguneamiento,* the erasing of the personal identity, with which Felix, who ironically seeks to be recognized by the operator whom he has all along ignored, must cope. Because his intrinsic identity is so weak, so insubstantial, throughout much of his career the highly insecure and anxiety-ridden Félix Maldonado quests for the father figure: the intellectual father in his mentor, the economics professor Bernstein; the idealistic, political father, first in the image of Lázaro Cárdenas and then in the seemingly altruistic Timón, modeled after the munificent protagonist of Shakespeare's drama, *Timon of Athens;* the benevolent father in the North American, Captain Harding. Félix's insistent search becomes symbolic of the national quest for the protective leader who will unify and redeem Mexico. But Fuentes sees the appearance of this patriarchal figure, which reaches its spiritual apogee in the cult of the god of life and love, Quetzalcoatl, as extremely unlikely. Instead, what always returns to Mexico is the mere mask of this peace-loving deity. First it is the brutal Hernán Cortés evoked by Fuentes in *Terra nostra,* whom many of the indigenous peoples, including for a time at least the Emperor Moctezuma, believed was a *teul,* a white god and an incarnation of the Plumed Serpent. Later in the nineteenth century, it was the blond and blue-eyed Maximilian von Hapsburg, evoked by Fuentes in his short story "Tlactocatzine, del jardín de Flandes" and in his drama *El tuerto es rey* (The One-Eyed Man Is King; 1970), whom the Indians also greeted in Nahuatl as the returning and grace-giving god Quetzalcóatl. Yet both of these foreign leaders, instead of fulfilling a redemptive prophecy, resorted to acts of massive violence and bloodshed, imposing upon Mexico a despotic rule. Similarly, each time the gullible Félix looks for the regenerative father, he finds only the harsh, dictatorial father or the father of death. The physical brutality and mental torment wreaked on Félix by the Director General are paralleled by the intimidation and emotional brutalizing of Félix by the very person in whom he places not only his confidence but his very life, Timón.

Timón is the prime example of the hydra-like multiplication of identities that characterizes *La cabeza de la hidra.* His real name and identity will be forever unknown. A master of duplicity and disguise, similar in many aspects to the insidious Ixca Cienfuegos, Timón plays the exacting and dangerous role as double agent, known as both Trevor and Mann. This novel of Fuentes is characterized not only by character and situational doublings (its ending repeats its beginning) but also by a doubling of the narrator and the structure as well. The narrative has two endings, the one that is imagined by Timón and imposed by him on Félix's narrative, a disastrous ending in which Félix slips into insanity and gives up his crusade, and the one that Félix actually lives—and that he will never know. Most of *La cabeza de la hidra* is narrated in the third-person singular from Félix's perspective, but two-thirds of the way through the point of view suddenly shifts to the first-person singular as Timón steps into the narrative. This abrupt structural shift corresponds to a thematic issue. Paralleling the sudden and brutal intervention into Félix's life by the nefarious Director General, who seeks to strip the protagonist of his identity in order to destroy and then re-create him as the Other, is the authorial intervention of Timón.

The powerful yet extremely insecure and impassioned Timón has once regarded Félix as his soul mate or spiritual twin, on the model of Castor and Pollux, the divine twins of Greek mythology. Yet their relationship disintegrates into that of two more fractious brothers, Cain and Abel. Failing to possess Félix emotionally and physically, the enraged and vindictive Timón possesses him authorially, reducing him to a narrative object and depriving the puppet-like protagonist, similar to the weak Ignacio Aguirre who also is controlled by both sides in a political battle, of even the right to complete his own narrative.

Not only in *La cabeza de la hidra* but also in *Gringo viejo,* Fuentes emphasizes the filicidal impulse present in Mexico. In the latter novel this destruction of the son by the father is exemplified in the way not only that Miranda, the wealthy father of the illegitimate Tomás Arroyo, refuses to acknowledge him as a son and heir, but also that the commander, Villa, poses as the "father" of Arroyo only suddenly to execute him for his disobedience. In *Terra nostra,* this Saturn-like father, one who constantly devours his children, is the señor, the ruler Felipe. Although Felipe has no issue, he stifles the development of his national "children," as he quashes the revolt of the *comuneros* (communal landholders) and constructs a death kingdom, building for himself a huge palace-monastery reminiscent of the Escorial, which functions both as his imperial center and as his living tomb.

In contrast with the national and epic concerns of authors like Yáñez, Fuentes, and Del Paso, a group of young authors, including José Agustín (1944–), Gustavo Sainz, and Parménides García Saldaña (1944–), referred to collectively as La Onda (The Wave), represent another and more personal direction. In his first novel, *Gazapo,* Sainz probes with sensitivity and humor a volatile, contradictory world of adolescence, a realm on the borderline between reality and drama, fact and erotic fantasy. Experience in *Gazapo* is presented indirectly, through the tape recordings of the protagonist Menelao and his *cuate* (buddy) Mauricio and through diaries, letters, and telephone conversations. The protagonist is depicted in the process of memorizing, reconstructing, and recording events from the recent past. The tapes enable him to freeze experience, to remove it from time as duration, and to control it by evoking it at will. Thus Menelao goes over the tapes repeatedly in an effort to derive order and meaning from experience that per se is fast-moving, problematic, and many times bewildering. Like the protagonist, the other adolescents delight in rehearsing the past, and the juveniles of the novel thus become authors, actors, and audience for their own productions. For them, ironically, the incessant re-creating of experience and the witnessing of the effect of that re-creation upon their listeners are more important than the original living of it. Thus, instead of advancing as a causal sequence of activities within a linear time scheme, this highly innovative work progresses through the reiteration or expansion of the themes struck in the initial "chapter."

The tape recorder in *Gazapo* represents a pathway to freedom for the adolescents, constantly restricted by the adult world. The youths fabricate not only a series of wildly improbable incidents and hormonal adventures, but also an imaginative existence as well. In the first part of this complex novel, episodes are developed at length through Menelao's painstaking reconstruction of scene and dialogue. But by the end of this conjectural work, the anecdotal has ceded to the impressionistic. Instead of complete scenes there are but embryonic chapters, outlines of dialogues and confrontations or mere isolated images. The fragmentation and incompleteness of the structure of *Gazapo* capture the fragmentary, hypothetical, and nebulous lives of its adolescent heroes. The ambivalence and ambiguity found throughout the narrative convey the extreme fragility and inconclusiveness of adolescent relationships, both with one another and with the adult world.

The narrative as a whole, which experiments with many different types of language, affirms the liberty of the author to create his own universe with its own laws and its own idiom. Like in so many of the works of Fuentes, a major theme in *Gazapo* is the quest for freedom. With its wordplays, antitheses, incongruities, burlesque of official language and high-flown rhetorical expression, with the variants and reversals in the plot and the scenes that contradict and undermine one another, with its dynamic spirit of imaginative exploration and spontaneous, untrammeled fantasy, *Gazapo*—whose very title has multiple meanings, including "young rabbit," "tall tale" or "whopper," "astute dissimulator," and "printer's error"—affirms once again the power of the novel as a force for creative, psychological, and social freedom.

The universe of *Gazapo*, like that of many of the works of the late twentieth century, is capricious, kaleidoscopic, protean, and unsettling. It does not consist of the imposition of a rational or casual patterning upon life, such as found in the traditional novel of the nineteenth century, which may clarify the narrative situation for the reader but ends up falsifying experience by molding it to conform to a pattern of beginning, middle, and end. Instead, Sainz's novel reflects a complex, ambiguous, unstable world in which values and norms, as in Julio Cortázar's *Rayuela* (*Hopscotch;* 1963) and Fuentes's *Cristóbal nonato*, must be sought after and created by the experiencing consciousness.

The humor of Sainz, a combination of drollery and sentimental irony, is new in Mexican fiction, where humor has traditionally appeared most often in the form of irony, cynicism, and sarcasm. The piquant wit of the author of *Gazapo* contrasts with the mordant satire found throughout Azuela and in *La vida inútil de Pito Pérez* (*The Futile Life of Pito Pérez*; 1938), by José Rubén Romero (1890–1952) (a picaresque novel in which the sardonic protagonist states at the end that he is going to embrace his own true love and is subsequently found dead in the arms of a skeleton), or with the wry, cynical, destructive, even gallows humor of Lucas Lucatero, the murderous protagonist of Rulfo's short story "Anacleto Morones." Another significant manifestation of puckish and irreverent humor is found in the early novels of another major author of the Onda, José Agustín, in *La tumba* (The Tomb; 1964) and *De perfil* (In Profile; 1966). Like Sainz, Agustín treats the foibles and painful growth of his adolescent characters in a bold style crackling with colloquial speech. Finally, Fuentes's mammoth *Cristóbal nonato* demonstrates his remarkable versatility, for it is one of his most humorous novels, laced with puns, farcical incidents, and comic characters, although, as in *Cien años de soledad*, laughter many times covers tears, and pranksterism almost inevitably cedes to violence and tragedy.

Testimony to the continued vitality of the narrative in Mexico as the twentieth century nears its close is *Arráncame la vida* (*Mexican Bolero*; 1985) by Angeles Mastretta (1949–). Written in a clear, direct, and forceful style, this confessional narrative both continues the novel of the Mexican Revolution, once again demonstrating the enduring quality of this important subgenre of the Mexican novel, and adds a new and incisive perspective, the "inside view" on the lives of prominent and powerful political leaders at the state and national levels as given by the irrepressible Catalina Guzmán, wife of the revolutionary general Andrés Ascensio, who becomes governor of the state of Puebla and a confidant of several Mexican presidents. Ascensio constantly betrays the ideals of the revolution, and Mastretta's bold and powerful work provides a corrosive examination and denunciation of the power politicking, corruption, and incessant violence that characterize his political career. On the personal level, the novel focuses on the intense and persistent struggle of Catalina to preserve and to assert her identity and to maintain her sanity in the ruthless machista world in which she finds herself entrapped.

The novel concentrates in detail on the Mexico of the thirties and forties and becomes a roman à clef as it evokes the policies of President Aguirre, who symbolizes the actualization of revolutionary goals, as he travels throughout the country holding marathon audiences to solve the problems brought to him by the Indian populace—a clear allusion to Lázaro Cárdenas. The opportunistic General Ascensio pays lip service to these policies but secretly opposes them. Catalina, like her husband, exemplifies a dramatic social mobility, as she is catapulted from being the daughter of a peasant with six children to assuming the role of governor's wife. Both she and her husband owe their newfound status and wealth to the revolution. And yet, similar to the feminist drama by Rosario Castellanos *El eterno femenino* (*The Eternal Feminine*; 1975), in which the fiery Adelita, the revolutionary fighter brought back to life in contemporary Mexico, comments that the revolution has not been successful since it has not liberated Mexican women from lives of drudgery and continued dependence on and subordination to the male, *Arráncame la vida* demonstrates the virtual incarceration of Catalina in the traditional role of dutiful, attentive, and obedient wife, which from her husband's point of view is the necessary adjunct to his career and which from the very start of her marriage the despotic Andrés imposes on her. Catalina is a child bride. Married at age fifteen to a man more than twice her age, Catalina throughout her marriage is treated as a child-woman, whose opinions concerning her husband's political machinations are condescendingly swept aside. Instead, she is compelled to perform daily as the perfect hostess, planning and supervising countless banquets and receptions for Andrés's political cronies and compelled also to be the mother and caretaker not only of her two children, but also of the five more brought to her by Andrés, products of his many extramarital relationships in several towns and in Mexico City.

The outspoken and at times acerbic Catalina presents a highly demythified view of motherhood. She undercuts the official Mexican enshrinement of the mother, cursing her pregnancies that drastically limit her athletic activities and not welcoming her being treated with false reverence by Andrés, who refuses to have relations with her while she is pregnant so that in frustration she is impelled to take her first lover. With both legitimate and illegitimate offspring to take care of, Catalina becomes increasingly alienated from all of her children, so much so that when she seeks once again, years later, to renew these relationships, both she and her children find it awkward and essentially impossible. In contrast to her husband, who incessantly dons the mask of revolutionary hero and national savior, even though there are persistent rumors that, during the government of Francisco Madero, Andrés was a staunch supporter of Victoriano Huerta, Catalina can tolerate only so much of the life of political charade that she is compelled to live. When requested by the president who succeeds Aguirre, Rodolfo Campos, to be a guest of honor at his speech inaugurating the immense Monument to the Mother in Mexico City, she dutifully attends but finally explodes and launches a scathing diatribe against motherhood with its burdens and sufferings—an attack that shocks the president's wife.

In her narrative, in which she functions as a social conscience, Catalina notes wryly the many incongruities in her husband's behavior. Because of his support for Calles and his participation in the war against the Cristeros, Andrés refuses to get married in a Church ceremony. Yet, ironically, years later, he insists that his eldest daughter have a formal and lavish church wedding. Although he demands that Catalina marry him on the spot and brusquely takes her to a civil ceremony, he later expresses his contempt for the spinelessness demonstrated by Catalina's father in allowing his daughter to be so contemptuously treated. Yet Catalina refuses to become the docile and subservient wife that Andrés perceives her as. Strong-willed and feisty, through a combination of her audacity and wit, she is able many times successfully to defy him. At the marriage ceremony, she questions why she is compelled to sign the marital document as "de Ascensio" (of Ascencio) when he is not required to make an equivalent declaration of fidelity by signing as "de Guzmán." She deeply resents his *machista* perception of her according to which she, in return for his lifelong protection and support, is reduced to the status of his "possession."

Ironically, what initially unites Catalina and Andrés is their status of being outsiders. Both of them loathe the smugness and the pretentiousness of the wealthy aristocrats of Puebla. But after Andrés is elected governor, in a contest in which he is the sole candidate, he takes vengeance against this privileged class by employing the same brutal tactics that Pedro Páramo uses to consolidate his lands and build his empire: intimidation and murder. For Andrés as for the cunning and ruthless Federico Robles and Artemio Cruz, the revolution is seen as an unparalleled opportunity for self-aggrandizement at the expense of the very populace whom he tirelessly evokes and idealizes in his political speeches and yet secretly betrays again and again, selling their lands to foreign investors like Heiss. The hypocrisy of Andrés is also evident in that while he is exploiting his wife and his mistresses in private, he publicly proclaims his support for women's suffrage and exhorts them to participate in the revolution. The same hypocrisy is evident in his actions of sending to the funerals of those whom he has ordered to be eliminated huge wreaths that will barely fit through the doorway.

At first Catalina, with her characteristic energy and idealism, throws herself into the role of governor's wife. She takes very seriously the responsibilities that Andrés gives her as president of Public Charity, even though the new governor has meant it to be but a titular position. She requests funds from him to better the squalid conditions at the insane asylum and the orphanage, and when her request is denied by a husband who will spend state funds only on projects that increase his influence and power, Catalina throws herself into personal fundraising, organizing dances, parties, and raffles to provide beds for the asylum and sheets for the hospital. She even succeeds in surreptitiously freeing two of the women interned in the asylum, one because her own brother has sought to appropriate her inheritance by declaring her insane. Catalina is appalled by her husband's irrevocable decision to sell the city of Puebla archives at three cents a kilogram of paper, presumably because he does not want official records validating property and other rights to exist. And with no historical record, Andrés is freer to impose his own laws and authority.

Andrés constantly covers up his crimes, as he concocts stories that his political enemies were eliminated in a brawl or killed by a drunkard or that the peasants who were slain while proclaiming their rights were only bandits disguised as peasants. The result is that Catalina, in order to preserve her sanity, isolates herself by retreating from both her husband and her children, who know much more about their father's ruthless activities than Catalina does. They become blasé as they speak to her of their father's command to his subordinates to "find a hole" for the rivals and enemies whom he wants eliminated. Yet what most shocks and terrifies Catalina is the story she hears concerning Andrés's killing of a young girl merely because she had once spurned him. After hearing this, she is terrified for her own life.

Catalina only once determines to escape from Andrés's control, by fleeing the house and taking a second-class bus to Oaxaca. Yet the realization that she is condemning herself to the same poverty and anonymity as the peasants who now surround her compels her to return immediately. The only defense that Catalina has against the obsessive philandering of her husband is to engage in a series of secret affairs. Ironically, just when Catalina has emerged from her state of "suspended animation" and is beginning to fall in love with the dynamic Carlos Vives, the director of the National Symphonic Orchestra, her capricious husband expresses renewed interest in her, even to the extent of naming her as his private secretary and taking her to all of his political meetings. The mortal terror in which many of those who surround Andrés dwell is evident when Juan, her husband's chauffeur, interrupts Catalina's romantic interlude with Vives by holding a gun at her ribs to compel her to return to her husband on time—apparently believing that any suspected complicity on his part in her affairs will mean his death.

The tragic climax of *Arráncame la vida* is the final, doom-laden interlude between the two lovers, Catalina and Carlos, in whom she finds the imaginative exuberance, sensitivity, and sense of humor absent from her dour and even saturnine husband. The lovers have been taken along on a vacation by Andrés, ostensibly because he wants his wife to play the role of spy to inform him about Vives's subversive political activities. Andrés either does not know or, for the sake of political expediency, pretends not to know of his wife's romantic involvement with Carlos. Both Catalina and Carlos sense that one or both of them will be killed, but both remain powerless to halt the tragic course of events. Catalina defensively attempts to joke about the threat of imminent death, suggesting to Carlos that her husband kill them both now and that they continue their lovemaking in the tomb as the ultimate defiance of Andrés. Slowly there occurs a multiplication of the signs and symbols of death, like Catalina's obsession with the *cempaxochitl,* the Aztec flowers of death. They make love on ground carpeted with the flowers of death, and Carlos is delighted at seeing her covered with the pollen and scent of the *cempaxochitl* and even speculates how much it would please him to have his tomb filled with these flowers. Although Catalina attempts to dispel this death wish, she is soon forced to carry it out, as Carlos is killed soon after, and she decides to bury her lover at Tonanzintla on November 2, the day celebrated by the Indian populace as one of communion with the spirits of the dead.

After their romantic encounter, Catalina picks the flowers with their pungent smell and brings them to Andrés's house. Her husband is repelled at seeing the flowers, perhaps because he does not want his guests to be reminded of his incessant dealings with death, perhaps because they aggravate his feelings of guilt over the deaths that he has ordered of both Carlos and his political accomplice Medina. Ironically, he condemns Catalina as crazy for converting his house into a tomb, yet this is what he himself has done, for fearing assassination, Andrés never dines outside his home, and his family is prohibited from leaving at night, so that they become virtually imprisoned in their own house. And fearful of being killed while he sleeps, Andrés never occupies the same bedroom two nights in a row.

The constantly evasive Andrés pretends to know nothing about the sudden and mysterious disappearance of Carlos, and when he is informed of Carlos's death, he again assumes the role of outraged innocent as he is the first to demand that justice be done. He even becomes histrionic in his calling for the immediate resignation of the police chief Pellico, who is blamed for the capture, detention, and final shooting of Carlos in the neck; Pellico is tried and imprisoned but later mysteriously escapes and flees the country, presumably with the aid of Andrés.

At the end of the narrative, Andrés suddenly dies—ironically by his own hand. Yet even here the narrative retains its ambiguity, for the cause of Andrés's rapidly deteriorating condition cannot be detected by the doctors, who attribute it merely to hypochondria. Andrés has retreated into isolation and moroseness, the direct consequence of his presidential ambitions being suddenly and permanently quashed, not only as he loses his privileged status as right-hand man of President Campos, but also as the latter designates as his successor the most bitter antagonist of Andrés, Martín Cienfuegos, who immediately begins a campaign to discredit the powerful former governor, dredging up incidents from the past, suddenly materializing witnesses who before were nowhere to be found to testify to Andrés's crimes.

Andrés seems to be the victim of the black lemon tea that he excessively imbibes, the tea introduced to him by his wife, who has received it from Carmela, one of the many wives whose husbands have been killed by the ruthless former governor. Catalina seems to be at least indirectly responsible for her husband's death, perhaps in vengeance for his execution of her lover. Knowing the extremely harmful effects that the tea can occasion if taken in large quantities, she encourages her husband to keep imbibing it and, to allay his suspicions, even pretends that she is drinking it along with him.

What is certain is that Andrés's death occasions her little grief. As if publicly to proclaim her emancipation and perhaps even her joy, she is at first tempted to scandalize those at the funeral by donning a red velvet dress but then decides once again to play the role of dutiful and self-negating wife and respectable matron. She goes through the last political charade of her life, as she travels with the funeral cortege to Zacatlán, the birthplace of Andrés, and weeps copiously at the ceremony as the bereaved widow is expected to. Yet at the close of her narrative her last emotions are those of relief and even joy, as at the end she anticipates a new beginning for her life. Her one request to the president is that all of Andrés's other women come to her regarding the distribution of her husband's vast estates. Yet it is not out of materialism that she does this, as she determines that the property shall be allocated by lottery. Her only wish is for a small house by the sea where she, for the first time in her life, can be her own master, where no one makes demands on her or criticizes her for failing to fulfill these imposed standards. It is ironic that one of her female companions declares that the ideal state for a woman is widowhood, when she can publicly pay homage to her deceased husband and privately do all the things she was prohibited from doing while she was in servitude to him.

In conclusion, *Arráncame la vida,* a reference both to a popular song and to the victimized state of Catalina, who begins genuinely to live only after her husband's death, presents a devastating attack against rampant machismo, symbolized by the arrogant and monstrously cruel Andrés. It also dispels many of the most cherished myths surrounding women in Mexico: the saintliness of motherhood; the expectation that the role of wife be one of martyr to husband and children; the hypocritical double standard by which the wife, the epitome of decorum and respectability, is compelled to remain bound to the house and children while in contrast the husband is given the freedom to engage in many affairs and even to maintain separate households for his mistresses and extramarital children. And, finally, Mastretta's searing novel undercuts the myth of the grieving widow, dressed in mourning black many times for the rest of her life and consecrating her identity to the memory of her beloved husband. Catalina's account is one of the outwardly complaisant but secretly rebellious wife, one who constantly struggles to free herself both from her domineering husband and her endlessly demanding children and to construct a life and find a happiness of her own. The astute Catalina, finding either divorce from or desertion of her husband impossible, fearing the retaliation that will be exacted, becomes very adept at knowing how to please her husband, protesting adherence to his ambitions without forfeiting her integrity and becoming reduced to a talking robot as are the wives of so many of the political associates of Andrés. Again and again Catalina secretly maneuvers to aid the victims of her husband's wrath. She even secretly encourages his daughter Lilia to marry the youth Uriarte, with whom the girl is genuinely in love, instead of the duplicitous Emilio, the suitor designated by Andrés because of Emilio's family connections. The anguished Lilia, who like Catalina has no choice but to accommodate Andrés's wishes, predicts that the fate of Uriarte will be the same as that of Carlos, a prediction confirmed when Uriarte is one day found dead after his motorcycle mysteriously crashes into a ditch.

Similar to Azuela and Guzmán at the beginning of the twentieth century, Mastretta toward the end of the century converts the novel into a powerful instrument to penetrate the social and political reality of Mexico and to reveal what the official, historical record often leaves blurry or glosses over entirely.

Several of the novelists prominent in the fifties and sixties, including Gustavo Sainz and Carlos Fuentes, have continued to create significant works in the 1980s and 1990s. In *El muchacho en llamas* (The Boy in Flames; 1988), Sainz provides a sophisticated novel-collage, allowing the reader glimpses into the intricacy of the creative process. Sainz skillfully combines fantasy making with the "raw materials" of the artist-creator, including quotations from the aesthetic principles of artists as diverse as Horacio Quiroga, the filmmaker Roberto Bresson, and Jack Kerouac, portions of interviews he has conducted with Rodolfo Usigli and José Revueltas, and even notes taken in a class given by Rosario Castellanos. In a sense *El muchacho en llamas* not only continues *Gazapo,* but also emulates the fascinating "Morelliana," an allusion to the eccentric novelist Morelli, a reclusive, experimental author, a minor character in the Argentine Julio Cortázar's *Rayuela,* and a persona of Cortázar himself. The "Morelliana" are fragmented chapters at the end of Cortázar's main text in which the myriad sources of his vision—literary references, articles for newspapers, cinematic works, jazz lyrics—are revealed, and the reader is invited to become a co-creator of the novel by relating these "raw ingredients" to the characters, themes, and structures of the main part of *Rayuela.* In *El muchacho en llamas,* the Menelao of *Gazapo* is transformed into the irrepressible Sofocles, a persona of Sainz himself. Gisela, the girlfriend of Menelao in *Gazapo,* becomes Tatiana, and the alienation between Sofocles and his father is a continuation of the generation gap so convincingly explored in *Gazapo.* In this novel, but above all in the mammoth eight-hundred-page opus that follows, *A la salud de la serpiente* (To the Health of the Serpent; 1991), whose title echoes the national resonances in Guzmán's work *El águila y la serpiente,* Sainz assumes the mantle of the dramatist and piquant essayist Salvador Novo (1900–1974). In works like *La vida en México en el período presidencial de Lázaro Cárdenas* (Life in Mexico during the Presidency of Lázaro Cárdenas; 1964) and *La vida en México en el período presidencial de Manuel Avila Camacho* (Life in Mexico during the Presidency of Manuel Avila Camacho; 1965), despite their official-sounding titles, Novo provides a lively, highly informative, witty, and perceptive account of current trends in literature, films, and social mores. Emulating the vision of Novo, who was designated the official chronicler of the city of Mexico, Sainz becomes a chronicler of the effervescent literary scene of the 1960s in Mexico. Yet in *A la salud de la serpiente* there are somber undertones as well, as the narrator includes fragments evoking the massacre of Tlatelolco and speculates that it was only by chance that he was not present in the Plaza of the Three Cultures on the fateful night in 1968. In this work Sainz extends the novel-collage even further by including entire letters actually written to him by associates like Fuentes and by literary critics, along with a series of articles that parody the way in which the salacious passages of his first novel scandalized the staid and prudish literary establishment of the time.

Contrasting with Sainz's highly personal, autobiographical visions, in works that have also become literary homages to major Mexican writers of the 1960s, is the development of the historical novel in Mexico during the last quarter of the twentieth century. One of the most fascinating works to exemplify this important trend is *Memorias del Nuevo Mundo* (Memories of the New World; 1988), by Homero Aridjis (1940–), a major contemporary poet who here enters the narrative realm for the first time and infuses historical incident and detail with a lyric style. Based on exacting and exhaustive research, with a bibliography of numerous primary sources of the conquest of Mexico included at the end of the novel, Aridjis develops an imaginative account of the voyage of the lay brother Juan Cabezón with Columbus to the New World, then his joining of the expedition to Mexico of Hernán Cortés. Similar to Fuentes in *Todos los gatos,* Aridjis combines both the Spanish and the indigenous perspectives on the conquest, and along with the sixteenth-century Spanish chronicles cited in the bibliography are the ancient indigenous codices. Cabezón flees Spain to escape persecution by the Inquisition; his wife and son flee to Italy. Ironically, he is compelled in the New World to witness the extension of despotism as he views an auto da fe, the burning alive of an Indian who has been condemned as a heretic. Written in a clear and direct style that contrasts with the baroque effusion of Fuentes's evocation of the discovery and conquest of the New World in *Terra nostra,* Aridjis penetrates the mysteries of the social, linguistic, and religious world of the Aztecs after the fall of Mexico-Tenochtitlán. Indeed, Aridjis carries to a grotesque and horrifying extreme the theme, so often evinced in Mexican literature, of the *conquistador conquistado* (the conquered conqueror), the conqueror who becomes a victim of the indigenous people whom he has exploited and terrorized. The grisly ending of *Memorias del Nuevo Mundo* occurs at the end of December in 1559, sacred year of the Aztec calendar, the year that completes the fifty-two year cycle and heralds the ritual sacrifice of the New Fire in order to ward off the malefic spirits of the *tzitzimimes* and ensure the continuation of the universe. A stunned Cabezón encounters his old companion in arms, Gonzalo Dávila, now totally assimilated into Aztec culture, transmogrified into a priest of the god of the Smoking Mirror, Tezcatlipoca, complete with a crown of plumes and obsidian rattles on his feet. The powerful and grisly ending of the work is reinforced stylistically by a sudden and dramatic change from the third-person narrative to the first person, as Cabezón relates the attempts by the guilt-stricken Dávila to flee Mexico and return to Spain, his capture by the Aztec priests and his blood sacrifice, as his heart is torn out and cast into the flames, to mark both the dominance at the end of Aztec time and retribution of the vanquished against the person viewed as a simulacrum of Hernán Cortés.

Continuing the emphasis on the fusion of history and fantasy and written at least in part as a response to the marked pessimism of the account by the Colombian Gabriel García Márquez in *El general en su laberinto* (*The General in His Labyrinth;* 1989) of the last years in the life of the severely disillusioned Simón Bolívar, Fuentes, in one of his most optimistic works, *La campaña,* evokes the crucial period in the birth of Latin America's nations, from 1810 to 1821, the period of the War of Independence from Spain. Fuentes traces the adventures of the protagonist, Baltasar Bustos, committed to the ideal of social equality as articulated by Rousseau, across a continent torn by conflict. After one last contact with the past, as he visits the hacienda of his aged father on the pampa and confronts his repressed sister who stubbornly affirms her allegiance to the Church and Crown, Bustos joins the rebellion, unlike his two lifelong friends who remain comfortably in Buenos Aires: Manuel Varela, the narrator of Bustos's adventures, and Xavier Dorrego, an adherent to the rationalism of Voltaire as opposed to the passion of Rousseau. As in Fuentes's *La cabeza de la hidra,* the sociopolitical quest in *La campaña*—the determination of Bustos to convert his ideals into immediate social action—is fused with the amorous one. Corresponding to the immense impact of Sara Klein on the vacillating and inchoate protagonist Félix Maldonado in the former novel is the tantalizing vision of Ofelia Salamanca, the beautiful wife of the fustian Marqués de Cabra. And just as the amorous relationship between Félix and Sara is never consummated, the love of Baltasar for Ofelia remains a platonic one, as he pursues her across the Latin American continent. Fuentes, in this novel as in his previous novel of Latin America as a whole, *Una familia lejana,* has been markedly influenced by the Cuban novelist Alejo Carpentier (1904–1980), who in epic works like *Los pasos perdidos* (*The Lost Steps*; 1953) and *El siglo de las luces* (*Explosion in a Cathedral*; 1962) evokes the Creole and the autochthonous cultures of Latin America. Also, in *El siglo de las luces*—an ironic reference to the "Age of Reason," the eighteenth century of the Enlightenment—Carpentier portrays the New World reacting to the French Revolution and on the verge of its own independence. Rapidly changing locales as it traces the odyssey of Baltasar, *La campaña* vividly evokes several major Latin American cities at the time of independence: Buenos Aires, the viceregal court in Lima, Santiago de Chile, Maracaibo and its racial pluralism, and, finally, Veracruz as the scene of the fierce battles between royalists and the insurgent priests: Hidalgo, Morelos, and their defiant successor, Anselmo Quintana—the first two historical figures and the last a creation of Fuentes. One of the most human of Fuentes's protagonists, the quixotic Baltasar, myopic, overweight, and bumbling, at first fails in his attempt to change a harsh and rigid reality. His desire immediately to impose the ideal of social equality by kidnapping the child of Ofelia and the Marqués and substituting an illegitimate black child results only in a disastrous fire and the death of the surrogate.

Brief, compact, highly readable, *La campaña* is even more straightforward and linear in development than the taut adventure-laden *Gringo viejo,* and it exemplifies a trend, characteristic of the novel of the post-boom period, toward less experimentation, more emphasis on character and plot, and far shorter length. Yet Fuentes in *Una familia lejana* states as part of his aesthetic philosophy that the solution to one mystery should be another mystery. Bustos finally encounters Ofelia in Mexico: it is an Ofelia wracked by cancer, far different from the enticing illusion that he has cherished for more than a decade. The true father of Ofelia's child is revealed at the end, as well as a clandestine relationship never suspected by the exceedingly naive Baltasar.

In accordance with the emphasis on multiplicity in the works of the boom novelists, Fuentes evokes independence from contradictory perspectives, including even that of the royalist Marquis, who cynically views the result as the mere substitution of one tyranny for another: instead of authoritarian Spain there will be the control exercised over the interior of Argentina by a powerful new Buenos Aires. The idealistic center of the narrative is the Argentine leader José de San Martín. Yet in contrast with the iconic aura of the superhero that surrounds the historical Simón Bolívar, Fuentes's San Martín is evoked as extremely wary of military heroes and dedicated to the establishment of constitutions and laws to achieve social justice. In contrast with the nobility of San Martín are the egomania and ruthlessness of another leader in the independence movement, Miguel Lanza, who in Alto Perú establishes a *republiqueta,* a false republic under his own despotic control. Emulating the defenders of Numancia, the fierce inhabitants of the Roman province who preferred to fall on their swords rather than surrender to the Roman conquerors, Lanza orders his followers to fight to the death for their territory, exerting a tyrannical control that results in the desertion of Baltasar.

In part a Bildungsroman, *La campaña* can be seen as a series of initiation rites experienced by Bustos: into sexual experience, encouraged by the libertine priest; into killing an enemy in battle, which revulses him; and, under the tutelage of Simón Rodríguez (an allusion to the historical mentor of Simón Bolívar) into a magic, visionary realm, allowed to glimpse El Dorado, an entire city, streets, buildings, clocks, carriages, of golden light. Fuentes poeticizes here a vision of the New World as a utopia, an intensely spiritual realm that is the opposite of the City of Gold so fiercely sought after by the avaricious conquistadors. It is significant, and ironic, that this City is illusory: again and again Fuentes's narrative underscores the chasm between revolutionary ideals and promises and the repeated patterns of betrayal and power grabbing, so that the enemy most feared by San Martín is not the Spanish authority, but the newly empowered and divisive Creoles who will be victorious over the Spanish but who will also betray the cause of independence.

The ideological pluralism of *La campaña* is evident not only in the differing viewpoints on the consequences of independence and in the vacillation that even Bustos experiences, as he is tempted by the alternative of compromise and conciliation between royalists and insurgents instead of relentless conflict and slaughter, but also in three different French philosophers with whom the three Argentine friends identify. Varela, the most ambiguous of the three, espouses the position of Diderot, with his emphasis on constant change, compromise, and choice—the philosophy articulated by Fuentes himself in so many of his novels, like *La muerte de Artemio Cruz, Cambio de piel,* and *Terra nostra.* The ideology of pluralism and openness, reiterated throughout *La campaña,* is also evidenced structurally. Fuentes has stated that the enigmatic Ofelia and her son will reappear in sequels to *La campaña* that will form a trilogy, to end with the Mexican Revolution of 1910. Here again the vitality of the revolutionary theme in the Mexican novel is underscored. The kidnapped child, who reappears at the end of *La campaña* and is adopted by Baltasar, plays a game of "firing squad" in which he becomes the pretended victim, perhaps an allusion to the constancy of violence in Latin America, as depicted throughout the centuries in Fuentes's *Cambio de piel,* or perhaps an allusion to his future fate as revolutionary martyr. The paradox and ambiguity that characterize this incisive novel are also exemplified by Ofelia, who emerges as both royalist and insurgent ally. Although Quintana and Varela both attest to Ofelia's commitment to independence, Baltasar is left with gnawing doubts as he recalls her legendary evocation as the seducer and assassin of insurgent leaders. This paradoxical nature is reinforced by Ofelia's link with both sensuality and allure and with the demonic, with the horrifying Gorgon and Medusa, so that she becomes a continuation of the ambivalent Aura and the mythic superstar Claudia Nervo, a persona of María Félix, in Fuentes's *Zona sagrada*. But by emphasizing the importance of women in the independence period, just as he has underscored the great importance of the Malinche at the time of the conquest, Fuentes once again restores the balance, rejecting the male-oriented vision of Latin American and Mexican history and society and affirming plurality and diversity.

BIBLIOGRAPHY

Agustín, José. *De perfil*. Mexico City: Editorial Joaquín Mortiz, 1966.

———. *La tumba*. Mexico City: Organización Editorial Novaro, 1964.

Aridjis, Homero. *Memorias del Nuevo Mundo*. Mexico City: Editorial Diana, 1988.

Aub, Max. *Guía de narradores de la Revolución Mexicana*. Mexico City: Fondo de Cultura Económica, 1969. Brief, incisively written volume with short entries on novelists from Frías to Yáñez. Illustrated with photographs of incidents from the revolution and its aftermath.

Azuela, Arturo. *Manifestación de silencio*. Mexico City: Editorial Joaquín Mortiz, 1979.

Azuela, Mariano. *Andrés Pérez, maderista*. Mexico City: Imprenta de Blanco y Botas, 1911.

———. *El camarada Pantoja*. Mexico City: Ediciones Botas, 1937.

———. *Esa sangre*. Mexico City: Fondo de Cultura Económica, 1956.

———. *Los de abajo*. Originally in supplement to *El Paso del Norte,* October–December 1915. El Paso, Tex.: Imprenta El Paso del Norte, 1916.

———. *Mala yerba*. Guadalajara: Talleres de la Gaceta de Guadalajara, 1909.

———. *Las moscas*. Mexico City: A. Carranza e hijos, 1918.

———. *Nueva burguesía*. Buenos Aires, 1941.

———. *Las tribulaciones de una familia decente*. Tampico, 1918.

Bell, Steven M. "Mexico." In *Handbook of Latin American Literature,* 2d ed., ed. David William Foster, 357–442. New York: Garland, 1992. Excellent, comprehensive overview of the development of Mexican literature from the pre-Columbian epoch to the present.

Brushwood, John S. *Mexico in Its Novel*. Austin: University of Texas Press, 1966. Thorough, authoritative work on the novel from the colonial period to the 1960s.

———. *Narrative Innovation and Political Change in Mexico*. New York: Peter Lang, 1989. An excellent study demonstrating how Mexican fiction has predicted political change, with emphasis on periods of Mexican literature in which innovative techniques have been employed by novelists like Revueltas, Yáñez, Rulfo, Fuentes, and many others.

———. *La novela mexicana (1967–1982)*. Mexico City: Editorial Grijalbo, 1985. Perceptively written update of Brushwood's fundamental *Mexico in Its Novel,* including year-by-year listings of major novels.

Brushwood, John S., and José Rojas Garcidueñas. *Breve historia de la novela mexicana.* Mexico City: Ediciones de Andrea, 1959. First part constitutes panorama of the Mexican novel from the colonial period through the nineteenth century; second part examines the novel from Azuela through the 1950s.

Carpentier, Alejo. *Los pasos perdidos.* Mexico City: Edición y Distribución Iberoamericana de Publicaciones, 1953.

———. *El siglo de las luces.* Mexico City: Compañía General de Ediciones, 1962.

Castellanos, Rosario. *El eterno femenino.* Mexico City: Fondo de Cultura Económica, 1975.

———. *La novela mexicana contemporánea y su valor testimonial.* Mexico City: Instituto Nacional de Juventud Mexicana, 1966. Brief, very insightful overview of works by Yáñez, Rulfo, Fuentes, and indigenous novelists, concluding with Hernández and Mojarro.

Cervantes y Saavedra, Miguel de. *El ingenioso hidalgo don Quijote de la Mancha.* Madrid: Juan de la Cuesta, 1605, 1615.

Cortázar, Julio. *Rayuela.* Buenos Aires: Editorial Sudamericana, 1963.

Duncan, J. Ann. *Voices, Visions, and a New Reality: Mexican Fiction since 1970.* Pittsburgh: University of Pittsburgh Press, 1986. Carefully written work offering precise analysis of authors who began publishing in the 1970s and who emphasize innovative techniques. Authors examined include José Emilio Pacheco, Carlos Montemayor, Humberto Guzmán, Esther Seligson, Antonio Delgado, María Luisa Puga, and Arturo Azuela.

Durán, Manuel. *Tríptico mexicano.* Mexico City: SepSetentas, 1973. Highly illuminating study of the works of Rulfo, Fuentes, and Elizondo.

Foster, David William. *Mexican Literature: A Bibliography of Secondary Sources.* 2d ed. Metuchen, N.J.: Scarecrow Press, 1992. Outstanding comprehensive critical bibliography from the colonial period to the present, citing both general reference works and studies on individual authors.

Frías, Heriberto. *Tomochic.* Mexico City: El Demócrata, 1892. Second augmented edition, Rio Grande City, Tex.: Imprenta de Jesús T. Recio, 1894.

Fuentes, Carlos. *Aura.* Mexico City: Ediciones Era, 1962.

———. *Las buenas conciencias.* Mexico City: Fondo de Cultura Económica, 1959.

———. *La cabeza de la hidra.* Barcelona: Argos, 1978.

———. *Cambio de piel.* Mexico City: Editorial Joaquín Mortiz, 1967.

———. *La campaña.* Mexico City: Fondo de Cultura Económica, 1990.

———. *Cristóbal nonato.* Mexico City: Fondo de Cultura Económica, 1987.

———. *Cumpleaños.* Mexico City: Editorial Joaquín Mortiz, 1970.

———. *Los días enmascarados.* Mexico City: Los Presentes, 1954.

———. "Disyuntiva mexicana." In his *Tiempo mexicano.* Mexico City: Editorial Joaquín Mortiz, 1970.

———. *Una familia lejana.* Mexico City: Ediciones Era, 1980.

———. *Gringo viejo.* Mexico City: Fondo de Cultura Económica, 1985.

———. *La muerte de Artemio Cruz.* Mexico City: Fondo de Cultura Económica, 1962.

———. *La nueva novela hispanoamericana.* Mexico City: Editorial Joaquín Mortiz, 1969. Fascinating study of the boom novelists and their precursors in terms of their mythic and epic vision, the quest for utopia, and the creation of a new language.

———. *La región más transparente.* Mexico City: Fondo de Cultura Económica, 1958.

———. *Terra nostra*. Barcelona: Seix Barral, 1975.

———. *Todos los gatos son pardos*. Mexico City: Siglo XXI Editores, 1970.

———. *El tuerto es rey*. Mexico City: Editorial Joaquín Mortiz, 1970.

———. *Zona sagrada*. Mexico City: Siglo XXI Editores, 1967.

García Márquez, Gabriel. *Cien años de soledad*. Buenos Aires: Editorial Sudamericana, 1967.

———. *El general en su laberinto*. Buenos Aires: Editorial Sudamericana, 1989.

Garro, Elena. *Los recuerdos del porvenir*. Mexico City: Editorial Joaquín Mortiz, 1963.

Glantz, Margo. *Repeticiones: Ensayos sobre literatura mexicana*. Mexico City: Universidad Veracruzana, 1979. Thought-provoking, original collection of essays, including important study defining the Onda (Wave) of the seventies and reconsidering its impact ten years later.

González, Manuel Pedro. *Trayectoria de la novela en México*. Mexico City: Ediciones Botas, 1951. Informative, broad-scoped study of the development of the novel, from the nineteenth century to 1950.

Guzmán, Martín Luis. *El águila y la serpiente*. Madrid: M. Aguilar, 1928.

———. *Las memorias de Pancho Villa*. Mexico City: Ediciones Botas, 1938–1940.

———. *La sombra del caudillo*. Madrid: Espasa-Calpe, 1929.

Harss, Luis, and Barbara Dohmann. *Into the Mainstream: Conversations with Latin American Writers*. New York: Harper and Row, 1967. Highly interesting, well-formulated study that incorporates commentary with extracts from interviews with leading Latin American novelists and short-story writers, including Rulfo and Fuentes.

Lafforgue, Julio, ed. *Nueva narrativa hispanoamericana*. Vol. 1. Buenos Aires: Paidós, 1969. Includes insightful analytical studies on works by Yáñez, Rulfo, García Ponce, Leñero, and Del Paso.

Langford, Walter. *Mexican Novel Comes of Age*. Notre Dame: University of Notre Dame Press, 1971. Lucid, convincing overview of major Mexican novelists from the nineteenth century to Agustín and Sainz.

Lawrence, D. H. *The Plumed Serpent*. London: Martin Secker, 1926.

Leal, Luis. *Breve historia del cuento mexicano*. Mexico City: Ediciones de Andrea, 1956. Well-documented panoramic study of the Mexican short story from the pre-Hispanic era to 1955; sound and informative.

López y Fuentes, Gregorio. *Campamento*. Madrid: Espasa-Calpe, 1931.

———. *Tierra*. Mexico City: Talleres de El Universal, 1932.

Magaña Esquivel, Antonio. *La novela de la Revolución Mexicana*. Mexico City: Biblioteca del Instituto Nacional de Estudios Históricos, 1964. Well-organized, perceptive, two-volume overview of the major novelists of the Mexican Revolution, from nineteenth-century antecedents (Rabasa, Delgado, Mateos) to Muñoz and Campobello.

Mastretta, Angeles. *Arráncame la vida*. Mexico City, 1985.

Mendoza, María Luisa. *Con él, conmigo, con nosotros tres*. Mexico City: Editorial Joaquín Mortiz, 1969.

Miliani, Domingo. *La realidad mexicana en su novela de hoy*. Caracas: Monte Avila, 1968. Brief, probing study of the modern novel in Mexico.

Monsiváis, Carlos. *Días de guardar*. Mexico City: Ediciones Era, 1970.

Morton, F. Rand. *Los novelistas de la Revolución Mexicana*. Mexico City: Cultura, 1949. Good concluding chapter on social, historical, and aesthetic characteristics of the novel of the Mexican Revolution.

Muñoz, Rafael. *El feroz cabecilla y otros cuentos de la Revolución en el norte.* Mexico City: Imprenta de la Cámara de Diputados, 1928.

———. *Se llevaron el cañón para Bachimba.* Buenos Aires: Espasa-Calpe, 1944.

———. *Vámonos con Pancho Villa.* Madrid: Espasa-Calpe, 1931.

Los narradores ante el público. Mexico City: Editorial Joaquín Mortiz, 1966–1967. Absorbing, insightful two-volume series of public lectures sponsored by the National Institute of Fine Arts in 1965 and 1966 and given by thirty-three contemporary authors on their lives and works.

Novo, Salvador. *La vida en México en el período presidencial de Lázaro Cárdenas.* Mexico City: Empresas Editoriales, 1964.

———. *La vida en México en el período presidencial de Manuel Avila Camacho.* Mexico City: Empresas Editoriales, 1965.

Ocampo de Gómez, Aurora Maura. *La crítica de la novela mexicana contemporánea: Antología.* Mexico City: Universidad Nacional Autónoma de México, 1981. Highly informative, well-written collection by both Mexican and North American critics of thematic and stylistic essays on the novel of the Mexican Revolution, the indigenous novel of the Chiapas cycle, and the narrative of the 1960s and 1970s.

Ocampo de Gómez, Aurora Maura, and Ernesto Prado Velásquez. *Diccionario de escritores mexicanos.* Mexico City: Universidad Nacional Autónoma de México, 1967. Thorough, comprehensive biographical and bibliographical (primary and secondary sources) presentation of Mexican authors from Netzahuacóyotl to Poniatowska.

Pacheco, José Emilio. *No me preguntes cómo pasa el tiempo.* Mexico City: Editorial Joaquín Mortiz, 1969.

Paso, Fernando del. *José Trigo.* Mexico City: Siglo XXI Editores, 1966.

———. *Noticias del imperio.* Mexico City: Editorial Diana, 1987.

———. *Palinuro de México.* Madrid: Ediciones Alfagusta, 1977.

Patán, Federico. *Contrapuntos.* Mexico City: Universidad Nacional Autónoma de México, 1989. An insightful collection of essays dedicated to Arturo Azuela, Sergio Pitol, Carlos Fuentes, Sergio Galindo, and Vicente Leñero.

Paz, Octavio. *El laberinto de la soledad.* Mexico City: Cuadernos Hispanoamericanos, 1950.

———. *Posdata.* Mexico City: Siglo XXI Editores, 1970.

Poniatowska, Elena. *Fuerte es el silencio.* Mexico City: Ediciones Era, 1980.

———. *Hasta no verte, Jesús mío.* Mexico City: Ediciones Era, 1969.

———. *La noche de Tlatelolco: Testimonios de historia oral.* Mexico City: Ediciones Era, 1971.

Ramos, Samuel. *El perfil del hombre y de la cultura en México.* Mexico City: Imprenta Mundial, 1934.

Romero, José Rubén. *La vida inútil de Pito Pérez.* Mexico City: Editorial México Nuevo, 1938.

Rulfo, Juan. *El llano en llamas.* Mexico City: Fondo de Cultura Económica, 1953.

———. *Pedro Páramo.* Mexico City: Fondo de Cultura Económica, 1955.

Sainz, Gustavo. *A la salud de la serpiente.* Mexico City: Editorial Grijalbo, 1991.

———. *Compadre lobo.* Mexico City: Editorial Grijalbo, 1978.

———. *Gazapo.* Mexico City: Editorial Joaquín Mortiz, 1965.

———. *El muchacho en llamas.* Mexico City: Editorial Grijalbo, 1988.

Sommers, Joseph. *After the Storm: Landmarks of the Modern Mexican Novel.* Albuquerque: University of New Mexico Press, 1968. Penetrating analyses of Yáñez's *Al filo del agua,* Rulfo's *Pedro Páramo,* and the early novels of Fuentes.

Spota, Luis. *La Plaza*. Mexico City: Editorial Joaquín Mortiz, 1972.

Torres, Vicente Francisco. *Narradores mexicanos de fin de siglo*. Mexico City: Universidad Autónoma Metropolitana, 1989. An incisive commentary and short interviews with six contemporary novelists: Ignacio Solares, Jesús Gardea, Luis Arturo Ramos, Hernán Lara Zavala, Silvio Molina, and Paco Ignacio Taibo II.

Trejo Fuentes, Ignacio. *Segunda voz: Ensayos sobre la novela mexicana*. Mexico City: Universidad Nacional Autónoma de México, 1987. Short, perceptive articles on Fuentes, Galindo, Fernández, Soita, Solares, García Ponce, Ibargüengoitia, and Del Paso.

Usigli, Rodolfo. *Corona de sombra*. Mexico City: Cuadernos Americanos, 1943.

Valle Inclán, Ramón del. *Tirano Banderas*. Madrid: Sucesores de Rivadeneyra, 1926.

Vasconcelos, José. *Hernán Cortés, creador de la nacionalidad*. Mexico City: Xochitl, 1941.

Yáñez, Agustín. *Al filo del agua*. Mexico City: Editorial Porrúa, 1947.

———. *La creación*. Mexico City: Fondo de Cultura Económica, 1959.

———. *Las vueltas del tiempo*. Mexico City: Editorial Joaquín Mortiz, 1973.

9

The Essay

MARTIN S. STABB

Anyone familiar with Spanish American letters is well aware of the essay's importance in Mexico. Indeed, several of Latin America's most celebrated essayists are Mexican: the names of Alfonso Reyes (1889–1959) and Octavio Paz (1914–) come to mind immediately as writers who have been read and discussed from Buenos Aires to Caracas to New York. But in addition to these giants of the genre, the sheer number of important Mexican essayists is impressive. When José Luis Martínez published the first edition of his anthology *El ensayo mexicano moderno* (The Modern Mexican Essay; 1958) he included some fifty-six authors; his collection, moreover, excludes essayistic work produced before 1870 as well as texts that have appeared in recent decades. Not surprisingly Martínez's book contains many selections by writers who are better known for their verse or fiction. In fact, in Mexico as elsewhere, the writing of essays is often a secondary activity of novelists or poets, not to mention historians, journalists, and academics. This situation and the multiform nature of the genre itself make the apparently simple task of determining which authors actually constitute the main line of Mexican essayists rather difficult.

In view of these problems and of the space at my disposal, I have established the following parameters for the present study. In the first place, all essayistic writing of the colonial period will be omitted since early Mexican letters are treated elsewhere in this volume; secondly, I shall emphasize ideological rather than aesthetic considerations in an attempt to put the major concerns of the writers discussed into a meaningful historical perspective. Many fascinating questions regarding such matters as the generic boundaries of the essay, the genre's formal, technical aspects, and the sociology of essayistic production will be treated only in passing or not at all. Finally, only a limited number of representative essayists will be discussed in detail.

Our survey begins during the period of Mexico's struggle for independence, with the work of José Joaquín Fernández de Lizardi (1776–1827), a figure who well illustrates some of the problems noted above. Best known as the author of the long, rambling picaresque novel *El Periquillo Sarniento* (*The Itching Parrot;* 1816) along with other works of didactic fiction, Fernández de Lizardi was also a prolific journalist and pamphleteer: his major efforts in this area were *El pensador mexicano* (The Mexican Thinker; 1812–1814), *Alacena de frioleras* (The Closet of Odds and Ends; 1815), *Conductor eléctrico* (The Electrical Conductor; 1820), *Conversaciones del Payo y el Sacristán* (Conversations between the Country Bumpkin and the Sexton; 1824–1825), *Correo Semanario* (The Weekly Mail; 1826–1827), and a host of uncollected *folletos,* tracts and pamphlets. Like his North American counterpart, Franklin, he even published several almanac-calendars. There is no single definitive essay nor book of essays in this vast production. Moreover, many of his expository texts defy generic classification: for example, he frequently uses "dialogues" as vehicles for his ideas. These pieces can hardly be considered theatrical art since they have little action, no dramatic tension, and were obviously written to be read. On other occasions he casts his "essays" into the form of barely fictionalized allegories wherein "Truth" or "Experience" appear to the author in a dream and proceed to guide him through the city or universe. A true entrepreneur, he was obviously concerned about the commercial success of his ventures: he even resorted to publishing letters from his subscribers with his own comments or replies. This aspect of his work is important as it underscores the fact that Fernández de Lizardi was, if not a "man of the people," a writer who endeavored to reach all socioeconomic groups of his day. Though he reveals vast readings and encyclopedic breadth in his subject matter, one notes a constant attempt to reach an audience of only modest intellectuality. His frequent and historically important use of slang, Mexicanisms, and the like is further evidence of this. Despite the fact that Fernández de Lizardi was seldom an essayist in the classical sense of the term, this substantial corpus of nonfictional, generically mixed prose falls under the broad rubric of *ensayismo* (essayistic writing) by virtue of the author's overriding desire to convince and to mold the opinions of his readers.

Few commentators would say that Fernández de Lizardi, although known as the Pensador Mexicano (the Mexican Thinker), was an original thinker or even very rigorous in adapting the ideas of others in his own writing. In general terms he reflects the eighteenth-century enlightenment, though he typically shies away from the more radical or revolutionary implications of the century's thought. His political thinking during the struggle for independence reflects that of many Mexicans of the period; that is, it is characterized by doubts, ambiguities, and compromise. While he could attack certain aspects of the Spanish colonial regime like the Inquisition (3:172–188), he nonetheless considered Hidalgo and the early insurgents as troublemakers, guilty of a "reprehensible lack of tact" (3:247).[1] Mexico's faltering attempts to gain independence and the vagaries of Fernández de Lizardi's political thinking during the period are too complicated to be discussed here in detail.[2] It is sufficient to note that after suffering censorship despite the promises of the liberal Spanish Constitution, and after his espousal of the ill-conceived Iturbide movement, Fernández de Lizardi emerges as a supporter of genuine independence. The establishment of the nation's first autonomous government and the adoption of the Constitution of 1824 led him to write some of his most inter-

esting political essays. Two of these, "Pragmática de la libertad" (Pragmatic of
Freedom) and the "Constitución política de una república imaginaria" (Political Constitution of an Imaginary Republic) appeared in his rather charming,
folksy periodical, *Conversaciones del Payo y el Sacristán*.

The "Constitución política" is a wonderful example of Fernández de Lizardi's strengths and weaknesses as a thinker as well as a writer. Like so many of
his texts it is framed as a dialogue rather than in conventional essay form. The
interlocutors, the almost Cantinflas-like *payo* (rustic, bumpkin) and the somewhat more cultured middlebrow sexton, are quite a pair to discuss political
theory, economics, penology, and the like. One suspects that Fernández de
Lizardi—always the educator—hoped that the ordinary Mexican of the day
could identify with these types and thus become more involved in public affairs. The opening pages reveal this intent clearly:

> *Payo.* With good reason I've been dying to be made a deputy, for it's a great
> thing to be able to serve your country with your talents.
> *Sacristán.* You're right. I too have been hounded by the same desire: and I've
> come up with a way for the two of us to soothe our itch to become legislators.
> *Payo.* And just how, old buddy, can this happen since we're just ordinary folks, a
> sexton and a rancher?
> *Sacristán.* That's no obstacle; . . . the job of reforming the world is as easy as can
> be, especially if reforms are made without opposition. Plato made his Republic,
> Fenelon his Telemachus, Thomas More his Utopia . . . and many others. What bar-
> riers, then, can you find to prevent the two of us from making our Mexican Consti-
> tution? From destroying abuses, from opening the doors of abundance and general
> happiness, all with our wise laws? (5:14–15)

When the more humble *payo* suggests that ordinary citizens might not possess the education or background to write laws and reform the nation, the
ebullient sexton informs him that patriotism and good intentions can make up
for any such lack: "I've seen *ranchers* that seem to be men of letters and men
of letters that appear to be *ranchers;* so heck! Let's get going and fix up our
republic just the way we want to!" (5:16).

Leaving aside questions of the essay's literary frame and the playful, quin-
tessentially Mexican idiom of the speakers, what are the main ideas set forth
in this piece? The 116 "articles" constitute a curious melange of serious, fundamental political notions along with many trivial, perhaps facetious details.
In a serious section on land tenure and reform, Fernández de Lizardi calls for
limiting holdings to a mere "four square leagues." He notes that in Mexico
there are many rich people who have "ten, twelve or more properties . . . some
of which take four days to traverse, while there are millions of individuals who
don't own a handsbreadth of their own land" (5:435). Alongside these matters
of substance, Fernández de Lizardi outlines a number of curious statutes such
as those pertaining to the colors (blue and white) and materials (silk) for what
he calls the "honorific badge of citizenship" (5:418–419). In his lengthy treat-

ment of the criminal code he establishes specific penalties for various crimes; these range from some very sensible suggestions—such as short periods of labor on public works for minor crimes—to some rather bizarre punishments like the amputation of the right hand of officials who have accepted bribes (5.519).

Despite these curiosities in the "Constitución política," the piece does reveal a great deal about Fernández de Lizardi's social and political thought, as well as his views on the Mexico of his day. The sections on government organization, crime and punishment, economics, freedom of expression, and the role of the military are especially rich. As for government, we find Fernández de Lizardi to be a strong proponent of the separation of powers and a militant monitor of legislative propriety: ecclesiastics, while they could be elected as deputies, would have to abstain on votes involving Church interests; legislators popularly elected could not serve two consecutive terms; lobbying and the dispensing of public posts by deputies would be prohibited; and as in the United States (to some extent his model) the judicial branch of government was to be clearly separate from the legislative (5:421).

In his detailed section on the criminal code and penology, Fernández de Lizardi reveals some very modern notions as well as the strange abberations noted earlier. He calls for prisons to be physically attractive, corrective educational institutions: they should have shops for teaching practical skills and even garden plots to be worked by and for the prisoners. Before release from prison, anyone who did not formerly have a trade would be required to earn a certificate of competency as an artisan (5:431). Fernández de Lizardi also addresses the question of female delinquents. In a rather colorful vignette he notes that "among women, especially of the lower classes, there is a scandalous amount of vagrancy. Every day one finds on our streets a multitude of women in rags who look like bunches of celery, thousands of them drunk and many given to early prostitution; and yet one can't find a servant girl who is worth anything. This means that they prefer miserable idleness to useful work" (5:432). Fernández de Lizardi suggests as treatment for these women that they be placed in prisons where they could work in the kitchens until they find employment, presumably as domestic servants. Clearly, Fernández de Lizardi's espousal of progressive ideas could not quite overcome his rather elitist, sexist attitudes typical of nineteenth-century Mexico.

The brief section on liberty of expression is typical of Fernández de Lizardi's middle-of-the-road rather than radical thinking. After proclaiming that "every . . . inhabitant is free to write, print, and publish his ideas by whatever means available," he proceeds to list the restrictions on this basic liberty. "Subversive, scandalous, and injurious" expressions would constitute punishable crimes: he then defines "subversive" rather vaguely as "all printed matter that directly attacks the established form of government in such a manner that leaves no doubt as to the intent of the author" (5:486). His definition of "scandalous" writing is similarly revealing: "All writing that directly attacks religious dogma would be scandalous, but keeping in mind that abuses are not dogmas" (5:487). Here, as elsewhere, he shows his religious orthodoxy as distinguished from his critical attitude toward abuses within the Church or those stemming from Church-generated institutions, such as the Inquisition.

The foregoing provides only a small sample of Fernández de Lizardi's vast essayistic production. Scattered through the pages of *El pensador, Alacena, Conversaciones,* and his many other works one finds evidence of an amazing range of interests: comments on reforming (not abolishing) bullfighting, critical notes on gambling, attacks on merchants who overcharge, discussion of the reform of the military, comments on the tyranny of fashion, darts aimed at doctors and pharmacists, thoughts on the benefits of free trade, and discussions on elementary education, as well as on a host of other topics. While he could produce some of the most stultifying prose to be found in Spanish, he could also write pages exceedingly rich in folksy humor. At times he reveals an upper—or middle—class disdain for ordinary people, yet he apparently relished depicting the everyday speech, foibles, and idiosyncracies of the *payos* and picaros that people his pages. A derivative thinker, a reformer rather than a radical, he nevertheless catches bits and pieces of the Mexican character at the very moment of the nation's birth. Finally, as Agustín Yáñez has observed, his unflagging emphasis on moralizing toward practical ends "is a constant that governs Mexican art [and] Mexican life" (*El Pensador,* xvi).

As the writings of Fernández de Lizardi suggest, Mexico's break from Spain was, except on the strictly political level, rather superficial. The colonial legacy of a conservative, economically well-entrenched Church, of a self-serving, ambitious military, and of a corrupt, inefficient administrative bureaucracy remained to plague the nation during the early decades of independence. In the work of historians, *pensadores* (thinkers) and essayists, certain key terms soon come to reflect the desire to improve the young republic: thus the words *liberalismo* (liberalism) and *reforma* (reform) dominate the work of many intellectuals. The late fifties saw the institutionalization of these concepts in the Reform Laws, the adoption of which Mexicans view as a watershed event in the history of the nation. There are a number of writers who reflect the *reforma* and the genesis of the Mexican Liberal Party: J. M. Mora (1794–1850), M. C. Rejón (1799–1849), and M. Ramos Arizpe (1775–1843). During the same period Lucas Alamán (1792–1853) raised a strong voice as a defender of traditionalism. But with the possible exception of Mora, these writers were essentially historians rather than essayists. By contrast, Ignacio Ramírez (1818–1879), nicknamed El Nigromante (the sorcerer), not only represents the reformist-liberal tradition in full flower, but also is a man of letters of considerable merit. Teacher, orator, poet, minister of justice under Benito Juárez, Ramírez has been called Mexico's Voltaire by Harold E. Davis (92)—perhaps an understatement in one respect since his scandalous profession of atheism, "Dios no existe" (God does not exist), goes considerably beyond Voltaire's comparatively mild deism.

Somewhat like Fernández de Lizardi, Ramírez was a poligraph: it would be difficult to find any single essay that sums up the essence of his thought.

Unlike the Pensador Mexicano, Ramírez did not identify linguistically or psychologically with the lower classes, though he appreciated the intellectual potential of the ordinary Mexican, especially the Indian. His literary style is correct, clear-cut, and perhaps more formal than that of his predecessor. As a member of Juárez's cabinet, he became deeply involved in politics and many of his journalistic articles, speeches, and letters reflect political concerns. Like Fernández de Lizardi he was also intensely interested in education. But what Ramírez is best remembered for is his unremitting attack on religion, more specifically that version of Catholicism brought to the New World by Spain. Indeed, it is often difficult to determine whether his primary target is the Church as a religious institution or as an expression of Spanish values. There is certainly no doubt regarding Ramírez's basic attitude toward *la madre patria* (the mother country): "One should have no illusions; the last nation in the world that other countries would wish to resemble are the Spaniards. . . . Just one drop of Spanish blood, when it has coursed through the veins of an American, has produced . . . the Santa Annas, has engendered traitors" (1:319) he proclaims in a significantly titled article of 1865, "La desespañolización" (The Loss of Spanish Identity).

What seems to anger Ramírez most about Spain's role in Mexico is that Iberian institutions, values, and attitudes represented an all-embracing alien culture imposed upon the native and emerging mestizo society. In one of his most significant texts, the Mazatlán speech of September 16, 1863, he makes this point very clear: "Mexico was the new Spain; Andalusian dances, the idolatrous festivals of Castille's villages, the ridiculous court dress, Góngora's literature dominating the pulpit and the forum . . . and saints, taking charge of our pleasures, our sorrows . . . our dining tables and our beds; everything was Spanish: to go to Heaven, one had to go by way of Spain" (1:152). In other contexts Ramírez berates the Church on the question of divorce, on celibacy of the clergy, and on other issues. As one of the principal authors of La Reforma, the Reform Laws, he insisted that the Church should only exist within and subordinate to the secular national government: he would withhold citizenship from clerics who might seek economic or political privilege by virtue of their special status. Finally, Ramírez even objected to the use of the phrase "In the name of God" at the beginning of Mexico's new constitution of 1857. He explains his position by noting that this invocation suggests that the document, and the government which it was to establish, existed by virtue of divine right. He points out that "the name of God has always led to divine right; and the history of divine right has been written by the hand of tyrants with the sweat and blood of the people" (1:188).

Ramírez's basic ideas on the form of Mexico's new government and its relation to society are closely linked to his reaction against the Spanish colonial heritage. Thus it is not surprising that he should support freedom of religion and of the press. But Ramírez went considerably beyond these rather typical liberal positions in pressing for children's rights, legal protection for illegitimates, and especially women's rights. His attitudes, while not advanced by contemporary standards, represent fairly open views for the mid-nineteenth century: "Everywhere people have tried to base the inferior social position of women on the inferiority of their makeup; to make this inferiority even greater they have confused . . . certain transient defects; and from this true or exaggerated inferiority they have deduced a lessening of rights which would not be applied to men except in the case of a scientific or judicial declaration of incompetence" (2:234). The critic Manuel González Ramírez notes that earlier, in his comment on the new constitution, he stated, "In matrimony women are the equal of men and have rights of petition that the law must guarantee" (40). And in his extensive writings on education he vigorously refutes those who hold women to be inferior when he declares, with only minor reservations, that "the education of women should be the same as that of men" (2:186).

On more technical matters of governmental form and function Ramírez pressed for direct election of officials (he feared the politicking of intermediate electoral bodies) and for the establishment of active, independent local governments. Ever wary of central administrations that might become oppressive, he consistently sought to ground Mexican political power at the municipal level, though he clearly understood that this was hardly in the Hispanic tradition. He cites many foreign models to support this view; he was especially impressed by the North Americans with their traditional town meetings, councils, and leanings toward federalism (2:238). He even sought prototypes for local autonomy in pre-Columbian Mexico (2:238). It is interesting to note that this discussion, like the analysis of the status of women, is part of his extensive essay "La Internacional de Paris" (1871). In effect, a good deal of what El Nigromante seems to be saying here is a kind of rejoinder to the challenge of early communism, a political theory that he viewed with considerable hostility. Some of his reservations stem from the fact that he associates (almost fifty years before the founding of the Soviet Union) the threat of overbearing centralization with communism: he states this view clearly when he observes that "administrative centralization is a kind of communism" (2:240).

He frequently underscores his basic notion that problems are best solved at the grass-roots level and that neither utopian regimes of the future nor existing central governments work very efficiently. On a specific issue he will, for example, ask, "Is there enthusiasm for draining the Valley of Mexico? An alliance of municipal governments or the townspeople themselves or landowners . . . will carry it out more certainly than the Ministry of Public Works" (2:144). In some of these texts one can almost sense an anarchistic tone. For example, in a short piece of 1868, "Principios sociales y principios administrativos" (Social Principles and Administrative Principles), he contrasts a kind of natural "sociability" or "association" with the artificially imposed administration of governments: "The development of association is spontaneous; the form of administration is capricious. . . . Association demands equality; administration is maintained by hierarchy. . . . Association is well being; administration is obedience" (2:5). Somewhat later in the same piece, he goes so far as stating that "it is difficult to prove the goodness and need for governments, but it cannot be hidden from anyone that this system of handing over communal affairs to . . . agents breeds corruption and tyranny" (2:7). In short, while he agrees that man cannot live in isolation, that "natural" productive associations are necessary, he believes that government, and especially central government, will always be at odds with these less formal but more genuine groupings.

It would be erroneous, however, to emphasize this seemingly anarchistic trend in Ramírez's thinking. Typical of nineteenth-century liberalism, his critique of government administration derives more from his faith in the progressive, "positive" role of untrammeled economic activity—laissez-faire—than from any dedication to genuine anarchism. While Ramírez feared big government, attacked the Church, and considered the embryonic communism of his day a threat to small "natural" associations, he apparently saw little danger in private enterprise. Indeed, he often expresses optimism regarding the role of entrepreneurs in the developing nation. In his revealing essay on the Paris International he admires the situation in the United States where even workers who consider themselves exploited can buy stocks in private companies and perhaps eventually become capitalists (2:216). In his article of 1868, "Ferrocarriles" (Railroads) he questions the right of the federal government to monopolize the railroad system, while he suggests that private enterprise, foreign investors, or even local governments might also build and operate this form of transportation (2:128). And in several articles on free trade he repeatedly calls for a "hands off" attitude: in one of these pieces he attacks protectionism and rejects the notion that government is obliged to assure work for all Mexicans (2:89). Perhaps his most extreme statement of this position, and one that reveals the growing positivism of the period, appears in the short, pithy essay "Principios sociales y principios administrativos":

> From now on the world will not study itself in kings or congresses, but in banks, in companies, in entrepreneurial organizations where even the very poor can become powerful, where the general welfare is not translated into royal celebrations nor in showy monuments . . . but rather in railroads, in scientific enlightenment, in asylums for the unfortunate, in educational institutions for our youth, and in the amassing of capital. (2:89)

It is significant that Ramírez hopes that one of the areas to benefit from economic progress will be education. His mention of teaching institutions in the essay cited above is not an isolated example of this interest; in fact it is a major concern. This is not surprising since education for many nineteenth-century liberals and their close kin, the social Darwinists, played a fundamental role in the dynamics of any society. This was so since they viewed the social structure as a pyramid with the masses at the base and an elite, or "aristocracy of merit," at the apex: ideally, competition and social mobility would permit the truly gifted to rise in the system and eventually assume the directive positions they merited. But for this selective process to work efficiently and fairly, it would be required that all citizens have equal opportunity to demonstrate and develop their abilities: in other words, a broad-based accessible educational system would have to be provided. While Ramírez did not spell out these beliefs in any single, succinct statement, these ideas dominate his educational thinking. His essay on "Instrucción primaria" (Elementary Education; 1867), for example, calls for the government to go far beyond providing basic education for even the most humble Mexicans. Moreover, the government should not assume that working-class children learn only a trade: "The instruction of those whom we call the working class should not be aimed solely at the training of good apprentices and skilled workmen, but also toward the possibility of producing supervisors and directors" (2:174). To insure equal opportunity in education and the recognition of the practical problems of the lower classes, he even calls for the government to feed and clothe the children of the poor, especially the campesinos and Indians, during their education (2:175). It should be pointed out, however, that along with providing opportunity for all, Ramírez held vigorously to his selective notion of education: after age ten or twelve, he warns, "the least diligent will be dismissed" (2:176).

In several essays El Nigromante describes the details of his ideal curriculum. Like others of his liberal persuasion he favors the sciences, physical education, practical arts, and modern languages. He would de-emphasize metaphysical inquiry and rote learning. He questions the value of classical studies—at least for the general student—and he suggests that the history and literature of the ancient world can be read in translation (2:168–169). He makes a strong case for the study of the Indian languages of Mexico, not only for the country's Spanish speakers, but also for the indígenas, indigenous peoples, themselves with a view toward perfecting their knowledge of their native languages in order to be educated "in the natural instrument of the tongue in which they think and live" (2:177).

Unlike some of the social Darwinists of the late nineteenth century, Ramírez believed the native American to be fully educable. He felt, moreover, that the melioration of the Mexican Indian, whose lot had not improved under independence, was clearly a major responsibility of the nation. While he appears to be genuinely interested in preserving the indigenous cultural and linguistic heritage, he would not wish the Indian to pursue a life of picturesque isolation: "They should participate with their intelligence . . . in industry, in agriculture, in commerce, in politics, and in the theater of civilization and progress" (2:183). To accomplish all this he advises that they not be taught catechism, metaphysics, or classical history. Rather, the Indians—women as well as men—should have a modern education centered on science, law, civics, and so forth. Finally, in a note that prefigures the basic outlook of twentieth-century indigenista (indigenist) thinking, Ramírez suggests that "the Indians must know themselves" (2:184).

It would be appropriate, if space permitted, to analyze in detail the essayistic work of Ramírez's contemporary, Ignacio Manuel Altamirano (1834–1893). Though he is remembered more for his poetry and narrative prose, Altamirano—a pure-blooded Indian—shared many of Ramírez's political views. As editor of the important weekly *El Renacimiento,* he made important contributions toward the development of the national consciousness during a crucial period in the nation's history. His strong views on the uniqueness of Mexican customs, language, and letters provoked conservatives, but they had a catalytic effect on others, especially younger intellectuals like Justo Sierra, who would control the nation's affairs during the latter years of the century.

During the two decades from the Reforma of 1857 to Ramírez's death in 1879, Mexico underwent an important transition. The complex details of the period cannot be discussed here: it is sufficient to note that by the end of the 1870s an authoritarian regime, based upon a loosely defined but pervasive sociopolitical philosophy, positivism, became firmly entrenched under the leadership of Porfirio Díaz and his advisors, the *científicos* (men of science).[3] A concise, objective assessment of the *porfiriato* (rule of Porfirio) is rather difficult to make. For some it stands for the exploitation of the poor, the suppression of native cultural values, and a return to an era of special privilege reminiscent of colonial days, while for others it represents a necessary stage in the economic, technological, and political development of modern Mexico. Given these conflicting views of the period, it is appropriate that we choose as its spokesman Justo Sierra (1848–1912), a major essayist who held important positions within the regime and was yet one of its more articulate critics. A historian, educator, and creative writer, Sierra was without doubt the leading intellectual of the *porfiriato,* though many important writers were active during the period. Intellectual life was sparked by the activities of the National Preparatory School, the Preparatoria, an elite institution more like a university than a secondary school in its impact on national affairs, and by a goodly number of periodicals providing a lively forum for literary as well as political discussion. Sierra was one of the master teachers at the Preparatoria, a contributor to or director of several important periodicals (*El Renacimiento, La Libertad, La Revista Nacional de Letras y Ciencias, El Mundo Ilustrado,* etc.), for several terms a member of the national Chamber of Deputies, a Supreme Court justice, undersecretary and then minister of public education, and finally, one of the founders—if not the guiding spirit—of the National University, what would later become the National Autonomous University of Mexico. In addition to all these achievements, his collected works fill some fifteen volumes. Today, he is perhaps best known for his interpretive history, *La evolución política del pueblo mexicano* (The Political Evolution of the Mexican People; 1910), and his historical biography, *Juárez, su obra y tiempo* (Juárez, His Work and Time; 1905). Sierra can hardly be considered a genuine literary essayist in the sense of his Uruguayan contemporary José Enrique Rodó or of his twentieth-century compatriot Alfonso Reyes; yet his historical writings, his speeches, and especially his journalistic pieces reveal qualities typical of the best essayistic writing, especially the ability to see specifics in a broad context. Two themes will serve as focal points about which we may analyze the vast corpus of Sierra's work: his position on positivism and his ideas regarding education for a developing nation.

At first glance Sierra seems to be a typical proponent of that distinctive blend of positivism and social Darwinism that came to dominate much of Latin American thought during the latter decades of the nineteenth century. Citations from his texts would appear to support this point strongly; note for example: "The term *social organization* is not a metaphor; it is the expression of a biological fact: society is an organism in the real sense of the word" (5:213). On closer examination, however, it becomes clear that Sierra viewed humanity and society in much broader terms than those associated with a narrowly conceived scientism. His polemics with certain hard-core positivists—Gabino Barreda, for example—bear this out. In a well-wrought essay of 1874 dealing with the question of including philosophy in the Preparatoria's curriculum, he accepts positivism as a method but not as an all-embracing world view: "We believe in the existence of the spirit. . . . For, to put it succinctly, there is something spontaneous and original in man, there exists that *quid propium* of which the eminent Claude Bernard speaks . . . that which doesn't pertain to chemistry, nor to physics . . . something that enters into the realm of ideas . . . these things are in the province of spirit" (8:23). And, in the same context, he approvingly cites Littré: "That which lies beyond is absolutely inaccessible to the human spirit, but inaccessible does not mean null or nonexistent" (8:23). It is significant that the foregoing was written when Sierra was only in his mid-twenties; his distrust of orthodoxy, whether philosophic or scientific, was evident throughout his career. Some thirty-five years later his magnificent "Discurso en el Teatro Arbeu" (Speech in the Arbeu Theater; 1908), often referred to as the "Dudemos" ("Let Us Doubt") speech, illustrates the persistence and development of this basic attitude (5:387–396). In it he expresses some remarkably modern ideas regarding the limitations of science, the need for "perpetual discussion" and revision of scientific concepts.[4]

Sierra's intellectual honesty and basic open-mindedness are especially evident in his analysis of Mexico's educational needs. This subject, moreover, can be seen as the key to his thought, since in a very real sense El Maestro, as he was called, saw the entire nation as a vast classroom: his political thinking, his ideas on society, and his view of future Mexican culture were all inextricably linked to this basic vision. Underlying his many essays, articles, and speeches on education is a simple idea: people, virtually all people, are educable. As we shall note, this apparently innocent notion could be, and was, disputed in nineteenth-century Mexico. Closely related to this belief was his conviction that education should be obligatory in any viable democratic society. Recalling Mexican experience during the early years of independence, Sierra notes that where formal democracy exists without effective, free, obligatory education, it quickly degenerates and the people fall into the hands of corruption and tyranny. Education was central to Sierra's thinking in another very fundamental way: as one who accepted social organicism—with reservations—he held that for the selective process to function properly a broad-based primary educational system must be provided, along with its secondary and higher components. Moreover, he held that the only entity capable of establishing and maintaining this system was the State, that indeed a modern state could not simply serve as "judge and policeman," but must take an active role in many areas as a "civilizer" and as a "promoter of evolution" (8:250).

It was noted earlier that the United States often served as Sierra's model for development and modernity. His admiration for this country, however, was not unqualified, and he clearly saw Mexican identity as something which must be protected and nurtured. Here again, the role of education was decisive. In a pithy essay, "Americanismo" (1884), he discusses a plan of the government of Coahuila, a border state, to invite a North American Baptist group to establish teaching-training institutions in the city of Saltillo. While he frequently endorsed freedom of religion and the right of all religious groups to offer instruction, he foresees a possibly divisive effect in having Yankee Protestants take on a responsibility that he feels belongs to a Mexican state. Aside from the legal questions involved, Sierra was deeply concerned because this act would violate the "much more sacred law of patriotism." His sense of *mexicanidad* (Mexican identity) was offended by the image of young Mexicans kneeling in awe before the foreigners: "No, we will not permit the money of Mexicans to be spent . . . in training teachers who might learn to kneel before American greatness and to disdain their homeland. . . . We desire, by contrast, that they be taught not to take as their ideal the unfamiliar prosperity of the United States; this would be fatal and would result in producing hopelessness and desperation" (8:139). He goes on to urge that Mexicans content themselves by developing "their own things" in order to gain self-respect and honor. It should be noted in passing that an important detail in this defense of Mexican culture is Sierra's insistence that Spanish not be substituted for by any other language.

In his copious writings on education Sierra was very much aware that the presence of Indians, often culturally and linguistically isolated from the rest of the nation, posed special problems for a developing country. He was convinced that this group could not be ignored or relegated to second-class status. Most importantly, as I observed in my general survey of these themes, his adherence to social Darwinism did not lead him to accept the then widely held, essentially racist, view that the native American was "inferior" and hence condemned by nature to live beneath the heel of "superior" or "more fit" groups (Stabb, *Quest,* 35–57). In opposition to this notion, he considered the Indian to be fully educable and the mestizo to be indeed "the dynamic factor in our history" (9:131). Perhaps Sierra's most eloquent defense of his racial views surfaced in his 1883 polemic with Francisco G. Cosmes, a journalist and *positivista* (positivist) of conservative leanings who attacked the view that obligatory education was practical in the context of Mexico's social and ethnic complexity. In refuting Cosmes, Sierra reveals his firm conviction that the "inferiority" of any group is not an innate characteristic but simply a matter of inferior education: "given equality of circumstances, of two individuals or two groups of people, the one that is less educated is inferior" (8:110). Sierra, in explaining his views that the Indian is educable and that society may be thus modified and shaped by human effort, demonstrates a remarkably critical attitude toward the doctrinaire social evolutionists, many of whom held essentially racist views. If it is recalled that the reaction against orthodox positivism in favor of more idealistic, less mechanistic views of humanity and society has been considered typical of twentieth-century thought in Mexico, the historical significance of Sierra's attitude assumes major proportions:

> There is a school of thought . . . that, carrying to extremes the consequences of the sociological premises set forth by the most distinguished thinker of our time, Herbert Spencer, believes that laws, to be truly considered as such, should be held applicable to the needs of society from the very moment in which they appear; that the social state being the result of physical, biological, and sociological factors, which operate inevitably, as everything in nature, the efforts of the legislator are in vain, and with or without them, social phenomena will follow their inescapable course. This theory of systematic inactivity strikes me as contrary to the dignity of our species, to historical truth, and to science itself. (8:111–112)

On balance Sierra demonstrates intellectual breadth and vision that clearly transcend the limitations of his times. His intelligent rather than blindly mechanistic understanding of evolution, his preoccupation with the total development of the Mexican nation, his recognition of the Indian's worth, and his appreciation of the country's essentially mestizo culture all prefigure a twentieth-century outlook. It is not surprising that the historian Henry Schmidt should say of Sierra's work that "this conceptualization of Mexican experience as an evolutionary process would underlie the preoccupation with national identity in the twentieth century and characterize a substantial movement in the history of ideas" (45).

Sierra's death in 1912 coincides with the dramatic political and cultural reorientation of the nation set into motion by the revolution of 1910–1917. We have already noted, and Sierra's work bears this out, that even in its heyday positivist thinking was questioned. By 1910, however, Mexican followers of Comte, Darwin, and Spencer were in full retreat: younger intellectuals— writers born in the early eighties—were discovering new mentors among European thinkers seeking more vitalistic, metaphysical, and spiritual explanations of humanity and society. This group of youthful Mexican writers, known as the Ateneo de la Juventud, includes several major essayists: José Vasconcelos (1881–1959), Antonio Caso (1883–1940), and Alfonso Reyes. It would be difficult to characterize either the basic tenets or the overriding spirit of the Ateneo in a few lines. However, on the philosophical level these writers were striving to give humanity a chance to live as free agent, to act creatively and disinterestedly. They sought to refute the idea that human beings were simply cogs in a machine, that freedom was an illusion, and that creativity could always be explained away by showing preexisting determinants. Their antipositivistic attitudes are reflected not only in their essays but also in their devotion to specific tasks facing the nation. The young men of the Ateneo were active in establishing a broadly humanistic curriculum at the new National University and in the outreach activities of the experimental University of the People, the Universidad Popular Mexicana. In short, they became the leading spokesmen of the nation's new spirit, rekindled enthusiasm, and reborn humanistic faith.

The oldest of the three, José Vasconcelos, is an ambiguous figure for many contemporary Mexicans. After several years' activity as one of the leading Ateneo essayists, Vasconcelos performed impressively as minister of education during the cultural renaissance of the twenties. More than any other single individual he was responsible for reorienting Mexican culture in the direction of nativist values and toward an appreciation of the nation's importance as part of mestizo America. He took an active role in reorganizing the National University, even to the point of creating its motto. In his attractively titled essays, *La raza cósmica* (The Cosmic Race; 1925) and *Indología* (Indology; 1926), he presents arguments for racial mixing based upon aesthetics and his own somewhat idiosyncratic understanding of the anthropology of the times. While these rambling, broadly focused works have appealed to many, students of intellectual history will find that his most rigorous work was that produced during the early years of the Ateneo. Thus his essay of 1910, "Don Gabino Barreda y las ideas contemporáneas" (Gabino Barreda and Contemporary Ideas), is one of the best presentations of the group's intellectual position. In it, he draws heavily on the metaphysics of Schopenhauer and the vitalism of Bergson. He was especially fascinated by the latter's concept of the "life force," which he interprets as the "distinterested act" par excellence, since it "is only produced in violation of all 'laws of the material realm" (1:49). Vasconcelos's early interest in this theme bore rich fruit in the work of his colleague, Antonio Caso, perhaps the most impressive philosophical mind of the group. A man of mystical faith in the common people, a devoted nationalist, a dedicated proponent of popular culture (his sponsorship of the celebrated Mexican muralists attests to this), and undeniably one of the great figures of the postrevolutionary decade, Vasconcelos's image has nonetheless been somewhat diminished because of his personal ambition and unbridled ego and because, in certain later works, his latent conservative, antirevolutionary thinking comes to the fore.

Caso's essay *La existencia como economía, como desinterés y como caridad* (Existence as Economics, as Disinterest, and as Charity; 1919) is one of the clearest expressions of the Ateneo's rejection of positivism and espousal of a new sensibility. Though published in 1919, it grew out of Caso's 1915 lectures at the Universidad Popular Mexicana, an institution which virtually owed its existence to the efforts of the Ateneo group. Caso frames his essay on the basis of two opposing concepts of life. The first of these, life in the "economic" sense, may be described by the phrase "the maximum benefit with the minimum effort." The second concept, life as "sacrifice," as "disinterest," or as "charity," is described as "the maximum effort with the minimum benefit" (134). Human existence, when viewed from the standpoint of the "economic" concept, remains irretrievably enmeshed in the determinism of natural forces. Man, as a producer and consumer of goods, is simply another natural object, simply a "thing" in a material world. The human will, however, may liberate man from the realm of material necessity. Caso implies that the will, ego, or humanized life-force, call it what we wish, can pursue *either* self-interested (i.e., "economic") ends, or certain completely "irrational," not self-interested, and even undirected ends. We have already noted that in the pursuit of "economic" ends, the will functions merely as an instrument of economic forces, and hence man remains simply another determined object in nature. When, however, the will—or the formalizing force, as Caso occasionally terms it— pursues that which is "disinterested," man assumes his distinctive, free, human character. In short, it is not simply man's will that liberates him, but his will directed toward acts of disinterest, charity, and love. Caso's attitude is consistent with this viewpoint. He acknowledges a great debt to Schopenhauer for having pointed out the "disinterested" and liberating nature of art and similar activities, but he rejects the Nietzschean concept of will with its accompanying moral code. Caso objects particularly to the equation of the "lamb morality"—the code of the weakling—with Christianity. He points out that sacrifice and charity require great strength of character and a kind of nobility that surpasses the "lion morality" of which Nietzsche was so fond (155–156). Though much of what Caso wrote in *La existencia* had been written before this essay, he writes with a warmth and conviction found neither in his own earlier works nor in those of his compatriots. Perhaps the conditions under which it was produced, conditions of strife and chaos that must have brought acts of self-interest and disinterest into dramatically sharp focus, influenced the essay's general tone.

Though Alfonso Reyes, one of the youngest members of the Ateneo, left Mexico for Europe during the revolution, his contribution to Mexican letters has probably been greater than that of any of his colleagues. Humanist, critic, scholar, and creative writer, Reyes's name is synonymous with the essay not only in Mexico but throughout Latin America. Given his prolific and varied essayistic production, it is somewhat difficult to choose a few representative texts. We begin, however, with one of his earlier pieces, the beautifully wrought "Visión de Anáhuac" (Vision of Anáhuac; 1917), an essay in which the young Reyes combines his love of history, his passion for Mexico, and his sensitivity toward nature. He states at the outset that while certain areas of the New World (the jungles, for example) may inspire "romantic" reactions to nature, the Mexican plateau is characterized by "sparse and stylized vegetation, an organized landscape, an atmosphere of extreme clarity" (2:16). In short, he finds a distinctly "classic" spirit pervading the countryside of his beloved Anáhuac. Although it would be misleading to consider Reyes a believer in rigid geographic determinism, the very antithesis of the classically humanist view of nature, he often speaks of man's "continuous reference to the natural ambience." Thus, in the "Visión de Anáhuac" he suggests that there is a real link, disregarding all questions of blood, between the Mexican of today and the pre-Columbian Indian. This link exists since both peoples had the same natural environment with which to contend and since "the everyday emotion produced by the same natural object" engenders a common spirit (2:34). Somewhat similar concerns dominate his "Discurso por Virgilio" (A Speech in Honor of Virgil; 1933). While this essay's title might suggest that it deals primarily with the celebrated Roman poet, it really reflects Reyes's attempt to define New World culture and especially the essence of his *mexicanidad*. True to his classical leanings, Reyes begins this essay by pointing out that humanity's social and individual nature shows a remarkable constancy across vast realms of time and space. Thus, he can relate a plan of the Mexican government to develop local viniculture and cottage industries with similar motifs in Virgil's *Georgics*. It is in this essay on the Virgilian theme that Reyes expresses his own broad Americanist faith, born of a profound love for classical literature and for his native Mexico.

The great literary works of the western European tradition, and especially those of Greece and Rome, are not "foreign" or "exotic" to the American scene, he tells us. Properly associated, they are means by which our own indigenous world can be better revealed (11:160). In the context of Mexico's vigorous but often superficial indigenism of the 1920s, Reyes's comments on the relationship between nativism and Old World culture were extremely timely. First of all, he wisely observed that what is genuinely autochthonous will manifest itself in the work of a writer, painter, or thinker of its own accord. Since *lo autóctono* is part of the very makeup of the person, one need not be deliberately "nativist": "this instinctive tendency [nativism] is so evident that to defend it with sophisms is to deprive it of its greatest virtue: its spontaneity" (11:161). He then warns his compatriots not to deceive themselves, for although "the autochthonous element [is] in our America an enormous lode of raw material, of artifacts, of forms, of colors, and sounds" (11:161), only the barest fragments of the world of the pre-Columbian is known today. He stoutly maintains, moreover, that "until now the only waters that have bathed us are. . . . Latin waters" (11:161).

Though Reyes does not carry his metaphor any further, it is not unreasonable to view these "Latin waters" as the agent by which the gold of the autochthonous mineral is revealed in all its purity, washed clean of its dross. Reyes's view of what he calls "the hour of America" is decidedly ecumenical: he frequently states that the mission of the New World is to overcome the divisive effects of racism and of cultural jingoism. Support for such a program may be found, he notes, in Vasconcelos's vision of an amalgamated "cosmic race" and in Waldo Frank's deep humanistic faith (11:172). Variations on these same themes may be found in several other equally impressive essays of Reyes, notably in the "Notas sobre la inteligencia americana" (Notes on the American Intelligence; 1937) and "Posición de América" (The Position of America; 1942).

Critics have noted that Reyes's interest in broad issues of *americanismo* tended to subsume his dedication to *mexicanidad*. This question may be debatable; however, there is little doubt that Samuel Ramos (1897–1957), considered one of the "children of the Ateneo," focused his work squarely on the themes of Mexican character and identity. Indeed his essay of 1934, the *Perfil del hombre y la cultura en México* (*Profile of Man and Culture in Mexico*) has become, in Henry Schmidt's words, a "classic interpretation of the national behavior," and its author "the first modern student of *lo mexicano*" (140). Ramos was also a philosophical essayist of considerable talent: his early debates with Caso and his impressive essay on Marxist humanism, *Hacia un nuevo humanismo: Programa de una antropología filosófica* (Toward a New Humanism: A Program of Philosophical Anthropology; 1940), attest his power as a thinker.

The *Perfil* takes as its point of departure an essentially psychoanalytic frame of reference: "Modern psychological doctrines teach us that it is not possible to define the personality of an individual if we do not know about certain childhood experiences. . . . Thus we must go back to the beginnings of our history" (*Perfil,* 30). The basic fact of Mexico's birth, and here Ramos reiterates the ideas of both Alfonso Reyes and Waldo Frank, is that Mexicans were "invited to civilization's banquet when the table had already been served." Ramos feels that this situation, together with the overwhelming effect of nature in the New World, produced in the early Mexican a sense of being "lost," of being swallowed up in an alien world. These feelings led, in turn, to a sense of inferiority. The other participant in the national birth trauma, the Indian, also receives much attention. Ramos does not accept the notion that the Indian's passivity, or what he interprets as "rigidity," is simply the result of the treatment given him by the conqueror. Rather, he argues that this characteristic was apparent in the pre-Columbian Indian. Ramos denies any inferiority in the Indian, but he does hold to a notion of fixed native "differentness" which, "as if by magic," has spread to all Mexicans (40–41). This "rigidity," working in conjunction with the inferiority complex, makes the modern Mexican fundamentally inflexible and highly resistant to any demand that he alter his nature. However, and this point has provided much leavening for later studies of *mexicanidad,* the Mexican will adopt "masks" that produce a superficial change in his character while preserving his unalterable "spiritual bedrock" (39). This bedrock, the Mexican's sense of inferiority, is the ultimate term in Ramos's analysis, although it is never accepted as anything more real than a psychological complex. Ramos concludes the opening chapter of *Perfil* by noting a number of the specific masks that the Mexican has adopted: vanity, braggadocio, exaggerated individualism, and the like.

After a short discussion of "French Influence in the Nineteenth Century," a theme related to his thesis only in that the slavish imitation of European culture may be thought of as another typical mask, Ramos further develops the

main lines of his argument. Following the psychoanalytic method, he observes
that only by facing the truth, by airing the trauma that has produced the given
complex, can it be understood and thus removed. He makes clear his debt to
Adler, claiming that "what is proposed for the first time in this essay is the
methodical utilization of this old observation, but rigorously applying the
psychological theories of Adler to the Mexican case" (67). Ramos's study of
the Mexican is centered upon the *pelado*—the poor, lower-class, uneducated
male. He calls the *pelado* "an explosive being" whose "explosions" are usually
verbal. The *pelado* will typically resort to strong language and especially to a
rich vocabulary of phallic terms to express his violent nature. He is touchy,
defensive, and exhibits a marked lack of confidence in his dealings with others. All of this, as one might expect, is viewed as a mask for his deep-seated
sense of inferiority. In his attempt to play the *valiente* (tough guy), the Mexican will indulge in blatant patriotism and in the cultivation of a national mythology based on power and *hombría* (manliness). Moreover, he will deceive
himself into accepting the reality of the false image that he has created (85).
The poor *pelados* are not the only victims of this self-deception; Ramos argues
that even the more sophisticated bourgeoisie has been contaminated. They too
have accepted "archetypes as stimulants to overcome the problems and difficulties of life" (89).

The final chapters of Ramos's essay are concerned directly with the Mexican
as an individual. Echoing one of his favorite mentors, Max Scheler, he states
that "the ultimate objective of human activity [or "spiritual activity," to use
the Schelerian term] is not the production of culture, but rather the development of personality" (155). Above all, he calls for an attitude of individual
sincerity, of honesty: Mexicans must "have the courage to be themselves."
Ramos repeatedly makes the point that the national culture be understood as
"universal culture made ours" and that the only way to achieve this synthesis
is to recognize that which is essentially Mexican. For example, the artist who
wishes to achieve universality in his work must search his being for his "most
individual notes." When they are finally discovered, "in that very instant his
work will acquire universal transcendence" (157–158). The fact that Ramos
set forth these thoughts on *mexicanidad* as early as 1934 is as significant as the
ideas themselves. No studies of *mexicanidad* comparable in scope or penetration to the *Perfil* appeared until the late forties and early fifties, when an important group of writers picked up the threads of Ramos's work.

The leading figure in this group by any standards and certainly from the
perspective of the present study was Octavio Paz (1914–), an intense young
poet who had begun experimenting with expository prose early in the thirties.
During that decade he produced a number of curious pieces that were published in the ephemeral reviews *Barandal, Taller, Ruta,* and later in *El Hijo
Pródigo.* These writings defy precise literary classification and provide an insight into the genesis of many of the fundamental attitudes that were later
expanded in his major essays. Titled "Vigilias: Fragmentos del diario de un
soñador" (Vigils: Fragments from a Dreamer's Diary), they explore several

themes: man's existence in a fundamentally alien world, the redemptive function of Eros, and the rationalistic view of the world versus the irrational. Specific concern for *lo mexicano* is absent in his work of this period. Yet Paz did not escape to the ivory tower: his political position was often expressed in writing as well as in deed. What must be stressed is that this aspect of Paz's thought as well as certain aspects of his quest for *mexicanidad* are derived from his worldview and particularly from the role accorded therein to poetry.

In these early texts Paz frequently examines the realm of the erotic, which like poetic experience involves disinterested, "nonproductive," irrational activities and could never be accommodated to the values of bourgeois-capitalist society. The conviction that either this society must reject them or that they must be distorted to suit the demands of the "establishment" is implicit in much of Paz's work. And since the cultivation of *lo poético* (the poetic) and *lo erótico* (the erotic) are indispensable for the realization of that which is essentially human, it follows that the achievement of this ultimate objective is profoundly frustrated in the contemporary Western world. Given this rejection of things as they are, what positive positions are open to a thinker such as Paz? Clearly he must be a revolutionary, and, at least during much of the thirties, Paz did embrace the Third International. Later he abandoned orthodox communism for the less rigid but more radical camp of the surrealists.

Paz confesses at the outset of *El laberinto de la soledad* (*The Labyrinth of Solitude*) that for many years the concern for defining the uniqueness of *lo mexicano* appeared to him to be "superfluous and dangerous" (*Laberinto*, 10). It was his opinion that a creative work, be it literary or graphic, could do more to define the Mexican essence than any direct attempt to describe it. Paz conceived of *Laberinto* while on a trip to the United States. Although it would be unfair to maintain that the essay is merely a justification of Mexicanism produced under the pressure of the antithetical Yankee ethos, it is well to remember that relations between the Mexican Americans in the Southwest and the non-Latin population of the area were quite strained in the late forties. Indeed, Paz's interest in discovering what it was about the pachuco that made him an immiscible element in the North American melting pot provides the point of departure for the entire book.[5] It was this curious experience of noting the vaguely defined *mexicanidad* that seemed to "float in the air" of Los Angeles that led Paz to ask "the same questions that Samuel Ramos asked himself in the *Perfil*" (12).

The first chapter of *Laberinto* deals specifically with the character of the pachuco; although Paz sympathizes with him, he states that he is not interested in the pachuco per se. The reason for studying him, Paz claims, is that he represents one possible extreme of Mexicanism: an extreme that is very revealing since the pachuco when persecuted (presumably by the police or by belligerent North American street gangs) "achieves his authenticity, his true being, the supreme nakedness of a pariah, of a man who belongs nowhere" (16). Two propositions underlie this analysis. In the first place, although the pachuco's radical isolation—his solitude—is to a degree explicable in terms of his environment, Paz always considers solitude as a basic condition of man or, better stated, as one term in a dialectical view of human existence. Secondly, he posits this dialectic of "solitude-communion" as a universal process by which the individual not only becomes aware of his genuine essence, but actually creates this essence. In Paz's essay, solitude (perhaps the English word *aloneness* translates *soledad* better) occupies a position somewhat analogous to "inferiority" in Ramos's earlier work. Man in general, and the Mexican in particular, is not necessarily aware of this solitude and even less aware of the need for communion, for resolving the imperfection of aloneness into the state of wholeness or health characteristic of communion.

When Paz shifts his attention from the pachuco to the ordinary Mexican, as he does early in the *Laberinto*, he analyzes first the deliberate techniques employed by the Mexican male to obscure his sense of "solitude-sin." Paz then studies the inadvertent indications of genuine *mexicanidad* that crop up in language, customs, and folklore. A listing of the subterfuges that the Mexican uses to hide his radical aloneness (and his concomitant feelings of insufficiency, vulnerability, and so forth) provide a rich description of the national character. The Mexican tries to defend his intimacy by being *ensimismado,* or self-contained, or he cultivates a code of not "opening himself up," of not allowing the exterior world to penetrate his intimate being. He who permits this penetration is looked upon as something less than a man. The Mexican's attitudes toward women and his sexual mores are consistent with this fear of being vulnerable, of being "open to attack." Hence the "openness" of the female must be viewed as a defect, as an imperfection if not an evil. The Mexican further protects himself by a complex system of formalities and "courtesies," and his tendency to lie is more a self-deception than a deception of others (26–38). Perhaps most important, he is a "dissimulator," one whose mimetic talents are of such an order that he loses his own identity completely in his desire to blend into his surroundings (38). He becomes, to use Paz's ingenious figure, Mr. Nobody (*Ninguno*), a being so unidentifiable that he even treats himself "as a nobody." So general is this Mexican trait of self-negation that there is a strange pall of nothingness over the land: "stronger than our pyramids and sacrifices, than our churches, our popular songs and uprisings, a silence older than history again reigns in our land" (41).

Paz's discussion of the inadvertent indicators of Mexican character is equally interesting. In the third chapter of the *Laberinto* the national love for the fiesta is discussed as a ritual during which "the Mexican does not amuse himself: he wishes to transcend himself, to scale the wall of solitude that isolates him during the rest of the year" (44). The term "ritual" as applied to the fiesta is not to be taken lightly. Paz is well acquainted with contemporary theories regarding the nature of myth and the function of ritual. This is seen in his knowledgeable citation of writers like Malinowski and Frazer, as well as in his approach to the specific nature of the Mexican fiesta: "Everything takes place in a magic world: time is *other time* (situated in a mythic past or in pure presentness); the space in which it takes place changes in nature, it becomes detached from the rest of the Earth, it is bedecked and converted into a 'festival place' " (45). The analysis of the fiesta as ritual helps illuminate Paz's conception of being and existence. The individual Mexican who "scales the wall" of his aloneness and enters into the fiesta's communion is, as Paz puts it, returning "to a remote and undifferentiated, prenatal, or presocial state, so to speak" (46). There is a fascinating vagueness about the phrase "so to speak" (*por decirlo así*) in this context. Is Paz speaking metaphorically, or does he hold to the view that there is or was another world existing parallel to the "real world"? Certainly this is the same realm to which poetry leads us: the atemporal state of wholeness, of primordial being where such terms as *the one* and *the all* seem to lose all meaning. Perhaps Paz should not be pressed into answering such questions, for even when he is writing prose he is a poet at heart, and his work is grounded upon a fundamentally poetic vision of the world.

Paz's ability to probe the smallest details of Mexican life and to extract from them insights into the national character is very well demonstrated in his analysis of the *mala palabra*—the strong language of insult, curse, and invective. It will be recalled that others have found this kind of linguistic psychology rewarding: in Mexico, Paz's direct predecessor was Samuel Ramos, who in his *Perfil del hombre* analyzed the inferiority complex of the *pelado* on the basis of his compensatory use of phallic terms. For Paz, however, obscene words are more than simple psychological mechanisms. They comprise the "only living language in a world of anemic words—poetry within the reach of everybody" (67). And most important, these words "confusedly reflect our interior nature" (67). Paz frequently refers to the obscene as a "social language," as a set of terms imbued with ritualistic magic.

The specific word that he analyzes, in all its Mexican shadings and variants, is the verb *chingar* (to fuck, to violate). Why should this particular term be so valuable a key to *lo mexicano*? The answer is found in the fact that, aside from its literal meaning, the basic relationship denoted by the word is one of violence, of "forcible penetration into another" (69). Although the verb is always "tinged with sexuality" its significance goes beyond the merely erotic—"it stands for the triumph of closedness of the male, of him who is strong, contrasted with that which is open (and vulnerable)" (71). Paz argues that the relationship implied by the verb defines much of the Mexican's social environment—a world of "the strong and the weak," of *chingones* and *chingados* (the screwers and those who get screwed).

Paz then shifts his attention to history in an attempt to analyze the traditional Mexican battle cry, "¡Viva México, hijos de la Chingada!" ("Long live Mexico, sons of the violated woman!"—to put it delicately). Inquiring into the identity of La Chingada, Paz notes that she is, above all else, a mother—or, more precisely, an archetypal figure of the mother. Moreover, as the "violated mother" she represents the Indian woman of the conquest, the Malinche, the mistress of Cortés. It follows that the Mexican is the product of an illegitimate union and, as such, is fatherless and disinherited. In this sense La Chingada is "the mother of orphans" (71). To sum up, the "aloneness" of the Mexican has a historical dimension: as the product of the casual union of the conquistadors and the violated Indian woman, he is in a sense an orphan; his "accidental" birth has placed him in a fundamentally hostile world wherein he has been forced to live defensively, circumscribed by a complex armor of mask and dissimulation.

Paz's presentation of Mexican history, which occupies several chapters in the *Laberinto*, is organized in terms of this same myth. For example, the Reforma of 1857 is viewed as the definitive "rupture" with the mother, similar to the manner in which the adolescent breaks away from home and family. Perhaps the best example of Paz's dialectical application of myth is seen in his discussion of the Revolution of 1910–1917.

> The Revolution is a search for ourselves and a return to the mother. And thus it is also a fiesta . . . an excess and a waste . . . an orphan's lament and a cry of jubilation, of suicide and of life, all intermixed . . . it is the other Face of Mexico . . . the brutal and resplendent face of the fiesta and death. . . . It is a burst of reality: a revolt and a communion. . . . And with whom does Mexico join in communion in this bloody fiesta? With herself, with her own being. Mexico dares to be. The revolutionary explosion is a portentious festival in which the Mexican, drunk with himself, meets at long last in mortal embrace the other Mexican. (79–80)

The closing chapters of the *Laberinto* deal with problems that recur frequently in any discussion of national essence: how may the specific expression of a country's experience—whether literary, political, artistic, or philosophical—be universal and yet genuinely "native?" Is there any meaning in such terms as *Mexican art, Mexican essence,* and *Mexican philosophy?* Paz answers these questions in several ways. He argues that to look for distinctive philosophy in Mexico would be fruitless, for the modes of thought employed by Mexicans have clearly been eclectic and copied from Europe (133–134). But he qualifies this view when he notes that the contemporary world is one in which the ideological fount of the Western world has become exhausted. This puts Mexico, and many countries like it, in an unprecedented position: "For the first time Mexico does not have available a set of universal ideas to explain our circumstances. Europe, that storehouse of ready-made ideas, now lives as we do: in the present. Strictly speaking, the modern world no longer has any ideas. For this reason the Mexican, like all men, finds himself facing reality alone" (151). Thus, the Mexican must and will discover a genuine universality rather than merely copy European viewpoints. There may, of course, be a certain local flavor or style in Mexican philosophy, but this, like so many other external trappings, will eventually disappear: "*Mexicanidad* will be a mask which when it falls off will at last reveal (only) man. . . . Mexican philosophy . . . will simply and plainly be philosophy" (153). Paz sums up this point very neatly when he adds, shortly afterwards, "Our labyrinth is that of all men."

In words of eloquent sincerity Paz expresses the wish that the Mexican's quest for essence will resolve itself positively in the creation of "a world in which neither deceit, bad faith, pretense, greed, violence, nor subterfuge hold sway. A society that will not make of man an instrument. . . . A human society" (173). Finally the Mexican and certainly all men must have faith: faith that when all masks are shed, when all subterfuges are abandoned, when he is alone and naked he will find that "out there, in the open solitude, the hands of others who are alone are awaiting us" (174).

Paz's leading position as Mexico's foremost essayist during the fifties, sixties, and beyond should not disguise the fact that a host of talented writers also cultivated the genre during these years. Leopoldo Zea (1912–), though more an historian of ideas than a literary essayist, produced several important texts such as *América en la conciencia de Europa* (America in the European Conscience; 1955), and Abelardo Villegas (1934–), another essayist of a philosophical bent, wrote a number of fine essays including the *Filosofía de lo mexicano* (The Philosophy of Mexican Essence; 1960), while such writers as the historian Daniel Cosío Villegas (1898–1976), the journalist Francisco Benítez (1912–), and young followers of Paz like Jorge Carrión (1925–) and Emilio Uranga (1921–) all made substantial contributions to essayistic writing. Paz, nonetheless, must be considered the genre's dominant voice during this period: the quality of his rich prose, the breadth of his interests, and the sheer quantity of provocative essays he produced all support this assessment.[6] Among the emerging writers (people born in the late twenties and the thirties) his position as a mentor is very clear. Carlos Monsiváis (1938–), an essayist whose work we shall discuss shortly and who can be considered the central figure of this generation, wrote in 1965, "For me, and as I see it, for my generation Octavio Paz is today Mexico's most important writer and thinker. . . . The *Labyrinth of Solitude* has gained in validity with the years" ("Nuevo fracaso," iii). Similar acknowledgments of Paz's role among essayists of this generation are not difficult to find.

The privileged position enjoyed by Paz has been gradually eroded. This phenomenon may well be part of a common generational process: the brilliant ideas of yesteryear's mentor become overly familiar and well worn. Typically the iconoclasm and radical positions of the thirty-year-old grow into the conformism and cynicism of the more mature individual—or, at least, so the process is viewed by rising new writers. Thus, by the seventies a number of the younger essayists began to find Paz and his more recent political positions quite vulnerable to attack. This trend may have begun even earlier: in 1968 the philosopher and scholar Luis Villoro (1922–), writing of the younger Mexican intellectuals (not exclusively of the essayists), observed, "A characteristic symptom of the moment is the lack of concern, especially among the younger generation, for those themes that so interested my generation" (ff. 18). The themes referred to as not concerning the younger generation are those of "self-knowledge" and the "philosophy of *lo mexicano*," key issues in the writings of Paz and his *Hiperión* group of the preceding decade. Of course, this observation suggests not a strong critical attack on Paz, but simply that the concerns of one generation no longer interested another. The novelist Fuentes, writing a bit earlier, sheds further light on the question when he discusses the new "sensibility" of the sixties. The writers of the decade, he notes, may be characterized as "delving into, not the abstraction of *lo mexicano*, but rather that concrete reality of Mexicans, considered as a group or individually" (vi). What Fuentes appears to be saying here is of considerable help in understanding the emerging essayists of the period. Unlike earlier generations who, at least in retrospect, seem to have been dominated by a controlling idea such as positivism at the turn of the century, these essayists were not ideologues. Rather, they responded to concrete situations and current trends in the world of accelerated change that characterizes the second half of this century. At times, the new essayists appear to be almost flippant in defining their generational outlook: thus Monsiváis, writing in 1967 on the new generation in Mexico, will enumerate their concerns as "fashions, songs, protesting writers, neckties, dance styles" ("México 1967," iv). Of course, the early and mid-sixties were a unique period in Mexico as elsewhere: the youth movement, from Berkeley to Paris to the Pedregal was in its heyday; high fashion (the miniskirt, "swinging London," etc.) had become a worldwide cult; pop culture—especially rock music—was making unprecedented inroads on the general society, and on a somewhat more serious level, the Spanish American boom in fiction was underway.

This rather freewheeling frivolous mood of the mid-sixties was perhaps superficial and was certainly short-lived. As in Europe and North America, the new freedom claimed by the younger generation was to lead to an inevitable confrontation with the establishment: in the case of Mexico, this took the form of the Tlatelolco student massacre and its aftermath. These events and their background became central themes of the new essayists and major determinants of their generational identity. The mood of the times is best appreciated in the light of Mexican political history since the mid-century, a period that witnesses the continuing if not accelerating growth of power by the ruling PRI, the Institutional Revolutionary Party, a political force whose pervasive style has become unique in Latin America. The presence of a highly bureaucratized, manipulative regime whose "revolutionary" rhetoric often seemed hollow in the light of its specific policies and its parade of mediocre chief executives was becoming increasingly irksome to the intellectuals, especially since many of them earned their livelihood either directly or indirectly through government-funded positions.

Like the political situation, Mexico's economic environment, with its accompanying social and demographic changes, has played an important role in shaping this generation. In this regard, the central phenomenon of the sixties and seventies was *desarrollismo*—"development" in the technical sense of the social scientist. Not only have these essayists examined the concept itself, but also they have pondered the physical and social changes resulting from the developmental process. Thus, such matters as the migration of rural population to the city, the growth of peripheral slum areas, the impact of technology on humans, and issues related to ecology appear in their work. Closely related to these interests is their fascination with new lifestyles and subcultures. While the world of celebrities, the liberation of women, or the emergence of a "rock culture" are certainly not limited to one country, given the essentially traditional nature of Mexican society and institutions, it is not surprising that writers should be especially sensitive to these phenomena.

No one more than Carlos Monsiváis reflects the broad interests of this generation. A prolific writer, his books and numerous essays in periodicals deal with popular culture (cinema, comics, Mexican foibles, celebrities, popular music), high culture (especially poetry), politics, the youth movement, generational conflict, sexual revolution, technology, urbanism, and a host of related subjects. This extremely broad range of themes makes it difficult to generalize about his fundamental positions and attitudes; all the more so since his authorial tone runs the full gamut from that of a kind of literary stand-up comedian to that of the intense, angry young man. However, even in his comic mode this self-professed "mixture of Albert Camus and Ringo Starr" has much of substance to say. Perhaps the unifying themes found in his work have been the affirmation of change and of what might be termed a defense of cultural populism versus the establishment. Clearly these are the underlying motifs in his successful book-length collection *Días de guardar* (Days to Cherish; 1970). Note, for example, the chapter "Yo y mis amigos" (Me and My Friends) in which he lashes out against *el México visible* (visible Mexico), "The sum total of titles . . . honors, prizes . . . academies . . . model households . . . Rotarians, Lions . . . union leaders, ex-ministers. . . ." (*Días,* 70). His joyful recounting of the triumphs of La Onda (The Wave) during the sixties youth movement is another facet of the same theme. In this regard, representative texts would be his piece on neologisms and youth slang, "Sobre el significado de la palabra 'huato'" (On the Meaning of the Word *Huato;* 103); his comments on one of several Mexican rock concerts of the period, "Para todas las cosas hay sazón" (There Is a Season for All Things; 118–130), or his earlier overview, "México 1967," a rich analysis of the mood of the times wherein Monsiváis, still in his twenties, boldly proclaims, "The hip scene is the new spirit, the rejection of conventions and prejudices, the creation of the new morality . . . the advance of social militants . . . their longing for another Renaissance" ("México 1967," v).

Monsiváis, true to a long tradition among essayists, is quite capable of seeing both sides of the coin. Thus his positive attitude toward La Onda—the new life-styles, new perspectives, and new morality of youth—is undercut by serious doubts. Chief among these is that in the Mexican manifestation of the movement there was much false posturing, much playacting by bored middle-class kids who were simply copying another exotic fad. Not surprisingly these reservations seem more apparent in Monsiváis's writing of the seventies, after La Onda had run its course. Thus in his later book, *Amor perdido* (Love Lost;

1978), his comments on the Avándaro festival, the Mexican Woodstock of the
early seventies, are to a considerable extent negative:

> As a search for alternatives [Avándaro] is a confirmation of dependency. Avándaro
> is an autonomous and original reply, and is also a fact of colonialism, not because a
> rock festival may only be exclusively North American, but because of a basic objec-
> tion: the untroubled duplication of someone else's experience; that is, once again,
> to be up to date by virtue of servile imitation. (*Amor,* 252)

Questions of politics, demography, La Onda, and the nature of youth culture all seem to converge in the dramatic events of 1968: not only are the
specific details of Tlatelolco described by many of the essayists, but also the
reaction to the tragedy has become a defining theme of the entire generation
under discussion. What actually happened during the summer of 1968 and on
October 3 of that year is more a matter for historians than for students of
literature. Very briefly, after months of mounting tension between demonstrating secondary and university students and governmental authorities, a violent
confrontation occurred at the Plaza of Three Cultures in the Tlatelolco section of Mexico City. A substantial number of young people—the exact figure
has become a matter of heated discussion—were killed by federal troops.
While several immediate issues were involved in the confrontation, essayists
like Monsiváis and others have attempted to analyze the entire affair with a
view toward understanding its causes and assessing its long-term effects. He
has unequivocally stated that 1968 is "un año axial" (year of a turning point;
Días, 15) and that much of Mexican life during the years preceding this moment of truth was, in great measure, inauthentic: "This was the situation before July of '68: devalued years, when self-deception was the rule and forced
us to believe. Years of minimum intensity, forged by receptions, cocktail parties, laudatory notes" (*Días,* 74). Similar statements are not difficult to find
elsewhere in Monsiváis's writing. Note, for example, his comments on Mexican society and literature in a long essay published in 1973: "From the formal
point of view, the massacre of the Plaza of Three Cultures reveals that the
Mexican Revolution has died, and this is a political and cultural fact . . . thus
genuine literature has and must fulfill a function: to determine exactly the
extent of our rejection and the magnitude of our dissent . . . politically, socially, culturally, morally, etc." ("Notas," xvi).
    While the somber shadow of Tlatelolco colors the work of an entire genera-
tion of Mexican essays, the distinction of having written the most dramatic,
most widely read, and most unusual account of the event belongs to Elena
Poniatowska (1933–), journalist, critic, novelist, and if we accept a broad
definition of the genre, a major contributor to the Mexican essay. Her unique
La noche de Tlatelolco (*Massacre in Mexico;* 1971) is not easily described: an
experiment in new journalism, the book is a collage of short texts, transcriptions of posters, official pronouncements, graffiti, photographs, and most im-

portant, taped statements by victims and their families. Poniatowska herself writes only a few brief comments, yet her skillful ordering of the rich material establishes a clear authorial presence.

There are, of course, no questions regarding Poniatowska's sympathies and interpretation of the events of 1968. Like Paz, Monsiváis, and others, she decries the massacre itself while emphasizing the fact that Tlatelolco reveals the bankruptcy of the Mexican sociopolitical establishment. Thus we "hear" the voices of university students, of the armed forces, and of others. Note the comment of a family man: "If the one thing the Student Movement has accomplished is to strip the Mexican Revolution bare, to show that it was a filthy, corrupt old whore, that alone is enough to justify it" (*Noche,* 147). Statements like these abound, but what gives Poniatowska's work its unprecedented impact are the fragmentary, if anonymous, outbursts that her tape recorder and text capture. Thus the mother of a slain student cries out: "Don't spirit my son's body away the way you have all the rest! You can't do that to me! Even if he's been killed, if he's here among the dead somewhere, I want to see him!" (273). On balance *La noche de Tlatelolco* appears to be a far cry from what is usually thought of as a genuine essay. However, even though the technology of modern photography and the tape recorder play an important role in its composition, it retains basic essayistic characteristics. Poniatowska clearly wants her readers to join in her denunciation of the system that produced Tlatelolco, and despite the innovative techniques, the author's creative persona is very evident.

Before leaving the matter of Tlatelolco, we must return to Octavio Paz to consider one of his most provocative essays, *Posdata* (1970), not only because this relatively short text deals with the massacre and student movement in broad terms, but also because it illustrates Paz's declining role as an unchallenged mentor of Mexico's young intellectuals. The essay itself begins with a sympathetic analysis of the student movement, the atmosphere surrounding the 1968 summer Olympics, and the underlying tensions created by the manipulative, self-serving governmental establishment. While Paz notes the number of deaths resulting from the confrontation and the injustice of the authorities' violent overreaction to it, he refrains from highly colored descriptions of death and suffering. At the close of the first section he makes a point that serves as the keynote for the balance of the essay: "Like those neurotics who upon being confronted by new and difficult situations regress to instinctive, infantile or animalistic behavior, the government regressed to former periods of history. . . . The correlation with Mexico's past, especially the Aztec world, are fascinating, frightening and repulsive. The Tlatelolco slaughter reveals that a past that we thought buried is still alive and has erupted among us" (*Posdata,* 40). In the next chapter Paz traces the development of Mexico after the Revolution of 1910, giving special attention to the PRI's consolidation of power. These considerations lead him to examine the relationship between development in the technical sense and the current "Mexican crisis." The basic national problem, the existence of an underdeveloped marginal Mexico along with a developed relatively prosperous sector, can only be solved through what he calls a "democratic solution" (93). He expresses strong doubts regarding revolutionary solutions in areas where integrated development has not been achieved: thus he dismisses all revolutions that aim at accelerating development with the observation that they inevitably "degenerate into bureaucratic, more or less oppressive regimes" (95). He includes in this sweeping denouncement the Mexican, the Russian, and, indirectly, the Cuban revolutions. In short, it is in this essay that Paz's growing disaffection for Marxism emerges with greatest clarity.

Unquestionably this sharp critique of revolutionary praxis has not set well with many younger writers. But it is when Paz turns from the very pressing problems of modern Mexico to explore his notion of the "eruption" of the Aztec world into contemporary national life that he really arouses their intellectual ire. His interpretation of Tlatelolco, at the conclusion of *Posdata,* as a "ritual act," as a "text" that must be deciphered (114–115), was apparently too much for one of the most outspoken men of the younger generation, Jorge Aguilar Mora (1946–), who notes in his *La divina pareja* (The Divine Pair; 1978) that Tlatelolco was not a "metaphor," as Paz would have us view it, but a very real tragedy (30). The relegation of the violent events of 1968 to a mythic, timeless zone of identity with the Mexico of Aztec ritual sacrifice is for him simply another example of Paz's characteristic tendency to juxtapose "history" and "myth" and to opt for the latter. Stated somewhat differently, Aguilar Mora finds that his former mentor's recourse to myth leads him to value the aesthetic, poetic realm over historical reality. This position leads in turn to Paz's essential detachment from real events: "His entire process has consisted of this, of situating himself outside the historical storm because what disturbs him is that history is in fact a violent storm, that enunciates vital propositions that are incomprehensible and painful for someone who only wishes to metaphorize" (69). It should be noted that Aguilar Mora's critique of Paz is not limited to comments on *Posdata;* indeed Aguilar finds the same unacceptable tendencies in most of Paz's work, with the exception of his essays on poetry and aesthetics. Yet it is significant that the writings following Tlatelolco should elicit some of the sharpest attacks: clearly Paz's detachment, preoccupation with style, and distancing—elements that some feel are essential to the creation of genuinely literary essays—become suspect when violent events seem to demand authorial immediacy if not outrage. This interesting matter cannot be pursued here; raising it simply underscores the fact that 1968 is a watershed year and that the way writers reacted to its events helps define the generation under discussion.

Paz's concerns regarding *desarrollismo* have been paralleled by Monsiváis as well as by a number of other contemporary writers such as Carlos Fuentes (1928–), who must be considered an essayist of importance, his position as Mexico's leading novelist notwithstanding.[7] Space does not permit, however, a full discussion of this theme and related issues in the work of more than one essayist: Gabriel Zaid (1934–). An articulate voice among the generation to emerge in the sixties, Zaid has examined this theme along with the related issues of urbanism and demographic shifts with the freshest viewpoint and sharpest eye. A native of the bustling industrial city of Monterrey, Zaid combines the rare gifts of a poet with the hard-nosed pragmatism of an industrial engineer who has spent a good deal of his life only a few miles from the U.S. border. By comparison with his fellow essayists of more traditional origins and background, Zaid's thinking is iconoclastic, independent, and, like his birthplace, eccentric in the literal sense. His writing career begins in the mid-sixties with several contributions to major journals such as the *Revista de la Universidad de México,* two books on poetic interpretation, *La máquina de cantar* (The Singing Machine; 1967) and *Leer poesía* (Reading Poetry; 1972), followed by collaboration on important periodicals such as *Diálogos, La cultura en México, Plural,* and *Vuelta.* The charmingly titled *Cómo leer en bicicleta* (How to Read While Riding a Bicycle; 1975, 1979) and *El progreso improductivo* (Nonproductive Progress; 1978) would appear to represent his most significant essayistic work to date.

As these titles suggest, Zaid's interests are extremely broad: poetics, economics, politics, and Mexican culture are all major concerns. But it is when he brings his unique viewpoint and wry humor to bear upon such things as popular beliefs, contemporary fads, middle-class pretensions, and especially the unthinking worship of *desarrollismo* that this work is most impressive. At first glance his *El progreso improductivo* appears to be a rather technical treatise: its pages contain statistical tables, considerable economic terminology, and chapter headings that might deter all but the most devoted students of the Dismal Science. However, on closer inspection it becomes clear that we are dealing not with a typical social scientist, but rather with a spirit more akin to a Jonathan Swift or, if a contemporary comparison is needed, a George Will. Like that of his eighteenth-century soulmate, Zaid's writing is rich in "modest proposals." At one point he asks why not help the economy by taxing the traditional Mexican *mordida,* a bribe paid to a person in authority (177). In another context he wonders if the logical conclusion of much meliorist thinking should not be the elimination of all those who do not have a real chance to be wealthy: "castrate anyone who cannot demonstrate that he is a millionaire" (76). In his sly piece on "Los niños como negocio" (Children as a Business) he writes of children as "the product" and even suggests a cost analysis of reproduction among the rural poor compared with the university-educated class:

> Let us review the major cost differences that are involved in the economic production of two not-well-defined prototypes: the rural farmer and the university graduate.
>
> a) The time spent in coitus, in both cases, involves no costs, because it is not done (normally) during working hours and it is considered (normally) as a pleasure.

> But in the case of university graduates, in addition to time, there are other cost factors. Industrial expenses, such as books on lovemaking without fear, contraceptives, deodorants, perfumes, lingerie, etc. Professional services, such as psychoanalysts, orientation conferences, courses on interpersonal sensitivity, and even sessions directed by doctors and nurses in order to have better orgasms. (32)

Despite this tongue-in-cheek authorial voice, or perhaps by virtue of it, Zaid is a serious critic of his times and of his country. Though the underlying critical ideas in *El progreso improductivo* are not in themselves very unusual, in the context of contemporary Mexico bent on growth, industrialization, and modernity, they certainly provide a refreshing counterbalance to those who pursue progress for progress's sake, developmentalists who fail to recognize the nature of the Third World's basic needs, and planners who forever design increasingly complex projects. His thinking is all the more impressive since the alternatives he proposes are not typical ones. Neither a Marxist nor a reactionary nor a flower-child, Zaid combines ideas from many sources. Eclectic and pragmatic, he shuns ideology for its own sake; he espouses ideas that work, that offer a reasonable hope for social or economic improvement. Thus, at times he echoes the "small is beautiful" minimal technology of a Schumacher (133–134), while on one occasion he suggests that, instead of providing "make work" for the poor, cash be distributed among the lowest economic strata—a kind of "negative income tax" plan (92–93).

Much of Zaid's attention is directed toward the problems created by the influx of poor, uneducated campesinos into the city. Here again his thinking is quite unorthodox: while he is very much aware of the fact that modern urban bourgeoisie—especially Latin Americans—have a deep-seated disdain for rural life, though they may of course enjoy a weekend in the country or own a rustic vacation home, what he finds most disturbing are the efforts made to convert every campesino into a modern consumer of automobiles, university educations, urban housing, and so forth. As a result, the cities have become overcrowded, and the insufficient supply of jobs, housing, and educational services produces severe social problems, frustrations, ecological damage, and the growth of slums. He points out that by making country life attractive in the first place the absurd cycle of country-to-city-back-to-country, a process that might take many generations, could be obviated:

> A curious cycle of aspirations: leave the country, go to the city, have a university career, get a car and become prosperous enough to get to own a house in the country. . . . Is this the long round trip that we propose to the country people over two, three, or a thousand generations? . . . Wouldn't it be more practical and even cheaper to provide for a fully human life in the country right now? (61)

Zaid is somewhat vague in explaining what should be done to achieve this goal. However, his fondness for Vasco de Quiroga's sixteenth-century vision of a utopian society in rural Mexico perhaps hints at the nature of this ideal social order (64) as do his frequent references to "appropriate technology" for the rural masses. The notion that a relatively poor country can be modern to only a limited degree and still be happy runs through much of Zaid's thinking. Similarly, he apparently holds to the idea that not everyone can or should attempt to rise to the apex of the socioeconomic pyramid. Yet this seemingly elitist view is balanced by faith in individual effort and talent to overcome the "disadvantage" of living in less than modern circumstances. After all, he observes, "practically all the dignity, culture, and elegance that humanity has produced for thousands of years has been the work of people without cars or university degrees" (61).

Zaid frequently appears to be a voice crying in a wilderness of contemporary trendiness, impersonality, and hypocrisy. Yet he is hardly a desperate or anguished writer. As we have already seen, his distinctive tone is more often than not that of a humorist. This aspect of his work is especially obvious in *Cómo leer en bicicleta,* a collection covering over ten year's contributions to such journals as *Siempre, Plural, Vuelta,* and others. Here Zaid's targets are the radical chic, or *rábanos* (radishes, i.e., red on the outside, white on the inside) as he calls them, as well as his own kind—the literati and other intellectuals. Such pieces as "A quien corresponda" (To Whom It May Concern), an apocryphal want ad for an ideal literary critic or "Sobre la producción de elogios rimbombantes" (On the Production of Pompous Eulogies), on the need for a computerized program for the efficient production of eulogies, an item evidently in great demand among Mexican intellectuals, illustrate Zaid's wit at its best. Similarly, his sly critique of modish Marxism is perhaps best exemplified in a delicious put-down titled "De cómo vino Marx y cómo se fue" (On How Marx Came and How He Left). Zaid's work after the publication of *Cómo leer en bicicleta* reveals a similar use of poker-faced humor to jibe the Left. A good example appears in the journal *Vuelta* in a very "scientific" study, "Carta polimétrica" (A Polymetric Letter). In this piece Zaid analyzes apparently real statistics that demonstrate a direct relationship between wealth and districts registering the highest percentage of Communist votes: "Mexico is a country where radicalism increases with income. . . . To be a leftist and live in the Pedregal, have a house in Cuernavaca, travel abroad . . . is something forgiveable" ("Carta," 46–47).

In keeping with the general intent of the present volume, this survey of the Mexican essay has examined a limited number of crucial texts in some depth. Obviously the choice of one writer over another involves a degree of discretionary selection: this is especially true with regard to twentieth-century writers where no clear-cut canon obtains. Some students of Mexican letters may, for example, note the omission or only passing mention of important figures such as Salvador Novo, Francisco Benítez, Daniel Cosío Villegas, Carlos Fuentes, and Jorge Cuesta—to name just a few writers of expository prose who might well be included within the bounds of essayistic writing. The problem of choice is especially difficult with regard to very recent *ensayismo,* such as the work of such people as Enrique Krause, Hugo Hiriart, or H. Aguilar Camín which has, regretfully, been omitted. Unfortunate, too, is the exclusion of certain writers and works that illustrate what might be called the "new aesthetics" of the Mexican essay. I am thinking here of essays by such figures as Juan García Ponce and Salvador Elizondo and of several of Octavio Paz's more experimental texts. An adequate treatment of this kind would lie beyond the stated bounds of this study and would require many more pages than are at my disposal.

Similarly, the matter of thematic focus may raise some questions. Given the wide range of writing that the term *ensayismo* can cover, readers may be struck by the fact that I have excluded from this study essays of literary criticism, philosophic meditation, or of what has been called the "essay of fantasy, wit, or ramblings." While I have not attempted to define my thematic boundaries narrowly, in retrospect it is apparent that my emphasis has been on social comment, cultural interpretation, and above all on the question of *lo mexicano*. Indeed, by way of conclusion I must agree with José Luis Martínez who observed some thirty years ago, "In Mexico . . . our essayists are inclined insistently and tenaciously to explore a single question, the national reality and the national problematic, regardless of what each writer's individual perspective or field of expertise may be" (1:19). This observation, made before essayists like Monsiváis or Zaid published their work, continues to be valid.

NOTES

1. Unless otherwise indicated, all translations are my own.

2. Fernández de Lizardi's attitude must be seen in historical perspective: his early hesitancy to accept the revolution was due in part to the belief—held by many—that the Spanish king-to-be, Ferdinand VII, would uphold the liberal promises of the reformist Constitution of 1812. Regarding his position, see "Sobre la exaltación de la nación española y el abatimiento del antiguo despotismo" (On the Praise of the Spanish Nation and the Destruction of the Old Despotism; 3:47–52).

3. There is an abundant bibliography on Mexican positivism. See especially Leopoldo Zea and, for a somewhat different "revisionist" view, William D. Raat.

4. Regarding Sierra's position on the limitations of science and positivism, see Raat, 73, and Yáñez, *Justo Sierra,* 174–176.

5. The term *pachuco,* of uncertain origin, was common in the Southwest, especially California, in the period following World War II. It denoted a Mexican American juvenile gang member—a kind of latino "zoot-suiter." The term seems to have disappeared in recent decades.

6. A partial listing of Paz's major essays would include, in addition to the works discussed here, the following: *El arco y la lira* (1956), *Las peras del olmo* (1957), *Cuadrivio* (1965), *Claude Lévi-Strauss, o El nuevo festín de Esopo* (1967), *Corriente alterna* (1967), *Conjunciones y disyunciones* (1969), *Los signos en rotación* (1971), and *Los hijos del limo: Del romanticismo a la vanguardia* (1974).

7. Regarding Fuentes as an essayist, see Stabb ("New Essay," 51–52) and Reeve (2–3).

BIBLIOGRAPHY

Aguilar Mora, Jorge. *La divina pareja: Historia y mito.* Mexico City: Ediciones Era, 1978. Important critique of Paz's methodology; representative of recent thinking of younger generation.

Caso, Antonio. *La existencia como economía, como desinterés y como caridad.* Mexico City: Secretaría de Educación Pública, 1943.

Davis, Harold E. *Latin American Thought: A Historical Introduction.* Baton Rouge: Louisiana State University Press, 1972. A standard, authoritative work on all Latin America; considerable material on Mexico.

Fernández de Lizardi, José Joaquín. *Obras.* 10 vols. Mexico City: Universidad Nacional Autónoma de México, 1963–1982.

Fuentes, Carlos. "La máscara de esta década." *La Cultura en México,* January 3, 1963, i–viii.

González Ramírez, Manuel. *Ensayos de Ignacio Ramírez.* Mexico City: Universidad Nacional Autónoma de México, 1944. A short selective anthology of González Ramírez's prose. In the Universidad Nacional Autónoma de México's series "Biblioteca del estudiante universitario."

Martínez, José Luis. *El ensayo mexicano moderno.* 2 vols. Mexico City: Fondo de Cultura Económica, 1958. Standard anthology with comments by Martínez. A more recent edition has been published, and an English translation is available: *The Modern Mexican Essay,* trans. H. W. Hilborn. Toronto: University of Toronto Press, 1965.

Monsiváis, Carlos. *Amor perdido.* Mexico City: Ediciones Era, 1978.

———. "Con un nuevo fracaso Carlos Monsiváis ayuda resquebrajar la máscara funeraria del mexicano." *La Cultura en México,* December 29, 1965, ii–xvii.

———. *Días de guardar.* Mexico City: Ediciones Era, 1970.

———. "México: Notas sobre literatura y sociedad." *La Cultura en México,* January 17, 1973, ix–xvi.

———. "México 1967." *La Cultura en México,* January 17, 1968, iv.

Paz, Octavio. *El arco y la lira.* Mexico City: Fondo de Cultura Económica, 1956.

———. *Claude Lévi-Strauss, o El nuevo festín de Esopo.* Mexico City: Editorial Joaquín Mortiz, 1967.

———. *Conjunciones y disyunciones.* Mexico City: Editorial Joaquín Mortiz, 1969.

———. *Corriente alterna.* Mexico City: Siglo XXI Editores, 1967.

———. *Los hijos del limo: Del romanticismo a la vanguardia.* Barcelona: Seix Barral, 1974.

———. *El laberinto de la soledad.* 2d ed. Mexico City: Fondo de Cultura Económica, 1959. An English translation is available: *The Labyrinth of Solitude,* trans. Lysander Kemp. New York: Grove Press, 1961.

———. *Las peras del olmo.* Mexico City: Imprenta Universitaria, 1957.

———. *Posdata.* Mexico City: Siglo XXI, 1970. An English translation is available: *The Other Mexico: Critique of the Pyramid,* trans. Lysander Kemp. New York: Grove Press, 1972.

———. *Los signos en rotación.* Buenos Aires: Sur, 1965.

Poniatowska, Elena. *La noche de Tlatelolco.* Mexico City: Ediciones Era, 1971. English translation: *Massacre in Mexico,* trans. Helen R. Lane. New York: Viking Press, 1975.

Raat, William D. *El positivismo durante el porfiriato.* Mexico City: SepSetentas, 1975. Penetrating study of positivism as seen in work of many major and minor Mexican writers of 1877–1910. Raat frequently takes issue with Zea on matters of interpretation.

Ramírez, Ignacio. *Obras completas de Ignacio Ramírez.* 2 vols. Mexico City: Editorial Nacional, 1952.

Ramos, Samuel. *Hacia un nuevo humanismo: Programa de una antropología filosófica.* Mexico City: Casa de España, 1940.

————. *El perfil del hombre y la cultura en México.* Mexico City: Imprenta Mundial, 1934. An English translation is available: *Profile of Man and Culture in Mexico,* trans. Peter G. Earle. Austin: University of Texas Press, 1962.

Reeve, Richard. "Carlos Fuentes como ensayista." *Revista de la Universidad de México* 24.5–6 (January–February 1970): 2–3. Short article in which author expresses belief that Fuentes will be remembered as Mexico's leading essayist of the mid-century.

Reyes, Alfonso. *Obras completas de Alfonso Reyes.* 19 vols. Mexico City: Fondo de Cultura Económica, 1955–1968. An English translation of several representative essays is available: *The Position of America and Other Essays,* ed. and trans. Harriet de Onís. New York: Knopf, 1950.

Schmidt, Henry C. *The Roots of Lo Mexicano: Self and Society in Mexican Thought, 1900–1934.* College Station: Texas A & M University Press, 1978. Important study of theme of *lo mexicano* in period leading up to and including Ramos; essential for understanding the latter.

Sierra, Justo. *Obras completas del maestro Justo Sierra.* Ed. Agustín Yáñez. 14 vols. Mexico City: Universidad Nacional Autónoma de México, 1948. A more recent edition was published by the Universidad Nacional Autónoma de México in 1984.

Stabb, Martin S. *In Quest of Identity: Patterns in the Spanish American Essay of Ideas, 1890–1960.* Chapel Hill: University of North Carolina Press, 1967. General study of subject in period indicated. Chapter 7 (182–217) deals specifically with Mexico.

————. "The New Essay of Mexico: Text and Context." *Hispania* 70 (March 1987): 47–61. Survey of the Mexican essay from 1960 to 1980. Includes discussion of several contemporaries of Zaid and Monsiváis.

Vasconcelos, José. *Obras completas.* 3 vols. Mexico City: Libreros Mexicanos Unidos, 1957.

Villegas, Abelardo. *Filosofía de lo mexicano.* Mexico City: Fondo de Cultura Económica, 1960.

Villoro, Luis. "El sentido actual de la filosofía en México." *Revista de la Universidad de México* 22.5 (January 1968), unpaginated insert ff. 18.

Yáñez, Agustín. *Don Justo Sierra: Su vida, sus ideas y su obra.* Mexico City: Universidad Nacional Autónoma de México, 1962. A well-documented analysis of Sierra's life and works.

————. *El Pensador Mexicano.* Mexico City: Universidad Nacional Autónoma de México, 1940. A standard and very valuable study of Fernández de Lizardi.

Zaid, Gabriel. "Carta polimétrica." *Vuelta* 40 (March 1980): 46–47.

————. *Cómo leer en bicicleta: Problemas de la cultura y el poder en México.* Mexico City: Editorial Joaquín Mortiz, 1975.

————. *Leer poesía.* Mexico City: Editorial Joaquín Mortiz, 1972.

————. *La máquina de cantar.* Mexico City: Editorial Joaquín Mortiz, 1967.

————. *El progreso improductivo.* Mexico City: Siglo XXI Editores, 1979.

Zea, Leopoldo. *América en la conciencia de Europa.* Mexico City: Los Presentes, 1955.

————. *Apogeo y decadencia del positivismo en México.* Mexico City: El Colegio de México, 1944. A classic work on the subject. Zea provides the point of departure for virtually any discussion of Mexican positivism.

10

Literary Theory and Criticism

DANIEL ALTAMIRANDA

I

The inventory of Mexican critics and researchers who deserve attention is extensive and permanently open to new incorporations; in this sense it is a faithful index of the cultural production of that country. However, the majority of the pertinent figures have yet to receive anything approximating adequate metacritical examination. One reason for this circumstance may be found in the prevailing attitude of Latin American critics toward criticism as an academic or intellectual undertaking. Years ago, Guillermo Sucre paused to wonder what creative order criticism belongs to, and he stated: "Criticism only lives on the works of others, although it is also true that it makes them live. It is not an autonomous (*autotelic,* Eliot would say) activity like poetry. Criticism is a creation, then, not of the same type as that of poetry, but perhaps, yes, of the same structure" (*Latin America,* 202). Even admitting this somewhat idealized possibility, critical activity has been defined as at best a parasitic practice, a motivated, secondhand, ancillary writing. In a sense, it is redundant.

Despite this constitutive trait and the fact that, in the guise of different modalities, literary criticism is as old as the world—at least the world of literature—this century has witnessed an explosion whose scope we are not completely aware of yet. We are on the verge of a new abyss; perhaps we are about to burn Alexandria again, this time to protect ourselves from texts so as to have a second opportunity at re-creation. Meanwhile, we seem to be condemned to move in an environment saturated by texts and by metatexts, so different among themselves that any order one tries to impose on them will necessarily be aleatory. Nevertheless, it will be useful to consider briefly the general development of literary studies during the twentieth century.

José Luis Martínez (1918–), Jaime Torres Bodet (1902–1974), Emmanuel Carballo (1929–), Luis Leal (1907–), José Pascual Buxó (1931–), Manuel Durán (1925–), José Emilio Pacheco (1939–), Ramón Xirau (1924–), Juan García Ponce (1932–), Xavier Villaurrutia (1903–1950), Jorge Cuesta (1903–

Note: Where no English version is available, the translations of quotes in this essay are my own.

1942), Antonio Alatorre (1922–), Ermilo Abreu Gómez (1884–1971), Arqueles Vela (1899–1977): the list of Mexican critics who deserve consideration is not complete. The aspects their works correspond to are extensive: academic criticism, aesthetic analyses, structuralist, psychological, or sociological inquiry, and so on. To avoid producing a lengthy catalog of names and titles, we will approach Mexican criticism through a small sample of only a few major names.

Located in its immediate context, Mexican literary criticism as a whole is a reduced version of the various streams of thought of the entire cultural continent that is Spanish America. It is, therefore, susceptible to the same general objections that have been raised in recent years regarding this activity. On the one hand, Spanish American criticism "has been, rather, an external criticism, impressionistic or vaguely sociological; rarely has it structured itself upon a true vision of the world or around a notion of literature as the aesthetics of language" (Sucre, 208). In most cases, critics have availed themselves of imported theoretical paradigms, and often those paradigms have been applied to literary texts in a mechanical way, without any kind of "acclimatization" (Bueno Chávez, 82).

As a consequence, one of the problematic elements of criticism seems to be its derivative nature: "Concepts of aesthetics and criticism, vigorous enough to create an independent criticism or to influence universal literary criticism, have not yet been produced in Mexico" (Jasso, "Algunos problemas," 294). The aforementioned "universal criticism" is, to be sure, a hypostasis of Western thought, of what has been called "Eurocentrism": "a literary and aesthetic thought whose 'center' of generalizations is at times European and North American art and literature, and at other times exclusively Western European ones, while at the same time reducing the rest of world arts and literatures to a 'periphery'" (Navarro, 80).

On the other hand, as Jasso has maintained, Mexican criticism did not move sufficiently forward to "establish the nature of analysis and . . . the validity of literary values in terms of how we reach them" ("Algunos problemas," 297). This is a major problem due to the nature of values and the fact that the critical techniques in use are not always reexamined.

II

Within the context of the foregoing demanding conceptualizations of Latin American criticism, the presentation of Mexican critical production leads to at least two undesirable choices. On the one hand, a scrupulous account of those who have engaged in significant critical activity would generate a lengthy catalogue of names and titles. On the other hand, the lack of metacritical studies militates against the elaboration of a dispassionate and selective coverage. This essay attempts to mediate between both extremes, offering first an overview of well-known figures and then a more detailed study of only a few principal names.

We begin with a tendency in scholarship related to the manifestations of a widely extended nationalism during the early twentieth century, a foundational movement in literary studies that produced the initial national histories and anthologies in several countries. The starting point in this regard in Mexico is undoubtedly *Poetas nuevos de México* (New Poets of Mexico; 1916), a memorable anthology compiled by Genaro Estrada (1887–1937). In 1928, Carlos González Peña (1885–1955) and Julio Jiménez Rueda (1896–1960) published two widely reprinted histories, both under the same title: *Historia de la literatura mexicana* (History of Mexican Literature). Angel María Garibay K. (1892–1967) belongs to the same generation of literary historians. A monumental two-volume *Historia de la literatura nahuatl* (History of Nahuatl Literature; 1954) is a reliable sampling of his endeavors to recover pre-Columbian cultural texts. Other forms of the same nationalist affirmation are the editions of Mexican classics prepared by Ermilo Abreu Gómez, one of the most respected commentators of the works by Sor Juana Inés de la Cruz and Juan Ruiz de Alarcón (see the section on colonial literature).

During the early decades of the century, four influential figures emerge. Xavier Villaurrutia and Jaime Torres Bodet, best known as poets, both made valuable contributions to the study of turn-of-the-century poetry produced under the aegis of *modernismo* (modernism). Luis Leal, by contrast, concentrated his activity in the area of short fiction. His *Breve historia del cuento mexicano* (A Short History of the Mexican Short Story; 1956), *Historia del cuento hispanoamericano* (A History of the Latin American Short Story; 1966), and *Breve historia de la literatura hispanoamericana* (A Short History of Latin American Literature; 1971) are only a few of the essential titles from his extensive critical output. María del Carmen Millán (1914–), the first woman to become a member of the Mexican Academy of the Language in 1975, authored another history entitled *Literatura mexicana* (Mexican Literature; 1963) and an extremely useful *Antología de cuentos mexicanos* (An Anthology of Mexican Short Stories; 1977).

Another prominent group of Mexican scholars were not born in Mexico. Rather, as a consequence of the Spanish Civil War (1936–1939), their families sought asylum in Mexico, where these scholars completed their education. After obtaining a degree in philosophy from the National Autonomous University, Ramón Xirau (1924–) produced some notable books on poetry: *Tres poetas de la soledad* (Three Poets of Solitude; 1955), in which he studies the works of Xavier Villaurrutia, Octavio Paz, and Carlos Gorostiza; *Poesía hispanoamericana y española* (Latin American and Spanish Poetry; 1961), a collection of essays; and *Genio y figura de Sor Juana Inés de la Cruz* (Genius and Figure of Sor Juana Inés de la Cruz; 1968), a biobibliographical presentation of the colonial poet, with a selection of her writing. Manuel Durán is a prolific scholar whose scope of interests includes not only Spanish Golden Age writers, but also modern Spanish poetry and recent Mexican narrative as well. *El superrealismo en la poesía española contemporánea* (Surrealism in Contemporary Spanish Poetry; 1952), *La ambigüedad en el Quijote* (Ambiguity in Don

Quixote; 1960), and *Tríptico mexicano: Juan Rulfo, Carlos Fuentes, Salvador Elizondo* (Mexican Triptych; 1973) are among his best-known studies. It is worthwhile to mention here José Pascual Buxó, whose articles and monographs are built around a knowledgeable accommodation of concepts and techniques drawn from semiotics and Jakobsonian poetics, and Tomás Segovia (1927–), essayist, critic, and translator of Ungaretti and Rimbaud.

The names brought together here serve as a bridge to current trends in Mexican criticism. Although it has been possible to speak, for example, of academic criticism, aesthetic analysis, structuralist, psychological, or sociological inquiry, it is not always possible to single out leading figures. Moreover, these separate critical paths intersect. Consequently, instead of offering a premature balance sheet, we will proceed to a detailed presentation of the critical emphases of Alfonso Reyes, Octavio Paz, Carlos Fuentes, José Revueltas, and Carlos Monsiváis.

III

The common denominator of the majority of the different tendencies of modern criticism in Spanish America seems to be the postulate of the immanent meaning of the literary work. In Mexico, this principle was proposed by one of its major figures, Alfonso Reyes (1889–1959), who left his personal mark on Spanish criticism and literary theory through his vast and multifaceted works.

The initial period of Reyes's intellectual formation included his reading in his father's library in Monterrey and his studies in Mexico City, where he was a member of the Ateneo de la Juventud (Atheneum of the Young), made up of the Dominican Pedro Henríquez Ureña and the Mexicans Antonio Caso and José Vasconcelos, among others. Also as part of his main critical tasks in those years, Reyes dedicated himself to the analysis of the texts of some Mexican poets: "Los poemas rústicos de Manuel José Othón" (The Rustic Poems of Manuel José Othón) and "El paisaje en la poesía mexicana del siglo XIX" (Landscape in Nineteenth-Century Mexican Poetry). But his interests in world literature began to appear soon after in *Cuestiones estéticas* (Aesthetic Topics), published in Paris in 1911.

Two years later, Reyes arrived in France on a diplomatic mission, where he began to contribute to Raymond Foulché-Delbosc's *Revue Hispanique* while studying the works of Luis de Góngora and publishing the results of his research in some of the most important critical journals of the time (*Boletín de la Real Academia Española, Hispania* [Paris], *Revista de Filología Española*). Those articles—philological, bibliographical, historical, and critical studies—together with some unpublished notes, constituted the famous *Cuestiones gongorinas* (Topics on Góngora), a book that Reyes offered as his personal contribution to the celebration of the Generation of 1927.

In Madrid, where he spent ten years beginning in 1914, Reyes worked at the Centro de Estudios Históricos (Center for Historical Studies), whose president was the Spanish medievalist Ramón Menéndez Pidal. He engaged himself primarily in philological research dealing with the works of Diego de San Pedro, Juan Ruiz, Góngora, and other Golden Age writers like Lope de Vega, Quevedo, Gracián. He also prepared editions of Spanish classics and of the modern Mexican poet Amado Nervo. His investigations at the Centro were published later in *Capítulos de literatura española* (Chapters on Spanish Literature; 1939), *Entre libros* (Among Books; 1948), and the already mentioned *Cuestiones gongorinas* (1910). His studies on Góngora stand out among his other production of this period. In them, Reyes anticipated the directions that research on the poet would follow up to the present: determination of definite texts, analysis of poetic techniques, interpretation of difficult passages, and other related issues.

Once he completed his diplomatic career, Reyes returned to Mexico where his critical thought reached its apex. In those years he published three series of books: one related to the Hellenic and Latin culture, which includes *La crítica en la edad ateniense* (Criticism in Athenian Times; 1941), *Junta de sombras* (Meeting of Shadows; 1949), and *La filosofía helenística* (Hellenist Philosophy; 1959); another on the position and sense of Spanish America in the framework of universal culture and history (*Ultima Tule* [Farthest Thule; 1944] and *Tentativas y orientaciones* [Attempts and Orientations]); and a final one exploring basic topics on literary theory (*La experiencia literaria* [Literary Experience], *El deslinde* [Demarcation; 1944], and *Al yunque* [To the Anvil; 1960]). His theoretical contributions, primarily developed in the last series, reflect a certain subjective thinking in many aspects indebted to the aesthetics of Benedetto Croce.

La experiencia literaria, whose original version was ready for the publisher in 1941, is a series of articles in which the author considers linguistic themes and literary concepts. In the first essay, "Hermes, o De la comunicación humana" (Hermes, or Concerning Human Communication), Reyes mixes literary curiosities, historic anecdotes, and all manner of supplementary information toward reconsidering some conceptual elements like the notion of the sign, related to the Saussurian linguistic theory, and the classification of communicative phenomena. In "Marsyas, o Del tema popular" (Marsyas, or Concerning the Popular Theme), a definition of this elusive notion is given: "We will understand for our purposes that the expression 'popular theme' corresponds to all linguistic forms, whether derived or not from previous cultivated or artistic forms—all that has entered into the anonymity of people, into the undivided estate" (54). Immediately after, he lists the characteristics of this form: popularity, anonymity, traditionality, variety of versions, and brevity. The internal articulation of this essay is based on two moments. The first one, as we have seen, is devoted to establishing definitions and general considerations, which are mainly descriptive. Thus, this conceptual field has to be put aside in favor of a historical field, which will permit the critic to revitalize theory with examples (77).

One of the most interesting articles of the book is "Apolo, o De la literatura"

(Apollo, or Concerning Literature), where literature is considered part of the main activities of the spirit, together with philosophy, history, and science. "Literature has a value of significance, the semantic value, and one of linguistic expressions, the formal value. The common denominator for both values lies in the intention. The semantic intention refers to the fictitious succession of events; the formal intention refers to the aesthetic expression. Literature only exists when the two intentions fuse together" (82). As a consequence, the widely known distinction between content and form is elaborated with a new denomination: fiction and form.

Reyes's adherence to the diffuse notion of intention is the crucial point of his exposition. According to him, in terms of fiction, "the intention has not been to tell something because it actually happened, but because it is interesting in itself, no matter whether it happened or not" (83); in terms of form, "without aesthetic intention there is no literature" (83). Next, Reyes attempts to distinguish between ordinary language and aesthetic language: he notes that language in general possesses three values—grammatical (syntax and the meaning of words), phonetic (rhythm, sound), and stylistic—and that "literature is the activity of the spirit which makes the best use of these three values" (84), so that the difference lies in quality and not in quantity. This complex constitution of language is reconsidered in El deslinde: "The transformation of these notes [communicative, acoustic, and expressive] in values is the result of intention, which in turn polarizes the attention: intention of the one who produces the verbal formula and attention of the one who receives it" (233).

With respect to the reader, Reyes writes that "representation of the world, psychological implications, and verbal suggestions are different for each being, and they determine the personal essence of each man. Thus the study of the literary phenomenon is a phenomenography of the fluent being" (83 +). This literary phenomenography—in a previous version Reyes had used the word phenomenology and then decided to change it because the term evoked the philosophical ideas of Husserl—defines three functions (drama, novel, and lyrical poetry) and two modes (prose and verse), among which it is possible to find all sorts of combinations. In El deslinde, Reyes's phenomenography is identified with a literary theory that "considers the main forms in which the mind confronts postulated beings and objects: dramatic function, epic or narrative function, and lyric function, which are not to be confused with the genres they characterize, which are pure stratifications of the habits of each period" (30).

In another article from La experiencia literaria, "Aristarco, o Anatomía de la crítica" (Aristarchus, or The Anatomy of Criticism), Reyes writes that this activity is "an insolence of second degree" (104). The approach to the literary texts consists of a threefold process: impression, exegesis, and judgment. The exegetic stage allows the application of a small number of specific methods, but "only through the integration of these methods does [criticism] acquire the right to aspire to the qualification of science: first, historical methods; second, psychological methods; third, stylistic methods" (112). This methodological eclecticism, one of the constant elements in his thought, reappears many times in *El deslinde* (28, 179). Finally, Reyes conceives judgment as the culminating stage of criticism that "places the work in the balance of human acquisitions" (113).

Another interesting essay included in *La experiencia literaria* is "Las jitan-jáforas," a designation Reyes applies to certain verbal forms with little or no semantic meaning—onomatopoeias, nonsense, and tongue-twisters, which have served as the basis for a whole range of literary, mostly phonic, games— and he provides examples covering many languages and periods.

The exposition of Reyes's thought is more systematic in *El deslinde,* where he tries to establish the parameters of the literary object in contrast to the rest of theoretical objects, like the historical and the object of sciences, including mathematics and theology. But this was not the final point of Reyes's inquiry, since he continues to deal with these topics until his death, writing some articles that were published posthumously under the title *Al yunque.*

Literature conceived as an exchange between an active attitude, that of the creator, and a passive one, that of the critic, is the starting point of *El deslinde.* The passive attitude has two dimensions: one deals with particular objects covering the activities we usually recognize as criticism (impression, impressionism, exegesis, and judgment); the other considers literary phenomena in general as an organic totality (literary history, prescriptive schemata, and literary theory). According to Reyes, the first step toward literary theory is to establish a clear demarcation between literature and nonliterature. Therefore, he first admits the notion of aesthetic value as something essential and already known, and then he defines the set of conceptual instruments he will use: literature, poetry, poetics ("a craft that is applicable to all types of verbal utterances, regardless of whether they are literary or not" [38]), and semantics ("the topic alluded by the verbal or poetic expression" [38]). Subsequently, he proposes a new distinction between literature "en pureza" (in purity) and ancillary literature: "In the former case—drama, novel, or poem—the expression depletes its object in itself. In the latter case—history with rhetorical seasoning, science pleasantly presented, philosophy in a pleasant form, the sermon or religious homily—the literary expression is a vehicle for a nonliterary content and goal" (40). As a conclusion Reyes states that "literature expresses man as a human being. Nonliterature expresses man as theologian, philosopher, scientist, statesman, politician, technician, and so forth" (41).

IV

Belonging to the tradition inaugurated by Alfonso Reyes, but subscribing to a form of subjectivism in which the metaphor becomes the explanatory center of theoretical reflection, Octavio Paz (1914–) has created in his essays a universe in expansion, one that covers a whole range of areas: aesthetics, cultural anthropology, Eastern philosophy, modern poetry, politics. From this universe, we have selected a sample made up of three major works: *El arco y la lira* (*The Bow and the Lyre;* 1956, second edition 1967), *Los hijos del limo* (*Children of the Mire;* 1974), and *Sor Juana Inés de la Cruz, o Las trampas de la fe* (*Sor Juana Inés de la Cruz, or The Traps of Faith;* 1982).

Paz's concept of poetry was developed over a period of many years, beginning in 1942 when he was invited to participate in San Juan de la Cruz's Fourth Centennial. One year later, he published his view on poetry in an article, "Poesía de comunión y poesía de soledad" (Poetry of Communion and Poetry of Solitude), which contained some of the ideas he had included in *El arco y la lira,* "the best developed and most readable volume on poetic theory that Latin America has produced" (Fein, 6). In 1967, Paz presented a revised version that included as its epilogue his manifesto "Signos en rotación" (Signs in Rotation). The differences between both editions were outlined by Emir Rodríguez Monegal who showed that the time Paz spent in Asia greatly influenced his reconsideration of some basic ideas: "In the thinking and in the living experience of the East, Octavio Paz has found the key to dissolve the contradictions of Western thought: a system that allows us to accept the existence of the Other and the elimination of the I; a religion that restores the divine, and not a god, to the center of its beliefs; a conception of time as something that is cyclic and not linear" (45).

The discovery of Asia is a foundational act of Paz's conception of poetry because, for him, "Western history can be seen as the history of an error, a going astray, in both senses of the word: in losing our way in the world we have become estranged from ourselves. We have to begin again" (*The Bow,* 87). Poetry is a human experience, a scandalous contact with the essence, and the manifestations of poetry are numerous: "Poetry is polarized, assembled, and isolated in a human product: painting, song, tragedy" (4+). Therefore, the immanence of the poem is stressed because "each poetic creation is a self-sufficient unit" (6). The poetic process reproduces analogically the rhythmical processes of language: "The dynamism of language leads the poet to create his verbal universe by utilizing the same forces of attraction and repulsion [of words and phrases]" (42).

It has been proposed that the conceptualization of poetry in Paz's thinking is constructed with a set of constants that can be stated in a series of paradoxes: "The poet writes only for himself but must communicate to an audience. The poem is a mystery whose creation can never be accurately described, yet man cannot receive it without thinking about the process that created it. Language is a defective but indispensable instrument for conveying what is incommunicable. Poetry is an ecstasy that both denies and transforms reality, although it cannot be grasped, it is essential to man's concept of himself and to the functioning of society" (Fein, 6+).

For Paz, poetry is an experience that takes us to the limit. Like an erotic or a religious experience, it is a getting out of ourselves, the discovery of another reality, an instant when we are changed and become Others. But there is a difference between these experiences because the objects to which each one is directed are different. Chiles summarized this doctrine by establishing that "in the erotic experience . . . it [the object] is in union with the loved one; in the religious experience it is the union of the purified soul with God or the divine; and in the poetic and similar nonreligious mystical experiences, it is the reintegration of man with his deeper self" (132).

This reintegration is one of the most complex and original concepts of Paz, because in human beings the deeper self is otherness. The starting point for his notion of the constitutive otherness of humanity's being can be found in one of the maxims of Zen Buddhism: the other shore, Paramita. The experience of the other shore implies a mortal leap, "a change of nature: it is dying and being born. But the 'other shore' is within ourselves. Motionless, still, we feel ourselves being drawn, stirred by a great wind that casts us out of ourselves. It casts us out and, at the same time, pushes us into ourselves" (*The Bow,* 106). And as it has been said, "the connection of this philosophical formulation with its poetic application is, as everywhere in Paz's works, the word" (Díez, 107).

Another recurrent theme in Paz's works, not only in his essays but also in his poetry, is the notion of circularity, intimately related to the ideas of participation and re-creation. As an instrument of distinction, it appears in a chapter of *El arco y la lira,* "Verso y prosa" (Verse and Prose), where Paz compares the prose to the line and the poem to a circle or sphere: "something that is closed on itself, a self-sufficient universe in which the end is also a beginning that returns, is repeated and re-created" (*The Bow,* 57). The verse is, for him, an instance where "rhythm, image, and meaning are given simultaneously in an indivisible and compact unit" (58). If we probe further the communicative aspect of literature, we will find the idea of circularity again: "Poet and reader are two moments of a single reality. Alternating in a manner that may aptly be called cyclical, their rotation engenders the spark: poetry" (28). Thus, when the reader relives the poem, he or she reaches a poetic state, an experience that "is always a going beyond oneself, a breaking of the temporal walls, to be another" (14+).

Let us consider his theory of the meaning and function of poetry in the modern world from another point of view. A conception of myth derived from eclectic sources that include the knowledge obtained from the works of anthropologists, philosophers, psychologists, historians of religion, literary critics, and other writers (Chiles, 11) occupies a central place in Paz's theory. For him, "modern poetry has grown out of myth and has perpetuated it, and . . . it is the modern poet's task as myth-user and myth-maker to transform the ancient myths into the new myths of poetry" (Chiles, 12). For Paz, as we have seen, the modern human condition, characterized by feelings of alienation and isolation, is the result of an error. As a consequence, poetry becomes the new myth of humankind.

From an individual perspective, the postulation of a poetic tradition to which Paz's poetry belongs is an undercurrent in *El arco y la lira.* In the epilogue, "Signos en rotación," Paz writes that "since German romanticism, the history of Western poetry has been one of breaks and reconciliations with the revolutionary movement" (*Bow,* 234). Paz developed this idea in his lectures on modern poetry at Harvard University in 1972. The Spanish text of *Los hijos del limo* is a modified and amplified version of those lectures.

For Paz modernity is an exclusively Western concept. It corresponds to that period of history initiated in the eighteenth century when a new conceptualization of time was built on the foundation of change. "The Western world has identified itself with change and time, and there is no modernity other than that of the West" (*Children,* 20; the Spanish version omits the word "change"). The principle of change so conditions modern humanity that all the efforts to construct new thought systems—the Enlightenment, critical reason, liberalism, positivism, and Marxism—are rooted in it. By contrast, ancient religions and philosophies grew from atemporal principles.

There is a continuity—the sequence of breaks—beyond the many changes and aesthetic revolutions that have been produced during the last century and a half. Paz states that "the same principle inspired the German and English Romantics, the French Symbolists, and the cosmopolitan vanguard of the first half of the twentieth century" (*Children,* 7). In the literary sphere, modern poetry has been a reaction against the Modern. "Modern poetry's theme is twofold: on one hand, it is a contradictory dialogue with and against modern revolutions and the Christian religions; on the other hand, within poetry and each poetic work, there is a dialogue between analogy and irony" (*Children,* vii).

All the poets who lived during this critical age when the enormous philosophical and religious constructs inherited from the past broke apart are characterized in the *Children of the Mire.* Hölderlin, Blake, Richter, Yeats, Rilke, Eliot, and many others witnessed this collapse. It was necessary for them to invent personal mythologies, pieced together with snippets of philosophies and religions. However, all great Western poets—Goethe, Baudelaire, Mallarmé, Yeats, and the surrealists—shared a common belief in analogical thought, the belief in the universal correspondence among all beings and worlds. "Poetry is one of the manifestations of analogy . . . If analogy makes the universe a poem, a text made up of oppositions resolved in correspondences, also makes of the poem the universe. Thus, we can *read* the universe, and *live* the poem" (*Children,* 56).

The extensive essay by Octavio Paz on the Mexican nun and poet of the seventeenth century, *Sor Juana Inés de la Cruz, o Las trampas de la fe,* is a detailed commentary on her poetic work and, at the same time, a major contribution to the history of ideas and attitudes.

The guiding purpose of *Trampas* was to study the life of Sor Juana, her literary works, and also the period when both aspects developed. The superimposing of the personal on the historical circumstances that surround it constitutes an axial notion in Paz's conception of culture: the melding of the individual and the historic. "The life and the works [of Sor Juana] dispersed in a given society are only intelligible within the history of that society; in its turn, that history would not be the history it is without the life and the works of Sor Juana" (*Trampas,* 15).

In relation to the period, Paz elaborates a reconstruction that is literary rather than historical, although this observation does not mean that his book is undocumented or impressionistic. On the contrary, he presents in a very reasonable manner the characteristic features of the kingdom of New Spain on its diverse levels: latifundism and mercantilism in economics, patrimonialism in politics, and the tremendous weight of the Church and the viceregal court in the cultural realm.

The religious policy in the seventeenth century endeavoured to establish a bridge between the Indian and the Christian world. This form of synthesis, in contrast to the popular syncretism of the aboriginal people, sought prefigurations and signs of Christianity in the vernacular paganism. Paz observes that this syncretism, one of whose manifestations is the worship of the Virgin of Guadalupe, "was a huge task of theologians and chroniclers of the Society of Jesus and intellectuals close to it, like Carlos de Sigüenza y Góngora" (56).

The viceregal court, Paz remarks, "exerted a double civilizing mission: it transmitted a model of European aristocratic culture to the new world society and proposed a type of sociability for collective imitation, distinct from the one offered by the two major new world institutions, the Church and the University" (43). The court's influence was cultural and aesthetic. The literary activity, varied though in minor key, academic and profoundly dogmatic in its religious aspects, was developed in the court. New World literature was "hermetic and aristocratic," "written and read by men only" (69). Under these circumstances, the possibilities for partaking of the world of culture were, for women, limited; they could scarcely try "to slide through the half-open door of the court and of the Church" (69).

But Sor Juana circumvented both. The inquiry on her life is based on the few biographical documents we have, basically the famous *Respuesta a sor Filotea* (Reply to Sister Philothea, translated with the title *A Woman of Genius*) and the rest of her literary works. Paz is completely aware of the fact that "her work tells us something; but in order to understand that *something* we must realize that her telling is circumscribed by silence: *that which cannot be said*. . . . Such silence is not the absence of meaning; on the contrary: that which cannot be said alludes not only to the Church's orthodoxy but to the ideas, interests and passions of its princes and its orders" (16 +).

Paz believes that the crucial moments in the poet's life—the decision to devote herself to the Church, to leave off writing, and so on—can be explained by the confluence of the conditions that the historical period imposed on her and by certain elements of her personal past. "In her experience as an infant [the absence of the father, the uncertain relation to her mother and her step-father, and the secret reading of her grandfather's books] were already inscribed all the steps of Sor Juana's destiny: her renunciation of marriage; the cell-library of her maturity; her rebellion against authority and even the plot of the *Primero sueño* [First Dream]" (124).

Contrary to the opinion of most Catholic critics, who believe that Juana took vows due to an authentic vocation, Paz believes that, without casting doubt on her orthodoxy, she chose the religious life as an occupation that would allow her to develop her inclination toward knowledge and literature. "In the situation of Juana Inés during those years I can see three basic and permanent circumstances, beside others that, though temporary, finally were no less decisive. The basic circumstances are bastardy, poverty, and the father's absence. None of them was *the* cause of taking the veil, but all contributed powerfully to this resolution" (152).

Referring to her literary activity, Paz examines not only the principal works—her philosophical poem *Primero sueño,* the dramatic plays, and the personal poems—but her circumstantial poetry, as well, developing in each case personal and valuable readings. Perhaps the most interesting and controversial element of Paz's readings is the emphasis he gives to Neoplatonic hermetism, which Sor Juana could have received by reading the works of the German Jesuit Kirchner, whose ideas were the result of a combination of three different elements: syncretic Catholicism as represented by the Society of Jesus during the seventeenth century, "Egyptian" Neoplatonic hermetism, inherited from the renaissance, and new astronomical and physical hypotheses and discoveries. It is not easy to accept Paz's conclusions without raising some objections; yet his powerful prose is nonetheless highly convincing, and future studies on Sor Juana will begin with a careful reconsideration of his opinions.

V

Two lengthy essays on narrative and a book—a compilation of articles on art and literature—constitute the contribution of the novelist Carlos Fuentes (1929–) to literary criticism.

In 1969, Fuentes published an essay on Spanish American narrative, *La nueva novela hispanoamericana* (The New Spanish American Novel), where he reviewed, through the study of five contemporary novelists, the social and linguistic factors involved in the novels of the boom. For Fuentes, the novelists of the sixties created a new language in an effort to break away from the traditional dependence on the European novel.

Adopting some of the ideas of the French critic Paul Ricouer, Fuentes describes the literary text as a mediating force between synchronic structure and diachronic event in language. It has been noted that "such a duality naturally attracts Fuentes, and he characteristically expands it into a series of oppositions, or 'universal antinomies' of language: the systematic versus the historic, anonymous versus individual speech, and so on" (Faris, 116).

The Mexican novelist's ideas on language and the function of the writer reappeared in the appendix, "Muerte y resurrección de la novela" (Death and

Resurrection of the Novel), of the first part of *Casa con dos puertas* (House with Two Doors; 1970). "It has been the awareness of language that has universalized the novel during the last decade, liberating it from servitudes that guaranteed rather than prophesied its death. Language is a common fact. . . . The novelist's primary task has consisted in structuring imaginarily the incessant call for actualization of the word" (80).

The innovation of the new Spanish American novel, according to Fuentes, is due to an extraordinary shift in three orders: time became no longer the linear measure of Western progress; space opened to include new areas and not only the traditional centers of Western culture; and ideology ceased to be the blind and mechanically optimistic faith of positivist thinking. So, "on accepting the universality of linguistic structures, the novelist of the sixties accepted also the assumptions of that universality: the multiplicity and the contiguous validity of languages in a historical and cultural sense, the dissolution of cultural distinctions between 'civilized' and 'primitive' peoples, the ecumenical extension of the space of thinking" (85).

Casa con dos puertas is a collection of Fuentes's essays, organized in four sections: "Tres maneras de narrar" (Three Ways of Narrating), which includes prologues to Mexican editions of novels of Jane Austen and Herman Melville and a study on William Faulkner; "Notas del tiempo" (Notes of This Time), most of them necrologies that appeared originally in a variety of Mexican reviews; "Gran teatro del mundo" (The World's Great Theater), articles on Shakespeare, Jean Genet, Alain Resnais, among others; and "Tres maneras de ver" (Three Ways of Seeing), a superb essay on Luis Buñuel and studies on Adami and Cuevas that originally appeared as part of exhibition catalogues.

Fuentes's next long essay, *Cervantes, o La crítica de la lectura* (Cervantes, or The Critique of Reading), is the printed version of a series of lectures he gave at the University of Texas at Austin. He outlines the complex elements that historically constituted the Hispanic world and, after discussing some early Spanish texts—especially the *Libro de buen amor* (The Book of Good Love) and *La Celestina*—he focuses on *Don Quixote*. He shows how Cervantes's novel revolutionized the Western way of reading and, because of this, *Don Quixote* according to Fuentes is the starting point for modern fiction. Also for Fuentes, Cervantes's revolutionary writing lies in the setting-up of a "multivocal" reading that is set in motion when the main character, Don Quixote, discovers that someone has already written part of his life: "Certainly, this is the first time in the history of literature that a character knows that he is being written about while living his fictional adventures" (*Don Quixote,* 76). This revelation establishes a new reading level: Don Quixote becomes "the first modern hero, scrutinized from various points of view, read, and forced to read himself, assimilated to his own readers that read him and, like them, compelled to create 'Don Quixote' in the imagination" (77).

Through this ironic situation, Cervantes unmasked the medieval epic, imposing on it a critical reading. But, as Fuentes points out, "by establishing the criticism of creation within the creation, Cervantes founded modern imagination" (93).

Fuentes's last chapters connect this multivocal reading with the idea of a similar plural kind of writing that Joyce develops in his major works: "In *Don Quixote* . . . that criticism of creation is a criticism of reading; in *Ulysses* and *Finnegans Wake*, it is a criticism of writing" (97). Joyce's criticism of writing is oriented, according to Fuentes, toward the individual writing, therefore, "the innovation of the *Joyce-ization* is that it inscribes the *des-I-ization* within the total process of linguistic economy" (108).

VI

After the Cuban Revolution, the Marxist tendency that had been appearing sporadically in Spanish American literary criticism gave rise to an important and widespread production of critical and theoretical texts. Despite differences in detail, Marxist criticism proposes itself not only as a method of analysis and evaluation of literary works, but also as a means to achieve the liberation.

According to A. F. Jasso, whose study on Marxist criticism is the basis of this section, most Mexican Marxist critics "have transformed Marx's ideas into formulas or inflexible paradigms that, instead of helping to understand Marx's thought on art, obscure it and, in most cases, eliminate it" ("La crítica," 4 +).

After the Mexican Revolution of 1910, social criticism, or openly Marxist criticism, became much more militant. The controversy it provoked when Marxist critics faced the group of critics of the aestheticaly oriented Contemporáneos (Contemporaries) is a historical testimony to its vitality. "Although the controversy constantly changes direction (Europeism versus nationalism, cosmopolitanism versus nationalism, universalism versus nativism), the main reason for the dispute is actually between two radically different concepts of literature: the Marxist concept or the concept of 'engaged literature,' no matter how elementary it may be, and a basically aesthetic concept" (8). This controversy was the first step for Mexican Marxist literary criticism, whose purpose during those years required that critics attempt to resolve aesthetic problems and to prescribe themes and styles. Later on, this attitude came to be known as "socialist realism."

Perhaps the most interesting Marxist critic in Mexico is José Revueltas (1914–1976). His literary activity covered two areas: on the one hand, the theoretical and critical and, on the other, the creative. Jasso has written that "Revueltas distinguished himself [among the Marxist theorists and critics, both inside and outside Mexico] because of the capability, the profundity and the consummate apprehension of what the Marxist aesthetic *should* be according to Marx and Engels" ("Crítica literaria marxista," 24).

One of the commonplaces of several Marxist critics is the consideration of realism as the "correct" form of art, because it is alleged that it corresponds more adequately to social relationships. Referring to socialist realism, Revueltas believed that it is a "reactionary theory," the result of a dogmatic attitude toward art that "is based, respectively, on two essential deformations of historical materialism and dialectical materialism. The first one reduces the relations between the social base and the ideological superstructure to the simple logic of a causal derivation; the second transforms the objective dialectics into a crude teleology" (*Cuestionamientos,* 154). Revueltas's critical postulates distanced him from traditional Marxist ideas on realism and allowed him to construct a new conception, both materialistic and dialectical, that helps the writer to reproduce the internal movement characteristic of reality.

The most complete collection of Revueltas's critical thought, *Cuestionamientos e intenciones* (Questions and Intentions), appeared in 1978. The essays cover some general problems of aesthetics and the analysis that Revueltas made of his own works, provoked by the accusations of his comrades. As a consequence this book reflects Revueltas's intellectual history which, as Evodio Escalante has pointed out, "abounds in contradictions, and does not shy away . . . from the aberrations of Stalinism and its sequels. Hence it is impossible to subscribe to the image of Revueltas as hypercritical and always a heterodox" (29). However, Revueltas was able to perceive certain aspects of Marxism—the possibility of retrogression even inside dialectical materialism, for instance—that had not been perceived before.

Revueltas's revision of the Marxist aesthetic led him to consider that the foundation, the real nature of art, is to be revolutionary. "Art is—in his own words—revolutionary due to the critical value it contains, but not because of the objective tendencies that it reflects from reality. It could be said that every art, in itself, is revolutionary from the first moment; because it is reality's highest criticism where critical content is always revolutionary" (272).

VII

With the enormous fluctuation of criticism and after years of consistent efforts oriented toward the discussion of literary specificity and, as a consequence, toward the legitimization of an intellectual position for a discipline whose serious, scientific status demanded acknowledgment, it seems that we are witnessing a promising breakdown of boundaries. During the last twenty years or so, an expansion of the field traditionally explored by literary critics has been conducted. A semiotic understanding of the concept of text has replaced the conventional belief in a discourse anchored in the written text with the one of texture, of a canvas of potential and multiple meanings. As this shift became accepted, very different aspects of social life acquired the right to be discussed in a way analogous to literary texts. Some critics, therefore, no longer sought to study only the high literary canon, instead orienting their research interests toward a comprehensive set of public discourses.

In Mexico this trend is exemplified by the works of Carlos Monsiváis (1938–), a writer on a wide variety of subjects, one of whose recurrent preoccupations has been to produce a critical chronicle of contemporary Mexican life. As can be seen in *Amor perdido* (Love Lost; 1977), perhaps his most provocative book, Monsiváis's purpose is to outline the cultural itinerary that led from the fin-de-siècle Mexico to the present, a present shaken to its roots by the 1968 massacre of students in Tlatelolco. Since 1968, "one is deeply aware— in a violent and synoptical fashion—of the manufacture of a public history and the forging of a true history" (44). Using the chronicle form, Monsiváis manages to stage social life, history, politics, and cultural myths.

In a recent article, "Notas sobre la cultura mexicana contemporánea" (Notes on Contemporary Mexican Culture), this historical journey is based on the contrast between the situation of intellectuals, their place in the culture and their mission, and the political ground accorded education, which is basically reduced to teaching people to read and write: "The big literacy campaigns teach people to read, but the Government does not pay attention to what the newly literate will do with that knowledge" (14). His cultural analysis reinserts itself in the literary field and in the process uncovers essential traits of modern Mexico: "What is, literarily speaking, modernity in Mexico? Above all, the method that combines the most aggressive version of Western culture (i.e., the American one) with the energy that, in spite of everything, maintains open spaces. This modernity is superficial and profound, it tries to fuse historical and cultural times, it is real and simulated" (16).

Monsiváis's chronicles are, in fact, more than a chronologically or causally ordered narrative. They begin with snapshots that enlighten each other via a technique of superimposition. Behind this procedure for the assembling of data, it is possible to find a view of history where humor and sadness merge, a view that proposes itself as a reexamination of the official (hi)story. Monsiváis's intellectual commitment leads him to write another version of the facts, an implicitly deeper version because it grasps the hidden mechanisms of cultural power in order to bring them to light. In this way, he is able to rescue a whole set of phenomena that the members of the dominant class, especially the bourgeoisie, relegated to the periphery: popular songs, so-called dirty language, and most important, marginal social groups.

In the essays in *Amor perdido,* this project of historical reconstruction is reinforced through a series of strategies destined to subvert the formal principles of intellectual discourse, producing a new ground where the writing may zigzag, in the sense that the text is built as a collage in which popular proverbs are juxtaposed with official declarations, a colloquial tone with a journalistic style, and graphic material with popular music and poetry.

As Cossío has maintained, "the work of Monsiváis is a radical protest against false middle-class consciousness, an exact analysis of the actual situation where he finds himself, a theoretical reflection that, by establishing relation with and within every element that forms social life and by describing the position that each work occupies in the totality, constitutes the context, the dialogical space, the verbal climate from which contemporary Mexican literature arises" (142). Monsiváis's writings are an invitation to read, to reread, the social text from a different point of view, one that demythifies our cultural background. After reading his version of history, nothing, neither the reader, the writer, nor the referents of the discourse, retains its original condition.

APPENDIX: SELECTIVE INDEX OF MEXICAN CRITICAL WRITING (INCLUDING ANTHOLOGIES AND LITERARY HISTORIES)

Abreu Gómez, Ermilio (1884–1971)
> *Sor Juana Inés de la Cruz: Bibliografía y biblioteca.* Mexico City: Secretaría de Relaciones Exteriores, 1934.
> *Semblanza de Sor Juana.* Mexico City: Letras de México, 1938.
> *Ruiz Alarcón: Bibliografía crítica.* Mexico City: Ediciones Botas, 1939.
> *Sor Juana Inés de la Cruz: Poesías.* Edition, prologue, and notes. Mexico City: Ediciones Botas, 1940.
> *Poesía completa de Sor Juana.* Compilation and prologue. Mexico City: Ediciones Botas, 1948.
> *Teatro completo de Juan Ruiz de Alarcón.* Introduction. Mexico City: Compañía General de Ediciones, 1951.

Aguilar Mora, Jorge (1946–)
> *La divina pareja: Historia y mito en Octavio Paz.* Mexico City: Ediciones Era, 1978.

Alatorre, Antonio (1922–)
> *Los romances de Hero y Leandro.* Mexico City: Dirección General de Difusión Cultural, 1956.

Batis, Humberto (1934–)
> *Lo que "Cuadernos del viento" nos dejó.* Mexico City: Diógenes, 1984.

Bermúdez, María Elvira (1912–1988)
> *Los mejores cuentos policíacos mexicanos.* Mexico City: Libro Mex Editores, 1955.
> *Cuentos fantásticos mexicanos.* Mexico City: Oasis, 1963.
> *El cuento policial mexicano.* Mexico City: Universidad Nacional Autónoma de México, 1987.

Blanco, José Joaquín (1951–)
> *Se llamaba Vasconcelos.* Mexico City: Fondo de Cultura Económica, 1977.
> *La paja en el ojo.* Puebla: Universidad Autónoma de Puebla, 1980.
> *Retratos con paisaje.* Puebla: Universidad Autónoma de Puebla, 1980.
> *Crónica de la poesía mexicana.* Mexico City: Editorial Katún, 1984.
> *La literatura de la Nueva España.* 2 vols. Mexico City: Cal y Arena, 1989.

Buxó, José Pascual (1931–)
> *Góngora y la poesía novohispana.* Mexico City: Universidad Nacional Autónoma de México, 1960.
> *Muerte y desengaño en la poesía novohispana (siglos XVI y XVII).* Mexico City: Universidad Nacional Autónoma de México, 1975.
> *Introducción a la poética de Roman Jakobson.* Mexico City: Universidad Nacional Autónoma de México, 1978.
> *Ungaretti y Góngora: Ensayo de literatura comparada.* Mexico City: Universidad Nacional Autónoma de México, 1978.
> *César Vallejo: Crítica y contracrítica.* Mexico City: Universidad Autónoma Metropolitana, Dirección de Difusión, 1982.

Las figuraciones del sentido: Ensayos de poética semiológica. Mexico City: Fondo de Cultura Económica, 1984.

Campos, Julieta (1932–)

Función de la novela. Mexico City: Editorial Joaquín Mortiz, 1973.

La herencia obstinada: Análisis de cuentos nahuas. Mexico City: Fondo de Cultura Económica, 1982.

Carballo, Emmanuel (1929–)

Cuentistas mexicanos modernos (1949–1956). 2 vols. Mexico City: Libro Mex Editores, 1956.

El cuento mexicano del siglo XX: Antología. Mexico City: Empresas Editoriales, 1964.

Narrativa mexicana de hoy. Madrid: Alianza Editorial, 1969.

Las fiestas patrias en la narrativa nacional. Mexico City: Diógenes, 1982.

Protagonistas de la literatura mexicana. Mexico City: Secretaría de Educación Pública, 1986.

Castañón, Adolfo (1952–)

Alfonso Reyes, caballero de la voz errante. Mexico City: Boldó i Climent, 1988.

Castro Leal, Antonio (1896–1981)

La literatura mexicana contemporánea. Mexico City: 1917.

La novela de la revolución mexicana. 2 vols. Selection, introduction, and notes. Mexico City: Aguilar, 1960.

La novela del México colonial. 2 vols. Preliminary study, selection, etc. Mexico City: Aguilar, 1964.

Repasos y defensas: Antología. Introduction by Salvador Elizondo. Ed. Víctor Díaz Arciniega. Mexico City: Fondo de Cultura Económica, 1987.

Chumacero, Alí (1918–)

Los momentos críticos. Ed. Miguel Angel Flores. Mexico City: Fondo de Cultura Económica, 1987.

Cuesta, Jorge (1903–1942)

Antología de la poesía mexicana moderna. Mexico City: Contemporáneos, 1928.

Poemas y ensayos. 4 vols. Mexico City: Universidad Nacional Autónoma de México, 1964.

Domínguez Michael, Christopher (1962–)

Jorge Cuesta, o El demonio de la política. Mexico City: Universidad Autónoma Metropolitana, 1986.

Antología de la narrativa mexicana del siglo XX. 2 vols. Selection, introduction, and notes. Mexico City: Fondo de Cultura Económica, 1991.

Durán, Manuel (1925–)

El superrealismo en la poesía española contemporánea. Mexico City: n.p., 1950.

La ambigüedad en el Quijote. Jalapa: Universidad Veracruzana, 1960.

Genio y figura de Amado Nervo. Buenos Aires: Eudeba, 1968.

Tríptico mexicano: Juan Rulfo, Carlos Fuentes, Salvador Elizondo. Mexico City: Sep-Setentas, 1973.

Elizondo, Salvador (1932–)

Cuaderno de escritura. Guanajuato: Universidad de Guanajuato, 1969.

Camera lucida. Mexico City: Editorial Joaquín Mortiz, 1983.

Estrada, Genaro (1887–1937)

Poetas nuevos de México. Mexico City: 1916.

Bibliografía de Amado Nervo. Mexico City: Secretaría de Relaciones Exteriores, 1925.

García Ponce, Juan (1932–)

Cruce de caminos. Jalapa: Universidad Veracruzana, 1965.

La aparición de lo invisible. Mexico City: Siglo XXI Editores, 1968.

Desconsideraciones. Mexico City: Editorial Joaquín Mortiz, 1968.

Robert Musil: El reino milenario. Montevideo: Arca, 1969.

Apariciones (Antología de ensayos). Ed. Daniel Goldin. Mexico City: Fondo de Cultura Económica, 1987.

Imágenes y visiones. Mexico City: Vuelta, 1988.

García Terrés, Jaime (1924–)

Panorama de la crítica literaria en México. Mexico City, 1941.

Sobre la responsabilidad del escritor. Mexico City, 1949.

La feria de los días y otros textos políticos y literarios. Mexico City: Universidad Nacional Autónoma de México, 1961.

Poesía y alquimia: Los tres mundos de Gilberto Owen. Mexico City: Ediciones Era, 1979.

Garibay K., Angel María (1892–1967)

Historia de la literatura nahuatl. 2 vols. Mexico City: Editorial Porrúa, 1953–1954.

Epica nahuatl. Mexico City: Universidad Nacional Autónoma de México, 1963.

Panorama literario de los pueblos nahuas. Mexico City: Editorial Porrúa, 1963.

La literatura de los aztecas. Mexico City: Editorial Joaquín Mortiz, 1964.

Glantz, Margo (1937–)

Onda y escritura en México: Jóvenes de 20 a 33. Mexico City: Siglo XXI Editores, 1971.

González Peña, Carlos (1885–1955)

Historia de la literatura mexicana desde los orígenes hasta nuestros días. Mexico City: Cultura, 1928. Recent edition: Mexico City: Editorial Porrúa, 1985.

Novelas y novelistas de México. Ed. Emmanuel Carballo. Mexico City: Universidad Nacional Autónoma de México, 1987.

Guzmán, Martín Luis (1887–1960)

Crítica y autocrítica. Ed. Emmanuel Carballo. Mexico City: Universidad Nacional Autónoma de México, 1986.

Jiménez Rueda, Julio (1896–1960)

Historia de la literatura mexicana. Mexico City: Cultura, 1928. Recent edition: Mexico City: Ediciones Botas, 1960.

Antología de la prosa en México. Mexico City: Publicaciones de la Universidad Nacional, 1931.

Letras mexicanas en el siglo XIX. Mexico City: Fondo de Cultura Económica, 1944.

Herejías y supersticiones en la Nueva España: Los heterodoxos en México. Mexico City: Imprenta Universitaria, 1946.

Historia de la cultura en México: El virreinato. Mexico City: Cultura, 1950.

Estampas de los Siglos de oro. Mexico City: Imprenta Universitaria, 1957.

Leal, Luis (1907–)

Breve historia del cuento mexicano. Mexico City: Ediciones de Andrea, 1956.

Antología del cuento mexicano. Mexico City: Ediciones de Andrea, 1957.

Bibliografía del cuento mexicano. Mexico City: Ediciones de Andrea, 1958.

El cuento veracruzano. Jalapa: Universidad Veracruzana, 1966.

Historia del cuento hispanoamericano. Mexico City: Ediciones de Andrea, 1966.

Mariano Azuela, vida y obra. Mexico City: Ediciones de Andrea, 1966.

El cuento hispanoamericano. Buenos Aires: Centro Editor de América Latina, 1967.

Mariano Azuela. Buenos Aires: Centro Editor de América Latina, 1967.

Breve historia de la literatura hispanoamericana. New York: Knopf, 1971.

Mariano Azuela. New York: Twayne, 1971.

Juan Rulfo. Boston: Twayne, 1983.

Leiva, Raúl (1916–)

Imagen de la poesía mexicana contemporánea. Mexico City: Universidad Nacional Autónoma de México, 1959.

León-Portilla, Miguel (1926–)

Los antiguos mexicanos a través de sus crónicas y cantares. Mexico City: Fondo de Cultura Económica, 1961.

Las literaturas precolombinas de México. Mexico City: Editorial Pormaca, 1964.

Trece poetas del mundo azteca. Mexico City: Universidad Nacional Autónoma de México, 1967.

Literaturas de Mesoamérica. Mexico City: SepCultura, 1984.

Magaña Esquivel, Antonio (1909–1981)

Imagen del teatro. Mexico City: Letras de México, 1940.

Medio siglo de teatro mexicano, 1900–1961. Mexico City: Instituto Nacional de Bellas Artes, 1964.

La novela de la revolución. Mexico City: Biblioteca del Instituto Nacional de Estudios Históricos de la Revolución Mexicana, 1964.

Martínez, José Luis (1918–)

"Situación de la literatura mexicana contemporánea." *Cuadernos Americanos* 42 (1948): 229–257.

Literatura mexicana del siglo XX. 2 vols. Mexico City: Antigua Librería Robredo, 1949.

La emancipación literaria de México. Mexico City: Antigua Librería Robredo, 1955.

La expresión nacional. Mexico City: Imprenta Universitaria, 1955. Recent edition: Mexico City: Oasis, 1984.

El ensayo mexicano moderno. Mexico City: Fondo de Cultura Económica, 1958. English translation: *The Modern Mexican Esssay,* trans. H. W. Hilborn. Toronto: University of Toronto Press, 1965.

Unidad y diversidad de la literatura latinoamericana. Mexico City: Editorial Joaquín Mortiz, 1972.

Mejía Sánchez, Ernesto (1923–1985)

Los primeros cuentos de Rubén Darío. Mexico City: Studium, 1951.

Exposición documental de Manuel Gutiérrez Nájera, 1859–1959. Mexico City: Universidad Nacional Autónoma de México, 1959.

Cuestiones rubendarianas. Madrid: Revista de Occidente, 1970.

Rubén Darío: Poesía. Ed. Caracas: Biblioteca Ayacucho, 1977.

Millán, María del Carmen (1914–)

El paisaje en la poesía mexicana. Mexico City: Imprenta Universitario, 1952.

Literatura mexicana. Mexico City: Editorial Porrúa, 1963.

Antología de cuentos mexicanos. Mexico City: SepSetentas, 1976. Recent edition in 2 vols.: Mexico City: Nueva Imagen, 1986 and 1988.

Monterde, Francisco (1894–1985)

Cultura mexicana: Aspectos literarios. Mexico City: Intercontinental, 1946.

Aspectos literarios de la cultura mexicana. Ed. Evodio Escalante. Mexico City: Universidad Nacional Autónoma de México, 1987.

Pacheco, José Emilio (1939–)
La poesía mexicana del siglo XIX: Antología. Mexico City: Empresas Editoriales, 1965.
Rojas Garcidueñas, José (1912–)
El teatro de Nueva España en el siglo XVI. Mexico City: Luis Alvarez, 1935.
Autos y coloquios del siglo XVI. Prologue and notes. Mexico City: Universidad Nacional Autónoma de México, 1939.
Bernardo de Balbuena, la vida y la obra. Mexico City: Universidad Nacional Autónoma de México, 1958.
Presencia de Don Quijote en las artes de México. Mexico City: Universidad Nacional Autónoma de México, 1968.
Ruy Sánchez, Alberto (1951–)
Al filo de las hojas. Mexico City: SepSetentas, 1988.
Schneider, Luis Mario (1931–)
El estridentismo: Una literatura de la estrategia. Mexico City: Instituto Nacional de Bellas Artes, 1970.
Segovia, Tomás (1927–)
Poética y profética. Mexico City: Fondo de Cultura Económica/El Colegio de México, 1985.
Cuaderno inoportuno. Mexico City: Fondo de Cultura Económica, 1987.
Torres Bodet, Jaime (1902–1974)
Antología de Rubén Darío. Mexico City: Fondo de Cultura Económica, 1966.
Rubén Darío, abismo y cisma. Mexico City: Fondo de Cultura Económica, 1966.
Tres inventores de realidad: Stendahl, Dostoyevski, Pérez Galdós. Madrid: Revista de Occidente, 1969.
Vela, Arqueles (1899–1977)
Teoría literaria del modernismo: Su filosofía, su estética, su técnica. Mexico City: Ediciones Botas, 1949.
Villaurrutia, Xavier (1903–1950)
Ed., *Poemas escogidos,* Ramón Lopez Velarde. Mexico City: Cultura, 1940.
Xirau, Ramón (1924–)
Tres poetas de la soledad. Mexico City: Antigua Librería Robredo, 1955.
Poesía hispanoamericana y española: Ensayos. Mexico City: Universidad Nacional Autónoma de México, 1961.
Genio y figura de Sor Juana Inés de la Cruz. Buenos Aires: Eudeba, 1968.
Octavio Paz: El sentido de la palabra. Mexico City: Editorial Joaquín Mortiz, 1970.
Poesía iberoamericana contemporánea. Mexico City: SepSetentas, 1979.
Antología. Mexico City: Diana, 1988.

BIBLIOGRAPHY

(Since these works are commented on in this essay, no annotations are provided.)

Bueno Chávez, Raúl. "Sobre la nueva novela y la nueva crítica latinoamericanas." *Revista de Crítica Literaria Latinoamericana* 9.18 (1983): 81–85.
Chiles, Frances. *Octavio Paz: The Mythic Dimension.* New York: Peter Lang, 1987.
Cossío, María Eugenia. "El diálogo sin fin de Monsiváis." *Hispanic Journal* 5.2 (1984): 137–143.
Cruz, Sor Juana Inés de la. *Primero sueño.* In *Obras completas,* ed. Alfonso Méndez Plancarte, vol. 1, 335–359. Mexico City: Fondo de Cultura Económica, 1951.

————. *Respuesta a Sor Filotea de la Cruz.* In *Obras completas,* ed. Alfonso Méndez Plancarte, vol. 4, 440–475. Mexico City: Fondo de Cultura Económica, 1951.

————. *A Woman of Genius: The Intellectual Autobiography of Sor Juana Inés de la Cruz.* Trans. Margaret Sayers Peden. Salisbury: Lime Rock Press, 1982.

Díez, Luis Alfonso. "Poesía y pensamiento poético." In *Aproximaciones a Octavio Paz,* ed. Angel Flores, 96–110. Mexico City: Editorial Joaquín Mortiz, 1974.

Escalante, Evodio. *José Revueltas: Una literatura del "lado moridor."* Mexico City: Ediciones Era, 1979.

Faris, Wendy B. *Carlos Fuentes.* New York: Frederick Ungar, 1983.

Fein, John M. Introduction. *Toward Octavio Paz: A Reading of His Major Poems, 1957–1976,* 1–10. Lexington: The University Press of Kentucky, 1986.

Fuentes, Carlos. *Casa con dos puertas.* Mexico City: Editorial Joaquín Mortiz, 1970.

————. *Cervantes, o La crítica de la lectura.* Mexico City: Editorial Joaquín Mortiz, 1976. English version: *Don Quixote, or The Critique of Reading.* Austin: University of Texas Press, 1975.

————. *La nueva novela hispanoamericana.* Mexico City: Editorial Joaquín Mortiz, 1969.

Gallo, Marta. "Historiografía e historias de la literatura hispanoamericanas." *Filología* 22.2 (1988): 55–73.

Jasso, Arturo. "Algunos problemas de la crítica literaria mexicana." In *Otros mundos, otros fuegos: Fantasía y realismo mágico en Iberoamérica,* ed. Donald A. Yates, 293–298. Report from the XVI Congreso Internacional de Literatura Iberoamericana. East Lansing: Michigan State University, Latin American Studies Center, 1975.

————. "La crítica literaria marxista en México." *Cuadernos Escorpión* 1.1 (1981): entire issue.

Monsiváis, Carlos. *Amor perdido.* Mexico City: Ediciones Era, 1977.

————. "Notas sobre la cultura mexicana contemporánea: Las élites que se masifican." *Mundo, Problemas y Confrontaciones* 1.3 (1987): 7–17.

Navarro, Desiderio. "Eurocentrismo y antieurocentrismo en la teoría literaria de América Latina y Europa." *Revista de Crítica Literaria Latinoamericana* 8.16 (1982): 7–26.

Paz, Octavio. *El arco y la lira: El poema, la revelación poética, poesía e historia.* Mexico City: Fondo de Cultura Económica, 1972. English translation: *The Bow and the Lyre,* trans. Ruth L. C. Simms. Austin: University of Texas Press, 1973.

————. *Los hijos del limo: Del romanticismo a la vanguardia.* Barcelona: Seix Barral, 1974. English version: *Children of the Mire: Modern Poetry from Romanticism to the Avant-Garde,* trans. Rachel Phillips. Cambridge, Mass.: Harvard University Press, 1974.

————. "Poesía de soledad y poesía de comunión." *Primeras letras (1931–1943),* ed. Enrico Mario Santí, 291–303. Mexico City: Vuelta, 1988.

————. *Signos en rotación.* Buenos Aires: Sur, 1965. Reprinted in his *El arco y la lira,* 253–284. Mexico City: Fondo de Cultura Económica, 1972.

————. *Sor Juana Inés de la Cruz, o Las trampas de la fe.* Mexico City: Fondo de Cultura Económica, 1983. English version: *Sor Juana, or The Traps of Faith,* trans. Margaret Sayers Peden. Cambridge, Mass.: Harvard University Press, 1988.

Portuondo, José Antonio. "Alfonso Reyes y la teoría literaria." In *Ensayos de estética y de teoría literaria,* 281–293. Havana: Letras Cubanas, 1986.

Revueltas, José. *Cuestionamientos e intenciones.* Mexico City: Ediciones Era, 1978.

Reyes, Alfonso. *La experiencia literaria.* In *Obras completas* 14.17–233. Mexico City: Fondo de Cultura Económica, 1962.

———. *Capítulos de literatura española.* Mexico City: Casa de España, 1939. First series.

———. *Capítulos de literatura española.* Mexico City: El Colegio de México, 1945. Second series.

———. *La crítica en la edad ateniense.* Mexico City: El Colegio de México, 1941.

———. *Cuestiones gongorinas.* Paris: P. Ollendorff, 1910.

———. *El deslinde.* Mexico City: El Colegio de México, 1944.

———. *El deslinde: Prolegómenos a la teoría literaria.* In *Obras completas* 15.15–422. Mexico City: Fondo de Cultura Económica, 1963.

———. *La filosofía helenística.* Mexico City: Fondo de Cultura Económica, 1959.

———. *Junta de sombras.* Mexico City: El Colegio de México, 1949.

———. *Tentativas y orientaciones.* Mexico City: Editoria Nuevo Mundo, 1944.

———. *Ultima Tule.* Mexico City: Imprenta Universitaria, 1944.

———. *Al yunque (1944–1950).* Mexico City: Tezontle, 1960.

Rodríguez Monegal, Emir. "Relectura de *El arco y la lira.*" *Revista Iberoamericana* 37 (1971): 35–46.

Stanton, Anthony. "Una lectura de *El arco y la lira.*" In *Reflexiones lingüísticas y literarias: Quinto Centenario (1492–1992),* ed. Rafael Olea Franco and James Valender, vol. 2, 301–322. Mexico City: El Colegio de México, 1992.

Sucre, Guillermo. "La nueva crítica." In *América Latina en su literatura,* ed. César Fernández Moreno, 259–275. Mexico City: Siglo XXI Editores/UNESCO, 1980. English translation: *Latin America and Its Literature,* trans. Mary G. Berg, 201–218. New York: Holmes & Meier, 1980.

11

Literary Reviews: A Bibliographical Essay

LUIS H. PEÑA
Translated by Roselyn Costantino

The emergence of periodical literature in Hispanic America—and Mexico is no exception—establishes a new type of relationship between writer, text, and public. Among other characteristics, this relationship reveals its awareness of its role in the historic moment in which it is produced. Mexican literature from its origins is written on the fabric of time and the hurried rhythm of a hostile confrontation with history. The writer and the reader interact in the space between the power and the culture that this literature evokes. This interaction has given constancy to texts via literary and cultural journalism since the dawn of the nineteenth century.

As José Luis Martínez has observed, the culture of the first century of life as an independent nation calls for men and women who are eager to dedicate themselves to the training, the organization, the articulation, and the concrete activity capable of fostering a culture expressing an emergent nationality ("México en busca," 2:1019–26). Nineteenth-century writers participated vigorously in the transformation of the economic, social, political, and cultural orders, defining partisan positions that responded to the ideological contest between liberals and conservatives recorded in all the cultural discourse of the time. Discourse in the mass media testifies to a succession of confrontations between ideologies, generations, and cultures that reflected the political oscillation of the country as seen in its periodicals, its daily newspapers, and its magazines.

In the nineteenth century, politics and poetics—republican liberalism and romanticism in its various forms—are intertwined in their commitment to the transformation and revitalization of texts that serve to indoctrinate and to confront: academic criticism, poetry, and the novel, all with obvious ideological underpinnings. The process of constructing a symbolic referent representative of "national" character in Mexican literature directly or indirectly reflects the history of a culture with a longing for self-regeneration. Toward this end, writing becomes a self-portrait: Mexico's periodical publications are a mirror of ink recording the successive manifestations of its critical historical and cultural biography—independence, the North American invasion, the War of Reform, the French Intervention. The revolution, for its part, confronts and rewrites previous symbolic discourse concerning culture and identity, transforming it into a new national mythology that corrects the previous propositions of "national identity" according to the pragmatics of its political program in the first decades of the twentieth century. The industrial transformation, the development of a middle class, access to higher education, the growth of industrial culture, the effects of mass culture, and the successive economic and social crises of the political system continually undercut the cultural propositions of the State. Thus, from the end of the 1960s there is a subtle yet visible demand for the opening up and expansion of an alternative and a plural cultural space.

This essay is interested in describing the development of Mexican literary magazines in relation to their historical context. We also propose to offer, as far as is possible, a panoramic view that will characterize the shifting topography of magazines and cultural supplements in Mexican literary history. Our analysis acknowledges its great debt to critics like José Luis Martínez, Carlos Monsiváis, Octavio Paz, Luis Mario Schneider, Francisco Monterde, Guillermo Sheridan, Boyd G. Carter, Porfirio Martínez Peñaloza, and Paloma Villegas. Concomitantly, we acknowledge the limitations of a broad point of view versus a detailed analysis. The omissions are not the result of a value judgment but rather of the partial nature of any general approach.

From the second half of the eighteenth century significant changes occur in the forms of organization, production, distribution, and legitimization of intellectual activity in colonial cultural centers. Within this context fall the literary and scientific academies, although they apparently conform to the model of the metropolis as they guide their attention to, interest in, and observation of the Latin American reality. As a result, "periodical pages" appear, initiating a new form of experience of public life that provides for the circulation of commentary and news items and allows for the airing of topics of general interest. Obviously, the dominant themes are those reflecting local and immediate regional reality. This is apparent in the *Gaceta de México* (Mexican Gazette; 1784–1804), predecessor of the first daily published in New Spain, and *Diario de México* (Mexican Daily; 1805–1817), founded by Jacobo de Villaurrutia and Carlos María Bustamante, the latter being a notable member of the revolutionary cause. The *Diario de México* becomes very significant, with 787 subscribers and sales in countless strategic points throughout Mexico City. This periodical succeeds in attracting a group of writers that debate artistic, philosophical, moral, and literary issues in its pages. For example, *Diario de México* carries the critical polemic between José Joaquín Fernández de Lizardi and José María Lafragua over national literature and the function of language. It is a debate that, as Schneider states (43–70), would continue to surface, with various nuances, in the cultural panorama of Mexico thoughout the nineteenth and twentieth centuries. As González Peña observes, "According to the calculations of D. José María Lafragua, up to one hundred and twenty poets wrote for the *Diario de México,* and the number of prose writers was probably the same . . . Special homage was paid to the cult of poetry" (113).

The weekly *El Pensador Mexicano* (The Mexican Thinker; 1812–1814), founded by José Joaquín Fernández de Lizardi, serves as a national tribunal, a point of convergence and intersection between oral culture and writing. This publication represents the first open and aggressive attempt to incorporate the expression of Mexicanness in literary journalism by distancing itself in its pages from peninsular tone, form, language, style, and theme. Without a doubt, it signifies a worthy attempt to move from a colonial to an independent mentality.

With the triumph of independence in 1821, cultural journalism in this period of construction of a national identity becomes a vehicle par excellence for the diffusion and formation of cultural projects. These cultural enterprises were under the auspices of the two majority groups that sought to control the direction of the country, the liberals and the conservatives. Consequently, magazines, reviews, supplements, newspapers, and weeklies focused on previously unreported customs and expressions, enthusiastically articulating an emerging nationalism as attested to by the appearance of the *Semanario Político Literario* (Political and Literary Weekly; 1821). In this way, cultural journalism is disseminated through pamphlets, calendars, weeklies, flyers, reviews, and newspapers. Although ephemeral and erratic, these publications reveal the nature of prevailing literary discourse and the cultural project in the process of formation that seeks to imprint on national consciousness what is uniquely Mexican. Nationalism is forged in these journalistic mediums through narratives, poetry, speeches, short novels, chronicles, theater, mystery novels, and political and bibliographic criticism, as well as in stories, debates, short essays, and commentaries that urgently seek to consolidate a model of representation that identifies with the homeland.

In 1822 the political literary newspaper *La Sabatina Universal* (Worldwide Saturday Review) appears. Anselmo Aguilar published the newspaper, but Fernández de Lizardi is speculated to have been the editor. *El Iris* (The Iris; 1826) relied on the collaboration of the Cuban poet José María Heredia and principally targeted women readers. As a consequence of publishing political commentaries in disagreement with the regime, this magazine was destined to survive for only a few months, thus becoming one of the first victims of official censorship (Ríos, 13–46).

The Count D. José Gómez de la Cortina published both *El Registro Trimestre* (The Trimester Register; 1832–1833), a magazine of literature, history, science, and the arts, and *Revista Mexicana* (The Mexican Review; 1834–1835), which along with *El Mosaico* (The Mosaic; 1837–1842) contain a collection of the works of Mexican and Iberian writers. These publications formulate the political creed of their participants and look primarily toward nationalistic cultural journalism with the goal of establishing a tradition of their own. At the end of this decade, *El Recreo de las Familias* (Family Entertainment; 1838), edited by Gondra and Anastasio Ochoa, shows a marked autochthonous emphasis, thus integrating the entire country into this project. It brings together contributions from the interior of the republic and focuses on the cultural debate of the day. This exchange is central to the discussion of the advantages and disadvantages of the models of literary representation, both neoclassical and romantic.

It is at this time that we see a relative expansion of newspapers and literary magazines in the provinces. These include the first provincial literary newspaper, *El Ensayo* (The Essay; 1838), founded by José María Lafragua, and weeklies which were directed primarily toward women readers, such as *Semanario de las Señoritas Mexicanas* (Young Mexican Women's Weekly; 1842) by Mariano Galván and the *Semanario de las Señoritas* (Young Women's Weekly; 1841) by Vicente García Torres. Although these publications maintain a traditional European format, they strive for a local stamp. For its part, *El Museo Mexicano* (The Mexican Museum; 1843–1845) attempts to amplify the thematic range of Mexican experience without ignoring topics of foreign literature, art, and culture. At this time, *El Liceo Mexicano* (The Mexican Lyceum, 1844) seeks to record Mexican daily life via portraits and writings on everyday urban and rural life.

One fundamental aspect in the cultural history of Mexico is the founding of literary societies to support the intellectual production and diffusion of their own cultural programs by way of journalistic publications and/or cultural reviews with a regular audience. Thus, for example, the Academia de Letrán, founded in 1836 and surviving twenty years, brings together Guillermo Prieto, Ignacio Rodríguez Galván, Fernando Calderón, José María Lafragua, José María and Juan Nepomuceno Lacunza, Ignacio Ramírez Pesado, Manuel Carpio, José Bernardo Couto, Francisco Manuel Sánchez de Tagle, Andrés Quintana Roo, and Manuel Eduardo Gorostiza. These intellectuals endeavor to forge a distinctly Mexicanized literary activity. This same impulse is evident in the annual *El Año Nuevo* (The New Year; 1837–1840), *El Ateneo Mexicano* (The Mexican Atheneum; 1844–1845), the voice of the society of the same name, and *El Registro Yucateco* (The Yucatán Register; 1845–1847), published by the Society of Friends and inspired by Justo Sierra O'Reilly. Other prominent examples include a new *El Mosaico* (The Mosaic; 1849–1850), published by the Academy of Sciences and Literature, and *El Ensayo Literario* (The Literary Essay; 1850–1852), the publication of the literary society Falange in the capital of Jalisco (Martínez, "México en busca," 2.1019–1071).

During the first six decades of the nineteenth century political confrontations constantly interplay in the cultural media. At the same time the cultural media witness the appearance of individuals, groups, and generations impelled to formulate and to carry out important changes in the cultural programs of the day out of a desire to broaden the dialogue around the question of national culture. Circumstance, the theme of national identity, and modes of registering information interact at a moment of political instability in the country, resulting in a literature of ideological combat, essays of indoctrination, defensive autobiographies, poetry, and sentimental novels of mystery, all of which are filtered through the particular vision of each diverse interest group of the period.

These first ideological confrontations are consolidated in the foundation of significant newspapers and cultural supplements such as *El Siglo XIX* (The Nineteenth Century; 1841) and *El Monitor Republicano* (The Republican Monitor; 1844). In spite of precarious economic conditions and the critical political situation of the moment, these periodicals resolutely present the most varied and colorful aspects of the Mexican cultural tapestry. Innumerable national writers frequently contribute poems, short stories, historical studies, miscellaneous articles, and writings on everyday life to both dailies during their respective time periods. These contributions based on some fashionable theme appear regularly and include novels or other books by national and foreign authors.

With the restoration of the republic in 1867 comes the desire to create an atmosphere of cultural conciliation that would allow everything from courteous disagreement to open opposition, thus fomenting critical discussion and polemics. The famous literary soirees organized by Ignacio Manuel Altamirano take place at this time, between November 1867 and April 1868. The participants include Guillermo Prieto, Manuel Payno, Ignacio Ramírez, Vicente Riva Palacio, Luis G. Ortiz, José Tomás de Cuéllar, Juan A. Mateos, Justo Sierra, and Juan de Dios Peza. These soirees, along with other literary circles, cultural societies, and academies, promote cultural programs consonant with a project for national harmony. Inspired by the enthusiasm of those gatherings, Altamirano founded a magazine whose principal objective was to produce means of integration and conciliation for the different political, cultural, and literary factions of the moment. The cultural project to give national and universal resonance to Mexican literature is without a doubt reflected in Altamirano's *El Renacimiento* (The Renaissance; 1869). Edited by Gonzalo A. Esteva and Ignacio Manuel Altamirano, it includes the collaboration of Ignacio Montes de Oca, Joaquín Arróniz, Guillermo Prieto, José Peón y Contreras, José María Roa Bárcena, Isabel Prieto de Landázuri, and Vicente Riva Palacio. This cultural medium outlines the characteristics of a literature seeking to establish its own tradition. At the same time the cultural review proposes a global cultural project that synthesizes the affirmation of a national consciousness and pride—thematically circumscribed by Mexican culture—with cultural production abroad.

Another notable society participating in the debate over the nature and function of Mexican literature and culture is the Liceo Hidalgo (Hidalgo Lyceum), which in 1888 becomes the scene for the famous polemic between Ignacio Manuel Altamirano and Francisco Pimentel (Schneider, 71–119). It is important to note that the newspaper *El Federalista* (The Federalist; 1811–1878)—which Payno and Altamirano helped to found and on which Manuel Gutiérrez Nájera and Justo Sierra collaborated—published the *Edición Literaria de los Domingos* (Sunday Literary Edition; 1872–1877), Mexico's first literary supplement.

The last third of the nineteenth century brings with the government of Porfirio Díaz a relative "peace" that, combined with the improvement of economic and social conditions and with the promise of progress, inaugurates a variety of literary publications. These include *La Linterna Mágica* (The Magic Lantern; 1872), *El Artista* (The Artist; 1874–1875), *La Alianza Literaria* (The Literary Alliance; Guadalajara, 1876), *La Aurora Literaria* (The Literary Dawn; Guadalajara, 1877–1890), *La República Literaria* (The Literary Republic; 1886–1890), and *La Juventud Literaria* (The Literary Youth; 1887–1888). The latter publication represents the intersection of traditions, generations, and sensibilities that were uniquely to characterize literary and cultural activity in Mexico at the end of the nineteenth century and the beginnings of the twentieth. *La Juventud Literaria* enjoys the collaboration of a workshop of writers that includes Luis G. Urbina, Jesús E. Valenzuela, Manuel Gutiérrez Nájera, Manuel Puga, Salvador Díaz Mirón, Federico Gamboa, Carlos Díaz Dufóo, and Manuel José Othón. *El Parnaso Mexicano* (The Mexican Parnassus; 1886), under the direction of Vicente Riva Palacio, is seriously dedicated to promoting the production of Mexican poetry, offering creative works, critical essays, biographical information, and sketches of the most famous contemporary poets.

Literary movements appear, disappear, and are established and legitimized through the cultural and literary reviews and the cultural supplements that publicize and sanctify them. Modernism in Mexico is promoted for the most part through two reviews, the *Revista Azul* (Azure Review; 1894–1896), founded by Manuel Gutiérrez Nájera and Carlos Díaz Dufóo and a Sunday supplement to the newspaper *El Partido Liberal* (The Liberal Party), and the *Revista Moderna* (Modern Review; 1898–1911). It is the *Revista Azul* which marks the convergence of diverse tendencies, styles, and aesthetic theories characterized by the echoes of a previous literary experience with centrifugal forces in response to the cultural reality of the moment. This literary review becomes the agent of a generation of writers who have a resounding impact on the models of subsequent literary expression. Some of the collaborators include Manuel Gutiérrez Nájera (El Duque Job), Luis G. Urbina, Angel del Campo (Micrós), Porfirio Martínez Peñaloza, Salvador Díaz Mirón, Emilio Rabasa, Luis González Obregón, Jesús Valenzuela, and María Enriqueta Camarillo de Pereyra (Carter, 47–80)

One hundred and twenty-eight issues of *Revista Azul* were published, incorporating the work of Mexican and other Spanish American authors, along with translations from pieces written in French, prose, poetry, and a variety of articles. These ranged from debates about art to critical commentaries on poetry and articles polemicizing the function of cosmopolitan or national aesthetic expression. At the same time the review brought prominent French and Spanish writers such as Charles Baudelaire, Marcel Prévost, Emile Zola, Benito Pérez Galdós, Gaspar Núñez de Arce, and Salvador Rueda to the Mexican readership. The historical value of the *Revista Azul* is unquestionable because it gave concrete form to the confluence of national and Hispanic American expression in the last decade of the nineteenth century. It included works from modernist writers whose talent had been recognized throughout Latin America and much of Europe, such as Rubén Darío, Julián del Casal, José Santos Chocano, and José Martí. It is important to note that within their limitations, *El Renacimiento,* inspired by Altamirano, and *Revista Azul* conveyed a search for continuity, for a tradition that would strive to support the transcendental value of the articulation, promotion, and development of the critical analysis of a national culture and literature, as well as the integration of the national culture into the universal culture.

Revista Moderna, which voices the innovative spirit of the consolidation of modernism, compliments *Revista Azul* by gathering creative works and translations of manifestos and foreign creative writing and compiling proclamations on the absolute autonomy of art from the perspective of aesthetics. Beginning with its ninth issue, important polemics are covered, including the debate over nationalism versus cosmopolitanism, with Victoriano Salado Alvarez against the modernists Amado Nervo, Juan José Tablada, Jesús Urueta, and Jesús Valenzuela (Schneider, 120–158). The artistic director of the first issue is Julio Ruelas, whose collaborators include José Juan Tablada, Antenor Lezcano, Bernardo Couto Castillo, Rubén M. Campos, Alberto Leduc, Francisco M. de Olaguibel, Jesús Urueta, Ciro B. Ceballos, Rafael Delgado, and Jesús Valenzuela. This review encourages a cooperation between those dedicated to the plastic arts and those working within the literary field. *Revista Moderna* is an exception to other nineteenth-century publications that served to promote and display illustrations independent of the literary text under consideration. Ninety-six issues were published in two different periods, one under the direction of Jesús Valenzuela (1898–1903) and a second one with both Amado Nervo and Jesús Valenzuela at the helm (1903–1911), during which time the name was changed to the *Revista Moderna de México* (Modern Mexican Review).

Moving in a direction similar to that of *Revista Moderna* and *Revista Moderna de México* is *Savia Moderna* (Modern Impulse; 1906), founded by Alfonso Cravioto and Luis Castillo Ledón. This publication first appeared in 1906 and published six issues. It expressed the goal of fostering contemporary Mexican literature by bringing writers together. These included the poets Alfonso Cravioto, Eduardo Colin, and Luis Castillo Ledón and prose writers such as Antonio Caso, José J. Gamboa, Carlos González Peña, Jesús Valenzuela, and Emilio Valenzuela. The valuable contributions of essayists like Alfonso Reyes, Max Henríquez Ureña, and Pedro Henríquez Ureña, all of whom represent the unease of a new generation—the Atheneum of Youth—were also included.

The outbreak of the revolution brings with it the resurgence of a "spiritual nationalism" that sees in culture the necessary mirror for a new Mexican identity. Culture is thought to be the instrument to promote, voluntarily or involuntarily, serious debate over a new criteria for the representation of what is considered to be "national." From this moment on, literary and cultural reviews present a variety of interpretations of cultural nationalism, focusing on the models of *criollismo,* nativism, regionalism, indigenism, avant-gardism, and social realism. In the turbulence of the revolutionary movement the magazine *Nosotros* (We; 1911) appears, bringing together the collaborators of *Re-*

vista Moderna under the direction of the poet Francisco González Guerrero. It defines itself primarily as a "review of art and education" and initially has pedagogical focus but subsequently concentrates on the diffusion and propagation of literary materials. It is a review published with great sacrifice, due to the political, economic, and social circumstances in which it is produced.

One curious yet important event in the historiography of journalistic literatures is the appearance of the humor weekly *Multicolor* (Multicolored; 1911– 1914), the offspring of political caricature directed primarily at a male public. It is later modified to incorporate the publication of burlesque verse and prose. Also in this decade of political instability a group of preparatory-school students attempt to promote the plastic arts, music, and literature. They include the distinguished future poet-laureate Carlos Pellicer and the untiring cultural promoter Octavio G. Barreda. They succeed in obtaining a subsidy from the secretary of education, Felix F. Palavicini, to publish *Gladios* (Gladius; 1916), directed by the poet Luis Enrique Erro and administered by Octavio G. Barreda. The sections on literature remain under the supervision of Carlos Pellicer, those of music under that of the distinguished composer Carlos Chávez, and plastic arts under Eduardo Chávez. A section on history is also included, as well as one of reviews and another of science.

In the stormy cultural context of the second decade of this century the vitality of poetic production gives impetus to the founding of the illustrated review *Pegaso* (Pegasus; 1917), which brings together the efforts of Enrique González Martínez, Efrén Rebolledo, and Ramón López Velarde. Some of the participants subsequently come to publish the *San-ev-ank* (1918), a student weekly of some twenty pages directed by the restless Luis Enrique Erro, administered by Octavio G. Barreda, and edited by Guillermo Dávila, Fernando Velázquez Subikurskz, and others. Innumerable artists and writers collaborate on the weekly, including Carlos Pellicer, Bernardo Ortiz de Montellano, José Gorostiza, Jaime Torres Bodet, and Enrique González Rojo, among others. The major value of the review lies in the risk it takes in promoting works of future writers of the Contemporáneos (Contemporaries) movement.

Under the guidance of Enrique González Martínez, *México Moderno* (Modern Mexico; 1920–1923) was an organ of the publishing house of the same name. Its original format was divided into sections on literature, music, and books, with Jaime Torres Bodet, Manuel M. Ponce, and Genaro Estrada in charge, respectively. Included in the list were also artists and intellectuals who were already known for their sophisticated work, such as Alfonso Caso, Antonio Caso, Alfonso Reyes, and Martín Luis Guzmán. It was a magazine open to the latest in philosophy and literature, and it was successful in presenting new Mexican values as well as translations of the best works on the international level in both prose and poetry (Monterde, 111–143).

El Maestro, Revista de Cultura Nacional (Maestro, Review of National Culture) appears in 1921 and includes Ramón López Velarde as one of its editors, along with contributors like José Gorostiza, Jaime Torres Bodet, and Carlos Pellicer. Under the auspices of José Vasconcelos, minister of education, and the direction of Enrique Monterde and Agustín Loera y Chávez, this review brings together sections on literature, poetry and history—works universal in scope by Hispanic Americans and Spaniards. These contributors were anxious to revalidate Mexican values as well as to publish "humanistic expression."

Without escaping the formal experimentalism that prevailed in Western culture during the twenties, a series of artistic declarations challenged the nature and function of aesthetic experience and expression. In this light, *Actual: Hoja de Vanguardia* (Present: Writing of the Avant-Garde) appears along with the first "Manifiesto estridentista" (Stridentist Manifesto), for which Manuel Maples Arce is responsible. The second manifesto, which appeared in Puebla in 1923, was endorsed by Manuel Maples Arce, Germán List Arzubide, Salvador Gallardo, and Miguel N. Lira, among others. The third came out in Puebla in 1925, the fourth in Zacatecas, and the fifth in Ciudad Victoria, Tamaulipas. This coming together of writers in a literary movement that sought to break barriers and minimize the prevailing cultural centralism makes evident the close relationship between writers of the provinces and those of Mexico City. (Benítez, 145–164).

As a result, writers affiliated with this *estridencia* (stridency) in the provinces also look to their own means of expression, which in Puebla takes form in the review *Ser* (To Be); in Jalapa, in *Horizonte* (Horizon; 1922–1925); and in Mexico City, in *Irradiador: Revista Internacional de Vanguardia* (Illuminator: the Review of the International Avant-Garde). These reviews of the avant-garde express their ridicule of and disdain for the official canon and sacred literary figures. They boast of their familiarity and concurrence with the European avant-garde movement, as well as their affiliation with the latest in the literary, artistic, and cultural fields of the metropolises of the Old World, including the Latin American ultraist and creationist avant-garde. They insist on their close relationship with the Mexican Revolution and emphasize their artistic commitment to the masses, holding firm to a mode of reading founded upon this new political poetics. There is a profound desire in their texts to fuse the political avant-garde with the artistic by means of formal experimentation and ideological shock.

At the beginning of the 1920s several publications distinguish themselves: *La Falange, Revista de Cultura Latina* (The Phalanx: Review of Spanish-American Culture; 1922–1923), under the direction of Jaime Torres Bodet and Bernardo Ortiz de Montellano; *El Libro y el Pueblo* (The Book and the People; 1922), a monthly bibliographical review published by the Department of Libraries of the Secretary of Education under the administration of José Vasconcelos, which adapted itself successively to different objectives, eventually incorporating literary criticism and then the essay; and the *Museo de las Letras* (Museum of Literature), the Sunday supplement of *El Universal.* In 1924 *Antena* (Antenna) emerged under the direction of Francisco Monterde.

It published five issues, initially reporting the radio programming of select music. It relied on contributors of high quality, such as Xavier Villaurrutia and Salvador Novo, and also published avant-garde books.

Ulises (Ulysses; 1927), a cultural review of intellectual defiance and subtle and playful criticism, promoted and produced scandalous, radical, sophisticated, and profoundly experimental literary projects. It brought together Salvador Novo, Xavier Villaurrutia, Gilberto Owen, Carlos Pellicer, Enrique González Martínez, Jaime Torres Bodet, Roberto Montenegro, and Jorge Cuesta. Open to both the national and the cosmopolitan, it announced a change of tastes and aesthetic sensibilities, putting out six issues, including supplements that are short novels, poetry, essays, and translations, thus distinguishing itself as one of the architects of the impending artistic renovation. In mid-1929 a group of young writers conscious of and concerned about existing social conditions in the country decided to dedicate their artistic and literary efforts to the masses and to the working class. They considered questions of technique and aesthetic theory as secondary, privileging above all the social and political dimension of art. For them, artistic production and social action inform each other in order to interpret daily national reality. These writers began with the publication of the review *Vértice* (Vertex), which would put out four issues between 1929 and 1930, and one issue of the review entitled *Agorismo* (Agorism). The publication of *Vértice* signaled the rupture with traditionalism and the bourgeois canon; it oriented itself culturally, aesthetically, and socially toward the masses and rejected the dehumanization of art. The review advanced the proposition that Mexican literature was critically too far removed from the Mexican Revolution and insisted that national literature must be made explanatory, educational, and politically confrontational by basing itself on contemporary events. Collaborating on the publication were Alfredo Alvarez García, José María Benítez, Gilberto Bosque, María del Mar, Rafael López, Gustavo Ortiz Hernán, and Rafael Lozano. Diego Rivera, José Muñoz Cota, and Germán List Arzubide also participated.

Within this ideological line the Block of Intellectual Workers found the magazine *Crisol* (Crucible), which brings out monthly issues from 1929 until 1938. The review examines national problems and attempts to characterize the ideology of the revolution by inviting literary production that expresses the national and international political reality and includes social, political, economic, and cultural studies. Those writers who support the close relationship between art and the social struggle predominate. Among some of the contributors are Enrique Schultz, Emilio Portes Gil, Luis L. León, Jesús Rangel, Heriberto Jara, Adolfo Ruiz Cortinez, Tomás Manjarrez, José María Benítez, Leopoldo Ramos, Germán List Arzubide, Francisco Rojas González, and Jesús Reyes Ruiz.

The program for expressing a proletarian culture is continued later on by *Frente a Frente* (Face to Face; 1936–1937), the main publication of the League of Revolutionary Writers and Artists, and by *Ruta* (Route; 1938–1939). Both reviews are a project of José Mancisidor and Lorenzo Turrent, who engaged the Contemporáneos in a furious debate. *Vértice, Crisol, Agorismo, Frente a Frente,* and *Ruta,* rooted in the 1910 Revolution, all channel social and political unrest. These reviews represent serious efforts in literature, art, and culture toward a greater awareness of social reality and the appreciation and evaluation of society. At the same time, these writers distance themselves from elitist audiences in order to communicate with a broader readership. Another cultural strand in the generative process of literary production of these times is woven by the review *Contemporáneos* (Contemporaries; 1928–1939). This group includes Jaime Torres Bodet, Bernardo Gastelum, José Gorostiza, Bernardo Ortiz de Montellano, Xavier Villaurrutia, Enrique González Rojo, Rubén Salazar Mallén, Salvador Novo, and Jorge Cuesta. The review undergoes several transformations during its life under the editorship of Bernardo Gastelum, Jaime Torres Bodet, Bernardo Ortiz de Montellano, and Enrique González Rojo. These founding editors expanded editorial control to include Genaro Estrada, Celestino Gorostiza, Samuel Ramos, Ruben Salazar Mallén, and Ermilo Abreu Gómez. Later Bernardo Ortiz de Montellano assumed the directorship (Forster; Paz, 2:17–176; Sheridan). *Contemporáneos* was a controversial review that took its name from the generation that created it and survived by becoming well known nationally and internationally. It was an eclectic cultural medium that promoted continued awareness of the tension between nationalism and cosmopolitanism, ever-present since the nineteenth century. The review accomplished this in part by disseminating the ideas and critical attitudes of the European avant-garde. Viewed with distrust for its lack of emphasis on Mexican themes and for its continually changing identity, the review's standing seems to have been determined primarily by the prestige of its contributors. *Contemporáneos* inspired other cultural media, injected life into Mexico's theater tradition, inaugurated movie criticism in Mexico, gave impetus to art criticism, renewed cultural and political journalism, and engaged in a critical and polemical dialogue with the controversial nationalistic positions of the time (Schneider, 381). *Contemporáneos* marked a transition in modern Mexico's literary and intellectual history and served as a link between several generations and artistic movements generating fertile guidelines not only for criticism, but also for the essay and creative writing.

Jorge Cuesta is the founding director of *Examen* (Scrutiny; 1932), a modern writer's magazine similar to Alfonso Reyes's *Monterrey,* a journal of general culture and literature, and Novo's and Villaurrutia's *Ulises. Examen* embraces philosophical, political, cultural and social ideas. Many of the concerns expressed earlier in *Contemporáneos* are now articulated by a new generation actively working on the review *Barandal* (Balustrade; 1931–1932). This group includes artists and intellectuals born between 1913 and 1915, such as Octavio Paz, Rafael López Malo, Salvador Toscano, Agustín Loera y Chávez, and Arnulfo Martínez Lavalle. The review publishes seven issues, including a poetry supplement devoted to Villaurrutia, Pellicer, and Novo, among others. Other contributors include Julio Prieto, Raúl Vega Córdoba, Humberto Mata, Manuel Rivera Silva, and Francisco López Manjarrez. The Barandal group published four issues of the review *Cuadernos del Valle de México* (Notebooks from the Valley of Mexico; 1933–1934) until its demise as a generation; one unique figure from this group was Octavio Paz. *Alcancía* (Piggybank), under the creative directorship of Justino Fernández and Edmundo O'Gorman, and *Fábula* (Fable), under Miguel N. Lira, appear at this same time, expanding the literary interests of the readership.

Taller Poético (Poetry Workshop; 1936–1938) succeeds in bringing together Mexican poets and, under the editorship of Rafael Solana, encompasses in four issues a broad range of trends, including both contemporaries and poets of other generations. It mainly focuses on poetry, serving as an outlet for the best works of Torres Bodet, Pellicer, Novo, Ortiz de Montellano, Villaurrutia, José Moreno Villa, and Federico García Lorca. *Taller Poético* also includes work by authors without any other affiliation, such as Elías Nandino, Anselmo Mena, and Enrique Asúnsolo, and introduces and promotes young Mexican poets like Efraín Huerta (Paz, 2:17–176).

Taller (Workshop) published twelve issues between 1938 and 1941. The first four issues were edited by Rafael Solana, the remaining eight by Octavio Paz. The magazine served as a platform for diverse artistic sensitivities: it welcomed recently arrived Spanish authors like Ramón Gaya, Juan Rejano, María Zambrano, Antonio Sánchez Barbudo, José Bergamín, and Francisco Giner de los Ríos. Like *Taller Poético, Taller* expressed a maturation of the cultural and aesthetic ideas first introduced in *Contemporáneos*.

Abside (Apse; 1937–1979), edited by Gabriel Méndez Plancarte, proves to be tenaciously uncompromising in its Catholic interpretation of culture and achieves its purpose as one of the nation's primary conservative platforms in this media. Also born in 1937, *Letras de México* (Mexican Letters; 1937–1947), directed by Octavio Barreda, succeeds in setting aside political and literary disagreements. The review publishes 132 issues and reaches the phenomenal production—by the standards of that time—of a thousand copies distributed. It embodies the texture of the intellectual movement of a whole decade, introducing promising young figures as well as giving space to those already established like Agustín Yáñez, Samuel Ramos, Xavier Villaurrutia, Bernardo Ortiz de Montellano, Carlos Pellicer, Eduardo Villaseñor, and Felipe Teixidor. *Letras de México* galvanizes the cultural affinities between a variety of literary tendencies and interests. It is subdivided into sections: "Anuncios y presencias" (Announcements and Presences, on future publications, visits of artists, information about Mexican culture), "Poesía" (Poetry, usually recent), "Artículo de fondo" (In-depth Essay, on one of the best books of the previous month), "Actualidad literaria" (Literary News, critical comments on Mexican books), "Bibliografía del mes" (Monthly Bibliography), and others like "Artes plásticas" (Visual Arts), "Teatro" (Theater), and so on.

Another review that strikes a balance between tradition and modernity is Alfonso Reyes's *Tierra Nueva* (New World; 1940–1942). Other magazines representing continuities or ruptures between groups and generations and highlighting the diversity of the poetic expression of the time are *América* 1940,

Tiras de Colores (Streamers), *Espiga* (Sprout), *Vórtice* (Vortex; 1954), *Firmamento* (Firmament; 1945), and *Rueca* (Spinning Wheel; 1941–1952). The latter serves as a voice for women's poetic production, with contributors like Carmen Toscano, María Ramona Rey, María del Carmen Millán, Pina Juárez Frausto, and Ernestina de Champourcin. At the same time in different provinces a number of pioneering magazines are published: *Prisma* (Prism; 1940–1941), *Eros* (1943), *Pan* (Bread; 1945–1946), and *Ariel* (1949) in Guadalajara; in Guanajuato, *Umbral* (Threshold; 1941); in San Luis Potosí, *Letras Potosinas* (Literature of Potosí; 1943) and *Estilo* (Style; 1945–1946); in Monterrey, *Armas y Letras* (Arms and Letters; 1944 to the present); in Saltillo, *Papel de Poesía* (Poetry Paper; 1940–1948); in Torreón, *Cauce* (River Bed; 1948); in Morelia, Michoacán, *Viñeta de Literatura Michoacana* (*Vignettes of Michoacán Literature*; 1944–1947), *Trento* (1944–?), *Gaceta de Historia y Literatura* (Gazette of History and Literature; 1947 to the present), and *La Espiga y el Laurel* (The Sprout of Grain and the Laurel; 1947–?); in Puebla, *Cauce* (River Bed; 1945–1946); in Culiacán, *Letras de Sinaloa* (Literature of Sinaloa; 1947); and finally, in Veracruz, *Hojas de Literatura* (Papers of Literature; 1948–1949) (Martínez, *Literatura mexicana,* 1:83).

In 1942 *Cuadernos Americanos* (American Notebooks) was founded by the Chilean Juan Larrea and directed by the distinguished Mexican intellectual Jesús Silva Herzog. The review responded to a continental vision of culture that sought points of contact between the Mexican cultural experience and international phenomena and also confronted the official cultural project with Latin American reality. Seeking to establish correspondences between reality and culture, it stressed an interdisciplinary approach based on both Mexican and Latin American social, economic, political, and cultural phenomena. Thus, *Cuadernos Americanos* achieved an authentic critical attitude which confronted, redefined, and transcended the national cultural discourse of the moment (Monsiváis, "Notas," 2:1375–1548).

El Hijo Pródigo (The Prodigal Son), directed from 1943 to 1946 by Octavio G. Barreda, establishes a platform for changes in literary taste. It integrates sections that include essays, narrative, theater, poetry, translations of relevant texts, critical commentary about recent works, and notes related to entertainment, all framed by an editorial divided into two parts: "Imaginación" (Imagination) and "Realidad" (Reality). Such outstanding figures as Xavier Villaurrutia, Octavio Paz, Antonio Sánchez Barbudo, Alí Chumacero, and Celestino Gorostiza comprised the editorial board. To appreciate the importance and the influence of this review on the cultural atmosphere of Mexico, it is enough to consider the works of literature and art, the national and foreign theater, and the chorus of voices and styles that reveal their potential in its pages and inspire future cultural projects.

By the middle of the 1950s, the economic benefits of "stabilizing development" begin to show up in educational and cultural spheres, and they continue to be felt into the 1970s. At the same time the centers of higher education provide a stable structure that will permit the production and dissemination of culture as well as the professionalization of intellectual activity. In these contexts, academic endeavors bring together a group of intellectuals that José Emilio Pacheco labeled the Generation of 1950. This ensemble includes Rosario Castellanos, Emilio Carballido, Sergio Magaña, Jaime Sabines, Miguel Guardia, Jorge Hernández Campos, Ricardo Garibay, Margarita Michelena, Juan Rulfo, Juan José Arreola, Rubén Bonifaz Nuño, Jaime García Terrés, and Jorge Ibargüengoitia. The latter worked also with the philosophical group Hyperión, which included Emilio Uranga, Joaquín McGregor, Luis Villoro, Jorge Portilla, and Ricardo Guerra. This generation brings about the examination, the study, and the interpretation of the concept of a national ontology, a task which leads the majority of them to collaborate in the production of *Revista Antológica América* (The American Anthology Review), which is under the direction of the poet Efrén Hernández.

This generation records the experiences of a country changed by economic development and by the emergence of growing doubt and skepticism about the official concept of nationalism. This situation produces sharp critical analyses of the concepts of tradition, canon, and the diverse modalities of form and content which convey this idea of questioning nationalism, proposing in its place an integration of the entire Western cultural experience. In the context of distrust brought about by the Cold War and its ideological repercussions, several organs appear for the dissemination of intellectual activity. They include the cultural supplements of *El Nacional* (The National), directed by Juan Rejano, and *México en la Cultura* (México in its Culture) of the daily *Novedades* (News; 1949–1961), directed by the active cultural promotor Fernando Benítez. Benítez later founds *Siempre* (Always), which becomes *La Cultura en México* (Culture in México; 1962) and is continued by Carlos Monsiváis. *El Suplemento de Novedades* is a weekly that invites serious discussion by underscoring the relationship between culture, history, and power and energetically criticizing traditions that mythify the recent past. Speaking about its importance, Monsiváis quotes Alfonso Reyes: "Cultural life in Mexico during this decade found reconstruction of its best aspects thanks to 'Suplemento de Novedades.' Those of us involved with it have much to be thankful for" (Monsiváis, "No quisiera," 2). The pages of *México en la Cultura* feature a register of voices characterized by their plurality, openness, and concern for the realization of Latin American cultural alternatives. It publishes texts by Alejo Carpentier, Juan Goytisolo, Augusto Salazar Bondy, Octavio Paz, Jesús Silva Herzog, Alfonso Caso, Augusto Roa Bastos, Agustín Yáñez, and Pablo Neruda.

A profile of the qualitative changes that would emerge in the new Mexican narrative is recorded in the 1950s and 1960s in the *Revista Mexicana de Literatura* (Mexican Review of Literature), under the direction of Carlos Fuentes and Emmanuel Carballo in its first stage and Tomás Segovia and Juan García Ponce in its second. This review seeks to integrate diverse literary traditions and to introduce new writers and new works, promoting debate on the relationship between nationalism and social realism. Criticism thereby assumes aesthetic and moral responsibility as its function, opening doors to Latin American writers and confirming the desire to experiment.

The transition to the decade of the 1960s is marked by the historic event that places Hispanic America at the center of the forum of intellectual discussion, singularly affecting the cultural perception and the role of intellectuals in the process of social transformation: the Cuban Revolution (Monsiváis, "Notas," 2:1375–1548). At that time, Mexico was experiencing an editorial boom, the result of an expanding cultural industry and the development of middle-class sectors. These latter phenomena are the product of mass education that was initiated during the presidency of Miguel Alemán (1946–1952) and continues to the present. The atmosphere of financial development promotes and inspires intellectual production, considerably increasing cultural activities that leave their stamp on mimeographed pages, reviews, and supplements, as well as in amateur editions by literary workshops. The importance of these magazines and literary supplements lies in their quantity and in their influence on a continually growing public that perceives this journalistic form as the cultural vehicle for the expression of belligerent attitudes. Due to these characteristics, it is impossible to identify, classify, and analyze these ongoing publications with any certainty. Because economic, political, and social circumstances conditioned the length of their lives in many cases, it is necessary to point out their relationship to each other in the cultural discourse of recent decades.

One product of this cultural context was the *Revista de la Universidad de México* (University of Mexico Review; 1946 to the present), which during its lifetime has had as directors such outstanding intellectuals as Jaime García Terrés, Luis Villoro, and Gastón García Cantú. By publishing excellent translations of theoretical texts and original analytical studies, they supported the dissemination of new critical paradigms, including Marxism, existentialism, structuralism, feminism, and deconstructionism. The *Revista* earned national and international recognition for its ability to identify and promote innovative currents of thought. It is also important to mention the bilingual publication of poetic production by *El Corno Emplumado* (The Feathered Horn), a literary review edited by Margaret Randall and Sergio Mondragón. This publication scrutinizes a range of poetic expression and also gives voice to works by women writers.

One of the most distinguished lists of contributors to any Latin American review of this type can be seen in *Diálogos* (Dialogues; 1965–1985), founded by Ramón Xirau as an organ of the Colegio de México. Among its researchers and collaborators figure André Malraux, Noam Chomsky, Raymond Aron, Henri Michaux, Jorge Luis Borges, and Octavio Paz. The analysis and criticism that appear in its pages give rise to a sustained dialogue on national and universal culture. Some of its distinguished editors have been writers such as José Emilio Pacheco, Homero Aridjis, Vicente Leñero, and Alberto Dallal. Outside Mexico City, *La Palabra y el Hombre* (Word and Man) of the University of Veracruz, excels in its systematic effort to disseminate critical and original works. This review was founded by Sergio Galindo and is presently under the direction of Raúl Hernández Viveros. Focusing on issues around specific themes like literature of the 1960s, *La Palabra y el Hombre* publishes studies about Mexican and Latin American literature and culture from a range of ideological perspectives. It also offers reviews of literary conferences and testimonials and provides the most complete and informative coverage of cultural issues.

The petroleum bonanza of the seventies spawns the appearance of an enormous quantity of publications under the sponsorship of government institutions, private cultural associations, and public as well as private universities. Support also comes from groups demanding their right to social recognition, such as homosexuals, women, and lumpen proletarians. The discovery of the reality of an increasingly complex Mexico and of a more specialized and diversified cultural realm create the need for critical voices that will generate discussion in order to amplify and redefine the role of literary journalism in the sociocultural context of Mexico. Examples of this tendency include *Plural* (Plural; 1971–1976), *Texto crítico* (Critical Text; 1975 to the present), and *Nexos* (Nexus; 1978 to the present). The 1968 crisis of the Mexican political system initiates the radicalization of many cultural projects, turning them into arenas of criticism which question the function of cultural discourse in various ways. Intellectual contributions are multiplied by the expansion of the universe of readers attracted through networks of relationships among literature, culture, popular culture, and sexual or political marginalization. At the same time, the avalanche of cultural projects reflects the transnationalization of culture, the inequality of social experiences, the disparity of access to culture, and the metamorphosis and democratization of public taste and language. These phenomena lead to a disjunction between journalistic production supported by the state and home-produced publications. In this setting of massive cultural projects it is worth noting the convocational power of *Vuelta* (Return; 1976 to the present) and the aforementioned *Texto crítico, Nexos,* and *Plural,* which were centers of generational convergence, as some still are. From this standpoint, we witness an expansion of the limits, an amplification of the various tendencies and contradictory forces in the tastes, sensibilities, necessities, principles, and cultural obsessions of the times (Monsiváis, "No quisiera," 6).

Under the direction of Octavio Paz, *Plural* and later *Vuelta* are successful in creating a blend of the traditional and the modern with regard to universal literary and cultural phenomena. Open to cosmopolitan currents, they look toward establishing allies, affinities, and correspondences, thus stimulating critical and independent thinking through the participation of established Latin American writers. Their influence and impact as bulwarks of the intellectual establishment—not only in Mexico, but also in all of contemporary Latin America and Spain—is undeniable. Some of the distinguished names have included Enrique Krauze, Adolfo Bioy Casares, Guillermo Cabrera Infante, Julieta Campos, Haroldo de Campos, José de la Colina, Salvador Elizondo, Juan García Ponce, Severo Sarduy, and Gabriel Zaid. Although *Nexos* is not a publication specializing in cultural phenomena per se, it has done its part to present an analytic discourse that establishes points of contact between cultural experiences and the array of sociopolitical experiences of the moment. *Nexos* is a monthly publication of the Centro de Investigación Cultural y Científica, founded by Enrique Florescano and presently directed by Héctor Aguilar Camín. One finds in its pages a continuing critical examination of and concern for the multidimensional relationships between writing, history, and power. Contributors include such important figures as Luis Miguel Aguilar, Lourdes Arizpe, Roger Bartra, Hermann Bellinghausen, José Joaquín Blanco, Guillermo Bonfil, Pablo González Casanova, Soledad Loaeza, Carlos Monsiváis, Alejandra Moreno Toscano, Carlos Pereyra, José María Pérez Gay, Ruy Pérez Tamayo, Arturo Warman, and José Warman. This review works to expand cultural options and methods of critical analysis of literary phenomena, focusing on establishing coordinates in interdisciplinary reflection that would attempt to capture the processes of transformation of cultural reality.

Texto Crítico is a publication based on articles about the diverse literary genres in Latin America. Founded in 1975 in Jalapa, Veracruz, under the auspices of the Centro de Investigaciones Lingüísticas y Literarias de la Universidad de Veracruz, it was originally edited by the Uruguayan Jorge Ruffinelli. Its models of research range from historical biographical studies to semiolinguistic approaches to literature. The essays included center around works by such well-known authors as José Revueltas, Julio Cortázar, and Juan Carlos Onetti. Special issues are dedicated totally or in part to a particular theme or author. The caliber of the critics and the intellectual maturity of the researchers brought together in this review have made it a very important forum for theoretical and critical analysis in the area of Latin American literary production. Of similar importance is the revitalization of cultural supplements to daily newspapers like *Excélsior, Novedades* (News), *El Día* (The Day), *El Sol de México* (The Mexican Sun), *El Nacional* (The National), *unomásuno* (One Plus One), and *La Jornada* (The Daily) (Foster and Peña).

This overview of the shifting topography of journalistic literary publications allows one to contemplate the vitality of intellectual production in Mexico and to appreciate the aspects of cultural history that they reveal. The literary review has been and continues to be a nexus of ideological, social, and cultural confrontation, a broken mirror which reflects the changing nature of the national cultural projects in Mexico's historical development. These reviews point to the continuities and discontinuities between literary groups and currents, bridging gaps between generations while recognizing, establishing, and advancing a tradition that sets a model canon of culture. The wide spectrum of literary publications is a manifestation of the heterogeneity of public tastes, needs, and sensibilities, all of which call for distinct modes of reading and writing. Thus they reflect the intricate richness of the multidimensional aspects of contemporary culture that expand and further complicate the traditional consumption of intellectual production. In the last two decades of intense social, economic, political, and cultural changes, Mexico has become the center of many important intellectual and political movements. New themes and approaches inspire the writer to fresh responses to a multitude of questions about an open and defiant present. The explosion of political, regional, social, and individual differences demands creative responses and intellectual honesty because these will have a significant effect upon the evolution and definition of universal culture. The fact that these new attitudes and responses have been textually registered will force the reevaluation of the conceptual apparatus that they sustain and will demand the analysis of the diverse forms of inscription that record them. At this time, for better or for worse, cultural expression is obsessed with exploring and deciphering the intimate relationship between power and writing.

BIBLIOGRAPHY

Benítez, José María. "El estridentismo, el agorismo, *Crisol.*" In Benítez, Carter, and Martínez, 145–164.

Benítez, José María, Boyd G. Carter, and Porfirio Martínez Peñaloza, eds. *Las revistas literarias de México.* Mexico City: Instituto Nacional de Bellas Artes, Departamento de Literatura, 1963.

Carter, Boyd G. "Revistas literarias del Modernismo." In Benítez, Carter, and Martínez, 47–80.

Cosío Villegas, Daniel, ed. *Historia general de México,* vol. 2. Mexico City: El Colegio de México, 1976.

Forster, Merlin H. *Los contemporáneos, 1920–1932: Perfil de un movimiento vanguardista mexicano.* Mexico City: Ediciones de Andrea, 1964.

Foster, David William, and Luis H. Peña. "Materiales para el estudio de la nueva narrativa hispanoamericana: Dos ensayos." *Revista Interamericana de Bibliografía* 35 (1985): 3–24.

González Peña, Carlos. *Historia de la literatura mexicana: Desde los orígenes hasta nuestros días.* Mexico City: Editorial Porrúa, 1975.

Martínez, José Luis. *La expresión nacional.* Mexico City: Oasis, 1984.

———. *Literatura mexicana: Siglo XX, 1910–1949.* 2 Vols. Mexico City: Antigua Librería Robredo, 1949–1950.

———. "México en busca de su expresión." In Cosío Villegas, ed., 2:1019–71.

———. *Situación de la literatura mexicana contemporánea.* Mexico City: Cultura, 1948.

Monsiváis, Carlos. "No quisiera ponerme muy solemne pero . . . " *La cultura en México/Siempre* 1457 (May 27, 1981): 2.

———. "Notas sobre la cultura mexicana en el siglo XX." In Cosío Villegas, ed., 2:1375–1548.

Monterde, Francisco. "Revistas literarias durante el período revolucionario." In Benítez, Carter, and Martínez, 111–143.

Paz, Octavio. *México en la obra de Octavio Paz.* 3 vols. Mexico City: Fondo de Cultura Económica, 1975.

Ríos, Eduardo Enrique. "Periodismo independentista." In Benítez, Carter, and Martínez, 13–46.

Schneider, Luis Mario. *Ruptura y continuidad: La literatura mexicana en polémica.* Mexico City: Fondo de Cultura Económica, 1975.

Sheridan, Guillermo. *Los contemporáneos ayer.* Mexico City: Fondo de Cultura Económica, 1985.

12

Mexican and Mexican American Literary Relations

MANUEL DE JESÚS HERNÁNDEZ-GUTIÉRREZ

Critics have in recent years studied Chicano literature using such diverse critical perspectives as postmodernist, poststructuralist, archetypal, and Macherean (Sánchez; Saldívar, *Chicano Narrative;* Cárdenas; Hernández-Gutiérrez, *El colonialismo;* respectively). Unlike work in the mid-1970s, this rich critical interest has not studied relations between Chicano and Mexican literature. However, an interest of both Chicano and Mexican writers in developing close ties between themselves has resurfaced (Paz, "Art and Identity"; Ramírez, "Imagen del chicano" and "Estudios Chicanos"; Mijares; Nieto and Flores; and Stavans). In the face of historically significant developments in both the Southwest and Mexico—including the rise of Mexican neoliberalism with a sociopolitical agenda that has now programmed radical change in Mexican society and the recognition on the part of some Chicano intellectuals in the United States that minority gains in the 1970s and 1980s have led to an advanced integration into United States society—a study of the relations between Chicano and Mexican literature has become necessary (Barrera; Gómez-Quiñones). Parting from the notion of the text as a multilayered object, this essay examines literary production, or discourse, in both societies, with a particular focus on ideology.

EAGLETON'S SIX STRUCTURES IN A LITERARY DISCOURSE

In *Criticism and Ideology* (1976), Terry Eagleton holds that six levels, or structures—through various and multiple junctures—produce any literary discourse: General Mode of Production (GMP), Literary Mode of Production (LMP), General Ideology (GI), Authorial Ideology (AuI), Aesthetic Ideology (AI), and the text itself. The critical task lies in examining the historically complex junctures between the various levels that play a structuring function in the production of a specific literary discourse, or text. The GMP rises from the unity of certain forces and social relations in material production. Throughout history, such unity has taken different forms, and bourgeois production, with its consumer society, is its most recent one. Several dominant LMPs, or literary modes, have established themselves at different periods in the course of history. For its part, each dominant LMP, an expression of the hegemonic GMP, presents a unity of certain forces and social relations of literary production as part and parcel of the particular social formation (Eagleton, 46). Notwithstanding, one particular GMP can host various LMPs, with one of them occupying a hegemonic space; that is, an LMP from a past material production can continue to occupy space in the modern literary apparatus.

Using a specific literary language, an LMP can express the struggles between a conqueror and a subjugated people, one nation-state and another, a region and a nation, or one class and an opposing one (Eagleton, 55). An LMP's language, the base of a literary discourse, contains specific ideology that, on the one hand, reflects a particular GMP and, on the other, contributes to future ideological production. In this way, an imperialist class—with its particular LMP—can establish its hegemony over a subjugated people, or a subjugated people with their own LMP can carry on a resistance struggle against, or "resist," the erosion of its identity. According to Eagleton, opposition between separate LMPs also appears in the case of a state and a class or a region (Eagleton, 55). Thus there can exist ideological opposition between Mexico, a nation-state, and the Southwest, a region within a second nation-state. As for ideology, it manifests itself both in the exterior and interior of an LMP, or literary discourse, with a specific code in the text itself.

As an extension of the GMP in that it depends on its forces of production to produce literary texts, the LMP also inherits the GMP's dominant ideological formation, or General Ideology (GI). At the level of language, such a formation is "a relatively coherent set of 'discourses' of values, representations and beliefs" that "reflect the experiential relations of individual subjects to their social conditions" (Eagleton, 54). A subject's ideological expression, however, involves "misperceptions" of reality that contribute to "the reproduction of the dominant social relations." In regards to the opposition Mexican literature/Chicano literature, each particular subject has ideological limits arising from its spatial anchoring, as coded in the signs *Mexico* and *Southwest*, in either a nation-state or a region. The limitations on the subjects become clear the moment the critic takes into account the structures Authorial Ideology (AuI) and Aesthetic Ideology (AI). The first involves the "author's specific mode of biographical insertion into GI": social class, sex, nationality, religion, geographical region, and others (Eagleton, 58). These structuring factors may appear inside and/or outside the literary text. Aesthetic Ideology, also a region of GI, involves theories of literature, critical practices, literary traditions, genres, conventions, devices, and specific discourses. Although there may be contact between these respective factors in two geographically different discourses, they all have a specific manifestation in one single literary apparatus of each discourse, Mexican or Chicano.

The last constituent in the discourse is the text itself. The object of literary study, it stands as a product—locus—structured by elements from the first five levels. Motivated by a GMP and produced in a specific LMP with a particular GI, such a literary space contains certain productions of ideology and itself contributes to more ideological production in relation to history (Eagleton, 69). In studying ideology in the opposition Mexican literature/Chicano literature, we recognize the text as a product of a specific literary discourse and pay particular attention to the ideological elements coded by the subject's writing act—GI, AuI, AI—on the signs *Mexico* and *Southwest*. In providing further critical tools for reading ideology in a text beyond those elements in the above five levels, we use two formalist concepts: *fabula* and *syuzhet*. Fabula, or story, "refers to the chronological sequence of events" (Jefferson, 39); syuzhet, or plot, denotes "the order and manner in which they are actually presented in the narrative," with "manner" alluding to specific devices utilized in the text (Jefferson, 39). Integral to the syuzhet, a narrative device produces in the reader a defamiliarizing effect that foregrounds specific ideological elements coded in the fabula yet not part of the reader's reified regional or national consciousness. In the case of the opposition Chicano literature/Mexican literature, two defamiliarizing devices, description and character, artistically manifest themselves time after time in the narration, each centering repeatedly the sign *Mexico* or *Southwest* in a historically new perspective. In effect, these narrative devices, on the one hand, foreground the ideology of a specific subject—Chicano or Mexicano—and, on the other, serve to help the reader distinguish common and opposing elements in Chicano and Mexican literature, both processes revealing the real historical parameters operating in such desired and necessary discourse as well as indicating the latter's future path.

SELECTED CHICANO AND MEXICAN TEXTS

Since Chicano literature only affirmed its international voice in the 1970s, a study of its production and ideology necessitates the selection of texts from contemporary literary production: for example, *Pocho* (1959) by José Antonio Villarreal (1924–); *Generaciones y semblanzas (Generations and Sketches;* 1976) by Rolando Hinojosa-Smith (1924–); *Heart of Aztlán* (1976) by Rudolfo Anaya (1937–); *El sueño de Santa María de las Piedras (The Dream of Santa María de las Piedras;* 1986) by Miguel Méndez-M. (1930–); and *The House on Mango Street* (1984) by Sandra Cisneros (1954–). Published between 1959 and 1986, as a group these narrative texts objectively address the history of Chicanos in the United States with a particular interest in symbolizing the Southwest as a spatial metaphor. They code a historical experience in the United States from the 1848 conquest to the 1980s that includes links to the 1910 Mexican Revolution and modern-day Mexican society. Their discourse centers the struggle against a subordinated integration on the part of Chicanos into United States society, though one narrative, *Pocho,* abandons resistance and seeks instead full assimilation into mainstream Anglo-American culture.

The selected Chicano texts lead to a subsequent necessary choice of comparative texts from Mexican literature. The search for contemporaries points to the generation of Mexican writers known as La Onda (The Wave), whose ranks include José Agustín (1944–), Gustavo Sainz (1940–), and Margarita

Daltón (1943–) (Poniatowska, 206). These authors begin publishing in the mid-1960s. Ages and start of careers coincide with those of contemporary Chicano writers (Leal, 202–203; Bruce-Novoa, *Chicano Authors*). That Joaquín Mortiz, a major publisher of La Onda writers, printed in Mexico the first two novels by the Chicano Alejandro Morales (1944–)—*Caras viejas y vino nuevo* (*Old Faces and New Wine;* 1975) and *La verdad sin voz* (*Death of an Anglo;* 1979)—stands as a direct link. Moreover, as director of the Department of Literature at Bellas Artes, Gustavo Sainz published supplements in the 1970s featuring Chicano literature from the Southwest and Chicago (Poniatowska, 200).

However, as a general rule, La Onda writers, with a scarce exception, avoid writing on national issues or the search for a national identity. As Luis Leal observed in 1985 in his essay "Nacionalismo y cosmopolitismo en la narrativa mexicana" (Nationalism and Cosmopolitism in Mexican Narrative), they have as a project inserting Mexican narrative into world literature:

> The young writers did not want to be identified as partisan to specifically Mexican causes, or accused of writing under the influence of the major national writers. They wanted Mexican literature to be considered as part of Western letters. It did not interest them to write exclusively for the Mexican people, nor the Spanish-speaking countries, but rather to be translated and read in other countries. More than of national writers (if we exclude such Cosmopolitans as Reyes, Paz, Fuentes and Arreola), they were under the influence of Borges and Cortázar, from among the Spanish American writers, and of many foreign writers, but above all of the North Americans.
>
> (*Aztlán,* 206; my translation)

Although the Tlatelolco massacre in 1968 did impact ideologically on La Onda's literary production and some writers do refer to the tragic events in recent works, like *A la salud de la serpiente* (A Salute to the Serpent; 1991) by Gustavo Sainz, their contribution to Mexican literature resides in innovation at the level of form. Thus, in agreement with the critic Emmanuel Carballo, whose studies of Mexican literature cover works before and after La Onda generation, this study holds Carlos Fuentes (1928–) as the most representative Mexican narrator (Delgado, 3-D). His first novel, *La región más transparente* (*Where the Air Is Clear;* 1958), stacked out a space among the most famous Mexican writers which he continues to hold. That same novel was reviewed in translation in 1960 by José Antonio Villarreal, and in 1990, the writer and publisher José Armas, from New Mexico, publically criticized Fuentes, calling attention to a lack of understanding of Chicanos on the latter's part. Both events indicate an exchange between the literatures.

From *La región más transparente* to *Cristóbal nonato* (*Christopher Unborn;* 1987), Fuentes has sought to become the Balzac of Mexican society by producing a specific corpus whose diverse themes and characters establish a continuity in the history of Mexico for the last forty years. He has been its faithful chronicler in the following texts: *La región más transparente, La muerte de Artemio Cruz* (*The Death of Artemio Cruz;* 1962), *Cristóbal nonato,* and the essay collection entitled *Tiempo mexicano* (Mexican Time; 1971). Juxtaposed, they constitute a coherent discourse on Mexican society, facilitating the study of the opposition Chicano literature/Mexican literature.

MEXICO'S LITERARY MODE OF PRODUCTION AND CHICANO LITERATURE

Whereas the GMP provides the forces and social relations of material production, the LMP level has information regarding the infrastructure that makes possible the production of each respective literary production in the opposition Mexican literature/Chicano literature. The GI, AuI, and AI all concern themselves with ideology whether found outside or inside the text. According to Eagleton, an LMP itself "is constituted by [sub]structures of production, distribution, exchange and consumption" (47). Because it brings into play certain forces in the labor-power relation, *production* determines and is overdetermined by the other three structures. Various factors have a role: producer, materials, instruments, techniques, publisher, printer, and the product itself. Mexico's contemporary LMP is one of the best organized and most productive in Latin America. It makes available to its producers, or writers, several large publishers and a distribution network that extends beyond Mexico to South America, the Caribbean, Spain, the Southwest, the Midwest, and New York. The Mexican literary market even has the participation of publishers from Madrid and Barcelona; for example, in the 1980s Editorial Joaquín Mortiz merged with Planeta, a publishing house from Spain. Whereas in the 1950s a successful work sold from five to ten thousand copies, a best seller now can expect sales around forty thousand copies ("Fue un año," 1 & 7-D). This last fact speaks to its consumption. As far as exchange goes, two of Mexico's leading writers, Octavio Paz (1914–) and Carlos Fuentes, have been translated into many languages, and their works are the subject of master and doctoral studies around the world. That Paz won the Nobel Prize in 1990 and Fuentes continues to be named as a candidate further attests to the national and world impact of Mexico's contemporary LMP. Lastly, in European form, Mexico's literary production goes back uninterrupted five hundred years and involves previous LMPs, to which can be added still more Mexican LMPs from the Nahua tradition.

In addition to publishing works by its own writers, Mexico's contemporary LMP has extended to help in the production of Chicano literary discourse. In chronological order, the following publishers, both private and state-sponsored, have played a role in the publishing and distributing of Chicano literature in Mexico: Editorial Joaquín Mortiz, Editorial Fondo de Cultura Económica, Editorial Latitudes, Editorial Diógones, the Secretaría de Educación Pública (SEP), the Centro de Estudios Fronterizos del Norte de México (CEFNOMEX), the Universidad de Guadalajara, the Consejo Nacional de Población, and Ediciones Era. Printing per book varies from one thousand to four thousand copies, with thirty thousand being exceptionally high. A major publisher of writers from La Onda, Editorial Joaquín Mortiz was the first Mexican publishing house to edit a Chicano novel, apparently with the Mexican reader in mind: *Caras viejas y vino nuevo,* by Alejandro Morales, at four thousand copies. As a matter of fact, Editorial Joaquín Mortiz also published the second Chicano work in Mexico, *La verdad sin voz,* also written by Morales and with a printing of three thousand copies. Not until 1980 did Fondo de Cultura Económica, the government's semiofficial publishing house, take part. With the anthology *Chicanos: Antología histórica y literaria* (Chicanos: Historical and Literary Anthology, 1980), edited by Tino Villanueva and issued in a printing of three thousand copies, Fondo de Cultúra Económica diversified the Chicano literary discourse available to the Mexican reader. In the same year, 1980, Editorial Latitudes publishes a Spanish translation of poetry by Gary Soto under the title *Como arbustos de niebla* (Like Fog Shrubs), translated by Ernesto Trejo, and distributes one thousand copies. Three years later, in 1983, Editorial Diógenes printed the short-story collection *Nueva narrativa chicana* (New Chicano Narrative), edited by Oscar U. Somoza, in one thousand copies. Ironically, the "Mexican-American" work with the highest printing and distribution in Mexico—thirty thousand copies—was not written in the 1970s or the 1980s. In 1984 SEP and CEFNOMEX reprint the novel *Las aventuras de don Chipote, o Cuando los pericos mamen* (The Adventures of Don Chipote, or When Parrots Learn to Suckle) by Daniel Venegas, which was originally published in 1928 in Los Angeles.

Since 1984, three other Chicano works have been published in Mexico. In 1986 the Universidad de Guadalajara printed *El sueño de Santa María de las Piedras* by Miguel Méndez-M. with two thousand copies. Two years later, in 1988, the Consejo Nacional de Población rekindles an interest in the Chicano short story with the collection *Antología retrospectiva del cuento chicano* (A Retrospective Anthology on the Chicano Short Story), edited by Juan Bruce-Novoa, in a printing of one thousand copies. Lastly, Ediciones Era reprinted *Peregrinos de Aztlán* (*Pilgrims in Aztlán;* 1974) by Miguel Méndez-M. with three thousand. Era has also published works by several major contemporary Mexican writers: Juan Rulfo (1918–1986), José Revueltas (1914–1975), Carlos Fuentes, and Luis González de Alba.

Some Chicano texts published by Mexico's contemporary LMP have been written by Chicana writers. In the anthology *Chicanos: Antología histórica y literaria,* we find texts by (among others) Lucha Corpi, Margarita Cota-Cárdenas, Angela de Hoyos, Yolanda Luera, Alivia Nada, and Bernice Zamora. The anthology *Nueva narrativa chicana* includes one short story by a Chicana: "La carta" by Gloria Velázquez Treviño. One other Chicana text exists in Spanish, a translation of the anthology *This Bridge Called My Back* (*Esta* [*sic*] *puente, mi espalda;* 1981), edited by Cherríe Moraga and Gloria Anzaldúa and translated by Ana Castillo and Norma Alarcón. However, it was published by

Ism Press housed in San Francisco, and there is no information as to whether Mexico has been targeted for distribution.

Other Chicano works have been published in Mexico; however, they represent efforts on the part of Chicanos to print there and distribute in the Southwest: *Muerte en una estrella* (Death on a Star; 1984) by Sergio Elizondo from Tinta Negra Editores, one thousand copies; *Los siete hijos de La Llorona* (The Wailing Woman's Seven Sons; 1986) by Justo S. Alarcón from Alta Pimeria Pro Arte y Cultura, one thousand copies; and *Suruma* (1990) by Sergio Elizondo from Dos Pasos Editores, one thousand copies.

EXCHANGE AND AESTHETIC IDEOLOGY: CRITICISM ON CHICANO LITERATURE IN MEXICO

A growing body of Mexican literary criticism on Chicano literature marks two things: the substructure exchange in Mexico's contemporary LMP and, more important, Aesthetic Ideology, particularly in the factors of critical practice, traditions, and specific discourses. Several Mexican institutions have been involved in criticism: the Universidad Nacional Autónoma de México (UNAM), Ediciones El Caballito, Editorial Signos, Siglo XXI Editores, the Cineteca Nacional, the Colegio de México, and the Colegio de la Frontera Norte.

Literary criticism on Chicano literature begins to appear in the 1970s. The journal *Revista de la Universidad de México* prints the essay "México en la literatura chicana" ("Mexico in Chicano literature," 1975) by Juan Bruce-Novoa, which addresses a growing interest in Mexico. The essay examines such themes as *pre-indigenismo* (pre-indigenism), *mestizaje* (mixed Nahua and Spaniard heritage), the 1910 Mexican Revolution, Mexico as paradise lost, and the demystification of the encounter between Chicanos and Mexicans. With the same Mexican reader in mind, Juan Rodríguez writes in 1977 the essay "El florecimiento de la literatura chicana" (The Renaissance of Chicano Literature), where he outlines a rebirth in the literature of the Chicano, or Southwest Mexican, in the 1970s (348–369).[1] Carlos Monsiváis, a leading Mexican critic, joins Rodríguez in the same year with an essay entitled "De México y los chicanos, de México y su cultura fronteriza" (Of Mexico and Chicanos, of Mexico and Its Border Culture), where he calls for greater interest in Chicano literature and border culture on the part of Mexicans (1–19). Perhaps responding to Monsiváis's call, two years later, in 1979, Javier Vázquez-Castro, professor at UNAM's Escuela Permanente de Extensión in San Antonio, Texas, publishes a short critical work entitled *Acerca de literatura: Diálogo con tres autores chicanos* (On Literature: A Dialogue with Three Chicano Authors), where he interviews Alfredo de la Torre, Angela de Hoyos, and Tomás Rivera. Vázquez-Castro's work leaves the message that Chicano literary production comes from a colonized people. In another example of exchange, a Chicano publishing house, M & A Editions, edited Vázquez-Castro's *Acerca de literatura*.

The 1980s witness a sophistication in the factors involving Aesthetic Ideology as the published texts in literary criticism rise to the level of theory. In 1983 Oscar U. Somoza becomes the first Chicano critic to publish in Mexico a critical text produced by a single author: *Narrativa chicana contemporánea: Principios fundamentales* (Contemporary Chicano Narrative: Fundamental Principles), published by Editorial Signos at one thousand copies. This text examines the values found in Chicano narrative, such as *curanderismo* (herbal medicine), religion, and the family. For its part, in the same year Siglo XXI Editores publishes in translation into Spanish *Chicano Authors: Inquiry by Interview* (1980) by Juan Bruce-Novoa, a collection of interviews with Chicano authors, under the title *La literatura chicana a través de sus autores* at three thousand copies. This work is seminal in both languages. Most recently, in 1990, Alta Pimeria Pro Arte y Cultura published *El arquetipo de la Madre Terrible en Peregrinos de Aztlán* (The Archetype of the Terrible Mother in *Peregrinos de Aztlán*) by Guadalupe Cárdenas at one thousand copies. It is a study based on Jungian archetypes. The same year in Mexico marks an interest in literature by Chicanas: the anthology *Mujer y literatura mexicana y chicana: Culturas en contacto* (Woman and Mexican and Chicana Literature: Cultures in Contact; 1990), edited by Aralia López González et al., at a printing of one thousand, includes fifteen critical articles on Chicana works, constituting about one third of the total contributions in the text; the Colegio de México and the Colegio de la Frontera Norte, two leading research centers in Mexico, figure as its publishers.

MEXICAN LITERARY PRODUCTION
IN THE SOUTHWEST AND BEYOND

In contrast to the participation of Mexico's contemporary LMP in the production of Chicano literature, Mexican literary production has not been a conscious element in the Chicano LMP. With a rare exception, such as the book of poetry *"Amor de lejos . . . Fools' Love"* (1987) by Rubén Medina that was printed by Arte Público Press, Chicano presses as a policy do not publish or reedit Mexican writers. In the Southwest or the rest of United States, Mexican literary production remains the task of the hereinbefore mentioned Mexican publishing houses or United States publishers who share a specific interest in marketing Mexican literature in translation. With all known Chicano presses and distributors participating in the sale of Mexican literature at conferences or through mail order, only the distribution factor in the Chicano LMP has contributed and continues to contribute to Mexican literary production.

As far as the availability of Mexican literature in the Southwest and the rest of the United States, Mexico's contemporary LMP remains the leading element, especially in its distribution. This distribution reaches Chicanos both in Spanish and English. For reaching Chicanos literate in Spanish, Fondo de Cultura Económica, Ediciones Era, Editorial Joaquín Mortiz, and other Mexican publishers rely on a network of bookstores specializing in books in Spanish that starts in several Mexican border cities (Tijuana, Juárez) and extends to major cities in the Southwest (Los Angeles, Houston, San Antonio). The network even reaches Chicago, and possibly New York. Most likely such distribution networks already existed prior to the 1970s renaissance in the literature of the Southwest Mexican. In being that wherever they travel to educational and literature conferences they display and sell contemporary Mexican works in both Spanish and English to the Chicano reader, Arte Público Press and Bilingual Press—the two major publishers of Chicano literature—form part of the distributing network featuring Mexican literary production in the Southwest as well as in the rest of the United States.

Beginning in the 1960s several publishers in the United States who share an interest, with Anglo-American and Chicano readers, in Mexican texts in translation have played a subsidiary role in production—the main producer being Mexico's contemporary LMP—among them: Farrar, Straus and Giroux; the University of Texas Press (Austin); Grove Press; Columbia University Press; the Noonday Press; Vintage International; the University of Indiana Press; and the University of Minnesota Press. Apparently, Grove Press initiated Mexican literary production in translation into English in 1959 with *Pedro Páramo* (*Pedro Páramo;* 1955) by Juan Rulfo (1918–1986). Then followed New York's Farrar, Straus and Giroux with a translation in 1960 of *La región más transparente* by Carlos Fuentes—the same work reviewed by José Antonio Villarreal. A year later, 1961, Grove Press published a translation of *El laberinto de la soledad,* by Octavio Paz, as *The Labyrinth of Solitude.* As an expression of the factor of exchange in the Chicano LMP, in the 1970s this text, due to an essay on the pachuco, becomes part of the curriculum in Chicano studies classes (Armas, "Octavio Paz," 4–21). Other works by contemporary Mexican writers that appear in English in the 1960s and 1970s are *Al filo del agua* (*The Edge of the Storm;* 1947) by Agustín Yáñez (1904–1980), *Los de abajo* (*The Underdogs;* 1915) by Mariano Azuela (1873–1953), *Confabulario* (*Confabulario and Other Inventions;* 1952) by Juan José Arreola (1918–), *El llano en llamas* (*The Burning Plain and Other Stories;* 1953) by Juan Rulfo, *Las tierras flacas* (*The Lean Lands;* 1962) by Agustín Yáñez, and *La feria* (*The Fair;* 1963) by Juan José Arreola. Other Mexican authors in translation are Rosario Castellanos (1925–1974), José Revueltas, and Elena Poniatowska (1933–). Apparently, the only writers from La Onda who have seen their work translated into English have been Juan García Ponce and Gustavo Sainz: respectively, *Encuentros* (*Encounters;* 1972) and *La princesa del Palacio de Hierro* (*The Princess of the Iron Palace;* 1985).

In this corpus of translation belonging to Mexican literary production, Carlos Fuentes occupies the pinnacle and enjoys the most distribution in the Southwest and the rest of the United States, reaching Chicanos literate in English. Initiating its project following the translation of *La región más transparente*, the Noonday Press has published in translation several other works by Fuentes, among them *La muerte de Artemio Cruz, Agua quemada* (*Burnt Water;* 1981), *Las buenas conciencias* (*The Good Conscience;* 1959), *Terra nostra* (*Terra Nostra;* 1977), *La cabeza de la hidra* (*The Hydra Head;* 1978), and *Una familia lejana* (*Distant Relations;* 1980). Noonday has even become a pioneer in publishing *Myself with Others* (1988), a work that Fuentes wrote originally all in English. Joining Noonday, in 1990 Vintage International published *Christopher Unborn*, a translation into English of *Cristóbal nonato* by Carlos Fuentes.

As stated above, the Chicano LMP has played an unconscious role in Mexican literary production. Its best contribution, quite indirect, has been the inclusion of selections by Paz, Fuentes, Rulfo, and Castellanos in grammar or reading texts in Spanish designed for students in bilingual classes (Lequerica and Salazar; Cramsie and Lladó-Torres). However, the editors of such texts have needed to rely on United States publishers who specialize in foreign-language texts and do not directly form part of the Chicano LMP. Published in 1972, the anthology *Literatura chicana: Texto y contexto/Chicano Literature: Text and Context,* edited by Antonia Castañeda-Shular, Tomás Ybarra-Frausto, and Joseph Sommers, marks a greater effort in that it includes in its pages excerpts from texts by fifteen Mexican authors as well as short pieces taken from the popular tradition (Mayan and Aztec texts, *corridos,* or ballads, and oral testimonies). Among the fifteen Mexican authors included are Bernal Díaz del Castillo (*circa* 1495–1584), Bartolomé de las Casas (1474–1565), Fernando Alvarado Tezozómoc (*circa* 1520–1610), Sor Juana Inés de la Cruz (1648–1695), José J. Fernández de Lizardi (1776–1827), Mariano Azuela, José Vasconcelos (1882–1959), and Leopoldo Zea (1912)—mostly from previous Mexican LMPs. As far as contemporary writers go, the reader finds excerpts by Juan José Arreola, Rosario Castellanos, Octavio Paz, and Carlos Fuentes. (As an interesting note, *Literatura chicana: Texto y contexto* includes ideologically parallel texts from Latin American literature like the Gaucho epic *Martín Fierro,* 1872, by the Argentine José Hernández, 1834–1886.) Once again, similar to the grammar or reading texts in Spanish, Ybarra-Frausto used the press Prentice Hall, housed in the East.

To date, Bilingual Press is the only Chicano press that has published Mexican texts, though few. In 1983 it edited a collection of Aztec poems in translation under the title *Poems of the Aztec Peoples,* edited by Edward Kissam and Michael Schmidt, and in 1985 it printed *Sor Juana Inés de la Cruz: Poems,* translated by Margaret Sayers Peden. Unfortunately, these texts do not form part of Mexico's contemporary LMP. In a significant development, in 1992 Bilingual Press published *Saga de México* (Mexican Saga), edited by Seymour Menton and María Herrera-Sobek, a reader for students in high school or college. *Saga de México* contains many of the same authors already present in the text by Castañeda-Shular, Ybarra-Frausto, and Sommers; however, selections are longer and richer. As far as new authors go, the reader finds excerpts by Manuel Payno (1810–1894), Juan Díaz Covarrubias (1837–1858), Federico Gamboa (1864–1939), José Mancisidor (1895–1956), Gregorio López y Fuentes (1895–1967), Martín Luis Guzmán (1887–1976), Francisco Monterde (1894–1985), Ermilo Abreu Gómez (1894–1971), Alfonso Caso (1896–1970), Rafael Muñoz (1899–1972), Héctor Pérez-Martínez (1906–1948), Celestino Gorostiza (1904–1967), Agustín Yáñez, Rodolfo Usigli (1905–1979), José Revueltas, Juan Rulfo, Miguel León-Portilla (1926–), Carlos Fuentes, and Elena Poniatowska—once again, mostly authors who are members of previous Mexican LMPs. Noticeably, *Saga de México* does not include a text by Octavio Paz or by a member of La Onda generation. Nonetheless, perhaps because it was designed with the intention of reaching high-school and university students, one can safely hold that this text represents the major effort in the history of the Southwest Mexican toward distributing Mexican literature among Chicanos.

Other forms of distributing texts from Mexican literary production in the Southwest have been a theatrical production of *Los de abajo* and the reading over the radio of Mexican short stories written by such authors as Rulfo, Fuentes, and Castellanos.

EXCHANGE AND AESTHETIC IDEOLOGY:
CRITICISM ON MEXICAN LITERATURE IN THE SOUTHWEST

A growing body of literary criticism on Mexican literature by Chicanos also marks the element of exchange in the Chicano LMP. This centers the role of the latter's Aesthetic Ideology in the factors of critical practice, traditions, and specific discourses. Although weaker and less numerous than the corresponding Mexican ones, Chicano institutions—for example, the journals *De Colores, Aztlán,* and *Third Woman* and the publishing house Bilingual Press— have published concerned criticism. At times, Chicano critics have even relied on foreign mediums such as the intellectual review *Cuadernos Americanos* in Mexico and the press Gunter Narr Verlag in Germany.

Although one can hold that Chicano literary criticism on Mexican literature began in 1960 with José Antonio Villarreal's review of Fuentes's *La región más transparente* in English, in which he described the novel as unpromising and noted no relevance to the Mexican-American experience (Villarreal, 21), it became a continuous discourse in the mid-1970s. In 1975, Guillermo Rojas published the article "La prosa chicana: Tres epígonos de la novela mexicana de la Revolución" (Chicano Prose: Three Epigones from the Novel of the Mexican Revolution), in which he holds that Tomás Rivera, Rolando R. Hinojosa-Smith and Miguel Méndez-M. write in a mode that is an extension of the novel of the Mexican Revolution (317) and compares them to Mariano Azuela, Martín Luis Guzmán, Gregorio López y Fuentes, and Mauricio Magdaleno. The article was published simultaneously in *Cuadernos Americanos* in Mexico and *De Colores* in New Mexico. Four years later, in 1979, the critic Salvador Rodríguez del Pino includes *El diablo en Texas* (*The Devil in Texas;* 1976) by Aristeo Brito in the tradition of the Mexican writers that follow the generation mentioned in Rojas's article:

> I selected *The Devil in Texas* as an example of a Chicano novel because in it the Mexican influence is clear; such an influence, however, does not alter the Chicano

world view in the work. . . . That implicit world in *The Devil in Texas,* which emanates from Mexican consciousness, is also found in such works as *Human Mourning* by José Revueltas, *Pedro Páramo* by Juan Rulfo, *The Edge of the Storm* by Agustín Yáñez, *Confabulario and Other Stories* by Juan José Arreola and *The Death of
Artemio Cruz* by Carlos Fuentes. In other words, Aristeo Brito falls within a tradition in the Mexican novel represented by the generation of Mexican writers
mentioned.

(369; my translation)

The critic Juan Bruce-Novoa not only has participated in the development
of literary criticism on Chicano literature in Mexico, but also has made a
contribution, especially in the 1980s, to the growing body of literary criticism
on Mexican literature in the Southwest. In 1986 he studied the image of the
Chicano in such authors as Martín Luis Guzmán, José Vasconcelos, Octavio
Paz, Carlos Fuentes, and the poet Francisco Segovia. For Bruce-Novoa, Mexican writers adopt an elitist position in relation to Chicanos at the level of
culture and language that leads to a lack of understanding on the part of both
cultures. Bruce-Novoa, however, does not limit himself to studying the reductionist image of the Chicano in Mexican literature. In 1991 he published in
Hispania a study entitled "La novela de la Revolución Mexicana: La topología
del final" (The Novel of the Mexican Revolution: A Topology of the Ending),
in which he holds that the novel of the revolution did not advocate the ideals
of the revolution; rather, the narrators reflected a disillusionment that resulted
from the failure of those ideals (Bruce-Novoa, "Novela de la Revolución Mexicana," 43). In this way, he criticizes a specific discourse previously praised by
other Chicano critics. Lastly, on October 12, 1990, in New York, Bruce-Novoa
served as moderator in a round table on Mexican literature whose participants
were Carlos Monsiváis, José Agustín, and Elena Poniatowska. Presentations
and subsequent dicussion centered on La Onda's literary production ("Escritores mexicanos," 4).

In regards to an interest in literary production by Mexican women, the journal *Third Woman,* edited by Norma Alarcón, published in 1989 the article "La
sexualidad en la narrativa femenina mexicana 1970–1987: Una aproximación"
(Sexuality in Mexican Feminist Narrative 1970–1987: An Approximation) by
the Australian Peggy Job. Her article studied works by various Mexican
women, such as Rosario Castellanos, María Luisa Mendoza, Elena Poniatowska, Olga Harmony, Beatriz Espejo, and Adela Fernández, and concluded
that, unfortunately, there has yet to appear the female protagonist in Mexican
feminist narrative that challenges the established order, succeeds in her
struggle to claim her own identity, and celebrates her female body and sexuality (Job, 131).

In Chicano criticism on Mexican literary production, Luis Leal has made
the most ambitious effort. He not only has addressed traditions and specific
discourses in common, but also has made a major contribution in critiquing

the work of writers from the last two Mexican generations. In his essay collection *Aztlán y México: Perfiles literarios e históricos* (Aztlán and Mexico: Literary and Historical Profiles; 1985), edited by Bilingual Press, in which twelve of twenty-three articles examine Mexican literature and culture, Leal establishes several links between Mexican and Chicano culture: Nahua myths, early literary periods in their respective traditions that share common texts, the Mexican Revolution, the *corrido,* or ballad, and journals. Furthermore, he examines other relevant elements such as women in Mexican literature, La Onda's contribution to Mexican literature, the Anglo-American in Mexican literature, and the impact of the Tlatelolco massacre on the writers belonging to Fuentes's generation as well as on those in La Onda. Perhaps this text decisively contributed to his receiving in 1991 the Aguila Azteca national prize from Mexican President Carlos Salinas de Gortari.

CHICANOS UNDER FUENTES'S AUTHORIAL IDEOLOGY

Because of his prolific, high-quality production as well as the translation of his work into many foreign languages, Carlos Fuentes has been able to symbolize Mexican society for the world. Even though anchored in Mexico, Fuentes's symbolic society consciously forms an integral part of the Latin American narrative universe. For example, the protagonist of *La muerte de Artemio Cruz* makes a cameo appearance in *Cien años de soledad* (*One Hundred Years of Solitude;* 1967) by Gabriel García Márquez. Unfortunately, however, multidimensional Chicanos are missing from Fuentes's works. In other words, Fuentes considers both Mexico and his own narrative discourse part and parcel of Latin American society—a society from which Chicanos are again absent. Under such authorial ideology, Chicanos are neither Mexican nor Latin American.

Fuentes's self-conscious identification with Latin America, and with its literary opposition to the United States and Western-European societies, remains patently present in the critical works he has published to date: *La nueva novela hispanoamericana* (The New Spanish American Novel; 1969) and *Valiente mundo nuevo* (Brave New World; 1990). A structuralist study of the Spanish American novel, the former heralds the search for a new literary language on the part of the boom writers, including Fuentes himself. This search is necessary in order for Latin America to be able to design its own model for development (Fuentes, *Nueva novela,* 98). According to Fuentes, the Mexican writers Agustín Yáñez, Juan Rulfo, Octavio Paz, and José Emilio Pacheco—alongside such Latin American writers as Miguel Angel Asturias, Juan Carlos Onetti, Pablo Neruda, Mario Vargas Llosa, Alejo Carpentier, Gabriel García Márquez, and Julio Cortázar—have participated in such a task. Fuentes holds in *La nueva novela hispanoamericana* that even writers from the United States have made a contribution to this Latin American search. Although he mentions one or two Afro-Americans (without stating their significance), the overwhelming majority are Anglo-American. As for Chicano writers, Fuentes does not mention a single one. In 1969, they did not figure in Fuentes's conception of United States society.

A poststructuralist study of Spanish-American literature in the context of the economic crisis and political instability of the 1980s, *Valiente mundo nuevo* demonstrates the need for Latin American writers to fashion a continuity for Ibero-America and calls for their collective participation. Keeping in mind the twenty years since the publication of *La nueva novela hispanoamericana,* Fuentes once again examines the work of the boom writers; yet he also now recognizes a contribution on the part of rising young Latin American writers such as the Peruvians Isaac Goldemberg and Alfredo Bryce Echenique, the Argentines Osvaldo Soriano and Luisa Valenzuela, and the Chileans-in-exile Ariel Dorfman and Antonio Skármeta. Among the new contributors to Spanish American literary discourse, Fuentes includes members of Mexico's La Onda: José Agustín, Gustavo Sainz, María Luisa Puga, Fernando del Paso, and Luis Zapata. However, once again Chicanos stand out for their absence in spite of the fact that Rolando Hinojosa-S. won the Premio Casa de las Américas in 1976 with his novel *Generaciones y semblanzas.*

In taking into account the AuI structure in Mexico's contemporary LMP, the critic can only conclude that Fuentes, despite his long residences and fame in this country, lacks an understanding of a United States society where minorities play a part in literary production. While showing much familiarity in his critical writing with the ideas and significance of such Anglo-American writers as Melville, Dos Passos, and Faulkner, he has yet to delve into Afro-American consciousness as it contributes to the evolution of the United States into a multicultural society in which the dominant culture lacks hegemony. As for Chicano writers, he has failed to see them as active agents in United States society. His AuI permits him a minimal understanding of their work from the 1970s, but not until 1992 did he begin to indicate an interest in these writers (Fuentes, "Hispanic U.S.A.," 341–355; Nieto and Rodríguez Flores, 3-E).

If Fuentes has been forced to mention Chicano writers as part of the world's literary map—something he likes to do in the case of writers from Latin America, various Western countries, and Eastern Europe—this forcing began on September 3, 1987, at San Francisco State University, where he read from his then-new work *Cristóbal nonato* while several Chicano writers were present. In answer to a question on the future of Chicano literature, Fuentes confessed to a lack of knowledge regarding not only Chicanos as a sociopolitical group, but also their literature, with the exception of works by a small number of writers like Tomás Rivera, Rudolfo Anaya, and Rolando Hinojosa-S. He then declared that, in his opinion, any future for Chicano literature was linked to the development of a multicultural United States. In advancing such a position, Fuentes faithfully adheres to his view of Mexican literature as part of Ibero-American letters, dismissing any role for Chicano works in such production. In this way, Fuentes's ideological limitations in relation to Chicano literature resurfaced. As solidly indicated by his novel *Gringo viejo* (*The Old Gringo;* 1985) and his essay collection in English, *Myself with Others,* Fuentes has a greater understanding of the Anglo-American mind than of that of Chicanos (Straitfeld, 3–4).

With the above understanding in mind, José Armas's recent remark continues to resonate today. In the article "Mexicanos y chicanos" (1990), written after Fuentes lectured at the University of New Mexico and again confessed a lack of knowledge regarding Chicano literature, Armas declares:

> He [Fuentes] wants to see bridges between the United States and Latin America, for sure. But he has made little effort in seeing us Hispanics as a natural bridge that both of us, those in the South and those in the North, so desperately need.
>
> (Sec. 1, 1; my translation)

Armas detected a similar disinterest in the 1970s on the part of Octavio Paz. When the Mexican poet taught a course on Latin American literature at Harvard University, Armas enrolled as a student; however, he soon became disillusioned and dropped the course. Armas recorded his experience in an article and an interview that appeared in the journal *De Colores,* where he notes Paz interested yet distant on Chicano literature and issues. Paz's and Fuentes's lack of knowledge on Chicanos parallels a similar noneffort on the part of several writers from La Onda (Mijares, 3-E). Ironically, on the day he was forced to admit his ignorance concerning Chicano writers and culture, September 3, 1987, Fuentes read from *Cristóbal nonato,* where in section 8, chapter 16, Chicano and Puerto Rican characters appear as members of an invading Yankee force in Veracruz, Mexico. In a satirical mode, they are symbolized as not caring about Mexicans and blindly interested in sexual exploits, images in line with the writer's reductive nation-state ideology.

Lastly, in calling further attention to Fuentes's ideological limits in relation to Chicanos, we can look to *Tiempo mexicano,* an essay collection with entries from 1956 to 1971, of which not a single essay deals with Chicanos.

THE SIGN MEXICO: A DEVELOPING SOCIETY UNDER THE HEGEMONY OF THE CENTER

Since its fabula presents in detail the betrayal of the principles of the 1910 Revolution by one of the very marginalized who managed to obtain social justice, and since the novel's space is 100 percent Mexican, *La muerte de Artemio Cruz* best serves our study of the ideology of a subject belonging to a particular nation-state, Mexico. Centered in the fictive universe by three narrative voices (first, third, and second person), the protagonist himself, Artemio Cruz, is marked with history, taking the reader further into a specific Mexican society.

Artemio is the bastard child of a mulatto slave woman and a *criollo* (Creole) hacienda owner. Throughout his life, he does not know he is a descendant of a hacienda-owning family, linked to the dictator Santa Anna and to European interests, and the murderer of his father's brother. A protégé of both a radical priest and a revolutionary general, Artemio Cruz participates in the armed phase of the revolution and subsequently benefits from the spoils, rising to become a top businessman and national leader. The innate will to survive and gain economic power from every situation facilitates his rise. Even though it serves as a medium to deliver a strong message against the abuse of power, Artemio Cruz's configuration, as a narrative device, calls the reader's attention to the geographic and social parameters of a Mexican society under the dominion of a few rich Mexicans at the top of the social order and with an outside hegemonic center. Up to *Cristóbal nonato,* Fuentes's symbolization of Mexican society has always featured this ideological closure.

A device in the syuzhet, the description of a map that covers a whole wall in Artemio Cruz's office, besides centering the sign *Mexico,* unfolds the geographic parameters in *La muerte de Artemio Cruz,* especially in indicating the places where the protagonist has his economic assets. Coding a synchronic unit, the second-person narrator states:

> One whole wall of your office is covered by the map that shows the sweep and inter-relationships of your business network: the newspaper in Mexico City, and the real estate there and in Puebla, Guadalajara, Monterrey, Culiacán, Hermosillo, Guaymas, and Acapulco. The sulfur domes in Jáltipan, the mines in Hidalgo, the timber concessions in Tarahumara. The chain of hotels, the pipe foundry, the fish business. The financing operations, the stock holdings, the administration of the company formed to lend money to the railroad, the legal representation of North American firms, the directorships of banking houses, the foreign stocks—dyes, steel, and detergents; and one little item that does not appear on the wall: fifteen million dollars deposited in banks in Zurich, London, and New York.

(Fuentes, *Death,* 10–11)

The cities where the protagonist has real-estate investments (Mexico City, Puebla, Guadalajara, Monterrey, Culiacán, Hermosillo, Guaymas, Acapulco) and sites where he has mining and lumber interests (Jáltipan, Hidalgo, and the mountain range Tarahumara) fill the space of this economic map. Forged under the value of exploitation, a vast financial empire geographically spreads across a Mexico that includes rural farms and Indian-owned land. Ideologically, the synchronic description reveals that Cruz profiteered—another value—from Mexican urbanization projects in the years between 1940 and 1959: "the pipe foundry," "the chain of hotels," and "the financing operations." Cruz's financial empire includes an international dimension: "the foreign stocks" and "fifteen million dollars deposited in banks in Zurich, London and New York." This last geographic extension codes a complicity with outside investors as another of Cruz's values. Although based on exploitation, we have here in Artemio Cruz's wall map—especially in its being situated inside his own business office—the concrete coding of a Mexican subject who consciously directs Mexico's development.

However, although the map includes sufficient Mexican cities and sites and gives the reader the impression that the sign *Mexico* is completely filled, two border spaces appear minimally in the space of *La muerte de Artemio Cruz*: Mexico/the United States, and Yucatán/Guatemala. This minimal representation of the two borders demonstrates ideological limitation on the part of the nation-state subject. In the subject's vision, moreover, the Southwest is totally absent.

Next to the one above, a second description, which again centers the sign *Mexico,* presents Mexican society. This device in the syuzhet, however, foregrounds Mexico's social parameters. There parade before the reader individuals who were involved in one way or another in Cruz's accumulation of wealth. In a critical tone, the second-person narrator states:

> Yes: you will light a cigarette, in spite of the warnings you have had from your doctor, and to Padilla will relate again the steps by which you gained your wealth: loans at short terms and high interest to peasants in Puebla, just after the Revolution; the acquisition of land around the city of Puebla, whose growth you foresaw; acres for subdivision in Mexico City, thanks to the friendly intervention of each succeeding president; the daily newspaper; the purchase of mining stock; the formation of Mexican-U.S. enterprises in which you participated as front-man so that the law would be complied with; trusted friend of North American investors, intermediary between New York and Chicago and the government of Mexico; the manipulation of stock prices to move them to your advantage, buying and selling, always at a profit; the gilded El Dorado years of President Alemán, and your final consolidation; the acquisition of *ejido* [collectively owned] farm lands taken from their peasant occupants to project new subdivisions in cities of the interior; the timber concessions. Yes, you will sigh, asking Padilla for another match, twenty good years, years of progress, of peace and collaboration among the classes; twenty years of progress after the demagoguery of Lázaro Cárdenas; twenty years of submissive labor leaders, of broken strikes, of protection for industry.

> (Fuentes, *Death,* 11)

A diachronic unit, in contrast to the above synchronic one, the description features the protagonist's odyssey, which began in the province and ended in Mexico City itself. At the start of Artemio's rise to economic power, peasants, urban dwellers, and Mexican Indians played a major role. The last two figures appear respectively in the form of synecdoches: "land around the city of Puebla, whose growth you foresaw," "acres for subdivison in Mexico City," "new subdivisions in cities of the interior," and "timber concessions." These urban dwellers and Mexican Indians were forced to sell either their natural resources or labor for Cruz, who made large profits in both cases. A rich texture surfaces in the synecdoches as the reader remembers specific phrases in the narrative placed immediately before the synchronic unit: "You will go to your office, crossing a city impregnated with tear-gas because the police will

have just finished breaking up a demonstration in the Caballito plaza," and
"You, through Padilla, will send sharp word to the manager of the *ejido,* telling
him to clamp down on them [Mexican Indians], for that's what you pay him
for" (Fuentes, *Death,* 10). In this language richly impregnated with ideological
elements that value exploitation, the reader becomes further aware of Cruz's
innate will to seize wealth and power, a desire abetted and aided by Mexican
presidents and North American investors.

In the above manner, Fuentes has thus expanded horizontally the social
parameters to their maximum limits. Mexican society includes past presidents
who championed free enterprise, a female writer of a social column, a newspaper editor-in-chief, and a competitor from Sonora named Couto. Aside from
the national figures, international ones also have roles, though based on exploitation: American investors, Cruz's Anglo-American partner, and the representative of a Latin American benefactor. Nonetheless, Chicanos have once
again no role in this vast social world. At the level of AuI, Fuentes's concerns
remain Mexico's exploitation by the few and its dependence on foreign capital.

In the form of characters, actions, and symbols, the remaining discourse in
La muerte de Artemio Cruz provides further specificity to the geographic and
social parameters established in the above two quotes from the first sixteen
pages. Only three additional narrative elements contribute any significance to
the diachronic and synchronic axes in the above quotes: (1) the death in 1939
of Lorenzo Cruz, the protagonist's son, who is serving as a volunteer soldier
in the Spanish Civil War; (2) a monologue based on the word *chingar,* to fuck,
that seeks to characterize Mexico's experience under foreign domination; and
(3) Artemio's reflection on his last will and testament. In the reflection the
critical reader can detect Chicanos among Cruz's inheritors. Unfortunately,
the narrator sees them as braceros or wetbacks:

> You will bequeath this country: your newspaper, the hints and the adulation,
> the conscience drugged by lying articles written by men of no ability; you will be-
> queath the mortgages, a class stripped of natural human affection, power without
> greatness, a consecrated stultification, dwarf ambition, a fool's compromise, rotted
> rhetoric, institutionalized cowardice, coarse egoism:
> you will bequeath them their crooked labor leaders and captive unions, their
> new landlords, their American investments, their jailed workers, their monopolies
> and their great press, *their wet-backs,* hoods, secret agents, their foreign deposits,
> their bullied agitators, servile deputies, fawning ministers, elegant tract homes,
> their anniversaries and commemorations, their fleas and wormy tortillas, their illit-
> erate Indians, unemployed laborers, rapacious pawnshops, fat men armed with
> aqualungs and stock portfolios, thin men armed with their fingernails; they have
> their Mexico, they have their inheritance.

> (Fuentes, *Death,* 269; emphasis mine)

In retrospect, the Chicano role in Fuentes's Mexican society has not moved
beyond the reductive one present in *La región más transparente.* The phrase

"their wetbacks," in fact, constitutes the complete Chicano configuration—superminiscule—in *La muerte de Artemio Cruz*. It is a frozen and marginal image, empty of past and present history.

Twenty-five years later, Fuentes's Mexican society has changed radically. Instead of featuring another critique of former revolutionaries who become opportunists and benefit from Mexico's development, as in *La región más transparente* and *La muerte de Artemio Cruz*, the farsical novel *Cristóbal nonato* dramatizes a deep crisis in the Mexican state. The work's sequence of events are as follows: due to repeated mismanagement of the economy on the part of a government and because of the resultant infinite foreign debt, the Mexican rulers have been forced to divide the country into several parts and award them to various foreign companies, with a sole rectangle whose longest sides extend only from Mexico City to Acapulco remaining under their control. The foreign companies and their military forces represent in the narrative the hegemonic center that seeks to appropriate to itself all of Mexico. As one solution to possible rebellions among the Mexican people due to the selling of their country, the government sponsors a contest and offers as a prize full lifetime benefits and the presidency at age 21 to the very first male child born on October 12, 1992, at 0:00 hours. A young couple, Angel and Angeles, heed the call and conceive Christopher Palomar, who not only narrates his parents' tribulations in a nine-month period, but also will be born at the desired exact instant.

Although the country is now only a third its 1848 size, the narrative subject's spatial consciousness has greatly expanded beyond the one in *La región más transparente* or *La muerte de Artemio Cruz*. Narrative space includes not only the remaining Mexico but also the occupied territories and reaches into parts of the United States such as the U.S./Mexico border, the Southwest, Chicago, and the East. Ideologically foregrounding the hegemonic center's economic and military extension into Mexico, one particular description, a key device in the syuzhet, features a mutilated Mexico—the central spatial sign in Fuentes's Mexican society. The territory of the Yucatán has been ceded to the Club Méditerranée, which has created the Peninsular Tourism Trust (PENITT); Chiapas-Tabasco-Campeche—now known as the CHITACAM Trusteeship—belongs to a U.S. oil consortium called the Five Sisters; Veracruz finds itself caught in "an incomprehensible war," or "a U.S. invasion"; and the lands of the Pacific (the entire coast to the north of Ixtapa-Zihuatanejo: Michoacán, Colima, Jalisco, Nayarit, Sinaloa, Sonora, and Baja California) have been ceded to unknown hands (Fuentes, *Christopher Unborn*, 18–19). The Mexican nation-state, that now stretches only from Mexico City to Acapulco, has not escaped dissent, as it is under siege from revolutionaries and secessionists. Such is the mutilated country that Christopher Palomar, fetus and narrator, will inherit from his father, Angel Palomar, whose own conception occurred on October 2, 1968—the day of the Tlatelolco massacre—as an act of social protest.

As expected from a writer belonging to a nation-state, the new subject's spatial consciousness still has its geographical limitations. In reading the presentation of a mutilated Mexico, the reader finds the following description that features the Southwest under the sign *Mexamerica:*

> That atrocious nation on the northern border: Mexamerica, independent of Mexico and the United States, in-bond factories, smuggling, contraband, Spanglish, refuge for political fugitives, and free entry to those without papers from the Pacific Coast to the Gulf Coast, one hundred kilometers to the north and one hundred to the south from the old frontier, from Sandy Ego and Auntyjane to Coffeeville and Killmoors: independent without the need of any declaration, the fact is that there no one pays the slightest attention to the government in Mexico City or Washington

> (Fuentes, *Christopher Unborn,* 19).

Besides that the given measurements, "one hundred kilometers to the north and one hundred to the south," reduce the Southwest to a relatively narrow border region, no further significant spatial specifying occurs in the text. As an effect of the defamiliarizing description, the Southwest continues to be a mystery to the Mexican subject. The only ideologically favorable element associated with the Southwest above resides in the sign *independent,* which indicates a recognition of the other as part of a specific region.

It took Carlos Fuentes twenty-five years to configure Chicano characters beyond the bracero type found in *La región más transparente* or *La muerte de Artemio Cruz.* However, as read by Southwest Mexican readers, Fuentes's Chicano characters in *Cristóbal nonato* carry two ideologically contradictory messages: they are, on the one hand, an instrument in the foreign domination of Mexico and, on the other, a symbol of hope. Chicanos as an instrument of foreign domination appear in chapter 16, part 8, "Why Are We in Veracruz?" where they—and the discourse does contain the signifer *Chicano*—form part of a Yankee invasion force led by Reverend Royal Payne, who is a veteran of Vietnam and the Contra wars in Central America and Grenada. Among the legions of "white and black gringos" who land in Villa Cardel the reader also finds "dark skinned gringos Chicanos Puerto Ricans":

> dark skinned gringos Chicanos Puerto Ricans who aren't noticed here in Veracruz and don't have to be rotated in accordance with the law since they are identical to the little boys who show their swollen bellies and tiny penises among the shacks and alleys of Villa Cardel.

> (Fuentes, *Christopher Unborn,* 486)

As a device from the syuzhet, character configuration here ideologically defamiliarizes the text in coding Chicanos as aggressors. Yankee soldiers, including Chicanos, are the main customers who patronize Villa Cardel, the local town, that has been turned into an area full of discotheques, cantinas, and bordellos. Appearing a page later in the discourse, the phrase "Chicanos from

Chicago" (Fuentes, *Christopher Unborn*, 487) reveals their place of origin is outside the Southwest. At the ideological level, such a character configuration indicates once again that Fuentes is unfamiliar with the history of the Southwest Mexican. In a further emphasis on the message of Chicano characters as an instrument of dominion, the narrator uses scatological language in coding their figure:

> There is only one room in Deng Chopin's bordello: it is divided by a vaporous but stained gauze curtain stained with what only God knows / semen from an onanistic Chicano, bat shit or beer or guacamole it's impossible to tell.

> (Fuentes, *Christopher Unborn*, 494)

Puerto Ricans are also included in Fuentes's ideological perception of Chicanos as an instrument of domination. A native from the Island of Vieques, Macho Nacho, carries a nuclear device "equivalent to 250 tons of TNT" (Fuentes, *Christopher Unborn*, 492).

As for the message of Chicanos as hope, the birth of a Mexican male child in Chicago—a Chicano space—codes it. This child's birth occurs simultaneously with that of Christopher Palomar, the symbol of hope for Mexico itself. The fetus-narrator declares:

> I quickly think before I forget everything: I see a powerful city, a big-shouldered city, windy, early snow, the hut of a mute Indian woman, a grandmother who didn't learn English and who forgot Spanish, receiving into her hands another child who appears between the dark and bloody legs of a blind woman, the blind father holds the woman's head to make her comfortable, the blind boy is being born in Chicago, my fellow, my brother, he frozen and me hot!

> (Fuentes, *Christopher Unborn*, 529–530)

In that they are fleeing poverty and injustice in Mexico, the Mayan parents seek an escape from both in Chicago. Like the hope for the Mexican people in the birth of Christopher Palomar, the Chicano newborn promises the same for the Midwest Mexican. Unfortunately, this last child-symbol emanates from a Mexican narrative subject—the voice of a nation-state. In ideological congruency, narrative signs structure the parents as recent Mexican immigrants, who have no historical understanding of Southwest Mexican resistance from the nineteenth century to the present and who therefore see themselves and other Mexicans as unintelligible in United States society.

CHICANO WRITERS: A FRAGMENTED VOICE INSIDE AND UNDER THE HEGEMONIC

Chicano writers have consciously sought to give a voice to the Southwest, a region within the United States—already latent in previous generations of

Southwest Mexicans. A text containing elements of the GI in the Chicano LMP, the introduction to the fifth edition of the anthology *El espejo/The Mirror,* edited by Octavio Ignacio Romano-V. and Herminio Ríos-C., at its closing lists writers not only from each Southwestern state (California, Texas, New Mexico, Arizona, Colorado), but also from the Midwest, the Pacific Northwest, and the East. Whether from inside or outside the region, they all share one common literary project: "re-creating" or symbolizing the sign *Southwest.* Some of the values of their project are: to establish Chicano writing groups and presses, to rescue the history of the region from prior to 1848 to the present, to center the barrio as an autochthonous narrative universe, to distribute consciously their texts among Chicano readers, and to mold images of economic, cultural, and gender affirmation. At the level of space, Chicano symbolization generally features a humanly rich Chicano barrio under threat from a hegemonic Anglo-American society. In recognizing these common values or this understanding as the project's base, this study now examines the attempts to recreate the Southwest on the part of five selected writers: José Antonio Villarreal, Rolando Hinojosa-Smith, Rudolfo Anaya, Miguel Méndez-M., and Sandra Cisneros.

In contrast to Mexican presses which are directly helped by participation from Mexico's private sector, most Chicano presses (Bilingual Press and Arte Público Press) began publishing with and have needed to rely on university and/or foundation grants. This has been the modus operandi for the past twenty or more years. Just this year Arte Público Press received as a start-up grant, 2.7 million dollars from the Rockefeller Foundation to recover, catalog, and reedit United States Hispanic texts published prior to the 1970s ("Footnotes," A-8). The overall project will take about ten years and cost around 20 million dollars. However, in a new development in publishing, Bilingual Press struck a deal, also in 1992, with Anchor Books by which they will co-publish four novels: *The Mixquiahuala Letters* (1986) by Ana Castillo, *The Devil in Texas/El diablo en Texas* (1976) by Aristeo Brito, *The Road to Tamazunchale* (1975) by Ron Arias, and *The Ultraviolet Sky* (1988) by Alma Luz Villanueva. This development may indicate a decisive future participation by private companies in the Chicano LMP.

Of the five writers chosen here, only three appear on the list in *El espejo/ The Mirror's* introduction (Hinojosa-Smith, Anaya, Méndez-M.), and this fact centers their conscious adherence to the Chicano LMP. Their production has been solidly linked to the Chicano publishers, distributors, readers, and critics. Villarreal, for his part, stands as a precursor to these three; his re-creation of the sign *Southwest* began at an unconscious level, since he started his career within the production of the dominant culture and only recently apparently accepted, without renouncing an assimilationist ideology adopted in the 1950s, the challenge presented by the Chicano LMP (Bruce-Novoa, "Prólogo," 11–27). In fact, in Villarreal's narrative universe, the protagonists continue to flee the Chicano barrio, opting instead for integration and assimilation into Anglo-American society. On the other hand, Cisneros, born and raised in Chicago but now a resident of San Antonio, belongs to the feminist strand in the Chicano LMP, starting her career as a poet and now developing as a nationally acclaimed narrator. Her earlier production was nurtured inside Midwestern Chicano writers' circles, edited by Chicano publishers and presses, and addressed by Chicano critics.

VILLARREAL: FROM MARGINALIZATION TO SELECTIVE INTEGRATION

At the levels of GI and AuI in both the contemporary Mexican LMP and the Chicano LMP, José Antonio Villarreal shares with Carlos Fuentes a concern for people of Mexican descent—their history—from 1910 to the 1980s. This is seen in his three novels: *Pocho, The Fifth Horseman* (1974), and *Clemente Chacón* (1984). The difference is that, from the levels of the Mexican GI and his AuI, Fuentes has limited his concern to events inside Mexico during this period. He has not considered those in Southwest Chicano history during exactly the same seventy years, such as the self-exile of a half-million Mexicans in the Southwest and other parts of the United States from 1910 to the 1930s, the Chicano experience in World War II as part of United States troops, and the massive Mexican immigrations in the 1950s and 1970s. A nation-state ideology limits Fuentes's historical and social parameters, preventing him from seeing three Mexican diasporas as an integral part of Southwest Mexican history from 1848 to 1992. For his part, Villarreal has at least addressed two massive migrations into the Southwest (1910 through the 1930s and the 1970s migrations), specifically in California and Texas.

A precursor to 1970s Chicano narrators, Villarreal distinguishes himself from them in having embraced in the 1950s assimilation into Anglo-American society (Hernández-Gutiérrez, "Villarreal's *Clemente Chacón*," 35–43). Part of this consciousness rises from the fact that he developed as a writer in a mainstream writers' circle. He also does not see any historical significance for Chicanos in the 1848 conquest or in the necessity of an ethnic struggle for civil rights. In a rare instance in *Pocho* in which the narrator does recall the 1848 conquest, he fails to return to it, coding a silence on this event. He does, nonetheless, symbolize Southwestern society from the regional consciousness of a Southwest Mexican.

Integral to the sign *Southwest, Pocho* does symbolize Mexicans as part of the Southwest from *circa* 1910 to the 1940s. The fabula has two parts, one featuring the father Juan Rubio and the other the son Richard Rubio. In the first part, the protagonist Juan Rubio flees Mexico into Texas after his leader Villa is defeated. Rubio becomes a migrant farmworker in Southern and Northern California and rises to labor contractor in Santa Clara. At the novel's end, he loses his family, whose women rebel against his unilateral patriarchal rule, marring his social mobility. In the fabula's second part, the protagonist Richard Rubio is born in the Imperial Valley, grows up in Santa Clara, assimilates ideologically inside the Anglo educational system, witnesses economic oppression and rebellion during the Great Depression, faces racism at the start of

World War II, and, disillusioned, seeks to escape by joining the Navy to fight in Europe.

Unlike Fuentes's symbolization of Mexican society in which time after time signifiers fill the sign *Mexico, Pocho*'s discourse contains no sign combination that does the same in the case of the Southwest. Only one geographical description foregrounds, though shallowly, the sign *Southwest*. It features Juan Rubio migrating into Texas at the end of the armed phase of the Mexican Revolution:

> Thus Juan Rubio became a part of the great exodus that came of the Mexican Revolution. By the hundreds they crossed the Río Grande, and then by the thousands. They came first to Juárez, where the price of the three minute tram ride would take them into El Paso del Norte . . . The ever-increasing army of people swarmed across while the border remained open, fleeing from squalor and oppression. But they could not flee reality, and the Texans, who welcomed them as a blessing because there were miles of cotton to harvest, had never really forgotten the Alamo. . . . and so they moved onward, west to New Mexico and Arizona and California, and as they moved, they planted their new seed.
>
> (Villarreal, *Pocho*, 15–16)

However, in spite of their appearance above, the signifiers *New Mexico* and *Arizona* disappear from the narration altogether. Such disappearance has a defamiliarizing effect in that the placing of the description early in the text suggests the fabula directly applies to the whole Southwest. In fact, California disproportionately occupies the sign *Southwest* in *Pocho*. And from inside California, the County of Santa Clara—an Anglo-American neighborhood—takes the center in the narrative universe.

San José represents the Chicano working-class neighborhood. However, since the protagonist grew up in Santa Clara, such space is alien to Richard, foregrounding his assimilationist ideology:

> Of the new friends Richard made, those who were native to San Jose were relegated to become casual acquaintances, for they were as Americanized as he, and did not interest him. The newcomers became the object of his exploration. He was avidly hungry to learn the way of these people. It was not easy for him to approach them at first, because his clothes labeled him as an outsider, and too, he had trouble understanding their speech. He must not ask questions, for fear of offending them; his deductions as to their character and makeup must come from close association. He was careful not to be patronizing or in any way act superior.
>
> (Villarreal, *Pocho*, 151)

The scarce and scattered signifiers—county courthouse, Mexican dance hall, bar, joint, city jail, orchard, twelve-acre cherry grove, new industrial district on the north side of the city, firehouse, street, and Willow Glen—describe an urban Chicano working-class barrio that is experiencing the early stages of development.

As is implicit in the phrase "welcomed . . . as a blessing because there were miles of cotton to harvest," Chicanos in Villarreal's Southwestern society, unlike the entrepreneur Mexicans in Fuentes's *La muerte de Artemio Cruz,* mainly supply labor power in a developing Southwestern agriculture—a role that, however, does not grant them basic services like housing or medical care. At *Pocho*'s close, the protagonist thus finds himself working in a steel mill in spite of the academic education he actively sought and earned in Santa Clara's schools. Appearing early in the text, the description below has already coded Richard's subordination as beginning at the moment of his birth:

> It was near Brawley, in the Imperial Valley, at a place where a dry creek met a tributary of the Canal del Alamo, that Richard was born. The Rubio family lived in a white clapboard house on a melon farm, on land that had been neardesert [*sic*] not too long ago. . . . The land had been reclaimed and the valley made *artificially green and fertile,* but the oppressive heat remained, and the people who tilled the fields, for the most part, came from the temperate climate of the central plateaus of México and found it difficult to acclimatize. Every day, one or two or three of them were carried, dehydrated and comatose, from the field, . . . Indeed, there were a few that year who died before they could receive help, and were carted off to El Centro, where they ended up in a pauper's grave or on a slab in some medical school in Los Angeles or San Francisco.
>
> (Villarreal, *Pocho,* 28–29; my emphasis)

Ideologically, such harsh marginalization foregrounds irony in the protagonist's assimilationist goal.

Although it is a fact that the father, Juan Rubio, does eventually rise to labor contractor, in such a position he plays a mere intermediary role in which he recruits migrant Mexican labor for the benefit of the Anglo farmer. It is the latter who benefits the most by being able to market his crops on the East Coast at a higher profit. This economic opposition between an Anglo and a Chicano—both products of the character figuration as a device from the syuzhet—exposes concretely, through defamiliarization, the limitations of Richard's assimilationist ideology. Unlike Federico Robles or Artemio Cruz, Juan Rubio does not share in the profits. Juan Rubio, a Southwest Mexican, earns only a sufficiently high wage to purchase a family house. As a message from the device of character structuring, he and his son Richard are excluded from lucrative benefits in a developing society, especially the son who continues to face many obstacles in obtaining a university education. Prejudice, racism, low wages, and an overpowering Anglo-American society frustrate his social aspirations.

Twenty-five years later Villarreal presents in *Clemente Chacón* a new and radical view of Southwest Mexican society. Its setting unfolds primarily in El

Paso, and narrative time spans from the mid-1940s to September 1972. In the fabula, the protagonist, a Mexican immigrant at the very young age of twenty-eight years, has been promoted—from head of all departments in the city to regional director of four Southwestern states plus Oklahoma—in recognition of his hard work, dedication, high moral principles, company allegiance, and the sale, in just one year, of one million dollars in insurance to industry, plus more in debit in El Paso and Isleta. A "Catholic and brown" Horatio Alger, Clemente is on his way to becoming a regional manager in a New England company founded back in Connecticut during the English colony. In a surprising twist in narrative events, while waiting for the ceremony to make him regional director, Clemente learns that, against company rules barring infidelity on the part of employees or spouses, his Anglo mentor and superior, Virgil Smith, has had an affair with Queli, Clemente's wife. The protagonist, of course, protests before Mr. Max Calhoun, the national vice-president, and upon the latter's recommendation, Clemente receives Virgil's own awarded position as regional vice-president of all the Western states (Villarreal, *Clemente Chacón*, 138). Such a position includes an office in Los Angeles and a house in an Anglo suburb, an environment in radical contrast to Clemente's prior residences: a Zacatecas village, a slum in Mexico City, another in Ciudad Juárez, and a Chicano working-class barrio in El Paso.

With the sign *Company* projecting the United States, the sign *here* denoting El Paso, and the sign *Los Angeles* recalling California, the following dialogue between Calhoun and Clemente foregrounds the latter's protest before the former as well as Clemente's self-advocacy in securing the second promotion:

> "All right," said Calhoun. "You're a salesman; sell yourself."
> Clemente thought, *you're smart, too, you bastard,* because Calhoun was forcing him to tell him what he wanted. Forcing him to somehow stand naked by stating that he wanted Virgil fired so that he would not stand in his way. "You know it isn't true," said Clemente. "I don't have to sell myself. You know my record, you know my growth potential, my capabilities, my worth to the Company. You want me to build a case against Virgil. I think I can. Aside from today, he's been banging his secretary for some time. A cardinal sin for Company executives. Of course that's not important in your decision. Just a little extra if you make your report. What is important is that Virgil has reached his level. One more step upward will place him beyond his ability. Here, because he has someone like me, directly under him, he has done a great job. When he goes to Los Angeles, people like me will be hundreds, maybe a thousand miles away from his base. And we will have others under us doing the real work. Virgil can make a decision on the spot, but he doesn't have the imagination necessary for a broad operation. Oh, his experience will carry him through, but at best he will only be adequate. The Company will not suffer if he goes to Los Angeles, but it also will not suffer if he doesn't. That's the case."

> (Villarreal, *Clemente Chacón*, 136–137; emphasis in text)

Unlike the protagonists in *Pocho,* here a Southwest Mexican has passed the point of merely selling his labor power to an Anglo farmer or factory owner. Ideologically, Clemente now heeds the words from the protagonist in *Hunger of Memory* by Richard Rodríguez: "I have taken Caliban's advice. I have stolen their books. I will have some run of this Island" (3). In comparison to Fuentes's Artemio Cruz, Clemente has begun to play a similar role in the Southwest: managing society. It is a position for which his mentor Virgil Smith has been preparing him, as the former so declared before Max Calhoun: "In the Southwest, a great deal of our business is with the Spanish surnamed" (Villarreal, *Clemente Chacón,* 68). At the novel's close the figure of the protagonist not only symbolically hovers over the Southwest, but also exercises a power that reaches to each and every Southwestern state as well as to the Pacific Northwest and back East, namely to Boston.

In spite of the above spatial projection, the signifiers in the sign *Southwest* remain few in number and primarily code spaces in Southwestern Texas and Southern California. When signs referring to Arizona or Colorado do appear in the discourse—respectively Phoenix, Colorado Springs, and Boulder—they are linked not to Chicano but to Anglo-American characters. Such crisscrossing of the devices description and character in the case of Anglo figures foregrounds a reduction in the heroic configuration of the protagonist. The sole appearance of the sign *New Mexico* in association with a Chicano character serves to code rural Canutillo where a young boy died—Clemente Chacón, from whom the protagonist, born Ramón Alvarez in Mexico, took his Southwestern name. The young boy's Texas Mexican family had gone there to pick cotton (Villarreal, *Clemente Chacón,* 87). These elements in the configuration of the protagonist as character fracture the assimilationist fabula in that the protagonist's shallowness surfaces.

Fear of poverty and barrio conditions motivate Clemente's phenomenal rise on the social scale. By crossing the border from Ciudad Juárez into El Paso, Ramón Alvarez leaves behind a squalid Mexican slum where his mother was a prostitute. Mr. Clemente Chacón, a maintenance man at the Fourth Street playground in the Second Ward in El Paso, finds young Alvarez sleeping by the trash cans. He adopts the protagonist, who in turn takes the name Clemente Chacón from his adopted father's son. The following description features the Chicano barrio known as Segundo Barrio, where the new Clemente Chacón (Jr.) lives up to the age of eighteen:

> They walked a block south and west toward the bridge. Halfway down the second block the old man opened a door of a dirty brick building. The structure covered an entire block, each door from the street was the entrance to the living quarters of entire families—one room, one tiny kitchen area. The second floor was reached from the inner patio. Rickety outside stairs where children and grown men had fallen went up to a platform which gave access to cubicles similar to those below. Downstairs, under the stairway to save space, was one flush toilet to serve

the eighty dwellings of the complex. The women washed clothes in tinas in the patio. The building had been constructed for Mexicans who had fled from their homeland to find a better life.

(Villarreal, *Clemente Chacón*, 76–77)

As in *Pocho,* once again the Chicano barrio figures as an alien space where youths become "defeated, exploited or corrupt." Ideologically, such description and characterization of the youth, as devices from the syuzhet, foreground the protagonist's rejection of barrio life as central in the text.

In line with the fabula, Clemente works hard and saves, at times selling drugs to earn extra income, and he soon moves Doña Amparo Chacón, his adopted mother, to a small cottage on Aurora in the Highland area—presumably an Anglo-American neighborhood. After this event, his job with and mentoring by Virgil Smith help him to purchase a house in the Anglo suburbs and eventually ascend to regional director in the insurance company. In *Clemente Chacón,* the Chicano barrio represents the underdeveloped, the exotic, the sexist, and the dangerous, while the Anglo-American communities stand for material privilege, marking thereby an ideology of acculturation and assimilation. Symbolized by the New England company, the Anglo-American hegemonic center imposes selection and exclusion on the barrio residents who may enter its society. That the image of the barrio stands in sharp opposition to that of the Anglo community points to the defamiliarization inherent in the device of description, which here ideologically foregrounds cultural suicide on the part of the protagonist.

HINOJOSA: BARRIO RESISTANCE TO LOCAL AND REGIONAL ANGLO HEGEMONY

Aware that Villarreal's narrative universe forsakes the Texas and California barrios and instead privileges hegemonic spaces, we now turn to the work of Rolando Hinojosa-Smith, a conscious member of the 1970s narrators. He is the most prolific and representative Chicano narrator from the state of Texas (José David Saldívar, ed.). In opposition to Villarreal's assimilationist project, Hinojosa-Smith has been an active participant in the Chicano LMP that has as its primary objective the symbolization of the Mexican Southwest. As an achievement, in the past twenty years the Texas Chicano has not only contributed to the development of a world-renowned literature, but also opened space for works by such assimilationist writers as Villarreal and Richard Rodríguez.

In light of the above, *Clemente Chacón* can never displace Hinojosa's Texas narrative universe, especially its message of resistance. For one, Hinojosa's work is more extensive and diverse than that of Villarreal. Writing a series in both Spanish and English entitled *Klail City Death Trip,* Hinojosa-Smith has published the following works, all part of the series: *Estampas del valle y otras obras (Sketches of the Valley and Other Works;* 1973), *Klail City y sus alrede-*

dores (*Generations and Sketches;* 1976), *Korean Love Songs* (1978), *Mi querido Rafa* (*Dear Rafe;* 1981), *Claros varones de Belken* (*Fair Gentlemen of Belken County;* 1986), and at least four other works. In a qualitative achievement, *Klail City y sus alredededores* won the 1976 Premio Casa de las Américas, a prestigious prize in Latin American letters and was published in Cuba. Subsequently published in the United States by Editorial Justa Publications under the title *Generaciones y semblanzas,* it best serves this study on the Chicano LMP and its intention: symbolizing the Southwest.

Featuring a fabula whose collective protagonist is the people, the narrative universe in *Generaciones y semblanzas* unfolds, from the 1940s to 1973, the daily struggles on the part of Chicano residents in Belken County's many barrios: Balde, El Rebaje, El Rincón del Diablo, Bascom, Relámpago, Flora, Klail City, Jonesville-on-the-River, and El Cantarranas. As a group, they house a specific Southwest Mexican society: migrant and factory workers, shopkeepers, a few small landowners, and some office helpers.

Belken County residents treasure a rich history whose beginnings go back prior to 1848. Barrio resistance arises from such self-consciousness. Chicano residents see themselves as Greeks among Romans, the latter being, of course, the descendants of the conquering Anglo Texans. The very second paragraph in *Generaciones y semblanzas* informs the reader that it is the multiple Chicano characters who occupy the center in the narrative universe: "The number of anglos—*bolillos* [literally, bread rolls]—which appear in these writings is relatively small" (Hinojosa, *Generations,* 2). That is, in an ideological exercise of resistance, Chicano figuration is multidimensional. On the other hand, most *bolillos,* or Anglos, appear as caricatures. Tom Purdy, who helps house migrant workers from Belken in Michigan, figures as an exception, indicating an alternative path available to the hegemonic culture.

In sharp contrast to its image as a corrupting influence in *Clemente Chacón,* the barrio in *Generaciones y semblanzas* symbolizes continuity and regeneration, two forms of resistance. Continuity allows barrio residents to leave and return of their free will. For example, a Belken native fought in the 1910 Mexican Revolution and came back. Viola Barragán, a Mexican refugee of the 1910 Mexican Revolution, grew up in Belken County and traveled throughout the world; yet, she has returned time after time, being now recognized as a town legend. Also, the barrio houses Chicano veterans who fought in Europe and/or Korea. In the case of regeneration, barrio residents readily open their door to Brother Imás, a Midwest-born Chicano, who is able to rebuild his Spanish language and cultural identity.

Notwithstanding the above two qualities, *Generaciones y semblanzas,* just like *Pocho* and *Clemente Chacón,* fails to fully signify the Southwest. No route leads to California. The signs *Nuevo México* and *Arizona* do not even appear in the narrative discourse. In the final analysis, the spatial signs limit themselves to figuring South Texas. The incomplete description of the Southwest, as a defamiliarizing device from the syuzhet, exposes the ideological limitations of the text in not thoroughly knowing the Southwest.

In further defamiliarization at the level of description, *Generaciones y semblanzas*'s discourse instead transfers the reader to the Midwest, the South, and several international sites. The Midwest (Illinois, Indiana, Wisconsin) and the South (Tennessee, Alabama, Mississippi) code an economic dependence on both hegemonic spaces on the part of Southwest Mexicans. As migrant workers, Belken residents fill a cheap labor pool for Anglo agribusiness in both regions, a relationship historically present in Belken County since 1848. As for the international links, most come about by force: the United States Armed Forces, a hegemonic entity, takes Belken residents to fight in Europe at the time of World War II and Korea in the 1950s, where many lose their lives. For their part, barrio residents, in line with the fabula, struggle against both conditions, sometimes getting help from others like Tom Purdy.

In their fight for survival and historical continuity, Chicano residents encounter Anglo-American society. The triple narration—by Galindo, Jehú Malacara, and Rafa Buenrostro—makes the reader feel Anglo hegemonic power, leaving a strong message of the need for resistance. For example, in the novel's last chapter, Jehú Malacara reviews his graduating class and lists its members according to economic and political rank: "the [six] wealthier anglos [males]," "the wealthy anglo girls," "the less rich [urban] *bolillos*," "two farm and ranch *bolillos*," "the Chicanos with land" (Hinojosa, *Generations*, 172 and 174), and lastly, all Chicano sons and daughters of farm and factory workers. Ironically, in this narrative universe whose center is Southwest Mexican society, Chicanos occupy the lower end of the hierarchy in Belken County. Ideologically, such a manner of presenting Chicano characters demystifies their dominant presence in *Generaciones y semblanzas,* foregrounding instead their subordinated integration into the hegemonic center.

Emphasizing the message of resistance, six paragraphs parade the multiple characters in *Generaciones y semblanzas* with the intent of detailing Belken County's hierarchical order (171). "The wealthier Anglos," who exercise hegemonic power, are J. B. Longley, Edwin Dickman, Roger Bowman, Robert Stephenson Pennick, Royce Westlake, Harv Moody, a woman named Elsinore, Molly Loudermilk, Liz Ann Moore, and Babs Hadley. They, above all others in Belken County, benefit materially from the social order. For example, Roger Bowman has the privilege of hosting the twenty-second anniversary of the Klail High School graduating class at his Green Gaulet restaurant and gardens. Featuring "two farm and ranch *bolillos*," or the next level below in the social hierarchy, the following description, as a device from the syuzhet, foregrounds the hegemonic power as it daily impacts Chicano residents in Belken:

> There are still two other groups of anglos, the farm and ranch *bolillos*. Those with the most land are friends of the Klail City rich and those with little land are friends of the Klail poor; for it's said that likes attract. The largest landowners have German names: Muller, Gottschalk, and Bleibst; those with small spreads have English surnames: Watkins, Snow and Allen, among others.

The Chicanos with land in Klail and the surrounding areas are the Buenrostros (not all), the Leguizamóns (all) and some of the other old families who joined forces to keep their lands: the Vilches, the Campoys, the Farias, etc.

Twenty years later almost all the groups with land will get fat, will stick close to home, and will see each other on Saturdays and Sundays at church and in the Klail City bars. After these twenty years or more, the children of these people will have their own cars and fill'er up 'cause we're going across the river.

(Hinojosa, *Generations,* 172 and 174)

Such hegemonic power excludes Chicano migrant and factory workers from basic benefits. Defamiliarization in the description lies in that, although the majority of the characters who occupy the center of the narrative universe are Chicanos, the seldom-seen land-owning Anglo characters, and some landed Chicanos, hold economic dominance. Thus, irony and sarcasm, narrative devices themselves, on the part of Chicano narrators and characters, especially the migrant workers, code resistance, a dominant principle in the Chicano LMP, as the resonant ideology in *Generaciones y semblanzas.*

ANAYA: A WAGE EARNER IN THE PLACE OF ORIGIN

Like Chicano writers from California and Texas, those from New Mexico have limited themselves to their Southwestern province: Sabine Ulibarrí, Nash Candelaria, Jaime Sagel, and Rudolfo Anaya. In the triology *Bless Me, Ultima* (1971), *Heart of Aztlán,* and *Tortuga* (1979), Anaya has best symbolized, in three phases, the modern condition of Chicano New Mexican society: exile from a pastoral community, labor exploitation and family fragmentation in urban Albuquerque, and lastly, total human dependence on technology. Anaya's work has been and continues to be at the center of the Chicano LMP. In 1972, he published an excerpt from his novel *Bless Me, Ultima* in the historic anthology *El espejo/The Mirror.* Because it offers a rich social specificity, *Heart of Aztlán* helps the reader understand Anaya's symbolization of the sign *Southwest.* As chronologically coded by the music of Bill Haley and Little Richard, which is modern and preferred by the young protagonists, *Heart of Aztlán* takes place in Albuquerque in the 1950s.

Its fabula features the protagonist, Clemente Chávez, who faces two severe challenges to his leadership skills: keeping his family united amidst drugs, delinquency, and a decline of parental authority; and leading a group of striking workers at the local railroad yard who seek higher wages and safe working conditions. As personal support, Chávez has a tradition in leadership that, based on land ownership, goes back as far as the early seventeenth century. The land factor stresses his personal crises in leadership, especially since Clemente is forced to sell the last piece of family-owned land in the novel's first chapter. In the process of proving himself, he codes through his personal actions a message of barrio resistance.

Although all twenty-one chapters in *Heart of Aztlán* take place in a working-class barrio named Barelas in Albuquerque, at its opening the very first chapter presents the last day of continuous land ownership in the Chávez family. In order to pay accumulated debts and seek greater opportunity for his children in Albuquerque, Clemente sells his ranchito, a small plot, situated at the edge of the town of Guadalupe. In turn, the Chávezes now must sell their labor power to pay for basic needs: rent, food, and clothing. In the following character configuration, as a device from the syuzhet, Clemente recognizes that, like many other rural New Mexicans, he has been reduced to an urban wage earner, a condition that leads some to migrate to elsewhere including California:

> He looked at his sons and knew there would be nothing left to pass on to them. Without the land the relationship a man created with the earth would be lost, old customs, and traditions would fall by the wayside, and they would be like wandering gypsies without a homeland where they might anchor their spirit. But he had to go because there was no work in Guadalupe, and because he had to be the leader in helping to create a new future for his familia. He was not the first to leave, many of his vecinos and compadres had already left to make a new life in the bigger cities of Las Vegas, Santa Fe, Albuquerque, and many had gone as far west as California. The people were dispersed, but as they left each one secretly vowed to return to the sacred land of his birth and heritage.
>
> (Anaya, *Heart*, 3–4)

Defamiliarization through the character device occurs in that the characters, including Chávez, continue to hold on—in an urban setting—to a pastoral ideology based on land ownership. Ironically, the reduction to wage earner already has a long history. Although the buyer is one Don José, a Southwest Mexican, Clemente understands that the family began losing its land in 1848, projecting the rise of Anglo-American hegemony—present in the signs *tejano, barbed wire,* and *new laws* from the quotation below—over the Southwest. He says to Don José:

> Somehow we began to lose the land a long time ago. The tejano came, the barbed wire came, the new laws came. A few survived, but death came and took so many of our family in such a short time—.
>
> (Anaya, *Heart*, 5)

In textualizing the downward mobility from landowner to mere wage earner, *Heart of Aztlán* remains, like other Chicano novels, spatially local. Its geographic signs configure primarily Albuquerque, New Mexico. As such, the sign *California* appears on only two other instances in the discourse—a mere total of three times; *Colorado* surfaces once. Both Southwestern signs establish that New Mexicans who have lost their property to land speculators migrated there in search of jobs, not pleasure or investment. As for Texas and Arizona, or the Midwest, their signs are absent. Once again, the symbolization of the sign *Southwest* remains fragmentary, which accentuates a defamiliarizing effect that codes geographic regionalism in this subject's world view.

As mentioned earlier, Barelas appropriates most spatial signs in *Heart of Aztlán,* although other Chicano barrios in Albuquerque are present. Barelas is a poor, working-class neighborhood, not much different from the others, whose Chicano residents depend on a railroad yard next door for employment. This last space, though, symbolizes Anglo-American hegemony, bringing into play defamiliarization on the part of the description device. In the broadest description that centers Barelas, the protagonist's son, Jason, sees the yard as nightmarish:

> Jason did not see them [two women]. His eyes were fixed on the huge, round water tank that rose out of the dark buildings at the end of the road. It towered above the barrio, so that Jason could read the letters on the faded cross. SANTA FE. The black tower of steel loomed over everything. Around it trains thrashed like giant serpents, and when they coupled the monstrous act gave unnatural birth to chains of steel. Jason cautiously approached the labyrinth of grimy buildings, steel tracks and boxcars. The houses near the yards were dark with soot and the elms trees withered and bare. A chain link fence surrounded the yards. Jason found the gate just when a blast of steam shook him from his daydream. The silence was ripped open by a thunder and lightning that spewed out of the dark forge.
>
> (Anaya, *Heart,* 22)

Supported by a union leader named Kirk, a local New Mexican store owner named El Super, a priest, and the police forces, faceless Anglos hold owner-ship and power over Barelas's main job source. Although Chicano workers overwhelmingly populate the narrative universe, they are mere wage laborers whose function is to produce greater wealth for the Anglo owners of the rail-road yard.

All barrio dwellers, including the Chávez family, share Jason's nightmarish vision, foregrounding their exploitation and exclusion from the benefits of a developed society. The simile "trains thrashed like giant serpents, and when they coupled the monstrous act gave unnatural birth to chains of steel," built on the plural nouns *trains* and *serpents,* suggests a lack of control over tech-nology on the part of Chicano workers. In denying them union representation, job security, and safe working conditions, this Anglo-American society super-exploits them and reserves for them a subordinate role. From the role of syu-zhet in structuring the narrative, the railroad yard, as a defamiliarizing sym-bol, represents the hegemonic center that controls the workers' incomes and very lives. For example, on the first day in Barelas the protagonist Clemente does secure employment at the yard, but only after another worker, who re-sembles him, dies instantly upon being hit "squarely on the head" by a giant crane chain (Anaya, *Heart,* 23). Ideologically, the dominant presence of Chicano characters in the narration does not mean an end to Anglo economic dominance. Lastly, the image "houses near the yards were dark with soot and the elm trees withered and bare" codes barrio dwellers as victims of industrial pollution.

It is this employee's death that leads workers to strike against the railroad yard and make demands, thus projecting in the text an ideology of resistance shared by Chicano characters. The demands include detailed safety measures, accident compensation, and higher pay. A new worker, Clemente Chávez initially avoids the striking workers. However, he soon realizes that they were truly "mistreated" (Anaya, *Heart,* 77) and attends one of their meetings where the union boss, Kirk, first pushes and subsequently fires him. The firing sharpens his leadership crisis. After living through a period of self-destruction, Clemente does return to become the workers' chosen leader.

That he was once a landowner in the New Mexican llano, or valley, becomes the source of constant inspiration for reaffirming his leadership role and skills. The Anglo owners now begin to fear him. Offering Clemente enough money to survive the rest of his life, the "shop bosses," "politicos," and some collaborators from among barrio dwellers seek to buy him out in an effort to leave the striking workers without a leader. The protagonist refuses. At the closing of the novel he leads a workers' march through the streets of Barelas with the intent of finally facing the yard's owners and resolving the strike favorably on the side of the workers. At the head of the march, Clemente Chávez ideologically symbolizes resistance in the narrative of the Chicano LMP—a principal element from the GI. Ironically, such description placed at the end of the text, with its open structure, leaves the reader ambivalent about the resolution of the workers' struggle against the railroad yard.

MÉNDEZ-M.: A CRITIQUE OF DEVELOPMENT

As Arizonan writers, the Chicano LMP has Alberto Ríos, Miguel Méndez-M., Justo Alarcón, and so forth. Méndez-M., however, models Arizonan consciousness in Chicano narrative discourse. He began writing in the late 1940s but did not publish until Quinto Sol Publications printed the first edition of the historic anthology *El espejo/The Mirror* in 1969. Although Méndez-M. has five short-story collections, the novels *Peregrinos de Aztlán* and *El sueño de Santa María de las Piedras* excel in their Arizonan symbolization of Southwest Mexican society. Of all the writers in the Chicano LMP, Méndez-M. has received the most recognition in Mexico. Both of his novels have now been published there, and in 1991 he was awarded the Premio Nacional de Literatura José Fuentes Mares for his short-story collection *Que no mueran los sueños* (Do Not Let Dreams Die).

Similar to the Buendía family in *Cien Años de Soledad,* the fabula in *El sueño de Santa María de las Piedras* features the Noragua family, which has played a significant role in the border town of Santa Maria de las Piedras in northern

Sonora. Since the beginning of the twentieth century to the 1980s, three family generations have already made contributions to the town. Taking place from the early to the mid-1980s, the latest contribution involves a journey by burro by young Timoteo Noragua, who crisscrosses the United States: up the West Coast, across the Midwest into New York, and down to Texas. In his journey, the protagonist sees places and events that demystify United States development. As Timoteo witnesses superexploitation in the Southwest and mass destruction from a nuclear attack in New York, the United States's world fame as a utopia crumbles. At the novel's close, Timoteo hurriedly and eagerly returns to Santa María de las Piedras.

As an innovation in Chicano narrative, space expands beyond the Southwest. Though sketchy, it includes Chicago, New York, and Boston. The expansion even takes the reader south of the Southwest, into northern Mexico and Mexico City. However, in spite of the broad geographical context of *El sueño de Santa María de las Piedras,* the symbolization of the sign *Southwest* remains elusive at the level of specificity. The fact that the dominant society takes up seven of the eight chapters detailing Timoteo's journey across the United States while Southwest Mexican society appears only twice in them (see chapter 18, 150–156) dramatizes the elusiveness. Though indirectly, *El sueño de Santa María de las Piedras* does feature Arizona signs (*Tucson* and *Yuma*), California ones (*Los Angeles* and *San Francisco*), and a Texas sign (*San Antonio*). However, New Mexico and Colorado are totally absent from the narrative discourse. And ironically, Santa María de las Piedras, a town in northern Sonora, not the Southwest, occupies the center in the narrative universe: twenty-three out of thirty-one chapters and most spatial signs revolve around Santa María de las Piedras.

Thus, before examining the symbolization of Southwest Mexican society in *El sueño de Santa María de las Piedras,* the reader needs first to understand Santa María de las Piedras's historical dependency first on a colonial and hegemonic Mexico City and now on United States development. In the following description at the outset of the novel, one of the many narrators maps the town for the Chicano reader, who expects a Southwestern site:

If it is true that Santa María de las Piedras did exist, here we are to demonstrate it with our presence, standing on these blurred streets. That imposing church was molded by Father Encarnación with his spirit and it has existed forever. There is the plaza where history, absurd and playful, plays in the mouth of talkative old men. . . . Another part of Santa María de las Piedras consists of the hills stretched out in the shape of a half-moon with jagged peaks at each end, facing the esplanadelike prominence where the dead rest. The Spaniards decided to call these hills the Cathedral, but the Indians had already named them Twin Tits. . . . You might well ask why Santa María de las Piedras is located in the middle of sand dunes and scraggly plants, with only sahuaros as sentinels, in an oasis of stones. Say a world of stones, although in the middle of this wasteland there is nothing more than a fistful of pebbles and sand. . . . Time in Santa María de las Piedras moves backwards because it knows this is a town condemned to oblivion, living only on the memories of memories made into dreams. Only one man from Santa María de las Piedras happened by chance to enter the future. Madness freed him from this petrified dream and led him to tread solid ground while navigating forbidden spaces that open onto profound mysteries. Crossing the United States of America, he stumbled onto God's tracks and devoted himself to seeking Him everywhere until he found Him.

(Méndez-M., *Dream*, 3–4)

The description's defamiliarization lies here in that the history of Mexico, not that of the Southwest, is central to Santa María de las Piedras, foregrounding a dilution of Chicano ideology. Historically, the town has been tied to Mexico: populated first by indigenous Opatas, Apaches, and Yaquis; mined by Spanish conquerors in the early seventeenth century; evangelized in the middle of the same century by Father Encarnación, who built the town's church; farmed and mined once again from the latter part of the seventeenth century to the early nineteenth by Spanish colonists, who slowly intermarried with the indigenous peoples; taken over in 1830 by latifundista and slave-owner Don León Marcial de las Colinas; redistributed through land reform after the 1910 Mexican Revolution; and overtaken by another gold discovery and boom in the 1930s. However, from the 1930s forward, a shift has occurred: like Southwest Mexicans since 1848, residents from Santa María de las Piedras now form part of a cheap labor pool supplying workers to a hegemonic Anglo-American society. The latter structurally represents the new hegemonic center whose wealth attracts town residents in search of a better life. Such promises move Timoteo Noragua to undertake the five-year journey across the United States. In the process, however, he becomes familiar with inherent contradictions in United States society. Part of them involve the Southwest.

As mentioned earlier, Southwest Mexican society does not appear until chapter 18, after the protagonist has witnessed two wonderful achievements: wonderful mechanical rides in Cosmicland, in Los Angeles, and the concert-like construction of a bridge across the bay in San Francisco. Timoteo then reaches an immense, fertile agricultural valley—possibly California's Sacramento Valley—where thousands of workers harvest fruits such as grapes, oranges, and peaches. To Timoteo's surprise, the laborers happen to be people just like those living in Santa María de las Piedras: Indians and mestizos. That these workers labor under the eyes of blond and intimidating guards stands as the sole difference. Thus the first contradiction chips Timoteo's utopian image of the United States.

As in the case of Cosmicland, Timoteo believes that the rich, agricultural lands belong to Huachusey—the personification of a highly developed United States. (In asking Anglo-Americans in Spanish the name of the person who owns the wonders he has seen and only being answered with the question "What did you say?", he phonetically adapts this phrase into the name Hua-

chusey and ingeniously assumes that this is the owner.) In asking for Huachusey's whereabouts, Timoteo listens to a young Chicano in the field whose
answer—a character device from the syuzhet—reveals the marginalized status
of the farmworkers at the hands of *gabas,* or Anglo landowners:

> . . . You know what, mister? These guys are really on their last legs, brother. Don't
> you know that all this belongs to the gringos? We work our butts off, and they pay
> us just enough to keep us from dying of hunger. We work for him from dawn to
> dusk, and we are still as poor as lizards. We go from one place to another, and the
> kids never get any schooling, and on top of it, they put them to work too. It's hell.
> We live in hovels while the gringos rule the roost with their lovely homes, soft
> clothes and cars you wouldn't believe.

> (Méndez-M., *Dream,* 105–106)

As coded in the phrase "lovely homes, [good food] and cars you wouldn't
believe," the Anglo owners reap the benefits of a developed society, while Chicano migrants work long hours daily, have a low standard of living, lack an
education, provide child labor, live in substandard housing, and lack good cars
and fine clothes. Ideologically, such opposition at the level of characters constitutes exclusion. Timoteo's naiveté, a character element, produces defamiliarization at the level of the fabula: although he comes from a benefactor
family in Santa María de las Piedras, Timoteo fails, despite the explanation
from the young man, to understand the exclusion of Chicanos from the benefits of a developed society, revealing in his configuration traces of Mexican
ideology which idealizes the United States.

Ironically, the young speaker happens to be the grandson of a former Mexican revolutionary from Michoacán who, under General Obregón, rose to lieutenant in the revolutionary forces. Projecting the social divisions in place in
Mexico after the revolution, the lieutenant chose to migrate north and work
for the gringos instead of accepting employment as a peon in a huge estate
acquired by his general from the revolution. As a character element, the former revolutionary's role as a farmworker in the United States, a role inherited
now by the second generation, foregrounds once again Santa María de las
Piedras's new dependency on United States development. The United States's
hegemonic influence not only is present there, but also has been present for
many years as part of Southwest Mexican communities.

In the same chapter 18 the reader becomes familiar with Chicano urban life.
Such description—as a device from the syuzhet—foregrounds the dominance
of Anglo America over Southwest Mexican society despite the protagonist
sympathetic toward Chicanos. After leaving the above fertile valley and continuing his journey through forests, mountains, rivers, and other cities, the
protagonist Timoteo, on top of his donkey, Solomón, arrives at "a monstrous
city" with "elegant suburbs" and "poor neighborhoods" (Méndez-M., *Dream,*
107). It is in one of the latter that he encounters "people of his same origin

and condition" (Méndez-M., *Dream,* 108). These residents are poor people
who "have served as the fodder of war and industry" (Méndez-M., *Dream,*
108). Timoteo knocks on the door of one of the delapidated houses, and a
Chicana grandmother and her daughter-in-law answer his question on the
whereabouts of Huachusey:

> What is the name of the man you are lookin for? Ah, the whole world knows him
> and everybody speaks his name. He's Huachusey. Modesta, do you think that's the
> name of your son's boss [my son and your husband's boss], the Huachusey that this
> man is talking about? I don't rightly recall . . . Huachusey . . . Huachusey, that
> name sure sounds familiar to me. But I can tell you that they call the foreman
> Bulldog, but maybe that Huachusey is the owner of the whole place, because my
> old man says that the boss's got all the things you mentioned: tall buildings and
> airplanes, and who knows what all else. Seems to me that he must be the one.
> What did you say the name of the man you're looking for is? His name is Huachu-
> sey, ma'am; he is like a god on Earth. Well, who knows, my husband says he's a
> real bastard who works them to death and pays them nothings, see, and then runs
> them off when they're too weak and useless to work anymore.
>
> (Méndez-M., *Dream,* 108)

As presented in the grandmother's answer (a character configuration), urban
Chicano workers do not fare much better than their rural counterparts. In
addition to lacking a union, job security, and retirement benefits, their low
wages restrict them to living in a slum where hunger is present. A defamiliarizing effect from the character device is that, although the text is from Chicano
narrative, these Chicano figures are faceless, ahistorical.

In a description that is defamiliarizing due to an absent sign, the urban
barrio has no name. By contrast, Santa María de las Piedras and its residents
enjoy a rich sense of history and continuity. In the Southwest, the ahistorical-
ness also forms part of the rural area previously discussed, whose name also
does not appear in the discourse. What is everywhere present, and in an even
stronger form than in Santa María de la Piedras, is Anglo-American hegemony
shown by figures who hold power—in both the rural and urban settings—
over land, buildings, factories, and people. The message unfolds that Timoteo
will warn Santa María de las Piedras about such a hegemonic relationship
reaching them.

Eerily, in *El sueño de Santa María de las Piedras,* Southwest Mexicans are
not the only targets of the hegemonic center. Although their signifiers, or
words, do not appear in the discourse and ambiguity marks their configuration, Chicago and New York also feel the center's dominance. In chapter 23
Chicago is the site of a peaceful antiwar protest whose participants are violently repressed. In chapter 29 New York has just experienced a nuclear attack
and lies in apocalyptic devastation. All dead and injured residents are Anglo-
American. The description of the events and of the dead in both cities pro-

duces a defamiliarizing effect in that the text contains a Chicano world view that includes some Anglo-Americans as themselves victims of the hegemonic center. Added to previous incidents in his journey, the events in Chicago and New York finally erode Timoteo's utopian view of the United States, leaving in its ideological place a critique of development. At the end of the novel, on his way home, he yearns for the solidarity of his own townspeople in Santa María de las Piedras:

> Timoteo continued his journey in the direction of Santa María de las Piedras. The moans continued to resound in his ears and the horrible scenes to burn in his eyes. The dilemma gnawed at the deepest roots of his judgment. When the evidence seemed the clearest, so much darker did the shadows of his doubts become. Confusion took hold of his spirit. He felt a strange fear that at times became terror, and he knew that it would not diminish with time. Thus he urgently covered the distance, to see if distance and the warmth of his own people could help him recover a little peace, because he could never forget, nor could he even laugh or hope to dream surrounded by tranquility.

> (Méndez-M., *Dream*, 169–170).

CISNEROS: THE SYMBOLIZATION OF CHICANO ROOTS IN CHICAGO

As evident in the inclusion of Alberto Gallegos from Illinois in the list of writers at the end of the introduction to the fifth edition of the anthology *El espejo/The Mirror,* Midwest Chicano writers share the literary project of symbolizing the sign *Southwest,* though their greatest contribution resides in placing Chicago on the map of Chicano literature. They have participated in multiple ways, among them forming their own writers' circles, editing local journals, founding Midwest presses, and contributing work to Chicano journals and presses with a national distribution. In *The Last Laugh and Other Stories* (1988), Hugo Martínez-Serros (1930–) has symbolized the Chicano experience in Chicago from the 1930s to the 1950s. A native of Chicago, the playwright Carlos Morton (1947–) even migrated in 1970 into the Southwest and has now written some of the best dramatic work about Texas and California. Moreover, the Chicano writers from Chicago are pioneers in the task of opening space in mainstream presses. Most recently, Random House reedited *The House on Mango Street* by Sandra Cisneros; and as mentioned above, Anchor Books, in cooperation with Bilingual Press, reprinted *The Mixquiahuala Letters* by Ana Castillo (1953). In 1991 Random House printed the first edition of *Woman Hollering Creek and Other Stories* by Sandra Cisneros. In these ways Cisneros and Castillo have helped expand the distribution and readership of Chicano literature beyond the Southwestern literary circuit.

In representing the feminist strand in the Chicano LMP, Cisneros developed as a writer through her interaction with members of the feminist journal *Third Woman,* organized in the Midwest in 1981 by Norma Alarcón and staffed by

Chicanas, Puertorriqueñas, and other United States Latinas. Although Alarcón now teaches and edits the journal at the University of California at Berkeley, she was an assistant professor at Indiana University in the early 1980s and interacted with writers from Chicago. Cisneros thus has a literary development different from that of Chicano writers from the Southwest. In fact, Cisneros has declared that in her formative stage as a writer she read few of the works by the founders of contemporary Chicano literature, and when Cisneros did read some later on, she did not find their works as inspirational as those by Latin American and European writers (Hernández-Gutiérrez, unpublished interview). On the other hand, she, unlike José Antonio Villarreal, does share with 1970s Chicano writers the value of symbolizing the barrio as an autochthonous narrative universe. Alarcón herself is the author of the essay "Chicana's Feminist Literature: A Re-vision Through Malintzin/or Malintzin: Putting Flesh Back on the Object" (1981), one of the founding texts in Chicana feminist theory. In perhaps assimilating Alarcón's thinking, Cisneros's writing contains one of the most highly conscious feminist narrative subjects in Chicano letters. Such narrative subject is present in all levels of her texts, especially the language. Cisneros's first narrative work, *The House on Mango Street,* brings together both the symbolizing of the barrio and the Chicana feminist world view.

The fabula in *The House on Mango Street* focuses on the protagonist's coming of age. Central to Esperanza's maturing is home acquisition and female identity. The narrative opens the year the family, tired of being renters, has finally been able to purchase a home in an apparently South Chicago neighborhood. It is an ethnically mixed barrio with Chicanos, Afro-Americans, Puerto Ricans, and Mexican immigrants. The protagonist's family is Chicano—her father is a Mexican immigrant and her mother presumably second generation. As far as narrative events, the reader witnesses Esperanza make new friends, play children's games, explore the neighborhood stores and schools, experience interethnic conflict, meet single mothers, criticize the irregular and decaying state of her family's house, attend family baptisms and first communions, visit the barrio *curandera,* or herb healer, meet estranged wives, learn about child abuse, hear of jealous and violent husbands, express her desire to become a writer, mourn family deaths, witness and experience adolescent sexuality, and see marriage as a prison for women. At the closing of *The House on Mango Street,* Esperanza confesses her wish to escape the barrio; however, unlike Richard Rubio in *Pocho,* she expects one day to come back and help those who, due to economic factors, cannot leave.

Similar to Hinojosa's and Anaya's work, *The House on Mango Street* contains a copious description of the barrio. In fact, no chapter takes place outside the ethnically mixed community. *The House on Mango Street* represents an unequivocal symbolization of Chicano roots in Chicago. The fact that the narrative perspective falls repeatedly on the new family house codes this intent. The descriptions from the Mango house involve three houses and their corresponding periods in the life of the family: residences prior to buying the house, the currently owned family house, and the narrator's future house.

Prior to living in Mango Street, the family has rented on three other Chicago streets: Paulina, Keeler, and Loomis. Little description appears in the text about the first two houses. The rental on Loomis is a third-floor flat with peeling paint and wooden bars nailed on the windows. The family eventually leaves the Loomis house on account of a callous landlord:

> We had to leave the flat on Loomis quick. The water pipes broke and the land-lord wouldn't fix them because the house was too old. We had to leave fast. We were using the washroom next door and carrying water over in empty milk gal-lons. That's why Mama and Papa looked for a house, and that's why we moved into the house on Mango Street, far away, on the other side of town.
>
> (Cisneros, *Mango Street,* 7)

Ideologically, such a description is a defamiliarizing device from the syuzhet to foreground the belief on the part of the family that house ownership guarantees protection from a hegemonic center that limits not only their place of residence and movement, but also their existence. Along with her family, the narrator-protagonist feels no need to pay rent, share the yard, keep noise down, or deal with an aggressive landlord.

Unfortunately, the protagonist's family soon faces disillusionment: "But even so, it's not the house we'd thought we'd get" (Cisneros, *Mango Street,* 7). Like her family, the protagonist-narrator expected the ideal house so often discussed at the dinner table prior to buying the one on Mango Street:

> And our house would have running water and pipes that worked. And inside it would have real stairs, not hallway stairs, but stairs inside like the houses on T. V. And we'd have a basement and at least three washrooms so when we took a bath we didn't have to tell everybody. Our house would be white with trees around it, a great big yard and grass growing without a fence. This was the house Papa talked about when he held a lottery ticket and this was the house Mama dreamed up in the stories she told us before we went to bed.
>
> (Cisneros, *Mango Street,* 8)

Ideologically, the hegemonic center has influenced their consumer expectations as coded by the simile "like the houses on T.V." Addressing repeatedly the family house as "sad and red and crumbly," the narrator-protagonist vacillates between the ideal house and the one on Mango Street. As seen in the following description, the family house is a far cry from the ideal one:

> It's small and red with tight little steps in front and windows so small you'd think they were holding their breath. Bricks are crumbling in places, and the front door

is so swollen you have to push hard to get in. There is no front yard, only four
little elms the city planted by the curb. Out back is a small garage for the car we
don't own yet and a small yard that looks smaller between the two buildings on
either side. There are stairs in our house, but they're ordinary hallway stairs, and
the house has only one washroom, very small. Everybody has to share a bedroom—Mama and Papa, Carlos and Kiki, me and Nenny.

(Cisneros, *Mango Street,* 8)

In spite of being homeowners, the family has not escaped its class status: lower
working class. The only qualitative change is the rise from renters to property
owners. The father continues to work as a gardener six days a week and the
mother as an unsalaried housewife.

Further description of the neighborhood defines unequivocally its class and
ethnic make up. As illustrated in the cover to the 1985 edition of *The House
on Mango Street,* older single A-frame houses with black-tarred roofs, "a row
of ugly 3-flats" (43), an apartment building, a tavern, a laundromat, a drug-
store, a nearby Catholic school, and two community stores house the barrio.
While a Chicano couple (Benny and Blanca) owns a grocery store, an older
Black man, Gil, owns a second-hand store. There is even one abandoned house
with an overgrown yard whose owner left for the South. The majority of the
barrio residents are renters. That people in single houses, whether owned or
rented, sublease the basement contributes to a high population density. In
such a basement apartment lives a Puerto Rican family made up of two parents, son Louie, several little daughters, and two cousins from Puerto Rico.
The university is "two trains and a bus" away (32). An old Anglo neigborhood,
its few white descendents are moving away.

Such social conditions move barrio residents, including the narrator-
protagonist, to look outside the community boundaries. Whereas the Puerto
Rican characters hope to return to the Island, Chicanos dream about Mexico.
In fact, in *The House on Mango Street* the sign *Mexico* has greater resonance
than the Southwest. Since he migrated from Mexico to Chicago and apparently
takes the family there for vacation, the protagonist's father, Mr. Cordero, has
the most direct link. The protagonist herself has happy memories from her
visits to Mexico. Although she repeatedly uses a phrase full of indifference to
refer to Mexico—"that country"—the memories do help her endure the social
conditions in Chicago:

One day we were passing a house that looked, in my mind, like houses I had
seen in Mexico. I don't know why. There was nothing about the houses that looked
exactly like the houses I remembered. I'm not even sure why I thought it, but it
seemed to feel right.

(Cisneros, *Mango Street,* 19)

Still, it is recent immigrants who feel the greatest closeness to Mexico. For
example, the neighbor from the third floor across from the protagonist's house

worked two jobs so that he could save enough money to bring his wife and child from Mexico. Lastly, there is Alicia, a university student and one of the protagonist's best friends, who immigrated from Guadalajara and plans to return there:

> I like Alicia because once she gave me a little leather purse with the word GUADALAJARA stiched on it, which is home for Alicia and one day she will go back there.
>
> (Cisneros, *Mango Street,* 99)

For her part, the protagonist feels she does not "have a house." That is, Esperanza considers herself landless whether in Chicago or Mexico. She lacks a sense of origin. Perhaps the direct absence of the Southwest in *The House on Mango Street* cedes such a sense of landlessness. In effect, the protagonist seeks to fill the lack of origin through her friendship with two friends from Texas.

As a synecdoche, Texas represents the Southwest. One of the earliest land bases for Chicanos, the state is present indirectly in the narrative. Rachel and Lucy, the protagonist's best friends, migrated from there to Chicago. Whereas Cathy, an Anglo-American girl, feared people of color and could be Esperanza's friend only for a few days before moving out of the barrio, Rachel and Lucy remain the protagonist's faithful friends throughout the narrative. Aided by their friendship, she can see the positive side of life in the Chicago barrio. Nonetheless, at the end of the novel Esperanza continues to feel landless as she confesses to Alicia:

> You have a home, Alicia, and one day you'll go there, to a little town you remember, but me I never had a house, not even a photograph . . . only one I dream of.
>
> (Cisneros, *Mango Street,* 99)

Several selections from *Woman Hollering Creek and Other Stories*—Cisneros's second narrative work—take place in California and Texas, which indicates that the Chicana narrative subject of *The House on Mango Street* has expanded its parameters and sought to further symbolize the Southwest. For now, Texas represents the source of a strong Chicano identity.

In *The House on Mango Street,* the protagonist's feminist identity leads the resistance to hegemonic Anglo-American society. In addition to being concerned with the future of the barrio, such resistance challenges the economic limitations placed on women and advocates an end to oppressive roles for women. The protagonist's desire for change rises from a rebellious spirit already present among women in the family from as far back as the nineteenth century in Mexico and as recently as barrio life in the 1950s and 1960s. From nineteenth-century Mexico, the protagonist extols the actions of her great-grandmother, Esperanza, whose name she carries:

My great-grandmother. I would've liked to have known her, a wild horse of a woman, so wild she wouldn't marry until my great-grandfather threw a sack over her head and carried her off. Just like that, as if she were a fancy chandelier. That's the way he did it.

And the story goes she never forgave him. She looked out the window all her life, the way so many women sit their sadness on an elbow. I wonder if she made the best with what she got or was she sorry because she couldn't be all the things she wanted to be. Esperanza. I have inherited her name, but I don't want to inherit her place by the window.

(Cisneros, *Mango Street,* 12)

From the 1960s and 1970s in the barrio, Esperanza has her mother. Recalling her own life as a housemaker and the fate of her *comadres* Isaura and Yolanda—*comadre* refers to the relation of a godmother to the parents of a child—her mother openly protests the economic limitations placed on housewives and advocates the education of women:

Today while cooking oatmeal she is Madame Butterfly until she sighs and points the wooden spoon at me. I could've been somebody, you know? Esperanza, you go to school. Study hard. That Madame Butterfly was a fool. She stirs the oatmeal. Look at my *comadres.* She means Izaura whose husband left and Yolanda whose husband is dead. Got to take care all your own, she says shaking her head.

(Cisneros, *Mango Street,* 83)

Armed with a feminist consciousness, the protagonist understands the conditions for women in the barrio. All around she sees barrio women who face physical abuse, date rape, jealous and violent husbands, spouse desertion, and single motherhood. Esperanza also decries that her friends, such as Sally, see marriage as an escape from physical abuse. Ironically, Sally goes from experiencing violence from her father to experiencing that from her husband. Exercising early in life her rebellious spirit in the form of refusing to cross the street, unlike her girl friends, when boys are approaching her, the protagonist resolves not to fall into oppressive roles. Teased by her mother that eventually she will make herself presentable to males, the protagonist affirms her self-determination:

My mother says when I get older my dusty hair will settle and my blouse will learn to stay clean, but I have decided not to grow up tame like the others who lay their necks on the threshold waiting for the ball and chain.

In the movies there is always one with red red lips who is beautiful and cruel. She is the one who drives the men crazy and laughs them all away. Her power is her own. She will not give it away.

I have begun my own quiet war. Simple. Sure. I am one who leaves the table like a man, without putting back the chair or picking up the plate.

(Cisneros, *Mango Street,* 82)

However, Esperanza's feminist consciousness does not practice separation. In addition to being committed to bettering women's condition, the protagonist would help marginalized males. For example, in her future house she will offer a room to "bums" who have been cast away by the hegemonic center. Esperanza feels solidarity with a *brazer,* an undocumented worker, who works hard to send money to his family in Mexico yet dies in a car accident without a person around to claim his body. The protagonist also feels the pain of her "brave" father who cries upon learning about the death of his own father.

The narrator-protagonist's destiny is solidly linked to the barrio. She knows that no outsider, including the mayor of Chicago, will improve its social conditions (Cisneros, *Mango Street,* 99). Change must come from within the barrio residents. Her personal desire of owning a house falls within such an ideological position: it will be a space for the oppressed to find liberation. Thus, although in chapter 41 she does still want to leave the barrio, Esperanza heeds the advice from three adult barrio women, all sisters, who ask her to return later:

> When you leave you must remember to come back for the others. A circle, understand? You will always be Esperanza. You will always be Mango Street. You can't erase what you know: You can't forget who you are.
>
> (Cisneros, *Mango Street,* 98)

CONCLUSION

Our study of both LMPs and their respective ideology does reveal a conscious and consistent relationship between Mexican and Chicano literature, one that has been continuous from the mid-1970s to the present. In its specific form in both Mexico and the Southwest, the bourgeois GMP has provided the necessary sources and social formations in material production to make available contemporary Mexican and Chicano literature. One difference distinguishes them: the former has the conscious participation of a private sector, while the latter still needs to rely on institutional support like university subsidies and foundation grants. Specifically, three substructures from each LMP bridge the relationship between Chicano and Mexican literature: production, distribution, and exchange. The substructure consumption, however, needs further study in order to reveal the targeted and real consumer of Chicano narrative produced in Mexico. It could be that Mexican publishers have targeted the Southwest consumer instead of the Mexican reader.

Based on the above structural links between both LMPs (those of Mexico and the Chicano), the relationship does leave behind four resonant messages that any future research must address.

Overall, Chicano texts published in Mexico contain a disturbing symbolization of the Southwest. Due to low printings of anthologies that do make available in Mexico a rich Chicano literary discourse (historical, regional, linguistically diverse, feminist, stylistically varied), the dominant symbolization of Southwest Mexican society has been reduced to two levels: one, as in *Caras viejas y vino nuevo* and *La verdad sin voz,* a marginalized urban society that suffers from youth gangs, street violence, alienation, family fragmentation, and racial prejudice; and two, as in *Las aventuras de don Chipote* and *El sueño de Santa María de las Piedras,* an Anglo-dominated society whose racial hostility to and superexploitation of the undocumented workers—read the Chicanos—leads them time after time to return defeated to their villages or towns in Mexico. This last type of symbolization holds most of the space in Chicano texts published in Mexico due to the fact that, in 1984, SEP and CEFNOMEX printed 30,000 copies of *Las aventuras de don Chipote,* while the combined printing in the 1970s and 1980s of all Chicano anthologies and novels reached only 17,000 copies. The symbolization of the Southwest Mexican as an undocumented worker prevails also in Fuentes's *La región más transparente, La muerte de Artemio Cruz,* and *Cristóbal nonato,* although in this last text a new Chicano appears who unfortunately forms part of an invading Yankee force in Veracruz.

In the second place, in sharp contrast to the above disturbing symbolization in Chicano texts published in Mexico, Mexican works available in the Southwest and the rest of the United States, whether in Spanish or in English, present a pluralistic and multidimensional Mexican society, particularly in works by Azuela, Yáñez, Rulfo, Fuentes, Paz, Castellanos, Poniatowska, and Sainz. From this group, only Azuela, Yáñez, and Rulfo present a rural and underdeveloped Mexico. As for the dominant Mexican symbolization available in bookstores across the Southwest, Paz and Fuentes have claim to a Mexican society that, although developing, has several rich qualities in its multidimensionality, among them urbanity, cosmopolitanism, and identifiable nationality. Unlike the reductive marginalized and inhospitable Southwest Mexican society, Mexican society cannot be reduced to a unidimensional simulacrum by the Chicano reader. Just reading Fuentes's works—*La región más transparente, La muerte de Artemio Cruz, Terra nostra, Cristóbal nonato, Myself with Others*—denies the reader in the Southwest such arbitrariness. The Chicano reader, moreover, cannot dismiss the many classic Mexican writers in the anthologies by Castañeda-Shular et al. and Menton.

Third, in combatting the disturbing symbolization in Mexico of Southwest Mexican society, Chicano literary criticism, whether from thematics or literary theory, has skillfully introduced the Mexican reader to the broad parameters of a rich and multifaceted literary production in the Southwest. As early as 1975, in "México en la literatura chicana," Bruce-Novoa called attention to a profound Chicano interest in Mexican traditional themes: *indigenismo* (indigenism), *mestizaje* (dual racial heritage), and the 1910 Revolution. As for leading Mexican critics, Monsiváis and Vázquez-Castro have recognized the significance of Chicano literature and rightly called for greater attention to and understanding of its anticolonialist message on the part of the Mexican reader. In its most recent development in Mexico, Chicano literary criticism reached new heights with the appearance of several works grounded in critical theory, among them *Narrativa chicana contemporánea, La literatura chicana a través de sus autores,* and *El arquetipo de la Madre Terrible en Peregrinos de Aztlán.* The most progressive work of this new phase includes feminist criticism, as seen in the book *Mujer y literatura mexicana y chicana: Culturas en contacto.* Chicano literary criticism has thus proven to be a necessity inside Mexico.

Finally, in the Southwest, criticism of Mexican works has remained consistent and critically significant. Beginning with Villarreal's 1960 review of Fuentes's *La región más transparente,* Chicano critics have specifically examined works on the 1910 Mexican Revolution. Ideologically, Chicano criticism has evolved from praising such texts to denying their revolutionary message. Rojas and Rodríguez del Pino have identified thematic links between several Chicano writers from the 1970s and various Mexican writers from two revolutionary generations. In the first one, we find Azuela, Guzmán, López y Fuentes, and Magdaleno; Revueltas, Rulfo, Yáñez, Arreola, and Fuentes represent the second one. At the height of identifying thematic links, Leal in *Aztlán y México* ambitiously compares both LMPs at the popular and literary levels, including a study of La Onda. However, in his article "La novela de la Revolución Mexicana: La topología del final," from 1991, Bruce-Novoa adopts a critical position and suggests instead that the novels of the Mexican Revolution present disillusionment with the revolutionary ideals, indirectly questioning Rojas's and Rodríguez del Pino's prior conclusions. Further, as seen in the journal *Third Woman,* Chicana critics have taken an interest in absent or passive sexuality in Mexican woman writers. Having such a corpus already in place, future critical articles should show greater depth and findings.

As for ideology at the level of the text, the selected works studied here mark differences between Mexican and Chicano literature. By surfacing and resurfacing in this narrative universe, Fuentes's nation-state ideology foregrounds the sign *Mexico,* especially in synchronic and diachronic descriptions that highlight a Mexican subject consciously participating in directing Mexican development. Yet this ideology's ideological parameters have limitations that code a lack of a historical understanding of the Southwest. This last region is absent in Artemio Cruz's historical consciousness and barely surfaces in Christopher Palomar's. In Fuentes's Mexican society, national resistance remains the primary concern. In fact, from reading *Gringo viejo* and *Myself with Others,* the Chicano can clearly see that Fuentes has a significantly greater understanding of Anglo-Americans and Spaniards than of Southwest Mexicans. Perhaps the reason lies in that he has lived in Spain and the East in the United States but not in the Southwest. As evident in his critical writings, the exclusion of Chicano writers from Spanish American literature further exposes the limits to Fuentes's ideological framework. Perhaps the last chapter in *The Buried Mirror,* "Hispanic U.S.A.," signals a beginning of an understanding in Fuentes's work of the Southwest Mexican.

As for Southwest Mexican writers, although each has fallen short in the complete symbolization of the Southwest—a region in the United States—

that was called for in the introduction to the historic anthology *El espejo/The Mirror,* they have amply succeeded in symbolizing the particular polyvalence present in each Southwestern province and do include in their works partial or tangential images of the Southwest. Only when the critic takes them as a group and juxtaposes their respective texts can a full symbolization of the Southwest appear, one dimensionally comparable to Mexico in Fuentes's *La muerte de Artemio Cruz* or *Cristóbal nonato.* At such a moment, Southwest Mexican writers do give a voice to the object region. Ideologically, Hinojosa and Anaya code the mainstream symbolization of the Southwest in Chicano literature: a resistance struggle against a hegemonic Anglo-American society, grounded in a subordinated working-class barrio and inspired by an autochthonous Southwest Mexican history. Although creating a Chicano space outside the Southwest, Cisneros succeeds in joining the symbolization of the barrio with a Chicana feminist world view. Also, unlike Fuentes, she successfully maps a literary space in the Midwest. That Villarreal advocates a break with the Chicano working-class barrio and opts instead for assimilation into middle-class Anglo America only points to ideological diversity among Southwest Mexican writers. For his part, as in *Peregrinos de Aztlán,* Méndez-M. continues to critique United States development, specifically its superexploitation of three types of Chicano workers (undocumented, rural, and urban), adding now an observation on the victimization of Anglos.

Both Fuentes and Chicano writers share one element: the recognition that one common hegemonic center has historically impacted and now determines their respective societies. A united opposition to such hegemony can play a significant role in bridging the differences between Mexican and Chicano literature.

NOTE

1. The author has developed the term *Southwest Mexican literature* for four reasons: (1) to establish that the category *Chicano literature* emanates from the conscious adoption of the term *Chicano* by writers and critics of the 1970s; (2) to correct the revisionist effect of including, without serious study, all literary production since 1848 by United States Mexicans under *Chicano literature;* (3) to call attention to the fact that any previous generation of United States Mexican writers has its own particular literary project, ideological representation, figuration, and idiom; and (4) to remind the reader that other ethnic groups lay claim to the Southwest as a literary space, namely, Native-Americans, Anglo-Americans, and Afro-Americans. The Southwest is a polysemic sign in which modern Chicano writers play a particular generational and ethnic role.

BIBLIOGRAPHY

Alarcón, Alicia. "Cuentos por el aire." *La Opinión,* September 19, 1991, 1 and 5-F. Informs on radio reading of Mexican texts.

————. "Lectura da vida a novela de Rosario Castellanos." *La Opinión,* October 26, 1991, 3-E. Reports on a radio reading of a novel.

Alarcón, Justo. *Los siete hijos de La Llorona.* Mexico City: Alta Pimeria Pro Arte y Cultura, 1986.

Alarcón, Norma. "Chicana's Feminist Literature: A Re-vision Through Malintzin/or Malintzin: Putting Flesh Back on the Object." In *This Bridge Called My Back: Writings by Radical Women of Color,* ed. Cherríe Moraga and Gloria Anzaldúa, 182–190. Watertown, Mass.: Persephone Press, 1981.

Anaya, Rudolfo. *Bless Me, Ultima.* Berkeley: Quinto Sol Publications, 1972.

————. *Heart of Aztlán.* 2d ed. Berkeley: Editorial Justa Publications, 1979. Orig. 1976.

————. *Tortuga.* Berkeley: Editorial Justa Publications, 1979.

Arias, Ron. *The Road to Tamazunchale. West Coast Poetry Review* 4-4, special number.

Armas, José. "Mexicanos y chicanos." *La Opinión,* October 31, 1990, Sec. 1, 1. Author criticizes Carlos Fuentes from a Chicano point of view.

————. "Octavio Paz." *De colores: Journal of Emerging Raza Philosophies* 2.2 (1975): 4–21. Author criticizes Octavio Paz.

Arreola, Juan José. *Confabulario.* Mexico City: Fondo de Cultura Económica, 1952. Translated as *Confabulario and Other Inventions* by George D. Schade.

————. *La feria.* Mexico City: Editorial Joaquín Mortiz, 1964. Translated as *The Fair* by John Upton.

————. "Prólogo." In Lucha Corpi, *Palabras de mediodía,* xi–xviii. Berkeley: El Fuego de Aztlán Publications, 1980. Arreola writes an introduction to work by the Chicana poet.

Azuela, Mariano. *Los de abajo.* 14th ed. Mexico City: Fondo de Cultura Económica, 1977. Orig. 1915. Translated as *The Underdogs* by E. Munguía, Jr.

Barrera, Mario. *Beyond Aztlán: Ethnic Autonomy in Comparative Perspective.* New York: Praeger, 1988. A comparative study between Chicanos and other ethnic groups in countries like China and Nicaragua.

Brito, Aristeo. *El diablo en Texas.* Tucson: Editorial Peregrinos, 1976. Translated as *The Devil in Texas* by David William Foster. Tempe: Bilingual Press/Editorial Bilingüe, 1990 (bilingual edition).

Bruce-Novoa, Juan. *Chicano Authors: Inquiry by Interview.* Austin: University of Texas Press, 1980. Contains fourteen interviews with contemporary writers and sets the parameters in Chicano literature.

————. "Chicanos in Mexican Literature." In *Missions in Conflict: Essays on U.S.-Mexican Relations and Chicano Culture,* ed. Renate von Bardeleben Briesemeister and Juan Bruce-Novoa, 55–64. Tübingen: Gunter Narr Verlag, 1986. Article studies a reductionist image of the Chicano in Martín Luis Guzmán, José Vasconcelos, Octavio Paz, Carlos Fuentes, and Francisco Segovia.

————. *La literatura chicana a través de sus autores.* Mexico City: Siglo XXI Editores, 1983. Translated as *Chicano Authors: Inquiry by Interview* by Stella Mastrangelo. Austin: University of Texas, 1980.

————. "México en la literatura chicana." *Revista de la Universidad de México* 29.5 (January 1975): 13–18.

————. "Mexico in Chicano Literature." In *Retrospace: Collected Essays on Chicano Literature,* ed. Bruce-Novoa, 52–62. Houston: Arte Público Press, 1990. Examines common themes: indigenism, *mestizaje,* and the 1910 Revolution.

————. "La novela de la Revolución Mexicana: La topología del final." *Hispania* 74.1

(March 1991): 36–44. Examines the disillusionment with revolutionary ideals in the novel of the Mexican Revolution.

———. "Prólogo: ¿Chicanos?" In *Antología retrospectiva del cuento chicano,* ed. Bruce-Novoa, 11–27. Mexico City: Consejo Nacional de Población, 1988. Differentiates and discusses generations in contemporary Chicano literature.

Cárdenas, Guadalupe. *El arquetipo de la Madre Terrible en "Peregrinos de Aztlán."* Mexico City: Alta Pimeria Pro Arte y Cultura, 1990. Pioneers in Jungian analysis of Chicano literature.

Castañeda-Shular, Antonia, Tomás Ybarra-Frausto, and Joseph Sommers. *Literatura chicana: Texto y contexto/Chicano Literature: Text and Context.* Englewood Cliffs, N.J.: Prentice-Hall, 1972. One of the earliest Chicano literature anthologies. Includes texts from other U.S. Latino groups and Latin Americans.

Castillo, Ana. *The Mixquiahuala Letters.* Binghamton, N.Y.: Bilingual Press/Editorial Bilingüe, 1986.

Cisneros, Sandra. *The House on Mango Street.* Houston: Arte Público Press, 1985.

———. *Woman Hollering Creek and Other Stories.* New York: Random House, 1991.

Cramsie, Hilde F., and Nitza Lladó-Torres. *Contrastes: An Intermediate Spanish Reader.* Englewood Cliffs, N.J.: Prentice-Hall, 1990. Contains selections from Mexican literature.

Cruz, Sor Juana Inés de la. *Sor Juana Inés de la Cruz: Poems.* Trans. Margaret Sayers Peden. Binghamton, N.Y.: Bilingual Press/Editorial Bilingüe, 1985.

Delgado, Javier. "Carlos Fuentes, el novelista mexicano más representativo: Emmanuel Carballo," *La Opinión,* June 7, 1991, 3-D. Reports on Carballo's presentation on the status of Mexican literature.

Diez-Canedo Ruiz, Juan. *La migracion indocumentada de México a los Estados Unidos: Un nuevo enfoque.* Mexico City: Fondo de Cultura Económica, 1984.

Eagleton, Terry. *Criticism and Ideology: A Study in Marxist Literary Theory.* London: Verso Editions, 1980. Orig. 1976. Offers a materialist theory for the study of ideology in literature.

Elizondo, Sergio. *Muerte en una estrella.* Mexico City: Tinta Negra Editores, 1984.

———. *Suruma.* Ciudad Juárez: Comercial Editora/Dos Pasos Editores, 1990.

"Escritores mexicanos se reúnen en mesa redonda neoyorquina." *La Opinión,* November 13, 1990, Sec. 2, 4. Chicano critic Bruce-Novoa chairs discussion on La Onda. Authors present: Carlos Monsiváis, José Agustín, and Elena Poniatowska.

"Footnotes." *The Chronicle of Higher Education* (January 29, 1992): A-8. Reports on a twenty-million-dollar grant.

"Fue un año de crisis para las editoriales latinas." *La Opinión,* December 30, 1991, 1 and 7-D. A report on book sales in the Spanish-speaking world.

Fuentes, Carlos. *Agua quemada.* Mexico City: Fondo de Cultura Económica, 1981. Translated as *Burnt Water* by Margaret Sayers Peden.

———. *Las buenas conciencias.* Mexico City: Fondo de Cultura Económica, 1959. Translated as *The Good Conscience* by Ivan Obolensky.

———. *La cabeza de la hidra.* Mexico City: Fondo de Cultura Económica, 1985. Translated as *Hydra Head* by Margaret Sayers Peden.

———. *Cristóbal nonato.* 3d ed. Mexico City: Fondo de Cultura Económica, 1990. Orig. 1987. Translated as *Christopher Unborn* by Alfred MacAdam and the author.

———. *Una familia lejana.* Mexico City: Fondo de Cultura Económica, 1980. Translated as *Distant Relations* by Margaret Sayers Peden.

————. *Gringo viejo*. Mexico City: Fondo de Cultura Económica, 1985. Translated as *The Old Gringo* by Margaret Sayers Peden.

————. "Hispanic U.S.A." *The Buried Mirror,* 341–355. New York: Houghton Mifflin Company, 1992. Attempts to interpret the reality of U.S. Hispanics.

————. *La muerte de Artemio Cruz*. Mexico City: Fondo de Cultura Económica, 1962. Translated as *The Death of Artemio Cruz* by Sam Hileman.

————. *Myself with Others*. New York: The Noonday Press, 1988.

————. *La nueva novela hispanoamericana*. 2d ed. Mexico City: Editorial Joaquín Mortiz, 1969. Offers a structuralist study of the boom in Latin American literature.

————. *La región más transparente*. Mexico City: Fondo de Cultura Económica, 1958. Translated as *Where the Air Is Clear* by Sam Hileman.

————. *Terra nostra*. Mexico City: Fondo de Cultura Económica, 1977. Translated as *Terra Nostra* by Margaret Sayers Peden.

————. *Tiempo mexicano*. 14th ed. Mexico City: Editorial Joaquín Mortiz, 1989. Orig. 1971. Contains Fuentes's essays on Mexico from the 1950s to the 1960s.

————. *Valiente mundo nuevo: Épica, utopía y mito en la novela hispanomericana*. Mexico City: Fondo de Cultura Económica, 1990. Offers a poststructuralist critique of the Latin American novel.

García Márquez, Gabriel. *Cien años de soledad*. 15th ed. Buenos Aires: Editorial Sudamericana, 1969. Translated as *One Hundred Years of Solitude* by Gregory Rabassa.

García Ponce, Juan. *Encuentros*. Mexico City: Fondo de Cultura Económica, 1972. Translated as *Encounters* by Helen Lane.

Gómez-Quiñones, Juan. *Chicano Politics: Reality and Promise 1940–1990*. Albuquerque: University of New Mexico Press, 1990. Studies Chicanos from the 1960s to the 1980s and suggests greater integration has occurred.

Gomez-Quiñones, Juan, and David Maciel. *Al norte del rio bravo (pasado lejano) (1600–1930)*. Mexico City: Siglo XXI Editores, 1981.

Hernández, José. *Martín Fierro*. 25th ed. Buenos Aires: Editorial Losada, 1991. Orig. 1872 and 1879.

Hernández-G., Manuel de Jesús. *El colonialismo interno en la narrativa chicana: El barrio, el anti-barrio y el exterior*. Tempe: Bilingual Press/Editorial Bilingüe, forthcoming. Presents a Macherean model for interpreting the establishment of a narrative tradition in Chicano literature.

————. "Villarreal's *Clemente Chacón* (1984): A Precursor's Accomodationist Dialogue." *The Bilingual Review/La Revista Bilingüe* 16.1 (January–April 1991): 35–43. Provides sociohistorical and textual evidence that Villarreal continues to distinguish himself from contemporary Chicano writers.

————. Unpublished interview, October 11, 1991. Reveals that Sandra Cisneros considers herself separate from the founders of contemporary Chicano narrative.

Hinojosa-S., Rolando. *Claros varones de Belken*. Tempe: Bilingual Press/Editorial Bilingüe, 1986. Translated as *Fair Gentlemen of Belken County* by Julia Cruz.

————. *Estampas del Valle y otras obras*. Berkeley: Quinto Sol Publications, 1973. Translated as *Sketches of the Valley and Other Works* by Gustavo Valadez.

————. *Klail City y sus alrededores*. Havana: Casa de las Américas, 1976. Reprinted as *Generaciones y semblanzas*. Berkeley: Editorial Justa Publications, 1977. Translated as *Generations and Sketches* by Rosaura Sánchez. Berkeley: Editorial Justa Publications, 1977, 1979 (bilingual edition). Symbolizes the subordination of Chicano migrants in the Texas Valley, the Midwest, and the South.

————. *Korean Love Songs*. Berkeley: Editorial Justa Publications, 1978.

————. *Mi querido Rafa*. Houston: Arte Público Press, 1981.

"Ideas." *Excelsior* December 6, 1991, 1–4-I. A special section, contains various interdisciplinary articles on Chicanos.

Jefferson, Ann. "Russian Formalism." In *Modern Literary Theory: A Comparative Introduction*, 24–45. 2d ed. London: T. T. Batsford Ltd., 1991. Orig. 1982. Surveys major critical methods and concepts.

Job, Peggy. "La sexualidad en la narrativa femenina mexicana 1970–1987: Una aproximación." *Third Woman* 4 (1989): 120–133. Studies sexuality in novels by Mexican women.

Kissam, Edward, and Michael Schmidt, trans. *Poems of the Aztec Peoples*. Ypsilanti, Mich.: Bilingual Press/Editorial Bilingüe, 1983.

Leal, Luis. *Aztlán y México: Perfiles literarios e históricos*. Tempe: Bilingual Press/Editorial Bilingüe, 1989. The book represents the most exhaustive comparative study of Chicano and Mexican culture. Includes "Nacionalismo y cosmopolitismo en la narrativa mexicana," 195–208.

Lequerica de la Vega, Sara, and Carmen Salazar. *Avanzando: Gramática española y lectura*. 2d ed. New York: John Wiley & Sons, 1986. Contains selections from Mexican literature.

López González, Aralia, et al., eds. *Mujer y literatura mexicana y chicana: Culturas en contacto*. Mexico City: El Colegio de México/El Colegio de la Frontera Norte, 1990. Represents first major work on literature by Chicanas and Mexican women.

Maciel, David. *Al norte del rio bravo (pasado immediato) (1930–1981)*. Mexico City: Siglo XXI Editores, 1981.

————, ed. *La otra cara de México*. Mexico City: Ediciones El Caballito, 1977. Contains multidisciplinary articles on Mexicano/Chicano relations.

Martínez-Serros, Hugo. *The Last Laugh and Other Stories*. Houston: Arte Público Press, 1988.

Medina, Rubén. *"Amor de lejos . . . Fools' Love."* Houston: Arte Público Press, 1987.

Méndez-M., Miguel. *Peregrinos de Aztlán*. Tucson: Editorial Peregrinos, 1974. Translated as *Pilgrims in Aztlán* by David William Foster. Tempe: Bilingual Press/Editorial Bilingüe, 1992.

————. *Que no mueran los sueños*. Mexico City: Ediciones Era, 1991.

————. *El sueño de Santa María de las Piedras*. Guadalajara: Universidad de Guadalajara, 1986. Translated as *The Dream of Santa María de las Piedras* by David William Foster.

Menton, Seymour, and María Herrera-Sobek, eds. *Saga de México*. Tempe: Bilingual Press/Editorial Bilingüe, 1992.

Mijares, Enrique. "Los intelectuales mexicanos y el TLC." *La Opinión,* January 5, 1992, 3-E. Contains comments on Chicanos by members of La Onda.

Monsiváis, Carlos. "De México y los chicanos, de México y su cultura fronteriza." In Maciel, ed., 1–19. Calls for greater interest in Chicanos on the part of Mexico.

Moore, Joan W., and Alfredo Cuellar. *Los mexicanos de los Estados Unidos y el Movimiento Chicano*. Trans. Aurora Cortina de Nicolau. Mexico City: Fondo de Cultura Económica, 1972. Orig. 1970.

Moraga, Cherríe, and Gloria Anzaldúa, eds. *This Bridge Called My Back: Writings by Radical Women of Color*. Watertown, Mass.: Persephone Press, 1981. Translated as *Esta [sic] puente, mi espalda: Voces de mujeres tercermundistas en los Estados Unidos* by Ana Castillo and Norma Alarcón.

Morales, Alejandro. *Caras viejas y vino nuevo.* Mexico City: Editorial Joaquín Mortiz, 1975. Translated as *Old Faces and New Wine* by Max Martínez. Ed. José Monleón and Alurista Monleón. San Diego: Maize Press, 1981.

———. *La verdad sin voz.* Mexico City: Editorial Joaquín Mortiz, 1979. Translated as *Death of an Anglo* by Judith Ginsburg.

Nieto, Margarita, and Juan Rodríguez Flores. "'Si Estados Unidos desea seguir siendo un país unificado deberá respetar la diversidad étnica y cultural', afirma Carlos Fuentes." *La Opinión* April 28, 1992, 3-E. Reports on Fuentes's changing views on Chicanos.

Ocampo, Aurora M., ed. *La crítica de la novela mexicana contemporánea.* Mexico City: Universidad Nacional Autónoma de México, 1981. Represents a major study of La Onda generation.

Paz, Octavio. "Art and Identity: Hispanics in the United States." In *Hispanic Art in the United States: Thirty Contemporary Painters and Sculptors,* ed. John Beardsley, 13–37. 2d ed. New York: Abbeville Press, 1987. Offers an existentialist/surrealist interpretation of United States Hispanic art.

———. *El laberinto de la soledad.* Mexico City: Fondo de Cultura Económica, 1973. Orig. 1950.

Poniatowska, Elena. *¡Ay vida, no me mereces!* 6th ed. Mexico City: Editorial Joaquín Mortiz, 1990. Orig. 1985. Examines the rise of La Onda generation.

Ramírez, Axel. "Estudios Chicanos, una disciplina en la UNAM." *Excelsior* December 6, 1991, 1-I and 2-I. Examines the rise and institutionalization of Chicano studies in Mexico.

———. "Imagen del chicano en el sistema político mexicano." *El Día Latinoamericano,* 2.65 (September 9, 1991): 11–14. Traces government efforts to establish relations with Chicanos.

Revueltas, José. *Los motivos de Cain.* Mexico City: Fondo de Cultura Popular, 1957.

Rodríguez, Juan. "El florecimiento de la literatura chicana." In Maciel, ed., 348–369. Introduces the Mexican reader to a rebirth in Chicano literature in the 1970s.

Rodriguez O., Jaime E. *The Mexican and Mexican American Experience in the 19th Century.* Tempe, Ariz.: Bilingual Press/Editorial Bilingüe, 1989.

Rodríguez, Richard. *Hunger of Memory: An Autobiography.* Boston: Godine, 1981. Contains an assimilationist and conservative view of Chicanos.

Rodríguez del Pino, Salvador. "Lo mexicano y lo chicano en *El diablo en Texas.*" In *The Identification and Analysis of Chicano Literature,* ed. Francisco Jiménez, 365–373. New York: Bilingual Press/Editorial Bilingüe, 1979. Links 1970s Chicano narrators to Mexican writers from the 1940s to the 1960s.

Rojas, Guillermo. "La prosa chicana: Tres epígonos de la novela mexicana de la Revolución." *La Luz* 1.4 (1975): 43–57. In *The Identification and Analysis of Chicano Literature,* ed. Francisco Jiménez, 317–328. New York: Bilingual Press/Editorial Bilingüe, 1979. Sees 1970s Chicanos narrators in the tradition of the Mexican novel of the revolution.

Romano-V., Octavio Ignacio. *El espejo/The Mirror.* Berkeley: Quinto Sol Publications, 1969. Represents the first anthology of Chicano literature in the world.

Romano-V., Octavio Ignacio, and Herminio Ríos-C. *El espejo/The Mirror.* 5th ed. Berkeley: Quinto Sol Publications, 1972. Contains a major manifesto—"Introduction"—in Chicano literature.

Rulfo, Juan. *El llano en llamas.* Mexico City: Fondo de Cultura Económica, 1953. Translated as *The Burning Plain and Other Stories* by George D. Schade.

————. *Pedro Páramo*. Mexico City: Fondo de Cultura Económica, 1955. Translated as *Pedro Paramo* by Lysander Kemp.

Sainz, Gustavo. *A la salud de la serpiente*. Mexico City: Editorial Grijalbo, 1991.

————. *La princesa del Palacio de Hierro*. Mexico City: Ediciones Oceano, 1985. Translated as *The Princess of the Iron Palace* by Andrew Hurley.

Saldívar, José David, ed. *The Rolando Hinojosa Reader*. Houston: Arte Público Press, 1985. Stands as the most exhaustive study and interpretation of Hinojosa's work.

Saldívar, Ramón. *Chicano Narrative: The Dialectics of Difference*. Madison: The University of Wisconsin Press, 1990. Represents perhaps the best theory and study of Chicano narrative to date.

Sánchez, Rosaura. "Postmodernism and Chicano Literature." *Aztlán* 18.2 (Fall 1987): 1–13. Succeeds in placing Chicano literature on the postmodernist map.

Somoza, Oscar U. *Narrativa chicana contemporánea: Principios fundamentales*. Mexico City: Editorial Signos, 1983. First critical text published in Mexico by a Chicano critic.

————, ed. *Nueva narrativa chicana*. Mexico City: Editorial Diógones, 1983.

Soto, Gary. *Como arbustos de niebla*. Trans. Ernesto Trejo. Mexico City: Editorial Latitudes, 1980.

Stavans, Ilan. "Se reúnen escritores latinos de Estados Unidos." *La Opinión,* May 3, 1992, 3-E. Reports on major conference attended by United States Latino writers to discuss the status of their literature and strategies for distribution.

Straitfeld, David. "La imagen de Carlos Fuentes en el espejo." *La Jornada Semanal,* 227 (November 17, 1991): 3–4. Reveals that Fuentes is versed in such writers and symbols as Henry James, William Faulkner, Margaret Mitchell, and Moby Dick.

"Tema central." *El Día Latinoamericano,* 2.65 (September 9, 1991): 11–14. A special section, presents three articles: Mexican policy on Chicanos, Chicana struggle, and history.

Vázquez-Castro, Javier. *Acerca de literatura: Diálogo con tres autores chicanos*. Introduction by Luis Arturo Ramos. San Antonio: M & A Editions, 1979. Exposes Mexican reader to colonized world view in Chicano literature.

Venegas, Daniel. *Las aventuras de don Chipote, o Cuando los pericos mamen*. Mexico City: Secretaría de Educación Pública and Centro de Estudios Fronterizos del Norte de México, 1984.

Villanueva, Alma Luz. *The Ultraviolet Sky*. Tempe: Bilingual Press/Editorial Bilingüe, 1988.

Villanueva, Tino, ed. *Chicanos: Antología histórica y literaria*. Mexico City: Fondo de Cultura Económica, 1980. Stands as the best anthology of Chicano literature published in Mexico.

Villarreal, José Antonio. *Clemente Chacón*. Binghamton, N.Y.: Bilingual Press/Editorial Bilingüe, 1984.

————. *The Fifth Horseman*. Binghamton, N.Y.: Bilingual Press/Editorial Bilingüe, 1974.

————. "Mexico's Big Novel: A Mixture of Styles." *San Francisco Chronicle,* "This World" (December 18, 1960): 21. Reviews *Where the Air Is Clear* by Carlos Fuentes, dismissing its relevance to Chicanos.

————. *Pocho*. New York: Anchor Books, 1959.

Yáñez, Agustín. *Al filo del agua*. Mexico City: Editorial Porrúa, 1947. Translated as *The Edge of the Storm* by Ethel Brinton.

————. *Las tierras flacas*. Mexico City: Editorial Joaquín Mortiz, 1962. Translated as *The Lean Lands* by Ethel Brinton.

Index